The Hippies

The Hippies

A 1960s History

JOHN ANTHONY MORETTA

McFarland & Company, Inc., Publishers

Jefferson, North Carolina

ISBN (print) 978-0-7864-9949-6
ISBN (ebook) 978-1-4766-2739-7

LIBRARY OF CONGRESS CATALOGUING DATA ARE AVAILABLE

British Library cataloguing data are available

On the cover Hippies and others at a "happening" in Golden Gate Park in San Francisco, 1968 Documentary *Revolution* (Lopert Pictures Corporation/Photofest)

Printed in the United States of America

McFarland & Company, Inc., Publishers
Box 611, Jefferson, North Carolina 28640
www.mcfarlandpub.com

Acknowledgments

Rarely does one earn the distinction of having written a book without the key support of relatives, friends, colleagues, and mentors. Thus, it is a pleasure to thank the many people who helped and encouraged me with this endeavor. My first thank you, as always, goes to Ira Gruber, Harris Masterson, Jr., professor emeritus of history, Rice University, who, since my days as a graduate student at Rice, has been one of my strongest supporters in all of my scholarly efforts. Ira is one of the most selfless, compassionate, genuine, and thoughtful human beings I have ever known and it is an honor to call him both mentor and friend. Ira continues to inspire me, for he is a great model for what it means to be totally dedicated to the life of the mind.

Within my home department of the Houston Community College System, I received the kind support that represents the best of my fellow historians and colleagues. I am especially grateful to Mike Botson, who in his own right is a first-rate historian and who took the time out from his own work to read not only the manuscript but offer insights and criticisms that forced me to go beyond where I was in my own thinking about the hippies and the book's overall intent. I would also like to thank our department chair, Bennie Ables, who is unequivocal in her support of our scholarly undertakings, doing all she can to sustain and promote our efforts to show the larger community that the HCC history department values the academic and intellectual pursuits and accomplishments of its faculty.

Along with several other HCC colleagues, I ventured to the Gulf state of Qatar in 2010 on behalf of HCC to help open the region's first community college. While in Qatar I came to know HCC folk that I had previously never met and two of them, Ms. Dana Fields and Ms. Helen McMillan, became not only colleagues and close friends but key individuals in the final delivery of this book. Both provided invaluable assistance in helping me to arrange the chapters, notes, and bibliography, along with meticulous proofreading and formatting. I thank them both most profusely. Another HCC/CCQ colleague who generously gave her time proofreading every page, offering stylistic suggestions along the way, was professor of political science and government Barbara Loggins. Barbara also helped me to "remember" aspects of hippiedom that I had forgotten! Finally, I would like to thank all the individuals—friends, colleagues, and relatives—who graciously discussed with me where they were, who they were, and what they were doing during the 1960s. Their stories, memories, and interpretations then and now of the events and people of that era proved invaluable in helping to shape the historical contours and landscape of this book.

Aesthetically, this book would not have been possible without the photographs that will give readers a wonderful pictorial image of the 1960s and the hippie movement. It is thus with the greatest appreciation and affection that I thank our two oldest daughters, Michelle and Christina Moretta, both of who took time out from their own busy work schedules to scour the photograph archives at the San Francisco Public Library and the Bancroft Library on the campus of the University of California, Berkeley, to find the never-before-seen photos from the period found throughout this book. From the SFPL collection, especially noteworthy were those taken by Dennis Maness, as he captured on camera hippiedom's early years as it was evolving in the Haight-Ashbury neighborhood in San Francisco, climaxing with the hippies' first major coming-out party, the January 1967 Human Be-In, celebrated in the city's famed Golden Gate Park. Thank you Dennis for your permission to use your photos in this book. I would also like to thank Ms. Crystal Miles of the Bancroft Library who was most gracious in helping Michelle and me to locate those photo collections at the Bancroft germane to the hippies and the 1960s in general. Some of the most exemplary were taken by Larry Keenan, who sadly passed away a few years ago. However, thanks to the kindness and generosity of his daughter Chelsea and his wife, Lisa, Larry's iconic photos can be seen in this book as they are indispensable to the telling of the hippie story and the 1960s.

Of all the encouragement I received to complete this undertaking, no one was more reassuring and confident in my ability to do so than my wife, Chris. From her understanding of this project's importance to her reading of every paragraph, she was always there, never hesitating to help in whatever way she could. She was my sharpest critic, most determined advocate, muse, best editor, closest friend and confidante. No written tribute could ever express my deep appreciation for the faith, patience, and love she has demonstrated throughout our forty years of marriage.

Table of Contents

Acknowledgments v

Introduction: The World of the Hippies 1

1. The Beats, the Culture of Consensus and Suburban America 7

2. The Haight-Ashbury and the Emergence of the Hippies 32

3. Hippies and the Emergence of the Drug Culture 57

4. The Hippies and Rock and Roll 82

5. The October 1966 Love Pageant Rally 114

6. The 1967 Human Be-In 117

7. Hippies Elsewhere 139

8. The Summer of Love 167

9. The Monterey Pop Festival, June 1967: The Summer of Love's Defining Event 197

10. Communes and the Counterculture 211

11. The Emergence of the Yippies and the 1968 Chicago Democratic Convention: The Beginning of the End for the 1960s Counterculture 258

12. Woodstock, August 1969: A Brief Ray of Hope for the Hip Counterculture's Survival 285

13. The Manson Murders and the December 1969 Altamont Calamity: The Roads to Hippie Perdition 303

14. The Counterrevolution to the Counterculture: The Middle Class Backlash to a Decade of Excess 335

Epilogue and Legacy 351

Chapter Notes 367

Bibliography (Including Articles by Chapter) 401

Index 417

Introduction: The World of the Hippies

Riding the train from Casablanca to Marrakech, Morocco, in February 2014, the lyrics of "Marrakech Express" repeated through my head, on the way to the North African city that had been a favorite hippie destination in the late 1960s and early 1970s. *It still is.* By the late 1960s, with the explosion of psychedelic drugs and a desire to be immersed in nature, a renaissance in exotic travel and the quest for the mystical and the authentic emerged among the nation's latest bohemians, the hippies. It was the same passion for boundless travel and *real* life experiences that drove the 1950s Beats to many of the same locations. Marrakech became a compulsory stop for seekers on the original hippie trail to India, which for many, was the ultimate destination. It was there, they believed, as the Beatles had in their sojourn to India in 1968, that nirvana could be found, along with some of the best hashish in the world. The search for dope defined the hippie trail as the often treacherous roads, through scorching deserts and high mountain passes led to the major hash-producing centers of the world—Afghanistan, Chitral, Kashmir, and Nepal. These were familiar names to hippies, who knew very little else about those countries and their inhabitants, other than that they cultivated some of the finest-grade, highest quality weed on the planet. At that time, Marrakech's allure was not only the ready availability of one of the counterculture's favorite hallucinogenic drugs, hashish, but bountiful amounts of *kef,* which smoked in a shisha or hookah pipe, gave an even more intense high than marijuana or hashish. Both were in plentiful and in cheap supply in Marrakech and locals were more than happy to sell the opiate.

During the late 1960s and early 1970s the underground hashish trade was a lucrative business for many Moroccans, including the police, who turned a blind eye to this most profitable enterprise in which American hippies invested heavily. Adding to the city's hippie mystique were visits by some of the era's most notable rock and roll celebrities, such as Jimi Hendrix and the Rolling Stones, with the former said to have spent a few days in the picturesque Atlantic-seacoast city of Essaouira, about two hours from Marrakech. In both cities, "hippies" could be seen–not originals of course. Even more fascinating were the signs of residual hippiness in the form of many younger Europeans in their twenties and early to midthirties decked-out head to toe in stereotypical hippie attire and look; caricatures of the originals. It was as if they had sprung from an old *Life* or *Look* magazine loaded with photos of the original hippies, now photo-shopped, air-brushed, slicked-up, and come to life on the streets of Marrakech. Their 2014 chic, hip appearance from clothing to hairstyle was not even remotely the equivalent of the rag-tag, rucksack look of the original hippies, who rarely had enough money for a meal let alone the latest in bohemian fashion. The original hippies might have scoffed, referring to them as "plastic hippies."

But still, while these dread-and-jewelry adorned seekers might have been playing at being hippies, they were responding to the same siren call of the legendary Red City and the yearning for discovery of the mystical and exotic. In many ways they were not unfamiliar; they were a reminder of friends who dressed up to play hippie for a weekend, dabbling on the periphery of hippiedom by momentarily consuming countercultural symbolic commodities or by acting in stereotypical hippie behavior: smoking dope, dropping acid, or indulging in wild sexual escapades. For many such individuals the momentary transformation reflected a personal desire for a voyeuristic experience of the "other." In truth, the majority of weekend hippies were hesitant to fully embrace the counterculture life for fear of being cut off from their affluent, secure (white) suburban upbringing. The appearance of the 2014 pseudo-hippies also reflects how mainstream business enterprises, particularly the fashion industry, easily co-opts and profits from the desire of so many young people, both then and now, to be seen as hip. As will be seen in this book, such was also the case for the thousands of young people who came to the Haight-Ashbury in San Francisco both during and after the momentous Summer of Love in 1967; most simply *played* at being hippie.

Suffice it to say for me, a baby boomer, this evolution of the hippie vibe was simultaneously surprising, humorous, and revelatory. It was unexpected to see such stylized, cleaned-up caricatures of the hippies as they never were. Yet, they were proof that over forty-five years after the original hippies first appeared on the streets of San Francisco's Haight-Ashbury neighborhood, the hippies' historical reach and legacy has transcended both their own time and place to virtually every corner of the world in some manifestation or another and continues through music, fashion, and philosophy, into the present.

The 1960s hippie counterculture was overwhelmingly a youth movement, unprecedented in American history and one that drifted out of the most studied generation in the American experience. The baby boomers, born in the immediate aftermath of World War II—circa 1946 until the year 1964–represents the largest generation ever to exist in the nation at one time and they are possessed of a mentality, temperament, and way of looking at life and the world in general that was much different from any previous generation of Americans. In truth, hippies completely redefined that favorite American adjective "free," giving it a meaning that still resonates with many current baby boomers, who could be accused of seeing themselves as "forever young." They feel free to come and go as they pleased and to choose to do whatever made them feel spiritually, emotionally, and sensually fulfilled. The hippies represented John Winthrop's nightmare of three centuries earlier come to pass—a wholesale redefinition of freedom as the renunciation of all authority.

By the close of 1967, scores of Haight-Ashbury–replicated mini-worlds had emerged in most of the nation's major cities, splitting American socio-cultural history into a momentous Before and After not seen since the end of World War II. Even though the hip dream ended almost before it began, for a brief moment the latent power of the hippie ethos, along with other countercultural affinity groups, helped to shift the foundations of American post-war culture while challenging the liberal consensus which had sustained those assumptions, expectations, and institutions since the New Deal. At that time if you were between the ages of fifteen and thirty it was virtually impossible to resist hippiedom's many appeals and attractions, whether they came in the form of sexual freedom, mind-altering drugs, rock and roll music, rollicking dancehalls and free concerts in the parks, flamboyant clothing, outrageous street theatrics, the occult, Eastern mysticism, or cooperative/communal living. The new counter-culture had something for everyone. In some form or another, the hippie phenomenon per-meated every facet of American culture and society, ushering in so many personal liberations and awakenings that people's lives changed forever, in balance, mostly for the better, but in many instances, unfortunately, for the worst.

Nonetheless, the hippies' impact on American culture and society was significant, leaving an imprint that many in subsequent generations continue to honor in look, behavior, and attitude. Because of the hippies' relatively brief visible presence (less than ten years) many have relegated the counterculture as having been nothing more than the perennial adolescent defiance of authority displayed by every generation, and thus many histories of the era reduce the hippies into a bundle of clichés. Even many liberal, left-leaning historians tend to represent the hip counterculture as a self-absorbed, naïve, if not delusional, drug-obsessed rebellion that was doomed to failure because of the hippies' apolitical mentality and quest for personal freedom rather than social justice.[1] Suffice it to say, such assessments or outright dismissal, fall far short of relating the hippies' significance in American socio-cultural history. The 1960s counterculture was a movement and ethos of changing values and norms that have transcended their own time and continue to resonate with many Americans on a daily basis in a variety of different manifestations. In most instances, the reflection is subtle; at other moments it is glaringly obvious that the look, behavior, attitude, even the vocabulary, is a direct throwback to the hippie counterculture. Joe McDonald (lead singer of the acid-rock band Country Joe and the Fish, and author of one of the era's greatest anti-war protest songs, "The Fish Cheer" or "I Feel Like I'm Fixin' to Die Rag," memorialized at Woodstock), maintains that hippie happenings such as the 1967 Summer of Love were seminal, becoming "the template for Arab Spring and Occupy Wall Street. And it became the new status quo. The [new] Aquarian Age! They all want sex. They all want to have fun. Everyone wants hope. We opened the door, and everybody went through it, and everything changed after that."[2]

As the hippies became associated with a burgeoning, spectacular new subculture, they naturally drew not only media attention but that of scholars, who flocked to the hippie scene like flies to honey, eager to analyze and interpret for the larger public what had caused this most recent phenomenon of *bohemia exotica*. Although most of the academic assessments of the time reflected a genuine desire to explain the hippie counterculture as objectively as pos-sible, there were still a significant number of publications that perpetuated or reinforced the stereotypical and exoticized notions of hippiedom popularized by the mainstream media. One notable contemporary exception was Theodore Roszak's *The Making of a Counterculture*, a classic primer for anyone interested in exploring the hippies' socio-cultural and ideological foundations. Roszak's thesis was straightforward: the hippie revolt reflected a sincere, col-lective fear of, and antagonism toward, the "technocratization" of American society and cul-ture, which was destroying humanism, authenticity, and personal relationships. To Roszak, the hippie revolt represented a genuine rejection of 1960s mainstream America that raised deep ethical issues that "delv[ed] into the very meaning of reality, sanity, and human purpose," from which "grew the most ambitious agenda for the reappraisal of cultural values that any society has ever produced."[3] It must also be remembered that the hippies did not simply appear out of nowhere in 1966 in San Francisco; they represented a countercultural historical trend in American history that even pre-dated the Beats, that of the those other non-conformists, the Romantics of the early to mid–19th century, embodied in the writings and lifestyles of Ralph Waldo Emerson, Henry David Thoreau and Walt Whitman, all of whom were deeply admired within the hippie community. Also inspiring the counterculture was the "critique of conformity" that had emerged among liberal intellectuals and social critics by the late 1950s and which gained currency during the political crises of the 1960s. By the late 1960s many hippies believed their revolt against the status quo reflected precisely what William H. Whyte wrote about in *Organization Man,* or Sloan Wilson in *The Man in the Grey Flannel Suit.*[4]

When writing about a socio-cultural movement as amorphous as that of the late 1960s hippies, it is crucial to observe the historical context from which this particular brand of dissenters emerged. The present work identifies the hippies as among the more significant contributors to 20th century American countercultural history. The historical literature on the 1960s in general is vast and seems to increase with each passing decade, reflecting the keen interest and fascination Americans have with that time period, one of the most pivotal eras in post–World War II United States history. Many of these accounts portray the decade as a ten-year fall from grace, the demise of the liberal consensus that had governed the nation since the New Deal, and the end of an Edenic epoch of shared values and accepted standards of behavior and civil discourse, even appropriate forms of disobedience. However, missing from the historical literature is a general history of the hippies, specifically a survey of the broad sweep of this great socio-cultural youth rebellion that variously intrigued and disgusted mainstream Americans. In the bulk of the larger anthologies the hippies usually receive a peripheral, one chapter synopsis. The majority of the authors of these works believe the hippies to have been of secondary importance to the much more socially and politically conscious activist-oriented groups, such as the SDS or the civil rights movement. Both no doubt played key roles in shaping the youth rebellion of the 1960s but often relegated to the fringe are the hippies, who in the end had a much farther historical reach than the student activists and the many other socio-politically charged affinity groups that emerged as the decade progressed.

Indeed, when many Americans think of the 1960s youth rebellion against conventional American society, more often than not, the images they conjure are those of the hippies, whom many believed reflected the mentality and behavior of the majority of 1960s young people. To be sure the hippies were the most visibly spectacular and recognizable social rebels of that era, but to claim them to be the quintessence of American youth protest, or *the counterculture,* is inaccurate. The hippies merely became the most easily identifiable, ready-made challengers to the established order to emerge in the 1960s. They became part of a larger countercultural impulse that had its origins among those white middle class youth who participated in the civil rights crusade of the early 1960s, or among the alienated who found sanctuary for their despair in the ephemeral Beat phenomenon. As the decade progressed and increasing numbers of disaffected white youth sought more meaning to their lives than what mainstream America had to offer, many found momentary escape and fulfillment by joining the burgeoning ranks of young dissidents, whose identity groups coalesced to become the "counterculture." The 1960s counterculture thus became a youth-oriented/driven anti-authoritarian, anti-status quo, anti-bourgeois movement encompassing a variety of affinity groups and ideologies, many of which shared a common ethos while displaying similar attitudes and behaviors in their respective protests against the Establishment. However, in any study of the hippies it is imperative not to conflate them with the era's other nonconformists, even though that is precisely how the majority of straight Americans came to view *all* of the decade's young renegades, especially those who looked the stereotypical part: a young male with longish hair, who smoked dope, was slovenly dressed, and who lived in some sort of communal arrangement, was surely a hippie. As the 1960s progressed and increasingly more "normal" American youth embraced aspects of the hip look, attitude, or behavior, many Americans believed that the nation's young had all "gone to hell in a handbasket"; they had all become *hippies*.

Many forget, or even lump into the same category as the hippies, the highly politicized student activists, represented by such organizations as the Students for a Democratic Society (SDS), who dismissed the hippies as spoiled, escapist bourgeois brats who would rather remain in a drug-induced stupor than crusade against the inequities and injustices that university campus radicals believed afflicted the nation during the 1960s. The student activists in general were much more vocal and visible than the hippies, especially as their protests against the Vietnam War and the failure of Great Society liberalism to deliver up the poor and disenfranchised intensified. So determined were the activists to stop the war, the draft, and to ultimately bring down the Johnson administration for who they blamed "Amerika's sicknesses," that they were willing to engage in direct, often violent confrontation with local police or the National Guard. All such encounters were graphically illustrated on the nightly television news. Despite both groups' media-enhanced and exaggerated presence, the hippies and the student radicals more often than not represented antithetical countercultural groups and neither represented the majority sentiments and behaviors of white middle class youth (from both white and blue collar communities) in the 1960s. The preponderance of young white Americans were "straight" and remained so throughout that most turbulent decade.

Interestingly the general socio-cultural conservative backlash that began in the late 1970s and is presently referred to in popular jargon as "the culture wars" has unfortunately resurrected an attitude of denigration of most liberal social movements in American history and the hippies remain a favorite target of reactionary derision. They have been relegated to have been "little more than an adolescent outburst," or as an historical aberration of "the children of the favored classes turning political tantrums into terrorism."[5] To such critics the word counterculture (by which hippie is implied) has become a pejorative; an epithet almost as menacing to them as the term liberal. Although most informed Americans dismiss such attacks, they nonetheless continue to see and define the hippie movement in the simplest, most comprehensible frame of reference: a naïve and indulgent party that lasted a few years, thrown by a group of white middle-class suburban youth, who focused their lives on the clichéd triad of sex, drugs, and rock and roll. However, it must be remembered that for those young men and women who embraced that mantra, the phrase meant much more to them than the pursuit of individual pleasure and collective liberation from the soul-crushing, mindless conformity and "uptight" attitudes, behaviors, and strictures of 1960s white middle class America. As the hippie movement proliferated throughout the land, these indulgences became important identifiers and bonds; manifestations of allegiance to, and membership in, an amorphous but *real* and growing countercultural community. While these dynamics no doubt shaped much of the hippies' behavior and ethos, they were largely stylistic and did not define hippie identity. The hippie impulse was much deeper, more complex, genuine, serious, appealing, and thus a more momentous "happening" than the mainstream media, critics, or the general public realized at the time.

Then, who were the hippies and what was the counterculture they represented? It is my hope that the following pages will convey that the hippie culture of the 1960s was a group of people who first identified themselves by what they were *not*, and then engaged in a way of living that they believed would lead them down the path toward the creation of a New Age; a society and culture that was more humane, spiritual, and free than any that had existed before. Hippie philosophy stressed the need for pacifism, quietism, creativity, gratification, and community. Hippies translated these values into a radical break with mainstream society's institutions, culture, and lifestyle. Instead of aggression, destructive productivity, obscene commercialism, and conspicuous consumption, the hippie ethos affirmed peace, love, sensuousness, environmentalism, and a simple, less materialistic life. Hippies envisioned the ideal community as one where everyone was turned on and happy and floating free. Their goal wasn't one long party but rather to create a new society that integrated art and life.

In the last twenty years interest in the hippies and their legacy has increased and concomitantly, so has the number of historical treatments, most of which focus on specific facets of the hip lifestyle, ranging from the street theatrics and anarchism of the Diggers; the hippies' identification with Native Americans; the resurrection of communal living; the importance of the music and hip persona of Jimi Hendrix as a countercultural icon; the emergence of hip communities outside of the Haight-Ashbury in San Francisco; and the reinterpreting of the role countercultural women played in shaping the hippie movement. These studies represent the work of those historians who have broken new ground in redefining the 1960s hippies and counterculture in general. In the process, they have contributed significantly to helping erase what had been for several years the standard assessment of the hippie movement, which had been the reduction of the hip narrative down to sex, drugs, and rock and roll. Indeed, the cliché has it that the hippies danced at Woodstock, self-destructed at Altamont, and woke up one morning sometime in the 1970s, looked in the mirror, concluded that they had deluded themselves into thinking that they could change the nation's socio-cultural landscape and ethos, and decided to rejoin the very bourgeois culture and society they had previously disparaged. Some re-entered mainstream life on a grand scale, becoming over time ice-cream moguls, media magnates, and triangulating politicians. Yet, for every ex–flower child who "sold out" to the post–1960s Establishment, thousands more, in some form or another, have remained true to the hippie spirit. This book is an interpretive synthesis, drawn from both primary and secondary source material that exams those individuals, ideas, and pivotal events in the making and unraveling of the hippies.

Although many tried, (and some are still trying), to make the hippie vision real there were too many countervailing forces arrayed against the hippies at the time for them to succeed. In the end those forces simply overwhelmed one of the most important countercultural movements in United States history; one whose legacy has become one of the most enduring in the American story.

1

The Beats, the Culture of Consensus and Suburban America

"By avoiding society you become separate from society and being separate from society is being Beat!"—Beat poet Gregory Corso

On the evening of October 13, 1955, around 11 Pacific time, twenty-nine-year-old Allen Ginsberg, wearing Levis and a navy sweater, made his way to the lectern at the Six Gallery, looking like a "horn-rimmed intellectual hepcat,"[1] to read his now-classic T.S. Eliot–Walt Whitmanesque epic poem "Howl." A renovated automobile repair shop located at 3110 Fillmore Street and named after six unrecognized artists, the Six Gallery opened in 1954, offering the perfect setting for an organized reading with the intent, as Ginsberg declared "to defy the system of academic poetry, official reviews, New York publishing machinery, national sobriety, and generally accepted standards of good taste."[2] A tangibly excited crowd of over 100 had assembled, marking the first time since the end of World War II that the scattered denizens of San Francisco's intelligentsia-bohemia had come together. Typical of such San Franciscan social events, the assemblage comprised individuals from all walks of life including college professors, political radicals, poets, carpenters, and civic leaders; the perfect composite of the city's avant-garde, the working class, and varietal "straights," who for decades had demonstrated an uncanny ability to get along, and despite lifestyle differences and socio-economic disparity, could come together at public functions and help promote their city's rich pluralistic traditions and diversity. The intimate 500-square foot place had white walls, dirt floors, and a makeshift dais erected before a backdrop of surrealist furniture made from orange crates and plaster dipped muslin. A semi-circle of chairs was set up for poets or others who wished to share with the community their particular aesthetic medium.[3]

Ginsberg had been working sporadically on "Howl" for the past two years but decided two weeks before his public reading that it was time to finish it, come what may. He plunged himself into a frenzy to complete the poem, working day and night, ingesting peyote, amphetamine, and Dexedrine to sustain his creative impulse. Rumor has it that Ginsberg was still tinkering with his opus until he stepped to the podium. He started his reading in an earnest but somewhat nervous voice, having never read publicly before. Fortified with several glasses of cheap California burgundy, Ginsberg's exuberance and voice's intensity grew as he fed off the crowd's enthusiasm. The electrified audience shouted "Go! Go! Go!" as Ginsberg's tranquil demeanor gave way to an evangelical jeremiad of helplessness and despair. Swaying rhythmically, waving his arms, taking deep breaths to sustain him through each of the long verse lines, he was a wild troubadour, and the audience had never heard such vividly raw language in public. "I saw the best of my generation destroyed by madness, starving, hysterical naked, / dragging themselves through the Negro streets at dawn looking for an angry fix, / angelheaded hipsters burning for the ancient heavenly / connection to a starry dynamo in the machinery of night / whose poverty and tatters and hollow-eyed and high sat up smoking in / the supernatural darkness of cold-water flats floating across the / tops of cities contemplating jazz / who bared their brains to Heaven under the El and saw Mohammedan / angels staggering on tenement roofs illuminated."[4] According to the evening's emcee, San Francisco aesthetic Kenneth Rexroth, by the time Ginsberg had finished reading his fourth stanza, the audience was "gasping, laughing, and swaying; they were psychologically had, it was an orgiastic occasion."[5]

From the poem's opening lines to its last verse—"in my dreams you walk dripping from a sea-journey on the highway across America in tears to the door of my cottage in the Western night"—Ginsberg graphically created menacing and despairing images of a 1950s mainstream culture that not only had made life miserable for himself as a Jewish homosexual, but for all the other outcasts, rebels, and down-and-outs who already had been "gobbled up," or spit out and forgotten by the rest of society. Christening 1950s mainstream culture "Moloch," after a Semitic deity who ate children, he ranted "Moloch! Solitude! Filth! Ashcans and unobtainable dollars! Children screaming under / the stairways! Boys sobbing in the armies! Old men weeping in the parks! / Moloch whose mind is pure machinery! Moloch whose / blood is running money! Moloch whose fingers / are ten armies! Moloch whose breast is cannibal dynamo / Moloch whose ear is smoking tomb!" Cold War paranoia had caused such repression, fear, and resignation to the status quo. Ginsburg and his fellow Beats tried to find solace and personal escape from such madness by "purgatory[ing]" their "torsos night after night with dreams, with drugs, with waking nightmares, alcohol and cock and endless balls."[6]

Ginsberg offered no resolution, political nor spiritual, for the state of affairs he had just described, believing redemption impossible. In the end, all would go mad: Americans, who had cried out against such soul-sucking oppression would become so alienated and full of despair that they would end up with all of the rest of history's mad seers and lost visionaries in insane asylums. "I'm with you in Rockland [New York's state mental hospital] / where you scream in a straightjacket that / you're losing the game of the actual pingpong of the abyss / I'm with you in Rockland / where fifty more shocks will never return your soul to its body again from its pilgrimage to a cross in the void."[7]

Ginsberg's poem was not only about his generation's sense of alienation from 1950s mainstream culture; "Howl" also openly promoted drug usage to help ease the spiritual, emotional, and psychological pain society inflicted on individuals unwilling to live by conventional standards. Most controversial was Ginsberg's use of graphic sexual imagery and language, especially when describing homo-erotic encounters. Ginsberg not only unveiled his own homosexuality in "Howl" but exalted as well gay sexual escapades. Ginsburg's explicit language and flaunting and exultation of homosexuality in an era when gays were often more vilified than communists outraged white middle class moral sensibilities and accepted standards of intimate behavior.

Emotionally drained after fifteen minutes of delivery, Ginsberg recalled that he dissolved in "tears which restored to American poetry the prophetic consciousness it had lost since the conclusion of Hart Crane's 'The Bridge.'" Rexroth, equally emotionally moved, later recalled that Ginsberg's reading "just blew things up." Ginsberg's peers all agreed that they had witnessed an individual's transformation. Poet/dramatist Michael McClure, who had read his work just before Ginsberg, believed "Howl" was "Allen's metamorphosis from a quiet, burning bohemian scholar, trapped by his flames of repressions, to epic vocal bard." The transfiguration extended beyond Ginsberg to accelerate the communal promotion of San Francisco's Beat community. McClure later recalled, "We had gone beyond a point of no return—and we were ready for it, for a point of no return. None of us wanted to go back to the gray, chill, militaristic silence, to the intellectual void, to the land without poetry—to the spiritual drabness.... Ginsberg left us standing, wondering, cheering but knowing at the deepest level that a barrier had been broken, that a human voice and body had been hurled against the harsh wall of America and its supporting armies and navies and academies and institutions and ownership systems and power-support bases. We wanted voice and we wanted vision," and Ginsberg had provided both to his fellow Beats.[8]

Perhaps the most important congratulation came from poet/bookstore owner/publisher Lawrence Ferlinghetti, whose City Lights Bookstore at 261 Columbus Avenue in the North Beach area, had become one of the City's bohemians' favorite haunts. Ferlinghetti had missed the evening's performance but had heard of its electrifying affect on all in attendance. In a telegram Ferlinghetti told Ginsberg that "I GREET YOU AT THE BEGINNING OF A GREAT CAREER. WHEN DO I GET THE MANUSCRIPT?" Interestingly, Ginsberg, who had arrived in San Francisco two years before his epic reading, had showed Ferlinghetti some poems he had been writing in a journal for the past several years and which William Carlos Williams had liked. Ferlinghetti was intrigued, for a young poet to have his work blessed by someone of Williams' stature was to be taken seriously. Ginsberg also mentioned his work in progress, "Howl." Neither man could have imagined that this poem would eventually expose both Allen Ginsberg and his patron, Lawrence Ferlinghetti and his little bookstore on Columbus Avenue in North Beach to international fame and notoriety. Nor could either poet have realized that they would be among the key players in igniting the "San Francisco Renaissance" of the Beat era.[9]

Ironically, *Howl's* initially notorious place in American culture owed most to Captain William Hanrahan of the San Francisco police department's Juvenile Bureau, and the United States Customs Collector for San Francisco, Chester MacPhee. Ferlinghetti published 1,000 copies of *Howl and Other Poems* (Number 4 in his Pocket Poet Series) in November 1956 knowing full well that "Howl's" explicit sexual imagery and obscenities would arouse the censors and other conservatives disturbed by the poem's "vulgarities." Ferlinghetti took some precaution with the text, placing asterisks "on the dirty words." Within a week of the collection's release, Ferlinghetti had sold all 1,000 copies. His local printer could not handle a larger order so Ferlinghetti contacted a British printing company who agreed to print 5,000 more. No sooner did the books arrive at the port of San Francisco (March 1957), than they were seized by Collector of Customs, Chester MacPhee, who hoped to not to let them see the light of day based on their obscene content. Despite MacPhee's attempts to confiscate the books, he eventually was forced to release them to Ferlinghetti who placed them on his shelves. Again, patrons lined up outside the door to buy copies, some purchasing several at a time. However, on May 21, 1957, Hanrahan ordered the arrest of Ferlinghetti and Shigeyoshi Murao, City Lights Bookstore manager, who had sold *Howl* to two plainclothes policemen,

City Lights Bookstore owner Lawrence Ferlinghetti holding the book of poems by Allen Ginsberg that put both his establishment and the San Francisco Beat scene on the 1950s countercultural radar. Photograph taken in August 1957 (courtesy San Francisco History Center, San Francisco Public Library).

on obscenity charges. The Beat literati were enraged and so were many of the nation's poetic establishment, such as William Carlos Williams who quipped, "Howl is an arresting poem."[10]

Not only did many of the nation's most prominent men and women of letters rally to Murao's and Ferlinghetti's defense but so did the American Civil Liberties Union, believing the matter to be a precedent-setting First Amendment case. During the trial, which began in the summer of 1957, ACLU attorneys marched literary experts one after another to the stand,

From the moment he read his seminal epic poem "Howl" until the day he died, Allen Ginsberg remained in the vanguard of the post–World War II countercultural rebellion against the United States' Cold War ethos. Photograph taken in October 1963 (photograph by Eddie Murphy of the *San Francisco News-Call Bulletin,* courtesy San Francisco History Center, San Francisco Public Library).

with many proclaiming *Howl* to be as monumental to American literature as Walt Whitman's *Song of Myself* and *Leaves of Grass*. One critic called "Howl" the "Waste Land" of the younger generation, and poet-critic Mark Schorer opined that Ginsberg's inclusion of street language and homosexuality and other alleged "obscenities" was necessary to convey to readers "the picture the author is trying to give us of modern life as a state of hell." To the shock of censorship advocates but to the delight of the Beats, the ACLU, and to the majority of the nation's literary community, Ferlinghetti and Murao were found not guilty. The trial not only provided a beacon of light for free expression but a spotlight trained on the Beats. Indeed, by 1958, 20,000 copies of *Howl and Other Poems* were in print; as of 2012, over one million copies have been sold worldwide.[11]

Both the Six Gallery and the epochal poetry reading held there that evening epitomized the burgeoning post–World War II avant-garde that had been percolating in cities like San Francisco and New York for several years. However, at the time of Ginsberg's reading, the overwhelming majority of Americans had never heard of the "Beats," let alone their personal and collective outrageous escapades, spiritual quests, and sexual explorations, all of which became the *raison d'être* of both their literature and individual lives. By 1955 a few, sporadic articles had appeared about the Beats in the nation's more progressive metropolitan newspapers such as the *New York Times* and in some of the nation's more radical journals. By the late 1950s, thanks in large part to Ginsberg's performance at the Six Gallery the Beat Generation would be out of obscurity and into mainstream popular culture. Although their star-power was brief, they would nonetheless become one of post–World War II's America's most influential countercultural forces, providing the template and inspiration for the most important countercultural phenomenon in post–World War II America, the hippies.

Indeed, for many hippies, Ginsberg would become one of the most sanctified gurus, the embodiment in spirit of their movement's ideals and purpose. According to Theodore Roszak, through his poems, Ginsberg became "the vagabond proselytizer of the new consciousness for the disaffiliated young of America and much of Europe."[12] Ginsberg believed as fervently as most hippies in the transformative power of psychedelic drugs and Eastern spiritual traditions, which Ginsberg and many of his Beat compatriots had embraced long before the first hippie quoted the sacred texts of Zen Buddhism. Ginsberg regularly attended the hippies' "gathering of the tribes" to recite his poetry, propagate Eastern philosophy and spirituality, and lead the crowds in Vedic chanting. Although a reluctant leader to the legions of hippies who venerated him, Ginsberg nonetheless took his role seriously as guru, doing all he could to ease the tensions between the countercultures of the Beats and hippies, as well as between 1960s New Left political activists and the hippies. True to his pacifist core and devotion to propagating the hippie love ethos, Ginsberg even believed rapprochement possible between a hostile straight world and the counterculture. Ginsberg continued to write poetry through the 1980s while he traveled the college circuit, passionately advocating to new generations of American youth the importance of spirituality, free speech, and the beauty of poetry. In 1997, one of the most revered countercultural icons died from liver cancer. Ginsberg's literary legacy is one of the most influential of modern American writers; his presence and activism during one of the most pivotal decades (1960s) in post–World War II America made him a socio-cultural and historical tour de force. Soon after Ginsberg's death, a reviewer for *The Economist* declared that "Like it or not, no voice better reflected his times than Mr. Ginsberg's. He was a bridge between the literary avant-garde and pop culture."[13]

Although he never embraced the hippie movement, dismissing its followers as effete wastrels, void of any intellectual or literary creativity or aesthetics in general, Jack Kerouac's classic *On the Road*, nonetheless influenced many a hippie. Kerouac based his characters on real individuals, and his personal relationship and experiences with them. For his protagonist Kerouac chose the revered Neal Cassady, who to Kerouac and other Beats was a vital force of raw energy and physical fearlessness. To Kerouac, Cassady epitomized "Beatdom," becoming Kerouac's real-life alter ego. Like Ginsberg and a handful of others Beats, Cassady would transition into the hippie counterculture of the 1960s, becoming a legendary member of Ken

Beat icon Neal Cassady with former girlfriend Anne Murphy, Oakland, California, 1966 (photograph by Larry Keenan, courtesy Bancroft Library, University of California, Berkeley. © 1997 Larry Keenan. All rights reserved).

Kesey's coterie of devoted acid-heads, the Merry Pranksters. Kerouac based his story on the actual cross-country car trip he and Cassady had taken together in the fall of 1946 in a silver Hudson Hornet, speeding here and there; stealing food or working as laborers or dishwashers to earn some gas money, sleeping in the outdoors or in their car, and of course picking up girls and having wild sex with as many as possible.[14]

For Kerouac the journey represented the search to find in motion what had been lost in time; that spiritually transcendent moment when mind and experience became one; what Kerouac referred to as "IT." He believed IT defined the essence of Beat as well as his own personal, perpetual restlessness. Only by physically moving, searching, and indulging in every real human experience could that amorphous but all-important IT be found and celebrated and enveloped. For Kerouac and his fellow Beats, as it would be for most 1960s hippies, finding IT also required one to disassociate themselves completely from white middle class hegemonic culture and its attendant acquisitive values, oppressive ethics, and rational analysis; its grand expectations, and phony aspirations. IT could only be found by living in the impulsive moment of immediacy; by engaging in ethereal flights of "fancy, sensuality, and community."[15] Perhaps most important to both Beats and hippies, their respective collective ITs could only be discovered by a devotion to authentic experience at all times in one's life.

For a variety of personal and professional reasons, it took Kerouac six years to get his work published, which Viking Press finally agreed to do in the fall of 1957. Much to Kerouac's and his Beat compatriots' delight, mainstream literary critics and reviewers, such as Gilbert Millstein of the *New York Times*, proclaimed *On the Road* "an authentic work of art," and "the most beautifully executed, clearest and most important utterance yet made by the generation Kerouac himself named years ago as 'beat.'" Millstein was so impressed by *On the Road* that he believed it to be in the same league as Hemingway's *The Sun Also Rises*, which he believed was the definitive work of the Lost Generation and was certain "that *On the Road* will come to be known as that of the Beat Generation."[16] Soon after Millstein's rave review, *On the Road* climbed onto the best seller list where it stayed for five weeks, peaking at number eleven. Within two weeks of publication it went into a second printing and by year's end 500,000 copies had been sold.

The publication of *On the Road* and *Howl*, brought the Beat movement out of obscurity and into popular culture. While some critics lambasted 1950s culture implicitly, the Beats challenged it frontally. To the surprise if not shock of many mainstream Americans, young people and others tired of middle American blandness and banality, welcomed the Beats' outrageousness, not only in their literature and poetry, but in their attitudes and behavior as well. Ginsberg, Kerouac and a host of less-celebrated Beats not only became the cultural heroes of the disaffected, but through their poetry and prose exposed many young Americans to their exotic, erotic, subterranean urban world. *On the Road* is a classic tale of wanderlust men seeking freedom from all societal restraints and personal commitments. Yet, for all their cultural and lifestyle exoticism, the Beats were solidly of the American fiber. Ginsberg's plea to "return to nature and revolt against the machine" echoed the American Romantics and Transcendentalists Ralph Waldo Emerson and Henry David Thoreau. Kerouac's main characters, Sal Paradise and Dean Moriarity were 1950s Huck Finns, preferring the freedom of the open road over civilization; Route 66 and the nation's other highways were their Mississippi River, and the Silver Hudson Hornet, their raft in which, like Huck and Jim, they experienced the liberation of open spaces; coming and going as they pleased wherever they wanted on the spur of the moment or not at all; whenever they felt like moving. Indeed, many Beats saw themselves carrying forward (as would many hippies) the mid–19th century Romantic countercultural movement against the onset of the American industrial revolution, when Transcendentalist writers such as Emerson in "Self-Reliance" (1841) and Thoreau in *Walden* (1854) warned of the dangers to the creative, the genuine, and the aesthetic unleashed by the burgeoning market economy with its increasing emphasis on profit and consumption. For the 1960s hippies it would be the fear of *real* life being obliterated by war and technology, which they saw as symbiotic, impelling them to reject the conventional bourgeois ethos of their time. Resistance to modernity, rooted in anti-materialism became one of the defining features of the 1950s and 1960s counterculture.[17]

The Beats were apolitical and fatalistic as a result of living with the prospect of nuclear holocaust. They believed the American political system had become so corrupt and controlled by corporations that it was beyond any sort of redemption, and thus participation in campaigns or crusades to try to return "power to the people" was delusional and thus futile. The Beats instead focused their energies on promoting and living a creative and aesthetic life. Instead of security, respectability, and careerism, the Beats searched for ecstasy, mystical experience, sexual release, and emotional honesty. Such notions were clearly unpopular in 1950s Cold War America, a time of profound individual powerlessness. Personal responsibility was rationalized in the interests of corporate growth and Americans became imprisoned in the new fetish of "togetherness," team work," "group-think," and "adjustment." In the Beat frame of reference such homogenization and conformity obliterated the ideas of individuality and the autonomy of private conscience. In their view, the United States had become a dehumanized, exploitive, bomb-shadowed, consumer driven, technocratic civilization beyond redemption and thus the Beats opted "to protest by disengagement—that is [they] did not fight the mainstream social order but ignored it. It was the early manifestation of 'dropping out.'"[18] This would also be the hippie perception of late 1960s American culture, society, and politics, and their response would also be one of complete detachment.

The word "beat" originally derived from circus and carnival argot to describe the hard-luck, dissipated, lives of nomadic carnies and their Big-Tent compatriots. In the hipster drug world of the 1940s and 1950s, beat meant robbed or cheated in a drug deal, whether it was loss of money or being sold "bad dope"—all reflected a "beat deal." It was Herbert Huncke, one of the white, urban underworld's first "white Negroes" or hipsters, who introduced the term to Ginsberg, Kerouac, and other Beat writers, who embraced and exalted the word to define the *raison d'être* of their art, literature, and existence as human beings. Ironically, Huncke never intended the word to be elevating, but the opposite: "I meant beaten. The world against me." But Kerouac believed Huncke's definition perfectly described his generation's feeling of discontent and estrangement from postwar America's acquisitive, materialistic mass culture. San Francisco poet Gregory Corso, who also became part of the Beat literary elite, reaffirmed that to be Beat one had to abandon completely conventional society, for "by avoiding society you become separate from society and being separate from society is being BEAT." By the early 1950s, Kerouac and Ginsberg began to emphasize the "beatific" quality of beat, imbuing the Beat existence with a mystical purpose and quest. "The point of Beat is that you get beat down to a certain nakedness where you are actually able to see the world in a visionary way," wrote Ginsberg.[19]

As the Beats inspired the hippies, so were the Beats informed by the world of 1930s and

1940s black hipsters. Since the days of slavery black folk have always been something of a counterculture in America. In white imagination, distinguishing blacks from whites was the alleged inherent inability of blacks to control their baser instincts, absurdly representing id run amok. In the aftermath of World War I, thousands of young Southern black men migrated to Northern ghettoes in hopes of finding not only greater economic opportunities but an environment in which they would have greater autonomy. Many found the lifestyle and behavior of the most recent manifestation of the black renegade, the hipster, to be especially appealing. The brash behavior and blatant contempt for white strictures of the legendary black prize fighter Jack Johnson energized the hipster, who was not only aggressively sexually driven and hedonistic, like Johnson, but openly disdainful as well of the white world that continued to exclude and oppress him. The hipsters insulated their world from white comprehension with the invention on Harlem street corners of "jive," an action language honed from its origins in the verbal art known as the "Dozens." Some jive words that became part of the hip lexicon were *cat, solid, cool, chick, square, groove, high, lay on, hip, fruit, The Man,* and *kicks. Ofay*, the jive word for white, meant foe in pig Latin. Favorite hipster attire was the zoot suit, an outfit consisting of long, loose coats with padded shoulders, ballooned pants pegged at the ankles, and wide-brimmed hat. A watch and chain and ducktail haircut completed the costume. It was a look, as hip garb would always be, to call attention to the individual while defying and outraging conventional taste. The hipster's favorite pastimes were listening to jazz music, smoking marijuana, and having sex, the most satisfying high of his indulgences.[20]

Nineteen-sixties hippies used all the same slang as their Beat and black hipster predecessors, adding somewhat new idioms such as "groovy" and "far out," to the lexicon. Beat and hippie slang combined and transformed the vocabulary of many subterranean worlds. Both incorporated into their vernacular, conversation, and written explications the argots of jazz and rock and roll musicians, drug users, carnival and circus workers, homosexuals, hipsters, and African Americans. Inside language creates community and belongingness to the isolated and disaffected while barring others from the clique. Both the hippies and their countercultural predecessors created a language and vocabulary of radical transgression; lingo and words that reflected their suspicion and hostility toward the status quo. Sixties counterculturists especially liked inflammatory words and expressions such as "revolution," which probably became one of the most worn bromides of the decade, for there appeared to be a "revolution" occurring every moment in some facet of 1960s life. There was a sexual revolution; a revolution in rock music; in filmmaking, the clothing industry, and fiction writing. As Todd Gitlin recalled, the word became a "supreme talisman."[21] Corporations, ironically, create their own special lingo, as do today's techno geeks and computer nerds, which many baby boomers often find as incomprehensible as their parents found their hip vocabulary during the 1950s and 1960s. Hip language became cliché by the early 1970s, as hundreds of words and expressions, previously considered countercultural became part of everyday, normal American parlance. But in its formative years, hip language came to define and express the countercultural, underground world of both the Beats and hippies.

Both Beat and hippie appropriation of black hipster vernacular and lifestyle reflected neither group's understanding of the historical factors that produced this particular manifestation of black expression of resistance to, or rejection of, white hegemonic culture. Few Beats and even fewer hippies had any interest in the civil rights movement, or even much of a desire to understand that much of what they admired and embraced as the quintessential countercultural life was born of deep, seething rage after decades of insult, degradation, and oppression. In effect, both the Beats and hippies selected those specific aspects of black deviance that they believed best described their similar feelings of alienation from mainstream white American society. Perhaps the best example of this reality was the phenomenal popularity of rock and roll music among the new white teenage generation that came of age during the late 1950s. Especially captivated by the new sound were suburbanites, who naively identified their own feelings of estrangement with the very different reality of the racism and discrimination encountered by rock and roll's African American progenitors, most of whose music had been appropriated and popularized by whites, who had become rock and rolls biggest stars by the late 1950s.[22]

As rock and roll would become the hippies defining medium of aesthetic expression, jazz was the most vital to the Beat lifestyle; a wholly, uniquely African American musical creation that emerged in the 1920s, becoming one of the most important, dynamic statements of the black creative impulse of that decade known as the Harlem Renaissance. From its inception, white mainstream culture condemned jazz for causing "a loosening of instincts that nature wisely has taught us to hold in check, but which every now and then, for cryptic reasons, are allowed to break the bonds of civilization."[23] Much to the chagrin of white critics, jazz attracted a significant white following, especially in the nation's larger metropolises such as New York and Chicago, where chic and hip upper class whites in particular, frequented the black jazz clubs such as the legendary Cotton Club in Harlem in the 1930s, enjoying Louis Armstrong or one of the many other black jazzmen's "hot," gritty trumpet or saxophone improvisations. Jazz changed however in the 1940s when a group of resentful renegade black jazzmen, led by saxophonist Charlie "Bird" Parker, created bebop. Prompting Parker, trumpeter Dizzy Gillespie, pianist Thelonious Monk, and others (most notably saxophonists Lester Young and John Coltrane), to originate the new genre was that fact by the 1940s much of their music had been appropriated by white big band leaders such as Benny Goodman and Tommy Dorsey, and commercialized into "swing" music. Bebop relied on small groups and complex improvisation, with long, introspective solos becoming the hallmark. The sound was "cool," the rhythm variable, the volume low, and the technical brilliance of its leading progenitors legend. Both black and white bebop musicians spurned the suburban middle class, sharing their highly personal vision with small audiences of rapt fans in smoky urban jazz clubs.[24] Considering bebop a form of dissent, the Beat generation considered the sound *the* countercultural music of the period.

Bebop ushered in a change in the hipster persona. Along with the sounds came the language, the dress, the pot, and the personal style affected by the black jazz musicians. The zoot suit disappeared along with other flamboyant attire, replaced by more conservative garb. Black became the favored color and jeans with a black sweater or turtleneck the preferred look, along with dark glasses. Loud, impulsive behavior became gauche; aloofness the required pose. A raised finger stood for a wave, brushed palms for a handshake. Indeed, the new hipster resembled that of feline indifference, and it was no accident that "cool cat" became the ultimate compliment. The new hipsters also borrowed marijuana as the drug of choice, but heroin, the ultimate "kick," was also widely used. Perhaps most important, by the 1950s, hipsters were no longer exclusively black. In New York and other big cities, disaffected white youth also embraced the hipster character, finding him to be the perfect embodiment for their own sense of alienation from and hostility toward mainstream white American culture. In novelist

Norman Mailer's view, thus emerged "the white Negro" who lived in an urban, subterranean world in which sex, pot, jazz, kicks—the daily pursuit for Dionysian ecstasy—defined his life.[25]

In a 1957 essay in the magazine *Dissent*, Mailer exalted and romanticized the new white hipster of the 1950s believing "years of conformity, oppression, and subsequently depression" gave rise to this latest manifestation of white deviance and rebellion. To Mailer, the "white Negro" (hipster) represented the decade's quintessential rebel, "an enfant terrible turned inside out," "a psychic outlaw," "the rebel cell in our social body," who emerged out of the metropolitan enclaves of disaffected white youth. It would be through the new hipster's quiet, rebellious, intrepid non-conformity, regardless of how dissipated the lifestyle, or "psychopathic" the behavior, that American "totalitarian society" would be resisted. Mailer saw the hipsters as inspiring people "to explore that domain of experience where security is boredom and therefore sickness, and to exist in the present, in that enormous present which is without past or future, memory or planned intention, the life where man must go until he is beat."[26]

This new breed of hipster represented a "ménage a trois" of the "bohemian, the [white] juvenile delinquent, and the Negro." In this amalgamation of deviance, "it was the Negro who brought the cultural dowry" because for decades African Americans (especially males) had lived with "the prospect of violence, perpetual oppression, and constant humility," creating the belief in many black urban males that "life was a war, nothing but a war." The result was the emergence of an individual who "for survival kept the art of the primitive," who lived in the present for "his Saturday night kicks, relinquishing the pleasures of the mind for the more obligatory pleasures of the body." Uniting all three was marijuana use, the hip vernacular, and bebop jazz, which gave expression to the "abstract states of feeling which all could share"; the "working philosophy" of America's "sub-worlds." As rock and roll would define the quintessence of the 1960s hippie, creating for many a euphoric, even an "orgasmic" experience, bebop jazz had penetrated "knife-like" into the soul of both white and black hipsters, giving "voice to the character and quality of [their] existence, rage, infinite variations of joy, lust, languor, growl, pinch, cramp, scream, and despair of orgasm. For jazz is orgasm, it is the music of orgasm, good orgasm and bad." In short, the new white hipster had "absorbed the existentialist synapses of the Negro and for practical purposes could be considered a white Negro."[27]

At the time of his essay, Mailer believed there were "not more than 100,000 men and women who consciously see themselves as hipsters." Despite their small numbers, Mailer was certain that they represented an "elite" cadre of rebels, who over time would increase in both stature and quantity as more and more adolescents embraced "the hipster's intense view of existence and their desire to rebel."[28] Mailer's forecast proved accurate; by the late 1960s millions of alienated white youth had adopted, in varying degrees and some completely, yet another manifestation of hip or "white Negro" persona, the hippie, who in many ways represented perhaps the crescendo as well as the metamorphosis on a grand, panoramic scale the nation's countercultural tradition.

By the early 1950s San Francisco had developed a bohemian and literary scene that paralleled the New York mood in its advocacy of the spontaneous, the primitive, and the outlaw. However, East Coast avant-garde intellectuals and writers dismissed their Bay Area counterparts as an eccentric collection of misfits and dilettantes not able to make it in the *real* literary province of New York. Despite such disparagement, many of the decade's most preeminent Beat writers and poets found the City by the Bay a mecca for a host of personal, professional, aesthetic, or academic reasons, and would continue to do so for several more decades. "In the spiritual and political loneliness of America in the fifties, you'd hitch a ride a thousand miles to meet a friend," wrote the poet Gary Snyder. "Whatever lives needs a habitat, a proper culture of warmth and moisture to grow. West coast of those days, San Francisco was the only city; and of San Francisco, North Beach."[29] Just as *Howl* and *On the Road* became literary focal points, North Beach became the San Francisco renaissance's geographic center and California in general and San Francisco in particular were fast becoming havens for the nation's bohemians. By the late 1960s, both the city and the state had become avant-garde retreats, and more importantly the progenitors of the country's most outrageous, ubiquitous, and popular countercultural movement in the Republic's history, the hippies.

By the late 1950s, thousands of gawking sightseers had made North Beach a must see on their visit to San Francisco. They came to stare and photograph America's latest manifestation of a counterculture, personified in the "beatnik," a term coined by *San Francisco Chronicle* columnist Herb Caen, six months after the October 1957 launching of the Soviet Union's sputnik, asserting that both the satellite and the new bohemian type were "equally far out."[30] Whether featured in *Time* or *Life* magazines or lampooned in *Mad*, the stereotyping became commonplace and publicly embraced. As presented by the media, the male version, the "cat," sported a goatee, the thinner and scragglier the better, had longish hair hanging loose over the collar, and no earrings or other piercings but occasionally a tattoo or two. No true beatnik male would be caught dead without his legendary black beret along with black jeans with a black turtleneck sweater, or in summer a white tee-shirt. On the feet were sandals of some sort, or hipster/jazzman pointy black shoes, or tennis shoes, usually black and white Converse, either high-tops or low-tops, and "shades" (dark sun glasses) completed the look. His favorite activities (other than sex), were smoking "reefers," playing the bongo drums, and chanting poetry as bebop played in the background.

The male beatnik's female counterpart was equally "out there"; a "chick" obvious in her waifish appearance, long, usually black straight hair, if not naturally that color, Lady Clairol did the trick; pale makeup, dark leotards and a dark skirt with either dark hose or leggings, and either sandals or very high-heeled black pumps. Her favorite pastimes were drinking espresso, attending poetry readings, and "consorting" with black jazz musicians. The beatniks' popular haunts were the dark coffee houses and dives of North Beach; or Venice in West Lost Angeles; the French Quarter in New Orleans; or New York's East Village. They lived in garret-like loft apartments, "pads," outfitted with shade-less lamps, a hot plate for warming espresso, and Mexican cow bells. They furnished their pads with bare mattresses, cheap prints, and dime-store cushions, phonographs on which bebop jazz records played non-stop. They appeared to function in a perpetual drug-induced haze with prolonged periods of languor interrupted by wild, manic euphoria. Most Americans would come to see hippies in a similar stereotypical light in the 1960s.

In the public mind and mainstream press, by the late 1950s, Ginsberg, Kerouac, and their compatriots had all become beatniks. Through various magazines such as *Time*, *Life*, and *Look*, the Beats were portrayed as not only anti-social deviants but as potentially subversive and anti–American as well. *Life* magazine summed up the Beats as "talkers, loafers, passive little con men, lonely eccentrics, mom-haters, cop-haters, exhibitionists with abused smiles, painters, who cannot paint, and dancers with unfortunate malfunction of the fetlocks." Even leftist critics who usually supported assaults on the 1950s status quo, dismissed the Beats as nothing more than "naughty children," whose alleged literature was not to be taken seriously and certainly not exalted because it was shrill, crude, and confessional. Writing in such journals as the *Partisan Review* and the *Nation*, they condemned the Beats for their anti-intellectualism, primitivism, and affectless manner of not caring about society and its problems.[31] Such criticism of Beat arts and letters led Kenneth Rexroth to conclude that "the Beat Generation may once have been human beings—toady we are simply comical bogies conjured up by the Luce publications."[32] Moreover, corporate America was fast realizing the commercial potential of the accelerating youth market, and thus both business and the mainstream media were assiduously transforming Beat lives and their work into commodities on which they could profit. Indeed, late 1950s media moguls and their corporate sponsors saw great financial gain to be made by promoting a lifestyle that threatened the era's domestic tranquility a la *Ozzie and Harriet*. By the late 1960s American corporate capitalism had become even more adept at reshaping, co-opting, and filtering the counterculture through the broader streams of business civilization; lessons-learned from their 1950s counterparts who shrewdly absorbed the Beat Dionysus into the dominant culture.

The beatnik became the embodiment of classic bohemianism, filled with a growing sense of restlessness and rebelliousness that represented a sweeping rejection of everything about 1950s America from TV dinners to Disneyland and the Organization Man. The same sense of alienation from mass culture, the quest for individual freedom from conformity, and the passionate search for self-expression and identity through the creative arts and literature that drove earlier American counterculturalists, generated the same inevitable response in the 1950s in the emergence of the Beat Generation. Similar impulses would also inform and energize the 1960s hippies in their quest for self-discovery and the holistic, anti-materialistic, and authentic lifestyle.

For all their admonishments for the people of their generation to revolt against the status quo by becoming "beat," the Beats' exhortations fell largely on deaf ears because their lifestyle was neither accessible nor hopeful. To the Beats art was life but life could never be art. By contrast, the hippies' aesthetic platform for change was optimistic, egalitarian, and community-driven, and thus they attracted a much wider, larger, and much more committed seeker, at least initially. Nonetheless, the Beats became for the hippies and many other 1960s rebels the "cultural signifiers for the promise of personal freedom.... Different as they were from each other, they stood collectively as a wild, alternative vision to the soul-deadening track of conformity. Their vision resonates deep in the American soul and the American past." They offered the hippies "a bold, forthright template for revolt and uncensored self-expression."[33]

Although the Beats were harbingers of the youth revolt that would explode in the mid–1960s in the form of the hippies and other manifestations of alienated young people, for the majority of white Americans, the 1950s was a time when they became a "People of Plenty," the beneficiaries of a postwar boom that ushered in one of the greatest, protracted economic growth periods in American history. Indeed, for many white Americans still alive and now in their seventies and eighties, few decades in the 20th century evoke greater nostalgia than the 1950s. Even among those Americans born in the post-fifties years, there lingers an image of the country and the majority of its citizens awash in innocence, tranquility, stability, and prosperity. A general feeling predominated that all was once again right in the United States. The depression and war years were finally behind Americans and from the 1950s forward, for the majority of white middle class Americans, that decade represented a period of financial security with unprecedented bounty and unbounded possibility. The luxury of material comforts was not only affordable but the lure of the novelty made them irresistible. Thus the 1950s became, above all, years of unimaginable consumption of goods, spawning a middle class ethos driven and defined by material acquisition and the preservation of security, stability, and prosperity as paramount to personal and collective happiness and fulfillment in America.

Nineteen-fifties American's concern for respectability, need for security, and wholehearted acceptance and promotion of the post-war capitalist system not only reflected their unflinching belief that a robust American economy was the best bulwark against the communist threat, but also the necessary prerequisites for participation in the reward structure of an increasingly affluent society. Conformism thus replaced individuality as the main ingredient for success. Americans' growing obsession with conformity during the decade resulted from a need to escape from confusion, fear, worry, tension, and sense of insecurity, largely stemming from the Cold War and the ever-present possibility of atomic annihilation. As a result, a consensus mentality developed, offering Americans an emotional, psychological, and ideological refuge in an anxious and confusing world. This mindset represented an attempt to shift the burden of individual responsibility for one's fate to an impersonal, monolithic whole. In short, 1950s white Americans' excessive conformity became for many a salve to smooth over their inability to control external conflict and the inner turmoil caused by Cold War tensions. These new standards of thought and behavior extended to all facets of American life during the 1950s, whether in the form of tract-built, identical, tidy little boxlike ranch houses on uniform fifty-foot plots bulldozed to complete flatness, or planning in the form of Levittowns or in the silencing of political dissidents. Creativity meant do-it-yourself painting by numbers; one created great artistic masterpieces by following directions. Occupying the Oval Office during these supposed halcyon years was an individual who personified this new ethos; whose great appeal was that he represented a politics of consensus, classlessness, and conformism—General Dwight David Eisenhower.

Nineteen-fifties prosperity and white middle class affluence resulted from a coalescence of several factors that crested by the middle of the decade. These included increasing middle class purchasing power, the result of wage and salary increases (particularly for blue collar workers); the insatiable demand for consumer goods among the expanding middle class; and the creation of new industries, especially in electronics, chemicals, plastics, aerospace, and aeronautics, many of which emerged because of the Cold War. All generated thousands of job opportunities. Adding to those factors was unprecedented population growth—"the Baby Boom"; urban/suburban expansion; technological innovation that led to a more productive and efficient workforce producing more goods at cheaper prices; and a Cold War containment policy that emphasized foreign aid, which in turn provided numerous foreign markets for American exports. Despite three mild recessions, large sectors of poverty, and uneven income distribution, 1950s prosperity was real and widespread. If few became rich, the great majority lived more materially comfortably and secure than at any time in American history and had more leisure time to enjoy the fruits of their labor.[34]

Right on cue, American industry consistently delivered brand new gadgets, devices, and machines designed to make life easier and more convenient. During the fifties factories presented Americans with such new items as the automatic car transmission, the electric clothes dryer, dishwashers, the long-playing record, the Polaroid camera, and the automatic garbage disposal unit. Americans also bought in record numbers older products such as vacuum cleaners, refrigerators (most stylishly in harvest gold and avocado green), electric ranges and freezers. Thanks to agri-corporations such as Green Giant and Birds-Eye Foods, frozen foods, initially mainly vegetables, were marketed widely for the first time in the 1950s. Eventually one could buy a frozen dinner—entrée and dessert—which went from freezer to dinner table, in less than 45 minutes. "TV Dinners" were the brainchild of the Swanson Company, another mass producer of processed foods, who provided families with complete frozen meals so they could eat their dinner while watching their favorite TV shows.

No respectable middle class home was without the latest black and white television set, placed center-stage in the living room as the most important and expensive piece of household furniture. From their favorite viewing spots, the family watched the nightly news with Chet Huntley and David Brinkley or their favorite sit-com such as the most popular *I Love Lucy* or *Father Knows Best*. One of the many paradoxes of postwar social change as witnessed by the advent of television and the middle class lifestyle that the "tube" helped define was that many suburban nuclear families lost cohesion and the kinship that the family dinner table had once fostered and sustained. Indeed, dinner time was often the only time during the day that *all* family members gathered in one place, shared food and drink, and reaffirmed companionate relationships. With the advent of television and TV dinners, such interaction in many suburban homes disappeared completely. Every night the household gathered for hours in front of the television, absently eating their frozen dinners and staring at a black and white screen, which not only entertained but also bombarded viewers with "ads," encouraging the purchase of even more "things"; must-haves for sustaining the modern suburban lifestyle. In that environment families became increasingly impersonal entities with relationships among members more superficial than genuine. The exchanges at this new dinner table revolved around what was being watched on television and discussions of the show's plot or the surprise of a particular episode's ending. Commonality extended to collective guffawing as Lucy Ricardo (Lucille Ball), engaged in yet another of her harebrained schemes, always ending up in catastrophic hilarity, as she tried to find a way to break free from the shackles of domesticity.

Ironically, for many suburban homes, the only traditional family dinner tables they saw were *on television*, as many of the most popular series, such as *Ozzie and Harriet, Leave It to Beaver*, and *Father Knows Best*, were created to reinforce the traditional nuclear family and attendant values. All portrayed dinner time as a family gathering, with members discussing the day's events and family issues, bonding as families once did in pre-suburbia, even though all these TV families lived in suburban neighborhoods, just like those of the majority of their viewers. Television thus became "a magic mirror on the world that both reflected and distorted reality, which nearly everyone lived a white, middle-class life."[35] Interestingly, many hippies, the majority of whom grew up in such bland, shallow, and homogenized suburban enclaves, tried to resurrect in their experiments in communal living, the traditional family dinner hour, which to them represented authenticity via the sharing of food and conversation; the bonding many hippies desperately sought from among themselves in their new families, an intimacy that had been sadly missing in many of their respective suburban homes.

Virtually all of the decades' sit-coms displayed an idealized image of suburbia and middle class family life and gender roles: supportive, apron-clad, pearl-necklaced, high-heeled housewives, à la June Cleaver; benign but sagacious fathers who materialized at dinner time in a grey flannel suit (the essential attire for corporate climbers) to resolve the day's petty crises and wise-cracking kids (almost exclusively boys) who get into amusing scrapes or trouble at school but ultimately recognize and accept their parents' (really father's) authority and wisdom. Moreover, all the families portrayed in the sitcoms were WASP; no families with ethnic last names had their own shows, even though increasing numbers of former immigrants were making their way to the suburbs and acculturating WASP values and expectations. In addition none of the families were blue collar (save Jackie Gleason's character as well as the rest of the cast of *The Honeymooners*), and of course none were African American, Hispanic, or Asian-American, nor were they urban apartment dwellers or single-parent or multi-generational families. In short, the America portrayed on television was suburban, white and white collar, Anglo-Saxon and Protestant. Indeed, to the leftist critics of mass culture, television was one more weapon in the capitalists' arsenal of class manipulation, numbing the masses to their own alienation thus furthering the elite's hegemonic control of society.[36] To people who vaguely fit the image, television confirmed their vision of America: that only white (mostly WASP) middle class suburbanites had access to and were entitled to such abundance and *creature comforts*. Those on the outside longed for the good life shown on television but they knew firsthand about the diversity, discrimination, and deprivation television ignored.

Nineteen-Fifties Hollywood was as guilty as the television studios in promoting and reinforcing this fantasy of the United States as one big, happy suburb and an American society in general whose citizens were devoted to family and traditional values. Despite the release of some menacing "monster movies" such as *Them, The Thing,* or *Invasion of the Body Snatchers,* or controversial pictures such as the 1957 classic, *The Defiant Ones,* the majority of films made were upbeat; frothy, silly, slap-stick comedies such as *Bedtime for Bonzo,* featuring future president Ronald Reagan as a parent of a chimpanzee or rollicking but lighthearted musicals such as the sexist *Seven Brides for Seven Brothers.* Five of the ten films awarded the best-picture Oscar in the 1950s were of such genre or escapist epics, including *An American in Paris* (1951), *Around the World in Eighty Days* (1956), and *Ben Hur* (1959).[37]

Not to be excluded from celebrating both domesticity and 1950s America as the land of opportunity and abundance, was the technologically brilliant but politically conservative Walt Disney, whose 1956 animated film *Lady and the Tramp,* had a mongrel street dog and his dainty pedigreed mate achieve a canine version of suburban domestic stability and bliss. Disney's movies as well as his weekly, prime-time Sunday night television show, not only promoted traditional family values but Americans' historic righteousness, virtue, courage, and heroism as well. Disney's spectacular theme park, which opened in 1955 in Anaheim, California, one of southern California's many suburban heartlands, became the physical manifestation of Disney's idyllic image of the United States. Indeed, at the time, there existed no other place in the country where one could literally immerse oneself in a mythic version of America as the ideal and untroubled society, past, present, and future, beginning with a nostalgic stroll down Main Street, U.S.A. (built to look like small-town America circa the 1890s), and ending with the technological utopia of Tomorrowland U.S.A. From its inception, Disneyland (and later Disneyworld in Florida), catered to a newly affluent, white clientele seeking leisure time diversion on a grand, sensory, and expensive scale.[38]

On the basis of income level, by the beginning of the 1960s, demographers claimed that 60 percent of white Americans had attained middle class status. Included in that category were many previously socially disenfranchised and culturally marginalized working class ethnics, who by the end of World War II had finally worked their way toward "whiteness." Some had achieved their improved status through professional sports such as baseball and boxing or through their participation in the war effort, either as soldiers or factory workers. Such engagement showed loyalty and patriotism and led to acceptance by mainstream WASP society. With wartime savings in their pockets, a GI bill offering low-interest loans, a booming economy that provided plentiful job opportunities and security, and most important, confirmation as "white Americans," the ethnic working class was ready to step into the previously WASP-dominated middle class. Indeed, by the end of the 1950s, the creation of the privately owned, single-family dwelling by William Levitt and other tract-home innovators and developers, and financed by banks whose risk was underwritten by the federal government (the Federal Housing Administration), had become the norm for working Americans. How easy was it for post-war white Americans to purchase a home? Compared to today, unfathomably easy: for only 5 percent down of the purchase (nothing down for veterans) and 30 years to pay, an ex–G.I. could buy a new tract home with no down payment and installments of only $56 a month on an average purchase in 1950 of $7,990. As *Time* magazine noted, at that time, white Americans could buy a house "more easily than they can buy a $2,000 car on the installment plan."[39]

Regardless of ethnicity or profession, the premier sign of middle class status was the financial means to purchase a brand new tract home in one of the myriad new suburban housing developments that proliferated throughout the United States in the 1950s. From the 1950s on, owning a new "ranch style" (in California) or "Cape Cod" (in the Northeast) single-family home in suburbia came to define middle class existence, becoming part and parcel of the American Dream and remaining so for the majority of Americans down to the present. The post-war partnership of government and private enterprise made home ownership available to Americans previously excluded from such a privilege, and in the process such policies resulted in a wider diffusion of traditional WASP middle class values. The provisioning of such a benefit as home ownership to working class Americans reduced any potential for class conflict in the post-war years and secured the loyalty of blue collar citizens to the government and to preserving the status quo for decades to come. In many ways, labor's access to land and home in the post war years represented writ large continued homage to the Jeffersonian republican ideal; that by extending property ownership to greater numbers of citizens, the number of individuals with a stake in society concomitantly increases, and thus the number of people willing to safeguard established socio-political and cultural institutions, values, norms, and mores. Even as late as the 1930s and 1940s this particular tenet of the Jeffersonian ethos still resonated with American political leaders, as both presidents Herbert Hoover and Franklin Roosevelt publicly affirmed the inextricable correlation between home ownership and vested interest in preserving the American way of life. According to Herbert Hoover, "The present large proportion of families that own their own homes is both the foundation of a sound economic and social system and a guarantee that our society will continue to develop rationally as changing conditions demand."[40] Moreover, pundits from the 1920s through the 1950s agreed that "Ownership of homes is the best guarantee against communism and socialism, and the various bad 'isms' of life. It is not an infallible guarantee, but owners of homes usually are more interested in safeguarding our national history than are renters and tenants."[41] Over a decade later, FDR reasserted his predecessor's commitment to ensuring that the United States would continue on its path toward becoming a nation of middle class home owners, for "a people who own a real share in their own land is unconquerable."[42] As will be seen in a later chapter, blue collar middle class Americans in particular viewed the hippie movement with the greatest contempt and fear, for they perceived the hippie ethos as a threat to all they had accomplished in the post-war years—their "stakes" in society—and their response to the hippie menace was to ignite one of the most determined backlashes in American history to eradicate from the nation's political and socio-cultural landscape all those they believed responsible for having defiled the sanctity of the American Dream. By the late 1960s and into the early 1970s, both blue and white collar middle America disdained all members and manifestations of the youth counterculture and referred to all such individuals and affinity groups as "hippies."

It was in these more affluent, predominantly WASP suburban enclaves where the majority of hippies would be born and raised and it was the mentality and lifestyle associated with suburbia that they came to reject; an alleged "plastic" environment in which an unbounded and crass acquisitiveness pervaded all denizens, transforming them into shallow, externally directed people, void of individual identity and driven by a passion for consumption and security. Soon-to-be hippies would flee from such an existence, searching in urban enclaves or in remote rural areas for a more authentic, spiritually uplifting, and communal way of living. It simply was not enough to be the beneficiaries of a "people of plenty." No doubt many suburbanites succumbed to this peer-dictated sociability and conformity, and despite the subsequent juvenile condemnations of such an existence, for the majority of white middle class Americans, suburbia met a need and fulfilled a dream. As millions of nouveau middle class citizens pursued their vision of the American dream, with which a new home in the suburbs became synonymous, they resented those who questioned that aspiration. To upwardly mobile white Americans, cultural critics, youthful rebels, and civil-rights protesters were unwelcome naysayers amid the abundance and optimism suffusing the decade's burgeoning consumer culture.

Although the lion's share of future hippies came from suburbia, comparatively few came from blue-collar, ethnic middle class neighborhoods, whether suburban or urban. Regardless of geographic location, in the less affluent working class suburbs, the majority of those young people retained their parents' traditional ethos, which became more conservative as their prosperity and security stabilized. Such parents were less inclined to indulge their progeny, insisting that their kids get jobs when not in school, and for the majority of such families, upon graduation from high school, obtaining a steady job in the local manufacturing plant or steel mill was more valuable than going to college. Serving in the military was also important for many such families as a way for the family to demonstrate their continued pride, patriotism, and loyalty to a nation that had so richly rewarded them with acceptance and bounty. Upon completion of service, young men usually returned to the neighborhood, got a job, perhaps married a high school sweetheart, and almost immediately started a family. Family bonds and obligations were strong in such ethnic enclaves and moving away from the community was frowned upon even if it meant an opportunity for upward mobility. Family traditions and values of ethnic working class suburban youth, coupled with limited experience and exposure to the countercultural movement, caused many to reject the hippie lifestyle and ethos. They felt only disdain for the hippie attempt to find an alternate existence that challenged the status quo, even though many working class youth desperately, quietly (and some not so quietly) questioned the same soul-sucking conformity from which their more affluent WASP counterparts were determined to break free.

Helping to drive increasing numbers of white middle class Americans to the suburbs was the desire for larger, more open living spaces to accommodate the surprising baby boom explosion of the years 1946 to 1964. This particular population increase was perhaps the most amazing social trend of the postwar era, and the generation of children born during this time gave rise to the future hippies. The family loomed large in 1950s American culture as postwar citizens, having put marriage and family on hold during the Depression-ridden 1930s and war-torn early 1940s were ready to resurrect with a passion, traditional family life. To this particular generation of Americans, who longed for stability, security, and traditional values, no institution better embodied such virtues than the nuclear family. By the close of 1946, one year after World War II had ended, 3.4 million babies had been born, the most ever in a one-year time period in United States history and there were more babies to come; more than 4 million every year from 1954 to 1964, when the boom finally subsided. As a result, the nation's population leaped from 130 million in 1940 to 165 million by the mid–1950s, the largest increase in the Republic's history. The total number of babies born between 1946 and 1964 was 76.4 million, accounting for almost two-fifths of the nation's overall population of 192 million.[43] The early boom was the result of millions of post–Depression, postwar Americans marrying young (late teens to early twenties), to start a larger family sooner, and to have two, three or four children in succession and perhaps even more later. The generation responsible for the boom's duration, however, was composed of younger folk, most of who were born in the early to mid–1930s and thus were in their late teens or early twenties by the late 1940s and early 1950s. These people were more likely to marry than young people had been in the 1930s, primarily because they recalled no deprivations (the Great Depression), and became young adults during one of the most secure and prosperous eras in postwar history. As in so many other capacities in the postwar years, the nation's economic vitality coupled with opti-mistic perceptions of sustained prosperity drove social change in postwar America, of which the ever-growing numbers of people moving upward into the middle classes reflected.[44]

Not only did suburban growth proceed at a sizzling pace in the 1950s but so did popu-lation migration as well, especially to the West. In the postwar years the nation experienced one of the most significant demographic shifts in history, as eventually millions of citizens poured into the "sunbelt" states of Texas, Arizona, and especially California. Returning GI's from the Pacific theater found the Golden State's beautiful beaches and mountains, temperate climate, exciting, avant-garde cities (most exceptionally San Francisco), and plentiful jobs too alluring not to stay and start their new life. They set to work in well-paying, cutting-edge industries such as electronics, plastics, and aeronautics as well as in construction—homes, schools, hospitals, and freeway systems. If any state became synonymous with suburbia, it was California, which witnessed the most explosive and all-encompassing suburban growth in the postwar period. In many ways and in the view of many Americans, by the end of the 1950s, California—particularly the greater Los Angeles area of southern California and the Bay Area surrounding San Francisco—came to define writ large the quintessential suburban lifestyle and mentality.

Although California became the ultimate definition of suburban America, it was a North-easterner, William Levitt, who paved the way to suburbia for the Golden State. Levitt pio-neered the process of suburban home construction on a massive scale, becoming the most renowned builder in the postwar era. During the war, Levitt, who never liked cities, witnessed the fantastic gains in productivity associated with assembly line techniques and believed he could apply such a method to home construction and thus deliver low-cost, one-story, single-family homes to tens of thousands of eager white Americans longing for their own freedom of space. To keep construction costs down, Levitt vertically integrated his entire operation and standardized every phase of the building process; from laying out streets, hooking up utilities, pouring concrete slab foundations and using prefabricated walls and frames assembled on site by non-union workers who Levitt paid well above the prevailing wage scale to avoid potential strikes. Consumers, depending on whether they were ex–G.I.'s or regular folk, paid $56 to $65 per month on a purchase price of less than $8,000 for roughly an 1100 square foot house—kitchen/dining room, living room, two bedrooms, one bathroom, and an expandable attic, on a 60' by 100' lot with small fruit trees or evergreens. In many instances, buying a tract house cost less per month than renting a city apartment. The houses were well-constructed and generous for that time in their amenities, providing central heating, built-in bookcases, closets, fireplaces as well as appliances, eight-inch Bendix televisions sets, refrigerators, stoves, and washing machines. Levitt developed his first suburban extravaganza—17,000 homes accommodating more than 80,000 people—on a onetime potato field 30 miles from New York City near Hempstead, Long Island.[45]

Out West, particularly in California, scores of William Levitts emerged, taking advantage of plentiful, undeveloped cheap land that seemed to be everywhere in the Golden State, perfect for new tract home construction on a more capacious scale than could be built in the Northeast. The "ranch-look," pioneered by Henry J. Kaiser and Henry Doegler in southern California, became the quintessential California-style suburban home. Defined by "picture windows" and sliding glass doors that opened to a grass back yard or to a patio or to a wooden deck and swimming pool, these homes were designed to showcase the possessions within as well as to open the house and family activities to neighbors' scrutiny. In order to foster community spirit, suburban developers added schools, swimming pools, tennis courts, athletic fields with Little League diamonds, shopping malls, and even hospitals. One of the first and grandiose of these all-encompassing community/tract home projects occurred in Lakewood, California, on an old sugar beet field about ten miles southeast of Los Angeles. There, a consortium of three different home construction enterprises combined to build what was heralded in 1950 as "the city they built in six months," as a new house was completed every 7½ minutes, 40 to 60 houses per day, with a record of 110 completed in a single day. As one of Lakewood's original residents told an interviewer in 2003, she watched "just bean fields" transformed into a complete community. "All these little houses had sprung up like mushrooms. I couldn't believe it; it was just like *The Wizard of Oz*. I mean it was just astonishing. Up one street and down the other were all these framed houses going up. It was really like seeing a fairytale take shape in front of your eyes. You just couldn't believe it went up that fast. Then all of a sudden the grass grew, the trees were planted, and here you were."[46]

For young members of the aspiring middle class, suburbia was a haven of security, stability, convenience, and sociability. Millions of Americans bought these houses as fast as the builders could put them up, to the point that by 1960, over one-quarter of the nation's population lived in what the Census Bureau defined as suburban areas. The nation's largest builders were answering the prayers of millions. By the close of the 1950s homebuilding had become one of the most important forces driving the post-war economic boom and middle class prosperity. As a result, a "suburban-industrial complex" had emerged, led by such individuals as William Levitt and his equally powerful California counterparts, who would over the next several decades, regardless of the environmentally destructive nature of their industry, keep *the bulldozer in the countryside*.[47]

Not all Americans agreed that suburbia represented the realization of the American dream. *House Beautiful* asked "Is this [suburbia] the American dream or is it a nightmare?" Regardless of locale, tract home builders, destroyed natural environments, upset ecosystems, and plowed under fruit orchards while turning fields and pastures into asphalt streets. Although the principal motivation for moving to the suburbs was affordable shelter, at times equally important to urban migrants was the opportunity to live in a more "natural" setting; to reconnect with the nation's pastoral history. Clever developers thus named their projects accordingly to reinforce or promote such nostalgia. Popular names for Eastern tracts were "Crystal Stream," "Robin Meadows," and "Stonybrook"; in California builders played upon the Golden State's idealized bucolic Spanish heritage, naming their projects "Villa Serena," or "Tierra Vista," or "Rancho Cordova," while they continued their routine destruction of the woods, meadows, and fields they honored in their place names. Architectural and cultural critics bemoaned the monotony of house after house with only the slightest differences in exterior look, size, and landscaping, and inhabited by people, the majority of whom were cut from virtually the same socio-economic cloth and race/ethnicity—white—and all willing to sign agreements to keep their suburban neighborhood as bland and as sterile as when they first moved in. Indeed, Levittown rules initially required homeowners to mow their own lawns every week, forbade putting up fences, and outlawed hanging wash outside on week-ends. As the decade of the 1950s wore on, owning a home in suburbia was insufficient proof that one had truly "arrived"; one's home had to be equipped with all the *latest* accouterments and thus peer pressure to "keep up with the Jones'" intensified the sense of mass conformity and conspicuous consumption that increasingly came to encompass and define middle class suburban life in America. In all this a profound irony existed: those who had left the city in hopes of finding greater privacy now found themselves enveloped in a form of group living that crushed privacy and undermined individualism as the vogue of togetherness and group participation reigned supreme. Perhaps the song "Little Boxes" (1962) by folksinger Malvina Reynolds best captured the growing fear among many that the suburbs reflected the homogenization of American society and culture; a place where homes ("little boxes"), and people were "all made out of ticky-tacky" and "they all just look[ed] the same."[48]

One of the harshest critics of suburbia was the cultural historian Lewis Mumford, author of *The City in History* (1961). Mumford maintained that suburban developers were destroying the modern city by turning them into sprawling megalopolises, as thousands of urban folk would move to the suburbs, empty the city of its most dynamic people, and cause over time the city's physical decay as well as its cultural, intellectual, and spiritual decline. Most alarming to Mumford was that suburbia was further homogenizing the American character, increasingly transforming individuals into self-absorbed, peer-driven, materialistic superficial conformists, who were fast losing their ability to see beyond their increasingly circumscribed existences. The daring and courage that Mumford believed had been the hallmark of American progress was fast melting into the asphalt of suburbia. "In the mass movement into suburban areas a new kind of community was produced, which caricatured both the historic city and the archetypal suburban refuge, a multitude of uniform, unidentifiable houses, lined up inflexibly at uniform distances, on uniform roads, in a treeless communal waste, inhabited by people in the same class, the same income, the same age group, witnessing the same television performances, eating the same tasteless pre-fabricated foods, from the same freezers, conforming in every outward and inward respect to a common mold."[49] If Mumford was correct about suburban life, it would only be a matter of time before many of the children who grew up in such environments would question such a soulless existence and rebel against all that was synthetic, superficial, bland, and standardized.

Equally trenchant in his criticism of suburbia and admonishment of middle class consumption, was the Harvard economist John Kenneth Galbraith. In *The Affluent Society* (1958), he expressed disquiet about Americans' penchant to accept whatever Madison Avenue advertised as they mindlessly spent their money on all manner of essentially useless products, which at the time of purchase were touted as the latest, must-have item. As Galbraith observed, "The family which takes its mauve and cerise air-conditioned, power-steered, and power-braked automobile out for a tour passes through cities that are badly paved, made hideous by litter, blighted buildings, billboards, and posts for wires that should long since have been put underground. They pass into a countryside that has been rendered invisible by commercial art. (The goods which the latter advertise have an absolute priority in our value system. Such aesthetic considerations as a view of the countryside accordingly come second. On such matters we are consistent.) They picnic on exquisitely packaged food from a portable icebox by a polluted stream and go on to spend the night at a park which is a menace to public health and morals. Just before dozing off on an air mattress, beneath a nylon tent, amid the stench of decaying refuse, they may reflect vaguely on the curious unevenness of their blessings. Is this, indeed, the American genius?"[50]

In his book, Galbraith called on Americans to curtail private consumption and support more public spending on infrastructure, cleaning up the environment, cultural activities, social services and other aesthetic endeavors. In Galbraith's view, 1950s white middle class Americans had become consumed by their own consumption, allowing a crass materialism and acquisitiveness to define their daily lives, becoming other-directed, bland, and self-absorbed individuals, with no sense of imagination, creativity, or individuality. According to the Marxist critical theorist Herbert Marcuse, American society and culture, was fast becoming "one-dimensional," a country of uniform people consuming standardized products, creating a mass culture by which capitalist elites marketed goods, muted class tensions, and in general legitimated the existing social order, with all its inequities, as wholly desirable and "natural." Marcuse asserted that white middle class suburban Americans' obsession with social status, "belonging," and material security had made them oblivious to their own despair and alienation.[51]

Contemporary indictments and subsequent rejection of suburban culture had little effect on white Americans' continued love affair with suburbia. Indeed, for millions of Americans suburban life was a dream come true. "Houses are for people, not critics," asserted Levitt. "We who produce lots of houses do what is possible—no more—and the people for whom we do it think it's pretty good." Indeed, as Levitt told *Time* magazine, "In Levittown 99% of the people pray for us." Perhaps Levitt's arrogance was not totally unwarranted, for as one Levittowner, ex–G.I. Wilbur Schaetzl, who had been living in a one-bedroom apartment with his wife and a relative before he moved to Levittown, told the same magazine, his previous living condition "was awful, I'd rather not talk about it. Getting this house was like being emancipated."[52]

Suburbia was far from utopia but it was not the social disaster some claimed. Americans in particular seem to require lots of space around them and by the 1950s more citizens could afford to fulfill that desire and the William Levitts were there to provide them with such an opportunity. Like Henry Ford, the post-war period's great tract home builders had found ways to offer "the great multitude" an essential component of the American Dream—afford-able home ownership—a feat that portended to remake the nation's socio-cultural, economic, and even political landscape.[53]

America in the 1950s concealed more turbulence and tension than a casual observer might have guessed. The America portrayed in mass media and promoted and reinforced by advertising, was that of a nation of affluent white people. They were all living in their own spacious suburban homes, complete with all the latest gadgets, reflecting the genius of Amer-ican corporate innovation and the bounty available to *all* (as long as they were white), because of the "wonders" of the capitalist free enterprise system. Indeed, the picture of 1950s Amer-icans as a prosperous, secure, proud, happy hard-working people, who had achieved the most enviable standard of living in the world, was considered by policymakers to be an essential component of the nation's Cold War ideology. If the fundamental premise of American Cold War policy was to contain communism on a global scale, then any threatening social aberra-tions or questioning of the status quo at home had to be suppressed by reinforcing at all times the gospel of domesticity, consumption, and clear gender roles. Both Democratic and Repub-lican politicians embraced this notion, committed to ideologically defending the "American way of life" from assault from abroad. For many American policymakers suburbia represented the promise and triumph of American capitalism, and that particular way of life had to be promoted and defended as the key bulwark against the forces of international communism. As the man most responsible for suburbia's creation, William Levitt, succinctly declared, "No man who owns his own house can be a Communist. He has too much to do."[54]

Nineteen-fifties corporate mass culture proved very adept at masking and manipulating reality: the nation was certainly not all white; the labor force had not transitioned to a com-pletely white collar workforce of college-educated technocrats and middle managers; and as Betty Friedan poignantly established in *The Feminine Mystique* (1963), a high percentage of suburban women were far from "fulfilled" housewives. Prosperity's by-products—rampant materialism, a standardized mass culture, and the growth of a desk-bound white collar class of "organization men"—created more anxieties than anyone dared reveal. Looking for relax-ation from such pressures and tension, many beleaguered middle class suburbanites—hus-bands as well as wives—found momentary solace in the nostrums of alcohol and prescription drugs—a good stiff martini or tranquilizers such as valium. Indeed, drinking rose sharply in the fifties and so did the sale of barbiturate drugs, which reached 1,159,000 pounds consumed by 1959. Seeking relief from a multitude of stresses by washing sedatives down with a "high-ball" became a respectable adult addiction. That such emotional and psychological distress should accompany affluence and material abundance surprised few psychologists or psychi-atrists; white Americans had been afflicted with the anxieties caused by rising expectations throughout most of their history, and thus for many 1950s middle class citizens, unrealized aspirations often resulted in depression requiring drugs or alcohol or both to soothe away the mental anguish of perceived failure. Suburbia offered white Americans a cherished dream with which they were supposed to feel fulfilled. But often "nothing is more hopeless than planned happiness."[55]

By the early 1960s the mainstream media had tired of the Beat "phenomenon"; their initial commercial cachet had run its course. The vast majority of Americans by then either seemed bored, disgusted, or mildly amused by Beat behavior; the Beats, like many other 1950s momentary diversions from the status quo, had been a fad. Nonetheless, during the placid 1950s the Beat scene was the only revolution around, and to the farseeing, it appeared a foretaste of more to come. By that time, many of the San Francisco poets had moved away, while the cops and tourists forced the rest from their old North Beach haunts. A few survived however, finding a safe sanctuary in another congenial San Francisco neighborhood, the Haight-Ashbury, a racially integrated community of 40 square blocks, adjacent to scenic Golden Gate Park. There, Beat old timers not only preserved the hip lifestyle but inspired a growing community of new hipsters—the "hippies"—to pick up where they had left off with their "Dionysian projects." Despite the Beats' fleeting fame, their literature, their reckless lifestyle, and perhaps most important, their wholesale rejection of middle class suburbia and its attendant values, they touched a spiritual restlessness in the hearts and minds of many more American youth than anyone dared to admit. In 1951 Allen Ginsberg wrote Jack Kerouac: "I can't believe that between the three of us [Ginsberg, Kerouac, and William Burroughs] already we have the nucleus of a totally new historically important American creation."[56] At the time, Ginsberg's self-congratulating sounded like youthful arrogance; over half a century later it sounds like bemused prophecy, for the Beat movement anticipated the counterculture of the 1960s.

2

The Haight-Ashbury and the Emergence of the Hippies

"We [the counterculture] long ago commenced, on our own, a total Moratorium on constructive participation in this society."—Raymond Mungo, co-founder of the underground Liberation New Service

It was in San Francisco's 44-block Haight-Ashbury neighborhood that the hippie was born sometime in late 1965, an amalgam of artists, Berkeley and San Francisco State students, and bohemian émigrés from the North Beach area, as well as an increasing procession and array of young drop-outs from across the nation. Interestingly, as the dynamics that would eventually form the hippie movement began to coalesce in the early 1960s, few predicted that this particular urban enclave would eventually become the counterculture's national epicenter or the new favorite haunt for the city's traditional bohemian subcultures. North Beach's Little Italy, not the Haight-Ashbury, seemed the natural place for the hippies to emerge, for the Italian-American community there had an already established reputation for embracing the city's avant-garde, most notably the Beats, as well as the new folk and jazz clubs, and, reluctantly but tolerantly, topless bars as well gay and lesbian taverns, and drag queen/female impersonator shows.

But it was not North Beach where 1960s counterculture history in the form of the hippies would be made; it would be across town, in the Haight-Ashbury, once one of the city's more fashionable residential areas noted for its grand, three-storied vibrantly painted Victorian-style homes. By the late 1950s and early 1960s the Haight had become populated by feisty, dispossessed black homeowners from the Fillmore, a district the city had targeted for the wrecking ball. In alliance with the other ethnic groups migrating to the neighborhood (mostly second and third generation Irish and Russian San Franciscans) they helped revitalize the area into a respectable, comfortable multi-ethnic and bi-racial middle class district. By 1960, the Haight had become one of the safest places for the city's African American community to live, finding acceptance among their white/ethnic neighbors. It was also during the early 1960s that many beatniks, artists, and other North Beach rebels began emigrating (resulting in steadily rising rent prices and gawking tourists) to Haight-Ashbury, bringing with them their brand of anti-bourgeois bohemianism and deviance, which they kept alive long enough for the new counterculturists to appropriate.[1]

However, as the 1960s progressed, many of the neighborhood's middle class residents

Countercultural icons, from left, Beat poet Michael McClure, singer/songwriter Bob Dylan, and Beat poet and hippie guru Allen Ginsberg, North Beach, San Francisco, California, 1965 (photograph by Larry Keenan, courtesy Bancroft Library, University of California, Berkeley. © 1997 Larry Keenan. All rights reserved).

decided to leave in protest to City Hall's plans to rezone the residential area for the construction of a freeway. Property values plummeted, precipitating a dramatic decline in rental prices. By 1965, a six-room elegant Victorian or Edwardian home, built after the 1906 earthquake, leased for $120 per month. The houses and apartments were large enough to share and thus cooperative living became increasingly common among the Haight's bohemian denizens.[2] When the deluge of young humanity overwhelmed the neighborhood during the 1967 Summer of Love, many of the flats became "crash pads" to house America's teenage refugees.

Besides the attraction of cheap, available, and open rental housing, the "Hashbury" area was situated on the periphery of Golden Gate Park, a verdant expanse of open meadows, formal gardens, statuary, and museums, one of the nation's finest city parks. Haight Street in particular became center stage for much of the action that was to take place over the next several years. Three blocks north, another green belt called the Panhandle, parallels the Haight neighborhood for about a mile. It was within the confines of these lush bordering parks, grand old Victorian homes with cheap rents, and a neighborhood tolerant of students and diversity that the hippie movement emerged. In many ways, the hippies became a *San Franciscan and uniquely* (but not surprisingly) *Californian event*, reflecting the importance of locale in American socio-cultural history. As eminent British historian Arnold Toynbee, visiting professor at Stanford University at the time of the hippie phenomenon opined, the reason the hippie movement first appeared in San Francisco was because "California is rich, and middle class wealth in one generation produces hippies in the next." Toynbee also sardonically observed that historically "California rather goes in for more innovations than the rest of the country. It is young and rich and it can afford to play the fool a bit more than other places."[3]

In a more rhapsodic assessment, Timothy Leary side-kick Richard Alpert, agreed with Toynbee that of all the cities in the United States, none was more uniquely "qualified" to serve as the epicenter of "the new consciousness emerging" than San Francisco and the Haight-Ashbury neighborhood in particular. "The Haight-Ashbury is, as far as I can see, the purest reflection of what is happening in consciousness, at the leading edge of society. There is very little I have seen in New York, Chicago, or Los Angeles that is giving me the hit that this place does because it has a softness that is absolutely exquisite."[4] Todd Gitlin agreed, observing at the time that San Francisco became a "wellspring, the headquarters in some sense" especially for Midwesterners, who "weren't looking to New York for cultural clues. They looked to San Francisco." For Deidre English, San Francisco "popularized an attitude. The attitude was one of seizing life, feeling free; feeling that if we do not like something we can change it; feeling there was this critical mass of people who wanted to reject inherited, authoritarian, conformist ideas and make the world our own." According to Kevin Starr, the hippie counterculture that emerged in the Haight "took San Francisco out of the mainstream of American cities and made it an eccentric alternative [cultural] capital"; a legacy and reputation that has remained down to the present.[5]

Indeed, from the city's founding, San Francisco was a wide open place, where behavior considered deviant or scandalous elsewhere in 19th century America was not only tolerated but frequently admired and promoted by the city's inhabitants. Well beyond its formative frontier years, San Franciscans displayed an unabashed predilection for sating their carnal desires, whether in the liberal enjoyment of fine wines and restaurants or by frequenting some of the most luxurious, high-priced brothels in 19th century America. Equally disturbing to Victorian sensibilities, which informed the behavior of the majority of the city's inhabitants, was the presence of one saloon for every 96 citizens along with untold numbers of opium dens. By the close of the 19th century, many San Franciscans took great pride in considering themselves to be the first white Americans to have liberated themselves from the nation's Puritan heritage.[6]

San Francisco was demographically unique compared to other major American 19th century cities in that early in its history (largely because of the California Gold Rush) the city became a melting pot of white ethnic diversity, as immigrants from Russia, Ireland, Italy, Scotland, Spain, England, Chile, Australia, France, and Canada, co-existed in relative peace and harmony with their native-born Anglo-American neighbors. At times WASP Americans were in the minority and consequently, unlike in Boston, Philadelphia, and New York, a nativist mentality of discrimination and policies of oppression never took hold of the city. The presence of so many white foreign ethnics compelled WASP Americans to be more tolerant of diversity than was their natural disposition. Unfortunately, such acceptance was not extended to Asian immigrants or African Americans.[7]

By the beginning of the 20th century, San Franciscans' accommodation of white newcomers and the morally deviant as well as a penchant for a life both sybaritic and refined, had become institutionalized, and over the course of subsequent decades came to inform much of the city's socio-cultural outlook and identity. In the post–World War II years San Franciscans continued their development of "a culture of civility," which, according to sociologists Howard Becker and Irving Louis Horowitz, set the city apart from its urban counterparts.

San Francisco became a "natural experiment in the consequences of tolerating deviance. Its inhabitants know that they are supposed to be sophisticated and let that knowledge guide their public actions, whatever their private feelings."[8]

San Francisco's location on the nation's western periphery isolated the city's residents from the traditional influences of the East Coast and from the rural, agrarian mentality of the Great Plains. This disassociation allowed San Franciscans the freedom to develop their own unique version of America, one that both predated and provided much of the inspiration, revelry, and ethos for the 1960s counterculture. Long before the first hippies appeared in the Haight-Ashbury, many of their 19th century forebears had dispensed with American assumptions about propriety and decorum, celebrating their disdain for convention as joyfully, flamboyantly, and as raucously as would their counterculture progeny in the Haight-Ashbury one hundred years later. "At the Parker House or the El Dorado women dealt the cards, a brass band or banjo music played, and gold nuggets were piled high on the tables. One could take a brandy-smash at the bar then stroll the crowded streets rakish in hussar boots, corduroy pants, red flannel shirt, and sombrero. Costume was posturing and romantic."[9] It was this particular era in San Francisco history that the future hippies found most appealing and relevant to their particular brand of bohemian style. According to Rock Scully, future manager of the Grateful Dead, "There was a huge romanticism around the idea of the Barbary Coast, about San Francisco as a lawless, vigilante, late 19th century town." The early new hipster males dressed "in old, stiff-collared shirts with pins, and riding coats and long jackets. Guys wore their hair long under Western-style hats, and young people decorated their apartments in old-fashioned castoffs." As early as 1963 the Haight assumed the feel and look of a uniquely late "Victoriana Americana," where costuming-as-rebellion became de rigueur. By 1965 the Haight-Ashbury had replaced North Beach as the center of the city's cultural radicalism. North Beach bohemian expatriates brought with them to the Haight the fixtures of their lifestyle—poetry, jazz, alcohol, and the clandestine use of marijuana and amphetamines.[10]

Until 1965, the Haight's avant-garde residents were referred to as beatniks. Indeed early media coverage of the Haight-Ashbury presented the burgeoning hippie movement as an evolution of North Beach's beatnik culture. However, the hippies increasingly colorful attire, flamboyant behavior and gregarious personalities contrasted sharply with the visibly drab, introverted, and cynical beatniks, and thus the local media believed a new appellation was needed to describe this latest manifestation of American bohemianism. According to Alice Echols, many veteran beatniks resented the new non-conformists, believing them to be usurpers and merely "playing" at being "other." The Beats thus came up with the term "hippie" as a way "to put down young [beatnik or hipster] wannabes, the junior hipsters."[11] Long-time Haight resident and founder of the Grateful Dead, Jerry Garcia, believed that "old-timers" such as himself always considered themselves to be fundamentally "cynical beatniks" but who "evolved into something nicer with the advent of psychedelics." Garcia however, maintained that "the media portrait" of "hippies" (including himself) as "innocent flower" children "was a joke."[12] Nonetheless, the label "hippie" stuck, thanks in large measure to a series of articles written by local journalist Michael Fallon for the *San Francisco Examiner* in the early fall of 1965. In his essays, Fallon used the term "hippie" to describe the "new generation of beatniks" who had emerged in the Haight and who congregated at such places as the Blue Unicorn Café on the corner of Ashbury and Hayes Streets. Given the strong popular connections at the time between the Beats and hippies, it was likely Fallon came up with "hippies," by which he still meant a with-it young person who knew what was "cool" and "happening" on the streets and elsewhere in the neighborhood, even in the city at large.[13] The majority of the Haight's new eccentric denizens eventually embraced the new designation and as the hippie phenomenon spread across the land over the course of the next several years, so did the tens of thousands of their counterparts in similar urban enclaves.

Although the majority of hippies referred to themselves as hippies, they also called themselves by other names, which changed over time and varied with location. "Seekers" were those dedicated to the quest to find their true selves by breaking free from the spiritually and emotionally suffocating middle class life; "heads" were so named because part of the seeker's journey to fine one's self usually involved dope use, particularly LSD, which promoted keener awareness and consciousness expansion. Or there was the "freak," a "far-out" person too odd, too abnormal to be part of mainstream society. Indeed, Haight photographer Bob Seidemann claimed that he and the majority of his peers called themselves "freaks, never hippies." Dave Getz, drummer for Big Brother and the Holding Company, agreed with Seidemann: "I never called myself a hippie, ever. I hated it. Call me freak, head, anything but a hippie." Jerry Garcia defined a hippie as "someone who is turned on; someone who's in forward motion; it's motion and creative energy at its best. It's just a better way for people who are in a creative community to look at things."[14]

Perhaps most important, the hippie counterculture was difficult to define because it included everyone, excluded no one. There were no real hippie leaders; no specific organizations, no age limits or race or gender requirements; no prerequisites; one did not have to engage in any expected or determined activities such as smoking dope or living in a commune or have long hair to *qualify* as a hippie; no minimum requirements to join the "counterculture club." Anyone and everyone was free "to do their own thing"; to find and define themselves as they saw fit because being a hippie was a very individualistic quest, a frame of mind. Becoming a hippie simply meant that one had chosen an alternative lifestyle that ran "counter" to that lived by the majority of their mainstream peers. As one southern California hippie told a *Time* correspondent, "You don't have to take LSD to be in the hippie brotherhood. You just have to try to live the best life you can." The young man then likened the hippie counterculture to "early Christianity. It's all characterized by love. Christ and Buddha were hippies. We're against violence. We're apolitical. I say 'we' but there are no hippie leaders. We have all the time in the world. We'll evangelize by example."[15] As the *San Francisco Oracle* declared, "The hippie movement is not a beard, it is not a weird, colorful costume, it is not marijuana. The hippie movement is a philosophy, a way of life." Being a hippie meant "to liberate yourself from the confining conventions of life and to celebrate the irrational side of your nature, kind of let yourself go."[16]

To the emerging counterculturists, affluence, the scientific and industrial revolutions, and the over two and a half centuries of the almost uninterrupted dominance of Enlightenment rationalism had produced an emotionally sterile mainstream culture, reflecting a Western society dominated by a desiccated intellectualism. However, 1960s counterculturists believed that the decade marked the "Dawning of the New Age," when the mystical, the intuitional, the aesthetic, the organic, and the sensual would be embraced rather than the industrial, the plastic, and the synthetic. In many ways the hippie movement was not a new socio-cultural impulse, not even in the United States, but rather a reflection of the ongoing dynamic in Western (Euro-American) civilization of the tension between a dominating classical Apollonian ethos and a recurring, reactive Dionysian creed. Viewed in this context, the emergence of the 1960s counterculture represented a manifestation of past romantic movements, most notably those of the early to mid–19th century in both Western Europe and the United States, in particular the aesthetics and the ethics of the American Romantics and transcendentalists. Henry David Thoreau believed that only by dramatically and completely disavowing the constraints and pretensions of "civilized" society and retreating to the solitude and "wildness" of Walden Pond, could he find his true self. Thoreau was certain that such an extreme

Conscripted for an unpopular war. U.S. Army Induction Center, Oakland, California, 1968 (photograph by Michelle Vignes, courtesy Bancroft Library, University of California, Berkeley).

act of separation from the mainstream America of his time and subsequent "self-reliance" was imperative if he hoped to have a more spiritually and emotionally fulfilling life. Only in a simple, natural environment could be found a "life of authenticity"; a life "without lies, without pretense, and without hypocrisy." Thoreau foreshadowed the philosophy of future hippies; living "organically" on Walden Pond provided him a place where "I can have a better opportunity to play life," and not "when I came to die, discover that I had not lived."[17]

While many hippies did lead dissipated, self-serving, and self-destructive lives, there were significant numbers who genuinely and passionately committed themselves to finding an alternative way of "being," of living in the United States without succumbing to the acquisitiveness, careerism, and conformity that had come to define white middle class life by the mid–1960s. The counterculture included a wide variety of dissenters, whose conscious decision to eschew the blessings of bounty, who directly challenged 1960s conformism, racism, sexism, and materialism. These individuals believed their "dropping out" of mainstream society and their pursuit of alternative lifestyles, would, by example, lead to a more humane world. In this regard, many hippies were indeed paying homage to their Romantic predecessors, many of whom sought the same ideals in their respective quests—a more egalitarian society, greater individualism, creativity, spirituality, community, and spontaneity as well as a reconnection with the natural environment.

Although a variety of dynamics coalesced during the 1960s to create the counterculture, the youth revolt was inconceivable without the Vietnam War's destruction of young people's belief in authority. Perhaps more important than hippie disaffection with the actual war and American foreign policy in general (which few hippies read much about or thought about on a daily basis) was the draft, which male hippie dropouts most definitely opposed. Being a young male in the late sixties was a different experience from being one in the early sixties, largely because of the draft—an expediency that pulled young men into a war in which Americans were killing and dying by the thousands without any perceivable gain. Moreover, the war itself, with its cruel and pointless violence was seen on television almost every night until 1968, when in that year, for a variety reasons, regular coverage ceased, and by the close of 1968, hardly appeared at all. No matter how much young people protested and reviled the slaughter, they could not stop it, and although males could be drafted at 18 they could not vote until they were 21. Despite repeated assurances from American military leaders that there was "light at the end of the tunnel," the war seemed to grind endlessly on. For the young men facing conscription, limited war was a nonsense term, and to be drafted to fight such a senseless war was considered involuntary servitude. Since they had abandoned school and mainstream institutions in general, hippies did not qualify for any deferments and thus became eligible for the draft—that Establishment dragnet that at any time could abruptly end their carefree ways, even their lives. If that was a possibility, then why not live fully for and in the moment and explore and enjoy all carnal and psychogenic pleasures? Many hippies consequently concluded they would rather "have their brains bashed out by a cop in front of an induction center for protesting against the draft, than by a grenade in the jungle."[18] For many in the hippie counterculture, Enlightenment rationalism had finally unraveled, revealing its inherent darker side. D.H. Lawrence once wrote that at its core, the American soul was "hard, stoic, isolate, and a killer." Hippies could not have agreed more with Lawrence's assessment.

Thanks in large measure to the Vietnam War and related "sicknesses and evils," by the mid–1960s many young Americans concluded that it was simply impossible to cope with the dominant culture any longer. To the emerging hip counterculture American society had become a perpetual "rat race" in which everyone was running as fast as they could to try to get ahead of everyone else, which meant getting a better job, more money and thus being able to buy more "things." American culture and society was awash in monolithic, meaningless, impersonal, and entrenched institutions that consumed the individual, eradicating all sense of humanity while churning out "products" both material and human. If the United States had become such a place, hippies asked the obvious question: what was there about "Amerikan" society and culture worth emulating or embracing? The pursuit of money? Supporting a senseless war? Buying the latest "plastic" gadgets or clothes? Taking meaningless courses leading to worthless degrees from authoritarian, bureaucratized "multiversities" and then getting a white collar, stultifying, monotonous, middle management job in a cubicle in a huge, impersonal military-industrial complex-related corporation, where everyone looked and acted just like you.

Those young Americans who joined the counterculture believed it was better to drop out and to "do your own thing" rather than continue to endure or try to make sense of such an afflicted society and culture. The hippies represented "a living protest vote, a declaration of choice—The Great Refusal to cooperate." Hippies were thus anti-traditional values, anti-consumption, and anti-materialism; in effect anti-capitalism and the American bourgeois/liberal ethic that sustained capitalism's power. What was more detestable, hippies asked, a nation wracked by racism and war or the alleged obscenity of "free love"—uninhibited sex? As one hippie wrote, "Is it obscene to fuck or is it obscene to kill? Why is free hate socially acceptable while free love is socially unacceptable? Which is really obscene?"[19]

Although hippies talked constantly of a bringing about "a revolution," few if any meant for such an insurgence against the status quo to be one of confrontation. Unlike their New Left counterparts, the majority of hippies opposed engagement with mainstream culture in any capacity, choosing instead withdrawal. To the hippie counterculture, conventional America could not be changed or reformed, especially through the existing political process. White middle class acquisitiveness and conformity had become such entrenched norms that they were now beyond redemption. If that were the case, then why waste time and energy trying to change such immutable individuals and institutions? Hippies were thus apolitical, anti-authoritarian, and anti-institutional. They embraced the values of egalitarianism, honesty, tolerance, personal freedom, and above all fun—"if it feels good, do it." Hippies believed that they had been charged by the Cosmos to build a healthy, peaceful society that loved and accepted everyone. That feeling of brotherhood was to be put to use building the new Eden. Hippies also believed they had a moral responsibility to propagate the use of mind-altering hallucinogenic drugs in order to reach the state of consciousness essential for American society's redemption from the crass selfishness and greed allegedly destroying the nation. They sought levels of spiritual and personal fulfillment and the intimacy they despaired of finding in mainstream society. As Hunter S. Thompson observed in an article for the *New York Times Magazine* in 1967, the "hippies despise phoniness; they want to be open, honest, loving and free. They reject the plastic pretense of 20th century America, preferring to go back to the 'natural life.'"[20] In short, the new bohemians were social rebels who preferred getting high on drugs rather than on radical politics. As journalist, writer, and Beat poet Lawrence Lipton observed in 1968, "The hippies have passed beyond American society. They're not really living in the same society…. It's not so much that they're living on the leftovers, on the waste of American society, as that they just don't give a damn."[21] Or, as Liberation News Service co-founder Raymond Mungo proclaimed, "We [the counterculture] long ago commenced, on our own, a total Moratorium on constructive participation in this society."[22]

Perhaps Beat-era activist and poet Tuli Kupferberg best captured the new hippie ethos and "politics" in an influential essay titled "The Politics of Love." Kupferberg was forty-four when he wrote his homage to the hippies' emergence and redemptive purpose for a nation increasingly wracked by violence, terror, and polarization. To Kupferberg, the politics of engagement as expressed by the student radicals and anti-war movement would in the end fail to bring about the desired socio-political reformation because "the society corrupts even those who would overthrow it," and in the end "they [the establishment] will not become like us—we will become like them." Rather, it was time for young Americans to embrace a "politics of love," in which young people would completely drop out of mainstream society, gather in "primitive communisms," live off the nation's bountiful "waste," and over time by sheer numbers and example, transform the country's malignancy through love. Although Kupferberg believed the struggle to bring such enlightenment to American society would be difficult—"we will lose many battles"—he nonetheless was confident that if American youth pursued this "flower-power" agenda, "the beauty of our youth will conquer the world…. We will make the ugly beautiful—the sick healthy—the poor rich—the soldiers peaceful." To Kupferberg, there was no one else who could redeem or save America from itself but these allegedly "stupid, insane, and naïve children" called hippies.[23]

Finally, hippies valued the process of experimentation, and thus the hippie ethos or social thought became an ever-evolving self-indulgent, if not narcissistic, code of conduct. As one hippie declared, "Change jobs, spouses, hairstyles, clothes; change religion, politics, values, even personality; try everything, experiment constantly, accept nothing as given."[24] Life was to be one endless, personally fulfilling venture in the pleasurable gratification of mind, body, and spirit. As Timothy Leary announced, sometimes "it becomes necessary for us to go out of our minds in order to use our heads."[25]

Although influenced to some degree by both the civil rights movement (which provided hippies with the techniques of protest), and by the New Left (to whom some hippies turned for the intellectual validation for their rebellion), without question the Beats had the most significant impact on the hippie ethos because they admired their forebears' renegade lifestyle and complete disavowal of mainstream American culture and its attendant values. The Beats were trailblazers, whose literature and brand of bohemianism inspired would-be hippies to reject white middle class security and pursue the liberated life of "self-awareness"; of living in and for the moment. By embracing much of the Beat lifestyle (sexual liberation and experimentation and drug usage in particular), the hippies propagated the Beat message and legacy by their sheer numbers.

Although similar in outlook, lifestyle, and behavior, there were some notable differences between them. Most Beats, born either in the 1920s or during the Great Depression, were much older and more seasoned by life than the majority of hippies by the time the latter had come of age. The Beats had experienced, in varying degrees, hard times and war, as well as postwar anti-communist hysteria as embodied in McCarthyism. Consequently their mood was pessimistic and their attitudes and behavior reflected those of fiercely independent outsiders. In Hunter S. Thompson's view many of "Hashbury's" new "denizens reject any kinship with the Beat Generation on the ground that 'those cats were negative, but our thing is positive.'" Thompson also believed that these "new bohemians" were not only younger ("their average age is about 20") but also were more "provincial" in a variety of capacities than their Beat predecessors. "The majority of beatniks who flocked to San Francisco 10 years ago were transients from the East and Midwest.... San Francisco was only a stop on the big circuit: Tangier, Paris, Greenwich Village, Tokyo, and India. The senior beats had a pretty good idea what was going on in the world; they read newspapers, traveled constantly and had friends all over the globe."[26] In Thompson's view, the Beats, like the hippies, rejected virtually all aspects of 1950s and 1960s "plastic" America. But Beats were more cosmopolitan, curious, imaginative, and extremely well-read, and thus far more intellectually sophisticated and creative than their hippie progeny.

Unlike the hippies, few Beats desired to develop a coherent Beat ethos. The Beats were reckless, hedonistic individualists, whose legacy was the cult of the rebel and the rejection of all post-war bourgeois values and institutions, especially the white middle class obsession with conformity, careerism, and responsibility. As Burton Wolfe noted, "They had no interest in building a greater America, in fighting communism, in working at a career to buy $100 suits and dresses, color television sets, a house in the suburbs, or a flight to Paris. They laughed at those goals. Some brew, a few joints, a sympathetic partner in the sack, a walk in the park, an afternoon of lying in the sun on the beach, a hitchhike trip to Mexico—this was all there was." Although many hippies shared this outlook with the Beats, there were just as many, if not more hippies, who worked hard, were responsible spouses and parents, who did not take drugs or engage in wild sexual orgies, but had simply decided to opt out of the rate race of the 1960s mainstream American existence and pursue instead an alternative life away from all the "noise" of suburban America. These more genuine hippies were solicitous of the environment and the human body; believed in resurrecting and preserving traditions and sensibilities, especially those of the nation's forgotten and oppressed people: Native Americans, Asians, African Americans, and Latinos. As for fighting evil, the hippies believed they were doing that every day by propagating their message of love and peace, and by living their lives detached from the acquisitiveness and corruption that bred such divisiveness and hostility. Having grown up in middle class affluence and security and thus less affected by life's vagaries, the hippies were more optimistic, vibrant, and overall less gruff than their Beat predecessors, and visibly and passionately devoted to changing the world for the better—at least initially. In effect the hippie movement that emerged in the Haight reflected yet another unique brand of American bohemianism of self-expression based upon "positive vibes," a functioning, cohesive community of dissenters, and a fervid personal liberation ethos that simultaneously promoted an equally strong sense of communitarianism. The Beats scorned such sentiments and as a result, history relegated them and their movement as having at most, a transitory cultural relevance. Holly George-Warren has aptly summed up the key differences between these two avant-garde movements of the post–World War II era: "The main contrasts between the Beat and hippie eras are in terms of isolation vs. community, opposition vs. separate-but-equal relationship to the Establishment, social apathy vs. activism, and pessimism vs. optimism."[27]

Mitigating many of these differences, however, was the universal language of music— a cross-generational form of creative expression that united the two countercultural movements. Although the Beats and their beloved jazz had faded from the aesthetic underground spotlight by the mid–1960s, the Beats' devotion to living in the "now" and the improvisational language of bebop reemerged in the hippies' consciousness as rock and roll, in particular, the acid-rock sound of San Francisco's hippie bands. Jerry Garcia of the legendary Grateful Dead, for example, often cited the Beats as being the primary source for his own creative impulses, especially their call to "try anything," and that his love for free-flowing art and his passion for touring and playing for live audiences rather than producing records in a studio to be akin to Kerouac's *On the Road*—one can almost hear Kerouac's breathless tale of adventure in Garcia's dynamic solos. The angst of Bob Dylan's protest-riddled lyrics and the orgasmic, psychedelic rage of Jimi Hendrix's guitar evoked images of connection to Norman Mailer's new brand of hipster, both black and white, to bebop jazz's esoteric flights of musical fantasy, and Allen Ginsberg's "swirling, rhapsodic verses." Similarly, Grace Slick, lead vocalist for the quintessential psychedelic band, Jefferson Airplane, credits the Beats for having inspired the hippie scene of the Haight-Ashbury: "I think it was a reaction against the Fifties which were extraordinarily boring and stiff. Compared to the Sixties, it was like being asleep."[28] As will be seen, 1960s countercultural rock and roll was built to last by a generation determined to use music as a medium through which to pursue and celebrate change.

Despite fundamental differences, the majority of hippies agreed with *Oracle* publisher Ron Thelin that "the beat scene was the father of the hippie scene. It was like they were the first real pioneers. The first group of artists that started to postulate in a new direction; started to point to the hypocrisy in ways that really made sense, started to really act out what they believed." Peter Berg, one of the founding members of the radical Diggers, agreed with Thelin about the hippies' lineage: "I don't think it happened in 1965 or 1966. When I read *Howl* I knew I didn't have anything to lose. That's what it did. That's what sent people out in search of experience." Gary Duncan, a member of one of the first hippie bands to emerge in the Haight, The Quicksilver Messenger Service, believed "The Haight-Ashbury scene was basically an outgrowth of the Beat generation. Poets and painters, every kind of drug imaginable and every kind of crazy motherfucker in the world."[29] Spontaneity, disdain for the values of the bourgeois American culture of their respective times, and the endless search for the more authentic life, linked the hippies and the Beats; a shared identity of living life fully in the moment because death was an omnipresent specter in Cold War America, either in the form of the jungles of Vietnam or in the image of the infamous mushroom cloud from a nuclear blast. To the narrator of the 2007 PBS documentary, *The Summer of Love*, the only differences between the hippies and the Beats were that the former "preferred sunshine to the dark coffee houses [the Beats' favorite haunts] and rock to cool, modern jazz."[30]

As the Beats had found a gathering place and support for their brand of bohemianism at City Lights Bookstore, the early hippies found a similar locus for their growing community at the Psychedelic Shop at 1535 Haight Street. The emporium was owned by the Thelin brothers, Ron and Jay, two college drop-outs who went to Lake Tahoe, high in the Sierra Nevada Mountains of northern California and one of the state's more high-end summer resort areas. There they opened a parking lot as well as a boat and beach umbrella rental business. The brothers did well and in 1965 sold their business and returned to their home in "the City by the Bay." With their profits they opened the Psychedelic Shop on January 3, 1966. Initially the store sold only a variety of books and magazines, and of course rock and roll records as well as some jazz and rhythm and blues. However, as the hippie movement unfolded on Haight Street in front of their store, the brothers "knew that a whole new world was opening up and we wanted to be part of it." They began stocking their store with staples that catered to and reflected the emerging hippie culture: paisley fabrics, incense, dance and other psychedelic pop art posters and prints, occult books, and all manner of drug paraphernalia, from colored Zig-Zag paper used for rolling marijuana joints, to roach clips and hash pipes. They also expanded their premises to include a "meditation room," which Thelin later admitted became nothing more than a place where couples went to have sex in its darkened interior. Thelin confessed years later, "Quite possibly a number of babies were conceived there." One of "The Psych Shop's" more innovative merchandising gimmicks was the placement of three folding chairs in its large storefront window where patrons could sit and read or simply stare out the window at all the passers-by. According to Thelin, "Our window was a live display of whoever was sitting there looking out at people looking in on them. It blew a lot of minds. Our display was a kind of mirror image of the street action outside."[31]

As reflected in the type of merchandise the Thelin brothers carried in their store, the Haight's burgeoning hippie community was founded upon two saleable cultural commodities—drugs and music, both of which came to define much of the hippie lifestyle. As the Haight's hippie community evolved, a definite, visible, collective look, attitude, and presence emerged, revolving around drugs, music, and fashion, which brought them together no matter where they were—San Francisco or the Bay Area, eventually nationally. Hippies best achieved community by becoming rooted (despite their alleged transient ways) to particular places. Thus a hippie community like that in the Haight-Ashbury was defined by place as much as by attitudes and behavior. For the Haight's original hip residents their respective lives became a concentrated social experiment rather than a diffuse set of styles. For this reason one of the signal events in the formation of the Haight-Ashbury community was the opening of the Psychedelic Shop. According to Thelin, "Things were happening in the Haight-Ashbury before we opened but it seems like the Psychedelic Shop brought publicity to what was happening. Suddenly there was a common fact that everyone could identify with. It was right in the middle of town, and it was called the Psychedelic Shop. People started coming in and then pretty soon it was like the whole Haight-Ashbury was the community."[32]

The Psychedelic Shop's success brought other hip entrepreneurs to the Haight, with many coming simply to tap into the potential financial gold mine the burgeoning hippie movement represented. By mid-year 1966, Haight, Page, Clayton, and Ashbury streets were lined with a variety of stores with colorful names all catering to hippie needs and wants: Far Fetched Foods, a health food establishment; In Gear, a "mod" clothing store; the Blushing Peony, a fancy, hip-chic boutique; and the I/Thou Coffee Shop. Later there would be the Print Mint, a posters and photographic picture shop; the Drog [sic] Store, a comparatively posh and expensive apothecary and ice cream parlor with paisley topped tables; and a pro-liferation of many others.[33] Hippie store owners and vendors protestations to the contrary, it would be naïve and delusional to believe, either then or now, that the various entrepreneurs noted above set up shop in the Hashbury *not to make money* off the "hippie thing." Many, such as the Thelin brothers, made relative fortunes while in business, frequently engaging in activities as capitalistically avaricious and opportunistic as the straight business establish-ments they roundly condemned for their profiteering. When hip merchants sensed that the hippie fad was beginning to wane, they sold their respective businesses, many for handsome profits, all at the expense of their love generation compatriots.

As the money rolled in so did the criticism from the larger hippie community, many of who believed that their shop-owner brethren were taking advantage of a captive market by charging inflated or even exorbitant prices for goods and services that would be much less outside of Hashbury. As Hunter Thompson observed, "Haight Street, the Great White Way of what local papers call 'Hippieland,' is already dotted with stores catering mainly to the tourist trade. Few Hippies can afford a pair of $20 sandals or a 'mod outfit' for $67.50." Most Haight boutiques sold mass-produced "antique," ready-to-wear clothing customized with psychedelic touches, ranging from $20 for a paisley men's shirt to $30 for a hippie sack dress.[34] Such unexpected reproach not only shocked the hip business community but forced many to publicly explain or justify their making money, which had become an anathema in the new hippie ethos. As hip essayist Guy Strait declared in an op-ed for the *Oracle*, "It has been demonstrated over and over again throughout history that it is the fight for money and pos-sessions and the prestige they bring that sets people at odds, and *that* is what makes the world hard." Strait further opined that it was a "security hypochondria, *this checking of bank books rather than pulses*," currently afflicting millions of adult Americans (especially the parents of white suburban youth), that was causing such widespread disaffection throughout the hip community. It was "this frantic concern for money" that was driving so many young (white) Americans "into the Haight-Ashbury. They [the parents] have thought so long in terms of money and possessions, that they have forgotten how to think in terms of people."[35]

Hip merchants called on Ron Thelin to speak on their behalf and convey to the "Tribe" (the term used by hippies in reference to their compatriots) their position on money making. Thelin believed that because he and his fellow hippies were embarked on the "evolution of a new culture" it was going to take time "to figure out how to do the right thing and have this money thing. It's hard because of all the bad habits we have. We have to find new means of exchange. We must free ourselves from all those other habits before we can discover how to deal with money intelligently. I understand that money is energy and that it has to flow, it's a matter of channeling. But it is also a matter of habit. This money thing like it's hard to figure out the economic mechanism that makes sense to the community."[36]

Thelin admitted that when he first opened his store, he personally "operat[ed] within the profit motive," and regardless of "how strong and beautiful the person is," if he allowed the desire for profit to dictate his business practices, then "you are going to get fucked up. That's the nature of it. That is what it does to you." To Thelin it was "greed," not money itself that was causing the outcry. "Almost all of us were exposed to this disease in childhood, but dope & love are curing us." Thus, in Thelin's view, the only way for himself and the other hip merchants to expiate their "afflicted past" and relieve themselves of the public scorn associated with "the money thing" was to absolve themselves of the "profit motive" (greed) by investing in the community to improve conditions for all and to "give away all we have beyond our needs, including money."[37] As bizarre as it sounded, Thelin made good his public declaration as he did indeed give away a lot of store items to the increasing hordes of vagrant street hippies. He also donated thousands of dollars to various hip enterprises and charities as did other hip merchants. However, Thelin continued to earn huge profits from his store, sufficient to afford him annual months-long trips to India and Europe and to be able to travel all over the United States for extended periods of time, visiting and staying for several weeks with various Native American tribes on their respective reservations.

Part of Ron Thelin's and the other hip shop owner's quest for a "new economy" for the Hashbury was to transform Haight Street into "a world famous dope center where every little store would be like fine tea shops where there are big jars of fine marijuana, where there are chemist shops with fine psychedelic chemicals, where there are real tea shops with fine tea, where there are fine restaurants with organic or macrobiotic, really good nutritious foods, where there are smoking dens, with a beautiful mall the length of Haight Street. Find foods and drugs all for free or trade." Suffice it to say, Thelin's vision for the Haight did not quite become reality, at least in the sense of "fine" or "quaint" or "refined," or "free."[38] Quite the opposite as will be seen, as thousands of wayward teens and other vagabonds inundated the area during the 1967 Summer of Love. They overwhelmed the Haight, despoiling its environs, depleting goods and services, and often ransacking homes and businesses, in their daily, desperate bid for survival. Many merchants, vendors, homeowners, and slum-lords, exploited the "flower children's" forlorn search for food, clothing, and shelter by continuing to charge exorbitant prices and rents for necessities. When most left in early September to return to the comfort and security of their white suburban neighborhoods, Thelin's dream of a charming, bustling, aesthetically pleasing psychedelic Haight Street lay in shambles. Nonetheless until that time, their shops were an integral part of the neighborhood; their businesses were what made the Haight a hippie community rather than just a place where hippies lived. Thelin and his fellow hip entrepreneurs saw themselves and their hamlet as a collective of artists and visionaries, who believed they were offering humanity an alternative way of living, one that was independent and self-sufficient in a society defined by crass materialism, mass consumption, and recurring spasms of violence.

For the most part, Thelin's and others' righteous indignation about the "money thing," fell largely on deaf ears as the majority of hip store owners, especially those who opened their doors at the beginning of the hippie/Haight-Ashbury phenomenon, made money, often quite a lot; they simply could not help it because the demand for their hip, cool products among their growing clientele was virtually insatiable and thus no matter how hard they tried to eschew the "profit motive" many found the temptation of financial remuneration too difficult to resist. It must be remembered that the majority of hippie merchants were the products of a very affluent American middle class. They had grown up with material abundance and consequently many, regardless of their condemnation of that culture, could not divorce themselves completely from its acquisitive ethos. Although none of the individuals who opened shops prior to 1967 expected to get rich off their enterprises, they did want to make money.

Bobby Bowles, owner of Peg 'n' Awl Leathers, who, like Thelin was very community oriented and donated generously to Haight initiatives, nonetheless recalls becoming very excited about the prospect of 100,000 hippies coming to the neighborhood during the summer of 1967: "Oh boy! If I can just get *one dollar* from each of them!..."[39] Thelin and many of the other hip merchants were capitalists in Bohemia, worse yet, capitalists who made money and thus, even as hippies, continued to live in relative prosperity.

The hip debate about money and profit reflected the first cresting of the post–World War II consumer marketplace and white middle class affluence. As early as the 1920s the mass production system promoted consumption rather than saving, indulgence rather than denial; depression and war only momentarily retarded these already entrenched impulses. The American economy's spectacular growth after World War II had not only brought an end to deprivation, creating unprecedented abundance, but also spawned the first generation in American history secure in the satisfaction of all material needs. Indeed, to this first wave of baby boomers, it was rarely a matter of how much, but rather *how many* and in what size, shape, color, flavor, or softness! Such freedom from scarcity and living in the rarefied and insulated suburbs with plenty of leisure time for introspection and brooding, interestingly created in many young white middle class youth a disdain for the way their parents lived. For alienated youth the Protestant ethic of self-denial, deferred gratification, and the disciplined life, had no relevance except in their parents' efforts to impose such a regimen. Perhaps it was inevitable that rejection of middle class comforts had to come from those having the most secure households; working class/poor youth at the time, had fewer if any material luxuries to rebel against.

Many hipsters concluded that the price paid for economic affluence and material security had been too high; the growth ethic was destroying or already had ravaged too many individuals' souls and psyche as well as the environment. As reflected in Thelin's comments, members of the hip community thus questioned the core values on which American capitalism was built. In rejecting the industrial corporate system and the ethos that sustained it, hippies potentially represented a real threat to that order. However, the counterculture's potential to undermine the nation's business/corporate civilization never materialized. No matter how determined hippie drop-outs were to eschew the growth ethic and its attendant values, they were children of affluence, and thus opting out meant having to live with scarcity; without all the material and creature comforts they had grown accustomed to having in their secure suburban environments. How long would someone from such a background be willing to live in such deprivation?

Also reflected in the debate concerning profitable hip-owned businesses was the remarkable speed with which American corporate capitalism seized upon the momentary popularity and chic of the hippie movement. Inevitably hippie vogue was translated into immense profits not only for local hip merchants, but more importantly for the huge companies that mass produced all manner of hip merchandise. Hunter S. Thompson saw this potential early on in the hippie movement, observing in 1967 that "everything genuine in the Haight-Ashbury is about to be swallowed—like North Beach and the Village [Greenwich]—in a wave of publicity and commercialism."[40] Such remunerative commercialization of the hip lifestyle never would have occurred if there had not been such white middle class prosperity at the time. As the hippie movement became more popular, increasing numbers of affluent white youth purchased all the appropriate apparel, emblems, and symbols associated with the hippie culture and lifestyle, reflecting their fascination and identification (though peripheral for many), with the movement. By the late 1960s, multi-million dollar hip-related industries had emerged. Many were completely new, hip-specific enterprises, such as the still–San Francisco based clothing conglomerate, The Gap Inc., founded in 1969 by the hip couple Donald and Doris Fisher. The Fishers' first store on Ocean Avenue initially sold only Levi jeans and rock and roll LPs—two of the decade's ongoing hottest items among consumers ages 13 to 30. Because of their enterprise's location near the Haight and the high demand among both hippies and "plastic" hippies as well as among day or weekend "trippers" (straights who transformed themselves into hippies on weekends, after living the square, suburban, corporate life for five days a week), for their products, in their first year of operation the Fisher's sold $2 million worth of merchandise, realizing enough profit to open a second store in San Jose, California, in 1970. It was in that year, in both of their establishments, that the Fishers introduced their first lines of hip clothing—paisley printed shirts and blouses, bell-bottom jeans, ankle-length madras skirts, and a variety of other hippie attire. Even though by that year the hippie movement was beginning to fade, the Fishers diversification into hippie garb saw their total sales triple from the year before as the desire among many young people to perpetuate the hippie look and identity remained popular. The Fishers were just one of many hip entrepreneurs who profited immensely from the brief but spectacular hippie phenomenon.[41]

Older, established mainstream corporations also seized upon the hippie fad simply by diversifying their product lines into production of hip commodities. Such businesses mass marketed all manner of colorful clothing, cosmetics, rock music, posters, and even drug paraphernalia. Most important, the rapid commercialization of hippie culture and lifestyle, especially by mainstream corporate America, reflected the Establishment's economic and political power to eclipse the potential for serious disruption the counterculture might have posed. By reshaping, co-opting, and filtering the counterculture through the broader streams of American business civilization, American capitalists absorbed Dionysus into the dominant culture. Thus the corporate establishment made it next to impossible for the hippie movement to remain uncorrupted by the very capitalist system they shunned.

The crucial role of the market reveals not only the limitations of the hippie critique of Establishment culture but also the powerful economic forces arrayed against the hippies' attempt to build a potential alternative society. In the Haight lived a community in opposition to bourgeois society yet it was suffused with commercialism. Here also was a subculture which sought collectivity yet passionately believed in the idea of each individual's right to "do your own thing." Finally, the Haight's hippie residents believed they had created a communal space within the city, encompassing a pastoral arcadia, yet surrounding and infiltrating and despoiling their ingenuousness were individuals from the urban technological nightmare from which they sought to insulate themselves. Yet, they needed these individuals to come to the Haight in order to sustain the community economically. In effect, a giant, cascading wave of consumerism came crashing down on the nation's first Hippieland, destroying everything genuine, and as the wave receded, what was left was only the movement's symbols: love beads, sandals, tie-dyed clothing, hash pipes, slogans, and flowers. But these objects no longer represented anything real or unaffected; the hippie's core philosophy had been obliterated by the capitalist system. These were the sorts of paradoxes that permeated the hippie impulse and community from the beginning, regardless of location. They also explain the movement's successes and failures. Theodore Roszak feared the hippies would soon be "swamped with cynical or self-deceived opportunists," especially from the media and fashion industries who presented themselves publicly (for purposes of profit), as the hippies biggest boosters but behind closed corporate doors pursued an agenda of subverting the counterculture by reducing hippies to "an amusing side show of the swinging society." Yet, Roszak was sanguine that "despite the fraudulence and folly that collects around its edges," the counterculture would resist co-optation and exploitation.[42]

If there was one prevalent enterprise that best translated the hippies' optimistic and exuberant spirit and concomitant desire to flaunt and mock convention by dressing outrageously, it was the apparel industry, which began in 1965 to adapt production to the increasing demand among young people for more eclectic, flamboyant, multiethnic, and just plain, old-fashioned attire, ranging from workmen's overalls to tie-dyed T-shirts and dashikis to Old Mother Hubbard or "Granny dresses. Sales of conventional suits, jackets, ties, elegant dresses, high heels, and white gloves plummeted, as hippies and many young people in general, viewed such clothing as the staid, unimaginative "uniform" of an "uptight" suburban bourgeoisie or the formality of their parent's 1950s generation—Ward and June Cleaver. As Andy Warhol observed, "The kids were throwing out all the preppy outfits and the dress-up clothes that made them look like their mothers and fathers."[43]

For young hippie men long hair, beards, or mustaches became the standard look, while their female counterparts also let their hair grow long or "natural," rejecting not only their mothers' permed hairdos but makeup, heels, hose, dresses, skirts, and even shaving armpits and legs. Naturalness seemed to define both male and female hippie appearance. Since many hippies believed that their movement was a resurrection of and homage to more elemental, tribal people, few should have been surprised by the hippie penchant for tattoos, ear and nose piercing, and other forms of bodily alterations. Expensive or traditional jewelry was also "out," considered to be symbols of petty, bourgeois self-indulgence. Hippies preferred cheap love beads along with other types of primitive necklaces, rings, and bracelets, reflecting their appreciation/fascination with non–Western, neo-pagan attire. As early as 1965, Tom Wolfe, who became one of the 1960s most avid counterculture chroniclers, anticipated the increasing youth penchant in clothing "from low places, from marginal types who carve out worlds for themselves in tainted undergrounds." Wolf was certain that it would only be a matter of time before teenagers and American enterprise transformed such attire into "high styles."[44] Not even the American flag or military was saved from hippie mocking or parodying. These "anti-uniforms" took on particular symbolic significance as the nation sent increasing numbers of young white males off to war. To show their contempt for such an "Amerika" and the war it was perpetrating in Vietnam, hippies wore all manner of military garb; some, to the great distress of straight or super-patriotic Americans, wore the American flag either in the form of a shirt or on the back of leather jackets, as the protagonists displayed in the 1969 counterculture movie classic *Easy Rider*. Hippies dressed for the public and their attire became an identifier for who they were, as clothes became costumes and costumes became clothes. To conventional eyes the hip look reflected slovenliness and sexual ambiguity; to hippies their dress represented freedom from the uptight, cramped, and contrived, to the loose and natural; the anti-uniforms had become uniform. As Jerry Rubin proclaimed, "Long hair, beards, no bras and freaky clothes represent a break from Prison America."[45]

Guy Strait was convinced that more than any other issue relative to the hippies, it was the way they dressed that caused "the straight community's angry, sometimes violent reaction to the hippies." According to Strait, hippies dressed the way they did "because they have thrown a lot of middle class notions out the window and with them the most sensitive middle-class dogma: the neutral appearance." Strait believed the drab attire of the middle class not only reflected the desire of its members for mass conformity but an equally passionate search for a secure "anonymity." To Strait and other hippies the larger straight world had become "a jungle of taboos, fears, and personality games," and "to survive in any jungle requires good protective coloring: the camouflage of respectable appearance." By contrast, since hippies "will not play the straight game of camouflage," unabashedly flaunting unusual and bright-colored clothing, their appearance "becomes alarm, a danger signal to the fearful [the straights]; a challenge that turns into fear and fear sours into anger." Hippies became targets of abuse and rage among straights, according to Strait, who believed "the oldest fallacy in the world: anything that makes you angry must be bad," because the hippies refused "to play the straight game of camouflage," the straight world considered their outrageous clothing to be manifestations of a sinister character lurking underneath that "Granny-dress" or "peasant shirt"—someone "capable of anything and therefore a danger."[46]

As Thomas Frank has observed, the 1960s and early 1970s men's clothing industry was especially affected by the hippie revolt and the revolution of the young in general, embracing the new "consciousness" as a way to revolutionize one of the most staid capitalist enterprises in the country. Progressive men's wear designers, corporate chieftains, and trade publications, most notably *Gentlemen's Quarterly*, allied with the hippie rebels in a crusade to liberate the men's fashion industry from 1950's conformity and conservatism, both in attire and mentality. By 1966–67, a "Peacock Revolution" was taking place in men's clothing, reflecting sartorially in attitude and rhetoric, the hip revolt and ethos. Increasingly men's attire became bold state-ments of defiance and radical transgression, which creative, "with it" advertising agencies, many of which had also welcomed the hip/youth revolt, celebrated as the apparel of men who chose to defy conformity and the mores of technocratic, plastic America. In effect, the revolution in menswear and the countercultural revolt became symbiotic as the men's apparel industry provided young rebels with the attire that befitted their liberation and new awareness. Indeed, according to GQ writer Jason McCloskey, "A new kind of cat was walking the land" and he must have the appropriate attire; garments that expressed his emancipation and new consciousness. As McCloskey further observed, while the youth revolt "was being pro-grammed through rock" it was simultaneously "manifest through fashion; the American fash-ion industry was one of the first to move to accommodate the change on a national level." Those clothing manufacturers who catered to the burgeoning youth market were genuinely excited by the new world of hip and thus helped to radicalize "one of the most reactionary industries." Indeed, to McCloskey and many others associated with the men's apparel industry, by the early 1970s, "the revolution [in men's clothing] had passed the point of no return. Many products long taken for granted would have to be overhauled or face outright rejection." As the president of Macy's department stores told *Esquire* magazine in 1965, "In our gener-ation you had to keep up with the Joneses. Today it's more important to keep up with the Joneses kids. In short, in the child-oriented society where we find ourselves, the teen-ager is the new influential." Andy Warhol seconded that observation, declaring that by the mid–1960s, the entire style industry had "reversed" itself, with "mothers and fathers trying to look like their kids." By the close of the 1960s a hip/youth inspired and oriented brand of capitalism had come to inform the policies, products, management, as well as the general ethos, vision, and direction of some of the nation's most important consumer industries, many of which down to the present have remained true to the ideas and practices first initiated during their late 1960s "Countercultural Reformation."[47]

For the majority of hippies, outrageous attire became a visual marker of shared countercultural identity, a way of recognizing other freaks. Clothing was a form of cultural communication and bonding among hippies, whose passion for romantic and flamboyant dress was also an assertion of power intended to shock and agitate mainstream America. Their penchant for the outrageous reflected not only their rejection of the white middle class obsession with conformity, but simultaneously a symbolic pledging of loyalty and kinship with each other and devotion to a different lifestyle. In short, hippie fashion allowed its adherents to project an identity of changing personas; an image that could be summed as "the many moods of me." The refusal to conform in dress and behavior, the rhetoric of revolution through love, and the belief that love could unite people in unexpected ways, came to inform much of the hippie ethos.

Although Thelin and other hip merchants suffered from cognitive dissonance relative to their business' success, there emerged in the Haight by 1966 a group of unabashed, flamboyant hippie radicals, the Diggers, who were uncompromising in their belief that property—land, money, ownership of anything—was theft and thus everything should be free: all goods and services, love, behavior, relationships. Indeed, the Diggers' motto was "Free," and the most apt term for their ideas and behavior was anarchism, albeit a proclaimed socially conscious and responsible type of insurgency but subversion nonetheless of the liberal capitalist system. They were anarchists of the deed and their outrageous antics and flair for the theatrical was to carry a romantic idea (anarchism) to its logical endpoint: the realization of a completely free society. According to ex–Digger David Simpson, "We were like a street gang and we really believed the socio-economic structure of America was completely unsustainable. We were trying to build a new, free society in the shell of the old."[48]

The Diggers despised the 1960s establishment liberal ethos as embodied in Lyndon Johnson's Great Society and the bourgeois culture that supported it, declaring that such a system was beyond reformation. They believed their mission in the Haight was to begin the uprising to liberate humanity from the "money nexus" that presently had captured the hearts and minds of the majority of white Americans, molding them into self-centered, acquisitive, and hostile human beings. Their goal was to transform the Haight into an autonomous community where people took care of each other and lived by their own visions, eschewing the profit motive poisoning America. To many in the Haight the Diggers became "the prime model of organized love," for in their various "Digger Papers"—typed, anonymous, mimeographed manifestoes put up on telephone poles, in storefronts, on walls, and even on door fronts throughout the Haight—the Diggers' declared that their existence was "to help motivate youth who move about without direction, to discover the rich creative potential inherent in them and to establish positive goal-directed activities for themselves." Another Digger decree announced that "Every brother should have what he needs to do his own thing." Also, since the United States had become a society beyond scarcity, it was time to live off the abundant fat of the land; or in the words of a Digger leaflet, "SEW THE RAGS OF SURPLUS INTO TEPEES." There should even be "Free Families," for every individual or group who desired to form such a kinship, whether they were the Black Panthers or radical street gangs, homosexuals, communards, whomever, regardless of their "orientation." Such associations, the Diggers believed, would become the vanguard for "Free Cities where everything that is necessary can be obtained for free by those involved in the various activities of the various clans."[49]

For a while the Diggers were one of the counterculture's most productive and fantastic communities. Unlike the tens of thousands of young people who would soon appear in the neighborhood, they had not run away to the Haight, but rather, believed that it was in that locale, at that specific moment (1966) that they were to ignite the cultural and spiritual revolution the hippies represented. In fact, the Diggers had the most thoroughly conceived, conscious ideology of any group in the Haight: a hybrid of bohemian–New Left politics filtered through psychedelic eyes. For a brief moment in the 1960s the Diggers became one of the most legendary avant-garde collectives in American history. Their principal founders, Emmett Grogan, Peter Berg, Peter Coyote, and Billy Murcott, had immersed themselves in the Haight's growing drug scene, sharing with the hippie faithful the belief that acid was the key to liberating individuals from the bourgeois "trips" that had been laid on young Americans by their parents, teachers, and all other human and institutional forms and manifestations of authority, restraint, and conformity. It was during an LSD trip that Grogan had a "flash of illumination": that property was theft, and therefore it was his and his followers' responsibility to Haight residents—and all others who came to Hashbury seeking "liberation"—to have what they needed for free. Grogan and company took the name Diggers from the 17th century English social dissenters, who appropriated common land and gave their surplus to the poor during Cromwell's reign.[50] Although claiming to speak for the Haight's *true* hip community, more often than not the Diggers' messages fell on deaf ears; their leaflets were frequently too intellectually sophisticated for the majority of Hashbury hippies to mentally digest or act upon.

Part of the Diggers' engrossing presence on Hashbury's streets was the literally theatrical way they implemented their ideas and challenged the Establishment. All of its founding members had been professional street actors with the legendary San Francisco Mime Troupe, founded in 1963 by Ron Davis, which had performed radical plays for free in public venues several years before the first hippie appeared on the Haight's boulevards. From the Mime Troupe's inception in 1959, Davis' goal was to use his company to push American society beyond what he called the "stagnation of the fifties." Davis found traditional "bourgeois" theater to be mindless, formulaic escapism, and the agitprop plays of the Old Left "pedantic pseudo-realism." "My own theatrical premise," wrote Davis, was that "Western Society is Rotten in General, Capitalist Society in the Main, and U.S. Society in the Particular."[51]

While still performing for the Mime Troupe, Digger co-founder Peter Berg coined the term "guerrilla theater," a concept Davis readily embraced and fanatically supported; it became the Mime Troupe's raison d'être. Davis and Berg required every company member, in addition to being artistically innovative or gifted, to be "politically oriented." The stage, wherever it may be or in what shape it came, must function as "a weapon" against establishment injustices and societal inequities. The Mime Troupe and their counterculture compatriots across the creative spectrum viewed art holistically; that is, politics, art, and personal life were all components of an interactive movement aimed at transforming the way people lived. Art *was* politics by the 1960s, and this mantra became especially true for the performing arts, whose creators were knee-deep in raising consciousness. Their works' priority was to move rather than entertain the audience. Every performance was designed to affect their audiences' lives profoundly, and in the process to express the joy of it all. This purpose required a "special" kind of actor and Davis had some types in mind: "I personally like to work with the kooks, the emotionally disturbed, the violent ones, the fallen away Catholics, non–Jewish Jews, the deviates.... They do what the well-trained actor can never do—they create." Thus, throughout the country an array of small, ephemeral street-drama groups emerged in college towns and metropolitan centers, all of whom embraced Berg's approach and methods. Their shows attacked racism, the Vietnam War, and establishment hypocrisy and abuse of the people. Their goal was to help individuals to liberate themselves from the bourgeoisie's psychological hang-ups about sex, materialism, and conformity. It was out of this rich compost of left politics, pot, LSD, and free love that the Diggers emerged, a rag-tag of street activists and cultural anarchists who would set much of the tone for the countercultural capital, Haight-Ashbury.[52]

Just as Davis had "split" from the Actor's Workshop for his colleagues' alleged sell out to the establishment, so were the Diggers' founders motivated to bolt from the San Francisco Mime Troupe when Davis refused to take his activism to where it counted: directly to the people on the streets. Hashbury's flowing, turbulent streets were the perfect venue for activist theater, preferred to the auditoriums and parks where the Mime Troupe usually performed. During the summer of 1966 Grogan decided it was time to provide the Haight with some politics and thus he and his compatriots began issuing anonymous mimeographed essays, and putting up posters and signs throughout the neighborhood, all expressing the groups' anarchist philosophy and all signed "Digger." Thus was born the "Digger Papers."

Grogan and company spared no one in their attacks on the Hashbury culture and its followers. They were particularly vituperative in their assaults on the Thelin brothers and other H.I. P. (the Haight Independent Proprietors, a consortium formed in early 1966 of the community's countercultural shopkeepers) merchants for their profiteering off the hippie fad—"prettified monsters of moneylust." The Digger Papers also condemned the hip *Oracle* for its "pansyness," while labeling the paper "an old rag of misinformation, outdated 'news,' psychedelic bullshit art and pre-masticated verbal masturbation about what we already know." Although the Diggers may have dismissed the *Oracle* as the mouthpiece of H.I.P. and of the Haight establishment, the paper nonetheless was mostly apolitical and documented the neighborhood's philosophy and culture with beautiful graphics, poems, and articles written by prominent underground members. According to founder Allen Cohen, the paper's main objective was to expose the mainstream print press as "a lie. We were going to make the newspaper format a joke that would show everyone that [conventional] newspapers were destroying sensibilities, causing paranoia and fear. We were going to fill our newspaper with art, philosophy, poetry and attend to this change of consciousness that was happening in the Haight Ashbury and, we hoped, the world." Despite the Digger's assault, the *Oracle* was popular with more than just the Hashbury's hippie population; at its peak, circa summer 1967, the paper had a circulation of 117,000 and boasted worldwide distribution, establishing its legacy as one of the largest community underground journals ever printed. It's avant-garde graphic style and printing methods "set the standards of graphic excellence for all underground papers to follow," and which were later coopted by such mainstream publications such as *Vogue* and *Playboy*.[53] As noted British journalist and underground press pathfinder John Wilcock observed of the *Oracle*, "Its creators [used] color the way Lautrec must once have experimented with lithography—testing the resources of the medium to the utmost and producing what almost any experienced newspaperman would tell you was impossible. It [the *Oracle*] is a creative dynamo whose influence will undoubtedly change the look of American publishing."[54] Most important, the *Oracle* provided a venue through which the community's residents could feel comfortable expressing views not publishable in the mainstream media, giving more insightful and usually more accurate, detailed accounts of "hippie happenings" than the established press. Mainstream reporters simply did not have intimate access to such events, and their jaundiced, conventional reporting could not match the authentic insider's view of the hippie community and how its members interpreted their complicated relationship with the dominant culture.

The Diggers also saw fit to disparage the New Left, referring to its leaders as "self-righteous" and "as full of puritanical shit as the country's right wing was cowardly absurd." New Leftists were "creep commies" on "power trips." Leary's drug culture was "naïve and devoid of moral direction." The Diggers even lambasted the rock stars they hung out with for being people "who can sing about the evils of the world while margining profits into war economies and maintaining [their] comforts on a consumer level of luxury." Grogan and company believed that most hippies were "cute, unserious, and innocent"; "white kids who weren't that hip." Indeed, the Diggers believed the hippie idea that love, peace, and a smile, along with a chestful of buttons and a psychedelic shop was all that was needed to transform the world, was just as much "bullshit" as the Swami's transcendental meditation. In a street manifesto titled "Sheep? Baa," The Diggers warned hippies to "Beware of leaders, heroes, and organizers. Any man who wants to lead you is The Man. Think: why would anyone *want* to lead me? Fuck leaders." "When Love does its thing," they declared in a broadside, "it does it for itself, not for profit. To Show Love is to fail." The Diggers were either/or: "If you're not a digger/you're property"; "If you Really believe it/do it."[55]

Suffice it to say the Thelin brothers and the other hip businessmen did not take kindly the Diggers' verbal pummeling and thus began the chronic war between the anarchists and the Haight merchants that agitated the neighborhood to the end of hippiedom in San Francisco. As *Oracle* co-founder Allen Cohen remembered, "The Diggers had a tendency toward anarchy that bordered on violence. The Haight merchants in defense against the Diggers demand to share their profits with the community accused them [the Diggers] of extortion and violence."[56] In Gear owner Tsvi Strauch was even more direct in her condemnation of the Diggers' radical Marxist approach to capitalism: "See, they believe in purity, which doesn't exist in the world. But dogmatic ideologies always claim to have that kind of purity like Catholics and the Communists and logical positivists.... They interpret the Haight-Ashbury according to their own economic doctrines, without any real knowledge of what's going on.... So they claim that we're selling love that we're dressing like hippies to sell our thing.... We're not straight people who saw something good, grew a quick beard, opened a store, and are trying to capitalize on that. You're not forced to buy anywhere. That's just Marxist bullshit."[57]

One of the Diggers' more participatory demonstrations was their September 1966 "street happening" to begin at dusk, at which time hundreds of hippies shined rear-view mirrors the Diggers had liberated from a local junkyard from Haight Street roof tops into the eyes of drivers going up the street to reflect the sunset. A group of women simultaneously began chanting on the street below and soon were joined by thousands of other street folk, who joined in the chorus. The police of course showed up and as they began clearing the crowds, they unwittingly became part of the "show." This was just one of the Digger's many theatrical public capers, all of which were designed to be "rituals of release through spirit" with "crowds [of] people pouring into the streets."[58]

To the Diggers, action, not words counted, and thus the need for perpetual, outrageous, poignant street theater, for such visual, physical displays of artistic expression could alter consciousness by altering frame of reference. In October 1966 the Diggers began handing out leaflets announcing that every day at 4 p.m. at the panhandle of Ashbury Street, free food would be distributed to all who came, so bring a bowl and spoon. Every day for the next year the Diggers made good their word. By the time the Diggers began their free-food crusade, the Haight was beginning to fill up with teenage refugees from suburbia, many dead broke, and thus they flocked to the Diggers' free feedings. The victuals weren't entirely free; those who wanted food had first to walk through a large wooden frame painted yellow called the "Free Frame of Reference." Their passage through the portal signified their supposed liberation from materialism.[59]

The quality of food was unpredictable, even suspect at times, but to hungry street urchins a bowl of hot soup of mysterious ingredients, complimented with two-day-old sourdough bread, went far to soothe a growling, empty stomach. The meat was usually fresh, although it was mostly butcher-shop trimmings or chicken wings. The vegetables were often wilted but in soups that made little difference. Most of the food was either begged or donated; some was just lifted. Digger cook Phyllis Willner was a 16-year-old runaway from New York when she arrived in Hashbury in 1966, broke and hungry. She remembered being fed by the Diggers: "Each week Phil, at the chicken warehouse, was good for two cases of chicken wings. Ray at the fish dock, provided a box of fish. And so it went. One day we received a message from a marine biologist from the Fish and Game Department offering a whale that had been illegally caught by some fishermen. The carcass had been stripped and the meat filled our Dodge truck. We pounded the shit out of that meat but it wasn't bad at all. It was OK and lasted a long time."[60]

As reflected in Phyllis Willner's account, Digger women did the grunt work that kept the movement alive while the Digger men had all the fun thinking up and staging all the pranks and spectacles. Rare was the moment when one would see Emmett Grogan or Peter Berg up at five a.m., driving the old truck around town scrounging for food for the day's free meal at the Panhandle. Digger women not only procured the meat, vegetables, and bread, but also did all the cooking, lugged the food out to the Panhandle in massive steel milk containers, and distributed it to the hungry hordes. In addition to feeding the masses, Digger women made all manner of clothing, often sewing for hours on end, and invented the tie-dying method of textile design—an innovation for which they never received proper recognition. As Emmett Grogan confessed years later, "If it hadn't been for those women there wouldn't have been the 4 p.m. Free Food in the park every day or any day. They were the real strength in the Haight-Ashbury community, the real Diggers. Cooking two or three twenty-gallon milk cans full of stew for two hundred people can be a goof, if you do it once a year, but try doing it for two or three days in a row, for two or three weeks, for two or three months. And not get paid—not make any money from it all. It's a bitch!"[61] As was more prevalent than not throughout the counterculture, hippie women were treated as less than equals, relegated and confined to traditional roles and often ridiculed and condemned when trying to establish their autonomy and self-actualization through a movement that allegedly cherished "individual freedom." Running through the counterculture from beginning to end, was an oppressive, sexually charged male chauvinism and dominance that blatantly contradicted the hippie message or belief in the freedom and equality of all humanity.

The Diggers topped their free-food jape by opening a free store in a converted garage on Page Street. They called their emporium the Free Frame of Reference, and after they were forced to move from their original locale, they named their new place The Trip Without A Ticket. At either location, anyone could rummage through boxes and barrels for clothes, pots, dishes, and food. The store reflected the Digger's contempt for all "things" the straight world held dear. When liberals gave money, the Diggers burned it; when someone asked who was in charge, he was told he was. As Michael William Doyle has observed, all of the Diggers' free ventures "parodied capitalism even while redistributing the cornucopian bounty of that system's surplus."[62] The media loved the Diggers and portrayed them as a hip version of the Salvation Army. Indeed, as New York's East Village Digger leader Abbie Hoffman declared, Diggers were hippies who had learned to manipulate the media instead of being machinated by them. "A modern revolutionary group," Hoffman explained, "headed for the television station not the factory." Interestingly, Hoffman also believed that both groups "are in one sense a huge put-on."[63]

The Diggers' exploits and escapades quickly gained national attention. Flocks of imitators appeared, not just throughout the Bay Area and in southern California, but nation-wide. All the Digger groups pursued the same agenda: displays of public contempt for the bourgeois capitalist liberal ethos and the use of street theatrics not only to promote their philosophy of free and win converts, but to defy as well all manifestations of establishment authority. They were the artist-politicians who the avant-garde had long envisioned. Although disdainful of the hippie ethos, the Diggers nonetheless felt compelled to inspire as many "flower children" as they possibly could to explore alternative consciousness by experimenting with new forms of social relationships. The Diggers embraced the use of hallucinogenic drugs, which they believed helped individuals to try on new costumes and to seek new identities. Freedom to the Diggers meant not being afraid to act out in front of others, of "doing your own thing," free of all inhibitions and restraints. They encouraged public displays of private desires and fantasies, which they believed represented the self-revelation of the totally free and autonomous person, unleashed from all the social controls imposed by a spiritually suffocating American culture.

As would occur with many of the counterculture's dreams and crusades for a better world, free from obsessions about money, career, and pursuit of the American Dream, reality would soon obtrude upon and shatter their illusions about humanity— especially the willingness of the poor, the degraded, the racialized, and the marginalized—to embrace their ideals. Such was the rude awakening Digger newbie Alex Forman experienced while working in the Diggers' free store. Forman "realized the absurdity" of what the Diggers were trying to do when a group of older black women came into the emporium and asked "'How much do these clothes cost here?'" We said, 'Oh, it's all free. You just take what you need, and then if you have extra, you give. They said, 'What do you mean, you just take what you need?' 'Well you just take what you need, that's all.' They said, 'Really?' So they came back with these big boxes and they started just taking tons of stuff off the racks. We said, 'What are you doing?' They said, 'Well you said take what you need.' We said, 'Yeah, well, you don't need all those clothes for yourself.' They said, 'No but we need the money so we're going to take the clothes and sell them.'"[64]

Peter Coyote had a similar experience on the day he was the Free Store's manager. "One day I noticed an obviously poor black woman furtively stuffing clothing into a large paper bag. When I approached her she turned away from the bag coolly, pretending it wasn't hers. In a conventional store, her ruse would have made sense because she knew she was stealing. Smiling pleasantly, I returned the bag to her. 'You can't steal here,' I said. She got indignant and said, 'I wasn't stealing!' 'I know.' I said amiably. 'But you thought you were stealing. You can't steal here because it's a Free Store. Read the sign, everything is free! You can have the whole fucking store if you feel like it. You can take over and tell me to get lost."[65]

Such encounters led Forman, Coyote, and others to the realization that outside of the rarefied confines of Haight-Ashbury and even within its environs, not all of its citizens had become enlightened seekers who could afford or were willing to extend such generosity to others; that scarcity, not abundance, was the order of the day for many Americans, particularly for African Americans and other socio-economically marginalized groups. Forman had bought into the "anti-money thing" expressed by Ron Thelin, Guy Strait, and the Diggers and thus naively yet sincerely, believed such a redemption possible. However, the black women and the other poor neighborhood folk who undoubtedly frequented the free store as often as possible and saw such bounty as manna from heaven for their own personal benefit, gave Forman a dose of the harsh reality for many of his neighbors: "they needed money, and here we were saying just take what you need for your own personal, immediate needs. But for them that wasn't reality. Their reality was, 'How are you going to get some money, and here's these foolish white people just letting us take whatever we need. Well, we need it all. We don't have anything.'"[66]

Although determined to change consciousness by an anarcho-theatrical-artistic approach, the Diggers' philanthropy and altruism should not be misunderstood as a hippie Goodwill Industries project. There was a darker underside to the Diggers, both personally and philosophically. They were significantly older than the majority of the hippies and radicals they associated with or tried to inspire. Many of them had had run-ins with the law, such as former junkie Emmett Grogan, who some have labeled as "sinister, paranoid, secretive, and often violent."[67] Even Peter Berg, who worshipped Grogan, admitted that "he [Grogan] was a little bit sociopathic toward other people. He even stole stuff from me."[68] To the Diggers, free was not about genuine charity but rather a tactic in the long political struggle to destroy the straight world's bourgeois capitalist system and replace it with an anarchist culture, which not only would liberate the human spirit but allow it to flourish to its fullest potential as well. However, the Diggers' often aggressive, confrontational style; hatred of all rules and convention; and their recklessness, all in the name of freedom, riled the Haight. Indeed, many of the Haight's original hippie denizens denounced the Digger creed and the Diggers' willingness to purposely provoke the city's Establishment (the police, politicians, and all straights) into acts of repression. The Diggers' anarchistic philosophy and refusal to accommodate any manifestations of normal society was antithetical to the hippie message of peace, love, and the brotherhood of all humanity and the respect for each person to be able to "do their own thing." Many hippies worried that the Diggers' outrageous antics and acts of deviance would give all hippies a "bad rap"; that straights would associate all hippies with the Diggers and believe that within every hippie lurked a dangerous and sinister political radical who was out to subvert, with violence if necessary, traditional American society and culture. Thus many hippies disassociated themselves from the Diggers, fearing any affiliation would provoke further straight disdain for their movement. Although only a handful of hippies joined the Diggers, they nonetheless had their partisans. One such admirer was yippie co-founder Abbie Hoffman, who described them as "slum-alley saints" who "lit up the period by spreading the poetry of love and anarchy with broad strokes of artistic genius."[69]

Despite the tensions already present in the Haight among many of the neighborhood's different groups, the overall population continued to grow throughout 1966 and into 1967.

For Alex Forman, who arrived in the Haight in 1966, "the city was just exploding with this counterculture movement. I thought 'This is it!' It was like paradise there. Everybody was in love with life and in love with their fellow human beings to the point where they were just sharing in incredible ways with everybody. Taking people in off the streets and letting them stay in their homes, breaking free of conventional morality." When walking down the neighborhood's streets, people "would smile at you and just go 'Hey, it's beautiful, isn't it?' It was like people were high on the street and willing to share that energy. It was a very special time. It was a whole other vision of what was possible."[70]

Such was also the experience and sentiments of native Indianan Larry Houchin, who left Los Angeles for the Haight in 1966. Upon arrival he too was "overwhelmed by how friendly, loving, sharing, and just high on life everyone was. I had never felt so welcomed by strangers." Houchin had saved up some money and was able rent a six-bedroom, four bath, three- level Victorian home complete with a huge "play room," for $200 a month. Houchin rented the rooms out to all manner of individuals over the course of the next three years but prior to the Summer of Love, Houchin "loved all the people who I rented to. They were real hippies, committed to what they believed in and lived by their philosophy as well. I never had any problems" Houchin also embraced the hippies' sexual liberation credo, in which he fully participated, to the degree that he not only "balled a lot of different girls who were just hanging out at my pad with nothing better to do," but also from whom "I got first a whole series of bad crabs but eventually really bad painful drippy dick [gonorrhea] that I had to go to the doctor for shots and medicine, penicillin. Man, no one wanted to use rubbers in those days; no protection needed we thought; all the girls were on the pill."[71]

It was also at this time that Houchin began to immerse himself in the drug scene, which in retrospect he believed caused the Haight's ultimate downfall, as well as his own: "I fried my brain pretty good then and now I have a hard time remembering recent shit or just staying focused very long!" But at the time, "Man, it was great; marijuana was everywhere and cheap and acid was too. I began to deal in both and made pretty good money but you didn't need a lot back then; everything was pretty cheap. I liked acid a lot more than weed. I had taken hundreds of trips by the time of the Be-In. Fuck everything else I said; job, career, money. There was plenty of dope for everyone and everyone loved each other; no hang-ups here. I wanted to stay in San Francisco forever."[72]

As reflected in Houchin's comments, the key to such early bliss in the Haight, and the main reason why the neighborhood was not simply North Beach transplanted, was LSD. Indeed, LSD became the Haight's best kept secret for euphoria. As one of the community's early initiates remembered, "Taking it was like being in a secret society. Hardly anything was being said about it publicly, and although not an illegal drug, people acted as if it were; it seemed illegal."[73]

No doubt the majority of the Haight's original hippie inhabitants shared Houchin's and Forman's sentiments and would continue to do so up to the Summer of Love, which began in June 1967. Unfortunately, by the time summer ended, the event had shattered the illusions about the neighborhood and the counterculture in general held by Houchin, Forman, and many of the Haight's original hippie founders. However, until that time, the Haight's hippies reveled in their moment in the sun, especially in their freedom to pursue Dionysian ecstasies, both bodily and mystic.

3

Hippies and the Emergence of the Drug Culture

"This [acid] is wonderful no doubt but it is a fake. I solved the secret of the universe last night, but this morning I forgot what it was."—Author Arthur Koestler's reflection of his first and last LSD trip

In early June 1963, twenty-eight-year-old Larry Houchin from Wabash, Indiana, arrived at the Hotel Catalina in Zijuantenejo, Mexico, ready to become a member of Timothy Leary's in-exile, International Foundation for Internal Freedom, and LSD-propagating enterprise. Leary had first organized his foundation at Harvard before being asked to leave by a wary administration and outraged colleagues for his unprofessionalism. Houchin had heard of Leary's LSD experiments at Harvard as well as the professor's other LSD-related escapades and knew of the experiences of others who had expanded their consciousness by ingesting the new wonder drug. By the time Houchin arrived, "there were about 25 or 30 others who had already come, all of us seeking to discover what we had all heard; that LSD would open up new worlds of perception previously unknown. We just hoped there would be enough LSD for all of us." Houchin did not have to worry about any shortages of the miracle tablet; Leary and his side-kick colleague and fellow tripper, Richard Alpert, had plenty, and according to Houchin, "gave them out like candy to anyone who wanted to trip, anytime, anyplace. It was amazing; most of us tripped for days on end; some left the place never really coming down." Leary not only had LSD tabs but sufficient supplies of mescaline and psilocybin as well.[1]

Houchin quickly became a Leary disciple and was certain "Leary had been sent by God to open up our hearts and minds to become better human beings. That was why we came, at least most of the initial crowd. " When not tripping on acid or some other hallucinogen, Houchin and company "laid around all day, really doing nothing or anything we wanted to do—swim, play the guitar, read, rap with others about our trips; it was all a stone groove." However, Houchin and the original group believed they were there for a higher purpose than just getting stoned: "We had all come to transform ourselves into more holistic, aware, and enlightened human beings and we were going to bring that awareness to others; that became our mission, and that's what Leary and Alpert told us all the time." In Houchin's view Leary in particular was "a new messiah; a prophet of enlightenment and someone who really believed in what he was saying. He was a most intelligent man but also real, down-to-earth, always smiling and happy and wanted all of us to share in his joy about his discovery. I really liked Leary and believed in him. Only years later did I realize it was all about him; that he was a fakir and showman. I guess he really believed he was God or the Biggest Guru of them all. But by then the whole LSD scene had become so popular; everyone was dropping acid but I had gone on to meth and other harder drugs. Do I blame Leary for how fucked up I became on drugs? No, not really, but maybe if he had not come along, many of us would not have gone down that path. I don't know. All I know is that I eventually blew a heart valve because of all the meth I took, the purest stuff around. I got it through a nurse for free."[2]

Unfortunately for Houchin and the other original seekers, Leary's little ersatz nirvana lasted for only about six weeks as a horde of unwashed, unkempt, and unemployed proto-hippies began washing up on their shores, begging for food, shelter, and "cosmic illumination"—free dope. Houchin stayed away from these "free-loaders," who "began showing up in droves and Leary became real concerned. He did not know what to do with them but we all knew they had to go. There were some real bad people who showed up, criminals and dope fiends [heroin addicts]. They were destroying the peace and love that was once all around the place." Leary had no choice but to turn them away. The disgruntled rejectees began spreading stories of the lurid doings at the Hotel Catalina, which, according to Houchin did occur, but "not the way it was told. Sure there was lots of free, easy sex, even among the guys, but not out in the open for everyone to see. Leary told us to keep such activities private and most of us did." Nonetheless, it was only a matter of time before such rumors reached Mexican authorities, who wanted no such individuals in their country. Thus, in late June 1963, Mexican officials ended the idyll, ordering the hotel closed and expelling Leary and his colleagues from Mexico.[3] For Houchin, his brief encounter with Leary and the LSD scene at the Hotel Catalina proved a turning-point and after his experiences he knew "I had to follow the path I was shown by my acid trips and that I could no longer live a normal life. I became a seeker and still am." Indeed, Houchin no longer drops acid or does meth, but confessed that he still "smokes a lot of grass; it's my medicine."[4]

The novelist Alan Harrington called hippies "no more than Beats plus drugs."[5] In the transformation from Beat to hippie and the psychedelic experience, hallucinogenic drugs, most notably LSD, played a key role. But the hippies were unlike the Beats and hipsters of the previous eras: dressed in black and hiding in dark cafes and jazz club dives, the Beats celebrated their heroin or reefer kicks quietly, privately. The 1960s LSD-energized hippies were out in the open, flamboyantly and confidently bringing their message of acid-enlightenment to a world that had forgotten how to "dream with the lights on." For the hippies, genuine spiritual and cognitively fulfilling awareness could only occur on an acid trip to a higher realm of consciousness where the impossible could be truly imagined; where reality became just another illusion. Perhaps most important to most hippies, acid trips erased the "dysfunctional programming" of old behavioral and mental conditioning. Creating this blank slate of new consciousness allowed people to eliminate old imprints, especially those that inhibited spiritual growth and sensual awareness, stimulating an elemental cleansing or purging of mind, body, and soul. Free of self-destructive preconditioned habits, individuals could recreate themselves according to a more spiritual, natural, drug-produced frame of reference. LSD became, in part, the dividing line that separated the hippie counterculture from the thrills of normal youth culture. *San Francisco Oracle* founder and chief editor Allen Cohen perhaps best captured the hippie attraction to LSD: "It was the rocket engine of most of the social or creative tendencies that were emerging in the 1960s. It sped up change by opening a direct pathway to the creative and mystical insights that visionaries, artists, and saints have sought and experienced and communicated throughout the ages." One's "own mind and their own senses" were "the only frontier left in America," and to explore that last frontier, acid was "the ticket to the ride." Grateful Dead leader Jerry Garcia agreed with his fellow Haightie: "Along came LSD and that was the end of that world. The whole world just went kablooey. It changed everything, you know, it was just—ah, first of all, for me personally, it freed me, you know, the effect was that it freed me because I suddenly realized that my little attempt at having a straight life and doing that was really a fiction and just wasn't going to work out. To get really high is to forget yourself. And to forget yourself is to see everything else. And to see everything else is to become an understanding molecule in evolution, a conscious tool in the universe."[6]

Peter Coyote agreed with his friend Allen Cohen that "LSD was the fundamental building block to a new way of thinking. Why is there war? What is the power of love? These were the ideas debated by young people. Drugs were going to change the world; if you took acid you would change, feel a cosmic oneness, a colorblind reality, and a sense of community. You wanted to know what was on the other side of the door, a sense of being brought into God's workshop. You wanted a peaceful planet, uncluttered, simple life, and a will to move the human race ahead."[7] For hippies like Cohen and Coyote, acid was the key for their collective vision of America's future as a clean slate.

One of the hippies' most profound legacies was the creation and legitimization among 1960s youth of the use of mind-altering drugs to find the bliss hippies longed for but believed unattainable in straight society. If any one of the many manifestations of the hippies' alternative way of being came to define the movement, it was the acid subculture. Indeed, dope usage and the counterculture became symbiotic, the hippies' "psychic staff of life." As Timothy Miller has observed, "The commitment to—as opposed to the furtive use of—dope was the single largest symbol between the counterculture and establishment culture." In the assessment of one *Time* reporter, there was "one sure way to distinguish a real hippie from his assorted sympathizers: hippies drop acid…. The chemical is a central theme to their way of life. Psychedelic drugs of various sorts always pave the way to hippiedom."[8] By the late 1960s, the use of hallucinogenic drugs—from marijuana to LSD—appeared to have so engulfed the counterculture, that even today when most people think of 1960s hippies, they stereotypically see a long-haired, patchouli-scented, shabbily garbed guy meditating cross-legged in a psychedelically painted room, a marijuana joint dangling from his lips and Jefferson Airplane's "White Rabbit" blaring.

To hippies drugs and dope were two distinct entities. Drugs encompassed substances that were both good and bad, ranging from valium to codeine to marijuana and heroin. Particularly bad drugs to hippies were amphetamines, especially speed or methedrine; opiates (heroin, morphine, and opium); and cocaine; all were considered "downers" because they did not expand perception. Hippies also viewed alcohol as a drug not only because it was addicting but also because it was the Establishment's most popular high. In effect, hippies opposed addictive drugs such as alcohol largely because they made the user stupid rather than expanding consciousness. Hippies embraced dope usage—marijuana, peyote, psilocybin, hashish, mescaline, even banana peels—because those substances led to a higher realm of sensory awareness and helped free the individual from hang-ups and the repressions of conventional society. For many hippies the "liberation of the senses" via dope use became the *raison d'être* of their movement.[9]

As a hippie explained in Atlanta's underground newspaper *Great Speckled Bird*, "Dope not drugs—alcohol is a drug, pot is DOPE; nicotine is a DRUG, acid is DOPE; DRUGS turn you off, dull your senses, give you the strength to face another day in Death America. DOPE turns you on, heightens sensor awareness, sometimes twists them out of shape and you experience that too, gives you vision and clarity, necessary to create Life from Death."[10] Acid rock legend Frank Zappa of the Mothers of Invention exhorted hippies not "to use speed and here's why: it is going to mess up your heart, mess up your liver, your kidneys, rot out your mind. In general this drug will make you just like your mother and father."[11] Although hippies professed disdain for addictive drugs, many in fact, transitioned to harder substances such as meth or speed, heroin or cocaine, and as a result, suffered severe, incapacitating mental and emotional breakdowns. Many died from overdoses or from adulterated dope, which became increasingly more prevalent on the streets of hippie neighborhoods as the decade wore on and as drug trafficking became too profitable for individual thugs, "burn artists," and eventually Organized Crime, to ignore as simply a "hippie thing."

The consumption and distribution of illegal and experimental drugs came to inform much of the nation's hip neighborhoods during the 1960s, significantly driving and sustaining many such communities' economies while simultaneously defining much of their socio-cultural order and disposition. However, as the decade progressed, drug usage did not remain an exclusive hippie identification for very long; dope penetrated mainstream white suburbia more rapidly than anyone anticipated, linking the comparatively small hippie counterculture with the vast majority of straight youth, many of whom became as enamored of acid or marijuana as their hippie counterparts. Not all hippies or even straight youth who smoked dope or took acid ascribed metaphorical importance to their activities; they simply enjoyed the momentary high or kick the drugs gave and looked forward to their next pleasurable turn-on. Nonetheless, for many, dropping acid or smoking a joint became the rites of a secret society, in which the proper "set and setting" was essential to the experience taking place behind drawn shades. Windows open, incense and candles burning, towels wedged under the door jamb to avoid detection, and rock cranked up full volume, were the standard backdrop to the event. Grass, more than LSD, according to one hippie, "opened up a new space for middle class white kids. An inner space as well as outer space. It became a ritual—sitting around with your friends, passing a joint from person to person, listening to music, eating, talking, joking, maybe making out—all the senses heightened."[12] As one University of Chicago student told *Time* magazine, "You take it when friends get together or when you're going to see *Yellow Submarine*. It's not to solve problems, just to giggle."[13] Despite popular media stereotyping of the time, *not all* hippies were acid heads. From the hippie movement's beginning to its end, the most common, preferred high of most hippies, student activists, and even of the many straights who dabbled in the drug culture and around hippiedom's periphery, was marijuana. By 1969 according to California psychopharmacologist Dr. Leo Hollister, pot usage among American white youth, regardless of their affinity, had become "entrenched in our society, with untold millions using the drug. We have passed the point of no return." As University of Indiana sociologist Alfred Lindesmith wryly observed, "If a kid goes to college these days and never develops an interest in marijuana, he's got a problem and you should worry. He may be a loner or not accepted by his peers."[14]

As early as 1967, 50 percent of the undergraduates interviewed in a survey conducted by National Institute of Mental Health throughout several West Coast universities, were already pot smokers. Despite attempts by the law and authorities to criminalize and vilify marijuana use, a position paper, released by the NIMH in 1967 which greatly reduced the "fear factor" among current and potential pot heads, reported that "The claims that marijuana is a dangerous drug, or a narcotic, or an aphrodisiac, or a stepping-stone to heroin is, as far as we are concerned, still unproven." For many young Americans the report was the green light of assurance that they would not turn into the "junkies" their parents had said they would if they smoked "reefer," and confirmed in their minds that they had been duped about marijuana's diabolic consequences. As far as *Time* was concerned, 1960s adults "must get used to the fact that their world has witnessed the growth of a separate youth culture, or 'counterculture,'" and smoking grass was "part of growing up and the great majority have no intention of freaking out for good."[15] Marijuana had many interesting side effects—the giggles, the munchies, motor mouth—but rarely did they lead to harder drugs. LSD, however, affected people's lives in ways marijuana rarely, if ever, did.

By the early 1960s, long before any hippies took their first marijuana toke or popped their first acid tablet, middle class white suburbia had become the nation's first large-scale, visible drug culture. Until the 1950s and early 1960s, widespread drug use, particularly of amphetamines and barbiturates, was unheard of in mainstream America. But by the close of the 1950s, thousands of suburbanites were drawn to drugs to numb the stress caused by a psychologically debilitating cognitive dissonance of status anxiety. They became addicted to a variety of prescription drugs, ranging from valium to amphetamines. For many the monotony and tedium of daily existence had become intolerable, and to cope each day they reached into the medicine cabinet for an "upper" or "downer," depending upon the physician's diagnosis of the mental/emotional state. By the end of the 1950s millions of Americans had become dependent on powerful substances to help them endure daily life. Few health care professionals challenged this perception and thus it came as no surprise when it was revealed in 1965 that doctors, led by psychiatrists, wrote 123 million prescriptions for tranquilizers and 24 million prescriptions for amphetamines. Surprisingly the overwhelmingly number of prescriptions written were to people considered to be normal functioning human beings. As sociologists William Simon and John H. Gagnon observed, "Modern medicine has made drugs highly legitimate, something to be taken casually and not only during moments of acute and certified stress. Our children, far from being in revolt against an older generation, may in fact be acknowledging how influential a model that older generation was."[16] Mom and Dad's drugs were considered legitimate because they had been produced legally by the pharmaceutical conglomerates and accepted by society because they had been certified by doctors as essential for their patients' mental and emotional well-being.

The drugs that vastly accelerated and redefined an already intoxicated America were mescaline, psilocybin and lysergic acid diethylamide (LSD). In the 1920s chemists synthesized the active ingredient in peyote, calling it mescaline, and in 1958 scientists did the same thing for the Indians' magic mushrooms, producing psilocybin. It was mescaline that brought forth the herald of the psychedelic revolution, the famed British novelist Aldous Huxley. Huxley, along with another Englishman, the psychiatrist Humphrey Osmond, created the term *psychedelic* to describe their experiences using mescaline and psilocybin. It was Osmond who first introduced Huxley to these drugs, "guiding" the author on his first mescaline trip at Huxley's Hollywood Hills home in May 1953. "It was without question," Huxley later wrote, "the most extraordinary and significant experience this side of the Beatific Vision." When he looked at a small vase of flowers, he saw what "Adam had seen on the morning of creation—the miracle, moment by moment, of naked existence; flowers shining in their own inner light and all but quivering under the pressure of the significance with which they were charged." Huxley even believed his trip took him to the "Pure Light of the Void" before he fled in terror from "the burning brightness of unmitigated Reality."[17] No doubt Huxley endured moments of being in a psychotic state, with paranoia being the most intense. But overall, he believed his journey to have been most illuminating for it allowed him to discover heretofore unknown mystical realms. Huxley's mescaline trip was so profound that both men believed "that the words we were using for these strange chemical instruments were idiotic" and thus the search began for a more appropriate description. Osmond, after consulting a guidebook of Latin terms, came up with the idea of combining two words, *psyche* and *delos*, "to reveal"; there it was: *psychedelic* would be the term, and Osmond coined a little rhyme to seal the deal: *"To fathom hell or soar angelic / Just take a pinch of psychedelic."*[18]

Huxley immortalized his mescaline trip in his book, *The Doors of Perception* (1954), in which he not only recounted his journey but lamented that the majority of the rich and highly educated white people of the world (such as himself) had become so consumed by their temporal existence and all the words, behaviors, and reason associated with that reality, that they had cut themselves off from mystic knowledge. Huxley believed the mystical had proven to be more beneficial to the human condition than conventional wisdom, especially those perceptions acquired through traditional academic or intellectual institutions and mediums. However, there was hope for Western man, and such salvation came in the form of the "gratuitous grace" of mind-expanding drugs.[19]

Huxley's clarion call to America's upper classes to expand their consciousness did not fall on deaf ears. One of the first of the nation's notables to embrace Huxley's message was *Time-Life* publishing magnate, Henry Luce and his wife Clare Boothe, both of whom had become serious users in Huxley's company. In 1957 Luce published a 17-page article in *Life*, "Seeking the Magic Mushroom," by the Wall Street banker R. Gordon Wasson, recounting Wasson's and his friend, New York photographer Allan Richardson's visit to Mixeteco, a remote Indian village in southern Mexico. According to Wasson, he and Richardson "were the first white men in recorded history to eat the divine mushrooms." Botanist had classified these fungi as *Psilocybe cubensis*, but the Aztecs called them *teonanacatl*, "the flesh of the gods." Psilocybin mushrooms and the secretive indigenous religion that surrounded them had been mostly unknown to the American public until Wasson's and Richardson's journey. With the guidance of two Mixeteca *curanderas*, the official shaman women who performed the ritual, Wasson and Richardson ingested 12 mushrooms each and within a few hours their trip was full blown, with both men having intense visions "whether our eyes were open or closed." Wasson's experience was especially vivid, with the banker feeling "suspended in mid-air viewing landscapes of mountains, with camel caravans advancing slowly across the slopes and mountains rising tier above tier to the very heavens. Then they evolved into palaces with courts, arcades, gardens, resplendent palaces all laid over with precious stones. Then I saw a mythological beast drawing a regal chariot.... I [saw] the archetypes, the Platonic ideas that underlie the imperfect images of everyday life." Wasson became convinced that "the effect of the mushrooms [was] to bring about a fission of the spirit, a split in the person, a kind of schizophrenia, with the rational side continuing to reason and to observe the sensations that the other side is enjoying.... The Indians believe that the mushrooms hold the key to what we call extrasensory perception. I am inclined to believe that they can take us to dimensions beyond."[20] If thousands read the Huxley book, millions read the Wasson article.

But it was in 1938 that Dr. Albert Hofmann of the Sandoz Chemical Works in Basel, Switzerland, fabricated a compound many times more potent than anything previously derived from a natural plant or fungus: LSD, which he culled from the ergot fungus that grows on rye bread. Believing the colorless, odorless concoction (diethylamide of lysergic acid) to be a useless substance, Hoffman shelved the compound for five years, ultimately returning to his creation for experimentation. Accidentally grazing his fingertips with the crystals, the LSD was absorbed through his skin, launching him into the world's first mini acid trip. The brief but "intense stimulation of the imagination and an altered state of awareness of the world," propelled Hofmann to want to try his elixir again, only this time it would be a legitimate, intentional experiment.[21]

Three days after the accidental dose, on April 19, 1943, Hoffman took 0.25 mg of LSD and about 50 minutes later the chemist jotted in his notebook that "there surged up from me a succession of fantastic, rapidly changing imagery of striking reality and depth, alternating with a vivid, kaleidoscopic play of colors." "My field of vision swayed before me," Hoffman would later record. "Objects appeared distorted like the images in curved mirrors. I had the impression of being unable to move from the spot, although my assistant told me afterwards that we had cycled at a good pace." Hoffman's condition worsened once he got home. "The faces of those present appeared like grotesque colored masks"; physically he alternated between "strong agitation" and paralysis" while his body and extremities felt off and on "cold and numb," and during the whole experience he believed he was suffocating. Yet, Hoffman persevered even though he was "overcome with fear that I was going crazy" and that he was "incapable of stopping it." At one point he "thought he had died." Hoffman eventually came down from his trip, much relieved that his body, mind, and soul were intact. Hoffman was a research scientist, and although obviously overcome by LSD's hallucinogenic qualities, he had no intention of marketing his discovery to the masses, hoping rather to see his company find use for his concoction as a profitable analeptic for migraine headaches and a variety of mental disorders.[22]

However, long before medicine or the behavioral sciences experimented with LSD's potential curative power for mental disorders, the United States government, via its respective intelligence agencies, believed the compound could become an effective weapon in its ever expanding Cold War arsenal. Beginning in 1947, the CIA (Project Chatter), ever alert for new ways to defend freedom and democracy from the communist threat, began experimenting with the chemical that it feared—and hoped—could "destroy integrity and make indiscreet the most dependable individual." In other words, the CIA hoped to develop the substance into a kind of mega truth serum. It was also hoped enemy soldiers could be drugged, hypnotized, and programmed to go back behind enemy lines and sabotage their compatriots. Perhaps LSD could be sprayed on enemy troops—a powerful weapon of *mass distraction*. The agency began testing LSD's effects on its own personnel and on unsuspecting patients in federal prisons and drug treatment centers (the MK-PILOT initiative), with many such experiments resulting in bad trips with subjects writhing in paranoid terror, or sinking into catatonic states. Taken with LSD's potential national security value, in 1954 the agency encouraged one of the nation's largest pharmaceutical conglomerates, Eli Lily, to begin synthesizing the compound. The CIA expanded its intelligence gathering relative to LSD by also awarding contracts to selected university scientists and private research labs, widening the circle of LSD initiates far beyond the Cold War defense community, and as the decade of the 1960s opened, LSD began seeping out of supposedly secret and secure laboratories and into the cultural underground.[23]

Timothy Leary, to this day remains the individual most identified with the psychedelic–LSD experience of the hippie movement. A UC–Berkeley Ph.D. in clinical psychology, Leary, at age 39, was doing research at Harvard when he discovered the magic mushrooms while on a family vacation in Cuernavaca, Mexico, in the summer of 1960. Until that time Leary was uninterested in mind-altering substances and in fact had little to no awareness of their potential to alter consciousness. True to his Irish heritage, Leary's only real addiction was to beer and whiskey and even in that capacity he was no alcoholic. He didn't smoke cigarettes; occasionally a pipe; and as far as "uppers" or "downers" were concerned, Leary eschewed them as well. All in all, until Mexico, Leary was "dope-free."[24]

It was in Mexico that Lothar Knauth, a University of Mexico linguist and anthropologist, introduced Leary to the mushrooms he had procured from a local Indian curandera, Crazy Juana, and Leary's life changed forever. On that hot August afternoon Leary and a few friends forced themselves to swallow a bowl of filthy, horribly tasting *crudos*, washed down with Mexican beer. "Five hours after eating the mushrooms it was all changed," Leary wrote. "The revelation had come. The veil had been pulled back. The classic vision. The full-blown conversion experience. The prophetic call. The works. God has spoken." Seven *crudos* and an ice-cold beer; that's all it took. As a result of his revelations, Leary now believed reality to be nothing more than a social fabrication and would later call his trip "the deepest religious experience of my life." It was his fervent belief that thanks to the mushrooms and other possible mind-altering drugs, "it [the human mind] can operate in space-time dimensions that we never dreamed even existed. I feel like I've awakened from a long ontological sleep."[25]

Upon his return from Mexico in the fall of 1960, Leary set up the Harvard Psilocybin Project with the purpose of testing the drug's effects on human beings, in collaboration with a younger Harvard colleague, Richard Alpert (the future Ram Dass). Leary was a scientist, not a therapist, and since his Mexico experience he was determined to show that hallucinogens, if administered properly, could benefit society. To prove his theory Leary needed a population that could be accurately measured and controlled and concluded there was no better place to find such a group than in a prison system rife with a history of rehabilitative failure. "What a boon to society—converting criminals into law-abiding citizens," Leary told a friend. "If we could teach the most unregenerate how to wash their own brains, then it would be a cinch to coach non-criminals to change their lives for the better."[26] The inmates of the state maximum security prison in Concord, Massachusetts, thus became the first sample group in a study to determine whether the drug would affect the recidivism rate. According to Leary's assessment, the follow-up tests showed what he had "expected": prisoners less depressed and hostile, more responsible and cooperative. He was certain such positive results were thanks to the magic mushrooms. He had cut the 70 percent recidivism rate in half; Timothy Leary had found a way to solve the nation's crime problem. But prison officials doubted Leary's rather arrogant proclamation, noting that there was no control group of inmates who were given that kind of attention but no mushroom pills. Disturbingly, Leary also encouraged all the graduate students assisting on the project to personally try out the drugs they would be giving the prisoners and to trip *with* their subjects.[27]

Convicts and graduate students were not the only people Leary and his associates were turning on. Both Leary and Alpert became confirmed trippers and salesmen for mind altering drugs, dispensing psilocybin to all manner of stray seekers who showed up at the door of their rather palatial rented home in Newton. Leary noted that "every weekend the Harvard resident houses were transformed into spaceships floating miles above the Yard." In truth, Leary was using science to disguise his real intention, which was to turn on as many human beings as possible. But drugs alone could not produce a state of blessedness; one' state of mind was almost as important in determining the psychedelic experience as the type of hallucinogenic taken. Leary therefore emphasized the importance of the proper "set and setting"; that is, the quality of a trip depended on the attitude of the tripper and the trip's physical and psychological surroundings (candles, incense, music, art, quiet) to help the seeker experience God. Leary and his associates' quest for the best "mind-blowing" environments led them to a variety of esoterica. They searched out past masters of the spiritual journey, finding particular visionary and mystical sustenance in Eastern religions, most notably Buddhism and especially the *Tibetan Book of the Dead*, which Leary believed offered a remarkable guide to the psilocybin or LSD experience. In Leary's view the Tibetan monks were working with the same visions that emulated an LSD trip; Leary and his followers wanted to follow their practices to ritualize and spiritually legitimize the use of psilocybin or any other mind-altering drugs.[28]

In late November 1960 Leary made his first connections with the hip underground in the person of Allen Ginsberg. Ginsberg had first enjoyed peyote and LSD in the mid–1950s as an LSD guinea pig at a mental research facility in California. During one session, at Ginsberg's suggestion, the experimenters turned on a stroboscope lamp while he was tripping on LSD. The flickering light caused Ginsberg's journey to become a terrifying encounter, creating the feeling that his "soul [was] being sucked out through the light into the wall socket and going out." Despite his ordeal, Ginsberg became one of the hippie counterculture's most fervid advocates of the power of LSD to change perception. Ginsberg had come to Leary's home in Newton to enlist the professor's support in his personal crusade to enlighten the world with the help of conscious-altering drugs. On the Sunday afternoon of November 26, 1960, Leary gave Ginsberg and Peter Orlovsky (Ginsberg's lover) 36 milligrams of psilocybin. The poets then repaired to their room, stripped naked, and while lying in bed listened to Wagner's *Götterdämmerung* on the record player. Suddenly Ginsberg began hallucinating with great fear and despair, "until Leary came in, looked in his eyes, and pronounced him a great man." Ginsberg arose, and still naked, entered the kitchen and declared himself the Messiah, destined to lead a revolution. "We will go into the streets and call the people to peace and love. We're going to walk through the streets and teach people to stop hating. I might as well be the one to do so. I pronounce my nakedness as the first act of revolution against the destroyers of the human image," Leary remembered him saying. So enraptured by his trip, Ginsberg not only wanted to call his closest Beat and other literary friends and share his euphoria and tell them of his epiphany, but also President John Kennedy and Soviet Premier Nikita Khrushchev and "settle all this warfare bit." Identifying himself to the operator as God, ("G-O-D," he spelled it out for her), "Get me Kerouac" and eventually she did. Ginsberg exhorted Kerouac to come immediately to Boston: "I am high and naked and I am King of the Universe. Get on the plane. It is time!"[29]

Sitting in the kitchen after the drug had worn off, Ginsberg and Leary plotted the psychedelic revolution. Ginsberg was convinced that psilocybin was the key to transforming the world's consciousness and that everybody should have the mushrooms, beginning with the most influential people, an idea Aldous Huxley would have endorsed. Such notables would not listen to him, a crazy beatnik poet, "I'm too easy to put down," but they might listen to "big serious scientist professors from Harvard. You're [Leary and Alpert] the perfect persons to do it." Before he left the Newton house, Ginsberg provided Leary with the addresses and phone numbers of some of the most important musicians, artists, publishers, poets, and writers in New York; all people who could spread the psychedelic gospel and help to alter the very basis of human perceptions. "We'll go right down the list and turn them all on," Ginsberg assured Leary. Leary was willing to become the drug's champion and proselytizer. "From this moment on my days as a respectable establishment scientist were numbered. I just couldn't see the new society given birth by medical hands, or psychedelic sacraments as psychiatric tools. From this evening on my energies were offered to the ancient underground society of alchemists, artists, mystics, alienated visionaries, dropouts, and the disenchanted young, the sons arising."[30]

Until late 1961 Leary believed psilocybin was *the* drug of the psychedelic revolution. He changed his mind when a tall, balding Englishman with a mysterious past named Michael Hollingshead showed up at Leary's house with a mayonnaise jar full of something new— LSD-laced syrup. Leary took some and so overwhelmed by its explosive effects that he declared his high to have been "the most shattering experience of my life," taking him far beyond any mental state that he had encountered on psilocybin. Leary believed his trip had taken him back to the beginning of life, a single cell of DNA and then thrust him at the speed of light outward to the cosmic vibrations where he became "the white light of nothingness." He also believed he experienced the "resurrection" of the body and became aware of the intensity as well as the repression of its more spiritual, sensual and carnal instincts. "Blow the mind and you are left with God and life—and life is sex," he announced. Leary believed LSD to be the most potent aphrodisiac he had ever felt, "probably the most powerful sexual releaser known to man.... The union is not just your body and her body but all of your racial and evolutionary entities with all of hers. It is mythic mating."[31]

One of Leary's major media coup's relative to the propagation of the supposed symbiotic relationship between sex and acid occurred in his now infamous (for its general absurdity and self-serving hucksterism) 1966 *Playboy* interview published in September of that year, in the same edition that featured a photo spread about the topless nightclub scene that had emerged in San Francisco's North Beach area. By 1966 *Playboy* had become not only the nation's number one selling men's magazine with the most alluring and explicitly nude photos of women, ranging from college co-eds to movie stars, but also the mouthpiece for its publisher's—Hugh Hefner—sexual freedom message. Not only did Leary tell the magazine's interviewer that he had taken LSD 311 times, but that in each instance he had sex (with a woman), which Leary declared "is what the LSD experience is all about. Merging, yielding, flowing, union, communion. It's all lovemaking. You make love with candlelight, with sound waves from a record player, with a bowl of fruit on the table, with trees. You're pulsating in harmony with all the energy around you. The three inevitable goals of the LSD session are to discover and make love with God, to discover and make love with yourself, and to discover and make love with a woman.... Sexual ecstasy is the basic reason for LSD."[32]

The interviewer then asked Leary if there was any truth to the claim that LSD brought to the surface the "acting out of latent homosexual impulses." Leary believed LSD had the opposite effect. "The fact is that LSD is a specific cure for homosexuality. It's well known that most sexual perversions are the result not of biological binds but of freaky, dislocating childhood experiences of one kind or another. Consequently it's not surprising that we've had many cases of long-term homosexuals, who under LSD, discover that they are not only genitally but genetically male, that they are basically attracted to females."[33]

It was only a matter of time before Harvard officials would begin to question the purpose of Leary's experiments with psilocybin and now LSD. Up until 1962–63, the university had allowed Leary, Alpert, and their increasing number of graduate assistants, to dispense both fairly freely to student volunteers. Interestingly, it was a group of disgruntled (and perhaps jealous) undergraduate students who were not asked to participate in Leary's and Alpert's Harvard Psilocybin project who led the crusade to get both Leary and Alpert ousted from Harvard. Andrew Weil, then an undergraduate reporter for the university's prestigious and powerful student newspaper, the *Harvard Crimson*, was especially vindictive for Leary had rejected him as a volunteer because of his undergraduate status. Whether out of jealousy, spite, or genuine concern, Weil told Joseph Russin, the paper's editor in chief, that he knew for sure that Leary and Alpert "were giving LSD to students who were undergraduates, including some who were psychologically on the fence, some of whom were going nuts. There was a guy on the *Crimson* staff who had been hospitalized for a mental condition after getting LSD from Leary and Alpert. There was more of this, and either way, they were not following the deal they made with the university, which was not to give the drugs to undergraduates."[34]

Perhaps most important to Leary by 1962 was LSD's transcendent agency and thus from the moment he became a devoted acidhead to his dying days, Leary vehemently opposed the use of psychedelics for kicks, insisting that they had been created for the higher purpose of helping individuals in their quest for God. Hallucinogenic drugs were thus "sacraments" and should "be treated and used as such." However, as Leary was learning, acid heads may have been temporarily blasted into a higher plane of consciousness, transcending their mental state and social conditioning but it was very difficult if not impossible, to imprint that insight on a permanent, behavioral-change basis. Writer Arthur Koestler told Leary after his first LSD trip, "This is wonderful no doubt but it is a fake. I solved the secret of the universe last night, but this morning I forgot what it was."[35]

Indeed, "reentry" became for *all* LSD users, their greatest dilemma: how to take the knowledge and insight, the beatitude of their LSD experience, and integrate such revelations into the reality of everyday life that quickly returned (sometimes more rapidly than anticipated) in the aftermath of every acid trip? Even the once-devoted acid head Richard Alpert became frustrated by LSD's non-cumulative, circular affects: "I had plenty of LSD but why take it. I knew what it was going to do, what it was going to tell me. It was going to show me that garden again and again and then I was going to be cast out and that was it. And I could never quite stay. I was addicted to the experience at first, and then I even got tired of that. And the despair was extremely intense at that point."[36]

By the spring semester 1963, Leary and Alpert's unorthodox experiments and personal lifestyles, both of which were becoming increasingly defined by an obsession with LSD that they were no longer willing to hide from the public, were being reported not only in the *Crimson* but in Boston's major newspapers as well. The *Boston Herald*, a Hearst tabloid, ran an article under the sensational headline: "Hallucination Drug Found at Harvard—350 Students Take Pills." Andrew Weil, the future MD who later became famous for his books on holistic health, did not limit his attack on Leary and Alpert to Harvard and the college newspaper. To the chagrin of the Harvard administration, Weil wrote an article for *Look* magazine entitled "The Strange Case of the Harvard Drug Scandal," in which he revealed all kinds of inside information about the Harvard drug scene and the details of Alpert's undergraduate liaisons. "One Harvard junior told a friend that Alpert had persuaded him to take psilocybin in a 'self-exploratory' session at Alpert's apartment," Weil wrote in *Look*. "There were stories of students and others using hallucinogens for seductions, both heterosexual and homosexual."[37]

In the spring of 1963, Weil and Russin wrote an editorial in the *Crimson* that proved to be the coup de grace for both Leary and Alpert. They accused both professors of being "propagandists" prone to "making the kind of pronouncements about their work that one associates with quacks.... Leary and Alpert fancy themselves the prophets of a psychic revolution designed to free Western man from the limitations of consciousness as we know it. They prefer mystical ecstasy to the fulfillment available through work, politics, religion, and creative art," and "they play these games to further their own ends." Newspapers across the nation reprinted Weil's and Russin's editorial, making Leary and Alpert celebrities, especially among the burgeoning hippie rebellion which they would help to define. However, more important, the Harvard administration could no longer tolerate all the negative publicity Leary and Alpert's shenanigans were bringing to the university. Thus in April 1963, with LSD selling for a dollar a dose in Harvard Square, the university fired Timothy Leary, ostensibly because he had cut classes but in fact because his work had become an academic scandal and embarrassment to the both the university and his discipline. A month later, Richard Alpert was fired as well. By the time of their dismal, both Leary and Alpert had "psychedelically outgrown" Harvard and its "antiquated" academic traditions and strictures, and thus probably would have left the university on their own accord sooner than later. Weil's investigative zeal only hastened their early departure.[38]

LSD's "Johnny Appleseed" Dr. Timothy Leary, circa 1966 (photograph by Larry Keenan, courtesy Bancroft Library, University of California, Berkeley. © 1997 Larry Keenan. All rights reserved).

Twenty years after his ouster from Harvard, Leary credited the Transcendentalists, most notably Ralph Waldo Emerson for being the inspiration for his 1960s mantra for everyone to "turn on, tune in, and drop out. They too were saying the same thing. Become self-reliant. Before Emerson came back to Harvard in 1838, he was in Europe hanging out with notorious druggies like Coleridge and Wordsworth," Leary said at a 1983 Harvard reunion. "They were expanding their minds with hashish and opium and reading the *Bhagavad Gita*.

Then he [Emerson] came back here and gave that famous speech where he said, 'Don't look for God in the temples. Look within.' Find God within yourself. Drop out. Become self-reliant. Do your own thing."[39]

Over the next several years, Leary's sense of self-importance and self-promotion knew no bounds, reaching a crescendo in the fall of 1966 when he appeared outside of a Loews Theater in New York's East Village, before a marquee proclaiming him as the "Reincarnation of Jesus Christ." By then he already had become notorious for his florid bombast and grandiose, if not absurd propagation of the miracles of LSD. According to Dr. David Smith, founder of Haight-Ashbury's Free Clinic in 1967 and a former tripper himself, "Leary was a charming and manipulative hustler for what he saw as the societal benefit of hallucinogens, particularly LSD. He was a merry medicine man ... peddling his message and his tabs of LSD from coast to coast, often just a step ahead of the law."[40] It was not surprising that Harvard University—founded by Puritans and cultivated over the centuries as the bastion of WASP elitism—refused to tolerate his personal eccentricities and avant-garde ideas about psychology. By 1963 Timothy Leary was "somewhere else." He was unemployed, professionally and academically disgraced, and homeless. Yet, he was determined to persevere in his quest to deliver the LSD experience to the masses, whether through "secular spirituality" or "renewal by the discovery of new mysteries."[41]

It was at this point that Leary and Alpert took brief refuge in Zijuatenejo, Mexico, until Mexican authorities closed the Hotel Catalina and expelled Leary and his colleagues from Mexico. At this juncture, both men were despondent, certain that their plan to turn on America was dead. Miraculously, salvation came in the person of William Hitchcock, a wealthy stockbroker with the Lehman firm of Wall Street bankers and brother of Tom and Peggy Hitchcock, two of Leary's most devoted disciples. The Hitchcocks were heirs to the banking and oil fortune amassed by the legendary Pittsburg industrialist/financier Andrew Mellon and his nephew, William Larimer Mellon, founder of Gulf Oil. All three Hitchcocks swallowed Leary's message, wanting their guru to spread the psychedelic revolution and the exaltation they had all experienced on LSD to the rest of humanity. So they bought Leary and his growing entourage a sixty-four-room Victorian/Gothic hodge-podge of a mansion built at the turn of the century by William Dietrich, a manufacturer of carbide lamps, located about 80 miles north of New York City in the village of Millbrook in Dutchess County. Capitalists' fortunes were now fueling the psychedelic crusade and the acquisition of the Millbrook refuge caused Leary to exult that "On this space colony we will attempt to create a new organism and a new dedication to life as art."[42]

For the next two years Leary quit proselytizing and presided quietly over a religious commune based on drugs. Millbrook would be a community of seekers and searchers, where the secrets of the inner world would be revealed through experiment and study. Leary's new organization, the Castalia Foundation, would publish these new manifestations of expanded consciousness and make them available to all mankind. On the model of past utopian communities, Millbrook would become a beacon of hope and redemption for all those still longing to escape the spiritual and sensual emptiness of their daily lives. The reality at Millbrook, however, was different. Tripping on acid consumed the lives of most of the residents and although they were to record as thoroughly and descriptively as possible their visions and journey, most of the time they were too spaced out to even move or eat. As authorities began clamping down on LSD access and distribution, Leary had to become more creative in helping people to experience consciousness expansion and thus he sponsored seminars in meditation, dance, yoga, breathing exercises, fasting, and sensory deprivation. But the majority of those who came to Millbrook came for one experience: the high provided by LSD, and thus many left feeling betrayed, duped, and hustled by Leary for his failure to deliver the goods.[43]

Millbrook's bucolic beauty masked a human environment that was orgiastic and chaotic. The permanent residents, including children and pets, remained stoned for days on end. Upon Leary's return in 1965 from a pilgrimage to India, Millbrook had degenerated from a community of committed, genuine seekers to a hedonistic Disneyland; a Fantasy Land where "all your orgiastic dreams could come true." The place had been taken over by misfits and druggies from New York who had heard about the libertine activities and plentiful drugs available at the estate and Leary had come home to a polarized "space colony." People pranced through the rooms, grounds, and corridors often naked, having sex at whim. By the end of 1965 Millbrook had become not only the avatar of the psychedelic era but was also helping to pioneer the sexual revolution as well.[44] Despite the increasingly unsavory character of its residents and the randy behavior of both old and new seekers, its founders still insisted Millbrook was a sanctuary for the revelation of the new ethic of spontaneity, the pleasure principle, and joy in idleness.

This new creed was a mixture of the serious and the clownish like almost everything touched by LSD. Acid and other psychedelics would be "sacraments" that would serve as the catalysts for "enlightenment," ex–Millbrook resident Arthur Kleps declared in 1967. Kleps, a former social worker from upstate New York, joined Leary and the other heads at Millbrook in 1964 but Kleps was too irreverent to fit comfortably into the community, and proved to be an even greater charlatan and self-promoter than Leary. In 1966 "the Mad Monk" (as Leary referred to Kleps) left Millbrook and founded the Neo-American Church, partly as a goof but mostly to gain a religious exemption from the nation's drug laws. Kleps made himself the high priest of his new religion in which acid and other psychedelics would be "the blessed sacraments." Kleps called himself Chief Boo Hoo and created as his church's symbol a three-eyed toad over the motto "Victory Over Horseshit." Kleps was honest about both his church's purpose as well his own. "Leary has a religion; he is a spiritual leader. I am functioning like a pope who is nothing more than a super-businessman." Church members, which totaled around 300 by 1968, referred to themselves as Boo Hoos. With the religious exemption they hoped to obtain from the government, the Boo Hoos would use LSD and other psychedelics as part of their worship based on the government's granting to members of the Native American Church the right to use peyote in their rituals. Was Kleps' enterprise's chief attraction that members just might get legalized dope? "Yeah," answered Kleps, "I think that has a lot to do with it. And why not? The Catholic Church certainly doesn't hesitate to use all kinds of arguments of the same kind to seduce people into joining." Naturally the courts denied Kleps' request, ruling that his "church" did not "merit" First Amendment protection, and that Kleps' attempt to represent the use of hallucinogenic drugs as a sacred ritual, "mocked established [religious] institutions." Moreover, how could the court take seriously any organization that had as its anthem "Row, Row, Row Your Boat."[45]

By 1966–67 Leary had become the self-appointed harbinger of the psychedelic revolution, telling packed houses at New York's Town Hall, that he knew "lots of languages. I can talk to trees and I do pretty well talking Holyman. You must be able to speak first to an amoeba, your father, a madman, Buddha, your lover." Most interesting, Leary told his audience

Berkeley acid/folk-rock singer **Country Joe McDonald** of Country Joe and the Fish giving Timothy Leary's hand-signals for his slogan "Turn on, Tune in, and drop out," Berkeley, California, 1967 (photograph by Larry Keenan, courtesy Bancroft Library, University of California, Berkeley. © 1997 Larry Keenan. All rights reserved).

that as more and more people took LSD, humanity would evolve toward "a better race of mutants" because LSD had the power to alter "the deepest and most basic chords of all human life, the DNA codes deep within each cell of living organisms," and thus "it was time to mutate." Such pronouncements only further alienated many contemporaries who saw him as a self-absorbed publicity hound whose antics and self-promotion were "putting out a lot of negative vibes," and "bringing on the heat" (attracting police attention). Some believed Leary's main motivation was his own self-aggrandizement. Even devotees such as Allen Ginsberg questioned Leary's sloganeering and showmanship, telling Leary "Everybody in Berkeley is all bugged because they say this drop-out thing really doesn't mean anything, that what your gonna cultivate is a lot of freaked-out hippies goofing around and throwing bottles through windows when they flip out on LSD." Leary had gained a reputation as a con man, who cut his message to fit his clientele's cloth.[46]

Unfazed by the criticism, Leary was determined to establish himself as *the* guru of the psychedelic movement. Most important, Leary knew that to advance his own image and persona as the hip counterculture's undisputed leader, he needed the news media. Journalists in turn, believed they needed Leary to help them figure out the direction the counterculture was tending, especially in its early years. In order to enhance his appearance while spreading the psychedelic gospel, Leary met with the reigning mass media expert of the times, the Canadian Marshall McLuhan, author of the best-selling *The Medium Is the Message.* Over lunch at the Plaza Hotel in New York, McLuhan advised the following: "You must use the most current tactics for arousing consumer interest. Associate LSD with all the good things that the brain can produce—beauty, fun, philosophic wonder, religious revelation, increased intelligence and mystical romance." Most important McLuhan told Leary, "Wave reassuringly. Radiate courage. Never complain or appear angry. You must be known for your smile." Soon after their meeting, Leary came up with an advertising slogan: "Turn On, Tune In, Drop Out," by which Leary meant, "Activate your neural and genetic equipment; interact harmoniously with the world around you; and pursue an active, selective and graceful process of detachment from involuntary or unconscious commitments." No sooner did he utter his now famous cliché than the press immediately interpreted his message as encouraging everyone "to get stoned and abandon all constructive activity."[47] Leary took McLuhan's advice seriously and by the time of the January 1967 San Francisco Be-in, he had become a major American media personality. Photos appeared of him in countless newspapers and magazines, and in virtually every shot, and regardless of what trauma may have occurred in his personal life, Leary had a radiant smile beaming across his face.

Beginning in December 1965 things began to go wrong for Timothy Leary. While on his way with his family to Mexico for a vacation, he was detained at the border and arrested with his daughter Caroline for possession of two ounces of marijuana. Leary later joked that he was probably the first person ever caught trying to smuggle pot *into* Mexico. There followed more arrests, trials, convictions, appeals. Millbrook also unraveled as news of the weird goings-on circulated in the neighborhood, prompting authorities to investigate for illicit activity. In April 1966, a young ambitious Dutchess County prosecutor, G. Gordon Liddy, staged a raid on Millbrook, and although loads of LSD and marijuana were found, the case was subsequently dismissed because in his zeal, Liddy failed to give the Miranda warning.[48] Not to be deterred, Liddy relentlessly pursued Leary and his followers, ultimately forcing Leary to abandon Millbrook and take his drug show to the West Coast where the Leary legend continued. For a while, the emerging hippie movement paid homage to him as the high priest of the psychedelic movement.

LSD became a big story in 1966. Congress outlawed it; possession and distribution were criminalized. National and local authorities overwhelmingly agreed that LSD use was dangerous both to individuals and to society. The majority of Americans agreed, dismissing Leary and others as delusional in their assertion that LSD opened the mind's eye to new possibilities; an outcome not worth the risks. *Newsweek*, *Life*, and the *Saturday Evening Post*, all did features on the drug's history, effects, and increasingly widespread use. Prompting the media coverage were doctors' reports of LSD-induced psychiatric breakdowns. As *Time* reported in March 1966, "The disease is striking in beach side beatnik pads and in the dormitories of expensive prep schools; it has grown into an alarming problem at UCLA and on the UC campus at Berkeley.... No one can even guess how many more self-styled 'acid heads' there are among oddball cult groups." The Food and Drug administration further stoked the media blitz by briefing reporters on the increasing number of "bad trips" they had been told about. The agency also sent a letter to 2,000 colleges warning of the drug's "widespread availability" and "profound effects on the mental processes."[49]

Those opposed to LSD use not only worried about the drug's potential adverse physical effects but its negative socio-cultural repercussions as well. Deeply disturbed by his research into this particular realm of LSD use was the psychologist Dr. Stanley Cohen: "We have seen something which in a way is most alarming, more alarming than death in a way. And that is the loss of all cultural values, the loss of feeling of right and wrong, of good and bad. These people lead a valueless life, without motivation, without ambition. They are de-cultured, lost to society, lost to themselves." In Cohen's view LSD did not bring the promised revelations of an expanded consciousness. Rather, users became delusional, self-destructive dissipated indigents, whose lives were all but physically over.[50]

While violent behavior and psychotic breaks were fairly rare among acid heads, researchers believed they had accumulated sufficient data by 1966 to show that LSD use was clearly dangerous. Interestingly, subsequent investigations revealed that most people who had bad LSD trips—severe mental or emotional trauma—had histories of established psychological breakdowns or instability. Nonetheless, acid heads were not surprised by the 1966 studies; they were aware that LSD was risky business. The problem, of course, was how many American young people knew the price they might pay for the adventure.[51] As far as former Beat-poet-turned-counterculture guru Gary Snyder was concerned, "Acid just happened to turn up as the product of this particular society, to correct its own excesses."[52] Snyder's insipid declaration outraged even the most empathetic of counterculture observers, individuals such as Theodore Roszak, who coined the term "counterculture" in his book *The Making of a Counterculture* (1969). Roszak believed Snyder's comment to be one of the "great absurdities" of "the psychedelic crusade" for it perpetuated the "facile assumption that there exists a technological solution [in this case, manufactured LSD] to every human problem ... by proclaiming that personal salvation and the social revolution can be packed in a capsule."[53] That simply taking a magic pill would transform an individual into a more sensitive human being and that a cadre of such enlightened individuals would then rearrange society to reflect the attainment of higher mass consciousness, was, in Roszak's view, delusional. Serious psychological and emotional disorders visited many persistent trippers, while far too many turned to heroin or meth to soothe a fried rather than expanded mind. In the 1960s the DuPont chemical conglomerate promoted its products by declaring they provided consumers with "Better Living Through Chemistry"; at the same time hippie street peddlers sold buttons and posters emblazoned with the same words.

Former tripper Bruce Hoffman witnessed first-hand through his friend's experience that acid could lead one to want even more intense "rushes": "I went to visit this colleague of mine who had been my guide for my first trip.... Much to my dismay, he was now experimenting with heroin and shooting up speed, and so was his girlfriend, his wife having left him in the meantime, and he was also engaging in shoplifting for the fun of it. He was one of the first clues I had that something was going wrong, because at that time [1965] I still had a rather utopian ideal of what psychedelics could bring about in our culture. I really had hopes that it was going to result in an awakening to inner values." A few weeks later Hoffman became even more despondent after overhearing a conversation "between a couple of kids I would have to call teenyboppers who must have been sixteen and seventeen." Most dismaying to Hoffman was that the two teenagers were going to take acid to get high for the hell of it; for fun and immediate pleasure and for nothing more. "They weren't searching," Hoffman lamented, "they were going to have a great party, and they were going to have great records, and they were going to have great sex." Hoffman took LSD as a "sacrament" but what he and other acid disciples were fast realizing as the 1960s wore on was that the psychedelic revolution had spawned a much larger, less than righteous, popular and increasingly sordid drug culture, where "drop[ping] LSD for the sheer partying of it" was more the reality than the search for expanded consciousness.[54]

Of course not all trips were bad nor were they taken just for the fun of it. Such was the case for Jane DeGenaro, who, while in high school "had been initiated into the drug culture—marijuana and hashish—and I wanted to see more. Especially I wanted to see some LSD." DeGenaro found the media blitz at the time (1967) especially alluring, as terms like "'heightening your perception,' 'seeing things like you've never seen them before,'" and "'playing with madness.' All that was just fascinating to me. I thought, Wow! Give me some."[55]

As excited as DeGenaro was to try acid, her first trip was a "bummer" but her second attempt proved to be what most trippers hoped the experience would be: "the expansion of awareness beyond the limited ego; a greater awareness that transcends the temporary, including the body." As DeGenaro and a group fellow trippers sat on the floor in the middle of a room she closed her eyes and found herself journeying through a spiraling tunnel where at the end she could see a gigantic eye, and at the moment she had to decide whether or not "to move down that tunnel. I decided to go." As she started traveling down the tunnel, the eye became "another eye, and a nose, and a mouth and a beard, and dark hair, and laughing eyes, and it was the most magnificent man I ever saw in my whole life." DeGenaro did not know who it was but "experienced religious ecstasy" as the man said to her "without words, 'We made it.' 'You're here.' 'We did it.' 'Here we are.' 'We're together.'" As DeGenaro came down from her trip she believed that what she had experienced "was what life was all about. I cannot express how fulfilled I was, how absolutely, totally happy."[56] DeGenaro had the kind of spiritual awareness encounter that acid propagators believed was the drug's most salient quality. Such was the view of a southern California hippie who was convinced that taking LSD was "a very religious thing, it is a religion in itself. It's like learning to accept God without question. When you start witnessing the universe all around you, you are aware of all energy levels. Things we can hear and feel, energies with the universe, just let it happen and become more enlightened."[57]

Although Bruce Hoffman's friend unfortunately succumbed to harder drugs, Hoffman's personal experiences with LSD were similar to those of DeGenaro; all of his trips were "beautiful" and were to be "cherished," even though it frequently took him several days to reenter reality. Nonetheless, there was always "an enormous sense of being a space traveler and you felt you were entering the frontiers of consciousness."[58] Despite Hoffman's and DeGenaro's "beautiful" trips, LSD remained an unpredictable drug; some people had pleasant experiences while others nightmarish cycles of mania, depression or paranoia.

LSD could be mass produced by simple processes, like bootlegged bathtub gin. It could be easily transported and easily concealed without notice. In liquid form it was odorless and colorless; in powder or pill it was minute. It was taken orally, requiring no needles or other paraphernalia, and thus left no "tracks" or other visible signs on the body. Although non-addictive, many hippies nonetheless became hooked, such as Larry Houchin, who admitted to have taken 300 tabs in a five-day period that "spaced him out" for several weeks while taking another several weeks for him "to finally come down."[59] A greater high than liquor, quicker for insights than college or psychiatry, the pure and instant magic of LSD captured not only the hippie mind but the mind of many straights as well.

Years before Leary had estimated that one million Americans would take LSD by 1967. According to *Life*, the nation had reached the million-dose mark in 1966. As for Leary, his status among heads declined rapidly after he went show biz, with his proselytizing making him the focus and the scapegoat for much of 1960s excesses. Leary loved to take the credit—but not the blame—for the drug revolution of the 1960s and 1970s. "Seven million people I turned on," he proudly announced near the end of his life, "and only one hundred thousand have come to thank me." Personally, Leary's life spun out of control from 1969 onward; broken marriages, the suicide of his daughter Caroline, constant arrests and flights from the law. In 1972, during his last year in exile in Kabul, Afghanistan, Leary went on a drug binge—marijuana, Quaaludes, cocaine, heroin, and mind-blowing doses of LSD. It was a wonder he was still alive when apprehended. In early 1973 federal agents kidnapped Leary and brought him back to California to stand trial for three prior drug convictions and for his 1970 escape from the California Men's Colony in San Luis Obispo. By April 1973 he was sentenced to thirty-five years in Folsom State Prison and three years later Leary walked out of Folsom a free man after agreeing to participate in the Federal Witness Protection Program. Word quickly spread among countercultural remnants that the high priest of LSD had become a government snitch. Former Learyites Allen Ginsberg, Jerry Rubin, and Ram Dass (Richard Alpert) convened a press conference in San Francisco in which they denounced their former guru. Leary's twenty-four-year-old son, Jack, was especially vituperative in his condemnation of his father, telling reporters that, "Timothy Leary lies at will when he thinks it will benefit him. He finds lies easier to control than the truth. And he creates fantastic absurd stories which he gets caught up in, and then cannot distinguish them from the truth."[60]

Leary spent the next twenty years of his life as a stand-up philosopher, preaching such profundities as: "the key political issue of our time is that every individual is entitled to complete and free access to his or her own brain." Before his death from prostate cancer in 1996, Leary requested that his remains be allowed to go on a final far-out trip into space. On April 2, 1997, a small glass vial containing seven grams of Leary's ashes was blasted into outer space aboard a Pegasus rocket launched from the Canary Islands. Accompanying Leary on this last adventure was a little bit of Gene Roddenberry, creator of the popular *Star Trek* television series.[61] Many acid heads were too young to know or remember that Leary had once been a serious, legitimate psychologist, with innovative ideas about curing mental illnesses. As far as the hippie counterculture was concerned, no individual did more to propagate and promote the psychedelic subculture; he had been the Johnny Appleseed of acid. Who was Timothy Leary? At the time of his death was he nothing more than a "twisted, angry, fucked-up old man?" Was he "a fool, drunk with his own 'celebrity-hood' ... a media clown" who "loved the limelight and relished his notoriety?" Or, was he a harbinger of a New Age; a brilliant, creative thinker; a man ahead of his times? Who was he? Perhaps his long-time friend and associate Richard Alpert said it best when he quipped, "You get the Timothy Leary you deserve."[62]

One person involved in the government-funded LSD research projects was a young writer and graduate student in the English department at Stanford University named Ken Kesey. Needing money at the time (1960), Kesey volunteered for the study at the local Veteran's Administration hospital in Palo Alto, California. At the time he and his wife were living in Perry Lane, a small beatnik community in Palo Alto. Doctors placed him in a room, gave him pills, and recorded his responses. One out of every three pills was LSD, and the effects were fantastic. Sounds had color, small objects appeared huge; figures glowed and pulsated. With his perceptions transformed by acid, Kesey put to words his experience with psychiatric treatment at a state mental hospital. In February 1962, Kesey's now-classic *One Flew Over the Cuckoo's Nest* appeared to rave reviews and made the burly Oregonian a literary celebrity, which Kesey parlayed into counterculture fame and legend. As he later recounted, "I mean the first acid I took was Sandoz, given me by the federal government in a series of experiments. What now, Uncle [Sam]? Don't give me that anti–American drug field bullshit: you turned me on and it was beautiful."[63]

Novelist and founder of the Merry Pranksters and the Acid Tests, Ken Kesey, 1966 (photograph by Larry Keenan, courtesy Bancroft Library, University of California, Berkeley. © 1997 Larry Keenan. All rights reserved).

Ken Kesey's "Magic Bus" *Further* that took the Merry Pranksters on a raucous, acid-infused epic cross-country pilgrimage in the summer of 1965. This photograph was taken in the summer of 1966 at the Artist Liberation Front Fair at the Panhandle in Golden Gate Park (photograph by Michelle Vignes, courtesy Bancroft Library, University of California, Berkeley).

If Leary spread the psychedelic revolution, Ken Kesey defined the movement's style, West Coast version, part Hollywood, part San Francisco bohemian. Because of LSD and drug use in general, Kesey perhaps became one of psychedelia's more tragic figures, forsaking a promising writing career for the sake of expanded consciousness. By the time of his second novel, *Sometimes a Great Notion* (1964), critics were hailing Kesey as being in the same literary league as Philip Roth, Joseph Heller, Bruce Jay Friedman, and Larry McMurtry. However, as Kesey told his chronicler, the novelist Tom Wolfe in a third-person parody of his life, "this young, handsome, successful, happily-married-three-lovely-children father" had become "a fear-crazed dope fiend in flight to avoid prosecution on three felonies and god knows how many misdemeanors and seeking at the same time to sculpt a new satori from an old surf— in even shorter, mad as a hatter." Kesey was honest about what had caused his fall from grace. "What was it that had brought a man so high of promise to so low a state in so short a time? Well, the answer can be found in just one short word, my friends, in just one all-too-well-used syllable: Dope!"[64]

Perry Lane was a hang-out for many Bay Area counterculturists and other avant-garde seekers. The Texas novelist Larry McMurtry came to visit as did Richard Alpert and a young, wild-haired musician named Jerry Garcia. Neal Cassady of *On the Road* fame not only showed up but decided to stay and become one of the leading men in the Kesey comedy about to unfold. The Perry Lane household was also completely turned on, with both guests and permanent residents consuming vast helpings of Kesey's LSD-laced venison chili and peyote buttons supplied by a mail-order house in Laredo, Texas. On acid, Kesey and his compatriots experienced "shell shattering ordeals" as they searched the Cosmos for that All-in-One energy field through which all humanity was interconnected. As David Farber succinctly stated, Kesey and his compatriots "took acid not so much to explore inner space as to re-negotiate social space."[65]

In the spring of 1964 Kesey and his entourage moved to a house in La Honda, California, about an hour's drive south of San Francisco, and there Kesey and company began the psychedelic style, creating their own concept of "set and setting." Neither Zen detachment nor Leary's carefully monitored environment had any acid relevance or purpose. Kesey and his compatriots used LSD to propel themselves out of their minds toward whatever realm of existence or being they were searching for at that moment; in "freaking freely." Rock and bebop jazz blasted around the clock from speakers strung tree to tree; fantastic mobiles and pulsating paintings dangled from bushes and limbs. Kesey believed it was his and his followers mission to help others "have some fun" with acid; to turn the whole world on spiritually, creatively, and cosmically. Kesey believed societal repressions were best challenged via the wacko style, or as Kesey put it, "tootle the masses." These escapades were for more than just kicks. Kesey saw himself as a religious prophet, preaching that no matter how zany the antics or insane the behavior, all was for the purpose of transforming America, as Michael Bowen declared, into an "electric Tibet."[66] Kesey believed it was time to see what the world looked like while perpetually loaded on LSD and bring such "enlightenment" to others in order to remake society according to their acid vision.

Kesey and his friend Ken Babbs renamed their LSD consortium the Merry Pranksters and decided they wanted to drive to New York to arrive in time for the publication of Kesey's new novel, *Sometimes a Great Notion*. For their journey the Pranksters bought for $1500 a 1939 International Harvester bus, which they completely refurbished and out-fitted with benches, bunks, a sink, a refrigerator, cabinets, and shelves. Although in mint condition, the Pranksters believed it wasn't quite right; it must look and feel appropriate for who they were. They completely repainted the vehicle with swirling Day-Glo mandalas, rewired it for speakers, tapes, and a microphone, and cut a hole through the roof so a passenger could sit on a raised platform with his head and upper body poking through the top. On the rear of the bus they affixed a sign that read CAUTION: WEIRD LOAD.; one in front said FURTHER; and in the refrigerator were pitchers of orange juice spiked with grade–A acid. In early July 1964 the Pranksters set off for New York. Before leaving La Honda they changed their names: Kesey was now Swashbuckler; Babbs, Intrepid Traveler; Mike Hagen was now Mal Function; Steve Lambrecht, Zonker; and others nicknamed Mountain Girl, Gretchen Fetchin the Slime Queen, Doris Delay, and Hardly Visible.[67]

The Pranksters were hip but in a new way. They were not alienated, "beaten" individuals, rejecting the materialism, conformity, and the values of 1960s American bourgeois culture. Nor did they curse their fate for not having been born black, nor did they even envy the "primitive naturalness" of other ethnic Americans. Indeed, according to Tom Wolfe, author of *The Electric Kool-Aid Acid Test* (a history of Kesey and the Pranksters), for this new breed of white hipsters, African Americans were no longer part of the hip scene, "not even as totem figures. It was unbelievable. *Spades*, the very soul figures of Hip, of jazz, of the hip vocabulary itself, man and like, and dig and baby and scarf and split and later and so fine; of pouring soul all over the spades, all over, finished, incredibly."[68] To Wolfe this new hip generation, these "hippies," were products of postwar affluence, most of whom spent their teen years safe and secure in their rarefied *white* California suburban neighborhoods, oblivious to the Black America that the Beats had so admired and from where and whom they had drawn their creative and aesthetic inspiration.

The Pranksters trip east is the closest rendition of a hippie epic. Kesey filmed the entire journey, perhaps as a future commercial venture and thus a record exists of the pranks, trips, encounters, and mishaps they experienced across 3,000 miles of American highways. Days were not comfortable and nights were even worse. It was hard to sleep going seventy miles an hour over pot-holed roads in a vehicle without springs. Such tribulations were hardly noticed by the travelers for all were perpetually strung out on acid, pot, and then for variety Benzedrine—speed. Good dope was not the only compensation in an overall rough road trip. There was good sex, or at least lots of it. There was a sleeping bag on the shelf of the "love bunk." That's where you crawled when you wanted to "ball" a fellow traveler, male or female, but mostly it was male-female, and the bunk was always occupied. Indeed, as Tom Wolfe observed, the sleeping bag "got such hard use that mere proximity was enough to impregnate any virgin."[69]

The Pranksters reached New York in mid–July and immediately wanted to see Allen Ginsberg and Jack Kerouac, an encounter made easy because of Neal Cassady's close relationship with the Beat generation's two most famous individuals. Interestingly, despite Cassady's association with both groups, the meeting of Beat and counterculture was not as "synchronistic" as Kesey and his disciples had hoped. The two groups eyed each other across the chasm of acid as well as a "generational thing." As Wolfe observed, "Kerouac was the old star. Kesey was the wild new comet from the West heading christ knew where."[70] There was no bonding between Beat and hippie. The Pranksters next stop was Millbrook and there as well, Kesey and friends were treated more like outliers than embraced fellow acid heads. After enduring a few days of cool-eyed appraisal and aloofness from the Millbrook folk, the Pranksters decided it was time to leave, convinced that their East Coast brothers and sisters were not kindred spirits; that their free-wheeling American brand of psychedelia, not Leary's set and setting amidst Far Eastern gewgaws, was how the future would go.[71]

Kesey and the Pranksters spent most of their time during the fall of 1964 and through the spring of 1965 making a movie out of the 45 hours of color film they had shot on their trip. They also became increasingly immersed in the acid dream. In the summer of 1965 Kesey met the Hell's Angels through gonzo reporter Hunter S. Thompson, and that August invited them to a "bonding" party at his La Honda commune. Suffice it to say, most of Kesey's compatriots believed their mentor had indeed finally lost his mind to acid, welcoming a group as notoriously thuggish and violent as the Angels to-sing-kumbaya-around-the-campfire-get-together seemed dangerously insane. The Angels, malevolent shaggy toughs, were the counterculture's resident bad guys, striking fear into even the hippest white middle class heart. However, making peace with the undisputed barbarians was a challenge no countercultural vanguard could refuse, for to succeed would represent a victory over the bogeymen of their white suburban, bourgeois past. To everyone's surprise, and thanks largely to the Pranksters' cool and ice chests full of beer and batches of acid in which the Angels freely indulged, all went harmoniously well, with both hippies and Angels, arm-in-arm, literally singing around campfires at night. At first thought the camaraderie seems improbable but upon further reflection, fitting. Both acid heads and bikers were persona non grata in the square-straight world; both built their lives around moving down the highway. When the Angels roared off two days later, an alliance of two outlaw cultures had been forged. By the time of the Human Be-In, the Angels had become permanent Haight residents, celebrated by Allen Ginsberg as the current version of the "saintly motorcyclists" about whom he had "howled" a decade before.[72]

The drug community, hitherto a small band of initiates, was fast swelling into a psychedelic nation. Leary and Kesey provided the psychedelic movement's software while the hardware was provided by a skinny, dark-haired character from Kentucky with a nasal voice and patrician pedigree named Augustus Owsley Stanley III, who liked to be called by just his middle name. Grandson of a former U.S. senator from Kentucky, he had inherited part of the family fortune, which came from distilling bourbon. After a stint in the Air Force, Owsley drifted to the West Coast to attend the University of California at Berkeley. However, traditional college life was not for Owsley, who became a thirty-year-old dropout. He quickly found a way to live rather well: he became, in the Kentucky tradition, a bootleg chemist. In partnership with his girlfriend Melissa Cargill, who was majoring in chemistry, Owsley set up a methedrine lab in his apartment near campus. After California narcotics agents closed down their operation, Owsley and Cargill shifted their activities to manufacturing acid. However, not until the entrance of Tim Scully, a Berkeley science whiz did the Owsley enterprise shift into high gear. Thanks to Scully, Owsley and company produced the purest, strongest acid anyone had ever seen. The Owsley tablets, color-coded for each new batch, which was supposed to be different from the previous production in quality or potency, established the standard and made Owsley a fortune, especially after Sandoz stopped selling LSD in 1966. By the close of the decade Owsley had made and sold an estimated 10 million doses of LSD. Thanks to Owsley, the psychedelic revolution accelerated faster than anyone anticipated. Although he made a ton of money, Owsley was in it for more than money and gave away as much as he sold. He and his compatriots saw themselves as benefactors and social engineers as much as psychedelic entrepreneurs. Tim Scully later described the messianic purpose of their enterprise: "Every time we'd make another batch and release it on the street, something beautiful would flower, and of course we believed it was because of what we were doing. We believed that we were the architects of social change; that our mission was to change the world substantially, and what was going on in the Haight [the burgeoning San Francisco hippie neighborhood] was a sort of laboratory experiment, a microscopic example of what would happen worldwide."[73] Indeed, by the beginning of 1966, Kesey and the Pranksters, along with Owsley, had become San Francisco's psychedelic wizards, showing mainstream Americans that LSD was the key to the discovery of their inner childlike, authentic selves.

From Leary, Kesey, and celebrity elites, drug usage spread to the population at large, especially to rebellious young people. Leary's crusading efforts on behalf of mind-altering drugs made life a great deal baser for many young people. As drug trips became more commonplace, less care was taken with "set and setting." Given a bad mind-set and careless physical environment, hallucinogens such as acid were capable of driving anxiety to a high pitch. "Drug tourism" led to bad trips—rare with marijuana, more common with hashish, and most common with LSD, particularly when amphetamine-laced or polluted with other compounds, increasingly common on the streets by the late 1960s. The press, of course, did embellish the catastrophic freak-outs but people did have bad trips and *did* jump out of windows, believing they could fly—even Richard Alpert had such a fantasy once. Groups of "chemical freaks" formed, with indiscriminate tastes for barbiturates and amphetamines—speed—as well as LSD, mescaline, or whatever else was available at the moment. Ultimately, Leary and other drug pushers were false prophets who left behind them a generational wasteland strewn with victims of brain damage, overdose, and tragic death.

As the 1960s progressed and drug usage accelerated in popularity, so did the public outcry, and the demand for the law to crack down on the alleged drug epidemic sweeping the nation and turning American youth into hopelessly self-destructive delinquents and drug addicts. However, as *Time* observed, "Pop drugs hardly portend anything as drastic as a new and debauched American spirit as some alarmists believe"; that "a joint today" did not signify "a junkie tomorrow." Rather, the increased use of pop drugs reflected "a persistent unwillingness of youth to accept the straight world" as well as "the social and political dislocations of the times: uncertain wars, a capricious draft system, inequitable distribution of opportunity and income, and institutions too immured against necessary change." Nonetheless, morally outraged parents and authorities condemned the drug culture, wanting to bring the full force of the law down upon even the most casual or recreational user, many of whom were arrested and sentenced to long prison terms, especially in the counterculture's early years. Such a heavy-handed dragnet prompted even some government officials to publicly denounce the current laws as "completely out of proportion to the dangers of the drug," particularly marijuana. To the director of the National Institute for Mental Health, Dr. Stanley Yolles, there was no "clearer instance in which the punishment for an infraction of the law is more harmful than the crime."[74] Perhaps more than any other feature of the hippie lifestyle, it was the drug culture the movement spawned that led the majority of adult Americans to fear and even hate the hippies.

The widespread appeal of LSD and other hallucinogens among 1960s youth is difficult to tell in one chapter. Perhaps Albert Hofmann best summed up his discovery's unexpected impact: "It was obvious that a substance with such fantastic effects on mental perception and on the experience of the outer and inner world would also arouse interest outside medical science. I had expected curiosity and interest on the part of artists outside medicine—performers, painters, and writers—but not among people in general."[75] As one physician said of the many young hippies he had met, "They are serious and good-humored and remarkably non-fanatical, except about one thing—and that's their drugs."[76]

4

The Hippies and Rock and Roll

"WE all know what's going to save the world. Rock, that's what."—Arthur
Johnson, *Distant Drummer*, 1968

Rock and roll music defined the hippie counterculture perhaps even more than drugs
and sex, even though all three formed the symbolic tripod upon which the hippie movement
rested; it was rock that became the most important medium for countercultural communication, interaction, and influence during the hippies' heyday. Indeed, as one historian has
asserted, "Though changes in the other arts reveal the sixties and expose its sensibilities, rock
was the culture of the sixties."[1] Most important, 1960s rock and roll affected an entire generation of young Americans both physically and emotionally, not just hippies. John Sinclair
perhaps best summed up rock and roll's across-the-youth-identity-spectrum appeal during
the 1960s: "For our generation … Rock and Roll is the great liberating force of our time. Its
most beautiful aspect is that it gets to millions of people every day, telling them that they can
dance and sing and holler and scream and FEEL GOOD even when they have to listen to all
those jive commercials and death news reports all around the music, everything's gonna be
all right as soon as EVERYBODY GIVES IT UP!"[2]

Even today, nearly fifty years later, when the legendary bands from the 1960s reunite to
play, concert halls are filled to capacity just as they were during that time when that same
group performed for the same baby boomers—both hippie and non-hippie. Both band members and the majority of the audience are significantly older now and grayer, and generally a
bit more worn, especially if either had also over-indulged in some of the decade's other
excesses. But ageing baby boomers are not the only attendees at these reunion gigs: The February 2014 Rolling Stones concert in Abu Dhabi sold out immediately to a crowd that was
an even mix of boomers, Generation X, and millennials—fans young enough to be the *grandchildren* of their original 1960s followers. Many of the top bands of the new millennium pay
public homage to the sounds of fifty years ago. Rock and roll, in all its lyrical varieties and
different sounds, appealed to both hippies and straights during the 1960s. For most 1960s
youth rock and roll was simply fun because the music allowed the celebration of adolescent
feelings and emotions; it was a sound that was not only specifically created for young people,
but "understood" by them as well. At the same time, rock allowed escape from the perceived
monotony, conformity, vagaries, and daily grind of mainstream American life. Lead singer
and lyricist Country Joe McDonald of the Bay Area band Country Joe and the Fish, one of
the early progenitor's of the acid/folk rock "San Francisco sound," perhaps best captured the

Regardless of locale, rock music was always the centerpiece of hippie tribal gatherings. Photograph taken in 1967 (Dennis L. Maness Summer of Love Photograph Collection (SFP51), San Francisco History Center, San Francisco Public Library).

symbiotic relationship between rock and dope when he said "You take drugs, you turn up the music very loud, you dance around, you build yourself a fantasy world where everything is beautiful."[3] Since hippies believed that the rock and roll songs of their era reflected the realities of their time, "the terror of [contemporary] life, about the need for love," listening to rock when stoned was "when the message really gets through—it's more difficult to evade these matters."[4] To the majority of baby boomers, but especially to hippies, rock was not just sound; it was part and parcel of a way of life; they lived it and breathed it, for rock was a declaration pivotal in their rebellion against the bourgeois values and lifestyles of both their parents and many of their peers. To this day hippies believe rock and roll, more than either drugs or sex, to have been their movement's most definitive cultural imprint and legacy.

It was "Negro music" that informed much of early rock and roll, captured by a host of white rock and rollers, but like jazz, the sound had become so thoroughly appropriated by white middle class youth, that by the end of the 1950s few, if any teenagers knew its origins. Rock and roll perhaps became the most commandeered of all African American expressions by whites in the history of American music both in a warmly appreciative but also coldly exploitive way. The simulation of black musical idioms, first by white rock and rollers, then by counterparts in Europe and around the world, represented, according to Robert Pattison, "the biggest cultural crossover since Moses parted the Red Sea."[5]

Since the days of slavery the black church had informed much in the lives of African Americans, especially for those living in the Deep South where the term rock and roll originated in the region's rural Pentecostal churches during the 1920s and 1930s. In these congregations, in the call-and-response interaction between the pastor and his flock, members "rocked and reeled" in the celebration of the Lord to fast, bluesy music played on guitars, horns, and drums. What was particularly unique about the various strains that coalesced to form rock and roll was that they were part of the overall racial and ethnic dynamics of American society. For example, many of the early white rock and rollers, the majority of who were from the South, found the "hillbilly" music of their Scotch-Irish Protestant forebears, who had settled in the region's piedmont areas, to be appealing and incorporated that sound into the melodies, chord progressions, and lyrics. Although reflecting the influence of the nation's other musical genres, rock and roll unquestionably originated in the African American community; a hybrid of predominantly black musical expressions, among which "rhythm and blues," an urban-based (Chicago) blues music played with electric instruments, pounding beat, and racy lyrics had the greatest impact. "R&B" was a new sound that reflected the gritty, grinding monotony of the daily lives of the growing class of African American urban industrial workers, who had migrated North in hopes of finding greater economic opportunities and personal freedoms in cities such as Chicago. To their despair, instead of Jim Crow they found his slick cousin "James Crow," who proved to be equally adept at marginalizing black life as his more blatant Southern counterpart. R&B found its most receptive audience among the black working classes in Northern cities such as Chicago, Detroit, and Cleveland because it was a sound that was "singularly expressive of the [Southern African American] encounter with industrial urbanism: expressive in lyrics, theme, and the juxtaposition of strong, southern-accented feeling with mechanized, routinized mass produced—that is, industrialized—sound and experience."[6]

As rhythm and blues emanated from the black enclaves within Northern industrial cities, reflecting the urban-industrial experience of African Americans, rock and roll would follow a similar evolutionary pattern, becoming by the mid–1960s a metropolitan-based and informed genre that had its greatest appeal among 1960s urban/suburban white middle class youth. As the urban R&B sound reflected the hard life of the Northern black working class and the search for cheap thrills to escape the daily grind of racism and economic oppression, so too did the words and music of acid rock echo the hippies' desire to escape through the pleasures of drugs and sex from the oppression of plenty, which in the counterculture mind had created a spiritual and emotional despair similar to that experienced by their urban black working class "soul brothers." However, the hippies' often self-absorbed, drug-induced lifestyles, which they claimed were spiritual journeys to find their true selves, could hardly be compared to the *real* psychological and emotional anguish suffered by Northern African American industrial workers; a condition caused by genuine deprivation and deep-seated racism. Few if any hippies came from such a background and thus despite attempts by hippies to reach out to their black "brothers and sisters," few African Americans could identify with the hippie ethos and consequently acid rock had few black followers. Nonetheless, urban R&B influenced many hippie bands and hippies believed as passionately as black folk that their music was as expressive of their feelings as Northern black workers had embraced R&B as the music of their souls.

Almost all the pre-eminent Chicago bluesmen were Southern born and raised before migrating to the Windy City in the 1940s. Leading this new movement in black music was the Mississippian Muddy Waters, who along with John Lee Hooker and B.B. King became legendary rhythm and blues artists, whose music and race hippies and other counterculture groups warmly embraced in the 1960s. Influenced by the acoustic blues sound of Robert Johnson and Son House, Waters was seminal in resurrecting and recreating a musical tradition that featured solo performances with a guitar within an ensemble arrangement that had as its staple a lead guitarist, a rhythm guitarist, pianist, harmonica player, drummer, and at times a saxophonist. This line-up of musicians established the template for many of the 1960s white rock and roll bands. Indeed, Waters and other rhythm and blues players made the guitar the centerpiece of their music, as would the majority of the 1960s rock and roll bands. The Chicago bluesmen also created a more danceable rhythm than bebop's more esoteric variations. In fact, one of the most important features of late 1950s and 1960s rock and roll was that it was music *made* for dancing.[7] For the increasing numbers of whites who flocked to rhythm and blues performances, the mythology of black music became, according to Pattison, a "screen upon which to project a montage of the primitive for at least three hundred years."[8] As the 1950s progressed, more and more white high school and college students were becoming aware of black popular culture, intrigued by its vibrant, raw, and sexually charged "otherness." The attraction was all the more captivating when they compared their insulated, homogenized, and boring suburban existence with that of the perceived genuineness and liberating effects of the African American hip/urban experience.[9] Thus, the three most important dynamics that coalesced to form rock and roll were *youth, blackness, and Southerness*, with the South coming North in a cultural carpet bagging in reverse. Southern music trailed demographics, but in the 1950s caught up in a hurry.

As the 1950s progressed, both white and black rock and rollers brought "race music" out of its black confines, delivering it full force to an increasingly larger white teenage mainstream audience. According to rock historian and pop music pundit Greil Marcus, Elvis Presley, along with Buddy Holly, Jerry Lee Lewis, the Everly Brothers, and a host of other white Southern rock and rollers, "proved white boys could do it all—that they could be as strange, as exciting, as scary, and as free as the black men [Chuck Berry, Little Richard, and Fats Domino, to name but a few] who were suddenly walking America's airwaves as if they owned them." Regardless of color, 1950s rock and rollers "brought home the racial fears of a lot of people [and] the secret dreams of others."[10] The meteoric rise to dominance of the new rock genre by the above white rock and rollers perfectly reflected T.S. Eliot's musing thirty years earlier that "immature artists imitate, mature artists steal."[11] Indeed, in American cultural history rock and roll's ascension to the realm of the holy was the direct result of an aggressive, and often unapologetic theft, which even the best songwriter of a generation, Bob Dylan acknowledged: "find a music you love, steal it, and make it your own."

Despite constant parental tirades and harassment, 1950s and especially 1960s youth refused to disassociate their lives from rock and roll. As 1960s hipster John Sinclair declared, "For our generation [rock] music is the most vital force in our lives.... We have to have it."[12] Or as the legendary disc jockey Alan Freed succinctly observed, "Let's face it—rock and roll is bigger than all of us.... It began on the levees and plantations, took in folk songs, and features blues and rhythm. It's the rhythm that gets to the kids—they're starved for music they can dance to after all those years of crooners."[13] Rock and roll existed almost exclusively for American youth, even more so than television, and thus the new music seemed to separate young Americans from their elders, ushering in a powerful youth culture, which would explode in the 1960s, affecting practically every facet of American life. Consequently, young people's response to their parents and other's disdain for their music became, in effect, "I'm hip, cool, and 'with it' and you, the old, the out-of-touch, the over-the-hill, are not; you are a drag on my fun and pleasure, and I will tune you out of my life (for the moment)."

Sustaining rock and roll was the same affluence that it challenged. Rock owed much of its rapid growth and appeal to middle class prosperity and the power of the consumer culture. With the economy booming, many high school students held part-time jobs, or if from more fortunate households, received allowances from their parents. Regardless of the source, millions of 1950s American young people had sufficient purchasing power to buy record players and the cheap 45-rpm vinyl disks that carried the new sound. Almost everyone could afford to feed nickels into the jukeboxes that played rock music wherever teenagers congregated, whether at the malt shop or local hamburger joint, or the many other oases that became favorite hangouts. Rock and roll invaded white middle class suburbia as few post-war dynamics of change would, beguiling its teenage listeners into an imaginary world of "dream lovers," broken hearts, fast cars, and a host of other teenage fantasies and delights. Even many of the songs' inane lyrics did not bother its captivated listeners, who were more attracted to the driving beat and fast paced rhythm than to words. The music played an important role in expanding the peer group; uniting teenagers as rock lovers into a huge sub-society of the "knowing"; a sense of common bond: only *they* could understand and appreciate its significance. As rock historian William Schaffer observed, "Rock, as folk music of the white middle class American, did more than fill a cultural void or provide aesthetic interests in otherwise constricted lives.... Rock dissolved the everyday rubbish of the young American and revealed his dream life. It flaked away the thin whitewash of outward conformity and docility and revealed the basic fears and desires of [a] generation.... The message of rock was hardly a secret—it was a rejection of middle-class America."[14]

By 1960 the initial frenzy surrounding rock and roll had subsided, thanks in large part to the emergence and subsequent rise to the top of the charts of carefully overproduced, manufactured, packaged, and sanded-down teenage crooners—Bobby Vinton, Bobby Rydell, Bobby Vee, Frankie Avalon, Fabian, and Paul Anka, to name but a few. Joining their male counterparts were a wave of female vocalists and groups such as Shelly Fabares ("Johnny Angel"); Joanie Sommers ("Johnny Get Angry"); Leslie Gore ("It's My Party" and "You Don't Own Me"); The Crystals ("Then He Kissed Me" and "He's a Rebel"); and The Ronettes ("Be My Baby"). Helping these artists to become all the rage was Elvis Presley's Army induction in 1958. Presley appeared on the cover of *Life* magazine, smiling, famous pompadour shaved down to a crew-cut; the epitome of the rock and roller's ultimate civilizing. That once reviled sneering, gyrating delinquent turned out to be a good boy after all who bought homes for his parents, said his prayers, and did not smoke or drink. In the history of rock and roll, only a handful of performers so rapidly and completely dominated the popular scene as Presley. Like many of his white peers, Presley demonstrated that white musicians could artistically and commercially replicate the energy, sexuality, and aggression of "race" music. Presley simply did it better than anyone else, including many of his African American contemporaries. Presley did not bleach the black sounds of R&B; he possessed an inherent, genuine ability, temperament, soulfulness, and savvy to forge a dynamic new sound out of all he saw, heard, and felt around him. Whether it was rockabilly, the blues, country, or gospel, Presley took from each what he believed to be their more salient features, fusing them through his voice to deliver a distinct sound that was his own creation. According to jazz artist and music critic Eddie Condon, Elvis took "the best parts of the old blues singers' tunes, stirred them up, mixed them with moonshine hillbilly songs, backwoods bawls and goat calls, and has come up with something that sells." Although Condon, like many other music "purists"/pundits of his time disdained Presley on a variety of levels, he nonetheless believed "the boy with the sideburns from Tupelo, Mississippi," was "the biggest sensation the music business have ever seen. I've never seen anything to equal the Charles Atlas grip he now has on kids." Presley admitted that he purposely tried to emulate as much as possible the sound and feel of the black bluesmen. "The colored folks been singing it and playing it for more years than I know. I used to hear old Arthur Crudup bang his box [guitar] the way I do now, and I said if I ever got to the place where I could feel all old Arthur felt, I'd be a music man like nobody ever saw,"[15] and Presley was; from 1955 until his Army induction in 1958, Presley dominated the charts, selling 28 million records by 1957 and appearing on CBS's *The Ed Sullivan Show*, television's premier variety hour, a record three times, with an estimated 60 million Americans—a staggering 82 percent of the viewing public—watching Presley's first show. It was the largest television viewing audience ever and set a record that would not be broken until 73 million viewers turned into the Beatles on the same show in 1964.[16]

As the new crooners rose to the top of the charts, the consensus among rock and roll true believers was that the *real* music went into cryogenic sleep for several years until the Beatles resurrected it in 1963, breathing life back into the sound, making it more multi-dimensional—raw and refined simultaneously—and bigger and more appealing than anyone believed possible since Elvis Presley and other artists who comprised rock's Golden Age (1955–58) had originated the sound. Indeed, in 1958, with Presley in the army, mainstream Americans could relax. Perhaps the nation's youth had become bored with rock and roll as they quickly had with many of the decade's other fads (hula hoops come to mind), and thus the music's appeal had been nothing more than a phase; just good, old-fashioned American cultural growing pains.

By the early 1960s not only had rock and roll been co-opted by the teenage crooners but another musical genre had also resurfaced, folk music, which became especially vogue among the more politicized, crusading, college-attending sectors of the nation's youth. By the early 1960s increasing numbers of white young people, affected by the civil rights movement and other progressive undertakings found inspiration for their causes in folk music. Exhorted by President Kennedy's moral admonishments for affluent white youth to serve the nation and other countries' less fortunate before pursuing the American dream, thousands of young white Americans immersed themselves in crusades such as the Peace Corps to help ameliorate the lives of the downtrodden and oppressed, both at home and abroad. Thus, for a while, popular youth-oriented music reflected this more socially conscious, idealistic, and purposeful moment in the history of 1960s youth, with songs and ballads expressing serious social issues such as racial injustice, the excesses of modernity, poverty, war, and nuclear annihilation. The protest music of Pete Seeger, the Weavers, and Phil Ochs, and a host of others, was full of such themes as well as lyrics reflecting an obvious anti-cultural Establishment message. According to Ralph Gleason, these "topical song writers" had "consciously transformed the medium of the phonograph record from pure entertainment to that of the communication of ideas and made the concert hall a political platform."[17]

Whether musicians or fans, the majority of 1950s folksters were leftists, who believed that since the 1930s, their particular musical genre had been for the dispossessed and the marginalized. Thanks in large part to McCarthyism and the politics of anti-communism in general, by the late 1950s the pre–World War II Old Left had become a defunct movement, a penumbra on the nation's political landscape. However, those old leftists still around hoped to use folk's revival and growing popularity among their progeny as a medium to revitalize the Left in American political culture.

Folk music shed light on the growing alienation of American youth from the nation's institutions and the folk resurgence reflected a desire among young people for an America that was somehow more authentic from the plastic version they saw offered in the mass media. Folk music became a way of declaring their distance from and disdain for mainstream popular culture. By 1960 folk had come out of its hermitage; Harry Belafonte; the Kingston Trio; the Limeliters; the Chad Mitchell Trio; Peter, Paul, and Mary and Joan Baez, to name but a few, were all in vogue, producing slick, upbeat covers of mostly classic American populist folk ballads originally sung by such icons as Woody Guthrie and Jack Elliot in the 1930s. Although Baez and a few other popular folkies "scorned the commercial" and even wrote some of their own ballads, the majority of the craze's biggest stars, such as the New Christy Minstrels and the Kingston Trio, produced "middle-of-the road fun music" that offended no one's socio-political conscience or sensibilities. Indeed, the Minstrel's founder and leader Randy Sparks told *Time* that even though he and his troupe could sing "as ethnically" as any of their contemporaries, the group "hewed to the public taste because the public pays our salaries." Even when recruiting singers, Sparks "looked for the all–American boy or girl who had no political complaints and no sexual problems anybody would be interested in." It appeared that as folk became a more appealing alternative to the teenage crooners, many of its more popular artists readily succumbed to commodification, becoming in the process as packaged and as sanitized in their music and performances as their "teen-feel" rivals. Nonetheless, even after folk had become passé (circa 1966), many hippies continued to play pre-electric Dylan, Baez, and other folk artists on their stereos, most of them oblivious to the historical folk roots of *their* music, which the folk revival of the late 1950s and early 1960s had helped cultivate. As rock historian Geoffrey Stokes has observed, folk was a pivotal, transitional genre for sixties rock, offering an alternative to the more banal sounds of the teenage crooners. Especially among the more progressive or avant-garde, coming-of-age boomers, searching for a sound more authentic and meaningful than the popular pap produced by the record Establishment, folk music momentarily filled the aesthetic void until rock's rebirth in the mid-sixties. As Stokes observes, "Faced with the choice between teen and treacle, a lot of young people turned to folk music," and from the energized folk scene major portions of the new rock emerged.[18] Yet, even as endearing and righteous a music as folk was, it was nonetheless cyclical in its relevance and too staunchly traditional to capture and sustain the passion and interest of the Baby Boomers' rapidly accelerating restlessness for something more vital; a sound that they could embrace as definitively their own, and one that reflected their growing fascination for the "other" as embodied in the emerging hip counterculture.

Without question the most compelling minstrel of the folk craze of the early 1960s was Bob Dylan. Born Robert Allen Zimmerman in Hibbing, Minnesota, he renamed himself after the besotted Welsh poet Dylan Thomas and the manly sheriff of television's *Gunsmoke* series, Matt Dillon. Dylan not only dominated the American folk scene at its apex but became simultaneously one of rock and roll's greatest stars and icons; a seminal figure in rock's transformation during the mid–1960s. In the opinion of rock pundits, historians, and aficionados, Dylan has become the greatest of them all in a pantheon that includes Elvis Presley, the Beatles, and the Rolling Stones. Dylan's meteoric rise to the top of the folk music charts rivaled that of Elvis Presley's domination of rock and roll; one year after arriving in Greenwich Village (1961), the nation's folk capital, Dylan became America's premier folkie and remains as popular today as he was in the late 1960s and early 1970s. In the past fifty years, after the Beatles, Dylan's songs are the most covered by other performers; the result of Dylan having been one of the first folksingers of the era to write and perform his own songs rather than relying on the traditional themes and ballads of other folk artists. Indeed, Dylan became one of the most prolific songwriters in both folk and rock history.[19]

Although consciously emulating Woody Guthrie, Dylan simultaneously voiced the specific concerns of his own generation as can be heard in such Dylan classics as "Blowin' in the Wind," which sold 300,000 copies two weeks after its release by Peter, Paul, and Mary; the chilling "A Hard Rain's Gonna Fall" (written during the October 1962 Cuban Missile Crisis evoking Armageddon), and his most famous countercultural song, "The Times They Are a-Changin'," which white civil rights activists and other young politicos embraced as their anthem. Unlike other folkies who wrote their own material but mainly from the newspapers or the nightly news reports, Dylan's songs, beginning with his second album, *The Freewheelin' Bob Dylan*, were his own unique creations. Whether expressing social or political outrage or personal bitterness, sorrow, longing, betrayal, or love, Dylan conveyed his themes in messages to his listeners subliminally; in symbolic or surreal imagery, allegory, or figurative language that was often harsh if not callous, all of which served to distill and define his contemporaries' anxieties, frustrations, and disillusionment with either the status quo or with themselves while hopefully arousing them to action to try to make things better. Indeed, Dylan's lyrics were "so riveting they transformed folk art." Or, as a fourteen-year-old female fan succinctly declared, "Bob Dylan says all the things I feel but can't say myself."[20]

To Ralph Gleason and other music pundits supportive of the emerging counterculture, Dylan, Baez, and a handful of other folkies represented a New Morality in their respective songs. Their "topical songs" cried out against "The Bomb, against capital punishment, hypocrisy, and death and deceit and in favor of love, truth, and beauty, unashamed in the face of the centuries of misuse which has worn those words thin." Their songs embodied both their sincerity and simultaneous anxiety; the result Gleason believed, of having "lived with the Bomb all their lives. It has been part of their consciousness ever since they were aware of anything at all outside of the home. They are the true fallout from the blast that changed the world, the real Bomb Babies." Their songs mirrored both the New Morality and their dissatisfaction "with the world they came into." and through their ballads they not only found "expression to their feelings" but in the process were "*revising* the priorities of the entire society." Their message was "simplistic and evangelical and millenary. They say the virtues are Love and Truth and Beauty and the ultimate sins are to hurt another human, to break trust, and not to love." According to Malvina Reynolds, what made Dylan in particular *the voice* of the New Moralists was the way he "ties it all together. He is *saying* something and saying it effectively." Reynolds believed that 1960s youth had been "betrayed by the good voices all their lives, have been told lies by the good voices, I mean social lies—that love is all, y'know, and if you're good everything will be wonderful." Then Bob Dylan appeared with songs and lyrics that shattered such illusions, prompting 1960s youth to gravitate to their new messiah, "rejecting so thoroughly the language, attitudes, and concepts of their elders." According to Gleason, what Dylan and the other "conscience singers" were saying was that "the Emperor [1960s conventional bourgeois culture, institutions, and societal values, norms and mores] has no clothes. We have believed too long that he has," and thus Dylan and his compatriots were "serving notice on their elders to get out of the way" for the New Morality for which they were its harbingers. Gleason also made it clear that although Dylan, Baez, and company were "the poets and troubadours heralding a revolution," they were nonetheless "highly rewarded by the very society against which their revolution [was] aimed." Indeed, by 1965, both Dylan and Baez albums "ranked among the best sellers in the music trade sales reports, fully the equal and sometimes the superior in sales volume to the recordings by Frank Sinatra and Elvis Presley."[21]

As Dylan told a friend in the early 1960s, "My songs speak for me. I write them in the confinement of my own mind. If I didn't write I think I would go insane."[22] The high point of Dylan's folk fame came in August 1963 in Washington, D.C., where he joined with a handful of other folk singers to perform at the same massive demonstration For Jobs and Freedom where Martin Luther King, Jr., gave his now famous "I Have a Dream" speech before a significantly integrated crowd of 250,000 marchers of whom 60,000 were white. The audience's composition instilled hope in many Americans, especially the young who came away from the gathering sanguine that perhaps the nation was at last on its way to extinguishing racism. King's oration offered that nation a vision in which the spirit of brotherly love would heal the wounds of racism and the scars of slavery. Dylan, however, was not so optimistic; toward the end of the day he grumbled to a compatriot, "Think they're listening? No they ain't listening at all."[23] Interestingly, Dylan rejected the pedestal of leadership on which he had been placed by American youth by 1963, confessing in his autobiography that he had "ominous forebodings" when introduced and held aloft as such at folk festivals. Dylan's enigmatic guise can be interpreted as a defense against mainstream expectations. As a musician Dylan portrayed the dark realities of social injustices, yet when he slipped off his acoustic guitar, he bewildered his fans by professing that perhaps his music and all that it was supposed to represent, was just a cruel joke. Nonetheless young people increasingly looked to him to lead them to the Promised Land. As Todd Gitlin observed at the time, whether he liked it or not, Dylan sang for an entire generation: "We followed his career as if he were singing our song; we got into the habit of asking him where he was taking us next."[24]

Perhaps more important for the future, throughout all his early folk fame, Dylan never lost his teenage enthusiasm for rock and roll, becoming the first artist to seize rock's power to change consciousness. Whatever Dylan may or may not have represented, he should always be considered a poet whose words had an uncanny ability to foretell the future. In a statement that would come to define rock's authenticity as a genre based on the artist's aspirations rather than those of an expectant culture, Dylan declared that "Being a musician means getting to the depths of where you are at. And most any musician would try anything to get to those depths."[25] Whether Dylan's revelation was synonymous with drug usage, political sentiment, or musical composition, *try anything* became the *raison d'être* for many 1960s musicians, who, like Dylan, seemed to appear from another realm as avatars ready to stamp their legacy on 1960s hip/rock culture.

While Dylan ascended to the top of the folk world and the aforementioned teenage crooners continued to dominate the pop charts, traditional rock and roll remained in its cryogenic state. However, out in southern California (Hawthorne), three brothers—Brian, Dennis, and Carl Wilson—along with their cousin Mike Love and childhood friend Al Jardine, were busy putting together a unique, new sound that helped to resurrect "classic" rock and roll. Borrowing heavily from 1950s rockers such as Chuck Berry, Buddy Holly, and the Everly Brothers, as well as from the cult of surfer music pulsating from the guitars of Dick Dale and the Del-Tones, the Chantays, the Challengers, and the Ventures, the Beach Boys delivered what many considered to be one of the most original and innovative genres in 1960s rock and roll. After Beatlemania engulfed the country beginning in 1964, the Beach Boys were the only American white band (ironically an African American Motown "girl" group, the Supremes, led by Diana Ross, had several top ten chart-busters during this time), who challenged the Fab Four's dominance both in commercial and critical appeal, with three of their songs, "I Get Around" (1964), "Help Me Rhonda" (1965), and their biggest hit, the quasi-psychedelic "Good Vibrations" (1966) all reaching number one on the decade's pop charts. Distinguishing the Beach Boys from early 1960s rock bands, both American and British, was not only their popularization of what had been a previously underground sound—surf music—but also their remarkable vocal harmonies, which reflected the folk influence of such groups as the Four Freshmen. Perhaps most important, was their ability to capture in song and lyrics, the personification of the "set and setting" of the nation's quintessential youth culture scene of the early to mid–1960s; of the sunny, warm beaches, surfing, cars, and romance of Southern California; a place like no other in the country at the time. Their popularity, unique sound, and ability to capture in music a way of life, earned the Beach Boys the position of number 12 on *Rolling Stone* magazine's list of the "100 Greatest [rock] Artists of All Time," the highest ranking for an American rock and roll band.[26] The Beach Boys' surf rock sound ended the teenage crooner's dominance of pop music, but perhaps more important they helped to open the door for rock and roll's revitalization, delivered to American youth courtesy of Great Britain and the Beatles, the greatest rock and roll band of all time.

In England, the black sound that had inspired rock and roll was being assimilated anew by several artists, most notably by four self-taught but inherently gifted young musicians from Liverpool—John Lennon, Paul McCartney, George Harrison, and Richard Starkey (Ringo Starr). During their long years of apprenticeship (1959–1963), through the coming and going of different band members, playing lower-class clubs and dives in Liverpool and Hamburg, Germany, and trying on a variety of names from the Quarrymen to Johnny and the Moondogs to the Beatals to the Silver Beetles, and finally the Beatles—Lennon, McCartney and Harrison explored the roots of rock and roll even as they slowly fashioned their own style. What perhaps made the Beatles, *the Beatles* was their keen and unhesitating willingness to experiment and synthesize and ultimately absorb into their own sound, all previous rock and roll genres and innovations. For example, their electric guitar riffs were pure Chuck Berry and Buddy Holly. The duet singing of Lennon and McCartney was reminiscent of the Everly Brothers, from whom they learned the importance of writing their own music and lyrics. From American gospel and blues vocalists they learned "how to mix harmony with rhythm while heightening the effects of their voices through a mid-tempo range." Lennon and McCartney's "falsettos" reflected the influence of Little Richard, several of whose songs, they covered. They also experimented with "skiffle" music, a black New Orleans street music, which taught the Beatles that self-instrumentation created a more genuine, raw sound than elaborate studio arrangements, which they eventually developed and took to a new level later in their career. In short, American black music informed much of the Beatles rock and roll sound. In a 1968 interview with *Rolling Stone* magazine, Lennon acknowledged how influential African American music had been in the development of the Beatles' own sound. "It was black music we dug. We felt we had the message, which was 'Listen to the music.' When we came here [the United States, 1964] nobody was listening to rock and roll or to black music in America. We felt as though we were coming to the land of its origin, but nobody wanted to know about it."[27] Lennon was not exaggerating about the significance of black music in shaping rock and roll, especially its impact on the Beatles.

By 1963 the Beatles style had fully matured. Thanks to the savvy management and cultivation of their image by Brian Epstein, who had signed on as their manager in 1962, the band was ready to hit the big time venues in England; their days of playing local dives and pubs were over. As Epstein reflected on the day he "dropped in at a smoky, smelly, squalid cellar," and "there were these four youths. Their act was ragged, their clothes were a mess. And yet I sensed at once that there was something there." Epstein completely transformed their look from blue jeans-and-leather jacket toughies to well-tailored suit-and-tie professionals with a distinctive hairstyle (Eton long), and charismatic stage presence, which Epstein also helped them to foster. No longer would they start and stop songs when they felt like it, or when an audience member requested a certain song. Epstein also insisted that they stop swearing, drinking, smoking or eating on stage. He exhorted them to develop a set repertoire of songs that they would perform, curtailing a propensity for too much spontaneity and improvisation. Epstein even choreographed their famous synchronized bow at the end of their performances, believing the more professional, refined, and organized the look and performance and non-threatening the music, the greater the chances for success. For his efforts, Epstein was to receive a management commission of 25 percent of the Beatles' gross income after a certain threshold had been reached. McCartney embraced Epstein's ideas without opposition as did Harrison and Starr, but Lennon balked constantly, finally capitulating as the money started rolling in. Lennon later said that "I'll wear a suit. I'll wear a bloody balloon if somebody is going to pay me," and pay the Beatles they did.[28]

No doubt Epstein's clever image promotion and the disciplining of their act helped catapult the Beatles to stardom. However, the band possessed some immense, inherent qualities that would have come to the fore, with or without Epstein's shrewd management skills. For one, and perhaps most important, the Beatles had one of the best and most prolific songwriting teams in pop history, John Lennon and Paul McCartney. Writing and producing their own songs made them appear more genuine to their fans, much in the same way Dylan and other folk artists and bluesmen appealed to their respective audiences. Augmenting their creative authenticity was the perceived uniqueness of their sound; a supposed new British adaptation of traditional rock and roll. No doubt the Beatles were creative geniuses in their interpretation of classic rock and roll à la Americana. However, in reality, they re-introduced white America to rock and roll's black heritage; a tradition most white Americans had forgotten but were now willing to embrace because four white boys from another country proudly and publicly acknowledged that African American music had been the inspiration for their "original" sound. As *Variety* observed, "The Beatles are dishing up a rock and roll style that was current in this country ten years ago and that is still typical of such groups as the Everly Brothers." Almost without exception the majority of English rock and roll bands that followed the Beatles as part of the mid–1960s "British invasion," reflected in some form or another, black influences as well as American rockabilly.[29]

Consequently, as the decade progressed, American rock and roll not only became more integrated, but increasing numbers of white youth also embraced both the Motown as well as the soul sound of such black artists as James Brown and Aretha Franklin. According to rock historian Charlie Gillett, the Beatles were "exciting, inventive, and competent; lyrically they were brilliant, able to work in precisely the right kind of simple images and memorable phrases that distinguished rhythm and blues from other kinds of popular music." The Beatles early music also provided a feel-good escape which "appealed in part to the innocence and good times American youngsters sought after the shocking assassination of President John Kennedy." Kennedy represented change, the perfectibility of the United States, and the American people's unlimited potential to transform the nation into a righteous, just, and moral society in which all the world would take pride and want to emulate. Such became the Kennedy vision and legacy (and even myth), and in death he became a martyr, who even his political adversaries could not help but grieve. His murder plunged millions of Americans, particular the young, into disquiet. The collective despair over Kennedy's loss "made American youth uniquely vulnerable to Beatlemania ... what Beatlemania achieved for many young people was a restoration of the feelings of hope and sheer intensity that many feared had died forever with John Kennedy." Like JFK, they embodied charisma and the triumph of youth. Neil Hamilton notes that although the early Beatles' lyrics appeared "trite, their music had a beat, the Liverpool sound, that challenged assembly line American rock, and the band's long hair made a statement (much as had Presley's sideburns a decade earlier) that young people would set their own standards."[30]

Adding to the Beatles' aura was a stage-presence vitality and energy not seen since Elvis, as the Beatles projected that they were having the time of their lives performing, and wanted to share their exuberance with their fans. It all came together for the Beatles in 1963, igniting "Beatlemania" and propelling them to stardom in Britain. In January 1964, the Beatles released "I Want to Hold Your Hand," and in less than a week's time the single soared to number one on the U.S. charts. A huge part of the Beatles' unprecedented commercial success was their prolific production of new songs, which allowed them to rarely lose popular traction and momentum. They thus quickly followed up "I Want to Hold Your Hand" with "She Loves You" and "Please, Please Me," which also became number one hits, rotating with each other for the top spot for several weeks; again, an extraordinary pop record event. In February the Beatles arrived for their U.S. tour, their first stop a record-breaking appearance on the pre-eminent American television variety series, the *Ed Sullivan Show*, watched by an estimated 73 million people, a feat yet to be repeated on American television, excluding Super Bowl Sundays. The hysteria continued as they performed before sold-out crowds in New York, Washington, and Miami. In the first week of April 1964, all five top singles in the United States were Beatles songs; in order one to five: "Can't Buy Me Love"; "Twist and Shout"; "She Loves You"; "I Want to Hold Your Hand," and "Please, Please, Me." On the albums' chart, no surprise, the top two albums were Beatles albums: *Meet the Beatles* and *The Beatles Second Album*. Neither feat has been matched by any other artist(s) to date. By the end of 1964 the Beatles had sold 25 million records in the U.S. market alone, and of that total, they had 15 million-selling-plus records (nine singles and six albums), a never-matched accomplishment.[31]

In July the first Beatles movie, *A Hard Day's Night*, hit the theaters and many critics found it surprisingly entertaining, admiring its élan and puckish creativity, thanks in large part to the visual media savvy of the film's director Richard Lester and screenwriter David Owen, both of whom believed that the best way to showcase the Beatles was to let the Beatles be *the Beatles*: the movie was actually a "day-in-the-life-of" plot-less black and white documentary, which Lester cleverly shot as if it were a series of commercial promos for the Beatles individually and collectively, and their songs, which he knew were all the teenage audience cared about. Even the Pulitzer Prize–winning historian and Kennedy/Johnson advisor Arthur Schlesinger, Jr., who initially disparaged the Beatles for their "idiotic hairdo and melancholy wail," came around to applaud *A Hard Day's Night* as a "smart and stylish film, exhilarating in its audacity and modernity."[32] Beatle fans delighted in the movie's humor and the showcasing of more new Beatles' songs. The Beatles commodification did not end with their movie: Beatles merchandise—everything from dolls to coffee mugs to posters—could be found in every major retail store in America, grossing over $50 million in sales. The Beatles' stupefying commercial success prompted Conservative Prime Minster Sir Alec Douglas-Home to quip that the Fab Four was his country's "best export" and "a useful contribution to the balance of payments."[33] Nothing comparable to Beatlemania had ever happened in the history of pop culture and by the end of 1964 it was clear that the Beatles had become not only the preeminent rock and roll band of the 20th century, but also one of the prime shapers of American music for the remainder of the decade and beyond.

Inspired by the commercial success of *A Hard Day's Night*, in 1966 NBC launched the television series *The Monkees*, clearly demonstrating corporate America's rush to exploit, commodify, and profit from the latest manifestation of youth culture. The Monkees weren't even close to the Beatles in any musically creative capacity; they were simply four random studio musicians and actors the network threw together and luckily they clicked as a band. According to *Time*, the Monkees were the product of "two wily promoters" (Robert Rafaelson and Bert Schneider), who "ran the Beatles through a Xerox machine and came up with the Monkees." Although critics considered the band "a dull imitation of the origin of the species [the Beatles]," they nonetheless had produced several smash hits by 1967 such as "Last Train to Clarksville," "I'm a Believer," "Pleasant Valley Sunday" (probably their best counterculture song), and the bubble-gum pop hit, "Daydream Believer." Thanks to the show's popularity and savvy promotion of their music by veteran record producers, in 1967 The Monkees outsold both the Beatles and the Rolling Stones. However, in that year both the Beatles and the Stones were in the process of redefining both their personae and music, and thus 1967 was not a heavy release year for either band until the summer. Nonetheless youth culture consumerism, which encompassed the purchase of an ever increasing variety of hip products— from records to rock concert tickets to posters to roach clips and pipes—became one of the most important macroeconomic forces driving and sustaining the decade's economy. As *Time* correctly observed, "the surest sign" that any rock band "will function comes not from TV or records but from the promotion department." For the Monkees it was "the inevitable flood of Monkee merchandise, from guitars to comic books and Monkee pants (of which J.C. Penney alone has ordered $670,000), which will gross $20 million this year [1966–67]."[34]

Neither British nor American conventional society perceived the Beatles to be a menace. Such had not been true for Presley and the term would also be applied to the Beatles' British rivals, the Rolling Stones, as well as to the Who, the Kinks, and the Animals, who were also part of the 1960s British invasion. These particular groups' songs and persona were viewed as subversive in contrast to the playful irreverence exuded by the Beatles. Indeed, thanks to Epstein's as well as producer George Martin's influence, by the time the Beatles had put out their first smash-hit singles, they had long discarded their earlier, raunchier, black-based rhythm and blues in order to rise as stars for the teenage audience. Despite becoming one of the most commodified icons of pop culture, the Beatles never lost their insouciance; their witty impiety and flip attitude, anti-intellectualism, anti-highbrow culture, and unpretentious self-deprecating humor. This especially appealed to an American white middle class youth that was growing increasingly weary from conformity and convention. Despite being millionaires several times over, the Beatles never forgot their working class heritage; they had simply transcended those roots by becoming pop stars. Indeed, with his first million Ringo Starr bought his "mum" several "beauty parlors" for her to own and to manage—but not to work in. She had done that all her adult life while Starr was growing up in Liverpool, the quintessential English working-class industrial/port city. "What do you think of Beethoven?" a reporter asked at the band's first American press conference. "I love him," responded Starr, "especially his poems." "Which do you consider the greatest danger to your careers: nuclear bombs or dandruff?" Ringo again replied "Bombs. We've already got dandruff."[35] Above all, the Beatles' songs, movies, and public engagement celebrated youth as they told their young fans to indulge their hormones and have fun. From 1963 to 1965 the Beatles' songs reflected carefree, light-heartedness as they turned out simple boy-meets-girl, "I'll-do-anything-for-you" puppy-love songs that threatened few adults if any. In fact, their clever self-deprecating bantering with reporters won over even their most skeptical critics. All of the band's early songs, from "Love Me Do"; to "I Want to Hold Your Hand"; and "Please, Please Me," were completely innocent and sexually non-threatening, reflecting the same restrained, sanitized lyrics and sound of 1950s white rock and rollers. *Newsweek* perhaps best captured the Beatles' overall mass appeal, referring to the group as "a band of evangelists. And the gospel is fun. They shout, they stomp, they jump for joy and their audiences respond in a way that make an old-time revival meeting seem like a wake.... The Beatles appeal to the positive, not negative. They give kids a chance to let off steam and adults a chance to let off disapproval. They have even evolved a peculiar sort of sexless appeal: cute and safe. The most they ask is: 'I Want to Hold Your Hand.'"[36]

However initially non-threatening the Beatles phenomenon was, there were inherent portents for concern. According to Alan Matusow, the almost crazed loyalty they engendered endowed them with enormous potential power "to alter lifestyles, change values, and create new sensibilities; a new way of perceiving the world."[37] Few, however, saw such intrinsic force as they sang their love songs. Ever on the lookout for countercultural messiahs was Ken Kesey, who attended the Beatles 1965 concert at Candlestick Park in South San Francisco (Daly City actually) and was astonished by the "concentration and power" focused on the Fab Four. He was just as amazed by the Beatles failure to exploit the frenzied multitude to a new level of "consciousness." "They [the Beatles] could have taken this roomful of kids and snapped them and they [the kids] would have left that place enlightened, mature people that would never have been quite the same again. They had the power to bring off this new consciousness to people, but they couldn't do it." A *Berkeley Barb* reporter had a similar view of the Beatles' personal power and attraction, likening the event to "a virgin sacrifice in its intensity. The girls pelted the band with jelly beans, which they [the Beatles] had mentioned liking in passing." The Beatles seemed "aware of the danger and were being careful not to look at any one group for too long—for fear of a rush." By 1966 the Beatles had attained iconic status virtually world-wide and along with such adulation came the customary consequences of being misinterpreted, misunderstood, and hounded for interviews. Their 1966 summer tour was played in huge stadiums, a venue not at all conducive to the acoustics of a rock concert. Tens of thousands of unrelenting screaming fans often made it impossible for the Beatles to hear their own instruments. They played their last concert for all time at Candlestick Park in San Francisco on August 29, 1966 (except, of course, their rooftop concert for movie cameras on January 30, 1969). More than two years of Beatle phenomena had finally taken its toll on the band members as they all suffered from mental, emotional, and physical exhaustion. From that point on their music was "sculpted in the studio, with little thought as to whether the songs could be reproduced in concert."[38]

What Kesey and other countercultural hopefuls failed to grasp about the early Beatles (pre–1967), was their unwillingness to use their immense popularity and power to manipulate their followers into another realm of consciousness; such thoughts rarely, if ever, entered their minds. As Morris Dickstein has observed, "the sixties were a period that believed in magic and innocence … [and] the Beatles were its most playful incarnation."[39] However, beginning in late 1966, both the Beatles' music and personae began to reflect the decade's accelerating fads, popular fashion, excesses, and along with their embrace of the hip ethos, the realization that they did indeed possess the collective imperium to change the world of 1960s youth.

However, there were artists who used rock and roll to change consciousness, and perhaps no one used better their extraordinary talents for that purpose than Bob Dylan. Many established folk and rock stars believed the Beatles would not last the hoopla surrounding their music and persona; that they would simply burn out after a year or so. Not Dylan and thus when they arrived, he was *listening*. "Everybody else thought they were for the teenyboppers, that they were gonna pass right away. But it was obvious to me that they had staying power. I knew they were pointing the direction music had to go."[40] Interestingly, by the time of the Beatles' first USA tour in 1964, the folk craze was in decline, and Dylan sensed this, referring to folk festivals as "witnessing the end of the traditional people."[41] Dylan contributed mightily to folk's demise while simultaneously initiating a new genre that critics labeled "folk rock" when he appeared on stage at the July 1965 Newport Folk Festival, no longer dressed in the attire of a bohemian-folky-biker, but as a rock and roll singer, outfitted in leather jacket and backed by an electric band. No sooner did Dylan start to sing "Like a Rolling Stone," than the crowd reacted with shocking hostility. In *No Direction Home*, Robert Shelton summed up "the Newport fiasco": "As Dylan led his band into 'Like a Rolling Stone,' the audience grew shriller: 'Play folk music! Sell out! This is a folk festival! Get rid of the band!' Dylan began 'It Takes a Train to Cry,' and applause diminished and the heckling increased. Dylan and the group disappeared offstage, and there was a long, clumsy silence. Peter Yarrow [of the popular folk trio of Peter, Paul, and Mary] urged Bob to return and gave him his acoustic guitar. As Bob returned on the stage alone, he discovered he didn't have the right harmonica. 'What are you doing to me?' Dylan demanded of Yarrow. To shouts of 'Tambourine Man,' Dylan said 'Ok, I'll do that one for you.' The older song had a palliative effect and won strong applause. Then Dylan did 'It's All Over Now, Baby Blue,' and singing adieu to Newport, goodbye to the folk purist audience."[42] Dylan's attempt at Newport to reveal his transformation to rock and roll proved seminal in the history of counterculture music, marking the end of folk's hegemony and the embracing of rock as *the music* of 1960s hippies and as the overwhelming preference of the majority of straight youth as well. Although leading folk artists such as Joan Baez and Pete Seeger would remain popular throughout the decade, they were no longer center stage performers; they had been supplanted by acid folk/blues bands who would dominate future youth festivals, beginning with Monterey and climaxing with Woodstock. That summer (1965) Dylan's rock single "Like a Rolling Stone," perhaps the greatest song he ever wrote, reached number one on the charts.

From 1965 to the end of the decade, Dylan's songs no longer echoed the idealism and optimism of early 1960s liberal politics; they now took on a far more personal, cynical, abrasive, and cryptic if not esoteric quality, reflecting both his identification with the increasing political and cultural radicalism of many of his peers as well as the influence of LSD, which Dylan began using while composing, even before Newport. Dylan had been smoking dope since 1962 so he already was familiar with a drug highs' potential for expanding creativity and introspection. A friend turned Dylan on to acid, which he believed proved to be a turning point in both Dylan's personal and professional life, certain that Dylan's trip marked "the beginning of the mystical Sixties right there."[43] Almost overnight both Dylan's perception of the world and his music changed rather dramatically. In Dylan's view, America was no longer a place of hope, justice, and decency, but a corrupt, chaotic, and violent society full of scared, desperate, alienated people, searching to find and free themselves (often with the help of hallucinogenic drugs), from the insanity, spiritual depravity, and vicious acquisitiveness that was all around them. Such were the themes pounding subliminally into the skulls of a generation, found in such Dylan classics as "Highway 61," "Maggie's Farm," "Desolation Row," "Ballad of a Thin Man," and "Gates of Eden." Critics hailed Dylan's new music as the genesis of yet another new genre in rock and roll, "folk rock." Perhaps even more than the Beatles, Dylan almost single-handedly made rock and roll *the medium* that both expressed the Sixties counterculture and defined it. *San Francisco Chronicle* music critic Ralph Gleason believed Dylan's songs were "saying, in short, that the entire system of Western society, built upon Aristotelian logic, the Judeo-Christian ethic, and upon a series of economic systems from Hobbes to Marx to Keynes, does not work."[44] Dylan's ingenious fusion of the two genres was not only unprecedented but forever changed the face of American music. From Dylan's transformation forward, the central purpose of much of the new rock sound was innovation rather than salability, and as a result, opened the doors to a whole new demographic of American fans, which ironically boosted the popularity and record sales of those artists who made such a risky transition away from audience-driven, formulaic productions. As rock documentarian D.A. Pennebaker observed in his iconic film *Don't Look Back*, Dylan's metamorphosis from folk musician to "one of the most storied figures in rock 'n' roll history, completely transformed the music and its expressive possibilities in the minds of those who played it and those who listened to it."[45]

As Dylan and the Beatles in particular were fast proving, rock and roll music during the 1960s had extraordinary potential power to change both individual and collective consciousness on a variety of socio-cultural and political issues, even though the message of the majority of rock lyrics was curiously apolitical. Without question, mid to late 1960s rock and roll reflected the decade's increasing turbulence but the mood conveyed was personal alienation from what was perceived to be a self-aggrandizing, anti-youth, consumer-driven callous environment. The majority of musicians were young and white, preoccupied with their own fears and anxieties, which they believed conventional America had caused. One of the more prevalent themes in 1960s songs was that of an American society that crushed individual freedom, suffocated creativity and repressed spontaneity, dictating to everyone how they should speak, dress, have sex, and publicly behave. Young audiences had come to see themselves as victims of a mendacious older generation, perpetually castigating its progeny for wanting to be free of restraints and dictums. "Down On Me," sang Janis Joplin of Big Brother and the Holding Company in 1967.

However, attempts by political activists to enfold rock and roll into their respective crusades and rebellion, rarely, if ever succeeded. This was especially true by the later years of the countercultural insurgence as witnessed by Yippie co-founder Abbie Hoffman, booed by the throngs at the 1969 Woodstock festival for trying to politicize the "celebration." He was physically driven off stage by the enraged lead guitarist of the Who, Pete Townshend, who whacked Hoffman with his instrument in order to silence the LSD-loaded radical. The overwhelming majority of 1960s rock musicians simply refused to enter into the decade's radical politics in any capacity and bitterly resented those activists who tried to use their celebrity status for causes they could not care less about. As Janis Joplin declared, "My music isn't supposed to make you riot, it's supposed to make you fuck."[46]

Dylan and others sang about the imminent demise of the nation's materialistic, self-absorbed bourgeois culture and the debilitating effects on body and soul of modern technological society. In general, to most 1960s counterculturists, rock's larger revolutionary purpose was not necessarily to engender political activism, but rather to create a greater awareness among its listeners that Western culture, epitomized by 1960s America, was a society void of humanity, spirituality, and love, and thus was on the abyss of self-destruction. But as the Jefferson Airplane (1966) and then the Youngbloods (1967) proclaimed in their respective versions of "Get Together," there was still hope. If people found such compassion and love within them for others then society could be changed for the better. Although many hippies embraced the message and tried to live a life of selflessness, the majority were apolitical. For them rock had no revolutionary or subversive purpose; as Country Joe McDonald declared in 1969, "One of the most revolutionary things you can do in this country today is have a good time and enjoy yourself."[47] Ron Jarvis, writing in Houston's underground publication *Space City*, seconded McDonald's declaration, asserting rock music "more than any other single factor" was responsible for "spreading the good news. For joy and ecstasy is the essence of rock."[48] Ralph Gleason reinforced McDonald's and other 1960s rock and rollers' assessment of rock's potential cultural revolutionary power, by quoting the 17th century Scot Andrew Fletcher of Saltoun: "Give me the making of the songs of a nation and I care not who makes its laws." To Glea-son rock music had been "the single most potent social force for change for several years now. That is why Dylan seems to me to be more important than the Weathermen. They blow up buildings in New York; he blew minds all over the world. Ginsberg's poems speak to more people than all the SDS pamphlets put together."[49] As rock became the "revolutionary ultimate," as one hippie opined in an editorial for Philadelphia's underground newspaper, *The Distant Drummer*, "WE all know what's going to eventually save the world. Rock, that's what."[50]

Although the majority of 1960s rock and roll songs remained apolitical, focusing on the concerns, anxieties, and pleasures of life, love, and drugs, occasionally a politically loaded record did come out and to the surprise, delight, and shock of listeners, moved people to think less about themselves, their hormones in particular, and more about the world around them. In August 1965 Barry McGuire, a former folk singer with the New Christy Minstrels, released such a blockbuster, "Eve of Destruction," written by a nineteen-year-old named P.F. Sloan. Within five weeks of its unveiling, the song surged to the top of the charts, becoming the fastest rising song in rock history. However, "Eve of Destruction" also became one of the decade's most controversial songs, engendering all manner of outcry among conservative groups while many radio stations banned it, including all of the ABC networks. Reactionaries believed the song was "obviously aimed at instilling fear in our teenagers as well as a sense of hopelessness," helping "induce the American public to surrender to atheistic international Communism."[51]

"Eve of Destruction" began with two funeral thumps of the kettledrum, leading into a pounding drumbeat. Then the surly, gravelly, despairing voice of McGuire boomed out his jeremiad. To be sure "Eve" was brooding, dissonant, and bitter, with blatant references to both the nation's and the world's many ills—no precedent for such candor, not even in Dylan's allegorical "Blowin' in the Wind." Interestingly, "Eve" was fundamentally a folk song, albeit not in the strictest traditional sense, but in structure with simple guitar strum, repeated refrain, and customary rhymes. McGuire's voice started out with a relative calm equilibrium but as he sang more of the verses, painting an increasingly grim and violent world, his voice became progressively more aggressive, even outright hostile, accentuated by the occasional rip of a Dylanesque harmonica. Impending Armageddon of course included the Bomb, and even civil rights, which, with the passage of the 1965 Voting Rights Act, had become a third-rail issue.[52] Much to the horror of conservatives and other alarmists, the song's popularity made it clear that for many young Americans rock music, regardless of the form it took, was indeed affecting hearts and minds, creating in many a consciousness that the United States was a nation and society rife with egregious inequities, and that a mass movement of American youth was about to descend upon the nation and attempt to alter the old collective consciousness responsible for such maladies before it was too late.

Although the omnipresent Vietnam War and the hated draft that sustained it was a key catalyst for the hippie movement, comparatively few 1960s rock songs assailed either issue directly and perhaps more revealing, only a handful made the top ten and none ever reached number one on the charts. Interestingly, the only Vietnam War era song to reach the top of the charts was a hearty *pro-war* ditty sung by Staff Sergeant Barry Sadler, "The Ballad of the Green Berets," which remained number one for five weeks in 1966. Nonetheless, popular among antiwar hippies and others were such songs as Buffy Sainte-Marie's "Universal Soldier" and Phil Ochs' "I Ain't Marchin' Anymore," songs about defying the draft and refusing to carry a gun. One of the most poignant antiwar songs was by the Byrds, "Draft Morning," in which a young man leaves his warm bed to take up arms against unknown people, asking why. One of the most popular hip antiwar folk-rock anthems was County Joe McDonald's sardonic "I-Feel-Like-I'm-Fixin'-to-Die Rag" (1968) about Uncle Sam's perverse propaganda hailing young Americans to help get him out of jam in Vietnam. There was perhaps no better song of the era that combined the whimsical, feel-good nature of sixties rock with folk music protest; the fusion of circus-like instrumentation with silly yet poignant lyrics that made one question the purpose of America's war in Vietnam; the absurdity if not insanity of the entire debacle. Also known as "the Fish Cheer," the song reached the height of its countercultural popularity at the legendary 1969 Woodstock festival.[53]

The popularity of songs such as McDonald's was understandable since the war was a real danger to the lives of those who either volunteered or who were drafted to fight and possibly die. What is somewhat perplexing, however, was that much of mid-to late 1960s music reflected the belief among the counterculture that American society and its institutions were so intolerably oppressive that complete disavowal by "dropping out," or escapism with drugs, or revolution, were the only ways to cope with such an afflicted society and culture. This alienation and hostility came overwhelming from young, affluent, middle-class whites, one of the most protected and indulged generations in the nation's history. This perception of an ugly, repressive, and conformist America represents an interesting generational dichotomy, for those who claimed to have such sentiments knew very little about *the real* poverty, suffering, despair, or any of the other physical and emotional hardships endured by millions of citizens outside of their rarefied suburban neighborhoods. Regardless of the sincerity among many hippies to reach out and try to bond with the nation's minority poor and disenfranchised, the response to such overtures or pretense, especially from African Americans, was rejection and hostility. The only discomfort most but not all hippies felt was that of self-inflicted brooding and introspection, largely caused by their own sense of self-importance, entitlement, and perhaps a tinge of guilt for having so much. Nonetheless, many hippies genuinely believed that the "Amerika" of their time was an awful place and thus found in rock music a way to express their outrage and contempt for the nation's ills and injustices.

Although Dylan believed the Beatles were "for real," and that they "were pointing the direction of where music had to go," the Fab Four were as intrigued by Dylan as he was with them, perhaps even more so. To the Beatles, Dylan represented a musical avant garde and trend that captivated them privately. But they were hesitant to embrace this ethic entirely because they were still developing artistically. It is hard to imagine today, but the Beatles at the time were in awe of Dylan, who was fast becoming a legendary musical iconoclast. Indeed, to the Beatles, Dylan had already arrived at the consciousness essential to take rock and roll to yet another aesthetic manifestation. Interestingly, it wasn't until John Lennon began experimenting with Dylanesque music ("I'm a Loser" and "You've Got to Hide Your Love Away"), that it became clear folk music could also be rock music. Nonetheless, thanks to Dylan and marijuana, which he introduced to the Beatles at their August 1964 meeting at the Delmonico Hotel in New York, the Beatles' reservations about their abilities to take their music in new directions, dissipated. From that first encounter on, the Beatles fully embraced the countercultural drug scene. Perhaps more important, they too began writing songs reflecting their increasing fascination with the countercultural ethos. By 1967, that initial allure had transcended into immersion and complete identification with the hip movement. In their next two best-selling albums, *Rubber Soul* (1965) and *Revolver* (1966) (which many critics have hailed as two of their all-time best) both their mounting obsession with drug use and support of the counterculture could be heard. *Rubber Soul*, for example, had a specific, thematic approach—a persistent sexual tone, while *Revolver*'s lyrics dripped with acid, especially the song "Tomorrow Never Knows," where the sounds were played backwards, a technique Lennon accidentally discovered while on an LSD trip. Prior to *Rubber Soul* and *Revolver*, Beatle LPs had been nothing more than random compilations of their hit singles; all that changed with *Rubber Soul* and *Revolver*. Both albums possessed a sound and coherence unimaginable two years earlier. Henceforth, Beatle albums would not only be thematic—usually hip and drug-related in content—but aesthetically experimental and innovative as well. The Beatles were in the process of "making history by anticipating it" and the rest of the rock world was along for the ride. In their personal lives the Beatles became devoted acid heads captivated by Eastern music and religion; they even took a pilgrimage to India to study Transcendental Meditation with Maharishi Mahesh Yogi. After a year's hiatus from music, and enlightened by Dylan and their other countercultural experiences, the Beatles returned to the studio ready to produce a sound that would catapult them to the head of the psychedelic parade. Indeed, John Lennon believed their forthcoming opus would make the Beatles "out to be a Trojan Horse…. The Fab Four moved right to the top and then sang about drugs and sex." The Beatles' realization of their power to change consciousness came to the fore with their next LP, prompting the usually quiescent George Harrison to remark that the intent of their new album was to "wake up as many people as we could" to love, happiness, and fun; to embrace spontaneity over the ordered life, which was seen as drudgery; to question their most fundamental assumptions about music, politics and culture. John Lennon was even more explicit about his band's power to change consciousness. "Changing the lifestyle and appearance of youth throughout the world didn't just happen—we set out to do it; we knew what we were doing."[54]

In June 1967 the Beatles released what many consider to have been the decade's quintessential countercultural musical expression, *Sergeant Pepper's Lonely Hearts Club Band*. It was a pure concept album, packed with clever, if not brilliant lyrics and social commentary, all reflecting in sound and words, the various manifestations of the countercultural creed and lifestyle with songs expressing getting "high with a little help from my friends," to "Lucy in the Sky with Diamonds" (the title reduces to the abbreviation LSD), to feelings of mournful loneliness and spiritual emptiness, introspection, and redeeming the world with love. The album's cover was pure psychedelic art (courtesy of pop artist Peter Blake); a cornucopia of countercultural interpretations of reality overlaid with a mélange of images of popular icons, including Karl Marx, Mae West, Marilyn Monroe, W.C. Fields, Marlon Brando, and Dylan. The Beatles not only wanted the album to reflect their own personal spiritual awakening and expanded consciousness, but their identification as well with other hip seekers. They created in music and lyrics, a split world in which fantasy and reality blurred, producing the "set and setting" of an extended trip through sound and words; "a sonic carpet that enveloped the ears and sent the listener spinning into other realms … it changed the way we listened to recorded sound forever."[55]

Since the Beatles wanted everything about the album to be unprecedented, they took rock and roll beyond traditional limits, incorporating crowd noises, screeching tires, crowing roosters, barking dogs, the use of different keys and tempos, and massed orchestral instruments. "These guys weren't just recording songs; they were inventing stuff with which to make this record as they went along." The result, according to recording engineer Geoff Emerick, was that, "everything was either distorted, limited, heavily compressed or treated with excessive equalization. We had microphones right down in the bells of the brass instruments and headphones turned into microphones attached to violins. We plastered vast amounts of echo onto vocals, and sent them through the circuitry of the revolving Leslie speaker inside a Hammond organ. We used giant primitive oscillators to vary the speed of instruments and vocals and we had tapes chopped to pieces and stuck together upside down and the wrong way around." In addition, a variety of genres were enfolded into the album, such as "Within You, Without You," which was Indian music; "Sgt. Pepper's Lonely Hearts Club Band (Reprise)" was good, old-fashioned rock and roll, and "When I'm Sixty-Four" was a tongue-in-cheek ode to such 1920s ballads. The Beatles broke all "the rules" of rock music with *Sgt. Pepper's* and thus henceforth rock and roll could be whatever its respective artists determined it to be.[56]

The result was a technological illusion of sounds and voices that perfectly captured the mood of the 1960s youth rebellion; all the grand expectations, anxieties, frustrations, and longings of the counterculture with remarkable accuracy. Indeed, *Sgt. Pepper's* could have only come about because the hippie movement and ethos had created the ethical, spiritual, and cerebral template upon which the Beatles could stamp their own persona and perspectives. The image of the world projected by the album's songs was a place rife with so many ills that the only way to cope and survive was to escape into a dream world of love and spiritual introspection. Perhaps most important, *Sergeant Pepper* revealed and validated that in the counterculture world, rock and dope were symbiotic; that dope was an essential ingredient among rock and roll musicians in determining "the direction music had to go." With *Sgt. Pepper's* release, the Beatles became the most important vehicle through which the hip ethos was transmitted, expanding the cultural revolution already a foot. However, to some rock culture pundits, it *was* the Beatles who "started the whole long-haired hippie business and who knows whether they developed with it or it developed with them. All those pages of analysis are a gauge of how important the Beatles have become to *us*."[57]

Shocking many in the rock world of the late 1960s, not all music critics lauded *Sgt. Pepper's* as the Second Coming on the pop music scene or "The closest Western Civilization has come to unity since the Congress of Vienna in 1815.... For a brief while the irreparably fragmented consciousness of the West was unified, at least in the minds of the young." One individual who disagreed with such exaltations was *The Village Voice's* pundit Richard Goldstein, who declared the album to be "busy, hip, and cluttered"; a work of "dazzling special effects but ultimately fraudulent," for in Goldstein's view in the Beatles' allegedly new sound could be heard "a touch of the Jefferson Airplane, a dab of Beach Boys vibrations, and a generous part of gymnastics from The Who." The "only evident touch of originality" was in the LP's structure, which had one song leading into the next without any pauses. To Goldstein the album reflected the Beatles "obsession with production" rather than in creating any new rock expression or genre. The result: "a surprising shoddiness in composition permeates the entire album. There is nothing beautiful on 'Sergeant Pepper.' Nothing is real and there is nothing to get hung about." Goldstein believed *Sgt. Pepper's* reflected the Beatles having become "cloistered composers" rather than continuing to be visibly active and present countercultural companions, touring the world and spreading their music's message via concerts. "In substituting the studio conservatory for an audience, they have ceased being folk artists, and the change is what makes their new album a monologue."[58] Suffice it say, Goldstein's excoriation was not well received by either the Beatles' adoring fans nor by fellow pundits, who retorted that Goldstein "got hung up on his own integrity and attempted to judge what he admittedly did not understand." Despite such outrage, Goldstein stuck to his guns, declaring a month after his initial review that in his opinion, compared to *Rubber Soul* and *Revolver*, both of which he had praised as the Beatles' greatest works to date, *Sgt. Pepper's* remained "Beatles baroque— an elaboration without improvement; a sarcasm masqueraded as hip, a dangerously dominant sense of what is stylish. *Sergeant Pepper* is not a work of plagiarism [which Goldstein had intimated in his previous assessment], but neither does it represent a breakthrough. It is an in-between experience."[59]

Although the Beatles produced several more critically acclaimed albums (including what became their all-time best seller, *Abbey Road*), soon after the release of *Sergeant Pepper's*, the Fab Four began to unravel. Causing much of the rift was the increasingly competitive creative differences between John Lennon and Paul McCartney, as well as ongoing friction caused by Lennon's omnipresent Japanese girlfriend, the artist Yoko Ono, to whom Lennon had become completely devoted, to the exclusion of his fellow band mates. Of course success and the public's ever higher and higher expectations of the Beatles to continue to remain in the vanguard of rock and roll music and the countercultural revolution produced even more tensions. Even though the official break-up did not occur until after the release of *Let It Be* (1970), by the time they had finished *Abbey Road*, a kind of reconciliation album arranged by their new manager, George Martin (Brian Epstein had died from a drug overdose in August 1967) the greatest rock and roll band of all time was on the verge of disintegration. Indeed, *Abbey Road* proved to be their final hurrah. John Lennon announced he was through with the band and went his own way, accompanied by Yoko Ono, and for the next several years remained an icon of the countercultural rebellion. The others as well pursued their own separate paths of pop music (Paul McCartney); an on-going quest for spiritual enlightenment (George Harrison), and all-around celebrity "regular guy" (Ringo Starr). After listening to *Sergeant Pepper*, Timothy Leary proclaimed the Beatles "evolutionary agents sent by God, endowed with a mysterious power to create a new human species."[60]

Some believed that this new version of humanity had already emerged in San Francisco, in the form of the burgeoning hippie bands who were developing their own brand of rock and roll. By the mid–1960s the Bay Area witnessed an explosion of literally hundreds of local bands, and because none of the major record companies had studios in the area, the groups developed their music free from the influences of the commercial mainstream. The result was the creation of a new sound, "the San Francisco Sound"—spacy, pounding, pulsating unbounded whorls of screaming electric guitars and lyrics that celebrated drugs and sex rather than protest or revolution. Indeed, it was a sound that embodied the psychedelic ethic. It was music to trip on, thus the designation, "acid rock." As Timothy Miller has noted, the confluence of drugs and music was not a new phenomenon in American musical history, and thus San Francisco's hippie bands "simply expanded on [a] musical heritage when [they] created acid rock, music that was intimately related to cherished dope."[61] Because they had developed their music within the insulated Haight environment, hippie bands identified with their fellow freaks and thus initially their music was for the exclusive enjoyment of their hippie brothers and sisters. It was music that had no other purpose than the promotion and cultivation of Dionysian ecstasy and revelry. Unlike the mainstream pop bands, "the rock bands of the San Francisco scene were less drawn to fame and fortune than to breakthroughs on the level of consciousness, creativity, and an unfettered lifestyle."[62] Perhaps Janis Joplin, lead singer for Big Brother and the Holding Company, best summed up the intimate bond between the early San Francisco bands and their devoted community followers. "I'm on an audience trip. When I go on stage to sing, it's like the 'rush' people experience when they take heavy dope. I talk to the audience, look into their eyes. I need them and they need me. Sex is the closest I can come to explaining it, but it's more than sex. I get stoned from happiness. I want to do it [perform] until it isn't there any more.... I'm untutored native folk talent."[63]

One rock critic described the San Francisco Sound as "revelatory roaring chills of ecstasy, hallucinated wandering, mystic-psychotic wonder. Not a trace of preciousness in this music; musicians in this city have knocked all the civility away."[64] Music pundit Richard Goldstein believed hippie rock and roll to be "the most potentially vital music in the pop world. It shoots a cleansing wave over the rigid studiousness of rock. It brings driving spontaneity to a music that is becoming increasingly conscious of form and influence rather than effort." The hippie bands had turned San Francisco into "the Liverpool of the West" and accordingly, as few understood or grasped the importance of the unique rock and roll sound that came out of that English city in the early 1960s, "Not many breadmen understand the electronic rumblings from beneath the Golden Gate. San Francisco is a lot like the grimy English seaport these days. In 1964 Liverpool rang with a sound that was authentically expressive and the city never tried to bury it. This is what is happening in San Francisco today."[65]

Perhaps the most distinguishing feature of the San Francisco bands and their sound was that they played their music live in dance halls where the musicians could jam as long as they wanted and the dancers came dressed in the latest hip attire—beads, painted faces, and flowered shirts. Interestingly the first of such venues did not emerge in the Haight or in San Francisco, but in a historic small town in the foothills of the Sierra Nevada mountains, Virginia City, Nevada. It was there, in the summer of 1965, that the owner of the Red Dog Saloon, Mark Inobsky, held the first psychedelic rock and roll shows featuring the first of the acid rock bands, the Charlatans. The light show was the handiwork of Bill Ham, a San Francisco painter who had been experimenting with "electrifying" his paintings by plugging his creations directly into a wall socket. Ham also had procured an Army surplus light machine that had been used to project images onto large screens. Ham used the apparatus to cast onto a large wall his concoction of watercolor pigments and oil solutions, which combined, produced a kaleidoscopic landscape. Ham then would hand synchronize the liquids with the rhythms of the music, creating "surging, pulsating effects that were downright psychedelic. Psychedelic lights. The whipped cream and the cherry for a rock 'n' roll show."[66] Ham and the Charlatans brought the concept back to the City where it became the symbiotic hallmark of the hip dancehalls and the legendary hippie bands that performed amidst such a sensory-overloading spectacle. As the city's hip music critic Ralph Gleason noted, "The important thing about San Francisco rock &roll is that the bands here all sing and play live, and not for recordings. You get a different sound at a dance, it's harder and more direct."[67]

Another pioneer of the dancehall concept was Chet Helms, a defrocked Baptist minister from Austin, Texas, who came to the Haight in 1965 accompanied by his girlfriend, an aspiring raw blues singer named Janis Joplin. No sooner did Helms arrive in the Haight than he began organizing weekend jam sessions at his commune at 1090 Page Street. Helms' promotion of local bands became instantly popular, encouraging Helms to expand and formalize his venue, which he did by having fifty-cent Wednesday night mini-concerts featuring Joplin with Big Brother and the Holding Company, a group Helms' personally help put together and who became his house band. Helms' Page Street forum lasted for twenty weeks and in that time, Helms showcased some of the greatest acid rock bands of the era, future international stars such as Janis Joplin and the Grateful Dead. By early 1966 Helms had out-grown his Page Street location and moved his rock/psychedelic enterprise to the Avalon Ballroom at Sutter

The Grateful Dead rehearsing in Sausalito, California, 1966. Of all the hippie bands that emerged in the Haight-Ashbury during the counterculture's heyday, none proved to have as enduring a legacy as the Dead, who down to the present remain the most popularly memorialized. Band members from left were Phil Lesh, Pigpen (Rod McKernan), Bill Somers, Jerry Garcia, and Bob Weir (photograph by Michelle Vignes, courtesy Bancroft Library, University of California, Berkeley).

Street and Van Ness Avenue. For the next two years Helms, through his company Family Dog Productions presented some of the best acid rock/blues bands in the area as well as bringing in for performances headliners such as The Doors and the Paul Butterfield Blues Band. Above Helms' office door hung the Avalon's motto: "May the baby Jesus shut your mouth and open your mind."[68] The dances sponsored by Helms and other dance hall/psychedelic entrepreneurs, in many ways, were the first "gathering of the tribes"; expressions of a sense of community solidarity developing among the city's new bohemians. These were events the Haight's counterculturists had "been waiting for without realizing it."[69]

By the fall of 1965, young people from all over the Bay area were flocking to the City's seedy dance halls rented by local promoters to feature hippie bands like the Jefferson Airplane, Big Brother and the Holding Company, Quicksilver Messenger Service, the Charlatans, Moby Grape, and the Grateful Dead. Most of the bands concocted their names from the sort of inspired and often inexplicable juxtapositions that had come to members in dope flashes. Such was the case for the Grateful Dead, who originally called themselves the War-locks. While on an acid trip the band's founder Jerry Garcia, had an "illuminating flash" in which he saw the band's new name hieroglyphically inscribed on an Egyptian tomb, which when translated read "Grateful Dead." In the new dances individuals didn't touch; they "communed"; they dug each other by occupying the same space. Tom Wolfe, who attended several of these massive celebrations of early hippiedom, believed the combination of acid and the barrage of lights and sound in conjunction with all manner of other sensory-stimulating paraphernalia hanging everywhere in the dancehalls, caused one to lose all inhibitions: "The dancing was ecstatic, a nice macaroni of braless breasts jiggling and cupcake bottoms wiggling and multiple arms writhing and leaping about," while "Thousands of straight intellectuals and culturati and square hippies, North Beach style, gawked and learned."[70] In his reviews of these events for the *San Francisco Chronicle*, music critic Ralph Gleason, one of the counterculture's most empathetic straight boosters, believed the dances were "a great deal more than a benefit." They were "substantiation[s] of the suspicion that the need to dance on the part of a great number of residents of this area [the Haight-Ashbury] is so great it simply must be permitted."[71]

Dancing became one of the most important physical expressions of hippie values and shared experience while simultaneously providing dancers a mode of rebellion against Cold War taboos relative to gender roles, sexuality, and conformity. Interestingly, the hip passion for such catharsis was not new; young people during the Swing Era of the 1940s and perhaps even more so during the "Roaring Twenties" with such dances as the "Charleston," displayed similar rejection of the day's social conventions and behavioral restraints. Indeed, in many ways hippie dancers were re-enacting on the dance floors of the Avalon or Fillmore ballrooms two analogous periods in American history. The wild dance floor abandon of hippie women reflected the letting loose of 1920s "flappers," while the Avalon, the Fillmore, and the other dance halls became the new speak-easies, where psychedelic drugs had replaced bathtubs full of gin.

Hippies not only came to dance but to listen, to just "be there and groove" to the music, usually stoned in the sensual assault courtesy of Ken Kesey and sidekick Owsley, who together provided what came to be known as the Trips Festival, the fusion of acid and rock with the dances, institutionalized at weekend freakouts at the Fillmore (West), Avalon Ballroom, and Longshoremen's Hall. The first of these sensory extravaganzas occurred in January 1966 at Longshoremen's Hall, the brainchild of Stewart Brand, a biologist and Keseyite, who would later go on to fame and fortune as the author of *The Whole Earth Catalog*, the bible for seekers of an alternative lifestyle. After a conversation with other members of "Kesey's circus makers" Brand became convinced that it was time to take Kesey's Acid Tests "indoors for better control" because "the decibel range," which "was very important" to the Tests, was simply not sufficient enough in the outdoors to blast one's mind into the stratosphere. According to Haight resident, "evolving hippie," and Brand contemporary Gene Anthony, Brand "could relate to that" because he was "a photographer and a visionary. He could see the new wave coming." Brand liked the idea very much but realized, that although he had "the vision" he needed the help of someone experienced in "show business" and thus turned to legendary hip entrepreneur and promoter Bill Graham for advice on how to pull off the event. Graham agreed to step in and run the show. He, Kesey and Owsley, combined to form a very lucrative Dionysian psychedelic consortium in which Owsley supplied the LSD and some of the money; Graham the promotional and business savvy, while Kesey generated the energy and the organizing (or often dis-organizing genius).[72]

The new mixture started out in what Kesey conceived and called the Acid Test, a sensory-overloaded ritual for spreading his version of cosmic consciousness; a total experience

Legendary capitalist/rock promoter and hip entrepreneur Bill Graham in his Haight office circa 1967. On his office walls hang several examples of hippie poster art (photograph by Michelle Vignes, courtesy Bancroft Library, University of California, Berkeley).

combining music, dance, lights, and images all galvanized in the mind by ingesting acid before or during the test. Kesey, the psychedelic angel to the San Francisco bands, donated both acid and money for their gigs, with multimedia psychedelic shows so mind blowing that many left such an experience not sure where they had been or who they were! To this day it is not clear what Kesey was testing other than an individual's mental and emotional stamina and stability. Nonetheless, to Kesey and friends, the purpose of the acid test was to create a "set and setting" so sensually overwhelming that celebrants (or subjects) would be able to transcend the present and plug directly into the Cosmos. After experimenting on the road with the Grateful Dead in comparatively small venues, with a variety of overpowering sensory/medium combinations, Kesey believed he had perfected the Acid Test and was now ready to take his show to another level. In the process of developing the Acid Test, Kesey and the Grateful Dead became symbiotic, with Kesey, via Owsley, not only providing the acid for both the band and the audience, but enough money for the Dead to buy the latest, most advanced electronic equipment. Soon no other group in the world had so many giant speakers, mixers, microphones, and control panels, all for the purpose of helping acid heads blast themselves into cosmic oblivion. Out of this amalgam of stimuli emerged "acid rock," the counterculture's special brand of rock and roll music.[73]

The Trips Festival of January 21–23 (Friday, Saturday, and Sunday), 1966, at Longshoreman's Hall in San Francisco put the acid rock scene and ballroom concerts on the hip map. Kesey and the Merry Pranksters produced and directed the event while Graham handled the business details and Owsley provided the acid. Lou Gottlieb, formerly of the folk group the Limeliters, was now working as a music columnist for the *San Francisco Chronicle* and provided free publicity. The timing was perfect: For over a year teenage dropouts and disaffected campus radicals had been migrating into Haight-Ashbury, searching for an identity and community, which the first Trips Festival more than amply provided. According to Gene Anthony, the Trips Festival was pivotal to the emerging San Francisco counterculture, for the event helped to "consolidate the new planes of consciousness that were emerging around the Bay area. There were a lot of people making some interesting discoveries, but the domains of these energies were widely separated. No one really knew how many people 'out there' wanted to be turned on." However the Trips Festival provided freaks with the opportunity and physical space in which "to celebrate [their] new feelings, the higher consciousness that people were trying to express. The time had come to commemorate all the good trips with a 'Trips Festival.' A new day was dawning."[74]

An estimated 20,000 "hippies" attended their coming out celebration. According to Tom Wolfe, "the heads pour[ed] in by the hundreds, bombed out of their gourds, hundreds of heads coming out into the absolute open for the first time. The Trips festival was like the first national convention of an underground movement that had existed on a hush-hush cell-by-cell basis. The heads were amazed at how big their own ranks had become—and euphoric over the fact that they could come out in the open, high as baboons, and the sky, the law, wouldn't fall down on them."[75] To Ron Thelin, "The Trips Festival was the first thing that got the larger, kind of whole community thing happening—everybody turning on. It was like we were all born at the same time in some ways. Like all brilliant children. And we liked to be around our fellow brilliants."[76] The hippies affirmed their emergence as a counterculture by wearing every variety of wild costume imaginable, from Victorian dresses to Civil War uniforms, to "serapes and mandala beads and Indian headbands and Indian beads." According

Not until Grace Slick joined the Jefferson Airplane did their sound "take off." Slick's soaring, piercing psychedelic voice, which can be heard most fully in the Airplane's biggest hit, "White Rabbit," helped to catapult the band to national stardom and to the forefront of the San Francisco Sound, especially at the commercial level. Photograph taken in 1968. (photograph by Michelle Vignes, courtesy Bancroft Library, University of California, Berkeley).

to Richard Goldstein, the attire worn by the attendees didn't "come from any mere bohemian quarter. Hip has passed the point where it signifies a commitment to rebellion. It has become the style of youth in the Bay Area, just as long hair and beat music were the Liverpool Look."[77] Live rock, performed by the Grateful Dead, Big Brother and the Holding Company, Jefferson Airplane, Wavy Gravy, the Loading Zone, and others, propelled dancers through an electronic whirlpool of strobe lights, movies, tape machines, and slide projectors. According to Tom Wolfe, "Lights and movies swept around the hall; five movie projectors going and God knows how many light machines, interferometrics; intergalactic science-fiction seas all over the walls, loudspeakers studding the hall all the way around like flaming chandeliers, strobes exploding, black lights with Day-Glo objects under them."[78] The strobe lights turned the dancers into unearthly mobiles. According to Gene Anthony, what Graham, Kesey, and the other promoters' wanted above all else was "audience participation. If the audience would participate as they had in the other benefits and at the Kesey Acid Tests, then everyone would come and have a good time. Everyone would be on his or her own trip."[79] High above the hall, directing the spectacle, making sure everything was in sync, was Ken Kesey. A few days after the event, Kesey fled to Mexico rather than face the possibility of five years' incarceration without parole for a second drug bust for marijuana possession. Kesey's flight from the law added to his growing legend among freaks, securing his place in countercultural history as the individual most responsible for pushing the hippie lifestyle to the edges of sanity.[80]

The festival was a huge success both in exposure for the San Francisco sound and the hip lifestyle, as well as financially for its promoters, grossing $12,500 with little overhead. The Grateful Dead emerged from the event to become the quintessential San Francisco band, as well as remaining on Kesey's trip and never getting over it. Indeed, from the Trips' Festival forward, the Grateful Dead, more than any other San Francisco acid/folk/rockers, including Jefferson Airplane, became *the band* most identified with the late 1960s hip Haight-Ashbury scene as both musicians and cultural icons. No group better captured the musical quality of an acid trip or matched their passion for live performances. They were perceived to be the musical embodiment of the hippie aesthetic; the musical prophets of the hip ethos, the "first among equals in giving unselfishly of themselves to hippie culture, performing more free concerts than any band in the history of music." As a result, they "permanently bonded to their audience," which over the years created legions of devoted, if not rabid followers, the "Deadheads." Such fan loyalty gave the band the luxury of "making their music and waiting for audiences to come to them." They thus "remained first and foremost a live band, a style conducive to their improvisational music."[81] To Jerry Garcia, the band's leader, the first Trips Festival "wasn't a *gig*, it was the greatest Acid Test to date, where anything was OK. Thousands of people, man, all helplessly stoned, all finding themselves in a roomful of other thousands of people, none of whom any of them were afraid. It was magic, far out, beautiful magic."[82]

Slightly more eloquent than Garcia, Lou Gottlieb in his Tuesday morning column waxed equally ebulliently, proclaiming the three-day extravaganza to have been "an event of major significance in the history of religion in this City of Saint Francis." According to Gottlieb, "the Almighty, in His infinite wisdom," was "vouchsafing visions" to "certain people in our midst [Kesey, the Dead, and most important, the hippies]," that far transcended "the rapturous transports of old Saint Theresa." Indeed, to Gottlieb, by comparison to the Trips Festival experience, Saint Theresa's visions and ecstasies were "but early Milton Berle Shows on a ten-inch screen." Gottlieb knew that his assessment of the festival would cause straights to tell him to "Drink this glass of warm milk slowly and try to get some rest." Gottlieb nonetheless believed the gathering to have been of seminal importance in the emergence of the counterculture and of San Francisco as its mecca; he was correct. Thanks in large part to Gottlieb's ringing endorsements, two weeks later Graham was running weekly trips at the Fillmore and was on his way to becoming the Florenz Ziegfeld of the rock business. Graham provided the Bay Area with six years of weekend concerts—297 dates—a continuous music festival featuring some of the best rock and blues bands from the era. For many rock music pundits, it was the "San Francisco" sound, performed at the Fillmore and other City venues that sparked the rock music explosion of the late 1960s. Gottlieb recommended attending the festivals to the city's clergy, intellectuals, the "man in the street," and even "the man in the ghetto." To the Chamber of Commerce he pointed out that the festivals represented a tourist attraction during the winter "slump season" and thus were "nothing to despise."[83]

A *San Francisco Chronicle* commentary echoed Gottlieb's assessment, stating that "the atmosphere at the ballroom appeared to please everyone. The Flower Children of the Hashbury in their sometimes outrageous street clothes partied right alongside straight folks wearing sports jackets and ties and sunglasses. It was an odd mix of people. It was a shocker but a fun trip was had by all."[84] Even the usually cynical, anti-counterculture *Chronicle* columnist Herb Caen was impressed by the Trips Festival's profitable success. "Was it true that one of the heaviest unions [The Longshoremen's Union] in the country had just let a bunch of scabs [Graham and company] run a profit-making enterprise inside their own mother-loving headquarters? Had the longshoremen really let non-union musicians [the hippie bands] play a sold-out concert inside their hiring hall? Hell's teeth, that had to be some kind of historical first."[85] In short, as Gene Sculati has observed the January Trips Festival at Longshoremen's Hall provided hippies with "a scene with rituals, rites, and revelatory touch-points that everyone could see, smell, and taste and say 'That's it. That's what it's all about.'"[86] For the thousands of seekers thinking about heading west, and for the legions of journalists and pundits in hot pursuit, all eager to be the first to report this new youth phenomenon, the Trips Festival and the Haight scene heralded the birth of the new consciousness rising; the beginning of the psychedelic era.

By the beginning of 1967 ballroom concerts had proliferated throughout the nation's cities, providing yet another "set and setting" in which hippies could turn-on. As one hipster observed, for himself and for other hippies, the dance halls became places where "salvation came through Hard Rock. Through total sensory involvement the mind became free."[87] Indeed, so important to hippies did this particular venue become that the names of the biggest halls took on a mythic aura, and to this day are remembered by both their hippie and straight attendees for both the music that was played and the humanity that gathered: Fillmore West, Winterland, and the Avalon in San Francisco were the first and remain the most legendary. There was also Fillmore East in the East Village, New York, which Bill Graham opened in 1968 as an East Coast companion to his already successful Bay Area Fillmore West. Although some of the era's biggest rock bands played at the Fillmore East (including Led Zeppelin, Crosby, Stills, Nash, and Young; Frank Zappa and the Mothers of Invention; Jimi Hendrix, Taj Mahal, and the Allman Brothers Band), for a variety of reasons the place simply did not consistently draw as well as the West Coast original during hip's peak years. With the hippie movement's demise by the early 1970s, hip rock promoters such as Graham had lost their main audience and in 1971 Graham closed both of his famous auditoriums. Although "never a great fan of high-volume rock and roll," believing most of the sound to be "nonsensical," Graham nonetheless believed he had an obligation to deliver to his profitable hip clientele what they wanted. "Well I took your ticket and you came here expecting something, and I want you to have that. I want the food to be hot and the drinks to be cold." How crucial was Graham to hippie dance hall jamborees? According to the Airplane's Marty Balin, Graham was "the star of the sixties. In the beginning there was great talent but there were no sound systems. No microphones. Graham came along and changed it. He made the performers a stage. He was what Alan Freed was to the fifties."[88]

For those baby boomers who can remember the 1960s, the names of these famous dance halls are forever etched in their memories, and it was in such environments that many 1960s youth had their first psychedelic experience. Most of the great rock and roll artists of the early to mid–1960s knew their music was innovative but few realized the extent to which their creativity and experimentation would impact the most prolific countercultural movement in post–World War II American history. These various musicians—Bob Dylan, the Beatles, and the Grateful Dead, to name just a few—were artists from completely different musical and cultural backgrounds but they shared one profound, overarching passion: to create a sound that was unique, dynamic, and most important, expressive of the new consciousness rising among many of the nation's youth during the late 1960s. Even America's darlings, the supposedly still innocent, clean-cut surfers, the Beach Boys, had embraced the new sound, producing in late 1966, the far-out yet seminal album, *Pet Sounds*, one of rock's most influential LP's that combined the Beach Boy's legendary sweet vocal harmonies with reverb-heavy psychedelia. The album reflected the creative genius of Brian Wilson and was recognized by the Beatles to be one of the greatest, most innovative LPs in rock history. Off the album came the Beach Boys' last number one hit, "Good Vibrations," which topped the charts in the fall of 1966.[89]

The hippie movement can be followed not only through its sounds but also through its sights. The overarching mantra of hippie art was that breakthroughs in consciousness—often with the help of acid—determined creativity and that the artist can produce his or hers most innovative medium when not encumbered by expectations or predetermined boundaries. According to one of the era's more famous poster artists, Wes Wilson, "When I started doing posters, especially posters in color, I think I selected my colors from my visual experience with LSD." Compatriot Lee Conklin agreed: "I made it my mission to translate my psychedelic experience onto paper." True to the hip ethos, hippie artists eschewed fame and fortune; jaded desires that hindered one's creative impulses. As *San Francisco Chronicle* art critic Thomas Albright observed at that time, "In the hippie sub culture art and life have become synonymous. Hippie art carries the idea of art as personal expression to the extreme…. [It] is flowing, lyrical, expansive, organic, and realistic, at least in the psychedelic vision. Beat art

Psychedelic poster artist Wes Wilson in his studio circa 1967. Wilson became the most nationally acclaimed of all the city's hip poster artists by the close of the decade (photograph by Michelle Vignes, courtesy Bancroft Library, University of California, Berkeley).

has yielded to an art of sensation—sound, color, and shape. Moreover, this new art is functional and integrated entirely into the daily life of the subculture."[90]

There is perhaps no better representation of the spectacle, movement, light, and color that combined to form the sensory elements of the new consciousness than the posters that advertised hippie "tribal gatherings," from rock concerts to communes, to be-ins, to even the Diggers' free food japes. Many album covers also reflected this new genre, such as Santana's 1970 *Abraxas*, which displayed Mati Klarwein's 1961 painting, *Annunciation*. The handbills, mass produced on mimeograph machines and widely distributed, and usually stuck on telephone poles, windows and street corners, have become valuable collector's items and the subject of major exhibitions. All of the dancehall promoters used posters to advertise their shows, with Helms and Graham the most prolific producers of such artwork. Both would drive up and down major Bay Area hip neighborhoods stapling their dance posters to telephone poles or placing them in store windows. As the dancehalls grew in popularity so did the posters advertising such events and they began disappearing from their locations as fast as Graham could place them there. By the end of 1966 the posters were beginning to be recognized as art among a growing poster-collecting public.

This new pictorial art was a fusion of various impulses: Eastern—predominantly Indian—motifs with bursting stars, flaming mandalas, and undulating lines of acid visions along with early 20th century art nouveau and Viennese artist Alfred Roller's fat, space-filling letters. Although this particular form of hippie art "recalled certain historic styles," it was "wholly by accident," and thus more accurately reflected an "individually motivated craft."[91] The acid-inspired swirls of the psychedelic posters were barely comprehensible, but that was precisely their point: they turned letters into art—objects themselves, liberating them from the burden of literal signification. Hippie poster artists intentionally rejected the direct, non-opaque styles used in 1950s advertising, using instead graphics "with an appeal to the sensory pleasure."[92] Wesley Wilson, who helped to pioneer handbill art, ran the low-cost Print Mint in the Haight as well as being the in-house artist for Bill Graham's productions. Through trial and error, Wilson gradually elevated the acid rock posters to fine art. Like several other leading countercultural poster artists (most notably Stanley Mouse, Bonnie Graham, Lee Conklin, Randy Tuten, David Singer, David Byrd, and Victor Moscoso), Wilson had little to no formal training (he had studied horticulture and philosophy, not art, at San Francisco State College), but nonetheless by the late 1960s had achieved significant aesthetic acclaim and commercial success, receiving a $5,000 National Endowment for the Arts award in 1968 as well as having his work and personal profile featured in such mainstream publications as *Life*, *Time*, and *Variety* magazines. In 1969 Wilson's creations along with those of the other artists mentioned, were displayed for several months as a primary exhibition at the Museum of Modern Art (MOMA) in New York City.[93]

The acid-influenced poster art merged with pop art in the late 1960s to produce a whole new aesthetic genre. Pop was an attempt to destroy the distinction between the everyday and high art. For instance, the pop art of Andy Warhol, Claes Oldenburg, James Rosenquist, and Roy Lichtenstein chose as its subject matter the most utterly banal—Campbell's soup cans, ice cream cones, giant hamburgers, automobile engine parts, silk-screened Marilyn Monroes—and presented such mundane topics in the most naïve, direct way—exactly how they looked in "real life." Pop art reflected the countercultural revolt against the cerebral while simultaneously mocking the plastic, commercial sensibility of mainstream culture.[94]

By 1967, thanks in large part to the trips festivals, the musical energies that had been gathering in San Francisco for two years burst onto the national scene. By that time some hippie bands—most notably the Grateful Dead (Warner Bros.) and Jefferson Airplane (RCA) had already succumbed to the lure of fat recording contracts. The Dead's deal with Warner Bros. was especially extraordinary because it gave the band complete control over material and production. As the group's rhythm guitarist Bob Weir boasted, "If the industry is gonna want us, they're gonna take us the way we are. Then, if the money comes in, it'll be a stone gas." Jerry Garcia seconded his band mate's declaration, telling an interviewer that "because we held out, because we thought we were worth something, now we can do anything we want." Stephen Stills of Buffalo Springfield agreed: "The Dead were the first people, I don't know whether it was acid or what, to come to that realization where they really didn't give a shit whether they made it or not." As Richard Golstein observed at the time, "talent scouts from a dozen major record companies are now grooving with the tribes at the Fillmore and the Avalon. Hip San Francisco is being carved into bits of business turf. Moby Grape is tinkering with Columbia [record company] and a fistful of local talent is being wined and dined like the last available *shikse* in the Promised Land."[95] Given the inescapable relationship of rock and roll to the youth market and therefore to money, it was inevitable that the capitalist record corporations would grab as many of the bands as they possibly could and profit from their sound. Indeed the record companies ended up making more from the music than hippie musicians, and the best bands, such as the Grateful Dead (Weir's nonchalance about money to the contrary), inevitably became profit-motivated. Ultimately, like most everything else related to the counterculture, if a particular hip commodity could be marketed for profit, the major corporations seized the opportunity. This became especially true for late 1960s rock and roll, which started out as "the language of a generation" but was quickly absorbed by the nation's mainstream capitalist enterprises. Indeed, Paul Kantner of the Jefferson Airplane believed that "the record companies sell rock and roll records like they sell refrigerators. They don't care about the people who make rock or what they're all about as human beings any more than they care about the people who make refrigerators."[96]

By the summer of 1967 the San Francisco Sound had made the city the new rock mecca and bands, such as the Dead and the Jefferson Airplane, rock's newest headliners. Jefferson Airplane had two hits in the Top 10 in 1967, "Somebody to Love" and "White Rabbit," which climbed to number four nationally. "White Rabbit" is to this day perhaps one of the most legendary of acid rock/hippie songs; a psychedelic rendition on an *Alice in Wonderland* theme. Ralph Gleason, San Francisco's hip music critic, understood well rock and roll's cultural significance. "At no time in American history has youth possessed the strength it possesses now," he wrote in 1967. "Trained by music and linked by music, it has the power for good to change the world." However, he added, "That power for good carries the reverse, the power for evil,"[97] which tragically will manifest itself within the general counterculture in the summer and late fall of 1969, in violent events, for which an increasingly antagonistic public will blame the hippies—the convenient, stereotypical label applied to all youth who identified in some way with the hippie subculture.

5

The October 1966 Love Pageant Rally

"It's just being. Human beings. Being together."—Richard Alpert on the Love
Pageant Rally

Another signal event in 1966 that further bonded the Haight's hippies into a more coherent and defined movement was the October Love Pageant Rally, organized by Michael Bowen and Allen Cohen to protest California's criminalization of LSD, which was to go into effect on October 6, 1966. The law imposed fines of up to $1,000 and sentences of up to one year behind bars for LSD possession. In June of that year the California legislature passed the bill and according to the measure's main sponsor, Republican state senator Donald Grunsky, "You cannot eliminate heroin and murder with laws, but you sure can cut down on them. A lot of kids would be tempted to fool with LSD, but will think twice if there is a law on the books." However, despite such mandates, for several more years getting the drug remained "as easy as it once was to buy a quart of bathtub gin." Many national lawmakers believed criminalization "would automatically place maybe 10% of college students in the category of criminals" and "would drive users underground, making it more difficult to find and treat those who suffer dangerously psychotic effects." Despite such concerns and opposition to such legislation, other states (Nevada, New Jersey, and New York) soon followed the California precedent, passing equally harsh penalties for LSD possession.[1]

Rather than organize the typical political protest à la UC Berkeley's anti–Vietnam War and free speech marches, Cohen and Bowen envisioned a new form of resistance, one that would challenge the Establishment but would not succumb to the "fascist reaction" that the "old forms" of demonstration inevitably encountered, rendering such action impotent. "Instead of protesting the moratorium on LSD," declared Bowen, "instead of protesting the law that was going into effect, our idea was to make a demonstration which would show the law's falsity. Without confrontation. We wanted to create a celebration of innocence. We were not guilty of using illegal substances. We were celebrating transcendental consciousness. The beauty of the universe. The beauty of being."[2] Allen Ginsberg wholeheartedly agreed and supported this new approach toward rebellion, expressing similar views a year earlier in an essay titled "How to Make a March/Spectacle." In his piece Ginsberg not only agreed with Cohen and Bowen but suggested some possible new tactics as well, such as having protesters bring flowers, musical instruments, toys, religious symbols, white flags, and little paper halos to be handed out to potential aggressors/suppressors.[3] Accordingly, the Love Pageant Rally was to be a psychedelic event, complete with rock and roll bands, outrageous costumes, and general freaky activity. The "carnival" was to commence at 2 p.m. on October 6, 1966 at Panhandle Park "between Masonic Avenue and Ashbury Street."[4]

In a letter to Mayor John Shelley and other city officials, whom the event's organizers invited to the Rally, Cohen and Bowen explained the reasons for their forthcoming "celebration": "Opposition to an unjust law creates futility for citizens who are its victims and increases the hostility between the governed and the governors. In the case of LSD prohibition, the State has entered directly into the sacrosanct, personal psyches of its citizens. Our Love Pageant Rally is intended to overcome the paranoia and separation with which the State wishes to divide and silence the increasing revolutionary sense of Californians." Cohen and Bowen were confident that their protest against LSD's criminalization would inspire "similar rallies in communities such as ours all over the country and in Europe. You are invited to attend and address our rally."[5]

Interestingly, despite Cohen's and Bowen's insistence on an alternative form of protest, to substantiate the righteousness of their cause, they referenced (parodied) one of the most sacred texts in American history: The Declaration of Independence, linking their idea of resistance to an unjust law to the American revolutionary tradition. "When in the flow of human events it becomes necessary for the people to cease to recognize the obsolete social patterns which have isolated man from his consciousness and to create with youthful energies of the world revolutionary communities of harmonious relations to which the two billion year old life process entitles them, a decent respect to the opinions of mankind should declare causes which impel them to this creation.... We hold these experiences to be self-evident, that all is equal, that the creation endows us with certain inalienable rights that among them are: the freedom of body, pursuit of joy, and the expansion of consciousness [the right to use hallucinogenic drugs such as LSD]."[6]

On the morning of October 6, a delegation from the *Oracle* and the Psychedelic Shop converged on City Hall in full golden-hued costume bearing morning glory seeds, flowers, and store-bought mushrooms, symbolizing psychedelic mushrooms, all gifts for Mayor Shelley, whom they hoped to "turn on." The press turned out for the show; the hippies were increasingly "making for good copy."[7]

The Love pageant rally was a huge success; thousands attended this latest hippie spectacle. Of course helping to attract such a throng was the music, provided by the Grateful Dead, Janis Joplin and Big Brother and the Holding Company, and Wild Flower. As Cohen and Bowen looked out upon the celebration, Richard Alpert walked by, and Bowen hailed him to join their conversation. "Isn't this far out," declared Bowen to his comrades. "People are sure hungry for some communicating. They love it. It's a joyous moment. What do you think Alpert?" Alpert agreed; the event was a success. "We should do it again," said Allen Cohen. Bowen agreed "But next time, I bet we could get ten times the people." Cohen then asked Alpert what he would have called the rally. "Well," replied Alpert, "it's a hell of a gathering. It's just being. Humans being. Being together." Bowen agreed: "It's a Human Be-In and we will just have to have another rally, only bigger and next time we will bring all the tribes together."[8]

Not to dismiss the January Trips Festival's importance in the history of the hippie movement, the Love Pageant Rally was nonetheless even more momentous. As reflected in the above conversation, as they watched their fellow freaks embrace the Pageant's vibes and revel in the scene, many hippies became even more sanguine that the evolutionary tides might be rolling in their direction. Maybe it was all the LSD that caused such euphoria and optimism but from the Love Pageant forward, a naïve optimism enveloped the Haight combined with a mystical faith that love would provide all for everyone. In fairly rapid succession throughout 1966 the neighborhood had its own newspaper, its own police force, the Hell's Angels, its own FM radio station, KMPX; its own Chamber of Commerce in the H.I.P. consortium of merchants, and its own social workers in the form of the Diggers. There was even discussion among Bowen and company to establish a hip employment agency and a hip hotel along with more hip restaurants serving only organic foods. As one middle-aged visitor from the East Coast remarked, "Why, you don't see anything like this [both the Haight neighborhood and the Rally she witnessed] in Philadelphia," at least not yet; in less than a year's time the City of Brotherly Love would have its own bona fide flourishing hip community. As Jay Stevens has observed, by the close of 1966, the Haight had become "a kind of sanitarium, an indigenous Baden Baden that offered a therapeutic regime of good vibes and drugs rather than mountain air and minerals."[9]

Like the January Trips Festival at Longshoremen's Hall, Cohen and Bowen had used spectacle and carnival to help galvanize their movement's sense of identity and community, while setting the stage for one of the counterculture's most important events, the Human Be-In of January 1967.

6

The 1967 Human Be-In

"We shall shower the country with waves of ecstasy and purification."—Statement by the Inspirers of the Gathering of the Tribes," *Berkeley Barb*, January 13, 1967

As Michael Stepanian, rugby player and recent graduate of Stanford Law School looked up into the sky above his end of the Polo Field in Golden Gate Park, he saw a parachutist drifting slowly through the late afternoon fog toward the opposite end of the field, where the man and his paisley chute immediately vanished into the sea of humanity that had been gathering since the early morning hours to celebrate "the Dawning of a New Age." As Stepanian arrived for his club's match against Oregon State University that Saturday morning, he was captivated by the parade of strange looking people, with day-glow painted faces and men with hair longer than his sisters,' dressed in all manner of outrageous attire, who had come to the park to assemble for a "Human Be-In," a "gathering of the tribes," which Stepanian had read on a poster stapled to a telephone pole in the Haight as he slowly drove his car through the neighborhood on his way to the field. The festival was to take place that Saturday, January 14, 1967, from dawn until dusk in Golden Gate Park. Stepanian's macho, straight teammates jeered at the freaks as they audaciously walked across the athletes' side of the park on their way to their celebration. However, unlike his peers, the event intrigued Stepanian and thus when his game was over he meandered over to the "happening" in his bloodied jersey and muddy cleats, wandering through the crowd, mesmerized by what he saw. Although he stuck out like a sore thumb in his rugby uniform, athletic body, and short hair, "nobody seemed to give a shit. The sun was shining, the kids were beautiful, the music was magic. That was the beginning of my education."[1]

Indeed, so illuminating and positive was Stepanian's experience at the Be-In that he used his legal talents later that evening to defend dozens of the attendees the police had tried to arrest on Haight Street for vagrancy and curfew violations. Stepanian, as a member of one of the City's most powerful law firms, also later represented the Grateful Dead in several attempted busts by the city's cops. Stepanian, like his mentor, rarely if ever failed to win his clients' acquittal. According to associate Brian Rohan, "When we [himself and Stepanian] started out, the city was anti-black, anti-gay, and anti-woman. It was a very uptight Irish Catholic city. We took on the cops, city hall, the Catholic Church. Vince Hallinan [the legendary defenses/civil rights/civil liberties lawyer] taught us never to be afraid of bullies."[2]

By day, Rohan and Stepanian were respected, establishment lawyers but during the

The gurus assembled: Dr. Timothy Leary (center right, seated), Allen Ginsberg (center, seated, beard), and Michael Bowen (center left, seated, sunglasses) on stage at the January 1967 Human Be-In, Polo Field, Golden Gate Park, San Francisco, California (photograph by Larry Keenan, courtesy Bancroft Library, University of California, Berkeley. © 1997 Larry Keenan. All rights reserved).

evenings they operated their own practice—The Haight-Ashbury Legal Organization (HALO)—hanging out their shingle at 710 Ashbury Street: the home of the Grateful Dead, from where they offered their services for free to runaways, draft dodgers, pot smokers, to anyone, to any hippie they believed had been wrongfully harassed or arrested in the police dragnets that seemed to be perpetually sweeping through the Haight during the late 1960s, beginning almost as soon as the January Be-In was over. The Haight's legendary rock bands, from the Grateful Dead to the Jefferson Airplane to Big Brother and the Holding Company, willingly and generously kept HALO afloat, for all of them at one time or another needed Rohan's and Stepanian's legal skills to keep them out of jail, which the attorneys successfully accomplished, often with great public notoriety and fanfare.[3]

What Stepanian witnessed on that unseasonably warm 68 degree Saturday afternoon was a unique and momentous event, even in a Bay Area underground long accustomed to the eccentric and outrageous. However, for the majority of Americans such as Stepanian, this particular spectacle represented their first glimpse, in full regalia, of these strange new counterculturists called "hippies"—the label given to the roughly 20,000 to 25,000 people who amassed for the first Human Be-In on the grass of the polo field at San Francisco's renowned Golden Gate Park. The event was dubbed "A Gathering of the Tribes" by its three main promoters, Allen Cohen, Michael Bowen, and Ron Thelin. Over the course of the next two years, these tribal gatherings increased in both attendance and in the prodigious exhibition of hippie culture, with the era's music the center piece of each subsequent celebration.

Attendees and sponsors were certain that after their display of "compassion, awareness, and love in the Revelation of the unity of all mankind," all violence and aggression would "be submerged and transmuted in rhythm and dancing; racism will be purified by the self of forgiveness. Spiritual revolution to transform the materialistic bruted body and mind of America is NOW, here with the young, budding."[4] Indeed, as Thelin told Art Kunkin, editor of the Los Angeles *Free Press*, another underground newspaper that had emerged by 1967, "the energy generated in gatherings like this could shift the balance enough to end the war in Vietnam and revitalize many dead hearts."[5]

The *Oracle* invited everyone "to bring costumes, blankets, bells, flags, symbols, cymbals, drums, beads, feathers, and flowers" to celebrate "the joyful, face-to-face beginning of the new epoch" in "the humanization of the American man and woman." "The Gathering of the Tribes" reflected the "new concert of human relations" based on "compassion, awareness, and love in the Revelation of the unity of all mankind." To Thelin and company, the Be-In represented the first massive unveiling to the rest of the country of "a new nation" that "For ten years has grown inside the robot flesh of the old. Before your eyes a new free vital soul is reconnecting the living centers of the American body."[6] To demonstrate the hippie's acceptance of all individuals, regardless of how tainted or questionable their past (or present) had been, the notoriously renegade and often violent Hell's Angels motorcycle gang was invited and agreed to guard the electronic equipment of the area's rock bands, all of who agreed to perform for free.[7]

The publicity for the Be-In reflected many of the cornerstones of the emerging hippie ethos: rejection of socio-cultural and political conventions, especially conformity to middle class norms and mores; the "humanization" of American society through more intimate personal relationships; consciousness expansion and spiritualism as an antidote to consumerism, and communalism. The Be-In was to be a massive affirmation of these values; a declaration to a national audience that the countercultural philosophy was a viable socio-cultural alternative to mainstream culture. In effect, the event's promoters hoped their celebration would not only bring about a mass "revolution of consciousness," but attract thousands more seekers to join their movement to help liberate Americans from themselves.

Although the spectacle drew the hoped-for national and international attention, the exposure resulted in un-anticipated and ultimately deleterious consequences, especially at the hands of the mainstream media, which, in the end, did more to marginalize and eventually sub-

For most hippies, tribal gatherings were a time for human bonding, tripping and the exultation of the free spirit and the new consciousness emerging. Photograph taken in 1967 (Dennis L. Maness Summer of Love Photograph Collection (SFP51), San Francisco History Center, San Francisco Public Library).

vert the hippie counterculture than any inherent self-destructive tendencies or potentialities within the hip community. Nonetheless, the Be-In's organizers had planned their gathering as a media event to represent the counterculture's national coming out celebration and in that purpose, they were successful. Television cameras were present to film the spectacle, "while photographers took pictures of photographers taking pictures of other photographers taking pictures." Unfortunately the organizers' exaltation of the Haight-Ashbury as "the spiritual center of a new consciousness," backfired as the local and national news media quickly put forth their own interpretations of the new counterculture.[8]

From the hippies' first rumblings, the media rarely if ever credited the movement with having anything remotely credible to offer the nation's citizens. From beginning to end, the media focused on hippiedom's style and hippie behavior, portraying and then dismissing hip gatherings and events as nothing more than debauched Dionysian revelries and juvenile escapades. In the process the majority of pundits delivered standardized, distorted images of hippies, reducing them to nothing more than hedonistic, self-absorbed, and reckless pursuers of drugs, rock music, and sex—the easily digestible sound-bite triad perpetrated by the media to define the hip lifestyle and priorities. Only a handful of reporters attempted or cared to dig deeper into the hip community to try to understand and convey to the larger public an objective assessment of the hippies' attempts to create a viable alternative way of life. It was the mainstream media's sensationalized identity that the majority of Americans bought during hip's heydays and such distortions contributed significantly to the movement's eventual demise.

The ceremonies were scheduled to begin at 1 p.m. but legendary Beat poets Allen Ginsberg and Gary Snyder, both of whom had come to embrace the new counterculture and had become two of its greatest propagators, showed up two hours earlier to perform a "purifactory circumnambulation" of the field, a ritual they had observed in India in 1963, to drive out demons. At precisely 1 p.m., while Ginsberg chanted a Buddhist mantra, Snyder blew on a conch shell to announce the Be-In's official opening. Snyder then declared that all assembled were "primitives of an unknown culture, with new ethics and new states of mind."[9] Almost 25,000 people covered the polo field like a human carpet in front of the makeshift stage. Indeed, the real show was the crowd. As *San Francisco Chronicle* music critic Ralph Gleason observed, "The costumes were a designer's dream, a wild polyglot mixture of Mod, Palladin, Ringling Brothers, Cochise, and Hell's Angels Formal." As Gleason further noted, "Bells tinkled, balloons floated, people on the grass played harmonicas, guitars, recorders, and flutes. Beautiful, often scantily clad girls handed out sticks of incense."[10] The *Oracle's* Stephen Levine was equally descriptive in his account of the celebrants, their attire, the day's activities, and general scene: "Barefoot girls in priest's cloaks, madras saris, and corduroy. Teenage braves stripped to the waist in a hot winter sun. Folksingers charting mountain ranges in their imaginations. Shamans and motorcyclists, lovers and voyeurs, cowboys and Indians, clouds of yellow incense geysers from the stage."[11]

One of the Be-In's more notable attendees was Timothy Leary, the momentary high priest of the psychedelic movement. For the day's event Leary came dressed in white pajamas, with beads around his neck, and a yellow flower tucked behind his ear to give the effect of a Buddhist holy man. Although loaded on 300 micrograms of LSD, Leary was aware and lucid enough to sense that the crowd was in no mood for sermonizing of any ilk, so he limited his usual loquacious proselytizing to his two holy imperatives: "Thou shalt not alter the consciousness of thy fellow man," and "Thou shalt not prevent thy fellow man from altering his own consciousness." However, in the end, he could not help himself; he closed his brief cameo by uttering his mantra of "Tune in, turn on, and drop out," the cliché that would follow him around for the rest of his life.[12]

Interestingly, by the time of Leary's appearance at the Be-In, many of the counterculture's most passionate supporters had begun to question the genuineness and reality of Leary's message of disassociation from established social structures by "turning on, tuning in, and dropping out." One of the acid culture's great paradoxes was that its sustainability actually depended on commodification; that is, although LSD could be cheaply manufactured, it was nonetheless a *processed* product, thus subject to the era's prevailing market forces. Leary thus preached a double standard: How could his acid head followers drop out of society if they needed to buy LSD to continue the illusion, or even purchase the raw ingredients to manufacture their own acid? One of the first to see through Leary's duplicitous pedagogy was gonzo journalist Hunter S. Thompson, who believed Leary had duped his legions of true believers, "those pathetically eager acid freaks who thought they could buy Peace and Understanding for three bucks a hit [a gram of acid]. What Leary took down with him was the central illusion of a whole life-style that he helped create ... a generation of permanent cripples, failed seekers ... lives of loss and failure."[13] At the moment, most of the Be-In's celebrants viewed Leary with adoring eyes; he was one of their most revered gurus.

One of the promoters' main objectives with Human Be-In was to try to unite the area's political activists with the acid heads and dropouts who had inundated and engulfed the City's Haight-Ashbury neighborhood by 1967; the Be-In would be a way "of unifying trips." Indeed, the promoter's press release had announced just such a union: "Berkeley political activists and the love generation of the Haight-Ashbury will join together with members of the nation who will be coming from every state in the nation, every tribe of the young (the emerging soul of the nation) to powwow, celebrate, and prophesy the epoch of liberation, love and peace."[14] Although many UC Berkeley and East Bay politicos showed up for the event, chatted, and gladly shared a joint with their "flower-power" counterparts, the hoped for alliance between the political left and the counterculture did not occur that day and never effectively would emerge. Reality for both groups had already set in at the event's first joint planning session. When Cohen and company announced that they expected between 20,000 and 50,000 people, the immediate politico response was, "Fine, now what are our demands going to be?" The hippies chuckled, politely telling their radical compatriot that they had no intention of "present[ing] *demands*." The radical, nonplussed, shouted, "It doesn't make any sense to get twenty or fifty thousand people together and not make any demands! We *have* to have some demands." The hippies placated the activist by giving him a piece of paper and then telling him, as to a petulant child, "to go in the corner and write down all the demands he wanted."[15] The hippies were making it clear to the Berkeley folk that although they welcomed their presence at the Be-In and embraced the idea of a possible alliance, the hippies were not about to allow their celebration to become politicized. Indeed, by the time of the Be-In, the Haight's psychedelic community considered itself to be beyond politics (bored actually) and thus uninterested in promulgating demands and formulating position papers. In fact, only sporadically and with little enthusiasm did hippies participate in New Left demonstrations or publicly support their causes. Instead, hippies believed their way reflected *the real* political power essential to change lives totally as witnessed by their ever-larger tribal gatherings.

As Theodore Roszak observed, the hip counterculture and the New Left represented opposing impulses during the period. "To one side, there is the mind-blown bohemianism of the beats and the hippies; to the other, the hard-headed political activism of the New Left. Are these not in reality two separate and antithetical developments; the one (tracing back to Ginsberg, Kerouac, & Co.) seeking to 'cop out' of American society, the other (tracing back to C. Wright Mills and remnants of the old socialist left) seeking to penetrate and revolutionize our political life?"[16]

In the Be-In's immediate aftermath, Ed Denson of the *Berkeley Barb* stated that although the Be-In had been "an event with national importance," it was simultaneously a failure because the counterculture had wasted a perfect opportunity, with thousands of people gathered, to transform the event into a political rally.[17] Even as the Haight scene and the hippie movement gained even greater traction and momentum in the months following the Be-In, Denson remained "very pessimistic about where this thing [the hippie movement] is going. Maybe this hippie thing is more than a fad; maybe the whole world is turning on but I'm not optimistic. Most of the hippies I know don't really understand what kind of world they're living in. I get tired of hearing about what beautiful people they all are. If the hippies were more realistic they'd stand a better chance of surviving."[18] Denson's former comrade-in-arms during the Berkeley Free Speech Movement, Steve Decanio, was even more distrustful of a prospective hippie-activist partnership, telling Hunter S. Thompson, "This alliance between hippies and political radicals is bound to break up. There's just too big a jump from the slogan of 'Flower Power' to the deadly realm of politics." In Decanio's view, the hoped-for union was already doomed because of the hippies' "obsession with drugs, which are the ready-made opiates of the people" that allowed hippies "to lie back in their pads and smile at the world through a fog of marijuana smoke, or worse, to dress like clowns or American Indians and stay zonked for days at a time on LSD. The drug culture is spreading faster than political activists realize."[19] Although Denson's and Decanio's comments proved prescient, at the time of the Be-In, both clearly missed the promoters' intention: the Be-In *was not* a political rally or protest but rather the celebration of an alternative culture; thousands came to simply *be* there; it was after all, a *Be-In*.

As the Jefferson Airplane's Paul Kantner perceptively observed, "The difference between San Francisco and Berkeley was that Berkeley complained about a lot of things. Rather than complaining about things, we San Franciscans formed an alternative reality to live in. And for some reason, we got away with it. San Francisco became somewhere you did things rather than protesting about them. We knew we didn't have to speechify about what we should and shouldn't do. We just *did*."[20] Nonetheless, the *Barb* remained momentarily sanguine, believing it would only be a matter of time before a rapprochement and partnership occurred, and when that happened, "We shall shower the country with waves of ecstasy and purification. Fear will be washed away; ignorance will be exposed to sunlight; profits and empire will lie dying on deserted beaches."[21]

"The gathering of the tribes" lasted until five o'clock. To the shock of many but to the delight of the 20,000-plus attendees, the San Francisco Police Department sent only *two* mounted patrolmen to police the event and the only time they interfered the entire day was when one of the cops rode through the crowd to deliver a lost child to the stage.[22] Throughout the afternoon, hip celebrities spoke from the stage between band sets; Leary, New Left political activist Jerry Rubin, and others sermonized. Most of the audience, however, ignored the official proceedings and just "grooved." Even those who came as dispassionate observers of the event could not avoid becoming swept up in the mood. Such was the experience of the 56-year-old veteran social worker Helen Swick Perry, who later published a book about her encounters on that day. "There was no program; it was a happening; It was people being together, un-programmed, uncommitted, except to life itself and its celebration. All seemed enchanted, happy, and smiled like a welcoming committee to everyone they saw. Sights and sounds turned me on, so that I had the sensation of dreaming," she wrote. "The air seemed heady and mystical. Dogs and children pranced around in blissful abandon, and I became aware of the phenomenon that still piques my curiosity: The dogs did not fight and the children did not cry."[23]

Ralph Gleason, the *San Francisco Chronicle's* popular and respected music critic, who had become one of the hippie's most passionate boosters, was equally favorably impressed by this latest hippie happening. "No fights. No drunks. No troubles. Two policemen on horseback and 20,000 people. The perfect sunshine, the beautiful birds in the air, the parachutist descending as the Grateful Dead ended a song. Saturday's gathering was an affirmation, not a protest. A statement of life, not death, and a promise of good, not evil.... This is truly something new and not the least of it is that it is an asking for a new dimension to peace, not just an end to shooting, for the reality of love and a great Nest for all humans."[24] Apropos for the day no one went hungry. The Diggers handed out free turkey sandwiches, homemade bread, and oranges. Local acid merchants made sure everyone was stoned, contributing freshly made LSD capsules to the crowd, handing them out like free candy to anyone who wanted one.[25] Those celebrants not on LSD were high on pot so that the whole event was filtered through a mind-altering haze that elevated the effect.

As dusk began to set in over the City, and after Beat poets-cum-hippies Michael McClure, Snyder, Ginsberg, and the hippie erotica, love poet Leonor Kandel read her passion poems in the silent presence of Zen master Suzuki Roshi, who was seated on the stage, and the hours of revelry wound down, Ginsberg turned toward the setting sun, led a Buddhist chant and asked attendees to practice "a little kitchen Yoga" by picking up their trash. City officials later declared that it had been decades since so large a gathering had left so little refuse in the park.[26] As Helen Swick Perry noted, the immaculately cleaned Polo Grounds "was more disturbing to the square community than a ton of refuse would have been."[27] Congregational youth minister Edward "Larry" Beggs, who also came as a "curious observer," was equally impressed by the people all around him who complied with Ginsberg's request, picking up "not only their own discarded items" but other people's trash as well, including cigarette butts, to the point that "The entire Polo Field, where thousands had sat and munched longer than [at] a baseball double-header, was now restored to its pristine green."[28] As Helen Swick Perry walked back to her car, she noticed that although "Most of the people looked tired and droopy, our eyes met in a secret delight. We had in common the sound of a different drummer."[29]

The next day a local TV station's news crew came to interview Leary, Bowen, Snyder, McClure, and as many of the hippies' other gurus as they possible could, for all of them were staying in the Haight at Bowen's house. Leary was to be their main focus, but when he appeared in a sports jacket and trousers they turned their klieg lights and cameras on Ginsberg, who was still dressed in his hippie costume; a far better visual for a piece on the hippies than a buttoned-down Establishment-looking Leary. Ginsberg told the interviewer that in his view, the Be-In "was very Eden-like, kind of like Blake's vision of Eden. Music. Babies. People just sort of floating around having a good time and everybody happy and smiling and touching and turning each other on and a lot of groovy chicks all dressed up in their best clothes and"— the interviewer interrupted Ginsberg to ask "But will it last?" "How do I know?" the poet responded. "And who cares."[30] Peter Coyote agreed with Ginsberg's simple appraisal: "It was simply a coming together, a gathering of the Tribes, 20,000 people there to reject the traditional path to success and drop out."[31]

The Be-In was a milestone; *Newsweek* had sent reporters and photographers to the "tribal gathering" and in a four-page, beautifully photographed exposé in its February 6, 1967, edition, proclaimed the event "a love feast, a psychedelic picnic, a hippie happening" that "affirmed one fact: San Francisco has arrived as the hub of the hippie world."[32] The January spectacle gave the counterculture scene national celebrity. By the time of the Be-In, millions of Americans—young, soon-to-be hippies to sociologists, pundits, politicians, parents—were asking themselves what had caused this particular countercultural phenomenon to emerge and affect in varying degrees, if not completely envelop, so many of the nation's youth. Thanks in large measure to the mainstream media's coverage of the Be-In, the event spawned one of the most intense public discussions among straights in post-war America to try to explain and understand this new socio-cultural phenomenon. The hippie impulse had to be understood. It was spreading through a generation of young people, who were embracing many of its tenets, causing them to challenge the traditional values of bourgeois culture, values still sustaining the liberal ethos and consensus that had dominated the nation's socio-economic and political disposition since the New Deal—reason, progress, order, achievement, and social responsibility.

To many bewildered adults, the youth revolt on display at Golden Gate Park represented one of, if not *the* most intense, vexing, and polarizing generational identity crises or gaps in the nation's history; one that had been percolating since the late 1950s and finally boiled over by the mid–1960s. The overwhelming majority of hippies were under 30 and among this age group there was a general distrust of anyone over 30, which gave rise to the popular cliché for young people to "trust no one over thirty." Depicted in both the popular and more serious literature of the time was the existence of a "generation gap" that many believed was the fundamental issue that had caused this latest youth uprising against the status quo. Such was the central thesis of Theodore Roszak's *The Making of the Counterculture*, which for several years was considered to be the defining book in explaining the emergence of the 1960s counterculture. In Roszak's view, the hippies represented the culmination and thus zenith of the nation's bohemian traditions. More important, Roszak was certain that the hippies' emergence reflected a seething discontent and rage in many young Americans toward the socio-cultural establishment. For Roszak, the counterculture represented American society's best hope for redemption from the crass materialism, mass conformity, vapidity, and spiritual sterility that had engulfed so many individuals by the 1960s: "The alienated young are giving shape to something that looks like the saving vision our endangered civilization requires." Charles Reich agreed with Roszak, confident that the hippies' new ethos would bring "a higher reason, a more human community, and a new liberated individual. Its ultimate creation will be a new and enduring wholeness and beauty—a renewed relationship of man to himself, to other men, to society, to nature, and to the land."[33]

Just how much of a chasm there was between older and younger Americans during the

1960s is still being debated. Nonetheless, at the time individuals on both sides of the divide believed it was real and the most significant in American history. In the minds of many older Americans the gap was undoubtedly real, for such socio-cultural tensions had historical precedent; there had been such generational splits before in history, with the most recent occurring in the 1920s and thus some 1960s parents could find an explanation and some consolation for their children's behavior by ascribing their progenies' rebellion to something historically but simplistically familiar. To many in the counterculture, their movement represented the vanguard of revolutionary cultural change about to envelop the country; one that would sweep away all that was old, moribund, and dysfunctional. Such was the scathing theme of an op-ed written for the underground newspaper, the *Los Angeles Free Press:* "You [the older generation] are standing on a generation that WILL NOT BE STOOD UPON! You have declared illegal virtually every establishment, event, gathering, device, and instrument we consider important and worthwhile. BUT YOU CANNOT STOP THE HANDS OF TIME AND YOU CANNOT STILL THE WINDS OF CHANGE! YOU ARE DYING! Time is removing you from the face of the earth."[34] To many in the older generation it seemed that all of a sudden, out of nowhere, a youth population considered docile and insignificant only a decade before, was trying to tear down every rampart of a once seemingly impregnable fortress of popular conservatism.

In a less disparaging and more interpretive tone, underground writer George D. Maloney believed 1960s American society had irrevocably separated into three distinct, antithetical generations: under thirty, thirty to forty-five, and over forty-five. The problem with many in the 30 to 45 category and certainly the issue with those in the over-45 group, was that a high percentage of individuals in those age groups simply could not shake themselves free from the confines of security, stability, and their perpetual quest for prosperity. How could they? They were products of the Great Depression and World War II; a time of unprecedented uncertainty and deprivation, materially, emotionally, and psychologically. During that time, for many, basic, individual survival was the order of the day, and thus when prosperity returned to their lives by the 1950s, they developed an ethos that made the attaining and sustaining of security and stability their life's priority, never much concerning themselves with "human values." By contrast, white suburban baby boomers had grown up amid unprecedented affluence, mass consumption, and material abundance, and thus believed an era of total freedom of choice was at hand. They could thus afford to take a hiatus for a few years from the quest for the economic assurance and its material rewards that had obsessed their parents' generation. They decided to put on hold career, family, and mortgage and instead pursue experiments in alternative living, in both their minds and bodies, which of course appalled and outraged older Americans who had allowed their preoccupation with obtaining the American Dream to inform if not define their lives. Hippies wanted to avoid becoming the Beatles' "Nowhere Man." To Maloney and his fellow counterculturists, an irredeemable gap had developed between "young" and "parental" generations, which he declared, "'Tis indeed the stuff of which revolutions are made."[35]

Such affluence, security, and boredom created a desire among many boomers to "sample and savor everything—music, underground comics, high-volume guitar assaults, delicate raga, anonymous sex, emotional commitment. This was, understandably, a little hard for parents to take; and the resulting generation gap, the first that didn't axiomatically appear to be 'just a phase,' was especially deep because on some level, the kids believed at least a little bit of the message their panicky parents were emanating. Combined with headiness of dope itself, it was easy for kids to think they *would* change, be completely and irrevocably different from their parents' generation.... Good-bye suburbs, good-bye barbecue, good-bye account-ants and loopholes, good-bye beauty salons, good-bye M1 rifles.... Hello peace, love, and understanding."[36]

However real the gap was to the many disconsolate parents of hippies, as well to many hippies, the fissure was not the main cause of the hippie protest. Indeed, more often than not, the perceived generation gap reflected more stylistic than profound ideological differ-ences between 1960s parents and their recalcitrant children. The hippies were searching for a personal fulfillment as old as the "free market and Protestant Reformation" and in the process believed they could find nirvana by ingesting all manner of psychedelic drugs and attending rock concerts which became, for most hippies, symbiotic. The hippies of course condemned corporate capitalism, the "warfare/welfare" state, and ironically 1960s liberalism in general for its alleged hypocrisy, but when pressed to come up with viable alternatives, few had much to say, for living in the moment was their priority, especially given their perception that all humanity could be extinct tomorrow by simply pushing a button (nuclear holocaust), or even a greater reality for males, via the jungles of Vietnam in a war that the majority of young Americans, regardless of lifestyle, came to fear and denounce.[37]

Others attributed the hippie rebellion to inconsistent parenting, which beginning in the 1950s, fluctuated between permissive neglect and meddlesome control. This was partly the result of white middle class affluence and the embracing by many parents of new child-rearing philosophies, most notably those expressed by Dr. Benjamin Spock in his 1946 best-selling *Common Sense Book of Baby and Child Care*. Indeed, many adults were convinced that the hippies were the result of those parents who had over-indulged their progeny's every need and whim; clearly they had succumbed to Spock's alleged call for pampering and spoiling in order to make their children more holistic, less neurotic, and less fearful adolescents and adults. According to Spock, it was imperative that children receive benevolent and consistent attention at home before school years and such solicitude must continue into adolescence. Spock believed that traditional child-rearing practices were not only antiquated but harmful to the child as well. Spock, in effect, wanted post-war parents to "spare the rod and spoil the child"; that is, stop the often humiliating punishments and spankings (if not physical abuse) for what he considered to be normal or typical childhood behavior. No doubt many boomer parents read Spock as gospel and consequently did indeed indulge to excesses their children's every desire, creating in the process the very pampered, spoiled, self-indulgent, yet secure and confident baby boom generation, which churned out the counterculture of the 1960s. But for all the criticism that Spock and other progressive social scientists received for allegedly promoting permissiveness and potential hedonism, it must be remembered that ultimately peers, not parents, most influenced the attitudes and mores of young Americans in the 1960s.[38]

Many of those looking for deeper currents in the hippie movement attempted to equate the impulse with that of a religious quest and revival. Such pundits saw the countercultural movement as one of individuals seeking greater ethereal meaning and value in their lives. Like many religious dissenters, the hippies were enormously hostile toward and therefore alienated from the nations' prevailing religious establishments and their traditional orthodox practices and beliefs, whether they were Catholic, Protestant, or Jewish. As Timothy Miller has noted, hippies considered mainstream churches and synagogues to be nothing more than "hoary Establishment" institutions of "self-righteous hypocrisy; wealthy organizations mainly interested in preserving themselves; havens for the narrow-minded and bigoted; anachronisms completely out of touch with modern life." Hippies thus sought outside of the dominant religious culture new and more transcendentally fulfilling ways to connect with God, or nature, or with whomever or whatever they believed could provide them with the soulful sustenance they despaired of finding within most mainstream Christian faiths. As one hip writer proclaimed: "The churches are as flagrant violators of the natural, real religious way, the way of man in harmony with earth, water, sky, and of course, his fellows as any other institution. These supposed houses of worship, where one would hope there might exist something analogous to an institutionalized conscience, are in fact just further examples of sham and hypocrisy. Rather than insist Christians as Christians in the barest sense the word conveys, refrain from supporting the golden calves of our government spawns, its campaigns, its waste, its wars, the church instead functions as a Sunday salve, assuaging the blunted senses of each cowardly congregation, dressed in its best for one more Sunday obligation."[39]

Interestingly most hippies chafed at being labeled as religionists of any stripe. However, outside observers, determined to find an historic niche for them or to ascribe greater significance to their existence, pursued such analyses. Historian Harvey Cox, for example, wrote shortly after the Summer of Love that, "Hippieness represents a secular vision of the historic American quest for a faith that warms the heart, a religion one can experience deeply and feel intensely. The love-ins are our 20th century equivalent of the 19th century Methodist camp meetings—with the same kind of fervor and the same thirst for a God who speaks through emotion and not through anagrams of doctrine. Of course, the Gospel that is preached differs somewhat in content, but then content was never that important for the revivalist—it was the spirit that counted. Hippieness has all the marks of a new religious movement. It has its evangelists, its sacred grottoes, its exuberant converts."[40]

California Episcopal Bishop James Pike seconded Cox's assessment, proclaiming that the hippie movement "represents almost a new kind of church. They have a lot of qualities of the early Christian church. They have no involvement with our society; they don't like it enough to care. They don't protest or demonstrate because they think it is *all* bad." Like the early Christians, whom Pike labeled a "dropout group" because they refused to obey the laws of Rome, the hippies were currently doing the same by rejecting mainstream culture and values. Pike made the stretch that the early church's founder, Jesus of Nazareth, was considered a danger "to the prevailing society and was crucified, so obviously He was a rebel."[41]

The hippies, of course, had no *Christus*, although there were abundant beards and sandals. From beginning to end no one leader emerged to forge the hippie movement. Indeed, for any individual to have attempted to assert such power or claim such status would have been considered an anathema to the majority of hippies, who prided themselves on their egalitarian ethics. Hippie disdain for and distrust of allowing any one individual or group of individuals to lead their movement reflected their larger fear of institutionalizing the counterculture, which many believed would result in "psychedelic fascism." Many hippies believed that if they became "established" they would mutate into their current enemies, with a structured, hierarchy-bound coercive power elite "instructing" seekers on how to be "proper" hippies. Hippie mandates would simply replace those currently provided by the bourgeois capitalists—clearly a self-defeating proposition. Thus, hippies had their gurus and other "advisors," but none of them ever assumed the title of "leader," or "leaders," but rather they referred to themselves as "*foci* of energy" (a Leary term), or as hipster Stewart Brand declared, "We are not directors, only *constellators* of energy," which the general hippie community approved.[42]

Hippie religiosity mixed scraps from a variety of faiths, becoming an intriguing eclectic creed that many hippies readily embraced. As one passionate believer exulted, "Our emerging religion is not borrowed but homegrown—and potentially planetary. Buddhism, Native American religion, various forms of psychotherapy (especially Gestalt and Jungian) Jewish, Christian, and Islamic mysticism, have all poured into and fused into a new brew, alive, nameless, and endlessly mutating." Or as *Time* succinctly declared, "the hippie faith is a weird blend of superstition and spiritualty that spans continents and centuries."[43] If the *raison d'être* of the hip rebellion was to herald "the new epoch" then adherence to old Christian institutions, orthodoxy, and practices had to be discarded along with all the other traditional restraints that had kept people for centuries from realizing their inherent humanity and spirituality. Suffice it to say, few mainstream churches welcomed hippies but the majority of hippies had little interest in joining anyway. The attempts by hippie apologists such as Cox and Pike, and the many others who tried to give meaning to the counterculture ethos were no doubt sincere. However, like their counterparts in the popular music scene, who tried to give deeper significance to rock music stream of consciousness lyrics, they were often merely projecting onto the movement their own familiar frame of reference in order to take the hippie ethos out of the realm of the inchoate and organize it into a recognizable, even admirable pattern of historical legitimacy and thus of socio-cultural importance and value.

Most popular media coverage of the time obsessed on "sex, drugs, and rock and roll," but especially on the first two dynamics, which were covered in the most sweeping and often outrageous assertions. *Newsweek* for example declared that "There are no hippies who believe in chastity, or look askance at marital infidelity or see even marriage as a virtue. Physical love is a delight—to be chewed upon as often and as freely as a handful of sesame seeds."[44] The mainstream media fixated equally on the hippie drug culture, with *Time* proclaiming "in its variety and virulence the hippie pharmacopoeia is the subculture's most valued possession … grass is the staple of hippiedom [and] lysergic acid diethylamide is its caviar." *Newsweek* expanded the "psychedelic smorgasbord" to include all manner of potential "household highs" that hippies could get from banana peels, nutmeg, cloves, glue, and cleaning fluid, in its characterization of hippies as insatiable "kick" fiends. In his coverage for *Life*, reporter Loudon Wainwright focused almost entirely on drugs, asserting that because of their "obsession" with dope, hippies were engaging in "a most disruptive sort of escapism" and a "headlong flight from reality." Because of their inordinate passion for drugs, sex, and rock and roll, and their alleged "professed aim" to subvert "Western society by 'flower power' and force of example," eminent British historian, Arnold Toynbee believed the rise of the counterculture to be "a red warning light for the American way of life." Judson Gooding of *Time* went even further in his foreboding of potential hippie vitiation of American society, equating, ironically, the hippies' "ideology" with that of totalitarianism; a bit of a stretch, to say the least. Nonetheless, Gooding asserted that "The hippies have an instinct for the jugular vein of society. They realize, perhaps from an atavistic consciousness, that if they can isolate the youth of a culture and prevent transfer of its value system from parents to children, they can end the culture. It worked under the Third Reich, and in the Soviet Union. It is presently being tried in Red China." Accordingly, it would be a grave mistake by straight Americans to simply "dismiss the hippies as a bunch of silly kids."[45]

Finally, the consensus among mainstream reporters was that hippies were naïve but sincere followers of a passing craze, a movement that "cannot last." *Newsweek* thus described hippies as "clownish" and "anti-intellectual" while *Time* labeled them as "almost childish" in their behavior and attitude toward life and in their "fascination in beads, blossoms, and bells." Martin Arnold of the *New York Times* believed a handful of activities defined the hippie movement: "LSD, marijuana, nude parties, sex, drawing on walls and sidewalks, not paying their rent, making noise, and rock 'n' roll music." To the urban sociologist and future senator from New York, Daniel Patrick Moynihan, the hippies were "lilies of the field—bearded and sandaled, they live on air and love and alas drugs. They do not seek to change our society, but simply have nothing to do with it. They seek experiences that are wholly mystical and eternal on the one hand and tribal on the other." If such assessments were accurate, then *Newsweek* predicted that the majority of hippies would soon "grow disillusioned, clip their hair, and rejoin the squares." Arnold Toynbee seconded *Newsweek*'s forecast, confident that "The hippie movement in a few years will be absorbed into a wider, more moderate movement. The extreme dress and the beards will have disappeared, and they will be more serious." Toynbee believed that in the end, it will be the hippies' "inactivity" and "maturity" that will cause their eventual demise; that in many ways hippiedom was nothing more than a typical, fanciful youthful moment of indiscretion. "It's very boring after a while not to work. Also, when you are outside society it becomes important to come back in—even on compromise terms. I can't imagine their continuing as hippies into their 40s, ad 50s, and 60s."[46] By superficially focusing on and distorting certain hippie behaviors and attitudes, while simultaneously dismissing the counterculture as nothing more than a momentary socio-cultural aberration of delusional miscreants, the mainstream media propagated and sustained a shallow and stereotypical image of hippies, which the majority of Americans accepted as accurate.

In an interview with the *Haight-Ashbury Maverick*, Psychedelic Shop owner and Be-In promoter Ron Thelin tried to establish a different image of hip, one that had nothing to do with drugs, sex, or rock and roll but rather with the counterculture representing the "budding spiritual consciousness, spiritual state, spiritual awakening" that was emerging in the United States among the nation's youth and "that seems very much at this time in history to be focused in Haight-Ashbury."[47] This was the message intended by the Be-In's organizers; neither in their press conferences or in their printed broadsides did they reference drugs, sex, or rock music. Yet, these were the images of the counterculture propagated by the mainstream mass media in the aftermath of the January Be-In.

Although widely criticized by the counterculture for having taken some "creative liberties" which resulted in some prevarications, Warren Hinckle's May 1967 article, "A Social History of the Hippies," in the leftist journal *Ramparts*, nonetheless contained some very keen observations about the hippie movement and subculture; insights dismissed by the majority of the mainstream media as fanciful and apologetic. Despite his questionable approach, Hinckle's piece provided an accurate, one-paragraph summation of hippie philosophy. "The utopian sentiments of these hippies are not to be put down lightly. Hippies have a clear vision of the ideal community—a psychedelic community to be sure—where everyone is turned on and beautiful and loving and happy and floating free. But it is a vision ... that necessarily embodies a radical political philosophy; communal life; drastic restriction of private property, rejection of violence, creativity before consumption, freedom before authority, de-emphasis of government and traditional forms of leadership." Hinckle's other key assessment was his assertion that the hippies' "profess[ed] distaste for competitive society" disguised a reality in which they were contradictorily frantic consumers.[48] This was an important, inherent paradox that the mainstream media missed about the hippie community: countercultural protests to the contrary, the majority of hippies remained avid middle-class consumers in a variety of ways; the result of a general, white generational affluence and materialism from which they could not fully break free because they were its by-products.

Novelist and adman Earl Shoriss had a similar view, observing that the hippies, after denouncing middle class values, then are free to "indulge in them without guilt" because their declaration served as sufficient proof of their disdain and thus rejection of all things associated with middle class life in 1960s America. For Shoriss the hippies' only "threat" to mainstream culture was the increasing appeal they may have had among other weary suburbanites and general middle class malcontents; a "solidly middle class dream" to escape from the banality and drudgery of everyday life in Middle America. "The preponderance of hippies come from the middle class, because it is there even among adults that the illusion of the hippies' joy, free love, purity, and drug excitement is strongest. A man grown weary of singing company songs at I.B.M. picnics, feeling guilty about the profits he has made on defense stocks, who hasn't really loved his wife for 10 years, must admire, envy, and wish for a life of love and contemplation, a simple life leading to a beatific peace. He soothes his despair with the possibility that the hippies have found the answers to problems he does not dare to face."[49]

By 1967 it seemed the nation was divided into two kinds of citizens: those who embraced the changes taking place, confident that most of them would prove positive in the end and thus at the time tried desperately to understand the "the flower children," or those who simply outright castigated the hippies as slovenly clad, doped-out malingerers; menaces to decent society, to whom work, cleanliness, and responsibility were to be avoided like the plague. Such was the perception of the counterculture held by California Governor Ronald Reagan, who in a 1967 news conference defined a hippie as someone who "dresses like Tarzan, has hair like Jane, and smells like Cheetah." The lack of intellectual depth in Reagan's assessment surprised no one, but many older Americans shared the governor's sentiments. Ironically, the hippie stereotype suggested in Reagan's comments was reinforced by the successful Broadway production *Hair*, "the American tribal love-rock musical" (1968), in which an assortment of male and female hippies sang and danced their way across the stage for two hours to a blaring rock beat, celebrating hippiedom embodied in the saga of a draft dodger as well in acid, oral sex, and peace. The musical opened at New York's Biltmore Theater to rave reviews. The message gleaned by many in the audience was that hippies do absolutely nothing and do it with an inexplicable—surely drug-induced—enthusiasm.[50]

The Be-In's success, magnified by the national media, finally prompted the question: where was this counterculture tending? A few weeks after the famous Be-In, four of the movement's celebrities—Timothy Leary, Allen Ginsburg, Gary Snyder, and Alan Watts—met on Watts' houseboat off Sausalito to exchange their respective utopian visions. The *Oracle*'s staff attended the gathering and tape recorded the entire discussion, eventually publishing "the fascinating party" in one of its later issues. To Watts, the evening's host, the fundamental question was "Whether to drop out or take over?" Plotting the next step proved no easy feat for a counterculture in which eschewing the future and reveling in the moment represented a state of grace. After about an hour of bantering back and forth amongst themselves on the issue, the four gurus finally agreed that it would be better in the long run for humanity for the current harbingers of change, "to throw all our energies into the subculture than to continue to maintain some communication network with the main culture"; in other words to "drop-out, to completely detach yourself from anything inside the plastic, robot, Establishment. We must have *nothing* to do with it. Drop out of school, drop out of college, drop out completely from the fake-prop-television-set American society." Leary was confident that "as soon as enough people do this—young people do this—it will bring about an incredible change in the consciousness of this country, and of the Western World."[51] Even though Leary and company agreed that "taking over" wasn't an option, that dropping out seemed more practical, they also concluded that the idea of the counterculture becoming something was inherently dangerous. They thus spent the rest of the "summit" offering their respective prognostications and forecasts about the counterculture's future without clear *directions* the movement should take.

Alan Watts then summed the predicament of the West: technological man had lost contact with himself and nature. Yet, Leary maintained, man need not despair because fortunately automation had progressed to such a level of sophistication that if used wisely, humanely, it could liberate man from work and enable him to live a simpler life, which of course to all four individuals, meant a return to a tribal, pastoral existence; to what Watts referred to as "going back to making arrowheads and to raising the most AMAZING PLANTS." Indeed, Snyder believed that as more and more people (especially "technologists and scientists") used "psychedelics" they would "become more interested in states of mind rather than things" and thus would want to use their knowledge to improve the quality rather than quantity of human existence. Technology would become so advanced that dropouts from megalopolis would form tribes and move back to the land. Snyder wanted to turn Chicago into a center for cybernetic technology and the rest of the country into buffalo pasture. However, as people "got so good" at making their own necessities and growing their own food, as life got simpler, "Chicago would rust away," and man's destruction of his natural environment would cease.[52]

Equally essential to the utopian vision was a change in the nuclear family structure, which all four men agreed would eventually give way to communes or tribes of extended families whose members would share food, work, and sex. Indeed, all forms of marriage would be accepted—group, polyandrous, polygamous, and monogamous. To Watts such a social arrangement relative to families was not only essential for tribal survival and procreation but also its natural state "because the family is an agrarian institution, which is not suited to an urban culture." In Watts' view, if the family concept was going to survive, it was imperative that it become "extended because the present model [nuclear] of the family is a hopeless breakdown. All the family consists in a dormitory where a wife and children are located, and the husband, who engages in a mysterious activity in an office or factory, in which neither the wife nor the children have any part or interest, from which he brings home an abstraction called money." To Snyder, the blueprint for such a drastic change in familial structure and associations, as well as living simply but bountifully and wholesomely off the land, was established centuries ago by the Native Americans, and thus all that was presently needed to begin the "new consciousness" was to embrace "their way of being." Already in Big Sur, Snyder continued, kids were using A.L. Kroeber's *Handbook of the California Indians* to learn the art of primitive survival, to learn how to be Indians. According to Snyder, "they're getting very sharp about what to gather that's edible, how to get sea salt, what are the edible plants and seeds. Kroeber tells you what's good to eat and how to prepare it. And also what to use for tampax: milkweed fluff and shredded bark for diapers. The whole thing is all there. It's beautiful man." Fine, countered Allen Ginsberg, who had become the Haight's most authentic voice, "but where are the people going to buy their Uher tape recording machines?" which were being used to record "the rap session."[53]

The "Houseboat Summit" revealed the counterculture's presentist, anti-ideological, and anti-materialist orientation. Hippies lived in a real world but their ideal remained a disavowal of the crass materialism that they believed had consumed middle class America by the late 1960s. Hippies were to lead the nation toward a new socio-economic order that, according to Jerry Rubin, would "free [people] from property hang-ups, free them from success fixations, from positions, titles, names, hierarchies, responsibilities, schedules, rules, routines, regular habits."[54] The hippie ethos that appeared to be evolving by 1967 opposed defining the human experience by conventional bourgeois precepts: causation and resolution; success or failure, present and future; being and becoming, or of even asking the question "where is the counterculture tending?" As Allen Ginsberg announced, "No one knows where it will go until its gets there."[55] The counterculture vision was to live in and of the moment; all other concerns were the irrelevant and anachronistic shackles of a dying culture. As Kenneth Keniston observed, the counterculture sought "new values *for living*, values that will fill the spiritual emptiness created by material affluence."[56] To straight Americans, especially among those of the working class, hippie anti-materialism and general disregard for money, work, and responsibilities; "success fixations," reflected the self-serving, naïve, and even self-righteous posturing of social privilege. Those hippies who talked the most about eschewing money and consumerism could literally afford to do so, because most of them came from affluent suburban middle class homes, and thus they had little awareness of the grinding reality of real deprivation. Blue collar or poor families could rest assured that few of their children would ever become hippies.

As reflected in the Houseboat Summit dialogue, the Native American way of life was a major cultural fount for hippies seeking to craft a tribal identity. They thus historically became yet another group within a long American tradition of whites "playing Indians." The hippies' embracing of American Indian culture was not a new dynamic within the nation's bohemian traditions. Indeed, throughout American countercultural history, attempted identification with and exaltation of one "noble savage" type or another became part and parcel of that particular bohemian impulse. For many 19th century Romantics, for example, it was the gypsy; for the Beats it was the black hipster, embodied especially in the bebop jazz musician. However, by the mid–1960s with the emergence of black power and black pride in the civil rights movement, African Americans were unwilling to serve as identity crutches for white people. The "holy primitives" for hippies thus became the American Indians and the Hells Angels.[57]

Those hippies who "went native" hoped to erase their identities as white middle-class Americans altogether; to repudiate a chauvinistic and violent American nationalism and imperialism responsible not only for the current Vietnam War but also for policies that had brutally subjugated Native Americans. To play Indian was "to become vicariously a victim of" United States aggression. However, this experiment in appropriation brought to the surface the racial tensions, stereotypes, and contradictions within the overwhelmingly white hippie movement.[58] Hippies embraced the authenticity of exotic cultures in attempts to find historical validation for their own quest for identity. Unfortunately in their enthusiasm to associate their movement with other groups, their approach was too frequently superficial, with little understanding of the true meaning of the appropriated symbols. The majority of Indiophile hippies merely played at being Indians, believing that they were honoring Native Americans by wearing their jewelry and clothing and by writing and speaking knowingly of their history and culture. Hippie publications were replete with homage to American Indians, whom the hippies believed would not only instruct them in how to live as a tribal people but would embrace them as well for wanting to emulate Native American ways. The *Oracle* published an exclusively "American Indian Issue" in the spring of 1967 featuring stories, art, poems, and discussions of all things "Indian." The paper's intent was to show the close associations and alleged mutual affinity both "tribes" had for one another through articles on treaties, Native use of sacred herbs, living with the land, and the tribal way of life.[59] Ironically, the mainstream media mirrored this approach in their cursory dismissal of the hippies, or perhaps more meaningful, the way in which the increasing number of Haight newcomers, the "teenyboppers" and "plastic hippies" (who the *real hippies* despised), only "played" at being "a hippie." Both hippie and pseudo-hippie substituted form for content, embracing the exotic and romantic versions of their idealized heroes in their search for an alternative identity as they struggled to find an authenticity and humanism they believed was woefully nonexistent in American mainstream culture and society.

American Indian culture provided hippies with a plethora of symbols, practices, and beliefs, ripe for counterculture appropriation. For example, the tribal nature of the Native American family presented hippies with an alternative model to the "white man's" concept of the nuclear family. Thus, the hippie reference to their community as a group of "tribes"; the Be-In had been advertised as a "Pow Wow" and "A Gathering of the Tribes," while posters promoting the event featured an Indian on horseback with an electric guitar. Native American costume was especially popular with hippies, as headbands, fringes, feathers, and moccasins became de rigueur attire among hippies because such clothing and accessories were considered to be more natural than commercial fashions. While many hippies earnestly appropriated aboriginal culture in an attempt to establish an alternative lifestyle to the technocratic culture of Cold War America, their actual knowledge of Indian life was rudimentary at best and more often illusory and delusional. For example communards in the Pacific Northwest built tepees for their homes because 1950s (and even through the 1960s) "cowboy and Indian" television shows and movies invariably depicted *all* Native Americans as Plains Indians, hunting buffalo and from the hides, making their dwellings, tepees. Tepees were completely unsuitable for the wet, Pacific Northwest weather. A hippie tribe called the New Buffaloes, called their cornbean-squash cultivation a "Navajo diet," which, in fact, the Pueblos had actually implemented. The real Navajo initially were neither hunters or farmers but rather raiders and traders for sustenance and later on turned to sheep and goat herding for survival.[60]

San Francisco Chronicle columnist Charles McCabe, known for his tongue-in-cheek satire, especially when it came to social issues or causes, believed the entire "Hip Revolution" was the "direct result of western movies and television programs" and because the majority of hippies grew up glued to the tube, they came to identify "with screen-heroes," which was not "only easy but encouraged for commercial purpose." "The western plot was at its popularity peak" during the hippies' formative years (the 1950s), and thus it was no surprise to McCabe that the hippies would be informed by such presentations of the Wild West and would find Indians rather the cowboys more appealing, especially since their "happiest, carefree moments were spent in tree tops and bushes, and grubbing in the dirt, the nature-worshipping Indians were natural objects of sympathy." Moreover, "They had no money, put-ting them on an economic par with the hippies, and [like the hippies], they obviously weren't worried about trivialities like bathing and tooth-brushing." The inevitable result of such media-shaping "was an Indian tribe of our very own, complete with feathers, beads, sacred plants, tribal customs and dances, and a religious fervor for independence." However silly or ridiculous the hippies appeared to McCabe, he, like many other pundits, believed them to be no cause for alarm as they would fade away, sadly much like the Native Americans. "This tribe inhabiting the Haight-Ashbury reservation poses as much threat to the established soci-ety as the extinct California coastal tribes whose territory we took over."[61]

Hippies found especially appealing the Navaho and Hopi, perhaps because they were two of the largest groups of indigenous people still alive and concentrated on fairly large reservations in Arizona and thus accessible to hippie sojourns. Adding to hippie attraction to Native American culture was the fact that both the Hopi and Navaho frequently used peyote or other natural hallucinogens to enhance their respective religious rituals or spiritual quests. As one Haight resident declared, "One of the reasons hippies are so fond of Indians is that acid [LSD] dissolves our European conditioning & turns us into temporary Indians. Unskilled, inexperienced, & untrained Indians, to be sure, but genuine Indians all the same, with fully functioning sensoria."[62]

The *Oracle*'s Ron Thelin perhaps best captured the hippies' affinity for and veneration of American Indian culture and the hippie desire to live accordingly. "Right here on our own continent we have a spiritual people, the Hopi, who I think are the spiritual heads of this continent, who know a way of life that is peaceful. And as a model of life we can learn from the Indians. We can learn a model of the way of life that is based on the tribal sense of family organization, of social organization, of how to survive off the land, how to make our own clothes, grow our own food, and how to live as a tribal unit. They have been doing all that for thousands of years and we can learn a lot from them and they will welcome us as brothers and sisters in the same journey back to being one with nature."[63]

While many hippies became symbolic Indians, they remained largely disassociated from Indian people. Hippies searched the reservations for affinity and inspiration, but their encoun-ters rarely went well as the majority of the Native Americans hippies tried to befriend grew impatient and ultimately dismissive of the flaky counterculture seekers who showed up on their reservations to learn native ways. Most hippies simply did not have the attention span or commitment to learn about Indian folkways. In the end, most hippies were content to "play Indian" by embracing the symbolic life of tepees and buckskins; to truly go Native required a mindset and physical toughness few hippies possessed, coming as the majority did from rather pampered "tribes" and protected suburban "lodges and villages." Nonetheless, hippies consumed the Indian identity indiscriminately, often insulting and angering Native American communities in the process.[64]

Much to the hippies' chagrin, the majority of Native American tribes despised the Love Generation and consequently wanted no affiliation with them in any capacity. In the spring of 1967, Allen Ginsberg and Richard Alpert wanted to meet Hopi leaders in Santa Fe, hoping the tribe would agree to help them sponsor a Be-In in the Grand Canyon. Much to the two guru's embarrassment, the tribal spokesman dismissed them out of hand, telling them "No, because you mean well but you are foolish. You are a tribe of strangers to yourselves." Causing Indian outrage was the hippies' sexual impropriety and sacrilegious behavior: they blithely and carelessly removed sacred tribal masks from their hallowed places, allowing uninitiated native children to play with them, to whom they also gave gifts of marijuana and LSD; pranced around naked, and engaged in outdoor, highly visible sex, which they believed was one of the Indians' "natural' practices." Several of the masks were later discovered missing.[65]

Even more disparaging in his assessment of the hippies while simultaneously upset with the mainstream media for associating hippies with Native Americans, was Rupert Costo, chief of the California Cahuilla Band, and president of the American Indian Historical Society. In a letter to both the San Francisco *Chronicle* and *Examiner*, Costo not only made it clear that "The way of the hippie is completely at variance to that of the Indian," but also that he and the majority of Native Americans believed the hippies were "the most corrupting influence in American life today." Particularly disturbing to Costo was a recent column in the *Chronicle* that began with "Hippies are American Indians," declaring that the hippies were the reincarnated children of "all those Redskins who were murdered" by American imperialism. The article ended by asking readers that when you greet a hippie, "Do you say 'Ugh! How! Pow! Or Wow!?'" Costo rightly condemned the article as "disgusting and demeaning," believing it portrayed both Indians and hippies as "bums," which Costo asserted Native Americans "are not now, nor were in the beginning—Bums." In Costo's view, the hippies were indeed "Bums" and to have white people believe that the hippies were even remotely similar to Native Americans was "a shameful insult to the Native American way of life." As Costo pointed out, "Indian life, even in aboriginal times, was highly ordered. Everyone worked. To beg is the greatest sin a man can be guilty of. To use drugs in order to induce hallucinatory experiences for their own sake is a crime against God, and foreign to our religions." Costo concluded his letter by unequivocally disassociating Native Americans from the hippies, believing them to "exemplify fraud and hypocrisy" and to have "completely corrupted the meaning of American Indian culture and history." As both Indian leaders made clear, if not strangers to one another, the hippies of Haight-Ashbury were hardly a tribe, especially not one in the Native American tradition.[66]

Soon after the Hopi incident, the Diggers took Haight hippies to task for being so "hungry for rituals and tribal touch" because they "lack[ed] elders to initiate you into the magic of yourselves. You are starving!" To the Diggers hippie Indiophiles had become "romantically Indian struck!" and were suffering from "Anglo Entertainment Syndrome. *Who the fuck are you anyway?* Sitting there in lotus, chanting Anglo Super-Culture Prostitution of Hari Krishna to uninitiated children?" The Diggers condemned the hippies for "looking into another man's world" and for "consuming someone else" in order to find themselves.[67]

With everyone wanting a piece of the sensationalized hippie pie, Hollywood quickly joined the print media and jumped on the hippie popularity parade as well, releasing in late 1966 (December) a 90 minute, disjointed, horribly directed, atrociously acted, gory, drug-infused film, *Hallucination Generation*. The picture's claim to fame: the first LSD movie, in which the acid trips were filmed in color—red, blue, and orange—while the rest of the movie's scenes were in black and white. The film was the brainchild of two enterprising producers, Nigel Fox and Edward Mann, who, like everyone else at that moment, wanted to exploit for money, the public's increasing fascination with the hippie scene, especially the drug culture that seemed to define much of the hippie lifestyle. Legendary B-movie producer/director Roger Corman followed suit with an equally bizarre LSD film, *The Trip* (American International, 1967), starring Peter Fonda and Dennis Hopper, and written by Jack Nicholson (all three would later collaborate and star in the counterculture classic, *Easy Rider*), which, was a bit more tasteful and sophisticated than *Hallucination Generation*, but nonetheless focused on LSD's transformative Jekyll and Hyde effects on an individual, from euphoria to despair, to in the end, a broken person, psychologically, emotionally, and physically. Of course throughout the movie there was plenty of wild sex, rock music, and weird psychedelic scenes.[68]

Perhaps the most mercenary and shameless example of the early commercialization of hippiedom was the Grey Line Company's offering of bus tours of the Haight-Ashbury neighborhood. As the mass-media blitz of the Haight-Ashbury intensified in the months after the Be-In, tourists, captivated by the mainstream media's images of exotic and colorful characters with strange rituals, began gravitating to the Haight for snapshots and souvenirs of this ephemeral phenomenon before it disappeared. By early May, twice a day the company's buses journeyed out to the Haight from the downtown hotels, filled with visitors from all over the world. Indeed, it seemed foreigners knew more about Haight-Ashbury than they did about San Francisco. Even within the United States, more people knew the Haight-Ashbury was in California than knew the location of San Francisco. At six bucks a head, the tour was known as the "Hippie Hop" and was advertised as "a safari through Psychedelphia [the most recent name for the Haight coined by the *San Francisco Chronicle*], and the only foreign tour within the continental limits of the United States." Upon entering the Haight-Ashbury district, the token hippie tour guides would exclaim: "When someone creates a thing of beauty—an Eiffel Tower, a great painting, the public comes to it. We hippies have created something beauti-

What the tourists wanted to see: hippies hanging out and doing their "thing," which allegedly was nothing! Photograph taken in 1967 (courtesy San Francisco History Center, San Francisco Public Library).

ful—it's natural that the public comes to it." As the bus approached the Haight and throughout the "adventure ride" through the neighborhood, the tour guides would explain to tourists what they were about to see, as if they were on the Jungle Ride at Disneyland. Indeed, one of the more popular terms for the Haight was "Hippieland," an evocation of Disneyland and thus prompting the Haight's emergence as a tourist destination. "We are now passing down Haight Street, the very nerve center of a city within a city, the largest hippie colony in the world. Marijuana, of course, is a household staple here, enjoyed by the natives to stimulate their senses. Among the favorite pastimes of the Hippies, besides taking drugs, are parading and demonstrating, seminars and group discussions about what's wrong with the status quo; malingering; plus the ever-present preoccupation with the soul, reality, and self-expression, such as strumming guitars, piping flutes and banging on bongo drums."[69] For the mainstream media nothing proved better for capturing readers or viewers than transforming excess into parody. Similarly, nothing proved more profitable for savvy business enterprises than taking the aberrant and merchandizing it. Media obsession with the Haight and its hippie community turned both entities into spectacular commodities; exciting curios and "exotic" people to be "fascinated" by much in the same way Americans, Westerners in general, read about the strange lands and people in an issue of *National Geographic*. Suffice it to say, hippies resented such stereotyping, which had transformed their neighborhood into a "zoo" where the tourists gawked at the residents "like animals, not individuals."[70] Fortunately neighborhood pressure forced the Grey Line Company to cancel the tour after only two months operation. However, by the time the company ended its hippie sojourn, popular demand "to see the hippies" had become so great, that Grey Line had begun offering two trips a day to the Haight. The company of course cited traffic congestion as the main reason for pulling out rather than the hippies' relentless public campaign to maintain their neighborhood's integrity, which, sadly, was fast succumbing to the vagaries of commercialization and population inundation.[71]

As the numbers of newcomers to the Haight escalated in the months after the Be-In, older residents as well as the H.I.P. merchants worried that the continued onslaught would create tension and possible confrontations with the police. In March 1967, a delegation of H.I.P. business people and artists met with Police Chief Tom Cahill to reassure the chief that they wanted to have peaceful, cordial relations with the area's police and that they planned to speak with Allen Ginsberg to come up with some sort of warning signals to their fellow hipsters when a police altercation seemed imminent. They told Cahill that Ginsberg had devised a *mantra* (chant) and a *mudra* (finger symbol) for such purposes. Apparently Cahill was impressed by his visitors' sincerity, expressing a willingness to work with the Haight's residents and businesses to help keep the peace. At the close of the meeting, Cahill shocked the delegation by his query, "You're sort of the Love Generation, aren't you?" The hippies, who had been searching for a name to give their alternative society and culture, readily embraced Cahill's designation. They had previously been thinking of calling themselves the "New Community" but Cahill's ascription was universally applicable to all seekers of their generation.[72] That a police chief, and one who sadly would unleash brute force on the hippies only a few months later, would come up with the perfect name for the 1960s counterculture was one of the great cosmic ironies of the decade.

The Haight's original hippie founders developed a cautious, if not wary, but generally positive relationship with both their still-majority straight residents as well as with city officials and the police. They accomplished this interesting rapprochement by simply being themselves and doing what they did best: peacefully coexisting with their neighbors while daily displaying in action and deed, that their new ethos—as antithetical as it was perceived to be by 1960s bourgeois culture—was dedicated to the common good. Thus the peculiar characters who wandered the streets dressed in Victorian garb or flowing robes, carrying incense and flowers, while hawking drugs, playing flutes, chanting Hindu scripture or marching in bizarre psychedelic parades, was mitigated by the original hippies' general joie de vivre, optimism, and sincere commitment to the realization of their ideals and devotion to their neighborhood and community; to establishing the Haight-Ashbury as the epicenter for the new consciousness rising throughout the land among the nation's youth.

Thanks in large part to the media attention on the hippies, by late spring 1967 it became certain that come summer, when school let out, the Haight would be buried in a tidal wave of adolescents, coming to the neighborhood to witness first-hand the hippie phenomenon or to immerse themselves completely in the hippie scene. As one hip resident observed, "Every day you saw scores of people, maybe hundreds of people showing up, just gaping that this was the great place. And this was where they were going to be. Everybody was talking this love, peace; you know racism was supposed to be really unhip. It was just for a little short time, but it was really just like something that shimmered."[73] The anticipated migration soon had its own theme song, performed by Scott McKenzie but written by John Phillips of the Mamas and Papas, "San Francisco (Be Sure to Wear Some Flowers in Your Hair)." "San Francisco" was a million-seller in the U.S., reaching number 4 on Billboard's Top 100 by mid-summer 1967. Many boomers still feel a rush of fond nostalgia for the 1960s and conjure images of the Haight's emblematic "flower children" the moment they hear the song's wispy tinkle of the chimes and the soft acoustic guitar strumming. Indeed the song is indelibly etched forever on many boomer memory banks as *the tune* that defined the Haight-Ashbury and the Summer of Love experience.

The song's national popularity reflected the deluge of young humanity about to descend on San Francisco. Interestingly at the time, both Phillips and the Mamas and Pappas producer/manager Lou Adler, saw the siren song only as a potential money-maker, admitting later that they had little in common with the Haight-Ashbury bands, let alone with the community. "We were the total opposite of Haight-Ashbury. We were Bel Air, we were slick." Indeed, the song's simple structure, anthemic lyrics, and sing-along feel were deliberately contrived by Adler and Phillips to sell a soft-edged, aural snippet of San Francisco's burgeoning hippie culture to an apprehensive straight America. It worked; the song became a symbolic introduction to the nationalized Summer of Love. Grateful Dead manager Rock Scully could not have agreed more with the Angelenos' confession. "'Put a flower in your hair.' It didn't say 'Bring a blanket and some money; tell your parents where you're going. There were no redeeming features to that song.'"[74] Other songs, such as Donovan's "The Fat Angel," told young people to fly "Translove Airways," and "Jefferson Airplane" to arrive for the Summer of Love. Eric Burdon and the Animals produced an equally alluring but syrupy paean to the city in their hit single (the song reached number 9 on the U.S. pop charts), "Warm San Francisco Nights," exhorting their fellow Brits and other Europeans to fly to the city.

The hip merchants, the Diggers, community elders, and city authorities took precautions. The Diggers promised to provide food, information, shelter, and medical services to the expected throngs of humanity. The Haight's community leaders organized the Council for the Summer of Love to provide park concerts and other distractions for the arrivals. The San Francisco State College administration expanded its summer Community Works Program (an offshoot of the Great Society's Community Action Program or CAP) to take in the Haight, and everyone, from the mayor's office to the San Francisco Board of Supervisors, to Hashbury's original denizens, issued warnings about the dangers of big-city life. In May, Mayor John Shelley issued a proclamation, endorsed by the Board of Supervisors, advising hippies to stay away from the city. Police Chief Tom Cahill was even more direct in his message: Stay home or face "possible arrest and even injury. Law, order, and health regulations [will] prevail."[75] Nothing helped; already thousands of young people from across the nation had come to the Haight in search of the hedonistic abandon promised by the media, and thousands more would soon arrive and overwhelm the neighborhood during The Summer of Love.

7

Hippies Elsewhere

"Kick Out the Jams, Motherfuckers!"—The MC5

The Haight was not the only hippie community in existence by 1967. Across the Bay in Berkeley, near the University of California flagship campus, hippies established themselves along Telegraph Avenue and in many of the side streets off that particular main drag. In Los Angeles, hippies found an inviting sanctuary in the Sunset Strip neighborhood, but more appealing were neighborhoods in West Hollywood along Fairfax Avenue, Venice Beach, Topagana Canyon in the Santa Monica Mountains, and Laguna Beach. Unlike their northern California sisters and brothers, southern California hippies geographically had no fixed center, and, according to *Time*, were a much more amorphous polyglot of humanity "wedged in between the happy never-never land of the teeny-bopper and the dark kingdom of the old beats." Regardless of background, they were, in the *Time* correspondent's view, "a shifting and often shiftless lot," no different in look, mentality, and behavior than their Bay Area counterparts, driving psychedelic-painted Volkswagen buses out of which popped the same weirdly dressed, long-haired "barefoot men women," followed by lots of children and dogs. "They are typical of many of the new dropouts, the unarmed shock troops of flower power who are tuning in and turning on in a thousand guerrilla bases in the low rent areas across the country." Southern California hippie girls especially impressed the *Time* reporter, particularly those who came from outside the Golden State. "Time was when bright young blondes in Grand Rapids [Michigan] went out to California to get on the screen. Now they go there to get on acid. They still talk of love, but not love defined by Hollywood. Often their ambition is to drop out, not to succeed. The man they often seek is a bearded pothead in a tattered poncho, not an executive dreamboat in a convertible or a football hero aglow with aftershave." No doubt there was much truth to the correspondent's assessment of "So-Cal" hippies, yet as witnessed in the Haight and elsewhere, there were equal parts denigration, generalizing, and stereotyping.[1]

In Seattle, hippies congregated in the University District adjacent to the University of Washington; in "BossTown" (Boston) hippies set up housekeeping in Cambridge near Harvard and the Roxbury area; in Atlanta, in the neighborhoods surrounding present-day Georgia State University, and later many hippies migrated to Peach Tree Street and the Buckhead area, establishing communities there before those vicinities became gentrified, chic, and expensive.[2] In virtually every major American city there existed by 1967–68 a burgeoning hippie community. Although San Francisco and the Haight-Ashbury will forever reign supreme as hippiedom's first, and most idealized mecca during hip's heyday, there were other notable hippie enclaves. Outside of the Haight, perhaps one of the most interesting and unique hippie communities existed in Detroit, where the hulky poet-musician-activist John Sinclair almost single-handedly created the hippie movement.

Like many of his older countercultural compatriots, Sinclair had lived the Beat life before transitioning to hippie. Even before moving to the Motor City, Sinclair had become captivated by the Beat lifestyle, becoming a hardcore fan of bebop jazz as expressed by John Coltrane, and of Beat poetry, most notably the works of Allen Ginsberg, Lawrence Ferlinghetti, and Gregory Corso. He also discovered marijuana, which Sinclair believed "heightened his aware- ness" of the larger world around him and stimulated his creativity. Like his Beat compatriots, Sinclair embraced the urban African American hipster/bebop jazz culture. By the time he was a teenager, Sinclair believed he had become Norman Mailer's "White Negro in the pure sense. By the time that [essay] came out, I was on the streets, I was hangin' in the barbershops, in the pool rooms, coffee houses listening to cool jazz. I was doing it."[3]

Typical of the majority of Beat communities throughout the country, Detroit hipsters displayed the same isolationist mentality and disdain for the larger straight society. As Sinclair recalled, "Jazz, it's all we did. We used to sit around and smoke dope, listen to jazz, rap, smoke cigarettes, drink coffee, then more dope and rap some more about how bad the square life was and how cool we were."[4] Typical of most Beat enclaves was an elitism and chauvinism that drew a very fine line on who was "cool" or "hip" enough to be invited to participate in their creation of a new cultural existence; the idea of galvanizing the masses of American youth for a cultural insurrection was antithetical to the Beat credo, such as it was. But in Feb- ruary 1966 (while Sinclair was sitting in the Detroit House of Corrections, convicted of second-offense marijuana possession), the Detroit hip scene began to dramatically change, as a number of core members left the city for a variety of reasons while others moved to San Francisco where "it was all happening." Sinclair was upset by this exodus, believing that it was imperative for his compatriots to stay in the Motor City because he was certain that they could create in Detroit another Haight-Ashbury. Writing from prison, Sinclair exhorted his comrades not to leave. "You have it in your power now to create a vital living situation here in Detroit—if you have the will and commitment to such a situation. We are all going to have to start working with each other and take advantage of what our local possibilities are." Upon his release Sinclair put his words to action, bringing together all of Detroit's disparate coun- tercultural groups—students, "old" Beats, and all the other bohemian, avant-garde factions that were out there—into a hip consortium he called Trans Love Energies (TLE). The TLE was developed "on a real human basis. You'd meet someone who turned out to be a hell of a trumpet player, and you'd have a joint and you'd become friends and they they'd bring a friend and so on. It was an organic process," that could not happen today because "now we just sit around and watch 'American Idol' and we don't need any fucking poems."[5] Sinclair got the name for his organization from a line in a song ("The Fat Angel") by the Scottish folk-rock artist Donovan, who, sang about the wonders of the Haight-Ashbury dope scene, urging listeners to "Fly Translove Airways, to get you there [the Haight] on time."[6]

By 1967, two simultaneous phenomena greatly helped Sinclair's efforts to establish Detroit as the Midwest's hippie mecca: the arrival of LSD and the increasing numbers of Wayne State students embracing the hippie ethos, as they bonded with the older beatniks in a mutual, passionate taste for acid. For both groups, but especially for the beatniks, LSD proved transformative, for the drug ended Beat cynicism and pessimism that the country's alleged cultural stagnation was immutable. As Sinclair explained: "When beatniks started taking acid, it brought us out of the basement; the fringes of society—and just blew us apart; from being cynical and wanting to isolate yourself from the squares. One was suddenly filled with a messianic feeling of love and brotherhood. LSD made you realize that you had ties with the rest of humanity."[7] Beat detachment and elitism quickly disappeared as Beat and hippie embraced each other as fellow acid-heads in pursuit of the common goal of creating a self-sustaining, alternative econo-culture independent of mainstream Detroit society.

TLE's most significant mediums of cultural expression were rock and roll music and the underground press. By early 1967 Sinclair was writing regularly on a variety of topics for Peter Werbe, editor of the *Fifth Estate*, Detroit's hip community's underground newspaper. One of Sinclair's and Werbe's main objectives was to try to unite all of the nation's burgeoning *sub-rosa* publications into a national information acquisition and distribution system, which eventually emerged in mid–1966, when five papers—the *Los Angeles Free Press*, the *East Village Other*, the *Berkeley Barb*, East Lansing, Michigan's *The Paper*, and the *Fifth Estate*—formed the Underground Press Syndicate, or the UPS. As a result of the UPS's formation, the number of subterranean papers proliferated (80 by June 1967 when the consortium held its first national conference in Iowa City), disseminating a variety of countercultural news stories, political commentary, literary criticism, and cartoons, most of which lampooned political and socio-cultural convention. Most important, a wealth of material was available to even the most modest start-up paper.[8]

To Thorne Dreyer and the other progenitors of the underground press, the new journalism was "born of necessity" as a medium through which the counterculture could be "visible" and relate to readers "the strange breeze of discovery [that] was sweeping through the land, carrying with it the pungent odors of pot and cum. Kids began to smoke, fuck, to discover their heads and their bodies, and most important, their lack of freedom. These two states of mind demanded expression." Dreyer believed that the young people who joined the counterculture "weren't just indulgent hedonistic middle class mutants seeking inner peace," but rather a much more aware and politically savvy group "that named the institutions of the state the enemy" and "acted on that analysis" by joining the counterculture as a means of mass protest and rejection of the status quo. They needed a forum for their causes and thus the emergence of the underground press, which gave voice to the "kinds of changes kids were going through. The papers were merely extensions of the hip communities [and] mirrored these changes."[9]

The hippies fascinated the mainstream media but rarely did conventional reporters take the hippies seriously enough to provide them with much space to express their ethos, let alone fair treatment or even much balanced coverage of their existence, which was the main focus of the underground journals. Most Americans considered the underground papers to be "smut sheets," "Molotov cocktails thrown at respectability and decency in our nation.... These papers encourage depravity and irresponsibility, and they nurture a breakdown in the continued capacity of the government to conduct an orderly and constitutional society.... They [the publishers] know that the more obscene and dirty their newspapers are, the more they will attract the irresponsible readers whom they want to enlist in their crusade to destroy this country."[10] Such screeds by right-wing individuals such as Texas congressmen Joe Pool only further emboldened the UPS and the later Liberation News Service to continue publishing their "subversive" papers, many of which continued to move even further left.

According to Thorne Dreyer and Victoria Smith, the underground press had "evolved from the sweetness and light of its early days" to become by 1968 "culturally outrageous and politically revolutionary. It has produced anger and fear among those whose interests it opposes.... [They have become] fairly sophisticated and attractive tabloids, beginning to develop a synthesis of the cultural and political aspects of making a revolution in this country."[11] Right-wing attacks also pushed UPS and LNS to become "consciously subjective" in their reporting and articles, as well as churning out stories that were "rooted in personal experience." Dreyer proudly admitted that "objectivity [was] a farce," as far as he was concerned, a mainstream media contrivance of meaningless, vapid pap journalism, and that by contrast the underground papers made no pretense about their biases; they were "upfront" and unequivocal in their positions on the decade's key issues affecting young Americans such as the Vietnam War and the countercultural revolution. Although a few years later Dreyer would "confess" that UPS was organized "to create the illusion of a giant coordinated network of freaky papers poised for the kill,"[12] the underground press was no "illusion"; the papers played a vital and dynamic role in the 1960s cultural insurrection. As a result of these connections, Sinclair and Werbe were able to establish the *Fifth Estate* as one of the underground press' best informed and most extensive in its coverage and propagation of not only the hippie scene and ethos, but of the New Left, Black power, and other countercultural movements and trends as well.[13]

Sinclair's other major contribution to Detroit's hip community was his promotion of the city's burgeoning rock and roll scene by sponsoring through Trans-Love Energies a local band, the Motor City Five, or the MC5. The alliance between the band and TLE occurred in 1967. By that time, thanks in large part to Sinclair's exhortations and leadership, a legitimate hippie community had emerged not only around the Wayne State University campus, but in a specific neighborhood, which, to the chagrin of its developers, became something quite different from what they had originally envisioned. The majority of this younger, hip crowd moving into the University and Plum Street neighborhoods, were as fanatical about rock and roll as Sinclair had been about jazz, and Sinclair seized the opportunity to expand TLE's youth appeal by adding to the TLE fold the popular local rock band, MC5.[14]

Sinclair's affiliation with MC5 members Rob Tyner, Fred Smith, Wayne Kramer, Dennis Thompson, and Michael Davis began in 1966 when Sinclair allowed the band to use one of TLE's houses as a free rehearsal place. All five were teenagers fresh out of high school and hailed from the blue-collar Detroit suburb of Lincoln Park. Over the next two years, the MC5 would develop a distinctive hard-driving rock and roll sound, which many rock historians and music critics have contended was the precursor of the punk and heavy metal rock genres of the late 1970s and early 1980s. By mid–1967 the MC5 had generated a substantial local following and in early 1968, the band cuts its first 45 rpm single, comprising two original songs, "Borderline" (Side A), and "Looking at You" (Side B), produced by Sinclair's Trans Love Energies. Local rock and roll stations gave both songs significant playing time and as a result the first pressing sold out in a few weeks, and by year's end had gone through more pressings totaling several thousand copies, all sold to the band's growing Detroit fan base. Contemporary rock writer Robert Bixby declared that the MC5's sound was like "a catastrophic force of nature the band was barely able to control. Their music is as exhilarating as it is exhausting." Another critic noted that fans compared the aftermath of an MC5 perform-ance to the delirious exhaustion experienced after "a street rumble or an orgy. The band com-bines the kinetic flash of James Brown on acid with the raw musical dynamics of the Who gone berserk." In rock music pundit Jason Ankeny's view, more than any other hippie band of the era, the MC5, "celebrated" more raucously and with an "in-your-face" provocation and physical presence, "the holy trinity of sex, drugs, and rock & roll, with "their incendiary live sets offering a defiantly bacchanalian counterpoint to the peace-and-love reveries of their hippie contemporaries."[15]

Not only did Sinclair realize the MC5's hip potential, but so did the band, who, were equally attracted to Sinclair's vision. As lead guitarist Wayne Kramer later admitted, "Being the young hustlers we were, we started to see that this hippie thing was gonna go, man. So we figured the way to get the hippies to like us was to get the chief hippie to like us, who was John Sinclair." To the MC5 Sinclair became the linchpin in their desire for fame and fortune. The burly hippie was the most respected and widely known individual within the Motor City's counterculture community with invaluable hip connections in a variety of venues. According to Kramer, Sinclair "took our experience and articulated and defined it so it became something political."[16] Indeed, the MC5 was precisely the "revolutionary force" Sinclair had been search-ing for, certain by 1968 that rock and roll music was the ideal medium to turn on large numbers of young people to the possibility for change. When Sinclair offered to manage the group, the band accepted immediately. The extent of Sinclair's influence within the hip community became readily apparent to the MC5 with the 1968 opening of the Grande Ballroom, a large Detroit rock and roll dance hall modeled after the legendary Fillmore West in San Francisco. Thanks to Sinclair, who had befriended the club's hip capitalist owner, Russ Gibb, the MC5 became the Grande's house band, assuring the group weekly exposure headlining for the top British and American touring acts of the day. Indeed, so popular had the band become in the Detroit area, that audiences regularly demanded multiple encores, even when the featured bands were such legendary acid rock groups as Big Brother and the Holding Company with Janis Joplin or Cream, with Eric Clapton, Jack Bruce, and Ginger Baker, all of whom, according to music critic Don McLesse, "left the stage vanquished"[17] by the Detroit upstarts.

Thanks to Sinclair's efforts, the entire TLE commune became part of the act, providing psychedelic light shows, posters, handbills, and even emcee duties from one of Sinclair's African American brothers, the former blues drummer J.C. Crawford, who became the MC5's "warm-up man," working rock and roll crazed maniacs into a mindless frenzy even before the music started. "I wanna hear some revolution out there brothers and sisters! The time has come for each and every one of you to decide whether you are gonna be the problem or whether you are gonna be the solution. You must choose brothers, you must choose! It takes five seconds, five seconds of decision, five seconds to realize your purpose here on the planet. It takes five seconds to realize it's time to move. It's time to get down with it! It's time to testify. And I wanna know: are you ready to testify?" "Brother" Crawford's rantings were punctuated by Sinclair's equally provocative proselytizing in which he urged youth to pursue personal freedom to the utmost extremes. The crowd's roaring response was the cue for MC5 to begin their thunderous cacophony of eardrum-splitting guitar music; it was time to "Kick out the jams, motherfuckers!" Perhaps only a handful of other bands' music reflected the late 1960s as intensely as the MC5: rebellion, anarchy, psychedelia, sex, and of course, aggressive rock and roll.[18]

Thanks to Sinclair's influence, MC5 shows reflected the successful combination of two very significant countercultural dynamics that came to define, along with drugs, the essence of the hippie rebellion: "alternative, electric rock and roll music and the rhetoric of youth culture liberation." Perhaps Ken Kelley, a member of Sinclair's TLE commune, best captured the band's hyper-kinetic and frenzied effect on audiences: "I'll never forget the first time I saw the MC5 perform that hot June night in 1968 at the Grande Ballroom. The ozone scent of anticipation quickened my pulse as Rob Tyner jumped to center stage and shouted 'Kick out the jams, motherfuckers!,' the opening rant into The 5's anthemic underground hit song. As Tyner squirmed and sang, behind him were two sparkle-sequined guitarists [Fred 'Sonic' Smith and Wayne Kramer] who traded off lead in a fervid fusillade of fiery notes. When Fred played solo on his trademark tune, 'Rocket Reducer No. 62,' you knew why he got his name 'Sonic'— the only word that packed enough G-force into his performances. He leaped up and down in swirling orgiastic gyrations of musical frenzy. When Fred played, sex itself exploded on stage."[19]

TLE's economy was also unlike most contemporary hippie collectives. Thanks to the MC5, the TLE often had a substantial income upon which to sustain its existence; rarely did the commune experience hand to mouth deprivation. Not only did the MC5 provide a decent life for TLE's several core members but also for the band and for scores of other individuals, such as writers for the *Fifth Estate*. Contrary to the hippie ethos of anti-materialism, TLE members basked in relative affluence thanks largely to Sinclair's savvy financial dealings and shrewd, remunerative management of the MC5. As TLE member Lawrence Robert "Pun" Plamondon told a *Time* correspondent, neither he nor any of his TLE associates believed "people should go to tribal living again, for instance we want the luxurious living, radios, and records."[20] With such steady income, Sinclair was also able to organize and fund free Love-Ins, concerts, and benefits. Ultimately, Motor City hippies began to question Sinclair's sincerity and commitment to the hippie ethos of living simply, for too often they saw him and his TLE comrades running around the community with plenty of cash in their pockets and living in well-appointed "pads." Sinclair defended TLE's political economy by claiming that the MC5 was a true "people's band," playing for free or donating performance proceeds to as many hip causes as possible. Sinclair also asserted that the lion's share of the money coming from paid concerts was used primarily "to spread the word that there was another way of doing things; to bring the new world order into being."[21] Hippie pap and righteous rhetoric aside, Sinclair, like Ron Thelin and many of the other hip merchants in the Haight, simply made money off the hippie phenomenon; hip music was an even a more lucrative hip enterprise than drugs. In the minds of the majority of impoverished hippies, this relative prosperity reflected antithetical hip behavior and betrayal of the hip ethos, and that dilemma revealed the one issue that caused the most rancor and division within the hip communities: the question of hippies making money in bohemia.

Detroit hippies not only congregated in the Wayne State University area but also in the Motor City's short-lived art's community, centered at the corner of Fifth and Plum streets, in what was considered "old town" Detroit: badly deteriorated buildings, homes, and stores, dating back to the 1880sand 1890s. Revitalizing the neighborhood was the brainchild of developers Robert Cobb and Sherman Shapiro, who envisioned transforming the district into an artists' colony with upscale hip boutiques, shops, restaurants, and theaters; in many ways a Ron Thelin image of the Haight minus the dope stores, head shops, and other exclusively hippie-oriented vendors.[22]

They initially had the political support and enthusiasm of city officials, ranging from Detroit mayor Jerome Cavanagh to Governor George Romney, who pledged they would do all they could to sustain the area and its purpose. However, no sooner did Plum Street open for business and habitation in September 1966, than Detroit's hippies flooded into the area. To the developers' dismay, they quickly took over the neighborhood, driving away any potential straight residents and businesses as well as tourists, and perhaps most important, the promised political and economic support from city officials. Ironically, Cobb and Shapiro initially welcomed the hippie presence, naively believing they would help promote Plum Street's image as a hip and happening place, especially for young people, who, they hoped, along with the tourists, would spend their money in the shops and restaurants. Cobb and Shapiro allowed the hippies to paint trash cans, park benches, and even some building storefronts, especially those which sold hip clothing and other hippie paraphernalia, bright psychedelic colors. For the project's first several months all appeared to be proceeding as envisioned. However, as the hippie and general misfit influx increased, the area began to feel the effects of these less than savory individuals. By the Summer of Love 1967, Plum Street looked like a microcosm of the Haight, with hundreds of loitering, vagabond hippies panhandling and selling drugs on the streets, squatting in the unoccupied homes and business, and setting up communes and dope dens.[23]

A similar scenario occurred in Boston's hip community, where, according to *Time*, "proper Bostonians" had "bent over backward" to accommodate and "accept the flower children.... The destitute are bedded down in churches and private homes, [they] get free medical attention at Cambridgeport Clinic, and legal aid from volunteer lawyers." Unfortunately, as would occur in many hip communities beginning in late 1967, "hoodlums and narcotics peddlers" increasingly "infiltrated hippie ranks." According to a local cop, this new wave of hippies weren't "the classy hippies, the beatniks or bohemians. Many of them are just criminal types" who were "urinating, defecating, and fornicating in the Common. This must stop." It was only a matter of time before the inevitable occurred: violent confrontations between these "pseudo hippies" and the police, resulting in massive arrests and cracked hippie skulls. Such encounters became almost daily occurrences in the hip neighborhoods throughout the country. In Atlanta, city officials and the business community allied "to wage war against these so-called undesirables, treating them as the greatest threat to the city since General Sherman." The objective: to drive out "the 1,000 or so hippie types who congregate along Peachtree Street" where the police had "stepped up patrols in the area, often stopping and threatening those of unorthodox appearance. Young people are arrested on such specious charges as loitering, jaywalking, and obscenity." Hip shops and homes were also raided, allegedly in search of drugs, but in most instances hippies claimed harassment, which was probably closer to the truth than not. How ridiculous did this scene become in Atlanta? One hippie, arrested initially for loitering then spent nine days in solitary confinement for refusing to shave off his beard and cut his hair! According to one local hippie shop owner, "We've got a new nigger in our society, and the way to tell him is by his hair and his beard."[24]

Unlike the Bay Area, which was a much more overall affluent, rarefied part of Northern California, producing a more prosperous teenage consumer as well as a more pampered hippie, the majority of Detroit hippies came from working-class homes and did not have the disposable income essential to sustain the developers' vision. Motor City's hippies were in general a much more rough-hewn, street-wise bunch compared to their West Coast counterparts; less inclined to embrace the flower child image of gentleness and peaceful behavior. They were more hardened by daily life and more prone to engage in reckless conduct, especially when challenged by the police or authority figures. Adding to the developers' woes was the presence of the Outlaws motorcycle gang, who were even more renegade and confrontational than their California Hell's Angels brethren. The Outlaws not only terrorized Plum Street businesses and harassed tourists, but the neighborhood's hippies often became the targets of the gang's violent intimidation as well. This rarely, if ever, occurred in the Haight, where the hippies and the Hell's Angels had formed interesting bonds of mutual respect for one another's anti-authoritarianism and outcast behavior. In short, California was the land of "the beautiful people," while Detroit was a blue collar industrial city, noted for churning out automobiles, pollution, and racial tension.

Within one year's time Cobb's and Shapiro's vision for city refinement had completely unraveled. The majority of the Motor City's hippies were simply too steeled by their blue-collar roots and daily life to embrace the West Coast love message. As Sherman Shapiro reflected years later, "I wish we could have had the type of hippies who had gone to San Francisco with 'flowers in their hair' come to the neighborhood. That would not have been too bad. Instead, we got not only the dope but the worst kind of hippie at that time; not a peaceful 'flower child' but thieves, dope-fiends, and all manner of just bad kids and gangs. It seemed that all of the city's undesirables came to Plum Street."[25] However, to hipster Mike Marino, from beginning to end, "Plum Street was a fake. It was not a 'real woman' but a drag queen on a runway strutting her stuff, attractive maybe, but not the real deal."[26]

Inspired by the seminal San Francisco Be-In as well as by similar hippie gatherings and celebrations throughout the country, Sinclair and his TLE compatriots believed they could stage an equally impressive Love-In festival in the Motor City. The venue would be the large metropolitan park on Belle Isle, in the middle of the Detroit River between the Motor City and Windsor, Ontario, Canada. Sinclair hoped to use the event as an unveiling to the nation of the Motor City's flourishing hip community, which he believed was as legitimate as anywhere else in the country in the embracing of the "new consciousness." Sinclair and TLE promoted the event as an assemblage of "peace and love," where hippies and straights would be coming together to inaugurate the new society. The Belle Isle Park Love-In of April 30, 1967, represented the peak of Sinclair's and his follower's optimism for the Motor City's hippie movement. Both of the city's major metropolitans, the *Detroit News* and *Detroit Free Press*, gave the Love-In extensive coverage; in many ways the papers' reporting provided Sinclair with free advertising.[27]

The event's official opening occurred around 11 a.m. and by noon, when the first of the local bands began to play (the MC5, the featured band of course, was not to play until around 3 or 4 p.m.), a crowd of around 6,000 freaks were in attendance as well straights and other non-hippie street folk. Sinclair had promised city officials and the police department that of course his event would be peaceful from beginning to end and that the TLE would provide its own security, the TransLove Rangers, who would patrol the crowds and keep order. The police agreed and for most of the day only a handful of mounted officers were on hand in case anything outrageous happened, which it did not—until the sun went down. Prior to sunset, the police ignored the obvious "reefer madness," acid dropping, drinking, singing, chanting, and the crowd's general but peaceful revelry. Unfortunately not all in attendance were hippies and had they been the majority of the crowd, the ensuing police riot might not have occurred.[28]

Indeed, according to *Fifth Estate* reporter Sheila Salasnek, until she left the park at 5 p.m., despite the presence of increasing numbers of "crew-cuts and motorcyclists," who mostly congregated on the event's periphery, in the middle of the festivities were the *real hippies*, who had come out "in full force to celebrate their love. They wore their most colorful clothing and brought things to give away to their brothers." Everywhere could be seen or heard manifestations of genuine hippiedom: "A woman in a pure white nun's habit with a diffraction grid on her forehead is handing out slices of kosher salami and a gray-haired old man is passing out balloons. Their eyes meet and they stop to smile at one another"; "A stranger walks by and looks in your eyes telling you you're beautiful. Something hits you from behind and you turn around annoyed only to find that someone has thrown a carnation at you.... Everywhere there seemed to be a feeling of joy. It's a love-in! It worked!" However, as she left the festivities, Salasnek sensed that crowd's mood had changed, particularly among "the staring crew-cuts and motorcyclist tribes" through whose congregation she had to pass on the way to her car. Moreover these particular groups of "beer drinkers" had begun to penetrate the interior of the jamboree and were shoulder to shoulder with those hippies still gathered around the bandstand and in the middle of the celebration. "You begin to feel a little awkward. The robe hangs a little heavy now and the 'Love Balloons' look kind of absurd. You have to look very hard to find someone smiling. You reach the outskirts of the few thousand people and start looking for a crowd you can feel comfortamble with," which was becoming more difficult to find because most of the hippies had already left the Love-In. "Whatever happened on the island that night should not be allowed to overshadow the 6 or 7 hours of dancing, singing, and sharing that preceded it." Unfortunately for Detroit's hip community, the melee that ensued later that evening, for which the city's hippie community was blamed for having provoked, was all that would be remembered from the Belle Isle Love-In.[29]

As the day progressed, increasing numbers of non-hippie street thugs and other unsavory characters joined in the celebration as well as the motorcycle gang, the Outlaws, whose members wantonly and savagely beat many male attendees, both straight and hippie, for allegedly provoking them or for making untoward advances to their girlfriends. No one stopped any of the beatings and when the Outlaws had had enough fun pummeling the individual, friends or bystanders simply dragged the bloodied, battered victims away from the scene. Much of the Outlaw's violence was caught on film or captured in photographs. Unfortunately the police either did not see the Outlaw's savagery or they looked the other way, with many cops perhaps not caring because it was "only a bunch of hippies who probably deserved it."[30]

The Detroit Police Department already had a national reputation for being one of the most brutal and hard-hearted in the country and not at all disposed to helping the "weirdo's" even if they were innocent victims. It must be remembered, that ironically, like the majority of Detroit hippies, the police as well came from working-class/ethnic backgrounds, and thus had no understanding, empathy, or the slightest willingness to believe that those Detroit youth who had become hippies were anything but lazy, dirty, drugged-out losers who hated everything about America that the police cherished and were sworn to uphold.

Finally, around dusk, just after the MC5 had finished their last set, all hell broke loose when the police, at the request of the TransLove Rangers, arrested an Outlaw for yet another beating. Earlier in the day flamboyantly dressed hippies had passed out paper daisies, candy, and balloons to the crowd, but now, as night set in, leather-clad bikers menacingly roamed the crowd, terrorizing attendees and the Rangers needed help. The police agreed and arrested the biker as well as another Outlaw who began driving his motorcycle recklessly through the crowd. Despite the Rangers *request* for police help, the crowd, loaded to the gills on dope, began taunting and throwing rocks at the police and as well as firecrackers into a group of mounted cops until the centurions had had enough and all earlier restraint dissipated. One-hundred and fifty more officers were called to the scene, ready to "disperse" the crowd, using any and all force necessary. Officers on foot and those on horses formed a czarist-like Cossack line and moved toward the 2–3,000 revelers still in the park. Brandishing police shields and wielding riot batons, the police literally drove the crowd out of the park, onto the bridge, and off the island. The result was a full-scale riot with numerous arrests for property damage and police harassment. Once the crowd had reached the other side of the bridge, they ventilated their rage by smashing windows and looting stores on East Jefferson Street. A *Detroit News* reporter and cameraman were pelted with rocks and bottles as they tried to report and film the mayhem. Finally by 9:30 p.m. the debacle was over. Suffice it to say, the day's end was not what Sinclair had envisioned and the subsequent melee not only put Detroit's hippie community in a bad light but also greatly disillusioned Sinclair, who blamed the disaster not on the unruly crowd or the Outlaws, but on the straights and weekend hippies who had attended the Love-In. According to Sinclair, "all the real hippies had gone home by the time the rowdiness began." Public sentiment and the mainstream media unanimously supported the police while "portraying Sinclair and TLE as mindless hedonists, more interested in picking a fight with police than in peace and love."[31]

Sinclair might have been accurate in his assessment of who caused the day to end so badly. Certainly the non-hippie Outlaws motorcycle gang helped to provoke the incident and there were more than likely other street thugs and miscreants in the crowd as well who were not hippie true believers but who attended for the plentiful alcohol and drugs. When they had become sufficiently stoned they mindlessly attacked the police. However, to what degree were the police responsible for using excessive force in their attempt to restore order? Detroit police were notorious for being easily provoked into "riot mode" and had been for quite some time, especially toward the city's black community. The Belle Isle incident could be interpreted as simply one more example of the Detroit police department's desire to rid the city of its counterculture denizens. Such was the view of MC5 guitarist Wayne Kramer, who observed the entire episode first-hand. Kramer was convinced that the police had been waiting all day for any excuse to "bum rush everyone off Belle Isle as soon as the sun went down. They had restrained themselves until that time. I am guessing they had been rehearsing their lock-step and were overjoyed to have a chance to use it." Kramer believed perhaps naively, that "no one there posed any kind of threat. After all this wasn't a cadre of highly trained Marxists militants. We were a bunch of stoned-out weirdos and Budweiser-buzzed factory rats enjoying a free concert."[32]

Since most of the day went well, according to Kramer initially no one took the police line that moved across the park seriously, as scores of people thought it was a game and "would shriek and laugh and run away, but very quickly—when the first heads got busted—the humor drained out of the situation. The violence the cops used was ridiculously out of proportion to the 'danger' they faced. They seemed to be really enjoying the total overpowering dominance they had." Most appalling to Kramer was the mounted police's attack on the ground. "The mounted cops took a galloping start on running at people and clubbed them like they were playing polo. Giddy-up there horsy. Whack! Pow! Score! Women screaming, blood spurting, men yelling curses. Everywhere I looked, another creep scene [police violence] was going down in the darkness and glare, like an unholy Chinese shadow puppet show."[33]

The Belle Isle melee profoundly affected Sinclair and his followers, for it shattered their illusion that the capitalist machine would "rust away." Earlier, Sinclair had told *Time* reporter Frank Beaumier, that "the hippie way is an enduring way, that hippies will live and die—from youth to maturity—middle and old age—as hippies." Sinclair also told Beaumier that the counterculture will eventually become a political force, an important voting bloc, who will make the legalization of marijuana their first objective. Sinclair had no doubt hippies "will change the world." Sinclair also believed that technology, "cybernetics will make everyone a hippie. Everyone will make love, eat, sleep while the machines do the work."[34] However, after Belle Isle, Sinclair admitted his earlier naiveté. "We had a simplistic picture of what the 'revolution' was all about. We said that all you had to do was 'tune in, turn on, and drop out,' as if that would solve all the problems of humankind. What we didn't understand, spaced out as we were behind all that acid was that the machine was determined to keep things the way they were."[35]

Soon after the Belle Isle episode, Sinclair and TLE embraced and began propagating the cultural and political radicalism of the more extreme white New Left organizations, such as the Weather Underground, and most importantly the stridently militant agenda of the Black Panthers. Sinclair had always identified with black culture (especially its music) and the Artists' Workshop had been a multiracial coalition. Moreover, Sinclair and many TLE members admired and respected the Panther's armed self-defense posture and their disciplined organizational structure. To Sinclair's and other radicals' delight, the Panthers were actively cultivating alliances with the "white country mother radicals" in the New Left, politicized hippies (such as Sinclair), and the peace movements. A little over a year after the Belle Isle episode, Sinclair disbanded TLE and formed in its place the White Panther Party, calling for a "total assault on the culture," which to Sinclair and his compatriots meant not only the promoting of cultural radicalism ("rock and roll, dope, and fucking in the streets"), but also the politicization of the counterculture in general as well as alliance with the New Left in order to bring down the Establishment, both politically and socio-culturally. Using black-militant language to reinforce his organization's identification with the Black Panthers, Sinclair further proclaimed that "The white honkie culture that has been handed to us on a silver plastic platter is meaningless to us! We don't want it! All we want is our freedom, and we know we can't be free until everybody is free!" Sinclair's rhetoric reflected not only that of the Black Panthers but of the Diggers and Yippies as well. Sinclair also learned from both the Black Panthers and the Yippies the mainstream media's invaluable role in helping to promote the youth rebellion of the late 1960s; that there was a direct relationship between the level of profligacy and sensationalism in the message: "If you make it outrageous enough," "Pun" Plamondon later recalled, "the networks will pick it up."[36]

By 1968 Sinclair was convinced that American youth culture had become "a revolutionary culture and that we have to realize that the long-haired, dope smoking rock and roll street-fucking culture is a whole thing, a revolutionary international cultural movement which is absolutely legitimate and absolutely valid." Opposing the insurrection was the decaying, repressive, desperate "pig power structure" of the current Establishment. In Sinclair's view the Establishment was not only a "low energy" entity but a "death culture" as well that would not hesitate "to kill us if they can get away with it" because of "the threat we represent to their immoral, decrepit, and self-serving ways," which, according to Sinclair, they sustained with the use of excessive brute force. Sinclair wanted to portray the White Panthers as genuine revolutionaries, willing to meet violence with violence and to wage unrelenting assault on the capitalist power structure by using any and all tactics at their disposal, such as creating "high-energy rock and roll bands" for the purpose of "infiltrating the popular culture." Sinclair also wanted to make it clear that hippies had been "dragged into the struggle" against their will; that at heart they were still peace-loving people but because of "pig" (police) harassment, persecution, and violent repression, they had no choice but to fight back; "to meet fire with fire, we will use guns if we have to," even though such a stance was supposedly contrary to inherent hippie pacifism.[37]

Remove the militant rhetoric and other bellicose posturing, in the end Sinclair and his fellow Panthers simply wanted to "turn on" as many young people as possible to all facets of the countercultural lifestyle—drugs, rock and roll music, communal living, and uninhibited sex—as well as the political implications involved in seeking such an alternative existence. Of those dynamics, Sinclair believed that rock and roll music was the best medium through which to propagate the revolutionary message to millions of disaffected youth as well as recruit them for the impending mass insurrection. As Sinclair told Dean Latimer of the *East Village Other*, he believed the MC5 to be in the vanguard rock bands as revolutionary messengers. "So you listen to the band and you just go crazy and have a good time. Throw away your underwear, smoke dope, fuck.... Rather than go up there and make some speech about our moral commitment in Vietnam, you just make'em so freaky they'd never want to go into the army in the first place." For Sinclair politics and culture had become symbiotic and thus it would be through cultural events and mediums such as rock and roll concerts, drugs, and even sex that would create the youthful uprising against the status quo. Sinclair was convinced that such mind-blowing experiences would be far more effective in radicalizing the nation's youth than all of the New Left's earnest speeches, manifestoes, and marches, all of which Sinclair believed were still too political for the majority of disenfranchised youth to embrace and act upon. By declaring that high-energy, electric rock and roll rock music, drug use, and the flaunting of all conventional behavior would bring about revolution, Sinclair and the White Panthers added a new dynamic to the history of *white* American cultural radicalism. Such a combination would not only liberate young people from traditional societal restraints but bring about a new culture as well.[38]

The White Panthers' outrageous, menacing, and allegedly subversive rhetoric made them a lightening-rod for the authorities—the Detroit police, the FBI, and even the CIA. Indeed, one of Sinclair's closest comrades in the party, Robert "Pun" Plamondon (the party's "Minister of Defense"), made the FBI's 1970 Ten Most Wanted list for his involvement in the September 1968 bombing of a CIA recruiting office in Ann Arbor, Michigan. The entire WPP contingent was heavily involved in the alleged "Ann Arbor riots" of June 16–18, 1969, which saw three days of pitched battles between an assortment of counterculture radicals and hundreds of riot gear-clad police. Until that event the FBI's interest in the White Panthers had been cursory at best. However, all that changed after the confrontation as FBI Director, the legendary J. Edgar Hoover, became convinced that the Panthers had fomented the insurrection. Hoover also believed that the MC5 were part of the conspiracy because of their songs, which the director was certain contained not only "filthy" and "obscene" lyrics but incendiary political messages as well. After the riot, Hoover ordered agents to destroy the WPP, using whatever means at their disposal, including illegal wire-tapping. Indeed, by 1970 Hoover considered the WPP to be one of the most dangerous militant organizations in the country, even though its founder and leader, "Big John" Sinclair had been in jail for over a year, busted in 1969 for his third marijuana possession. For his "crime" (the possession of two marijuana cigarettes!), Sinclair was sentenced to ten years in prison.[39]

While Sinclair sat in his prison cell, his fellow Panthers and co-conspirators, Skip Taube, Jack Forrest, and David Valler, all went underground, with Plamondon eventually fleeing to Canada and then on to northern and central Europe, and finally to Algeria, where he met with Eldridge Cleaver, the Black Panther leader in exile who had been instrumental in helping to forge the alliance between white New Left radicals and the Black Panthers. Plamondon eventually returned to the United States and hid out in the woods of northern Michigan from where he continued to write inflammatory broadsides (as well as collecting weapons), for "this righteous revolutionary war." On July 23, 1970, the Michigan State Police, thanks to a Dennis Marnell, a government agent provocateur who had infiltrated the WPP, arrested Plamondon and the rest of the Panther's leadership. Over the course of the next several months it was revealed that Marnell not only had gained the confidence of WPP members but had also illegally wire-tapped the Panther's commune in Ann Arbor, which no doubt greatly assisted federal and state authorities in their locating and apprehending Panther fugitives such as Plamondon. So excited was the Nixon administration at the capture of WPP leaders that the president was certain that they never would have been caught had it not been for the "bugging" of their headquarters. Nixon, through the Justice Department, attempted to acquire Supreme Court sanction for an unconstitutional dragnet initiative to be used against all "home-grown" leftist organizations considered threats to national security. "The Mitchell Doctrine" as the program became called, asserted that the president possesses the "inherent constitutional power" to wiretap "domestic radicals" *without a court order* if he, and he alone, believed them to be a threat to national security. Fortunately the Supreme Court saw Nixon's maneuver as a blatant usurpation of executive power and in June 1972, voted unanimously (8–0) against the president's high-handedness in the landmark *U.S. v. U.S. District Court* (also known as the "Keith" decision in honor of U.S. District Judge Damon J. Keith of Detroit, who had approved of the Justice Department's wiretapping of the White Panthers). As a result, the conspiracy case against the WPP was dropped as were many other federal conspiracy indictments involving New Left organizations because of illegal government electronic surveillance.[40]

Thanks to the U.S. Supreme Court's decision, Sinclair and Plamondon were released from prison in 1971. They returned to Ann Arbor and established the Rainbow People's Party, a nonmilitant, grassroots coalition whose activities and platform reflected that of many other former radical New Left parties, who also dropped their former bellicosity and stridency and entered mainstream politics during the 1970s. Perhaps more important, Sinclair's initial incarceration for 10 years for marijuana possession prompted the Michigan Supreme Court to reexamine the state's laws relative to narcotics possession, and during that decade joined other states in the decriminalization of marijuana, in most instances reducing possession to a misdemeanor rather than a felony. Such reform owed much to the two and a half years John Sinclair had spent behind bars in Michigan. Indeed, while in prison, Sinclair's conspiracy case as well as his harsh sentencing for marijuana possession became an international cause célèbre, attracting to his "plight" a host of celebrities such as Jane Fonda, Donald Sutherland, and Allen Ginsberg, as well as two of the decade's most legendary trial lawyers, known for their successful defense of student activists and radicals, William Kunstler and Leonard Weinglass.[41] Despite the fanfare, by the time Sinclair was sprung in late 1971, much of the fun was over; the counterculture was dying if not dead, especially in many of its more recent haunts, such as Detroit.

To the pleasant surprise of hippies everywhere, Austin, Texas, nestled on the periphery of the state's majestic Hill Country, had a flourishing hippie community by 1968, chronicled by one of one of the counterculture's most informed underground newspapers, *The Austin Rag*, edited by Thorne Dreyer and Jeff Shero. Few counterculturists should have been amazed by the presence of their brethren in Austin: since the 1930s, the city, the state capitol and home to the University of Texas (one of the South's more progressive institutions), had had a reputation throughout the South, of nurturing a thriving avant-garde community of intellectuals, writers, musicians, and social renegades, all of whom had found a welcoming reception among Hill Country Texans. Since the 1850s, when the first German immigrants arrived in the area, this particular region of the Lone Star state had been a socio-cultural anomaly, whose eventual mélange of Anglo-Americans, *tejanos*, African Americans, and German/Eastern European immigrants, bonded, creating in the process a diverse, tolerant, and dynamic culture and mentality found nowhere else in the state.

For decades, one of Austin's more salient contributions to American popular culture had been music, as it is still. During the late 1960s and into the 1970s and 1980s, Austin artists such as Stevie Ray Vaughan, the Fabulous Thunderbirds, Johnny and Edgar Winter, Christopher Cross, and country-western legend Willie Nelson, frequently combined or borrowed from each other's respective genres and talents to produce a unique "Austin sound," a hybrid of rock and roll, country and western music and rhythm and blues (as well as a touch of south Texas *tejano* music), labeled and commodified by the mainstream media and record producers as "progressive country" or "cosmic cowboy" music. Such branding did not and does not to this day, accurately convey this type of fusion music found nowhere else. In the 1970s, Austin abounded with all manner of cooperative enterprises, ranging from natural food co-ops (from which emerged the present day Whole Foods conglomerate, founded by four Austinites and University of Texas graduates, John Mackey, Renee Lawson Hardy, Craig Weller, and Mark Skiles), to electrical co-ops and free schools, virtually all initially owned and operated by young UT students and graduates, all of whom had been affected by Austin's 1960s counterculture scene. In the 1960s Austin also became a "major transit center" for psychedelic wholesalers and retailers who smuggled across the Mexican border marijuana and hallucinogenic mushrooms. Until 1966 when peyote was declared an illegal substance in the United States, some Hill Country Texans had been among the nation's most prolific plant growers and processors.[42]

Perhaps most important and unique among the 1960s Texas counterculture was the alliance between Austin hippies and the New Leftists of the University of Texas. Such a merger rarely occurred during the 1960s and Austin was one of the few places where such a blending took place. Contributing to the partnership was the fact that although Austin had a most definite, flourishing counterculture, it was not large; especially when compared to the Bay Area or the East Village in New York, there simply were not as many Austin hippies or New Left radicals. UT SDS declared it had over 200 members by late 1968, but according to the official SDS papers housed in the Dolph Briscoe Center for American History on the UT campus, membership peaked in late 1967 at around 150.[43] Moreover, from the UT-SDS founding, its members engaged in the same countercultural activities as their hippie counterparts: they all "turned on" to marijuana and some New Leftists even to acid. As SDS-UT activist Marianne Wizard observed, "Basically, everybody turned on; basically, everybody smoked; very few people did not smoke dope." As Thorne Dreyer reflected, "Austin was a very funny scene. There weren't the real ideological-philosophical splits seen elsewhere at the time between politicos and hippies. We probably had the most political hippies and the most hip politicos around." As Dreyer told his fellow underground editors at the time (1966), "The Austin radical scene has the strongest sense of community of any I have come in contact with; hippies and politicos merge." Todd Gitlin agreed with Dreyer's observation, asserting that "there was a direct line from the expressive politics of the New Left to the counterculture's let-it-all-hang-out way of life."[44] Nonetheless, both Dreyer and Gitlin exaggerated somewhat the hippie–New Left affinity for there were indeed definite ideological differences between the two on how to best foment social change. New Leftists never abandoned their commitments to social justice and democracy and to confronting the existing political system. The centrality of these beliefs was what separated the New Left from the hippies and informed much of their criticism of the hippies' ethos. However, true to their Texas heritage, both groups proclaimed their distinctiveness whenever it was possible, and to the dismay of their respective national brethren, frequently publicly announced their mutual interests and camaraderie. In short, the conviviality between Austin hippies and student activists was real, which when compared to the other hippie-activists relationships nation-wide, was indeed unusual.

No doubt uniting both groups at the time was the fact that they were viewed by the state's conservative establishment to be one and the same; in other words, reactionary Texans did not distinguish between leftists and hippies, especially as activists increasingly began dressing like the hippies and adopting much of the hip personal style. Thus to the police and "rednecks" who persecuted both groups, they were all uniformly dirty, lazy, dopers and hedonists, even "communist traitors." "Redneck terrorist groups" were more dangerous to hippie/activist existence than the police, for as *The Rag* observed, "Rednecks run on hate and violence. They have been raised to hate queers, niggers, commies, and mainly themselves. The rednecks' traditional enemies have either gone way or fight back and now the only ones left to hate are the hippies. Well ten years ago it would have been the niggers, and twenty years ago it would have been the Jews, but now I guess it's Us [the hippies and their activist brethren]!" At times as menacing to both hippies and student radicals were the "Frat Rats," those "obnoxious products of instant social life. They are herd animals with herd mentalities—each tries to out masculine the other by seeing who can yell 'queer' the loudest with the greatest degree of a Texas accent." Indeed, to such right-wingers, long-haired male hippies and activists were "queers"; in one instance, after arresting two male hippies (or perhaps two male SDS'ers), the police officers, for good measure, inquired why these young white American men were "dressin' up like a bunch of Niggers." Interestingly, such harassment tended to strengthen the bonds between Austin hippies and UT student radicals, for both realized that they confronted common enemies, who saw them in the same light and were as determined to crush one as the other. Indeed, to Thorne Dreyer it was "us against THEM.... Hardly a week passes that some beatnik doesn't get bashed on the head by a beer bottle."[45]

To the surprise of UT-SDS members their willingness to embrace the Austin hippie community and to promote hippie socio-cultural radicalism, caused their more doctrinaire fellow New Leftists to question UT-SDS'ers commitment to New Left ideology. However, SDS Texans believed that it was time to establish a more inclusive policy relative to the counterculture, particularly if the organization hoped to expand its national membership. As UT-SDS member Judy Schiffer Perez poignantly reminded her New Left colleagues, there were "more hippies out there, and their numbers are growing daily, than there are of us. More young people find the hippie life and philosophy more appealing than our often boring, esoteric political discussions and position papers." The UT-SDSer's advocated such a policy at national SDS meetings as early as 1965 but still in control of the Movement at that level were the more hard-core New Left ideologues, who believed that hippies were incapable of submitting themselves to the kind of personal discipline and organizational structure required by SDS members. Indeed, by 1965, in attitude, behavior, and philosophy, UT SDS'ers represented the emergence of a new "Western breed" and influence within the New Left, individuals primarily from Western (and some Southern) universities and colleges who increasingly adopted key aspects of the hip ethos and personae. These new SDS members smoked dope, affected Pancho Villa mustaches, and wore blue work shirts, denim jeans, jackets, and boots. Perhaps most important, they were less "heavy" intellectually, less ideologically doctrinaire, less politically driven, and much more action-oriented and open to accepting hippies into their ranks. They were impatient with the old guard's "position papers" and constant wrangling about petty protocol, agenda and philosophical issues. These new "prairie power" members pushed the old guard into active resistance to the draft and the Vietnam War as well agitating for expanding SDS's "enemies" list to include repressive, antiquated, and "inhumane," university policies, curriculum, "fascist" administrators and their bureaucratic minions, as well as corporation and military recruitment on campus.[46]

As UT SDS member Jeff Shero asserted, because they operated in such a conservative, hostile environment, Austin counterculturists, both bohemian and activist, "were by instinct much more radical, much more willing to take risks. In Texas to join SDS meant breaking with your family, it meant being cut off—it was like in early Rome joining a Christian sect—and the break was so much more total, getting involved with something like SDS you had to be much more highly committed.... If you were from Texas, in SDS, you were a bad motherfucker, and you couldn't go home for Christmas."[47]

To SDS Texans, what differentiated the New Left from Old was the New Left's alleged commitment to "social radicalism"; a kind of individual reformation that extended into one's everyday life and affected all personal interactions. If this was truly part of the New Left vision, then why not try to incorporate the hippie counterculture into the Movement? The hippies, after all, personified this particular dimension of the socio-cultural insurgency taking place throughout the nation among increasing numbers of white middle class youth. In the opinion of one UT-SDS member, they represented the quintessential "victims of the process of demoralization; the reduction of the individual to a machine-producing entity." However, "they have chosen to opt out of this process that dulls the consciousness, and have sought instead an alternative existence that rejects such exploitation of mind and soul." UT-SDS president Robert Pardun became one of the New Left's leading proponents for welcoming the hippies into the Movement, believing that the young people who were embracing the left were doing so for the same reason they gravitated to the hippie counterculture: they were sick to death of consumer-driven, "plastic America" and its oppressive, soul-sucking acquisitive obsessions; they wanted to become "real individuals" rather than continue to be the "game-players of society." Pardun and other UT SDS'ers were certain that those young people feeling such despair would find salvation from such alienation in a movement that represented the fusion of countercultural and New Left "consciousness." Such an alliance would provide young seekers with "the options" for the "authentic" life they craved. To Pardun and other more progressive New Leftists, the quest for a qualitatively better way of life defined the era's youth rebellion, and by that standard, both hippies and New Leftists were on the same socio-cultural page.[48]

In the minds of both hippies and many New Leftists, a cultural revolution was possible in the United States by the 1960s because the nation had become the affluent society, and Americans in particular should have been eschewing the pursuit of material aggrandizement for greater spiritual and emotional fulfillment. Those Americans still trying to achieve the American Dream (poor African Americans, Hispanics, women), were considered to be victims of an unfair political and economic system that kept many people confined in an enforced scarcity and powerlessness. Therefore it was the moral responsibility of the counterculture—both hippies and New Leftists—through their activism and example, to help uplift not only those still suffering from scarcity but those still afflicted by what the French critical theorist Herbert Marcuse called "surplus repression"—individuals still in obsessive pursuit of consumer goods, "tokens" of success manipulatively doled out by self-serving political and capitalist elites to keep the masses controlled and mollified by shrewdly promoting rising expectations. The hippies and New Left cultural radicals viewed such prizes as "objects of inauthentic desire." Such driven acquisitiveness, promoted and sustained by the power elites of industry, advertising, and politics, diverted human needs for freedom and community into an insatiable hunger for "things." As Allen Ginsberg remarked to an Austin gathering in 1967, "Man's basic nature is that he's a pretty decent fellow when there's enough to go around," and by the late 1960s, in the view of both hippie and New Left Austinites, there was plenty to go around, especially for white middle class Americans.[49]

Indispensable to the counterculture-New Left alliance in Austin was the city's legendary underground publication, *The Rag*, founded by Thorne Dreyer and "funneled" (edited) by Dreyer and Carol Nieman. According to Dreyer, it was *The Rag* that brought Austin's "large underground scene together—the radical politicos, ethnic folkniks, academic left-libs, peyote freaks, and bearded bikers. They were all there, dispersed around the campus area, but there was nothing to pull them together, to give them political direction, to bring them into action, to give them a sense of identity. *The Rag* was primarily responsible for bringing together a coherent left-hip scene."[50] The paper's office became the gathering place for UT's and Austin's growing hip/activist community. "You called *The Rag* or dropped by to find out about demonstrations, busts, or lost dogs. Or just rap politics and often you got pulled into working on the paper. *Rag* benefits brought together hips and politicos for musical celebrations and gave a forum for young artists." Indeed, Abe Peck believed "*The Rag* was the first independent undergrounder to represent the participatory democracy, community organizing and synthesis of politics and culture that the New Left of the midsixties was trying to develop."[51] John McMillian echoed Peck's assessment of *The Rag*, calling the publication "a spirited, quirky, and humorous paper, whose founders pushed the New Left's political agenda even as they embraced the counterculture's zeal for rock music, psychedelics, and personal liberation." Hip-left Austinites came to regard *The Rag* as "a beautiful and precious thing."[52]

What perhaps made *The Rag* so appealing to both groups was that editors and contributors wove together a fine balance of serious left-leaning political analysis and counterculture events and philosophy, with ample doses of humor, providing the perfect forum for two of the most important 1960s underground graphic artists: Gilbert Shelton and Jim Franklin. Shelton's iconic Fabulous Furry Freak Brothers commix would be republished in papers—both mainstream and underground—all over the world, while Franklin's surrealistic armadillos helped create "the Great Armadillo cult" in popular aesthetic culture. Indeed, Franklin's caricatures of the ugly little armored critters, helped catapult the armadillo to the same status as the longhorn as the symbol of Texas. How important was *The Rag* in galvanizing Austin's hip and radical communities? According to Dreyer, paramount, for "the people who put *The Rag* together were the same people who conceived demonstrations and love-ins, who were among the leaders of confrontations with local authorities, and who were at the forefront of local cultural gatherings. Its pages reflected the thinking of the community while they served to pull it together around common issues. *The Rag* was the common ground of the Austin radical [and hip] communities."[53]

As reflected in Dreyer's comment, underground newspapers such as *The Rag* proved invaluable in helping to foster not only countercultural growth and awareness, but more important, hip community solidarity and identity through shared understandings and experiences. In the larger hip urban enclaves these publications became the crucial propagators and validators of the countercultural ethos, whose reach extended beyond the physical and ideological boundaries of a specific hip neighborhood. For many seekers still wondering whether to embrace the new hippie sensibility, the various news articles, essays, op-eds, and even the cartoons of these underground publications often proved pivotal in convincing one to make the transition from straight to freak. As exemplified by *The Rag*, many of these underground papers became the most important bastion of countercultural identity and purpose in their respective communities, and as such, frequently became places where some of the most critical debates over the definition of the counterculture occurred.

In alliance with the hippie community, Austin's New Leftists embarked on a course of action determined to bring individuals back to their humanity, which they believed had been sucked out of people by the oppressive weights of consumer capitalism and its attendant values. Because the hippies advocated spontaneity and the ecstatic search for the "real life," Austin's student radicals believed such an ethos should become part and parcel of a "new" New Left vision and agenda for change, and thus the hippies must be welcomed and enfolded into the "new" Movement; they would provide the brashness and joie de vivre sorely missing in an increasingly polarized, doctrinaire, and antagonistic New Left by 1968. In the view of most UT-Austin SDS'ers, only through an alliance with the hippies could the *real* cultural revolution take place. Although they maintained respect for each other's differences on many issues and pursued many activities separately, they nonetheless both realized that on the topic of fomenting cultural change they shared much of the same ideology and thus were willing to come together for the common cause. In this regard, the 1960s Austin countercultural community was unique.

Few Texans outside of Austin and the Hill Country were shocked to find that in their state's heartland a hippie community flourished in the late 1960s. Indeed, as co-founder and editor Ronnie Dugger of *The Texas Observer*, one of the nation's leading liberal state journals quipped in 1972, "What can I tell you about Austin? This town, this community is so organic people will turn to compost before your very eyes."[54] To this day, one of the city's favorite placards reads "Keep Austin Weird"; no doubt a slogan and tribute to Austin's hippie legacy.

To the disappointment of some leftists and even some hippies in the nation's other communities, only sporadically did the hip-radical collaboration and affinity for each other's ethos take place, which made the counterculture-student left alliance on the UT campus and in Austin in general that much more extraordinary. On the whole, in most hip-activist communities, there was little common ideological/philosophical ground between the two rebels. Yet, as the decade progressed, they came together at various events, enjoying their mutual passion for dope—particularly grass for the New Leftists, folk-rock music, and sexual freedom. For leftists, smoking pot was not only fun, but because it was illegal, its usage represented one more way to challenge and defy the establishment. To hippie Stan Iverson, the counterculture had "superficially influenced a broad spectrum of the United States, and is such an influence in the New Left that it is impossible—and I think undesirable—to draw a sharp line of distinction between the two movements." Indeed to hipster Ed Sanders the relationship was clear and simple: hippies and politicos had "a commonality of radicalism, smut, chromosome damage, marijuana, street fucking—we know each other."[55]

They also shared a demographic heritage: both student radical and hippie came from comparatively affluent, white upper middle class homes; in the activists' case—at least initially—from urban, ethnic households, while their hippie counterparts were largely from more conservative WASP suburban families. Although both groups disavowed white bourgeois values and lifestyles—their upbringing— they nonetheless went their separate ways when it came to dealing with or challenging the status quo. Few hippies were committed to causes outside of their own lives, while to New Leftists, life in general became one crusade after another against the Establishment, and many defined or circumscribed their lives by the statement "the personal is political and the political is personal." By contrast, hippies valued "passion and feeling, the search for awareness, the cultivation of responsiveness," and thus spent most of their energy pursuing "openness to experience, contact with the world, spontaneity."[56] Nonetheless, the two groups frequently overlapped much more than the youth "experts" at the time allowed.

Still, in the big picture, the political left remained uneasy about the hippies, believing them to be irresponsible and naïve; juvenile evaders and deniers. When the *Berkeley Barb* asked a Trotskyist leader what he thought about the "psychedelic revolution," he replied: "It is a means of escaping the restlessness imposed by everyday life upon everyone in this society. But it is sterile and infantile because it does not fundamentally transform those restrictions which afflict and affect every one of us.... The philosophy of the 'hippies' is a philosophy of politics that says there should be love toward everyone. Love is a good thing, but hatred of what is hateful is as necessary and important."[57] SDS member Carl Ogelsby was less disparaging but still skeptical, warning that at the center of the hippies "new love ethic" was "an intrinsic capacity for surrender." To Ogelsby, despite the hippies anti-bourgeois blustering, the new cultural revolutionaries remained "suburbanites with beads."[58]

Outside of Austin, the counterculture was equally suspicious and often hostile toward the New Left. Reflecting the sentiments of the majority of hippies, Timothy Leary told the *San Francisco Oracle* that "Mass movements make no sense to me, and I want no part of mass movements. I think it is the error that the leftist activists are making. I see them as young men with menopausal minds."[59] Mick Wheelock of the *Los Angeles Free Press* believed that the New Left's obsession with revolution had stripped the movement's ideology of its human-ity. "When you pick up a gun and learn to kill," declared Wheelock, "the part of you that loved flowers and simple things will die!" Raymond Mungo, co-founder of the Liberation News Service and hip critic of the New Left's revolutionary fervor, believed that not only were the leftists' political obsessions damaging the youth movement in general, but that they reflected a "character disorder" within the radical movement. Many hippies and even non-hippies—straight observers—believed that by the late 1960s the New Leftists had become so absorbed by politics and revolution that they had lost all sense of fun. Bill Finn of the *Berkeley Barb* opined that "The New Left writes so many position papers that they never have time for sex. They just take a position."[60]

For the majority of hippies, politics was simply not their "thing"; dope and goofing were. Hippies most definitely opposed the war as well as the Establishment's and bourgeois Amer-ica's other oppressions and hang-ups, but they chose to display their disdain not by marching or demonstrating, but by simply refusing to participate. Until the New Left figuratively and literally imploded, and until the mainstream media and American capitalism obliterated the hippies, the two groups co-existed in an uneasy relationship. Both groups continued to admire and embrace aspects of each other's ethos while simultaneously criticizing the other for its lack of discipline and commitment (the hippies) or for their "power trips," seriousness, and obsession with politicizing everyday life (the student activists).

Despite the proliferation of other hippie enclaves throughout the nation's metropolises, next to the Haight, the largest and perhaps most spirited counterculture community existed in New York's East Village. Thanks largely to the Beat legacy, as early as 1964–65, the East Village had already established a self-conscious alternative community, similar to the Haight in its mixture of drugs, free love, rock music, experimental theater, and increasing numbers of wayward suburban teenagers seeking to find themselves in a Shangri-La of peace, love, and dope. The Village's epicenter was St. Mark's Place, and along that main street, New York hip-pies congregated at the Dom, a converted Ukrainian recreational club, Stanley's on Twelfth Street, the Psychedelicatessen, and Ed Sanders' Peace Eye Bookstore. Sanders, like San Fran-cisco's Lawrence Ferlinghetti, had also been one of the country's early paperback purveyors and publishing pioneers of Beat literature, which put his store on the counterculture map. However, by 1967–68, Sanders, unlike Ferlinghetti, had diversified, not only selling still pop-ular Beat novels and poetry anthologies but all manner of hippie paraphernalia as well.[61]

The East Village was also home to Paul Krassner and to Allen Ginsberg, who had left San Francisco in the early 1960s when North Beach started to become too expensive for its bohemian denizens. Similar to what had happened in San Francisco to North Beach Beats and other avant-garde vagabonds, New York Beat's original settlement, Greenwich Village, now the West Village, had become too fashionable and thus financially prohibitive for its always-strapped Beat inhabitants. They migrated to poorer neighborhoods, in this case, the East Village, a dilapidated section of the Lower East Side. In contrast to the Haight, whose original hippie residents inhabited decently well-maintained, spacious, and relatively "clean" old Victorian homes; the majority of East Village hippies lived in the kind of tenements muck-raker and social activist Jacob Riis crusaded against in the early 20th century—overcrowded, dirty, hot in the summer and cold in the winter (few had any sort of air conditioning and heating systems), poorly ventilated, and badly lighted.[62]

One of the East Village's soon to be most legendary émigrés was Abbie Hoffman, who arrived from Worcester, Massachusetts, in 1966 to run a store selling Mississippi-made crafts for SNCC (Student Non-Violent Coordinating Committee). However, in 1966, under the leadership of Stokely Carmichael, SNCC publicly broke with Martin Luther King, Jr. Carmichael believed that King's program of non-violence had accomplished very little for African Americans (especially in the realm of economic equality), because racism was too deeply embedded in the white psyche for any type of meaningful change to occur in black Americans' status. Thus no amount of moral suasion was going to get white Americans to embrace black equality in any capacity—social, economic, or political. It was time, Carmichael and his followers believed, to promote Black Power, to not only force white Americans to grant blacks their civil and political rights but to henceforth resist, with violence if necessary, all white reprisals. Not only did SNCC leaders break with King with their promulgation of Black Power but they also decided that, in the name of black pride and solidarity, all whites had to be purged from their organization. Thus Hoffman and all his white civil rights activist comrades had to find new causes, which Hoffman pursued with reckless abandon and great fanfare. Indeed, Hoffman came to New York with a purpose: to pioneer a new type of radical hippie devoted to creating a paradise of dope and sex through revolution. Hoffman described himself as an "action freak and anti-intellectual," who, along with his best friend Jerry Rubin and the other East Village Diggers, wreaked mayhem on the streets of New York, engaging in a variety of protest activities so outrageous and absurd that the mainstream news media would be conned into carrying their subversive message free to the masses.[63]

From the beginning of its existence as a legitimate counterculture community, East Village hippies were factionalized into indigenous, self-serving, autonomous grouplets, who believed that their particular brand of hipness defined the New York counterculture scene. These 23 distinct "tribes" included consortiums of painters, writers, crafts artisans, film makers, and psychedelic light show producers collectively known as the Group Image; the Jade Companions; and the Family Store, who provided much needed social services. The Jade Companions was a bail bond company that provided assistance to busted hippies while the Family Store supervised the collection, cooking, and distribution of free food in Manhattan's Tompkin's Square Park. Unfortunately, only a handful of the tribes were willing to put aside philosophical differences in order to unite for the community's common good. Led by the "chief" of the Group Image, Marvin Fishman, the tribal council hoped to bring an end to the contentiousness amongst the 23 tribes by exhorting their more recalcitrant brethren to realize that their community's divisiveness and general hostility made it that much easier for the police and other "hippie haters" to destroy the hippies grand experiment in alternative living.[64]

Unfortunately for East Village hippies, efforts to end the factionalism failed. Too many of the other tribes—the "politicos" as Fishman referred to them—continued in their contempt for their more placid compatriots, frequently displaying their disdain with public acts of aggression and physical confrontation. Suffice it to say, such open rancor did not bode well for the propagation of the hippie message of peace and love.

One group in particular, The Black Mask Revolution (BMR), formed in 1966 and led by abstract impressionist painter Ben Morea and poet Dan Georgakas, epitomized this sinister, reckless, and increasingly violent side of the counterculture. Embracing as their ideology the anti-consumption theories of the Dadaist French Situationists, the BMR made a fetish of the "spectacle," dressing in black clothes and wandering the streets of the East Village snarling and verbally assaulting other hippies, accusing them of being "fakirs," "fags," and "capitalist consumers." Similar to the Haight Diggers (but with a far more fiendish twist), the BMR also performed derisive, anti-establishment comedic acts on East Village street corners to propagate their message of revolution and anarchism. In 1968, BMR changed its name to the scabrous "Up-Against-the-Wall Motherfuckers," a phrase taken from the poem "Black People!" by Amiri Baraka (LeRoi Jones). According to Baraka, "Up against the wall, mother fucker, this is a stick up!" was the most common expression used by "spade" thugs and hoodlums when they robbed white people at gun point on city streets.[65]

Emboldened by their new manifesto, Morea and his comrades rampaged around Manhattan setting fires to the mountainous trash piles that had accumulated during New York City's months-long 1968 garbage strike, disrupted a performance of the Living Theater at the Fillmore East, and in late April 1968, egged on the students at the Columbia SDS uprising. Abbie Hoffman characterized Morea and company as "the middle class nightmare, an anti-media media phenomenon simply because their name could not be printed."[66]

Fishman and the chiefs from the other peaceful, apolitical tribes not only wanted to disassociate their clans from the Motherfuckers and their activities, but also wanted to make it clear to those outside of the East Village that they did not consider the Motherfuckers to be genuine hippies but "pseudo-hippies. They look like we do and they talk like we do, but they don't think like we do. They live down here but they're just not hippies. They do not want to groove with us nor do they want to turn the whole world on to love and peace. They want to destroy the world. We want a better world too, but we believe in doing it by spreading love and peace not hate and violence like the politicos [the Motherfuckers]. They give all hippies a bad rap."[67]

That an often violent sectarianism emerged among East Village hippies should have surprised few people, especially those native New Yorkers who became hippies. Historically, from the 1850s on, neighborhood street gangs had been part of the city's demographic landscape. Most of New York's gang history reflected the never-ending nativist attitudes among the city's Anglo-American community toward the constant influx of non–WASP immigrants; whether they were Irish, Italian, Polish, Russian Jew, or Puerto Rican, none were welcomed. Neither were African American emigrants from the South. Over time, animosity among immigrant groups emerged (Irish versus Italian, for example), and in the ethnic ghettoes gangs formed and "turf wars" between respective immigrant communities became endemic. Thus in many ways, the inter-tribal tension and conflict among East Village hippies could be considered just another dimension in New York's long history of gang organization and violence.

Hippie in-fighting was not the only strife that afflicted the East Village. Similar to the Haight, where hippies had hostile encounters with African American thugs from the Fillmore district, New York hippies frequently clashed with "outsiders": local Puerto Rican toughs often entered the neighborhood to harass hippies, but unlike their Bay Area brethren, East Village hippies were inclined to fight back. The hippies' older Polish and Ukrainian neighbors complained about the noise, the dirt, and the drugs; few if any of the more established residents welcomed the hippies, let alone displayed any willingness to enfold them into the community. There were no straight hippie champions. As occurred in all the other hip neighborhoods, the police regularly engaged in hippie-bashing and unwarranted harassment of East Village hippies. Similar to the Haight, there were also good times: pageants, free rock performances at Tompkins Square Park, free food, and plenty of dope for anyone who wanted it. However, on the whole, East Village hippies possessed a more aggressive disposition than their Haight counterparts, or at least that was the impression southern California sociologists Lewis Yablonsky came away with after visiting the East Village during the Summer of Love. The general squalor, exploitation, and perpetual conflict appalled Yablonsky, especially in comparison with his own Arcadian West Coast.[68]

Despite New York hippies' angry behavior and internal dissention, much of the East Village scene was borrowed from the Haight. New York hippies paid tribute to their Golden State compatriots' psychedelic leadership by commemorating California's criminalization of LSD (October 1966) with a ceremony in Tompkins Square Park. Inspired by the January 1967 Be-In, East Village hippies convened their own version in Central Park's Sheep Meadow on Easter Sunday, March 26, 1967. Spearheading the event were Jim Fouratt, an actor, Paul Williams, the eighteen-year-old Brooklyn-born founder (and soon to be millionaire) of *Crawdaddy!*, the nation's first rock and roll magazine, Susan Hartnett, head of the Experiments in Art and Technology organization, and Chilean poet and playwright, Claudio Badal. With a $250 budget they printed 3,000 posters and 40,000 small Day-Glo handbills designed and donated by hip poster artist Peter Max, and distributed them throughout the city. The police and parks departments quietly and unofficially cooperated with the organizers, perhaps because they were willing to give the hippies the chance to prove that their message of peace and love could genuinely fill the hearts and minds of thousands of people and result in a day of tranquility and the joyful celebration of humanity.[69]

An estimated 10,000 people attended the Be-In, a much smaller crowd than that which gathered on the Polo Grounds two months earlier. The "happening" began around 7:00 a.m. and lasted until dusk. There was no formal summoning of the tribes as there was in San Francisco, and much to the disappointment of many, no rock and roll bands blasted their latest music from a stage; no Hell's Angels or any other renegade biker gangs showed up (probably a blessing); and only a handful of celebrity gurus appeared, the most notable of whom was Allen Ginsberg, who simply mingled with the crowd, performing none of his Eastern rituals and blessings nor addressing the gathering as he did in Golden Gate Park. In short, personalities dominated the first Be-In, and activity centered on the stage; the New York event was more spontaneous, with the action continually shifting from point to point and from group to group with people, according to the *Village Voice*'s Don McNeil, simply "grooving to their own thing or to the rhythms and music [played by individuals] and mantras from all corners of the meadow which echoed in exquisite harmony while thousands of lovers vibrated into the night." Others "joined hands to form great circles, hundreds of yards in diameter, and broke to hurtle to the center in a joyous, crushing, multi-embracing pig-pile. Chains of people careened through the crowds at full run. Their energy seemed inexhaustible."[70]

Although the majority of attendees were hippies, many straight white and Puerto Rican families also participated. The Puerto Ricans had read of the event on posters printed in Spanish, while the "squares" had wandered over to the park after watching the Easter Parade on 5th Avenue. They were curious, no doubt, to see "the freaks" called hippies, who came as outrageously dressed as their Haight counterparts two months earlier. According to Sally Ordway of the *New York Times*, the costumes ranged from "Easter Parade hats and morning suits to high mod gear to psychedelic robes. Many people painted their faces in wild designs and colors ranging from chalk white to glowing lavender. One man was dressed in a suit of long, shaggy strips of paper. Another person wore a jacket covered with buttons, all upside down. 'This isn't a day for slogans,' he explained. " Ordway also believed the crowd was more eclectic in composition than that which assembled at Golden Gate Park with "poets from the Bronx, dropouts from the East Village, interior decorators from the East Side, teachers from the West Side, and teeny boppers from Long Island, as well as nuns from a local convent all wearing Be-In buttons. Grandmothers and executives, hippies and housewives mingled together in harmony." According to McNeil, the event was "at once surreal and beautifully absurd."[71]

Much to everyone's surprise and great relief, New York's "finest," the police, who had already gained a reputation for hippie bashing in the East Village, kept their distance and cool that day, even when approached by carefree hippies, such as those who rushed a squad car and pelted it with flowers, yelling "Daffodil Power." The two cops inside the car calmly rolled down their windows, smiled at their "assailants," waited for the hippie wave to move on, and then drove away. Most of the time, the cops watched the Be-In from the edge of the Sheep Meadow, and only occasionally were their services required such as when two men ran naked through the crowd. The five policemen who finally cornered the "streakers" did not wrestle the men to the ground, handcuff them or arrest them for indecent exposure; the cops simply asked them to put their clothes back on, which they promptly did. By 7:30 p.m. most of the crowd of 10,000 had gone home with only a few thousand hippies scattered throughout the Meadow, remaining. By this time city authorities and the police believed it was time for the Be-In to be officially over. When scores of cop cars arrived, beamed their headlights on the meadow and used bullhorns to order the Be-In to disperse, they met no opposition; within about an hour's time, the Meadow was empty of all human beings.[72]

As Jim Fouratt exulted, "The police were beautiful. It was really strange and it [the Be-In] freaked them out, but they were beautiful." However, not so beautiful was the event's detritus aftermath, which took city workers several days to clean up. Perhaps Allen Ginsberg should have given his New York brethren one of his "kitchen yoga" speeches. Nonetheless, to New York Hippies' delight, their Be-In was an overall success, even though its sponsors didn't believe a Be-In can succeed or fail, "It just is," declared Fouratt, who also wanted to "remain anonymous. People would ask who was organizing it, and we would give them a Be-In button and tell them 'You are.'" Don McNeil provided a more eloquent assessment: "It was a feast for the senses; the beauty of the colors, clothes, and shrines, the sounds, the rhythms, at once familiar, the smell of flowers and frankincense, the taste of jellybeans. But the spirit of the Be-In was tuned—in time—to past echoes and future premonitions. Layers of inhibitions were peeled away and for many, love and laughter became suddenly fresh."[7]

Perhaps the most momentous import from the Haight was the Digger idea, which emerged in the East Village just prior to the 1967 Summer of Love onslaught. Organized by Abbie Hoffman, his new side-kick from Berkeley, Jerry Rubin, Jim Fouratt, and Paul Krassner, the East Village Diggers proclaimed themselves a de facto East Coast branch of their Haight counterparts, and announced that their agenda would be the same but that they might have to "improvise" their tactics in order to achieve the same objectives. Initially the East Village Diggers' faithfully replicated their Haight brethren's' assault on the Establishment: they provided free food to hippies in Tompkins Square Park, organized a communications company to freely distribute mimeographed broadsides, which were often reprints of the Haight's Digger Papers, and opened a free store at 264 East Tenth Street. They also adopted many of the San Francisco Diggers' street theater antics such as summoning hippies to block traffic in response to vehicular congestion in the East Village caused by gawking tourists, which had also occurred in the Haight. The New York Diggers also staged a "Sweep-In" (July 1967) on Third Street in the East Village, one of the neighborhood's chronically dirtiest streets. Bewildered police did not know what to do when the Diggers showed up with brooms and mops and began cleaning the street. One Digger even had the audacity (or courage) to walk up to a New York City cop and polish his badge! Fortunately for everyone the cop took the affront in good humor, laughed, and according to the *Village Voice*, "Everyone on the street laughed along with the cop." The *Voice* also called the "Sweep-In" "a typical Digger goof." Later that year the Diggers sponsored a "Smoke-In" in which people went to Tompkins Square Park and smoked marijuana, which was pretty much what the majority of East Village hippies had been doing anyway for quite some time.[74]

In late August 1967 the New York Diggers pulled off their most memorable caper when they invaded the New York Stock Exchange and showered money from the visitors' gallery onto the trading floor. The spectacle also marked the beginning of the break between the two Digger organizations. The group arranged for a tour of the Exchange by telling officials that they represented ESSO, the East Side Services Organization, a hip social services agency. The fact that they cleverly used the acronym for one of the nation's largest oil corporations (Exxon today) no doubt helped them to gain entrance to the Exchange. The Diggers had also advertised their foray and when they arrived at the Exchange, an alerted security guard was there to stop them. "You're hippies and you're here to burn money," he shouted. Hoffman indignantly denied the charge, declaring "I'm Jewish." Another Digger, Jim Fouratt, announced "I'm Catholic." Worried that he might face religious discrimination charges, the bemused guard backed down and let them in. No sooner did the motley crew reach the balcony than they began throwing fistfuls of dollar bills onto the trading floor below. All bidding suddenly stopped as traders frantically scrambled to pick up as many of the bills as they possibly could. Once they realized what they were doing, they began berating the Diggers, feeling humiliated at being manipulated into revealing publicly the fine line between the greed and self-interest that continues to pervade and pervert American finance capitalism. The spectacle continued outside the exchange as Fouratt announced "the death of money" and Hoffman declared to reporters "No one will ever be a millionaire again. The government owns it [money] and only lets you use it." When a reporter asked Fouratt where the Diggers had gotten the cash they had just thrown away, he replied straight-faced, "Catholic charities."[75]

Emboldened by the media success of their Wall Street escapade, the Diggers became even more audacious in their anti–Establishment assaults, taking their antics beyond the streets directly to their adversaries' places of business. In the fall months of 1967 they plastered "SEE CANADA NOW" signs on the Army Recruiting Center in Times Square; parked a giant Yellow Submarine in a tow-away zone, and incited thousands of jubilant young people to run through lower Manhattan streets one night to hug people, throw confetti, and shout "The war [Vietnam] is over!" One of the Diggers' more innovative and legendary japes that fall was their "Black Flower Day" spectacle performed at the Consolidated Edison building on Irving Place. They first placed a wreath of black ink-dyed daffodils on the ledge above the lobby entrance and then handed out black flowers to pedestrians. They also put up a large banner on the building that declared "BREATHING IS BAD FOR YOUR HEALTH." They then brought into the lobby soot from a pile they had dumped on the sidewalk. Meanwhile other Diggers threw soot in the air outside, some of them dressed in clown suits. As the police

Hippie survival during the 1967 Summer of Love: hawking underground publications on the major street corners of Psychedelphia (photograph by Larry Keenan, courtesy Bancroft Library, University of California, Berkeley. © 1997 Larry Keenan. All rights reserved).

arrived the Diggers hurriedly lit a couple of smoke bombs, threw those into the lobby as well, and within seconds were gone from the scene, as if they had evaporated into the street crowd. Don McNeill of the *Village Voice* witnessed the event and later wrote that "the Digger drama [was] improvised with the idea that a handful of soot down an executive's neck might be more effective than a pile of petitions begging for cleaner air." This Digger caper along with their Stock Exchange prank and many others demonstrated that the East Villagers, unlike their San Francisco counterparts, were willing (indeed they relished the idea and reveled in the action) to take their street theatrics directly to those capitalist institutions and other Establishment bastions that their organization hoped to bring down. The Diggers' high jinks were often tinged with menace, with the hint of violence. As Abbie Hoffman reflected, "Personally, I always held my flower in a clenched fist. A semi-structure freak among the love children. I was determined to bring the hippie movement into a broader protest."[76]

By the late fall 1967 and to the surprise of many East Village Diggers, their San Francisco brethren had become irritated by their tactics and "perversion" of the Digger manifesto. To the San Francisco Diggers, the East Villagers' behavior was little more than self-promotion, marking an irreconcilable rupture. The San Franciscans demanded that the New Yorkers refrain from all such further engagement and if they did not, they then forbade the East Villagers from continuing to call themselves Diggers. It appeared that the original Diggers were ideologically disposed to share everything freely with anyone except their good name. Most objectionable to the San Franciscan's collectivism and egalitarian sensibilities was the emergence of Abbie Hoffman and Jerry Rubin as the group's leaders or spokesmen. Indeed, from the moment Rubin showed up in the East Village in the summer of 1967, he and Hoffman immediately bonded and by the end of the decade they would become not only national celebrities but two of the most legendary individuals in post–World War II counterculture history.[77]

As Abbie Hoffman wrote later of his relationship with Rubin, "Just as Che needed Fidel and Costello needed Abbot, Jerry Rubin and I were destined to join forces. We both had a willingness to go beyond reason." Hoffman took care of "the goofing," while Rubin managed the political tactics and strategy. In Hoffman's view Rubin was better "in getting the cultural revolution incorporated into a broader structure." On New Year's Eve 1967, lying stoned on pillows in a Lower East Side flat, Hoffman, Rubin, and fellow Digger Paul Krassner and girlfriends contemplated their current association with the Diggers and that perhaps it was time to officially break with the West Coast. But then what? As Rubin remembered the sequence of events that then took place: "It's a *youth* revolution. / Gimme a 'Y.' / It's an *international* revolution. / Gimme an 'I.' / It's people trying to have meaning, fun, ecstasy in their lives— a *party.* / Gimme a 'P.' / Whattayou got? *Youth International Party.*" Paul Krassner jumped to his feet and shouted: *"YIP-pie. We're yippies!"* With such an epiphany came the end of the East Village Diggers and the birth of yet another manifestation of the nation's 1960s hip counterculture, the Yippies. The New Yorkers were now free of any contested associations and were also free to take their operation to anywhere and anyplace they so desired.[78]

What was a Yippie? "A flower child who's been busted," wrote Hoffman, "A stoned-out warrior of the Aquarian Age." Despite attempts by Hoffman and Rubin to forge a single movement out of dissent's feuding halves, Yippie was not a movement but rather a myth propagated by a pair of Jewish comedians with the aid of sympathetic organizers spread throughout the counterculture. Indeed, Hoffman, Rubin, and company were outrageous "tummlers," who felt bereft without an audience. The Yippies proclaimed intent was to create a new national organization to transform the mostly apolitical hippies into radicalized activists. These new "Yippies" would then join with the New Leftists and other uncommitted young people at various "youth festivals" (mass protest demonstrations against the Establishment) throughout the nation in which all manner of Digger/street theater mischievous pranks would be performed for the purpose of shifting the youth rebellion not just from protest to resistance against the state, but to a frontal assault on 1960s American culture. As Hoffman announced, one of the Yippies' objectives was to create "a blending of pot and politics into a *potlitical* [sic] grass-leaves movement—a cross fertilization of the hippie and New Left philosophies." Lured by a score of rock bands, hundreds of thousands of kids would flock to Yippie events where the Yippies and their more radicalized New Left allies would transform the youngsters into cultural and political revolutionaries. Of course, all Yippie celebrations would be broadcasted to millions of other Americans and even to audiences around the world, thanks to the news media's willingness (both television and print journalism), to send reporters to cover "the spectacles." On the surface it appeared that the Yippies wanted to use their gatherings and the media attention they attracted as a means of promoting the counterculture. However, Hoffman and Rubin had a much larger ulterior motive: they hoped their events would purposely foment a violent Establishment reaction, which would, in Rubin's words, "put people through tremendous, radicalizing changes" with the objective of stimulating a "massive white revolutionary movement which, working in cooperation with the rebellions in the black communities, could seriously disrupt this country, and thus be an internal catalyst for a breakdown of the American ability to fight guerrillas overseas." Hoffman and Rubin planned for their first Festival of Life to be held in Chicago in late August 1968, at the same time and place where the Democratic Party was holding its national presidential nominating convention, or as one Yippie presciently referred to the Democrats' event, a "Festival of Blood and Death."[79] As will be seen, the Yippies attempt to radicalize the hippies failed rather miserably and violently as their Chicago "Festival of Life" ended in a bloody police riot, which in many ways marked the beginning of the end for the 1960s counterculture in general.

8

The Summer of Love

"Love Generation! What Crap!"—Steve, "the Chemist"

Although disappointed that their Grand Canyon Be-In would not take place, Allen Cohen and company were nonetheless determined to inaugurate the Summer of Love with another massive celebration of the dawning of the New Age, evidence of which they saw in the massive influx of new seekers to the Haight. Although plenty of warning signals had already appeared that there could be serious problems ahead in a neighborhood and city ill-equipped to deal with the onslaught of humanity, veteran hippies remained confident that all would be well. Cohen did not see the impending tsunami of young people arriving in San Francisco as vagabonds or misfits, or momentary thrill-seekers but as searchers engaged in a "holy pilgrimage" to a city that was "alive, human, and divine." As one resident hippie declared, "What we have here is a healthy environment, [and] hippies are coming for a spiritual purpose. They are not vagrants, but creative beings providing for themselves. When the summer ends these people will all go back to their towns and turn on the entire country." To help welcome new hippies and to "affirm and celebrate" the "new spiritual dawn," Cohen and his friends, the H.I.P. merchants, and even the Diggers, put aside their differences and joined together to organize a summer solstice "gathering of the tribes." No doubt Cohen, Thelin, and their compatriots were surprised if not overjoyed to have the Diggers' support. A Digger rejection of participation could have led to disaster, for the Diggers were at the apex of their power and prestige within the community and could have easily used their considerable theatrical creativity and street savvy to turn the event into a complete fiasco. However, Emmett Grogan and his comrades announced such a "do-in," to be worthwhile, even though Grogan had earlier denounced the January Be-In as a "shuck." Grogan believed the forthcoming festival would be "the moment" when people would "build their courage and leave be-ins to the college students, ad men, and news media. They will look to their brothers and not men who claim to be their leaders. And they will never tell anyone what they saw."[1]

At 4:30 in the morning on June 21, 1967, the official advent of the solstice, over a thousand people gathered at Twin Peaks, the highest point in San Francisco, to watch the sun rise, signifying the ceremonial beginning of the Summer of Love. A teenager dressed in robes for the celebration, told a *Chronicle* reporter "I don't think anybody thought the sun was really going to rise but I stood up here and I pointed to where I knew it was and said, 'Get bright, get bright.' And everyone looked and there were chants and drums and incense and bells and

The eclectic, amicable Haight-Ashbury neighborhood before the Summer of Love. Photograph taken in 1967 (courtesy San Francisco History Center, San Francisco Public Library).

Hares and red smoke bombs and somebody even brought a portable record player and some Beatles records." Relieved that the sun did indeed rise, the gathering then walked over to Golden Gate Park, to Speedway Meadow, a long, tree-lined area next to the Polo Field, to continue the festivities, which of course included music performed by the Grateful Dead, Big Brother and the Holding Company, Quicksilver Messenger Service and a host of other up and coming local rock bands. Similar to the January Be-In, the solstice "do-in" had the feeling of a medieval fair, as archers, musicians, jugglers, and freelancers playing whistles, flutes, and guitars moved among the crowd while a lady in a tent painted faces. Food of course, was courtesy of the Diggers, who barbecued a lamb on a hand-rotated spit while frying hamburgers in shovels. Most important for the attendees, there were no speeches; to the Diggers' delight, people were just "doing it." At sundown the solstice was over but it had been "a beautiful day" inaugurating the Haight-Ashbury community's self-proclaimed Summer of Love.[2]

At least 75,000 young people inundated the Haight during the summer of 1967, transforming the neighborhood and the city into "a hippie Fort Lauderdale of the West."[3] As Carolyn Garcia, wife of Grateful Dead guitarist Jerry Garcia (known as "Mountain Girl" at the time), observed, "It was sort of like a farmer unloading a truckload of onions—once the onions start to move, there's no stopping them. That's kind of how it felt, that the streets were just filling up with people, vegetables yearning to be free."[4] San Francisco's Summer of Love was a spectacle, a performance, a saga, a tragedy, and a saturnalia as tens of thousands of tourists, hippie wannabes, and genuine seekers descended upon the neighborhood to consume the hippie identity in some form or another, which they had read about in the press or seen on television. While many visitors—the tourists—never left their cars or tour buses, content to gawk at the hippies through the security of their locked doors and rolled up windows, many more plunged headlong into the Haight scene, hoping to experience as much authentic hippieness as they possibly could. To the Haight's established hippie and straight residents, the majority of the newcomers were potentially troublesome because they were what *Newsweek* called "imitation" or "plastic hippies," transients of one kind or another, "looking for free sex, free food, free dope, and free housing."[5] The overwhelming majority of these individuals had minimal to zero understanding of the hippie movement and its ethos, other than the distortions and falsehoods presented in the mainstream media, and even less awareness of the community it spawned in Haight-Ashbury. Instead, most came for subsequent bragging rights—to be able tell friends (or their eventual children or even grandchildren) that they were part of the Summer of Love and that they had trekked across the country with "flowers in their hair" to the hippie mecca of San Francisco. The majority did not stay long; just long enough to say they were there, and the majority of those who did stay longer only played hippie as they dabbled in varying degrees in the various manifestations of the psychedelic experience and in alternative living. As *Washington Post* reporter Nicholas von Hoffman observed, "The Haight-Ashbury ... had plenty of these [plastic hippies]: frat kids from Rutgers, high school itinerants, rich girls from Funland U. who would come, stay for a week or a month and leave. You'd talk to them and they'd say they came without an intention of staying, that they'd heard about it [the Summer of Love, the Haight-Ashbury] and wanted to make the scene just for a while."[6]

For four months the Haight's bizarre cast of characters performed for a national audience, resulting in *Time* magazine's declaration that the neighborhood was "the vibrant epicenter of the hippie movement."[7] In many ways, the Summer of Love represented not only the zenith of the hippie movement but that of Haight-Ashbury as hippiedom's first and most memorialized ghetto. By the summer of 1967 hippies estimated their full-time population nationwide at 300,000 and imitation Haight-Ashburys proliferated throughout urban America. "The San Francisco sound" ascended the music charts; prestigious museums exhibited psychedelic posters; and doing one's own thing had become the national cliché. However, the real story that summer, unreported by the media, was that the Haight-Ashbury was already dying; the Summer of Love simply proved to be the death knell. Such was the assessment of *Look* magazine writer William Hedgepath, who spent several weeks that summer "underground" covering the Haight spectacle. "The Haight, like most other valuable social phenomena, probably reached its creative peak before people anywhere else were able to learn what *was* going on. What was going on prior to, say, the legendary summer of 1967." Robert Christgau agreed. By the summer of 1967, the *real* hippies had "disappeared in an avalanche of copy. Most of the originals who were living in the Haight in 1966, when the journalists started nosing around, had fled from the bus tour and LSD and the panhandling flower children who will be back in school next semester." Nonetheless, the hippies were center-stage; their presence in the Haight and in other locales represented "America's love affair with bohemia" and it "dominated teen-age life." The hip lifestyle not only appealed "to the lost kids" who migrated to the Haight in the summer of 1967 but to "everyone who was turned on by the hippies, in person and through the media, not only the dropouts but a lot of youngish liberals. It was college instructors who wore their hair kind of long, and lawyers whose wives like to show off their four years of modern in the flicker of a strobe, and all the people who read the *Los Angels Free Press* or the *Berkeley Barb*. It was everyone who smoked pot, and in California that happened to be a lot of everyone."[8] The hippie drama that unfolded that summer in San Francisco had everything: love, crime, madness, sex, squalor, drugs, and art. Most important, the event burned indelible countercultural images on the nation's social psyche while simultaneously slowing its forward momentum.

The Haight community did try to prepare for the impending adolescent tidal wave months in advance, and most revealing was that in their preparation efforts, the hippie's had the full support of the majority of the neighborhood's less eccentric denizens. One such individual was Frank Kavanaugh, a long-time Irish-American Haight resident and chairman of the Haight-Ashbury Neighborhood Council. In several letters to both of the city's newspapers as well as in appearances before the Board of Supervisors, Kavanaugh articulated not only his acceptance of his new neighbors but an understanding and embracing of their message. Kavanaugh prefaced his every missive or speech with the declaration that his views represented the majority opinion of the Haight's non-hippie residents. To Kavanaugh, what had made the Haight for several years one of the most unique and colorful urban environments in the country was the diversity of the "people—no country club estates where you can live among people of similar taste here. We've got all God's Children; black, brown, yellow, white, and pink [gays and lesbians]. We've got high priced professionals in their mansions on the hill, laborers and craftsmen spread throughout, struggling students, veteran welfare recipients, artists, and dropouts. We've got white collar, blue collar, frayed collar, and no collar. They represent a remarkable cross-section of America."[9] Then the hippies emerged in the Haight and Kavanaugh and his straight neighbors were "suddenly faced with a new kind of integration. Beards, sandals, off-mode clothing suddenly appeared among us. A new community had arrived, attracted by a tolerant neighborhood, and for many reasons known only to themselves, they became part of our lives," forcing Kavanaugh and other straight residents "into a painful kind of self-examination. If anything these new neighbors by their very disavowal of many things we held to be essential, caused us to pause and consider our own value systems. The new community by its rejection of certain middle class attitudes of comfort, security, position, and property, has pointed out to us our exaggerated concern for these material distractions. In their effort to create new lifestyles based on personalism and simple awareness of the basic joys of sensible creation, they make us aware of the overlooked pleasures of colors, sounds, trees and children's smiles."[10]

Typical of many native San Franciscans, especially those who lived in such "tight" neighborhoods as the Haight-Ashbury, Kavanaugh expressed a characteristic inner-city chauvinism not only about the Haight but one that disparaged the suburbs as well. To Kavanaugh, the Haight was "America—this narrow, tight, teeming neighborhood. For it has all the kinds of people [that are] in America. What suburb has? It has all the problems of the American people. What suburb has? It has all the rich talents and human powers of America. What suburb has? It has tradition and history, people who are willing to work for each other, an open invitation to any newcomer. What suburb has?" To Kavanaugh the suburbs were for WASP America's "frightened security-seekers," who hid themselves behind a "Stucco Curtain" while their tract home developers held "the torch aloft saying 'Give me your white Christians, your huddled middle class, your refugees from mixed neighborhoods; I will save you from the melting pot.'"[11]

Because of neighborhood pride, Kavanaugh and his hip neighbors such as Chester Anderson, the Thelin brothers, Allen Cohen, and several other hippie activists and straights who were members of the Council for the Summer of Love, rightly worried that if preparations were not made months before the arrival of thousands of teenage seekers, "this city would be faced with the greatest disaster in 50 years." Although many local churches and individuals had "pledged their support, material and professional, without help from City Hall, it will never be enough." The Council thus called on the city to relinquish for incoming hippies' use of "several large buildings in the area which aren't being used, and are ideally suited for our purpose of housing large numbers of people. If we can obtain use of these buildings, a great number of our problems will be solved, merely by keeping masses of people off the streets at night."[12]

Of greater concern to the Council than the influx of would-be hippies were the tourists, who already had inundated the neighborhood and were expected to come in even larger numbers by summer. As Frank Kavanaugh expressed before a Board of Supervisor's meeting, "We might agree that tourism is a good thing when people visit a place to learn about the people, customs and values of that place but when the tourists are of such great numbers that they noticeably alter the essential nature of the place, then effectively they have destroyed that which they sought. That is one of the dangers of this coming summer." Nonetheless, Kavanaugh vehemently opposed the proposal by some supervisors to erect "barricades on the freeways and bridges" and was against the "undue prosecution of laws against young people who have been seduced by the mass media to make the scene." Kavanaugh urged fellow straights to "turn off" their "fear and respond to the many needs which will become apparent this summer." Kavanaugh was sanguine that if both hippies and straights throughout the city worked together to address these issues, the Haight's future would be secure and harmonious and San Francisco's reputation for being one of the most progressive, tolerant, and enlightened cities in the country would endure.[13]

In a broadside to Haight residents fellow Council member Allen Cohen echoed Kavanaugh's belief that San Francisco would rise to the occasion and provide the leadership and resources necessary "to nourish this small part of a worldwide spiritual awakening." Cohen was convinced that San Francisco had been chosen by God "for this momentous role in the history of the American continent" and because it was a "holy city" it would "provide food for the soul and joy for the mind" as well as "food for the stomach and rest for weary feet."[14]

Much to Haight residents' relief the first month of the Summer of Love went surprisingly well, primarily because acid and pot were plentiful and thanks to the Council's exhortations, the police followed a hands-off policy, allowing hippies, both old and new, free reign in the neighborhood. However, by July, despite the best of intentions of all concerned, the sheer numbers of young human beings pouring into the Haight simply outstripped the community's ability to provide for their needs. By that time, portions of the neighborhood, especially the main drag, looked more like a Third World slum, old Calcutta, with hordes of teenage waifs and older vagabonds, barefoot with tinkling anklet bells and clad in brightly colored rags, squatting on the sidewalks begging or panhandling in the streets. Others for survival hawked the *Oracle*, the *Barb*, as well as all manner of tour brochures and hand bills for local restaurants and boutiques, which had proliferated since the Be-In. Hippies like everyone else needed money to live. Some survived on subsidies from home or came with money. Most sold a little dope, usually grass to other hippies and to the swarms of college students and young professionals who descended on the Haight on the weekends, once it had become the in place. The smell of incense, patchouli oil, and of course marijuana smoke permeated from practically every nook and cranny while street dealers pitched "Acid, speed, lids?" to passersby. To live in the Haight that summer meant to be surrounded by masses of people all the time, endless faces of humanity from all walks of life and from all over the country, even the world, with many desperately wanting to experience the media-hyped hippie lifestyle to its fullest sensory and sensual capacity with reckless abandon, regardless of the consequences.[15] By August, the mass of summer residents had reached an estimated 100,000, and as result, the "Haight-Ashbury had become an unpleasant place to live—a circus and a caricature of its original version. People took on hippie personas for the summer. The strain of mysticism can only work in small groups. Attitudes were getting tough and people were just there for the drugs, not for the idyllic vision of change."[16]

So "foreign" was the Haight that during the Summer of Love, that the Peace Corps decided to send 180 of its volunteers to the neighborhood for a week-long "survival training." Each worker was given $12 and "the good wishes of his teacher" and was expected to exist on his or her own for the week for no additional money. The agency believed that stationing its new recruits in the Haight for a week would give them a good introduction to "harsh living conditions and human deprivations" before shipping them off to the Philippine Islands, where they would be working either in the slums of Manila or on farms near Luzon. As one Peace Corps volunteer announced before going to the Haight, "Haight-Ashbury looks like a more difficult assignment than the one I am about to be sent to. I hope I can make it." As the independent *San Francisco Standard* fancifully opined, "The trainee may not learn very much about survival techniques in the Haight-Ashbury but they will learn about love. They know it though their directors don't. No one will lose. For in the end, Love is the best survival technique."[17]

By early July so many kids had settled in the Haight that the Diggers could no longer provide free food and closed down their program. The hordes of flower children created an acute housing shortage, with new arrivals forced to cram into tiny, squalid "crash pads" where sanitation was abysmal, and people lived and slept cheek by jowl while being gouged for exorbitant rents. Such living conditions created the perfect environment for infectious diseases as pneumonia, hepatitis, flu, and chicken pox spread rapidly from hippie to hippie. Hundreds, if not thousands of others, suffered from illegal abortion complications, skin infections, gum diseases, malnourishment, and intestinal disorders from eating rotten food. Such contagions and maladies were not ones people associated with a prosperous American tourist destination and they were certainly not ailments common to white, affluent middle class suburban Americans unless they willingly chose the dissipated life. Some help for the afflicted—either from illness, drug overdose, venereal disease, street contagions and injuries came from Dr. David Smith, who founded a free medical clinic in the Haight after finishing his medical internship. Smith had lived in the neighborhood while completing his medical training and felt a responsibility for its denizens. The clinic, on the corner of Haight and Clayton, opened its doors in early June 1967 and thereafter provided first aid and emergency care for hundreds of patients and served as a safe refuge and hang-out for many of the Haight's homeless and more desperate characters.[18]

Orphaned at nineteen and cursed with a heavy drinking problem he inherited from his father who drank himself to death, Smith overcame his alcohol addiction long enough to graduate from UC Berkeley and go on to medical school at the San Francisco campus. Particularly intrigued with his pharmacology classes, Smith began personally experimenting with acid, mescaline, and marijuana, all of which replaced alcohol as his new high. In subsequent post–1960s interviews, Smith candidly admitted that "taking LSD was an incredibly positive experience ... it was a religious experience.... To be truthful, I wouldn't have opened the free clinic if I hadn't been taking LSD. And I smoked marijuana every day for twenty years. I was part of that Sixties drugs-are-romantic thing.... I 'd never have done what I did in my life had I not had that spiritual experience on LSD."[19]

Also inspiring Smith to open the free clinic to treat drug-afflicted hippies and the dispossessed was the way mainstream medical care at the time so cavalierly dismissed "the voluntary indigent," often denying the hippies and other disadvantaged individuals treatment. The physicians at San Francisco General Hospital, the city's largest all-purpose health care center, "treated [the kids] like garbage" and would always ask them "'Why are you coming here? You're voluntarily poor. Besides you use drugs—and dress weird and listen to weird music.'" Witnessing the neglect and contempt of his peers at San Francisco General convinced Smith to open his free clinic because "not only *should* I do it, but I *had* to do it."[20]

As Smith developed his idea for a free clinic he realized he "was pretty naïve about health politics then but the concept of 'free' was all around me. I became the architect of the slogan 'Health care is a right, not a privilege.' That was the founding philosophy of the Haight-Ashbury Free Clinic. It was a very radical idea then. Now it's being debated in the mainstream. And it all came out of this area, the street university known as the Haight-Ashbury. I was learning more every day walking around in my neighborhood that I ever learned in a lab." With donations from various community leaders and with the help of an ex-physician-turned-private investigator-turned acid head named Robert Conrich, the Free Clinic opened its doors on June 7, 1967, in an old dental office on the second floor of a faded yellow Victorian at 558 Clayton near the corner of Haight Street. Joining Smith were volunteer doctors and nurses from around the Bay Area and local hippies who handled the administrative chores. Suffice it to say, Haight residents were overjoyed; Smith and his compatriots treated 250 patients on opening day; 350 the next. However, no sooner did Smith hang out his shingle, than he encountered opposition and resentment, not only among the medical establishment, but more importantly and potentially damaging to his cause, from hostile city officials, led by City Health Director Ellis Sox, whom Smith believed so hated hippies that he "wanted to isolate the Haight-Ashbury and let its young residents die." Smith so outraged the establishment that they accused him of being "a Communist." Smith responded to such outlandish accusations by telling his carpers that "All we were doing was giving health care to the poor. How is that un–American?" Smith had difficulty understanding such disdain for his idea and the free care he was administering; after all the majority of his patients were young people who "came from traditional backgrounds. They were the establishment's own sons and daughters. They didn't come to Haight-Ashbury to go to the Free Clinic. They came for the music, for the freedom. And if you didn't take care of them, they'd get sick and clog up hospital emergency rooms. They certainly wouldn't go home."[21]

Smith not only had to contend with hostile, anti-clinic doctors and city officials, but with the cops as well, who regularly harassed Smith, his staff, and his patients on the pretext that they were looking for runaways or illegal drugs. In order to stop the police raids and the excuses for them, Smith posted a very visible sign at the top of the stairs to the clinic's entrance that read "NO DEALING! NO HOLDING DRUGS. NO USING DRUGS. NO ALCOHOL. NO PETS. ANY OF THESE CAN CLOSE THE CLINIC. WE LOVE YOU." Even more menacing than the cops were the drug dealers, one in particular named Papa Al who had designs on the clinic as a base for his drug operation. Papa Al specialized in speed, which had become a very lucrative enterprise, enough to afford Al a Berkeley mansion. Al roamed the Haight's streets packing a .38 revolver along with a burly bodyguard named Teddy Bear. Both men "volunteered" at the clinic, posing as Good Samaritans and Smith, upon discovering their real intentions, ordered them to leave the clinic. Al responded by putting out a contract on Smith and his clinic's administrator, Donald Reddick, offering a $100 bounty worth of speed to anyone who knocked them off. Smith's complaint was predictably dismissed by the police, confirming Smith's opinion that "the police were no protection. If Papa Al moved, I'd be dead. The cops' attitude was, here's this insane asylum called the Haight, and whatever you crazed animals do in there to each other, we don't give a damn—just don't let it spill out into the rest of the city."[22] It was fast becoming apparent to many Haight residents that the city's law enforcement and civil authorities considered the 44-block neighborhood and its inhabitants a pariah to be quarantined, for all had become "infected" by a socio-cultural contagion called "hippieness." If hippies killed each other in the process, so be it; they would be saving the city time, money, and effort.

Reddick gave Smith a pistol and holster, uncomfortable for a doctor physically and psychologically, treating patients with a gun strapped to his body and looking over his shoulder every time he left the office. Out of desperation Smith turned to the Hell's Angels, whom the community had already embraced as their protectors from all manner of abuse and violence, be it from the cops, sinister drug dealers, Fillmore black thugs, gangsters, or other rogue characters, who happened to show up in the Haight. However, there was always a potential price to pay for the biker's favor or protection; their mercurial behavior could just as easily turn on the hippies as anyone else. Fortunately for Smith, all turned out well. He contacted the Angels' leader Sonny Barger and told him of the contract out on himself and Reddick. Two Angels visited Papa Al and told him of the

The hippies' "protector": Freewheelin' Frank of the Hell's Angels motorcycle gang, San Francisco, California, 1966 (photograph by Larry Keenan, courtesy Bancroft Library, University of California, Berkeley. © 1997 Larry Keenan. All rights reserved).

new "arrangement" between Smith and the Angels. "You're David Smith's insurance policy. If anything happens to him—if he's hit by a car walking across the street—you're dead." The hit on Smith and Reddick was soon thereafter rescinded and Papa Al vanished from the Haight's streets. The Angels' reputation and historical legacy is far from positive but as far as David Smith is concerned, "They saved my life."[23]

Worry about his own safety was not Smith's only concern; his clinic was in constant financial straits. However, thanks to the *Chronicle*'s science reporter David Perlman, who featured Smith and his clinic in a front-page article titled "A Medical Mission in the Haight-Ashbury"; and to Bill Graham who held benefit concerts; and to the local celebrity rock bands such as Big Brother and the Holding Company who raised money for the project along with Kathryn Crosby, Bing Crosby's wife who frequently donated her time at the clinic as well as gifts of money, furniture, food, and medication; the Haight-Ashbury Free Clinic survived and is still in operation today. Inspiring Graham to become one of Smith's greatest fans and benefactors was the constant police harassment of his main "customers and clientele"— the hippies. Graham told Smith that "These kids have made my business possible. They don't deserve this treatment. Now I want to do something for them. We need the clinic. Its humanity—and the least I can do." In two benefit concerts, Graham raised $10,000 dollars for the Free Clinic, a substantial sum of money in 1967. An appreciative Smith rightly noted that, "Without Bill Graham, the clinic would not have survived its fragile infancy that summer.... We literally built this clinic on rock 'n' roll."[24]

Of greatest concern to Smith was the Haight's drug problem, which by early July had become very serious because both the pot and acid wells had run temporarily dry. Many hippies were so desperate for dope that they began taking Methedrine, an amphetamine that produced a rapid rush followed by a sharp emotional down and then, after prolonged use, hallucinations with a brutal paranoid twist. STP, a fast version of mescaline with high freak-out potential, was another alternative as well as the ultimate extreme. From beginning to end, the Haight's economy floated on drugs. According to Smith, once "Speed hit the Haight, it *all* went wrong" and "terrible violence" ensued. "I know how bad it was. I lived through it. Any philosophical movement fueled by drugs is doomed to fail. Janis Joplin helped save the Free Clinic in 1967 and then died of a drug overdose in 1970. I know all of the bad stuff."[25]

The Haight was the West Coast's major production and trading center for high-grade LSD. Other brands of acid circulated the Haight as well, including a trashy, dangerous concoction reputedly manufactured in Italy and sold by the Mafia.[26] The older, established dealers sold "righteous" (pure, clean) acid or pot, but there were scores of cheats, "burn artists," who adulterated, diluted, or misrepresented their wares. They were among the community's most despised citizens and if caught, were severely punished by their more "honest" peers. As the grass and acid disappeared and hippies became more desperate for their highs, the number of burn artists proliferated, especially those selling speed, which became the most widely used substitute for hippie dope users and—the most polluted. Veteran acid heads inveighed against meth, putting up signs warning people that "SPEED KILLS." The stuff was mixed with baking soda, tooth powder, talcum powder, and even such substances as battery acid. "What they do is grab anything, put it in the packet, and sell it," said one "legitimate" speed merchant named Rod. "They'll run into the street, get liquid out of the car battery, put it on a saucer, evaporate it, and what's left looks like real crystal. When I get hold of a burn artist, he's going to have pain. I make 'em take their own stuff, overamp [overdose] till they scream. I put 'em in the hospital, not for a couple of days either. I put 'em in the hospital for six or eight months because I don't break their bones, I break their joints and that snaps their tendons and rips their muscles."[27]

A similar fate awaited bad acid peddlers. According to a Papa Al's bodyguard and hit man, "Teddybear," a burn artist named "Lucky," was caught dealing "bad shit" by Teddybear and his "brothers," the Hell's Angels and dealt with "the hippy way, with love": Lucky was forced to ingest "60,000 mikes in three STP capsules, and he doesn't burn anybody anymore. He came out of that trip a beautiful human who only sells good shit now. See, that's how we hippy people do it with love."[28]

Contributing to the Haight's serious drug problem was the mainstream media's continuous touting of the neighborhood as the nation's dope capital, where there awaited a "psychedelic smorgasbord" for all those who came seeking thrills. However, as harder drugs such as STP and speed replaced the traditional staples of marijuana and acid, there was a shift in the community as the new arrivals increasingly came purely for kicks; spiritual enlightenment was of little consideration. The debasing of psychedelics' higher purpose by the plastic hippies greatly dismayed the community's true-believer acid heads. Unfortunately the thousands of pretend hippies who swarmed through the Haight that summer, looking for cheap thrills, shattered into oblivion the psychedelic utopia the neighborhood's original hippies envisioned the Haight-Ashbury would become as a result of the Summer of Love.

According to Dr. Smith, the Haight's drug issues were the result of "society not treating drug abuse as a health problem but as a police problem. My biggest criticism of the straight community is that they don't try to understand why the kids do it, and it's not just a few kids. Do you know that in the month of July we treated over two thousand of them [for drug abuse]. They are what I call a 'generation at risk.'" Smith believed the Haight had "tremendous energy" but was "crumbling at the edges" because so many of its inhabitants were "hung up on drugs, too many of them; they're not moving on to something else. I am appalled at the number of teeny-boppers who've taken LSD three hundred and four hundred times. They stay stoned all the time. What are we going to do with them? Drag them back by the hair? I don't know. I guess you could go down on Haight Street tonight and arrest half the boys as draft dodgers. It's getting frightening."[29]

Prior to the youth invasion, the majority of the community's founding members turned people on to dope expecting no compensation for their generosity; they viewed dope usage part and parcel of their identity and a reflection of their anti-materialism and anti-profiteering ethos. To the Haight's original hippie founders, dope should be free or the return should be minimal; just enough to buy life's essentials: another "lid" or tabs of acid from a brother or sister hippie with the same mentality toward dope and money. Marijuana and LSD were frequently given away to dancehall audiences, Acid Tests participants, and to the thousands of hippies gathered at such events as the Be-In, where huge profits could have been easily made if dealers so desired. But now not only was the Haight's population composition changing dramatically because of the Summer of Love; so was the community's attitude toward drug usage as newcomers created an opportunity for drugs to be bought and sold for a profit on the open market. The new arrivals brought with them from their white suburbs a capitalist consumption mentality based on the fundamentals of supply and demand.[30]

As the thrill seekers flooded into the neighborhood during the Summer of Love, the previous spirit of giving gave way to an aggressive, violent, profit-oriented drug trafficking business and a "Mafia mentality" toward drugs engulfed the Haight, at least according to the *Oracle*. "Whenever we attach value or worth or wealth to any external object whether gold or dope or property or country, that object in the pursuit for happiness becomes an object of contention more important than the human mind that is the original source of all wealth or value." The *Oracle* reminded readers that "Dope is valueless," but the newcomers and even some of the community's older members had made drugs "a glittering game of buying and selling" and creating a "Mafia state of mind" among brothers and sisters, many of whom now see dope as means to "buy status and things, which will hurt the community and change us into the very people we have come to the Haight-Ashbury to avoid." Hippies must absolve themselves "of this attachment" and if they do and return to their previous "spirit of giving and loving" then "there will be no Mafia control no murder no profiteering." It was essential for all hippies to "not buy or sell dope anymore! Let's tell our friends not to buy or sell dope any more—Let's detach ourselves from that material value—Plant dope and give away all you can reap.... Let's disengage ourselves from the commercialization and bottomless desire for more dope."[31]

Bad trips and strung-out teenagers were not the only health problems affecting the Haight during the Summer of Love. Equally alarming to Smith and other Haight physicians was the spread of hepatitis from speeders using dirty needles and venereal diseases such as gonorrhea, syphilis, and crabs that ran wild through the hippie population. Indeed, in the 10-month period from November 1967 to August 1968, Smith's Free Clinic reported 1250 cases of STDs and 1,922 diagnoses of "obstetric-gynecologic problems." A high percentage of the latter maladies was the result of botched abortions; trips by young, pregnant teenage girls to Tijuana, Mexico, for back-alley procedures. One of the clinic's more famous patients who suffered the consequences of a mishandled Mexican abortion was Janis Joplin, who was so grateful for Smith's care that she became one of the Free Clinic's greatest benefactors. Gonorrhea, Smith noted had "reached epidemic proportions." Indeed, because "there was a lot of group and communal sex, it would be an understatement to say there was a spike in STDs. That's like saying a hurricane is a strong wind. So we often said 'Well let's just bring in a gallon of penicillin and inject everybody." What had caused the scene to degenerate from carefree experimentation into a disease-ridden mess? In Smith's view, "we went from idealism to despair."[32]

Free love, even in 1967, carried some high risks, often the result of hippies preying on their own kind—desperate, lonely, hungry, cold young teenage girls and boys willing to become someone's "old lady" or "male companion" in exchange for a roof over their heads and food in their stomachs. For many male hippies and even for some of their female counterparts, but certainly not all, sex was about immediate sensual gratification and excitement—ecstasy through orgasm. Most Haight encounters were one night stands. Janis Joplin, the great white blues singer of Big Brother and the Holding Company, whose legendary onstage performance and persona effused sexual ecstasy ("she sang like she was fucking"), and whose personal life reflected much of the worst of hip's pleasure seeking, perhaps best summed up much of the hippie ethos regarding sex. "How was your vacation on St. Thomas"? a friend asked a year before she died of a heroin overdose. "It was just like everywhere else," she replied. "I fucked a lot of strangers."[33]

According to one of Joplin's lovers, Country Joe McDonald of Country Joe and the Fish, what really killed the great white blues singer was sexism because most of her male friends saw her not only as a woman, but also as "one of the guys," who could hold her own with them when it came to sex, drugs, drinking, and swearing. According to McDonald, "Everybody wanted this sexy chick who sang really sexy and had a lot of energy … and people just kept saying one of the things about her was that she was just 'one of the guys.' … That's a real sexist bullshit trip, 'cause that was fuckin' her head around … she was one of the women. She was a strong, groovy woman."[34]

The stereotypical association of hippies and sexual liberation and the exaltation of sex (primarily heterosexual) in general would never have come about had it not been for the introduction of "the Pill," an oral contraceptive licensed in 1960 by the Food and Drug Administration, which doctors could then legally prescribe to their married female patients who did not want to get pregnant. By the late 1960s unmarried women were also finally able to obtain prescriptions for the pill. The impact of the Pill on the late 1960s and early 1970s sexual revolution was profound, for the Pill relieved a single woman's greatest fear relative to premarital sex: pregnancy. STDs, although always a risk, were not yet as frightening or as widespread a consequence. As David Allyn observed, "It is almost impossible to overstate the impact of the pill on American culture. It gave women the freedom to have sex when and where they wished and made contraception palatable to the prudest of the prude. It put birth control on the covers of family magazines and symbolically represented scientific support for the sexual revolution. The pill promised a return to the rationalism and optimism of the Age of Enlightenment." A sexual culture had thus emerged before the first tie-dyed teenage runaway hitched a ride to the Haight-Ashbury during the Summer of Love.[35]

For all of the counterculture's proclamations about "transcendence," self-actualization, intimate personal relationships; community, and uninhibited emotional and physical expression, sadly, when it came to gender equality and sex, hippies, especially males, remained traditional, if not regressive in their views and practices than they would have ever dared to confess, and as a result women continued to be commodified sexual objects. The mainstream press helped perpetuate and reinforce this image by focusing on the hippies' alleged obsession with wild sexual behaviors. Indeed, "free love" became one of the defining characteristics of the counterculture identity. In his article for *Ramparts*, Warren Hinckle described the Haight as a place where hippies enjoyed "sleeping nine to a room and three to a bed, seem to have free sex and guiltless minds" and where "women don't seem, from the outside, to belong to any particular man." *Time* claimed that hippies had sex "however and with whomever they can find (including 'group grope')."[36]

Although claiming to offer Americans an alternative lifestyle, liberated from all bourgeois "hang-ups"—of which sexual repression was paramount— a very familiar heterosexual, male-dominated ethos prevailed in the counterculture movement. Many straight Americans ridiculed their long-haired, bearded, thin, weirdly dressed hippie counterparts as effeminate "sissies"; casting real men in the traditional, white jock image of the randy playboy. Hippie males, however, viewed themselves in quite the opposite context: they considered their long hair, jewelry, and flowing clothing to be symbols of their sexual potency and a bold statement of their rejection of mainstream gender norms—an "androgynous drift."[37] Many saw themselves as the vanguard of redefining American maleness; that the New Age would deliver a new American male free from all the machismo and ego-driven aggression, competitiveness, conformity, and consumption that had come to inform white American masculinity in the post-war years. The hippie male was the harbinger of a more sensitive and benign form of manliness; a radically new personae who would not run scared from intimacy and sensuality, and who would understand and treat women more equitably, respectfully, and lovingly because they were not afraid to embrace their anima. In reality, few hippie males practiced what they preached, and consequently, from beginning to end, the majority of counterculture males adhered to dominant notions of male sexual prowess and superiority; and counterculture women continued to be perceived as sexual commodities.

When it came to sex, the majority of male hippies and their straight counterparts shared similar views: both had been raised to equate sex with their masculinity. For both, sexual liberation meant that women were now (thanks to the Pill) allegedly more inclined to have sex with them, at any time or place, without the specter of unwanted pregnancy, reservations, or hang-ups. However, much to the disappointment of both straight and hippie men, many women continued to be affected by their own rearing and the message that sex reflected commitment and emotional intimacy. Although by the late 1960s many young women had absolved themselves of guilt for random sex relative to being labeled a "loose woman," many nonetheless still found it difficult to overcome their hesitation in the face of pressure exerted by self-interested men, who chided them for not "putting out" because they were still repressed about sex. "There was this ethic that it was good for you to have as much sex as possible and you were uptight and hung up if you did not," admitted native Ohioan Susan Keese, who came to the Haight as a twenty-year-old during the Summer of Love. "Some women seemed comfortable with that, but I was not. Years later I found out many of the other women did not want to either. We felt like we had to work on ourselves if we didn't like it."[38]

Many hippie men exploited the vulnerability of hippie women who hoped that physical intimacy would lead to a more emotionally stable and exclusive relationship. Commonly, in the hip heterosexual community, hormonally restless men who were bored with their partner for whatever reason, rarely hesitated to walk away, frequently accusing their abandoned mate of harboring hang-ups about sex and relationships rather than being open and understanding of male wanderlust. For such men (or boys), "the whole scene became too heavy" to endure and they "split" with little remorse or guilt. A SCUM (Society for Cutting Up Men) Manifesto declared hippie males to be nothing more than sex-crazed manipulators, predators, and slackers, who were "excited by the thoughts of having lots of women accessible" to them but who "rebel against the harshness of the Breadwinner's life and monotony of one woman." The counterculture's denunciation of the sexual double standard and proclamations about gender respect and equality rang hollow, often conveniently applied only to women with little expectation of behavioral change on the part of hippie men. Most hippie women were far from fools or as desperate to be "loved' as the popular media portrayed. Indeed, the hip sexual ethos helped many counterculture women to absolve themselves of "waiting for the right man syndrome," while simultaneously encouraging sexual explorations, which helped many to discover their "power [at] that time because women started to become aware and confident of their sexual natures, to feel that it was all right." Naturally, over the course of the movement, these women saw through the male hypocrisy and moved on long before they got "dumped," in the process, developing a more confident self-image and a more holistic, mature, and practical understanding of the sexual revolution they helped ignite. Perhaps most important, they found their inner strength to say no to coercive male demands.[39]

Hippie men nonetheless took advantage of hippie women. Despite all the talk of a "new society" the Haight had its fair share of misogynistic, chauvinist males and their female victims. Hippie "chicks" were often pathetic runaway waifs who found themselves defenseless against the male hustlers who congregated in the Panhandle, waiting for such desperate innocents to hop off the bus. Stories abounded of girls drugged comatose and then used as communal sexual resources by all comers. As one Haight hippie observed, "There are a lot of young girls who are coming in from the suburbs who really want to get laid and be liked and loved. And they're getting fucked but they're not getting loved. And that's because young males have their own hang-ups. They can't love everybody. I know a couple of communal places that have more and more meth-heads going all the time, and girls getting stoned on meth and get fucked for couple of days until they freak out. But that's not sexual freedom, that sexual compulsion."[40]

Shamefully, the commodification of counterculture women as sex objects went largely unchallenged, as both the mainstream and underground media perpetuated and re-enforced female objectification. Both currents presented stereotypical images of female hippies as innocent "Flower Children" who "give and take love at the drop of a petal,"[41] or as alluring, exotic goddesses; sexually charged sirens and temptresses, who "lounge in the grass, clad in nothing but beads, and bells, and feather headdresses"[42] waiting for the next young man to come along to entice with the prospect of copulation. The mainstream media also liked to present hippie women as wayward victims or as naïve and trusting innocents, lured into the counterculture by rapacious males and oblivious of the perils that awaited them as they plunged unwittingly into the pleasures of the flesh.

As such stereotypes of hippie women emerged, many of the most important mediums for propagating the counterculture message, such as the underground press and the commix (both male-dominated enterprises), betrayed hippie women's attempts at liberation as they put forth their own equally distorted, shallow, and highly insulting caricatures of counterculture women. The underground press' main readership was young, white middle-class males, who retained traditional attitudes toward women and sex and found the misogynistic and denigrating images of women in such journals appealing. At times hip newspapers were even more vulgar and demeaning in their objectification of hippie women than the mainstream press; witness the *Oracle* writer (a female!) who described the young women at one hip event as "sweet pretty pussy."[43] Apparently this particular hip female had no problem with identifying her sisters as sexual objects.

Underground comix in particular became legendary for having the most graphic and debasing depictions of hippie women and of women in general. Perhaps in no other underground medium did male sexual fantasy and perversion abound than in the comix. For the male cartoonists, nothing was taboo. Virtually all the women in the strips were either uncontrollable nymphomaniacs, seductive, sadistic vamps, or naïve, drugged-out hippie "chicks" willing to do anything involving sex. The readers, editors, male artists and others associated with comix productions claimed such presentations represented "revolutionary journalism," designed to outrage and challenge the mainstream media and bourgeois propriety. According to female cartoonist Trina Robbins, who tried to break-in with *The East Village Other* that particular underground publication was "loaded down with graphic rape scenes and every other degradation toward women that the writers/artists could think of. Entrails, usually female were scattered over the landscape in a phenomenon of violence to women that I believe has never been equaled in any other medium."[44] Offensive language and obscene sexual stereotypes further bolstered male chauvinism and misogyny, which were the hallmarks of the underground press during late 1960s and early 1970s.[45] As Gretchen Lemke-Sanatangelo has noted, by so exploiting women, the underground press, the comix, and even hippie poster art so objectified and marginalized women that they were "placed outside of the cultural revolution" and thus "their thoughtful and very deliberate commitment to counterculture ideals" were "completely ignored."[46]

As a result of such demeaning oppression, a more resistant and combative feminist consciousness emerged within the hip counterculture, that rightly declared that much of what was touted in the name of liberation, was nothing more than business-as-usual female exploitation that had been cleverly reformulated to reflect the new hip ethos and concealed and promulgated in the hip rhetoric of the underground press. In a liberation manifesto published in the New York underground the *Rat*, titled "Goodbye to all That," Robin Morgan took head-on the blatant chauvinism, misogyny, and sexual exploitation that was endemic throughout the hip and general counterculture scene. Morgan asserted that the counterculture's supposed sexual liberation ideology was a sham that reinforced male dominance and traditional gender roles and expectations, especially when it came to sex. In Morgan's view, "the so-called Sexual Revolution, has functioned towards women's freedom as did the Reconstruction toward former slaves—reinstituted oppression by another name." Morgan not only condemned the hip sexual liberation ethos but also those "sisters" who she believed had sacrificed their feminism in a "desperate grab for male approval." Thus it was time for women to say "Goodbye to Hip Culture," particularly to the movement's obvious perpetuation of female objectification and consequent oppression and sexual manipulation. As reflected in Morgan's manifesto, it did not take long for many women to realize that the sexual freedom championed by the hippie movement did not necessarily change their role in mainstream America—they just wore different costumes.[47]

Because both the mainstream media and the underground press presented hippie women in such contexts, it was no surprise that many believed the Summer of Love was nothing more than an orgy of "free love," and thus most of the new arrivals were men. Uppermost in their mind was the pursuit of guilt and consequence-free sexual escapades.[48] Also contributing to the male population's increasing demand for sex was the fact there were significantly more men than women in the Haight during the Summer of Love. The social consequences of this situation became alarmingly obvious by July 1967 as the Haight-Ashbury community witnessed dramatic increases in sexual assault against women. The Diggers, always ready to fix the blame on the H.I.P. Merchants and their "co-conspirators," the editors of the *Oracle*, for the media hype which had drawn such "vultures" to the Haight and that was destroying the Summer of Love in general, published a broadside through Chester Anderson's Communications Company that expressed the magnitude to which their community had degenerated. "Pretty little sixteen-year-old middle class chick comes to the Haight to see what it's all about & gets picked up by a 17-year-old street dealer who spends all day shooting her full of speed again & again, then feeds her 300 mikes [micrograms of acid] and raffles off her temporarily unemployed body for the biggest gang bang since the night before last. The politics and ethics of ecstasy. Rape is as common as bullshit on Haight Street."[49]

Countercultural women's sexual subordination and the continued denigrating of a woman's worth, made it all the easier to perpetuate traditional gender norms, and thus the majority of hippie women were expected by their man to remain within the confines of domesticity of cooking, cleaning, sewing, and childrearing. Interestingly, counterculture women had greater difficulty breaking free from these particular shackles and stereotypes than from popular sexual objectification and personal inhibitions relative to sexual experimentation. Acceptance of these particular gender constructs required herculean efforts on their part—at least among those women courageous enough to do so— to redefine a woman's role in the larger hippie community, let alone to break free from such constraints all together. Both male and female hippies accepted the reality that men and women were different; that women were more intuitive, nurturing, cooperative, nonaggressive, immediate, and defined or circumscribed by their emotions and bodies. If such was a "woman's nature," then it made perfect sense that they continue in their "natural," traditional roles—albeit in a different "set and setting"—as wives, mothers, caregivers, and helpmates. The majority of hippie women not only personally embraced such traditionalism but publicly promoted and reinforced such roles for women within the hip culture. Such was the outlook of Maggie Gaskin, who asserted that "The women in the hippie community are very very female. There are a lot of children that are there because they're wanted, and the women are going back and doing very feminine things, like weaving and cooking with a lot of pride, doing it as a woman thing."[50]

Hippie "siren" and libertine, the legendary hip love poetess, Lenore Kandel, whose *Love Book* contained some of the most erotic, explicit, and at times profane descriptions of heterosexual loving making ever written in American poetry, concurred with Gaskin that "A woman is always in relation to a man, really. I don't know any woman who digs being a woman who doesn't want her man a touch stronger. A woman who isn't happy being a woman for

Feminism on the march, late 1960s, San Francisco, California (photograph by Larry Keenan, courtesy Bancroft Library, University of California, Berkeley. © 1997 Larry Keenan. All rights reserved).

one reason or another runs into a lot of problems." Men, according to Kandel, were to continue in their natural roles as providers and protectors while a woman's job was to "feed her man" while making sure she took care of herself so that she could "radiate the feeling of warmth"; of security and solicitude for all those in her charge. "I don't think it's a man's role to go around changing the diapers. He should be able to when necessary. A woman takes care of the washing and putting the kids to bed."[51] Out of such sentiments emerged one of the male counterculture's most revered women, the receptive, nurturing, supportive Earth Mother or Madonna, who promised her man immediate gratification in the form of unconditional emotional and physical sustenance.

Suffice it to say, hippie men were euphoric that their female counterparts willingly and happily embraced traditional gender roles. As one young communard opined, "Chicks, mystical chicks: being witchy and spiritual [code for sexual] was the main contribution women were supposed to make to communal life. That and dinner." Digger founding member Peter Coyote was equally forthcoming about Digger women responsibilities. "Roles were generally divided among traditional male-female lines, with the women looking after the food, houses, and children and the men looking after the trucks and physical plant." Coyote expected his girlfriend, Jessie Barton, who followed him to San Francisco, to be as subservient to his needs as the rest of the Digger women were to their men, while he and his pals roamed the Haight's streets, free from any domestic charges that could prevent them from providing the street theater for which they became legendary. Part of those activities included "sexual diversions" in which Coyote and his sidekicks regularly engaged. In his memoir as his time as a Digger, Coyote admitted the Digger "division of labor" (gender roles) was "archaic, especially for a visionary community."[52] Despite such strictures, counterculture women nonetheless broke with many of the white middle class conventions and domestic expectations that had defined and circumscribed their mothers' alienated, atomized lives of quiet desperation in their suburban neighborhoods. Hippie women pursued their lives outside of such an oppressive environment and in the process participated in a movement that had significant ideological ramifications for subsequent generations. One of the most important was the placing of a positive and respected valuation on femininity and womanhood in general. As Nicholas von Hoffman observed in the Haight during the Summer of Love that even though "the essential feminine role" was "intractably the same," with "the old ladies of the Haight" doing the same drudge work as "the young matrons in the suburbs," as well as walking "one step behind their men, submissive," von Hoffman could not help but notice that they "retained a ferocious protection of their idea of womanliness."[53]

Young females were not the only young people who came to the Haight that summer who suffered sexual exploitation at the hands of male sexual predators. The boys found that some of the free crash pads were operated by homosexuals who expected them to put out in return for food and shelter. Trading sexual favors out of desperation to survive stunned and disoriented them, engendering intense feelings of guilt or shame, for so egregiously had they violated the morality of their white middle class upbringing and sense of propriety. Trying to find a way "to put his disjointed head back together," one young man remarked, "I didn't think I'd feel that way when I balled a guy. My friend said 'Do it because this old guy wants a young boy and we should share each other.' But I didn't like it, I didn't like it and I can't forget it. Maybe I was stoned. I guess I must have been. I must have been stoned to come to San Francisco."[54]

Although the majority of Beats embraced homo-erotic sex, the hippies were even more accepting of homosexuality, to the point of publicly supporting gay and lesbian rights, a crusade the Beats never outwardly endorsed. The counterculture's sexual ethos, with its emphasis on sexual freedom and acceptance of all forms of human interaction and relationships, helped energize gay consciousness and pride, which came to the fore in the late 1960s and into the 1970s, as one sector of the rights revolution fomented, ironically, by the 1960s liberal establishment via the Great Society and their main antagonists, the hippies. As far as most hippies were concerned, homosexuality was "natural and good," and true to their personal freedom creed, all individuals should have the right to enjoy sex with whomever they so desired and that no one should be discriminated against for their sexual preferences. To hippies, like everything else, sex was an individual's prerogative and thus all private acts between consenting adults should be respected not only by others but by the law as well. The majority of hippies believed it was time to legalize (like drugs), free sexual choice. As a Houston gay hippie declared, "All we hell-raising hippie homosexuals want is humanness. And we will have humanness when every man understands he is more similar to, than different from, his fellowmen and is willing to contribute a little effort to insure the same quality of life for everyone in the community."[55] Although generally accepting of homosexuality (Allen Ginsberg being a case in point), hippie sexual thought and orientation remained predominantly heterosexual and to the overwhelming majority of both male and female hippies, sexual freedom automatically meant male/female pairings. Most male hippies, despite their "feminine" appearance and liberated attitude toward sex and relationships, remained as homophobic as the majority of their straight counterparts.

The Haight's notorious orgies became even more sordid and misogynistic affairs. One episode occurred at the Glide Street Methodist Church, where naïve clergy allowed their sanctuary to be used for an arts festival, a symposium on obscenity, and a rock concert. However, according to Digger Emmett Grogan, once those events were over, the sexual escapades and debauchery began. A drag queen performed in the vestibule, Hell's Angels gangbanged a woman dressed as a Carmelite nun, couples fornicated on the main altar while prostitutes serviced their clients, and blood dripped from a statue of Christ "from a dude who had just got his head cracked during a scuffle." No doubt real love existed somewhere in the Haight that summer but as the season progressed, incidents such as the gang rape of the shot-full-of-speed sixteen-year-old girl became the more prevalent reality.[56]

For some, the orgies, in combination with drugs, were exhilarating. "I like Mazola orgies," a hippie named Frodo declared one day. "See, what you do is get stoned but before you get stoned you get sheets of plastic or something like that and put them on the floor, then you pour a gallon of Mazola oil on it and everybody takes their clothes off and has a group grope. It really feels good. You don't get as much fucking done as you would otherwise. It's hard to get purchase." Frodo could enjoy such romping in good health and so could the Berkeley coed who said, "Oh, those big cluster fucks! I can't stand them. I think it's revolting, you know, more or less getting punked by anybody who happens to be standing near you, man, woman, child, or dog. But four people, friends, good friends, spending a lovely quiet weekend together having nice sex every imaginable way, slowly in the same bed, well, that's long-drawn-out pleasantness."[57]

The Haight was supposed to float on love; it was charged with strife. Hippies prated much on love; everywhere symbols of their alleged gentle and peaceful ways could be seen:

flowers, butterflies, fairy wands, and the like. Hippie gurus like Allen Ginsberg, the *Oracle's* Allen Cohen, the Communication Company's Chester Anderson, and a host of other original Haight hippies, flooded the neighborhood with handbills, articles, posters, and pamphlets reminding everyone but especially the newcomers, that the hippie ethos was one of giving, kindness, communalism, and oneness with nature and the earth. However, as the summer progressed and the scene degenerated dramatically in drug-crazed mayhem, violence, and even death, it became increasingly more difficult to maintain the love charade. The smiles were often "through clenched teeth."

Although very few 1960s African Americans joined the hippie movement and in fact disdained the hippies' povertarian act, many nonetheless found the integrated scene intriguing and frequented hippie happenings. Photograph taken in 1967 (Dennis L. Maness Summer of Love Photograph Collection (SFP51), San Francisco History Center, San Francisco Public Library).

In the Haight the word "Negro" was almost never used. White New Leftists used the term "Black" to demonstrate their empathy and political understanding but the most common word was "spade." Even African Americans, who had acculturated into the Haight scene, invariably used the term when referring to themselves—a designation used without prejudicial meaning in the bebop jazz world for many years—but in the Haight its use was ambiguous. The descriptive connoted nothing more than an in-group vocabulary; most of the white kids of the Summer of Love were not in that category and consequently for them the word carried a mildly derogatory, hostile meaning. Perhaps nowhere was the "hate in the Haight" more revealing and potentially explosive than in black and white relations—not surprisingly, since the hippie movement was overwhelming white and suburban, which was especially true for those who came to the city during the Summer of Love. The new flower children brought with them fears and prejudices relative to African Americans. Despite living in the Haight with African American neighbors, many original hippies also feared the "spades" and wanted nothing to do with them. Blacks, they said, were "programmed for hate." Such hostility was not based on hippies knowing their black neighbors; such interaction was almost nonexistent in the Haight. Indeed, many hippies did not even realize that most of the black people they saw lived next door and not in the Fillmore, the city's black ghetto, which was defined as "dangerous territory" for the white hippies.[58] Like so much of the rest of white America at that time, the hippie community believed most black men had the rape of white women constantly on their minds; that they were still the uncontrollable, lustful, lascivious "beasts" portrayed by the KKK. Many of the flower children had been nurtured in the same social soil as everybody else, and their drugs did not expunge the fears and stereotypes.

Indeed, older hippies such as Chester Anderson were acutely aware of the inherent bigotry toward blacks among the recent arrivals, believing that the vast amounts of acid they had been ingesting had brought to the surface "their deeper straight prejudices" toward blacks. In Anderson's view they were "little more than freaked-out WASP's." It was thus up to Anderson's generation of hippies, "those of us who dropped out before acid and have lived/loved with spades & know where it's at," to "educate our new young hippies before they involve us in a race riot on the wrong side."[59]

As far as Chester Anderson was concerned, "The Negro community & the hippies are fighting for the same thing: FREEDOM." However, the Man (the white Establishment in all its various avaricious, capitalist manifestations) did not want either hippies or African Americans to be free because "He wants to own us, like a farmer owns cows; he wants us to be afraid so that we'll do what he says. He wants us to work for him so that he won't have to work. He wants us to be poor so he can be rich. He wants slaves that he doesn't have to take care of." However, according to Anderson, the Man knew his days would be numbered if or when black and white (spades and hippies) united, for "the Man knows we are brothers" but had worked assiduously "to keep us separated, because if we get together, he's in trouble. He wants the Negro to resent the hippy because if they get together, work together, share their resources and their experience, he's had it." Until "Black Power and White Power" merged, the Man would continue "his game" of fomenting fear, distrust, and hate between white and black, which could eventually erupt into violent confrontation between the two groups. Anderson concluded his broadside by reminding his black brothers that as long as the hippies and blacks remained polarized and fearful of each other "the Man wins." But he was "afraid of Black Power and White Power getting together because he can't beat that kind of army. Each Negro is Black Power; each hippy [sic] is White Power, and together—and only together—they make Freedom Power. Freedom Power is Soul Power is an Army of Brothers. Let us love each other and be free."[60]

In Anderson's somewhat delusional view, blacks and hippies "have the basic same problem: we are both oppressed minorities with a common enemy. But there are more of them than us and if the Fillmore erupts again this summer, and most likely it will, and we haven't reestablished our brotherhood with the Fillmore people, if we're not standing by their sides, they will erupt against *us* and WE WILL BE BURIED." Anderson called upon his fellow hippies to "meet with the spades; talk with the spades, share lives with the spades. Send ambassadors to the Fillmore. Throw parties; make friends. Do it all now before it is too late."[61] Anderson reminded his hippie brethren that they would not have become who they were had it not been for the spades, "our spiritual fathers. They turned us on. They gave us jazz & grass & rock and roll, in the early beat days they provided a community for us. From the beginning they were our brothers deeper than blood. If it weren't for the spades, we would all have short hair, neat suits, glazed eyes, steady jobs & gastric ulcers, all be dying of unnameable[sic] frustration."[62]

Ron Thelin was even more apologetic than Anderson in trying to promote good will and empathy between blacks and hippies. Thelin reflected the attitude prevalent among many white middle class youth: a sense of guilt and shame for being white and affluent, while most blacks remained mired in poverty and despair. To expiate his guilt, Thelin engaged in the rhetoric of confessional politics, declaring that it was time for white America to "apologize and confess to the black man that I have been wrong and stupid, that I have been a fool, and then when you get beat up [by a black person] you say you are right to that black man for doing that to you." To Thelin, it was too late for white Americans to say to black Americans "'I am sorry for 400 years of bullshit. I made a mistake, let's be friends. That's too easy, that's too superficial," and in Thelin's view "meaningless" to black Americans. If hippies were a truly "holy" people which, Thelin believed they were, then whites should "prostrate" themselves before blacks, "confess they were wrong, and if they burn down my house nonetheless, I should say thanks for showing me the way." Suffice it to say, few hippies let alone white, mainstream Americans were willing to engage blacks to the degree Thelin's apology demanded.[63]

Why such a paucity of black hippies? One reason might have been LSD. "Man, I feel enough as it is. I don't wanna know any more than I do," declared one Haight black who tried acid.[64] African Americans were the last people in 1967 America to need drugs to express themselves or realize their feelings. Some had used heroin or marijuana when their despair was too strong to tolerate. Moreover, black Americans had for decades the catharsis of art; it was black America who gave the 1960s drug world its language, its music, its visuals. Thus the hippies cast black people as whites always have in America: as the people who are truly affective, sensual, emotional, and uninhibited. Breaking out of white middle class restraints had always required going among African Americans or imitating them. The colloquial language of the Haight was the speech of the black ghetto interspersed with a few expressions from other renegade minorities. "Like man, you ain't gonna make it with that chick so like you'd best split," was all (and remains) black ghetto idiom.

At a time when African Americans were fighting off dope, trying to escape the urban ghettoes, and trying to obtain the material goods and secure life the hippies eschewed and dismissed as "so much plastic," it was almost impossible for black Americans to empathize with white kids who had all that blacks wanted. To African Americans it was incomprehensible that the hippies wanted to build a new ghetto and lock themselves in it and take dope. The hippies thus became an affronting put-down to black Americans, transforming into virtue every vice black Americans had been accused of—dirt, shiftlessness, sexual promiscuity, improvidence, and irresponsibility. Such attitudes had prevented black Americans from entering mainstream white American life. For these same disorders the hippies, the white sons and daughters of white collar America, became exalted as culture heroes, as holy povertarians. So privileged, they despised the money, the cleanliness, the comfort, the security, the balanced diet, the vitamins, the living room carpets black people had been aching for decades to obtain. Thus, poor blacks from the adjacent Fillmore district resented the suburban white kid's poverty act. It seemed phony and disingenuous. They also found it hard to resist the cornucopia of "white chicks" and the drugs the hippie scene thrust under their noses. The opportunities soon translated into hassles, fisticuffs, beatings, break-ins, rip-offs, and rapes. The rather observant Chester Anderson understood black resentment toward the hippies, admitting that "Spades resent us because we have so lightly abandoned what they have worked & fought so long to obtain. We have, if nothing else, cheapened their victory. They resent our freedom, both as hippies and as whites. They resent our dipping so blithely into their ghetto; we can get out by cutting our hair; most of them know they can never get out."[65]

Although random black street thugs would continue to harass and terrorize hippies throughout the hippies' urban enclaves, politicized black militants, most notably the Black Panthers, agreed with Anderson that the hippies represented potential allies in African Americans and hippies mutual struggle against the white Establishment, and thus the Panthers warned their brethren to "stop vamping the hippies. They are not your enemy. Your enemy, right now, is the white racist pigs who support this corrupt system.... Your enemy is not the hippies.... WE HAVE NO QUARREL WITH The HIPPIES. LEAVE THEM [the hippies] ALONE. Or the BLACK PANTHER PARTY will deal with you."[66]

A potentially explosive racial confrontation between hippies and blacks was not the only problem undermining the initial euphoria of the Summer of Love. By August the presence of so many "summer plastics" had especially outraged the hippie business community, which, led by Daric Jerome, president of H.I.P., and owner of two Haight Street clothing stores, the Blushing Peony and the Blushing Peony Skinnidippin, railed against "the hundreds of phonies using Haight Ashbury as a summer resort. Most of these people are either tourists or phony teen-agers who let their hair grow long the last week of school and blasted to Haight Ashbury with a couple of hundred bucks in their pockets and purses." Despite having money to burn, most often given to them by their parents, the "plastics" engaged in all manner of petty theft and shoplifting, which to Jerome and other H.I.P. store owners was especially galling since these kids obviously came from very affluent middle class homes. Indeed, Jerome was shocked to find that when he caught shoplifters and made them pay, "they open their wallets and a hundred dollars is sitting there."[67]

Interestingly many straight store owners were not as upset as Jerome when hippies stole from them, especially if it was only food. Such were the sentiments of one local grocery store owner, who felt sorry for the thousands of wayward and forlorn seekers who had come to San Francisco, attracted by the media hype of the Summer of Love, expecting to have all their needs taken care of by their loving brothers and sisters. Of course nothing could have been further from reality and thus many store owners, both straight and hippie took pity on these teenage waifs and vagabonds and usually turned a blind eye when they stole food.[68]

Most egregious to old guard hippies like Jerome was that, "most of these kids feel no responsibility toward the community. Six months ago you would have never seen the littered streets and broken glass that you see now." The "summer plastics" had also overwhelmed other community services and resources, most notably the Free Clinic, and as a result, "Sick residents who need immediate medical attention are often unable to obtain it." Interestingly, to the surprise and relief of the H.I.P. merchants, their straight counterparts were also experiencing the same issues and wanted to discuss the possible formation of a hip-straight merchant guild, to unite and try to ameliorate the problems before their respective business enterprises went under, the result of not only too many "summer plastics" in the Haight but humanity in general.[69]

On Sundays, it was virtually impossible to walk on Haight Street's sidewalks, so thick with human beings that many eventually found themselves squeezed on to the street. Driving through the neighborhood was an even more futile endeavor; by 10 a.m. on Sundays the traffic was at a dead crawl and passage through the area to the entrance of Golden Gate Park could take up to three hours. The multitude of tourists had come to gawk at what and whom they despised: the hippies and all the trappings and paraphernalia that surrounded them, and of course their lifestyle. Those tourists who deigned to get out of their cars, spewed verbal venom at all they saw around them, whether it was a person—a hippie—or merchandise; even the food served incurred their disdain. The idea of tourism helping to stimulate the Haight was an illusion that summer, as visitors rarely bought anything except Lenore Kandel's *Love Book*, and the now iconic photo poster of the street sign at Haight and Ashbury. By July tourism and the tidal wave of "plastic hippies" had turned the Haight into "a Coney Island tourist trap"; the neighborhood was no longer "hippie haven" but "a sort of honky-tonk Ghirardelli Square, catering to squares in search of hippies."[70] It had become clear that the affluent middle class hippie-wannabees had come to the Haight to *purchase* a countercultural experience.

By August the Summer of Love had become a complete fiasco and charade, at least in the view of long-time Haight booster Chester Anderson, who believed that he and many other hippies had been duped and betrayed by their own kind, especially by the H.I.P. merchants and Timothy Leary, both of whom Anderson held accountable for the Summer of Love's perversion and degeneration into a sordid, squalid disaster. It was Anderson's assessment that "Kids are starving on the street. Minds & bodies are being maimed as we watch a scale model of Vietnam. There are people—our people—dying long hideous deaths among us & the Council [of Love] is planning alternative activities and the Oracle continues to recruit for this summer's Human Shit-in. Haight Street is uglyshitdeath & Alan Watts suggests more elegant attire." Anderson was convinced that the Summer of Love and the Haight along with it had degenerated because of the H.I.P. merchant's greed who for the sake of their business profits, "sold our lovely little psychedelic community to the mass media, to the world, to you, and are blithely & sincerely unaware of what they have done. They don't see hunger, hip brutality, rape, gangbangs, gonorrhea, syphilis, theft, filth. They walk in their own beauty down Haight Street & if they see shit at all, they deplore it & say that somebody should do something about it. They do not realize that they and Uncle Timothy [Leary] have lured an army of children into a ghastly trap from which there is no visible escape." Neither Leary nor the H.I.P. proprietors cared about the collateral damage they were causing among "a whole generation of American youth" with their self-aggrandizing propagation of false hopes and promises.[71]

To Anderson the crux of the issue was that the H.I.P. shopkeepers had come to believe "their own bullshit lies" and that taking acid was the panacea for all human ills and shortcomings. "'Have you been raped?' they say. 'Take acid & everything will be groovy.' 'Are you ill? Take acid & find inner health and discover your own warmth. 'Are you hungry'? 'Take acid & transcend these mundane needs. 'You can't afford acid'? 'Pardon me, I think I hear somebody calling me.'" As far as Anderson was concerned, the real culprit was Leary, "the man who *really* did it to us. Why doesn't Leary help out? Because he is now hard at work on another touring Psychedelic Circus at $3.50 a head, presumably to raise enough cash to keep himself out of jail, and there isn't even a rumor that he has contributed any of the fortune he made with the last circus toward alleviating the misery of the psychedelphia [the Haight-Asbury scene] he created, who turned you on & dropped you into this pit." Anderson, although obviously bitter and hostile toward Leary and the H.I.P. proprietors, believed all was not lost, yet; salvation of the Haight and possibly even the Summer of Love could occur if the community turned to the Diggers, who, although despised by many (especially by the H.I.P. merchants), were the only group in the Haight "acting in anything like a responsible manner in this growing tragedy." Even though the Diggers "hardly ever talked about love," it was because "they're too busy doing it to talk about it. They are Real Men who think you're something more than an easy source of fast bucks. For all their messy imperfections the Diggers are the only human beings in the psychedelic ghetto." At this juncture in the Summer of Love debacle, Anderson would "be very much surprised" that "if anyone but the Diggers undertakes to feed the hungry, comfort the sick, shelter the homeless, clothe the naked, & restore some measure of dignity to Uncle Tim's [Leary] children."[72]

These were not the only conflicts and tensions. The police and the flower children frequently clashed despite the Council of Love's efforts to come to an understanding with police chief Thomas Cahill and other city officials. By July, with the drug shortage causing increasing crime and violence in the Haight, Cahill and the police reneged on their earlier rapprochement with the Council and began cracking down on the lawlessness that seemed to be escalating in the Haight. Police began routinely roughing up hippies, health officials harassed their communes, and narcotics agents infiltrated the neighborhood. Meanwhile, black toughs from the nearby Fillmore district continued to menace the streets, threatening violence and rape, and frequently descending on hippies and beating them up while other hippies stood by and watched. Indeed, in late July rumors circulated the Haight that Fillmore blacks were planning an uprising, similar to those that had occurred in Newark and Detroit, where scores of citizens had been killed. Interestingly, some white hippie apologists welcomed the insurrection, believing it would be the moment when "hippie and spade" would unite and "start at one end of Haight street / we [whites] at the other / and we start towards each other / burning everything between; / the tourist in their cars. / the cops. / the hippie shops / everything!" After laying waste to the neighborhood, then the black and white rebels, men and women, would "meet somewhere in the middle, in the broad daylight, strip naked, black and white flesh sweating in the sun and fire, and fuck in the hard bed of the street," giving "seed to children so holy and beautiful." However, they had to make the country "pure enough for them to walk on," thus "every rotten building, in every rotten block, in every rotten city in this whole rotten country will have to be burned to the ground."[73]

On the afternoon of the night the insurrection was supposed to begin a lithographed flyer appeared on the streets of Haight-Ashbury, warning hippies "to get the fuck out of their [rioting blacks] way. If you hamper them in anyway, you will be their enemy and they will shoot you. During the riot the only help they want from you is your gun; if not that then we say again, get the fuck out of their way." Hippies also feared the police's reaction to the riot, certain that they would use the event as an excuse to unleash their own rage against the hippies that they had been keeping in check. So, "don't fuck with them either. A hippie in the hands of frightened, shot-at police [by black snipers] will be the victim of sadistic and vicious assault."[74]

Fortunately for everyone and for the city of San Francisco, the anticipated riot never occurred; instead a police-hippie confrontation erupted at the intersection of Haight and Ashbury, the result of a supposed traffic jam caused by hippie panhandlers and other unsavory individuals "hassling" innocent tourists in their cars. The cops waded in with clubs and arrested nine people; four were badly injured. The Diggers continued to be a source of strife, constantly criticizing the H.I.P. merchants for exploiting the community, putting them on the defensive. The Diggers also clashed with the Krishna Consciousness, a newly arrived Hindu-based religious sect, whose beliefs the Diggers considered to be "absolute bullshit." Although the general public saw all the fringe groups as one and the same, the Diggers and the Hare Krishnas were very different. The Diggers favored the flesh; the Krishnas renounced the senses. A more important source of rancor between them was that both handed out free food and competed for the hearts and minds of Haight residents. Finally, the beguiling images of Haight-Ashbury marketed by the media attracted not only an invasion of gawking tourists but a floating population of all manner of miscreants, from the psychotic to the criminal to the down and out. By the end of the year, *reported* crime in Haight-Ashbury included 17 murders, 100 rapes, and nearly 3,000 burglaries. Interestingly, the majority of these crimes took place during the Summer of Love. As *Time* observed, "Love didn't necessarily fit if you hadn't had a meal in two days."[75]

Since the majority of summer hippies were high school and college kids, the Summer of Love would have ended after Labor Day in any case when it was time to return to their respective high schools or universities. However, the decomposing process was powerfully accelerated by two terrifying and demoralizing crimes: the murder in early August of two Haight acid dealers, Shob Carter and Superspade. Carter had been stabbed twelve times and his right arm cut off at the elbow; Superspade, one of the few African Americans on the Haight scene, had been shot in the heart and head, his body stuffed in a sleeping bag and thrown over a cliff at Port Reyes along the northern coast. Both incidents sent shivers down hippie spines, for the killings seemed to confirm in the minds of many increasingly disillusioned hippies that their love ethos and lifestyle had been nothing more than a drug-infused illusion, and so dope-dependent was their community that competitors were willing to murder each other in order to corner what had become one of the most lucrative drug markets in the country. To this day no one knows who killed either of the two dealers, although at the time a twenty-three-year-old named Eric Frank Dahlstrom confessed to the police he had killed Carter over the bad LSD he had bought from the dealer. When questioned about the severed arm found in the backseat of his car, Dahlstrom replied that he was "very, very hazy about that arm. The principal reason I'm in jail is LSD." Later, Dahlstrom told a reporter that the reason he had Carter's severed forearm in his car was because "The hand is a man's history" and that he "hadn't had life in my hands before like that." Dahlstrom's lawyer pleaded his client's innocence on the grounds that Dahlstrom "had lost his mind to LSD." Many hippies at the time were certain it was the Mafia, wanting to take over such a potentially profitable market and were in the process of getting rid of independent operators like Carter and Superspade. Other hippies believed the murders were simply the wanton acts of desperate, drug-crazed losers. Such was the opinion of Steve, "the Chemist" (a low-volume Haight LSD manufacturer) who told Nicholas von Hoffman, "It was simply robbery. You don't have to go inventing gangsters. Three-quarters of those kids out there would kill you for $2 if they got you alone and they had a weapon. Love generation! What Crap!"[76]

The tidal wave of tourists, plastic hippies, and teeny-boppers, as well as the creeping commercialism and the consequential cheapening of their identity, proved too overwhelming for many of the Haight's original hippies to endure. They could no longer watch their beloved community become co-opted and perverted by the media and their culture and identity bought and sold by profit-driven merchants catering to everyone but the very individuals who had created this magical, mystical place called the Haight-Ashbury. According to the *Chronicle*'s Jeff Berner, the Haight had become "a sewer. Drug busts are increasing. Fashionable shops are springing up everywhere. Tourism and not tripping is becoming big business. I expect the merchants to have a contest to see just who is The Richest Hippie West of the Mississippi."[77] The *Berkeley Barb* was not surprised at what had happened to the Haight. "It all goes to prove what every veteran Haightie knew all along: most of the summer lovers were out for their vacation thrill. They were tourists, plastic hippies, pseudo-hip middle and upper class straights who came down to play the game."[78] For all intents and purposes the Haight had died and the press was writing the neighborhood's epitaph: "The Haight-Ashbury Scene is Finished!" announced the *Chronicle*, while the *Barb* asked, "So Who Mutha'd the

'Hippies'?"[79] Not wanting to watch their righteous experiment in alternative living further degenerate, many of the neighborhood's original denizens temporarily exiled themselves to the country, to the many communes that proliferated along the West Coast that summer.

By mid–September the panhandlers, the tourists, and the majority of the plastic hippies had disappeared from the Haight. It was no longer an ordeal to walk through the neighborhood, especially down Haight Street. There were fewer barefoot, grimy, malnourished, sickly, lost-looking teenagers huddled in doorways clutching equally bewildered-looking, straggly puppies or kittens. Quite a number of businesses were in the process of "going out of business," or were having "the sale of the century." Many had been replaced by larger commercial enterprises, some with a national scope that catered to tourists and teeny-boppers, selling them at cheap prices all the symbols and trappings of hippiedom. The original, small neighborhood merchants were fast disappearing. Restaurants that had been full, with lines reaching out the door and into the street, only a few weeks before, were now half empty or about to join the ranks of their "out of business" colleagues. Haight Street had the tawdry, exhausted air of a beach town at the end of summer.[80] As former Haight resident, ex-hippie, and author Elaine Mayes remembered, "As the summer progressed, the joyous freedom of the hippie ideal diminished. Harder drugs appeared and the Diggers couldn't feed everyone. You couldn't sleep in the park without being arrested, and the people whose lifestyle initiated the idea of being a hippie moved to the country or traveled to places like India…. Life in the Haight-Ashbury became a tourist attraction."[81]

The Summer of Love's unraveling and concomitant demise of the Haight, as well as the emergence in many of the nation's major metropolitan areas of other countercultural ghettoes, reflected an unprecedented measure of intergenerational alienation in the minds of many serious observers. Such was the take-away of novelist, essayist, and memoirist, Joan Didion, who spent several weeks in the Haight during the late spring and early summer of 1967 reporting for the *Saturday Evening Post*. Didion believed that what she was witnessing in the Haight "was not a traditional generational rebellion" but rather something much deeper: a potential "social catastrophe," a "serious social hemorrhaging," as "a handful of pathetically unequipped children" tried "to create a community in a social vacuum." To Didion the emergence of the counterculture represented the failure in the transmission process of sound social values to young people and helping them live by civilized rules of conduct. Describing in stark, clinical detail what was occurring in the Haight that summer—drug abuse, venereal disease, rape, and murder—Didion asserted that the "social dysfunction" that had emerged in the Haight actually began "at some point between 1945 and 1967" when parents and society, especially those charged with being its caretakers and purveyors of values, norms, and mores, "neglected to tell these children the rules of the game we happened to be playing. Maybe we had stopped believing in the rules ourselves, maybe we were having failure of nerve about the game. Maybe there were just too few people around to do the telling. These were children who grew up cut loose from the web of cousins and great-aunts and family doctors and lifelong neighbors who had traditionally suggested and enforced society's values." The result of this neglect was that young people were thrown to their own devices, which simply were not informed nor developed enough to prepare them for a mature and stable social life. Looking at the hordes of aimless and despairing young folk who inundated the Haight during the Summer of Love, Didion opined that "they are less in rebellion against society than ignorant of it, able to only feedback certain of its most publicized self-doubts, *Vietnam, Saran-Wrap, diet pills, the Bomb*."

Perhaps prompting Didion to have such an assessment of the Haight at that moment was her encounter with a five-year-old named Susan who was living in a Haight commune with her mother and her mother's boyfriend Otto, who told Didion that the little girl would "blow your mind." In her conversation with the child, Susan revealed to Didion that she was in "High Kindergarten," and when a perplexed Didion asked the little girl what that meant, Otto quickly chimed in that her mother routinely dosed her with acid and peyote. "Five years old," Otto boasted, "and on acid. I told you she would blow your mind."[82]

Equally appalled by the Summer of Love's degenerative effects on the Haight was Beatle George Harrsion, who, along with his girlfriend Patti Boyd, visited the hippie mecca in early August 1967. Typical of the naiveté of most European visitors to the neighborhood, Harrison expected to see an American version of the quaint, charming, clean, and tidy streets and shops of Kings Road in London, with smiling and welcoming hip shopkeepers ready to assist him in anyway he so desired. "I expected them [the hippies] all to own their own little shops. I expected them all to be nice and clean and friendly and happy." Rather, to his disappointment and disgust, all around him he saw squalor, dilapidation, and sullen, desperate faces; "hideous, spotty little teenagers" who "were all terribly dirty and scruffy. It was all too much." The scene so depressed Harrison that he and his entourage only lasted about half an hour on the Haight's main drag, eventually running back to their waiting limo followed by jeering hippies. Apparently neither Harrison nor any of his companions could hide their aversion to such a sordid scene nor from the eventually insulted and consequently hostile hippie crowd that gathered and followed them on their brief sojourn through Psychedelphia.[83]

Look writer William Hedgepeth had the complete opposite experience to that of Didion and Harrison, and thus a more favorable assessment of the Haight and its hippie denizens. Hedgepeth not only personally took "drugs on behalf of the American people in order to tell them the truth" about the hippie lifestyle, but concluded that "the new phenomenon of hippies was part of a religious movement" because hippies were at all times "sympathetic and loving toward others. They handed out flowers to tourists and naysayers, and to people who demeaned them." After having engaged in "participatory journalism," for the entire Summer of Love, Hedgepeth became "so entranced" that he believed the hippie lifestyle to be "a perfectly good alternative universe to me. I mean you don't need money, you know, you don't need anything. I can, I could stay here if I wanted to. It was as benign an expression of the finer angels of people's nature than I have ever seen before."[84]

On October 6, 1967 (the first anniversary of the California anti–LSD law), disillusioned Haight elders conducted a Death of Hippie ceremony to announce the end of the media-hyped Summer of Love. To old guard hippies such as Ron Thelin, the establishment mass media had destroyed the hippie movement, "what could have been a beautiful thing." In retrospect, Thelin now realized that the January Human Be-In ironically, marked the beginning of the end for the Haight's hippie community, for from that moment on the Haight was "portioned to us by the Media-Police and the tourists who came to the Zoo to see the captive animals … we growled fiercely behind the bars we accepted and now we are no longer hippies and never were." Thelin acknowledged that the mainstream press was not solely responsible for the end of the Haight; Thelin and his comrades were just as culpable for their own demise, as he and other community members helped to perpetuate if not bolster the media's distorted image of the neighborhood. The mainstream media had "our own hungry consent" as "we tried to give the newcomers what they wanted instead of insisting that they do their own thing."[85] They realized too late what they had unwittingly done and thus became powerless against the media attention, the commercialization, and the legions of plastic hippies who panhandled for change or tripped for the six o'clock news.

Thelin, Allen Cohen, and a host of other original hippies had never accepted the media image and hated the press for perverting both their reality and their message, and for ruining both the Haight and the potential for propagating their ethos via the Summer of Love. According to Thelin, it was the mass media "that changed us from men into hippies, and then when they've done it they write these terrible editorials against us.... We wanted to be free men and build a free community. That word hippy turned everybody off, even most of the Indians. Well, the hippies are dead." The New York Times agreed, boldly declaring that "LOVE IS DEAD" and that "The hippie movement is over—the alternative to the 'computerized society' has proved to be as unsatisfactory to its adherents as the society that gave birth to it." According to William Hedgepath, by the early fall 1967, the mainstream media had not only become bored with the Haight/Summer of Love phenomenon but had dismissed it all together as a momentary aberration of youthful rebellion, and consequently "the press and the public retooled for new explorations into fresh areas of social outrage, and the Haight was allowed to continue its slow rot in relative privacy." On the counter of the venerated Psychedelic Shop, which Thelin closed on October 6, 1967, was a high stack of black-bordered cards inviting everyone to a "funeral": FUNERAL NOTICE / HIPPIE / In the Haight Ashbury District of this city, Hippie, devoted son of Mass Media / Friends are invited to attend services beginning at sunrise, October 6, 1967, at Buena Vista Park.[86]

The funeral ceremony began with a wake at All Souls Episcopal Church and ended three days later with a procession of costumed mourners carrying a coffin through the Haight. The box contained beads, feathers, posters, buttons, fake beards, and two kilograms of marijuana—all the supposedly false emblems and paraphernalia of the hippie movement, the "body of Hippy." At the end the mourners set the coffin on fire. A plume of black smoke marked the end of the Summer of Love. The Death of Hip Parade witnessed the final attempt of the Haight's original hippie community to challenge the media's deconstruction of their identity and culture. For such a cause, the various factions, whose rancor had helped to polarize the neighborhood and contribute to its demise, put aside their philosophical and political differences and united in one last effort to reclaim their true hippie identity. According to the Chronicle's Michael Grieg, the event represented a "titanic effort to save the dream from its publicity."[87]

"Hippy" did not die on October 6 but was merely, temporarily, "put to rest." For many true believers, to have truly buried Hippy would have meant the permanent end of their movement and of themselves and that was still unacceptable for the majority of hippies. According to the Haight-Ashbury Eye, "to say that hippie is no more, is like saying evolution is finite." That was precisely how many hippies interpreted their end; not a final death but rather an evolution beyond the Haight scene. They were now ready to take their message of "love and hope (dope)" to the larger society. Many ex–Haight hippies saw their reentry into mainstream society "not as a new conformity, but a contributing of what has been gained in a challenging, beautiful experience" during the Summer of Love and their Haight existence. Now, "in the light of evolution" that experience would no longer be confined to the Haight. The Haight expatriates hoped that the outside world was ready "to hear the findings and know the truths of a newly aware and intellectual movement on the reality of living together, in a new way."[88]

In an interview with *Washington Post* reporter Nicholas Von Hoffman, the older hippie "Teddybear" (he was 33 at the time), perhaps offered the best assessment of the Summer of Love and the hippie movement in general at that moment. "There never were any flower children. It was the biggest fraud ever perpetrated on the American public. And it's your fault, the mass media did it. This wasn't a 'Summer of Love,' this was a summer of bullshit and you, the press, did it. The so-called flower children came here to find something because you told'em to, and there was nothing to find." According to Teddybear, the press controlled the Summer of Love from beginning to end, to the degree of even telling young people how to be a hippie, "how to dress, how to behave, what to say. They only had to turn on their television sets or open a magazine and read; it was all there for them" even though in Teddybear's view (and he was more than likely correct), it was all a sensationalized media contrivance. Perhaps most honest was Teddybear's frank's admission that the Haight was a "community based on dope, not love"[89] and thus destined to degenerate, caused by the influx of thousands of desperate and dissipated seekers, much to the bitter disappointment and humiliation of the community's original true believers.

Not only did the mainstream media destroy the Haight-Ashbury phenomenon but so did the weight of population pressure, which few of the old-time hippies realized until the hordes of newcomers overwhelmed them in a tidal way of humanity, cresting by early July 1967. As observed in *The Summer of Love*, "The utopian dream of the hippie counterculture and the vision of changing the world through peace and love was threatened by such a mass exodus centering on San Francisco. People were coming just for the drugs, not the spiritual awakening, straining the resources of the city."[90] Veteran hippies believed that if the new arrivals just took enough acid, they would soon be "tuned in" to the Haight vibe and all would be "groovily" in sync. However, what the original hippies failed to grasp was that their trip was the result of many experiences, both psychedelic and real, which the younger, suburban plastic hippies had never sampled until coming to the Haight. Consequently, very little bonding took place between old and new hippies, as the latter was a transient swarm playing hippie for the summer rather than genuinely investing themselves in the community, embracing its spirit and vision. Many did however immerse themselves to the extreme in the Haight's dope and sex scene, consuming an impressive variety of drugs and tripping for days on end while trying to have sex with as many individuals as they possible could; "feats" most seasoned hippies rarely accomplished or were even interested in doing. In the final analysis, the Haight simply became just too densely populated with the wrong sort of people to work.

However, the hippie counterculture did not end in the fall of 1967 and the Death of Hippy Funeral; not only did the movement continue on in the Haight but in other cities as well and would continue to do so for several more years in various manifestations. However, hippidom's high point was no doubt the Summer of Love and the whole Haight-Ashbury experience. What was lost that summer in the Haight was flower-child gentleness, innocence, and perhaps most important, the hope that the hippie movement could inspire the rebirth of a better America by producing a better human being. By the beginning of 1968, many of the Haight's original hippies had either fled to rural communes or had "split to Zen monasteries," thus depriving the neighborhood of an "indigenous leadership-cluster." The new flower children according to San Francisco Parks Superintendent Frank Foehr, were "a different element—young hoodlums, misfits who can't make it. They put garbage in Albert Lake and break the rhododendrons. They once loved blossoms." The Haight's "night air," once filled with the sweet smell of marijuana smoke, patchouli oil, and the cooking of organic cuisine, now wreaked "of decay and anger." In the view of one of Los Angeles' underground papers, *Open City*, "Hippies are dead—the whole thing went out to lunch." As one Haight hippie observed in 1968, his brethren's panhandling had become aggressive and menacing. "Attitudes on the street," he wrote, "weren't like the summer before when everybody was acting so enchanted."[91]

9

The Monterey Pop Festival, June 1967: The Summer of Love's Defining Event

"I think there's a lot of heavy stuff going on here, acid, emotion, everything."—Grateful Dead guitarist Jerry Garcia's view of the Monterey International Pop Festival

For the majority of hippies no other form of tribal gathering was more crucial in energizing and sustaining the counterculture than the giant outdoor rock festivals. These events became the definitive hippie happening as culture, music, and ideology momentarily came together in a consonant, celebratory vision. It was through the rock festivals that hippies celebrated spontaneity, community, and music as a peaceful means of revolt against the status quo. Although the music was the initial and enduring appeal, for many festival-goers the most important attraction became the sense of community these jamborees provided for hippie true-believers; a bonding that could not be found on such a large scale in any other hip environment. For attendee John Bassett McCleary these celebrations were not "just musical events" nor were they "just an excuse for young people to come together to do frivolous, youthful things"; they marked "the beginning[s] of a new kind of gathering" that was both spiritual and political that "altered our world from the inside out…. In each generation there are defining moments. For example, Pearl Harbor may be that point. To others it could be 9/11. For me it was Monterey and Woodstock." For McCleary these outdoor events germinated "the society that was soon to enlighten the world on many levels."[1]

By 1967 rock music had dramatically transformed, eschewing its earlier mainstream boy-band innocence and entering into one of its most eclectic phases, producing a proliferation of new music that reflected not only the influence of all the various genres that had originally inspired rock and roll, but some recently discovered new expressions such as Indian raga and other non–Western sounds. However, the most important new dynamic to affect rock music was psychedelia, the quintessence of the hippie movement. Psychedelic rock not only reflected rock's fluid creativity but also the continued appropriation by 1960s white musicians of the work of other artists both living and dead. For example, the Doors' sexually provocative hit single, "Light My Fire," was a direct augmentation of John Coltrane's exotic Jazz album, *My Favorite Things*, which was influenced by Ravi Shankar's free form sitar improvisations. In one song three distinct musical styles coalesced along with three sources of technical innovation all compacted into the new genre of acid rock.[2] As John Bassett McCleary

197

observed, "In all cultures, music is the fuel for our emotions. Psychedelic music elevated our awareness of the world around us."[3] To be a psychedelic rocker meant to be an interlocutor between two realms of perception, deciphering mystical prophesy from the unconscious mind and translating that message into a musical composition for the masses. By the summer of 1967, psychedelia and rock and roll music had fused, creating a rock culture with its own unique sound; an amalgam of many of rock's previously most innovative strains that created for listeners the auditory experience of an acid trip.

Part and parcel of these changes was the emergence of the outdoor rock festival, inspired by Bill Graham's and Chet Helms great dancehall extravaganzas. The explosion in popularity of the live musical performances at the Fillmore and the Avalon reflected the "growing appetite for rock music in an unconfined, unrestricted setting. [Rock] music was a dynamic force ideally suited to bringing people together." The dancehall shows had "a profound effect on both the youth-propelled counterculture and the possible staging of a larger, [outdoor] rock-oriented festival."[4] Thanks to entrepreneurs such as Graham and Helms, it was the perfect moment for someone to come along and take their concept to the next level in the great outdoors. The festivals also became concrete indications that rock and roll was not just a fad but had become by the late 1960s an integral and enduring dynamic of the American Experience; "rock and roll was here to stay"—forever.

The first attempt to bring the Fillmore and Avalon experience outside occurred on the weekend of June 10, 1967, at the Magic Mountain Festival held on Mount Tamalpais, across the Golden Gate in Marin County. Sponsored by local radio station KFRC, the festival was an attempt to cash in on the increasingly commercialized and profitable Haight-Ashbury phenomenon, as various Haight shopkeepers and outside vendors set up a shopping concourse featuring dozens of kiosks and booths selling hippie paraphernalia and novelties, including "acid shakes" for fifty cents. Overall, however, the event was "a bust," failing to draw the countercultural crowd the promoters believed would show up in droves. In fact, the majority of attendees were "very straight" and "had trouble grooving."[5]

Interestingly, the only local bands to appear were Country Joe and the Fish, The Steve Miller Band, and the Jefferson Airplane, at the time, the only Haight group to have gained national stature. The majority of the performers were from southern California; many were on their way to stardom such as the Doors and the 5th Dimension. Others, such as the Byrds and the Grass Roots had already achieved notoriety. By the time of the festival the Jefferson Airplane had become the most commercial of the City's hip bands; from their inception the Airplane had been the most persistent in their pursuit of fame and fortune. One of their early promotional gimmicks had been the sale of "Jefferson Airplane Loves You" bumper stickers as well as a series of highly remunerative ads for Levis. By the late spring 1967 they had also appeared on the Bell Telephone Hour, the Smothers Brothers Show, and American Bandstand, all of which not only made them lots of money but also the most commodified hippie band in the country.[6] Although disappointing on many levels, Magic Mountain nonetheless generated the desire for a bigger and better festival. As would become endemic with such events, financing and location would be the most crucial upfront issues to resolve.

Monterey was the first of the "Big Three" most legendary rock festivals of the late 1960s (followed by Woodstock and Altamont in 1969). Although the Haight-Asbury scene was a phenomenon of energy and appeal, it was the Monterey Pop Festival and the performers and their music which would transcend the limitations of time and social fashion. One did not have to have been a hippie in order to enjoy the experience or relish the event's legacy, or appreciate the rock music that catapulted the "happening" into one of the defining moments in the history of the 1960s counterculture. However, above all else, it was the music and some of the performers who will be most remembered. Indeed, as one of Monterey's main promoters Lou Adler reflected, "At Woodstock people remember the weather. At Altamont people remember the murder. For Monterey people remember the music."[7]

Often forgotten in the euphoria of the Monterey Pop Festival's enormous success was that behind its initial conception and promotion were two very successful southern California venture capitalists—Ben Shapiro and Alan Pariser—who saw such a massive gig to be a fantastic profit-making enterprise. The two partners raised substantial money to book the Monterey County Fairgrounds and then pursued as much popular talent as they possibly could. To their surprise and chagrin, they had difficulty signing the acts they believed would make Monterey a profitable gambit. Many of the hip bands they approached apparently were "turned off" by the "capitalist" approach antithetical to the hip ethos of living and working without the profit motive! Frustrated by their inability to attract big-name performers, Shapiro and Pariser turned to John Phillips, front-man of the Mamas and Papas, whose connections in the rock music world were extensive, unusual, and enviable. According to rock critic Robert Christgau, what made Phillips such a rarity was that he was "a quasi-bohemian in a position any bohemian would envy—he can screw 'the establishment' and get away with it. There is so much money in rock that its big names have almost unlimited power, like the top movie stars. They are more like, you guessed it, hippies: fond of money, perhaps, but not enslaved by it; more loyal to their generation than to their business."[8]

Phillips got his own manager Lou Adler to join him and, with donations of $10,000 each from record producer Terry Melcher, Paul Simon, and Johnny Rivers, they raised enough money ($50,000) to buy out Shapiro and Pariser, so Monterey became a strictly non-profit show. Phillips and Adler then created a board of directors to advise them on whom they should solicit to appear. The board was an impressive array of some of the rock industries most legendary stars and promoters: Donovan, Mick Jagger, Paul McCartney, Roger McGuinn, Terry Melcher, Andrew Oldham, Johnny Rivers, Phillips, Adler, Smokey Robinson, Paul Simon, and Brian Wilson. Also contributing to Monterey's attraction to potential performers was the city's already established musical heritage. Monterey is still home to the longest running (1958 to the present) jazz festival in the country, as well as having sponsored in 1963 the Monterey Folk Festival, which eventually gave way in June 1967 to the now historic Monterey International Pop Festival, which became the template for future rock celebrations, including Woodstock.[9]

Phillips, Adler, and company put the show together in just seven weeks. Phillips envisioned the event as the perfect venue to showcase "the trends in popular music. The festival could bring together pop, soul, rock, folk, and jazz musicians from all parts of the world to jam and perform, with the proceeds going to a charitable cause"—a scholarship fund for popular music education, which was what Phillips told an anxious Monterey citizenry, mayor, and city council, all of whom worried that the proceeds would go to hippie "organizations" such as the Diggers.[10] According to Adler, he and Phillips "went to a lot of City Council meetings, we had to win them over. John Phillips was very charming and quite a good liar, actually, so we were able to promise them anything. He wasn't really a liar but he 'made up' a lot answers to questions we didn't have answers for."[11] In the end, Phillips convinced the burghers that all would be just fine, for he and Adler had designed the show "for those in the nineteen-to-thirty-five age group" by "omitting acts that draw the real young kids." In fact, their publicity had "solicited family groups. We haven't invited the sort of acts that inspire acting up on the part of the audience. If that happens we'll pull them off the stage."[12]

Perhaps most important Phillips and Adler realized that the key to their endeavor's success would be to feature the "San Francisco Sound," which was the hottest new music in the nation, thanks in large part to Jefferson Airplane's meteoric rise to the Top Ten with hits such as "Somebody to Love" and "White Rabbit." Both promoters grasped the grassroots authenticity of the Haight-Ashbury music scene; the bands such as the Grateful Dead had become community-oriented and connected to their neighbors in the great dancehalls of the Fillmore and Avalon ballrooms. This relationship contrasted dramatically with the caged "go-go" girls of Los Angeles' Sunset Strip, the closest equivalents of the Fillmore and Avalon. Indeed, *Village Voice* pop music critic Richard Goldstein believed the 400 miles that separated the two cities marked the difference between "a neon wasteland" and "the most important underground in the nation."[13] Wanting to capitalize on the Haight's aura, Phillips promoted Scott McKenzie's "San Francisco (Be Sure to Wear Some Flowers in Your Hair)." Phillips, one of the 1960s' most commercially savvy rock promoters and producers, released "San Francisco" as advance publicity for Monterey while making clear his and Adler's desire to have the San Francisco contingents' participation. As writer Barney Hoskyns observed at the time "the key to the whole event lay with the San Francisco fraternity."[14]

Phillips was aware of the "rivalry and antagonism between the Los Angeles and San Francisco camps. We had trouble even getting them to talk to us."[15] Indeed, the San Franciscans were very leery of the LA scene's "commercialism," which they believed Phillips and company personified, and whom they were certain were trying to co-opt and commodify their music. According to Chet Helms, "Basically we all resisted Monterey Pop because we felt it was kind of slicko L.A. hype. We felt that they were coat-tailing a bunch of L.A. acts on the success of what was happening in San Francisco."[16] As Paul Kantner of the Jefferson Airplane told Richard Goldstein of the *Village Voice*, "Everything is prefabricated like the rest of that town [Los Angeles]. Bring them [the L.A. bands] into the Fillmore and it just wouldn't work."[17] Lou Adler admitted decades later that he and Phillips were indeed much more "business-minded" and that rock music "wasn't a hobby. They [the San Franciscans] called it slick, and I'd have to agree with them. We couldn't find the link. Every time John and I went up there, it was a fight—almost a physical fight on occasions. And that was right up to the opening day of the Festival."[18]

The San Franciscans eventually capitulated and Monterey had its hippie stars—Jefferson Airplane, Grateful Dead, Quicksilver Messenger Service, Moby Grape, Big Brother with Janis Joplin, Country Joe and the Fish, and the Steve Miller Band. In the end, motivating the bands to participate was the incredible mass public exposure they would all receive and protestations to the contrary, the possibility of securing a lucrative recording contract with one of the major record companies. Interestingly, the San Franciscans' L.A. counterparts were more pop oriented acts with little to no countercultural cachet: the Mamas and the Papas, the Association, Johnny Rivers, and Lou Rawls. Despite the friction the Monterey International Pop Festival was a tremendous success and represented a turning point in both counterculture and popular music history. As hoped for by the promoters and the bands, the recording industry finally embraced the new "hippie rock" sound and rushed to sign as many of the bands as they could to contracts. Indeed, by the end of the weekend Columbia Records had signed Janis Joplin and Big Brother; Capitol Records struck a deal with the Steve Miller Band and had offered $40,000 advance to Quicksilver. After Monterey, Warner Bros. established a San Francisco office, endowing the operation with $250,000 with which to comb the Bay Area for new bands and sign them before any of their competitors could do likewise.[19] Monterey catapulted the San Francisco psychedelic sound to national prominence in popular music and legitimated rock as an art form in the same realm as jazz and folk, both of which by the 1960s had achieved status as uniquely *American* aesthetic expressions. Monterey helped to put rock and roll on the same path toward cultural, artistic, and popular acclaim.[20]

By the time the first band appeared (the Association, a band from Hawaii with three top–10 hit singles, "Along Comes Mary"; "Cherish," and their most recent hit, "Windy") on Friday evening June 16, 1967, a crowd of about 30,000 had gathered to hear not just the Association, but over the course of the weekend some of the most legendary bands and individual artists in rock and roll history ever assembled in one venue from both the U.S. and Great Britain: The Who; Simon and Garfunkel; Janis Joplin (with her band Big Brother and the Holding Company); Jefferson Airplane; the Grateful Dead; Johnny Rivers; the Animals; the Byrds; The Mamas and Papas; and a U.S. Army veteran making his first important American appearance, Jimi Hendrix, to name just a few of the eventually more famous. Monterey launched the careers of many who played there virtually overnight, including stars such as Hendrix and the Who, both of whom had already become sensations in Great Britain. Other artists rising to popularity following their Monterey appearances included Janis Joplin, Laura Nyro, Canned Heat, Otis Redding, and Steve Miller. All played for free with gate receipts going to charity; only the renowned Indian sitarist Ravi Shankar received $3,000 for his afternoon, three hour-long performance for which he received one of the most enthusiastic rounds of applause at the festival— a several minute standing ovation.[21]

According to Talitha Stills, sister of Stephen Stills, Shankar's virtuoso "created a veritable state of bliss. Everyone in the crowd was swept into a dreamlike state by the lilting, exotic music sinking into hearts and souls, imagining faraway places and encouraging all present to lift their spirits above that earthly place. We did." Equally

Monkees drummer/singer Mickey Dolenz "playing Indian" at the Monterey Pop Festival, June 1967 (photograph by Larry Keenan, courtesy Bancroft Library, University of California, Berkeley. © 1997 Larry Keenan. All rights reserved).

"blown away" by Shankar's artistry was Jim Thomas of Loveland, Ohio, who "most remembered the thunderous applause and the simultaneous rising of the audience to its feet. We were in awe of not only what we had just heard and felt, but how deeply we had been awakened and moved spiritually." Kathy Klawans-Smith remembered "sitting there like children at his feet while he told his legend through his music. It was mesmerization of the collective consciousness. When he finished, no one reacted for a few seconds. We were all stunned and then the arena exploded with sincerely overwhelming appreciation." Shankar and his group was *the surprise hit* of the entire festival, significantly raising the performance bar for the rest of the final day's acts. Rock music pundit Michael Lydon, writing for *Newsweek* at the time tried to describe Shankar's impact. "There was an excitement in his purity, as well as in his face and body, and that of a table player whose face matched Charlie Chaplin's in its expressive range. For three hours they played music, and after the first strangeness, it was not Indian music, but *music*, a particular realization of what music could be.... It was all brilliant, and the moment he began a long solo from the sixteenth century Shankar had the whole audience, including all the musicians at the festival rapt.... To all appearances he had 90,000 people with him, and when he finished, he stood, bowed with his hands clasped to his forehead, and then, smiling, threw back to the crowd the flowers that had been showered on him."[22]

By Sunday the crowd had swelled to 90,000. Although many hippies had trekked south from San Francisco or north from Los Angeles to attend this latest gathering of the tribes, they were not the majority of the audience; straight white kids were, complete with penny-loafers, button-down oxford shirts, and comparatively short hair for men while the majority of young women wore similarly conservative, fashionable clothing, hair, and make-up. Nonetheless, there were plenty of hippies or at least "week-end hippies" and thus "the gawkers were not disappointed," according Robert Christgau. "Those of the invaders who weren't dressed in costume—cowboys and Indians was the favorite masquerade—wore spectacularly new or spectacularly old clothing, usually the latter. Bells, tambourines, beards, painted and decaled faces, bare feet and bare thighs were all in evidence." As Michael Lydon observed, "Everything the hippie needs to make his life beautiful was on sale: paper dresses, pins, earrings, buttons, amulets, crosses, posters, balloons, sandals, macrobiotic food, and flowers." Christgau also believed that "many of the celebrants looked under nineteen and not many were over thirty." The "families" whom Phillips had told city officials would be a significant part of the audience, were few in number and "were very new ones." The primary interest for the straights was the music but forming relationships and sharing common experiences were also very important and many left the festival feeling "transformed," embracing much of the hippie ethos. Naturally there was plenty of dope, courtesy of the ubiquitous Owsley, who manufactured a special LSD concoction for the occasion, dubbed "Purple Haze," which he handed out for free as he had at the January Be-In.[23]

Filmmaker D.A. Pennebaker's classic documentary, *Monterey Pop*, was the first film to capture such events for posterity. Pennebaker focused on the crowd and what was happening offstage; his panning of the audience clearly reveals a predominantly straight-looking white audience at Monterey, including scores of both uniformed and civilian-dressed U.S. Army soldiers from nearby Fort Ord. Nonetheless, Monterey's bill was truly multi-cultural, crossing all musical boundaries, mixing folk, blues, jazz, soul, R&B, pop, and classical genres. In Ian Englis' view, Monterey was "a time capsule of contemporary popular culture, [an] intersection of soul, psychedelia, commercial pop, rock underground, Civil Rights, expanded consciousness, southern and northern California, of the southern states, and the rest of the United States."[24] Indeed, Monterey provided a venue for both established rock stars and the virtual unknowns; for domestic rock bands as well as for their international counterparts; for literally any rock/pop musicians whose sound could be labeled in some form as rock and roll.

Despite Adler's and others' efforts to showcase more black artists, only Hendrix, Otis Redding, Lou Rawls, Booker T. and the MG's, and South African Hugh Masekela appeared. According to John Phillips, "Smokey Robinson and Berry Gordy [CEO of Motown Records] were enthusiastic about the Festival at first," but "then they never answered the phone. I think it might be a Jim Crow thing. A lot of people put Lou Rawls down for appearing. 'You're going to a Whitey festival man,' was the line. There is tension between the white groups who are getting their own ideas and the Negroes who are just repeating theirs. The tension is lessening all the time but it did crop up here, I am sure." The only other black artist Adler and Phillips had hoped to bring to Monterey was 1950s rock legend Chuck Berry, but once Berry was told "it's for charity," the rocker responded that "'Chuck Berry has only one charity and that's Chuck Berry. $2000.'" According to rock music historian Craig Werner, the paucity of black artists as well as attendees at Monterey was due to the fact that the majority of African Americans at the time "didn't much care" about either the San Francisco hip scene or the music it produced. As Werner rightly contends, "Monterey and the scene that gave birth to it [the San Francisco Sound] was mostly a white thing. You could see it—the *Monterey Pop* [the documentary film] crowd shots rarely manage to capture more than a couple of black faces in any frame—but you could also hear it. Janis Joplin, one of the few Southerners to perform, blew the crowd away with 'Down on Me' and 'Ball and Chain' partly because she didn't have to compete with KoKo Taylor or Aretha Franklin."[25]

Despite the non-presence of African American headliners or major artists, one of the most riveting and wildly theatrical performances of the festival's second night was that given by Otis Redding, whose sound was a slick combination of soul, funk, and R&B. Although having an established national reputation among the African American community, Redding was a relative unknown to those whites interested in traditional black musical genres. Monterey marked the first time Redding had appeared before an overwhelmingly white audience. Attired in a bright green suit, within minutes of his opening song, Redding captured the assemblage with a profoundly moving voice coupled with an immense stage presence. Michael Lydon was as captivated by Redding's soulful stylizations and physical swagger as were the rest of his white counterparts as he described the almost-crazed adulation Redding's earth-shattering performance engendered amongst his majority white listeners. "'Shake,' he shouted, 'shake everybody, shake,' shaking himself like a madman in his electric green suit. What was it like? I wrote at the time, 'ecstasy, madness, loss, total, screaming, fantastic.' He closed with 'Try a Little Tenderness,' and by the end of his performance reached a new orgiastic pitch. A standing, screaming crowd brought him back, and back, and back."[26] In a matter of minutes, Redding had gone from an unknown soul singer to a beloved icon of the white hip celebration, transcending the barriers of race and exotic music style, helping to establish Monterey as a great artistic success while reflecting the hip counterculture's desire to be an inclusive, color-blind movement.

Adler and company did a remarkable job of preparation, anticipation, and organization especially when compared to the "set and setting" of subsequent rock festivals, many of which degenerated quickly into disasters on a variety of levels because of poor planning and outfitting by promoters and sponsors. As Adler later reflected, "Our idea for Monterey was to provide the best of everything—sound equipment, sleeping and eating accommodations, transportation—services that had never been provided for both the artists and for the people who came. We set up an on-site first aid clinic because we knew there would be need for medical supervision and that we would encounter drug-related problems. We didn't want people who got themselves into trouble and needed medical attention to go untreated. Nor did we want their problems to ruin or in any way disturb other people or disrupt the music. If someone got into trouble they were taken care of as quickly as possible."[27]

Most astonishing, Monterey was incredibly peaceful, especially given the mass of humanity that attended. The sheer presence of nearly 90,000 potentially stoned-out hippies could have created serious crowd control problems for the small contingent of local police. However, much to city officials' and the cops' surprise and delight, their worst fears that the festival would explode into mayhem never materialized; the result of wisdom, restraint, and unusual good will on both sides. Realizing that they could not have coped with mass arrests police turned a blind eye to drug use, for how do you lock up 50,000 people? Indeed, according to Robert Christgau, "Though the good aroma of California grass was everywhere, Marinello's [the city's police chief] men did nothing about it. Nor did they seize any of the thousands of acid tabs that were distributed free all weekend." The cops simply walked "away from obvious turn-on sessions." For show they occasionally confiscated some dope, throwing it away while "shaking a finger at the offender, and intone 'Be cool.'"[28] Chief Frank Marinello reported on Sunday that he had sent half his force home, and that those officers who remained at the festival got into the spirit, draping their motorcycles with some of the 100,000 orchids Adler had flown in from Hawaii. By dusk there were quite a few be-flowered cops. The stereotype reflects cops rendered powerless by beautiful, blonde, scantily clad barefoot girls presenting them with daisies and orchids. Marinello also told reporters "We've had more trouble at PTA conventions. I have never encountered such peace-loving people. I feel the hippies are my friends and I am asking one of them to take me to the Haight-Ashbury. I will have a lot of friends there."[29] An interesting about-face from an individual who, according to Adler prior to the festival believed "the hippie and the Hell's Angel was the same thing. Everybody was a Hell's Angel that didn't look like the people of Monterey"—affluent, upper middle class white folk.[30]

Sam Karas of the Citizens Committee for the Monterey Pop Festival was equally impressed with the hippie visitors to his city. "We all agreed no arrests unless somebody was really stoned. My first thought was, all these people came here, and they were so wonderful. We hired football players to be bodyguards, but I could have hired kindergartners to do the same job. It was so peaceful."[31] In response to Marinello's request to visit the Haight, Adler and publicist Derek Taylor presented the police chief with a gift at the Monday morning press conference: a glass and leather necklace imprinted with a peace symbol. As he handed Marinello the necklace, Taylor told the chief, "Now you're one of us."[32] In Lou Adler's view, the peace and light-heartedness of Monterey was the result of "local law enforcement authorities never expecting to like the people they came in contact with as much as they did. They never expected the spirit of 'Music, Love, and Flowers' to take them over."[33]

Interestingly, the only violent acts that occurred at Monterey took place on the stage. First the Who's lead guitarist Pete Townshend smashed his guitar to pieces after the band had finished their act, which from Monterey forward became part of the Who's signature finale at their live performances. As one critic noted, "The destructiveness of the Who is consistent theater, deriving directly from the groups' defiant, lower-class stance."[34] Not to be outdone by Townshend's antics, Jimi Hendrix worked himself into a Dionysian frenzy that was so wildly, blatantly sexual that many in this supposedly hip audience squirmed in their seats. He played his guitar behind his back, then rammed it through his legs as if it were an extension of his penis, humped his amplifiers, and simulated oral sex on his instrument, until, thoroughly exhausted, he sank to his knees, doused the guitar with lighter fluid, set it on fire and then smashed it to bits. All of Hendrix's sexual theatrics were captured on film (Pennebaker's *Monterey Pop* documentary) as well as the two women sitting up front who looked stunned and more than a little frightened.[35] Both the Who's and Hendrix's escapades disquieted even the most unflappable person at Monterey, Ravi Shankar, who after witnessing Hendrix's spectacle declared "That was the limit! I couldn't take it anymore and left with disturbing sensations in my mouth, ears, and heart."[36]

Many in the emerging rock press excoriated Hendrix's Monterey performance, believing his erotic contrivances to be a blatant pandering to white teenyboppers. Few critics were more disparaging in their review than *Esquire*'s Robert Christgau, who believed Hendrix's on-stage sexual gyrations epitomized the quintessential "spade," allowing whites to feel sexually free while simultaneously conforming to black stereotypes that made whites comfortable with his phallic nuances. To Christgau, Hendrix was more than just a "Spade with a capital S"; he was a "psychedelic Uncle Tom." Christgau continued savaging Hendrix's performance: "He was terrible.... Dressed in English fop, with a ruffled orange shirt and red pants that outlined his semi-erection to the thirtieth row, Jimi really 'socked it to them.' Grunting and groaning on the brink of sham orgasm, he made his way through five or six almost undistinguishable songs, occasionally flicking an anteater tongue at that great crotch in the sky.... He had tailored a caricature to their [the white counterculture's] mythic standards and apparently didn't even overdo it a shade.... Anyhow, he can't sing."[37]

Before launching into his assault on Hendrix, Christgau astutely assessed the festival's racial composition, the affluent, white "Love Crowd," the majority of who, Christgau contended, were uncomfortable with black music. They thus had difficulty responding "appropriately," other than applauding because they *were supposed* to as a demonstration of their new "love ethos," which embraced diversity and racial equality. Such were the "warm responses" given to Otis Redding in particular.[38] Other than the Who and Janis Joplin, none of the other acts, either black or white, put on, what rock biographer David Henderson refers to as "The Show," until Hendrix. As far as Henderson is concerned, regardless of his profanity, Hendrix's theatrics should not have been so shocking, for they reflected a black stage presentational tradition that for decades had been "the staple of every [black jazz, R&B, and rock and roll] performance, especially on the southern tours and places like the Apollo. 'The Show' was when the artists or band would do some wild, wild, way-out stuff. 'The Show' was the height of the performance, and ... often put both the audience and the performer in a transcendental state where improvisation came to the fore and the unexpected took everybody out ... for the true followers of black music, it was this transcendental moment everyone waited for."[39]

It was during his one-year (1966–67) of "doing the London scene," that Hendrix developed his own "show," polishing its overtly sexual overtones and phallic allusions. To Hendrix's delighted surprise, the London rock underground enthusiastically embraced his eroticized, outlandish performance style, which, according to Eric Clapton, Hendrix shrewdly exploited. "You know English people have a very big thing towards a spade. They really love that magic thing. Everybody and his brother in England still sort of thinks that spades have big dicks. And Jimi came over and exploited that to the limit. Everybody fell for it; I fell for it."[40] Hendrix's onstage flamboyance was very much in the black musical performance tradition and he believed his signature "wild, way-out stuff" would be even more welcomed among more liberated white, hip U.S. audiences.

Hendrix adorned himself in the pastiche of *white* hippie attire, becoming at least in image, a "black hippie," of which, of course, there were very few. Although adopting the white countercultural look, contemporary British pop culture observer Neil Spencer believed that Hendrix's appearance suggested the potential for a new style for blacks, especially for hipsters. "With their mutton-chop sideburns, droopy moustaches and flowing hair, English rock stars were effectively spoofing the Victorian officer class whose finery they donned. But a grinning, crazy-haired Hendrix in hussar's jacket suggested something else entirely—a redskin brave showing off the spoils of a paleface scalp, perhaps, or a Negro 'buffalo soldier' fighting on the side of the anti-slavery Yankee forces in the US Civil War." Hendrix's hippie affectations engendered criticism in the black community. Some blacks accused Hendrix of having "sold out to whitey" for money and for trying to look and act white, playing white music in order to gain acceptance and notoriety within white popular culture as well as access to the white-dominated music industry and commercial culture in general. It is true Hendrix desired material success and believed he had to appeal to the larger white audience (as did all the other pop rock and rollers of the decade, regardless of their color). But Hendrix was no sell out. Rather, he attempted to create an image and a sound that he hoped would reflect the cross-pollination of the various musical impulses that had come to inform late 1960s rock and roll—R&B, blues, jazz, "rockabilly," soul, and even acid rock. This was a unique amalgam that was neither completely black nor completely white; a hybrid sound that was "a-racial" yet rich in both black and white musical traditions. As music and culture critic Nelson George contends, Hendrix should be considered a "cultural curator" or "historical critic" because he took "established black forms, preserving their essence but filtering these textures through an ambitious creative consciousness. He made astounding music that was in the black tradition yet singular from it."[41] Not all African Americans at the time believed Hendrix to be a white panderer or of simply wanting to appeal to young people; instead they regarded Hendrix, his music and image, as having revolutionary potential to change American culture.

Christgau's lambasting of Hendrix's Monterey performance was definitely a minority opinion at the time. Neither the majority of those in attendance or other rock critics shared Christgau's assessment of Hendrix's playing. Only a handful of Monterey acts so awed and delighted the crowd as much as Hendrix's bravura. His talent and unorthodox playing style, captured by Pennebaker on film, was pure rock guitar virtuoso and instantly elevated Hendrix to legendary status. Hendrix even left dumbfounded some of the most established guitarists present at Monterey—Steve Miller, Paul Butterfield, Mike Bloomfield, and Pete Townshend—with his technical ability; it seemed as if the instrument was an extension of his body, which, to the shock of many, it became as he played on. According to Michael Lydon, Hendrix "played his guitar left-handed, if in Hendrix's hands it was still a guitar. It was, in symbolic fact, a weapon that he brandished, his own penis that he paraded before the crowd and masturbated; it was a woman whom he made love to by straddling and eating it while playing the strings with his teeth, and in the end it was a torch that he destroyed." Lydon believed Hendrix's burning of his guitar was a symbolic "sacrifice: the offering of the perfect, most beloved thing, so its destruction could ennoble him further."[42] For any other musician such theatrics might have been considered asinine; but this was *Jimi Hendrix*, and the crowd consumed him, signifying their embracing of his stage presence and his music which were symbiotic and which they had never before experienced.

Unfortunately, Christgau was not the only music critic disdainful of Hendrix's lascivious live performances. Equally scathing was a review of his May 1968 show at the Fillmore East in the *East Village Other*: "The great Jimi Hendrix Experience blessed the stage of the Fillmore last Friday ... but what a drag it was that Hendrix was so penis oriented that night. The greatest musician in the world really doesn't have to hump his guitar. Playing with his teeth is cool, but doing his guitar is a little out of the question and kind of silly." Yet, the audience responded to Hendrix's sexual theatrics "with the closest thing to mass hysteria I've ever seen."[43] Although fans continued to embrace Hendrix's performances as triumphs for racial and sexual liberation, many still viewed his antics as pandering to commercialism and racial stereotypes. Consequently, Hendrix became uneasy about his eroticized image. According to historian Brian Ward, to no matter what degree Hendrix projected or monitored his "spade" persona, he "left white assumptions [about black male sexuality] unchallenged and tacitly endorsed." Not for a second did Hendrix believe his performance reflected "Uncle Tomism."[44] Rather, he concluded by early 1969 that crowds focused more on his gyrations than his music and that was never his intention. "I never wanted it to be so much of a visual thing. When I didn't do it, people thought I was being moody, but I can only freak when I feel like doing so. I can't do it just for the sake of it."[45] Such a realization forced Hendrix to come to terms with the racial implications of his act, which he previously consciously tried to ignore or downplay. By 1969 Hendrix found himself at a professional and personal crossroads; that his show had failed to communicate the *real* Jimi Hendrix Experience—his music—to either counterculture or mainstream audiences. It was thus time for a new "Jimi Hendrix Experience" to emerge, which, as will be seen, was precisely what took place at Woodstock.

Also putting on "The Show" was Janis Joplin, who Christgau and a host of other critics proclaimed "the best rock singer since Ray Charles—that means since the beginning brother—with a voice that is two-thirds Bessie Smith and one-third Kitty Wells [a renowned country music singer], and fantastic stage presence."[46] A reporter for *Time* was as enthralled by Joplin's stage presence as Christgau was at Monterey, seeing her a year later at the Fillmore in San Francisco. "When she stomps, quivers, flails her arms, tosses her mane of hair and swoops through a vocal chorus with hoarse croons and piercing wails, few listeners fail to get the message."[47] Joplin gave a show-stopping performance at Monterey that elevated her to stardom—that of the greatest *white* female blues singer of all time. Few if any since Joplin have been able to affect the sultry quality of her voice or her ability to scream into the microphone, seamlessly transitioning from high-pitched squeals to low, eloquent bellowing; she literally *preached* the blues. As she changed voices she also began her now legendary contortions and gyrations, all of which Pennebaker captured on film as well as the awestruck audience. Michael Lydon was as deeply moved by her premiere as Christgau, Pennebaker, and 60,000 other people. "In a gold knit pants suit with no bra underneath, Janis leapt, bent double, and screwed up her plain face as she sang like a demonic angel. It was the blues big-mama style, tough, raw, gutsy, and with an aching that few singers can reach. The group behind her [Big Brother and the Holding Company] drove her and fed from her. The final number 'Ball and Chain,' which had Janis singing (singing?—talking, crying, moaning, howling) long solo sections had the audience on their feet for the first time. 'She is the best white blues singer I have ever heard' commented S.F. *Examiner* jazz critic Phil Elwood."[48]

For many women in the audience, Joplin's rendition of "Ball and Chain," proved to be a moment of inspiration, revelation and liberation, prompting many female listeners to eventually free themselves from the shackles of mainstream life and domesticity and embrace the burgeoning feminist crusade. Such was the impact Joplin had on Jasmine Tritten, who "When Janis Joplin came on stage and started singing, I got up from my seat, transfixed. I walked to the stage and stood six feet away, looking up at this amazing image.... When she started singing 'Ball and Chain,' half of my being was thinking, 'You can't do that!' The other half was saying 'Right on girl!' She was sexual, self-confident, and demanding her rights as a woman. I became a feminist that day. At that hour. I went back to L.A. and within a few months, I left my job [Tritten had been an account executive with a prominent Los Angeles advertising agency] selling worthless things to people who couldn't afford them. I became a hippie," and she remains true to that lifestyle in Corrales, New Mexico.[49]

Not surprisingly, the Grateful Dead also impressed Lydon, who declared their show "beautiful," playing "at top volume what Shankar had done softly. They played pure music, some of the best music of the concert. I have never heard anything in music which could be said to be qualitatively better than the performance of the Dead Sunday night." Most important, the Dead was the only band (other than solo performer Otis Redding) who called for audience participation, which had become the key to their immense popularity in the Haight and their strong connection with the neighborhood's hip community. They were the City's quintessential dance-hall band and thus from the moment they started playing, they called on the spectators "to dance. You're sitting on folding chairs, and folding chairs are for folding up and dancing on," shouted guitarist Phil Lesh. As several in the audience heeded Lesh's call to dance, they were restrained by ushers and nervous stagehands, "one of the few times the loose reins of the Festival were tightened," much to the Dead's disappointment. For the Dead such crowd rapport and interaction was the vital gauge by which they judged the success or failure of their performances. "Man it was impossible to know how we were doing without seeing people moving. We feed on that, we need it." But Lesh was confident that the band had "did our thing, we did our thing."[50]

Interestingly, Scott McKenzie's "San Francisco," the song which opened Pennebaker's documentary and helped to promote the vibe of a special coming-together, is also the film's swan-song. Perhaps Pennebaker consciously ended his classic with the Summer of Love's official anthem in order to bring down the intensity of Hendrix's flaming guitar encore to a manageable level or maybe, in the words of Jacques Attali, the song represented "the herald of times to come."[51]

Monterey was a huge success on a variety of levels, creating the template (at least on paper) for future rock festivals. Although Woodstock two years later would become the most legendary of such events, Monterey, according to music writer Rusty Desoto "was a seminal event: it was the first real rock festival ever held, featuring debut performances of bands that would shape the history of rock and affect popular culture from that day forward."[52] To Michael Lydon "The Monterey International Pop Festival was a dream come true. An odd, baffling, and at times threatening dream, but one whose main theme was the creation and further growth of rock 'n' roll music, a music as young, vital, and beautiful as any being made today." Lydon also believed that the hippie mantra of "flowers and a groovy kind of love" was out of sync with the realities of hippie rock, a sound in which "there is a feeling of stringent demand on the senses, an experimenting with the techniques of assault, a toying with the idea of beautiful ugliness, the creativeness of destruction, and the loss of self into whatever may come." Artistically, Monterey engendered the creation of a community of "rock musicians," who, regardless of "their bag, came together, heard each other, praised each other and saw that the scene was open enough for them to play as they liked and still get an audience. They will return to their own scenes refreshed and confident. The whole hippie-rock scene was vindicated."[53] For many of those who attended, whether straight or hippie, Monterey "seemed like one moment in time where people forgot about the war in Vietnam, protests, and civil rights clashes. Everything terrible about the 60s was gone from our memories for three days. There are no words to explain it; you just had to have been there."[54] Such were the sentiments of Dan Chavez, at the time, a twenty-seven-year-old straight employee of the Firestone Rubber Company in nearby Salinas.

For The Animals lead singer Eric Burdon, "Monterey wasn't a pop music festival. It wasn't a music festival at all, really. It was a religious festival. It was a love festival. It was a demonstration of what we can do if we put our minds to it and how we can impress people who think that we are incapable of doing things like behaving ourselves and listening to music and acting like human beings instead of acting like savages." What prompted Burdon to make such a statement (despite its rambling triteness) was Police Chief Marinello's comment about how the hippies had become his friends and that because of their warm and fuzzy relationship they were going to give him a personal tour of the Haight. According to Burdon, "When you can impress a guy like a police chief [especially in the United States at this time] and leave a mark on his memory, it just won't stop. If you can impress a guy like that, you can impress anybody." Earlier in the same interview, Burdon had stated that "We don't have the same kind of police force in England as you do in the United States. They're much more easy going," largely because "We don't have the same kind of problems with our kids as you do here. American kids are much more liable to riot. Everything in England is much more relaxed."[55] Unfortunately, Burdon's indictment of American youth came to the fore two years later at another pop festival called Altamont.

Listening to the music—rock and roll—was the common link that for three days united all in attendance regardless of background, age, race, or gender. It was the sound that defined a generation and which down to the present, is remembered and honored as "the music of the 1960s," one of the most memorable and informative decades of the 20th century. The Monterey International Pop Festival of June 1967 was the crescendo of the Summer of Love, becoming an integral part of that history, while some of the bands who played at Monterey have since been enshrined as some of the greatest progenitors of rock and roll music ever. Monterey was a remarkable event for its time. For three days an eclectic mixture of people (cops included), music, and politics formed a community. Prejudices were momentarily put aside as the music transcended socio-cultural stereotypes, dissolving human barriers previously considered intractable and helping to create an environment in which all in attendance temporarily experienced a universal sense of peace and harmony. Indeed, for hippie true-believers, Monterey represented that magical moment in time when they believed that it would be possible to redirect and reframe the nation's popular culture because enough youthful minds trusted the inherent power of goodness and community.

As John Sincalir told *Time*'s Timothy Miller, in Monterey's aftermath, it was "hard to describe the feeling we [hippies] had. Everybody was taking all that acid and dancing and screaming in the music and uniting on every level with everybody else around him. We had a whole new vision of the world, and we knew that everything would be all right once the masses got the message we were sending through our music, our frenzied dancing, our outrageous clothes and manners and speech, our mind-blowing consciousness-expanding, earth-shaking dope." Unfortunately such euphoria and optimism dissipated rapidly as the commercial visionaries of the big record companies, who also attended the festival, quickly "bought off all the musicians," with many bands signing huge contracts right there on the spot, seduced by the capitalists' promises of instant fame and fortune. The result: the music was "adulterated and repackaged and sold back to us like hamburgers."[56]

Monterey's "Love and Flowers and Music" theme would be channeled into the penultimate Woodstock and the denouement of Altamont. Given the weather and number of human beings at Woodstock which taxed festival resources beyond despair, and the violence at Altamont, and the subsequent attempts in later decades to replicate the 1960s rock jamborees, the majority of which ended in complete debacles, was Monterey Pop the greatest American music festival? That is up for debate. But as Michael Lydon observed, "Many of Monterey's offspring much outgrew their mother, but none had her tentative innocence, her blushing first-time exuberance." As Robert Christgau observed, "the Monterey International Pop Festival became the first powwow of the love crowd, the perfect pastoral, chocked with music and warmhearted people. Its success was so unprecedented that it took everyone a little by surprise. You see, at the beginning nobody was really sure the love crowd was out there." In up-and-coming actress Candice Bergen's view, there was no doubt that the "love crowd" had emerged, for Monterey clearly reflected that at that moment, "the Hippies are getting power and the Establishment's getting worried."[57]

10

Communes and the Counterculture

"Good news! America [has] something to export besides war. Open Land!"—Bill Wheeler, founder of Wheeler's Ranch Open Land community in northern California

In summer of 1969 *Life* magazine featured a photograph of a family of hippies, gathered around a teepee before majestic tall firs and broad leaf oaks of the southern Willamette Valley of western Oregon. The caption below the photograph read "The Commune Comes to America," and within a five-page story heralded the arrival of the communes, implying that such pastoral communities were a recent phenomenon in American culture, having bloomed from the hippie movement. Everything about the story reflected the mainstream media's stereotyping of the counterculture, caricaturing those hippies who chose to live physically even further from the straight world as the most extreme type of hippie "fanatics" to be approached with caution, *especially* if sighted in their remote, isolated rural enclaves. No exposé of a hip commune would have been complete without the gratuitous photos of hippies meditating as the sun set; or nude-but-happy hippie children frolicking in woods or meadows; or of hippie women wearing bright colors or perhaps nothing at all, preparing a typical hippie macrobiotic meal of rice, vegetables, and fruit. Even commune members' names were strangely "un–American"—Twig, Ama, and Evening Star—and their language equally unfamiliar if not unintelligible: "The energy we perceive within ourselves is beyond electric; it is atomic; it is bliss." Like the majority of their counterparts throughout the nation, this group of communards revealed as little as possible about their way of life, wanting to stay out of the media limelight. They referred to their commune as "The Family" and described their habitat as "somewhere in the woods." This particular assortment of new-age pioneers actually called themselves the Family of Mystic Arts.[1]

As the media's fascination with the urban hippie movement began to wane by the late 1960s, focus shifted to the rise of the rural commune, which in many ways, marked the high point of American communitarianism; those experiments in alternative group living arrangements that date back to the early 19th century. Although the communal tradition had been part of the American story for well over a century, to this day communes are associated with hippies and remain part of the counterculture stereotype. Comparatively few citizens were aware that the hippie communes of the 1960s were merely the latest expression of a centuries-old cultural motif that combined all sorts of social panaceas with utopian visions. Indeed, hippie communards were simply resurrecting (albeit with many bold, if not outrageous initiatives), a longstanding impulse of cultural dissent, representing an old ideal recast within the hip ethos. These earlier communal societies in the United States were usually formed by individuals with common utopian or religious or political convictions, and thus had a clear ideological core and strong sense of purpose. Few of these endeavors lasted for more than a decade, but some like Brook Farm (Massachusetts), Oneida (New York), Amana Society (Iowa), the Hutterites (South Dakota), and the Shakers (New York), had a long record of independent, self-sufficient living.[2]

Northern California hippie commune The Guild, circa 1969–1970 (photograph by Larry Keenan, courtesy Bancroft Library, University of California, Berkeley. © 1997 Larry Keenan. All rights reserved)

Late 1960s and early 1970s hippie communards became "builders of the dawn," developing their alternative societies in a pastoral set and setting and referring to their new hip enclaves as communes, cooperatives, collectives, or communities, depending upon which name most aptly identified the members' purpose for establishing their particular alternative existence; living and working arrangements were forever fluid. It has been estimated that by 1970 there were 2,000 rural communes and 5,000 urban counterparts, home for approximately two to three million hippies. Reliable statistics are difficult to gather because most communards wanted as little contact with mainstream society as was possible, and to reporters or social scientists who visited, they were reluctant to reveal much about themselves or their lifestyle choice.[3]

Inherent in hippie social thought was the pursuit of an Arcadia, felt by many seekers to have been lost with the passage of time. This quest culminated in a return to a pre-capitalist attachment to the land by moving to the country or the desert, of getting away from the city, and by extension escaping modernity. Journalist William Hedgepath maintained there was "a serious mass-level motive behind this migration," and that "those communes lying out there somewhere in the fierce, snaky reaches of the wilderness," were "by no means hideouts" or "cop-outs from the world. Rather, they are outposts, testing grounds, self-experimental laboratories, starting points for [a] ... social life that more rightly fits the human form."[4]

As reflected in Hedgepath's observations, joining a commune represented a deliberate, wholesale rejection of mainstream society and its attendant values and norms. As Bill Dodd of the *San Francisco Oracle* opined, "Everywhere it seems people, even those far removed from such a way of life, are at odds with the regimentation, alienation from their society and from themselves, and the simple sheer drudgery of their lives. Equally it seems that means were readily available to drop out of this vicious cycle there would be no one who would not do so."[5] Genuine bonding and solicitude for each individual's well-being would define the new societal order; one hip writer declared that communes were "a way to bring our people closer together—closer to social freedom."[6] *Time* reporter Robert F. Jones maintained that those hippies who had moved to a rural commune "come closest to realizing the ideal of complete alienation." As far as Jones was concerned, the rest merely "talk continuously and rapturously about the virtues of dropping out, but few, if any manage to sever all ties with straight society." Whether they panhandled or sold dope, or simply "turned on in doorways," they were "still linked—however remotely—to the macro-economy."[7]

Although there were several country communes that predated the counterculture movement, many of the 1960s communes were founded by disgruntled urban hipsters; "Haight-Ashbury and New York's East Village turned loose on the land."[8] Some of the more famous ones were established by hippies leaving their original metropolitan enclaves, many of which by the late 1960s had deteriorated into cesspools of hard drugs, violent street crime, and increasing establishment repression of dissident lifestyles. As communard Gwen Wheeler observed, "As 1968 unfolded, a new chapter of the New Age began with a hardening of the lines between the 'freaks' and the 'straights.' The colorful, gentle vibrations gradually disappeared and were replaced by a more militant, angry attitude. Brothers and sisters were being jailed by an establishment power structure that defined hippies as outlaws. The hard-edged old ways were rubbing against the soft Aquarian life-style and creating a callous."[9]

The economic recession and conservative backlash of the late 1960s and early 1970s dashed hippie "expectations ... that American society could be radically altered, whether by politics, revolution, or alchemy...." As a result, rural communal living became the favored new "countercultural mode," with the hope that the new forms of human relationships that had not come to fruition in the cities, could be better realized.[10] As their old urban haunts decayed, many "community-oriented hippies left the city" for the countryside where they hoped to recreate the hip vision; "to routinize hippiedom."[11] As William Hedgepath noted at the time, the explosion of country communes in the post–Summer of Love years reflected "the fact that these young people's mass readjustment to their parents' world simply did not take place," despite all the media's "epitaphs" that such a shift back had occurred. Instead hippies found "Another, quieter alternative"—rural communes—"of every imaginable genre ... silently cropping out of the earth by the hundreds," and prompting "alienated young folk to set off in a collective exodus once again."[12]

Inspiring many hippies to transport their experiment in alternative living to the country were the Beats, who saw the great outdoors as an antidote to the toxic conformity of suburbia. This was the theme of Jack Kerouac's 1958 novel *The Dharma Bums*, in which one of the *bums* soliloquized the coming of the hippies; a new generation that will refuse to stay "imprisoned in a system of work, produce, consume, work, produce, consume. I see a vision of a great rucksack revolution, thousands or even millions of young Americans wandering around with rucksacks, going up to mountains to pray, making children laugh and old men glad, making young girls happy and old girls happier, all of 'em Zen Lunatics who go about writing poems that happen to appear in their heads for no reason and also by being kind and by strange unexpected acts keep giving visions of eternal freedom to everybody and to all living creatures."[13]

The majority of hippies had been raised in the suburbs, an environment designed, ironically, to foster a more open and natural habitation and existence. Until they were fully developed, suburbs provided kids with plenty of unspoiled expanse where they could safely play from sun-up to sundown in forests, fields, or orchards just beyond the edge of development. The most memorable and carefree times for many baby boomers growing up in the 1950s, were in the great outdoors of their suburban neighborhoods. Not until suburbia became enclosed—the tract home project complete with schools, parks and playgrounds, and of course shopping centers—did young people begin to feel that their lives had suddenly become physically and spiritually circumscribed and homogenized, and they began rejecting the lifestyle and place that had originally been a wide-open fun-land paradise. Salvation from sterility and confinement came as many affluent suburban families loaded up the station wagon with camping, hunting, and fishing gear and headed to parks and campgrounds where kids once again could feel free. Later in the 1960s, unprecedented numbers of baby boomers went to college or university, many of which were set in serene, "green" environments, the likes of which they had not seen since childhood. Four years of walking across tree-lined quadrangles and studying and playing in that setting only further whetted an appetite for such natural environments where they believed they could become their better, truer selves.[14]

The great rock festivals also helped fuel the desire for greater self-awareness and spirituality through community and pastoralism, especially those tribal gatherings such as Woodstock set in the bucolic countryside. Regardless of set and setting, rock festival participants exulted at the sense of community they felt at these celebrations and were inspired to pursue more enhanced and intimate shared experimentation. Rock pundit Greil Marcus, moved by Woodstock's bonhomie became convinced that, "a free people" could create "instant communities" where they would be able to "live on their own terms." Tuli Kupferberg was even more hopeful in Woodstock's aftermath relative to rejuvenation through communalism. Kupferberg was certain that "We are moving towards a conscious community of artists and lovers who live together, work together, share all things—smoke dope together, dance, fuck together, and spread the word together every way we can—through our dress, our freedom of movement, our music and dance, our economy, our human social forms, through our every breath on this planet."[15] Although by the time of Woodstock scores of communes already existed nationwide, the festival confirmed that a new cultural reality could be realized and that the spirit that had pervaded Woodstock could be recreated throughout the hippie community.

Because rock music was a "tribal phenomenon immune to definition," many bands such as San Francisco's the Grateful Dead, the Charlatans, and Big Brother and the Holding Company, as well as Detroit's MC5, all lived together in communal arrangements, reflecting their identification with and immersion in the activities of their respective hip neighborhoods. Their commune's purpose was simple and specific: to produce rock and roll music. Chester Anderson called the SF bands living in such collectives "super families," believing they were "far more intimately interrelated and integrated than corporate ensembles in the past."[16] By example and through their music they encouraged other hippies to explore that possibility for themselves.

Dope also played an important role in the rise of rural communes; acid-heads and other dope-using freaks bonded the moment they started passing the joint around the circle or tripping together on acid. Since dope was illegal hippie users became outlaws and shared the common goal of staying out of jail. They believed their chances of avoiding that fate increased if they stuck together and remained out of the law's sight (and grasp) in the country, and in fact, most rural communes were isolated enough from mainstream civilization that they were safe from the law in dope cultivation and usage. No doubt the search for remote areas in which to grow marijuana motivated more than a few hippies "Going Up the Country" as Canned Heat urged fellow freaks to do.[17]

For many hippies too, back to the land was an opportunity to continue their veneration of the Native American way of life; an existence "white man" America had ruthlessly obliterated by the beginning of the 20th century. Many country hippies believed they were honoring Indian wisdom and solicitude for the earth by resurrecting Native American traditions and practices such as living in tepees; wearing buckskin loincloths; planting corn with a stone or wooden hoe, living on an "Indian diet"; performing sun dances and powwows. As homage was paid sitting in a hot-rocks steam bath for hours for purification and in peyote rituals, many country hippies believed they had become as close to Mother Nature as the Native Americans; both believed that "Parceling up Mother Earth" was "a foreign and ludicrous concept."[18]

The early communes attracted the more genuine, purposeful counterculturists; true seekers of a New Age in pastoral miniature. As one member of the movement reflected, "given both our despair over the social injustices endemic to our political and economic systems, and our optimism about our own ability to come together and create better environments in which to live, it now seems inevitable that so many of us would try to form communes in the late sixties and early seventies."[19] Another communard agreed: "I had done the political trip for a while but I got to the point where I couldn't just advocate social change, I had to live it."[20] "Right now, I'm trying to keep from being swallowed by a monster—plastic, greedy American society," a nineteen-year-old wrote to the members of one rural commune. "I need to begin relating to new people who are into taking care of each other and the earth."[21] Communal seekers wanted to feel the flow of the seasons, to grow things, to walk naked; to breathe-in, to soak up, to envelop themselves in as much nature as they possibly could; to affirm "Life," a word they often used that encompassed everything they valued. Indeed, as one Northwest communard told *Harper's* reporter Sara Davidson, who spent the fall of 1969 visiting intentional communities in California, Oregon, and Washington and interviewing their inhabitants, "I like it here [Tolstoy/Freedom Farm in Davenport, Washington established in 1963 by Huw Williams and one of the first to embrace open land] because I can stand nude on my porch and yell fuck! Also, I think I like it here because I'm fat, and there aren't many mirrors around. Clothes don't matter and people don't judge you by your appearance like they do out there [mainstream society]."[22]

Communing with nature or playing Indian were not the only reasons hippies fled to the countryside. Apocalyptic visions of the "end of days" for urban/industrial society compelled many to seek refuge in rural areas. Many hippies determined that the United States had finally reached a point of no return after decades of greedy excess and abuse of the nation's natural environment. The warning signs of the impending collapse were all around by the late 1960s—smog alerts, water shortages, pesticide scares, power outages, traffic snarls, over-crowding—clear indicators that the urban scene soon would be deadly to body and soul. To Lew Welch it was "quite clear that gluttony, greed, lack of compassion" was fast destroying "this generous and undemanding Planet. We face great holocausts, terrible catastrophes, all American cities burned from within and without. And there will be signs. We will know when to slip away [to the country] and let these murderous fools rip themselves to pieces."[23] As another communard explained, "our ecological sophistication told us that the cities and everybody in them were doomed. 'Don't drink the water and don't breathe the air' is pretty sound advice these days in the places where most Americans live."[24] Once hippies had staked out their "co-lively [communal] retreats" in the country, it was imperative to Welch that they "learn the berries, the nuts the fruit the small animals and plants. Learn water," so that when the day comes when all the "good men and women" who had taken refuge "in the mountains, on the beaches, in all the neglected beautiful places," gather together, "we will be prepared to go back to ghostly cities and set them right, at last."[25] Huw "Piper" Williams agreed with his compatriots, certain that doomsday was imminent and thus now was the time to prepare for "the end." "When the country is wiped out, electricity will stop coming through the wires, so you might as well do without it now. I don't believe you should use any machine you can't fix yourself." One of Williams' fellow communards Steve, told Sara Davidson that "Technology can't feed the world" and thus if "you don't want to starve to death, better know how to plot a garden."[26]

Rural communards were not the only hippies who believed the end was near. Many hip rock stars incorporated such apocalyptic visions into their songs, thus endorsing the back-to-the land movement. At the January 1967 Be-In, Jerry Garcia sang a song ("Morning Dew") about nuclear annihilation written by folksinger Bonnie Dobson; the cover of the Jefferson Airplane's *Crown of Creation* (1968), showed the mushroom cloud from an atomic bomb, while their "House at Pooneil Corner" evoked images of a deserted and scarred earth devastated by nuclear holocaust; Neil Young's "After the Goldrush," depicted a doomed planet as well, with himself "lying in a burned-out basement." Some hip musicians, most notably Frank Zappa, wrote songs about the devastating effects of industrial pollution, but rarely if ever did his work reflect any nostalgia for an arcadia that characterized the work of many of his contemporaries in the rock field. For Zappa it was man's destruction of nature rather than a longing for, or an escape to, an Edenic place where purity and innocence could be reclaimed. To Zappa it was more important for his work to expose the villains responsible for wreaking mindless environmental havoc upon the land: the military-industrial complex and the consumer society that sustained such self-serving and destructive entities. Zappa poignantly summed up the hippies' back-to-the-wilderness mania by likening their cause to children's fascination with nature. "Kids have a natural sense of mysticism, and a feeling of being connected to nature; the natural world is very exciting when it's all brand new." He then added a clever but pointed dig at those whose enrapture with the natural world was naïve, if not delusional. "For example kids have an appreciation for snow which is generally not shared by the guy who has to shovel the driveway. The older you get the more you take nature for granted (unless you're Euell Gibbons and you want to eat everything that's lying on the ground until you die from it)."[27] Despite their popular image at the time of being weird, naive nature freaks, the hippies' environment call to arms now seems visionary and cannot be dismissed as the silly notions of a bunch of "long-haired leaping gnomes."

Contrary to popular myth, few hip communards were either drug and sex-crazed hippies or general miscreants. Although some communes did become sanctuaries for the casualties of psychedelia or its sickies, vagabonds, and other unsavory characters opportuning on hippie gentle hospitality, the majority remained from start to finish, the home for mostly young, white affluent Americans, many of whom had a college education or degree. They were disenchanted writers or artists; disillusioned and alienated Vietnam veterans, rebellious outsiders; women searching for liberation, and myriad others, all longing for an alternative to bland suburbia or the drudgery, busyness, and impersonality of big-city living.[28] As William Hedgepath observed, these new "young migrants" were "not just displaced veteran hip gypsies who set forth on this second wave" of hippiedom. Joining them in this new migration were "thousands more hippie-symps and until-just-recently straight kids who were finally sensing the *Angst* of living in official America," and most important they were "more sophisticated and a damn sight more serious about why they were leaving and what they were headed for."[29] Regardless of who they were, or what they were searching for in communal living, "they all had in common the highest human aspiration: to be free."[30]

Without question the most salient feature of hippie-era communes was their diversity. There was an array of anarchistic retreat groups in which members agreed to reject all forms of "Establishment" organization, habits, and behavior considered "archaic" and where *anyone* was welcomed. There were also service or intentional organizations or cooperatives, in which communards pooled resources and agreed to live within certain but limited guidelines based on the philosophical purpose of people coming together to create a "lifestyle that reflected their shared core values."[31] Such a varied assortment made *defining* communes difficult as one Oregon communard noted at the time. "Each commune is different. There are communes that live on brown rice, and communes that have big gardens, and communes that buy white bread and frozen vegetables at the grocery store. There are communes with no schedule whatsoever (and no clocks); there is at least one commune where the entire day is divided into sections by bells, and each person states, at a planning meeting at 7 a.m. each morning, what work he intends to do that day. There are communes centered around a particular piece of land, like us, or travelling communes like the Hog Farm, or communes centered around a music trip or a political trip, like many of the city communes. This diversity raises certain questions. A piece of land that is simply thrown open to anyone who wants to live there, or a place where each family lives entirely in its own house but the land is owned jointly: shall we call these places 'communes' or not? Communes differ greatly."[32]

The majority of communes were generally small, perhaps a dozen people who lived on a farm or ranch or simply squatted on some land or occupied some abandoned buildings in an isolated, primitive, rural area. However, regardless of the type of commune and its purpose, land was the key and thus a mundane problem soon confronted those desiring a return to nature: where does a group of voluntary young povertarians find—buy—land to live on? Suffice it to say, few hippies had the requisite funds readily available for purchasing property. Coming to the rescue were hip philanthropists such as the fairly wealthy former Limeliter folk group member and music critic, Lou Gottlieb, who, during the Summer of Love, purchased a 31-acre apple orchard in Sonoma County, northern California's wine country, about an hour and a half drive north of San Francisco. Gottlieb initially established his commune for disaffected Haight hippies but eventually opened his gates to anyone who wanted to live on open land, which to Gottlieb and Ramon Sender Barayon, Morning Star's manager, meant that *any individual or group* at any time had *free* access to Morning Star's land upon which to live. Indeed, Gottlieb proclaimed that his land was not owned by him or anyone but was the possession of all who lived at his ranch; that the universe had decreed that private property was to be abolished. Morning Star also at the outset was to grow and provide organic vegetables for the Diggers' free food happenings in the Haight. "We give them food," one member declared, "and they give us beautiful young people." "Hippies hard at work—rarest of all hippie trips," so impressed *Time* reporter Robert F. Jones that he later commented that "The new-found trip of work and responsibility reflected in the Morning Star experiment is perhaps the most hopeful development in the hippie philosophy to date."[33]

Unlike many of their compatriots, Morning Star communards welcomed the publicity "because we felt we had to tell the world that this kind of experience was possible." However, as Gina Stillman further observed at the time, most of the journalists who came to the ranch "were looking for 'yellow journalism' stuff" while only a handful "tried hard to understand" or had an "open, positive attitude." Nonetheless, "the community decided to have a completely open policy in regards to the media. They felt that the good will of society must be promoted, and that one way to achieve this was through an open door to the media. Reporters were frequently amazed at the hospitality they encountered." Bill Wheeler, owner of Wheeler's Ranch or "the Ridge" and Gottlieb's neighbor, who became an open land convert, believed "the idea of Open Land had to be communicated. For once, America had something besides war to export. We had no fear of revealing our location, identity or activities to anyone who would listen." As a result of the media coverage, "More and more people came, to visit, to settle in, or just to stay for a while before moving elsewhere." Throughout the summer of 1967, "the flow of visitors" to Morning Star was "intense" but the communards "accepted it as the price of educating others to the new life style." The constant influx of the curious, the gawkers, the true believers, and even the less than savory individuals, who frequently showed up, convinced Sender that, all "were eager to find new ways to live, to relate to one another and bring up their children!" "People came pouring in from everywhere," exulted Lou Gottlieb. "I know of one young man who read the [*Time*] article as an inmate of a New York mental hospital. He split for Morning Star that same day saying, 'This is what I'm looking for and these are the people I want to be with.' His father had been paying a hundred dollars a day for his treatment. At Morning Star he got it for free.... The hippies should get the Nobel Prize for creating this simple idea."[34]

After spending several days at Morning Star, journalist Sara Davidson wrote perhaps one of the most objective assessments of not only the commune craze of the late 1960s and early 1970s, but the direction hip true believers appeared to taking the counterculture movement. There was no doubt in Davidson's mind, that mainstream culture had "absorbed so much of the hip style ... that it has obscured the substance of the movement." However, she believed, the folk at Morning Star were trying manfully to keep the ideal real and alive. These hippie purists, who had dropped out completely from the straight world, seemed to have found "another way of living, to support oneself physically and spiritually" without becoming "a company freak, working nine to five in a straight job and roaming the East Village on the weekends" playing hippie. They have said "no to competition, no to the work ethic, no to consumption of technology's products, no to political systems and games." They instead chose to "trek to rural land where there would be few people and life would be hard," and there, practice joyfully and earnestly "voluntary primitivism" and "re-tribalization." They built "houses out of mud and trees, plant and harvest crops by hand, roll loose tobacco into cigarettes, grind their own wheat, bake bread, can vegetables, deliver their own babies, and educate their own children. They gave up electricity, the telephone, running water, gas stoves, even rock music, which of all things, [was] the cornerstone of hip culture. Instead they sing and play their own music—folky and quiet."[35]

Neither Morning Star nor Wheeler's Ranch was a commune in the traditional sense or concept. Rather, they were a "loose community of individuals" who lived either by themselves or in "monogamous units" or "cliques who eat together, share resources" but who rarely mixed with the other communards. Wheeler opposed establishing his ranch as a conventional commune because he believed "trying to get too many different people under one roof doesn't work." As one member recalled "At [Morning Star and Wheeler's Ranch] a 'separate but equal philosophy' prevailed. Each participant was free to do his or her individual thing apart from everyone else's but no one's thing was more important than anyone else's. The only important thing was that everyone was doing their own thing together, somehow, somewhere, in spirit, on the land."[36]

Hashbury refugees and other seekers came to a functioning community of tents, gardens, main house, and communal dining room, where everybody shared the chores, at least initially. By the time he founded Morning Star, Gottlieb had long since shed his clean-cut, coat-and-tie geeky folkie image; he had transformed in look, attitude, and behavior into that of a bona-fide hippie, and thus Morning Star, in concert with the hippie ethos of openness and acceptance of all people, ideas, and things, had a no-exclusions policy. Gottlieb was confident his ranch and its purpose would attract the right kind of seeker, one with a "high capacity for community and toleration of others." Moreover, "From the first, the land selected the people. Those who couldn't work hard didn't survive. When the land got crowded, people split. The vibrations of the land will always protect the community." Bill Wheeler agreed: "The land was open only insofar as the people on it were themselves open. When they committed 'closed' acts they closed the land to themselves. When a person couldn't trust the Morning

Star consciousness, when they did violence of one kind or another, they did not remain but returned to the greater society which offered specific remedies for amoral and asocial behavior—prison or the hospital. In the first five years of Open Land, during which time many thousands from every stratum of society passed through the Ridge, I did not have to tell anyone to leave or remove them myself more than five times." According to Gina Stillman, for several months Morning Star did indeed attract the right sort of communard. "The people who came fit in. There was plenty of room and there was no reason to tell anyone to leave. As it was, a group of very talented people showed up—artists—people who liked to spend a lot of time in thought and contemplation. Somehow the land itself encouraged meditation, peace, and happiness.... I wanted to dedicate myself to be part of a huge, loving, giving, motherly force. I gave up my concern for my personal welfare and concentrated on a concern for the community, for the group consciousness rather than on my individual self."[37]

Gottlieb's vision for his commune was simple: he hoped Morning Star would serve as an inspiration for "a community style of life suited to the needs of a society in which cybernation will have rendered leisure compulsory.... Therefore new avenues of experiment must be explored to find out what to do with all this leisure time. Along this line, I see Morning Star as an open, intentional community with tremendous potential for psychological and sociological discovery." Gottlieb also believed that Morning Star represented the hippies' fight "against the territorial imperative. Open land has no historical precedent. When you give free land, not free food or money, you pull the carpet out from under the capitalist system." Communard Wilder Bentley agreed. "The necessity to pay to use land makes you sell your work. This is turn draws you into a servile conformity and no art is ever produced out of that state of mind."[38]

Gottlieb, like many of his countercultural peers, had come to believe that the United States had attained such a level of technological advancement (cybernation) that now individuals could devote more time to their spiritual and psychic well-being, which they had seriously neglected in their pursuit of the American Dream; open land would give them a chance to be "reborn by living in harmony with the earth.... "Why did no one think of it [open land] before the hippies? Because hippies don't work, so they have time to dream up truly creative ideas."[39]

By the close of the Summer of Love, hundreds of hippies were grooving at the ranch, boldly displaying the hip devotion to spontaneous, uninhibited living, complete with nudity, free love, and plenty of dope, especially acid, which became Morning Star's signature, favorite high and sadly one of its most defining "qualities." Indeed, the ranch's communards viewed LSD as the panacea for all that ailed individuals or groups in the community and thus mass LSD sessions were commonplace, especially among people having difficulty accepting one another, either collectively or personally. One such antagonism cured by a mass LSD trip was between "the budding community of Hindu-oriented yogis" and a group of "Jesus-freaks"—actually Bible-thumping fundamentalists—led by Don and Sandy King. The King family followers "felt uncomfortable in a group chanting 'Hare Krishna' while the others who had Jesus stuffed down their throats as children did not want any more Christianity." So Ramon Sender believed that the best way to bring the two factions together and promote tribal toleration and peace, was to hold "A group LSD trip on the hillside below the Lower House" with the hoped for result. "About thirty people *came together* in the morning sunshine. For me [Ramon Sender, head yogi guru] the highlight of that experience was the moment

Don and I embraced, tears streaming down our cheeks. It was the healing moment of the Christian-Hindu rift within the group. The Morning Star consciousness [with the help of several tabs of acid] was higher than any of the traditional antagonisms between old faiths."[40] Newcomers felt especially inclined to stay as loaded as possible for as long as they could, for as one such initiate remarked, "You sort of have to be stoned to get through the first days here, then you know the trip."[41]

Morning Star's most legendary LSD group trip occurred on "Black Sunday," June 1967, when several communards joined with a wedding party and drank "some very special punch" that contained only two quarts of fruit juice but was laced with five hundred tabs of "pure Owsley LSD" with "a little psilocybin for flavor and some mescaline for color." On that day about fifty people took the acid trip of their lifetimes. Fortunately no one died or freaked-out so badly that they blew their mind completely or had to be hospitalized, although plenty of people "couldn't walk, but could only crawl"; thought they had been "poisoned"; bit anyone "near them between screams"; saw "the end of the world"; "tried to jump off a cliff to see if I could hurt myself"; and "covered themselves in shit and ran around trying to hug everyone." According to Gwen Wheeler, "crawling, writhing, naked, muddy, stoned hippies" were everywhere as were heard many "unearthly screams" for several hours. She believed she "was visiting the wildest mental hospital on earth. Within the invisible walls of each person's 'cubicle' a different crazy human drama was unfolding." As Bill Wheeler wryly observed of the punch he and others drank that day, "This sure ain't Olympia beer!"[42]

Even a veteran acidhead such as Peter Coyote was "blown away" by the concoction and all the trips he witnessed. "For the record, I'll challenge anybody to an acid-eating contest anytime, anyplace, anywhere. I've tried every drug there is to try, and I'm All-American. The prize is the cosmos, of which I am currently the President. I'll give up my badge and trade positions if I lose. But when I tell people that Black Sunday at the Ridge was the greatest trip of my life, they don't believe me. They refuse to believe me. For some it was a demonic inferno. The Devil got loose that day. Ah, psychedelic splendor!" Fortunately for all involved, "no police came and no one [Wheeler's hostile straight neighbors] called town to come see what was going on. The Ridge community worked it through on their own in true Open Land tradition. Everyone in his own way had gone through some kind of hell and lived through it. Once again the lack of easy access to the outside had proved a blessing."[43]

One of the more interesting interpretations of "Black Sunday" came from community member "Zen Jack," another devoted acidhead. To Zen Jack, "Black Sunday" epitomized Open Land and such mind-blowing acid trips could only occur in an Open Land environment. The love of nature and acid became symbiotic; only on acid or some other hallucinogen, could the wonder and beauty of the wilderness, be truly experienced. On drugs, one felt in tune with the "stars, migratory patterns, planting cycles, the chirping of insects." Nature talked and stone country hippies listened in ecstatic communion. "The planet is a sentient companion! Everything that lives is talking to everything and communicating its response *back* to everything, without stopping, constantly!" For Zen Jack, Black Sunday "was something that couldn't have taken place probably anywhere else in the world, not in a state park, not in the city or in a private home somewhere. It only could have happened on a piece of land ruled by anarchy or not ruled at all. It had to happen where it was totally free to have whatever happened happen!"[44] For many rural freaks, acid did indeed make "it possible to have a decent conversation with a tree."[45]

To outside observers, drugs seemed to be the driving if not defining force behind communards' lives. Even meals were served with "hash; pot; acid; mescaline and TCP, a tranquilizer for horses." At one such "feast" at Wheeler's Ranch "a man in his forties with red-spotted cheeks" approached Sara Davidson and asked her if she had any "pills. 'I'll take anything. I'm on acid now.' I offered him aspirin. He swallowed eight." Although determined to free themselves from all processed foods and "manufactured medicinal drugs," most country hippies Davidson encountered saw "no contradiction in continuing to swallow any mind-altering chemical they are offered." Tragically, many communard parents gave their children acid as well. Indeed, according to "Fruits n' Nuts Nancy," who dosed her own children regularly, "many children have been on more acid trips than most adults at the ranch. They get very quiet on acid. The experience is less staggering for kids than for adults because acid returns you to the consciousness of childhood." Nancy also attributed her children's good health to all the acid she had given them. "They have not been sick in two years because a spiritually healthy, pure clean mind means a healthy body and acid cleanses the soul of all the impurities that cause sickness."[46]

One of Morning Star's more celebrated visitors was the famous blues singer Nina Simone, who came to the ranch in 1967 and overall was impressed by what she saw. However, she observed that "there aren't any black people here." Gottlieb, momentarily taken aback, responded "Well, what can I do? I want them to come but we don't invite people. They just show up." That the non-existence of black folk at Morning Star should have bothered Simone is perplexing. As noted in previous chapters, few African Americans joined the 1960s hip parade, finding little they could relate to in the hippie movement. Like most everything else related to the hippies at the time, the majority of African Americans, especially inner-city blacks, saw communes as just another manifestation of bored, spoiled, and crazy white people temporarily playing at being poor, and voluntary poverty, egalitarian or not, had little appeal among late 1960s urban black Americans. Neither did trying to eke out a living by working the land; a painful reminder for many African Americans of their ancestors' harsh and desperate lives as Southern sharecroppers or tenant farmers, or worse, plantation slaves. Nonetheless, both Gottlieb and Bill Wheeler remained committed to a non-exclusion policy to the very end of their respective Open Land experiments. As Bill Wheeler told all newcomers to the Ridge, "Within the community a man was neither black, tan or white but just another brother," and thus "most of the blacks who lived with us worked through any hang-ups they had about their race and made a positive contribution." Over the course of the ranches' respective histories a variety of interesting, mostly single African American males found their way to either Morning Star or the Ridge, with the majority easily integrating into an overwhelmingly white community. Unfortunately, as Zen Jack put it, occasionally a few "ghetto bad assess" would show up, happy to take advantage of hippie hospitality and generosity, whether it came in the form of free dope, sex, food, or a roof over their heads for a few days or weeks before moving on to the next hippie rural enclave, which for some served as temporary sanctuaries from the law. The transients, with their "hostile vibes" and behavior only exacerbated existing antagonisms while confirming in the minds of the communes' straight neighbors that both Morning Star and Wheeler's Ranch were nothing more than hideouts for criminals and other deviants, regardless of color.[47]

One of the first African Americans to show up at Morning Star was a World War II veteran named O.B. Ray, who had driven a cab in San Francisco for seventeen years, a job he labeled as "being forced into slavery." He quit, moved to Mt. Tamalpais in Marin County, immersed himself in Zen by Suzuki Rushi, meditated, and took tons of acid before migrating along with four of his "disciples" during the Summer of Love to Morning Star. There, Ray and his followers became "permanent fixtures." At Morning Star, Ray started the first "cult," that of the Gurdjief, building a large plastic dome, which served both as their "monastery" and place of residence. As Bill Wheeler observed, "Women or sex seemed to have no place within their tightly disciplined existence ... the 'Gurdjief Boys,' as we called them, proved extremely energetic and a fine addition to the community" and their leader O.B. regarded by all as "a font of wisdom and mellowness at all times, a great sage and much beloved tribal leader." Perhaps most important to the community, Ray was a "superlative good-karma marijuana farmer" who "gave away all he grew." Another equally embraced African American communard was John Butler, who "was extremely hospitable and generous with everything he owned." At his place "the radio [transistor] was always playing and there was always something to smoke, and people came to tell him their troubles." John was "A big-hearted brother with lots of soul, very devoted to the community, and felt that Morning Star was a dream come true, a place where he felt safe." Most important to his white brethren, John had "none of the bitterness and hostility of so many other Blacks who came."[48]

Unfortunately for all residents, not all of the African Americans who came to Morning Star or Wheeler's Ranch possessed the same desire to integrate and cooperate with the larger white community that O.B. Ray and John Butler displayed; a genuine willingness to "blend in" as inconspicuously and seamlessly as possible and interact with their white brothers and sisters on an equal hip basis of understanding and openness. Some who came were outright sociopathic or pathological in their behaviors and attitudes toward their white counterparts, causing serious racial tensions and dissension. Ramon Sender believed rather naively that such rancor between whites and blacks, was the result of African Americans' inability to take acid, the hippie panacea for all individual and group hang-ups about anything. Blacks simply "bummed-out" on acid, according to Sender. "They had been under the thumb of the White Man for so long that LSD only released all the bitterness and negative feelings" toward whites instead of "mellowing" them out and "reframing" their attitudes about racial acceptance and harmony. "The black man who dug acid was a rarity"; blacks "just couldn't cool out behind psychedelics. 'Hey man I'm not getting off, and just to show you how much I don't like it I'm going to rip you off.'" Despite Sender's absurd assessment, such was the disposition and response of "Dennis the Menace, a jive hustler inside a labyrinth of lies, with a jungle instinct for survival," whether he was on acid or not. He was especially "hung up on white women, hating them and obsessed by the need to rape them even if they were willing to submit voluntarily. When confronted with his deeds, he said 'Oh, that white bitch! I saw her going around balling all those [white] guys. She's a whore. She asked for it. She didn't want me 'cause I'm black.' ... If they resisted he smashed their faces in true ghetto tradition. For that matter, anyone who disagreed or crossed him invited violence." Dennis was also a thief, stealing not only from fellow communards, regardless of color, but also when in town. To Dennis, the Open Land community in particular was "a pasture of sheep" he "could fleece with no danger of being busted." After numerous complaints from both white and black community members, and despite numerous attempts to help Dennis find that "beautiful person struggling to emerge," Bill Wheeler had no choice but to expel Dennis from his ranch.[49] Despite the occasional presence of African Americans such as Dennis, the lion's share of blacks who found their way to Morning Star or The Ridge, either to escape the hostility and despair of inner city life, or simply to experiment with an alternative lifestyle for a while, had little difficulty living harmoniously and peacefully with their majority white neighbors.

Peter Coyote, an original Haight Digger, sought refuge at Morning Star as the Haight filled with thousands of wayward seekers during the Summer of Love. Upon his arrival, Coyote quickly discovered that "most who came up the road knew less about group life, hygiene, and labor than I did." However, since Coyote had been there longer than most he was "automatically elevated to the formless and far from invested role of patriarch"; a status both Lou Gottlieb and Ramon Sender eschewed. Thus in moments of lucidity, Coyote took upon himself "the struggle to instill a rudimentary sense of responsibility into each new arrival." In a handwritten broadside with huge letters that he posted so everyone could see, Coyote "encouraged" the following "Pearls of Wisdom from the Leader: If you let the baby shit on the floor and then eat it, you'll have a sick baby *and* a shitty floor. Free food doesn't mean that I cook and you eat all the time, asshole. It's fine if you want to take speed, just don't talk to *me*! I don't actually care that the insects are communicating with you. I *know* the Indians used moss for tampons, but you're picking poison oak."[50] Sara Davidson had similar observations relative to some community members' hygienic practices or lack thereof. "No one brushes his teeth more than once a week, and then they use 'organic toothpaste' made from eggplant cooked in tinfoil.... A girl says there are worms in the green apples. Another, with a studious voice and glasses says, 'That's cool, it means they were organically grown. I'd rather eat a worm than a chemical any day.' They eat with their fingers from paper plates, and when the plates are gone, directly from the pot.... Because of the haphazard sanitation system, the water at Wheeler's is contaminated, and until people adjust to it, they suffer dysentery. There are periodic waves of hepatitis, clap, crabs, scabies, and streptococcic [sic] throat infections."[51]

Despite Coyote's and others' admonishments, as 1968 progressed, and as increasing numbers of Haight fugitives and seekers from all over the country inundated Morning Star as well as Wheeler's Ranch, which had also become Open Land by that year, Gottlieb's and Bill Wheeler's best of intentions began to unravel. The new arrivals, more misfits and miscreants than wholesome hippies, refused to do any work and thus both communities, but especially Morning Star, began to rapidly deteriorate as "a great deal of anger came to Morning Star and was released in orchards and meadows" mostly by the single men and the "wine-drinking 'warrior caste'" who the ranch now attracted rather than families with children and other committed seekers. "Their drunken brawls, aggressive panhandling and thievery disrupted the community as well as further aggravating the neighbors." Garbage piled everywhere instead of becoming compost; latrines were not dug; the outhouses stank, the water supply dwindled, people became increasingly hungry and scavenged for whatever they could find, while a host of diseases, from STDs to hepatitis, spread through the community like wildfires; the latter more than likely caused by "the septic runoff in which the work crews had been digging" and which hit the community "like the Black Plague."[52]

By 1968 the ranch's most glaring "downside [could] be summarized in one word: hunger. Legal hassles were the other side of the downside, but our court problems had their spiritual upside at times. Hunger had no upside." Such were the reflections of Pam Read, who found herself "terribly hungry" all of the time that year, especially for protein. Pregnant with her second child, she simply could not get enough nourishment as the garden, which had been well-maintained the previous year, providing ample supplies of vegetables to feed the community, had literally gone to seed because no one any longer was willing to put in the required work to keep it productive. As a result, increasing numbers of communards experienced various manifestations of serious mineral and vitamin deficiencies/deprivation, and even mild forms of starvation. Sympathetic tourists and other "weekenders would often bring us food" and especially appealing was protein-rich or enhanced meats such as spam, which Pam Read, much to the chagrin of her vegan compatriots, sacrilegiously "covertly devoured," despite subsequent feelings of being "un-evolved" and "ashamed to be so unspiritual." Communard children also suffered from malnutrition and borderline starvation: Read's own son, Adam Siddhartha, much to Read's subsequent dismay, had "a distended belly" which she didn't "realize until much later [was] a sign of protein deficiency." Fortunately her child didn't appear "to have lost any brain cells because of this—it was nothing like the cases in Africa—but I'm convinced he was in the first stages of protein starvation." Read's most "shame-faced and miserable" memory of Morning Star's "starving times" was when she was so hungry that she gobbled up a bowl of "oatmeal with milk. Milk!" without giving any to her son. "That was a terrible moment. I was robbing my own child." It was soon after that episode that Read decided that it was time to leave Morning Star, at least for awhile, to try to improve her condition as well as that of her son at her parent's house in New York. With her husband Larry's blessing, Read flew to New York and stayed with her parents for over a month, and in that time, much to her relief, "Siddhartha's belly shrank back down to normal size and he was gobbling eggs and milk and cheese like crazy."[53]

By the close of 1968 Morning Star had become "unlivable, unworkable, impossible and dangerous because of the outlaw tribes living there," and many of the place's original inhabitants fled to Wheeler's Ranch, which, for a while, was a safe haven from the "troublemakers" who could not "find their way to the Ridge because of its isolation." At Wheeler's "A nucleus of responsible community members carried the burden of keeping things going" for as long as they possibly could, hoping "to create an example of Open Land which was safe, happy, prosperous, and a healthy place to raise children." However, it was only a matter of time before the troublemakers found out about Wheeler's and began settling there as well, and Wheeler soon found himself having to deal with the same issues and problems that were fast destroying Gottlieb's vision of Open Land. For many of the newcomers, Open Land meant "'Open Everything,' open house, open wallet, open bed, open car, open cupboard. Personal freedoms, so limited in most of society, became of primary importance. Personal privacy, minimal rules and the occasional need for decisive action played a constant tug-of-war within the basic anarchic framework of the community." One of the most disturbing and divisive developments at Wheeler's (which did not emerge at Morning Star), was the rise of a menacing cult led by a man named David of the Oak Grove. Wheeler attributed David's appearance to the "political vacuum" that existed in the Open Land concept, which often caused the experiment to be "a rudderless ship drifting helplessly and aimlessly in a storm," the perfect scenario for someone to "come along who saw Open Land freedoms as an opportunity to usurp power and become a self-appointed king." No sooner did David arrive at Wheeler's (summer of 1971) than "he gathered a following of people mesmerized by his Rasputin-like manipulative abilities, his hypnotic aura and his endless rap about astrology, love and God." He also had several run-ins with Wheeler purposely challenging Wheeler's supposed "authority" over the commune. At their every meeting Wheeler felt that David stared at him with "needles of hatred and competitiveness." Their relationship had become "an ego clash."[54]

Within a few months, David had a cult following of four men and six women, all of whom considered him "as an avatar or guru." He was constantly on the prowl for new recruits, especially women, all of whom were to be completely obeisant to the men "they slept with on a rotating basis" and who were seen "as the embodiment of complete and universal love." The women all wore the same clothing, "handmade, long, flowing paisley prints made from Madras bedspreads." They were not allowed to ever be by themselves and thus they walked about the ranch in groups "as New Age cloistered nuns." All of his followers had to sever ties with old friends and relatives and were forbidden any contact with the outside world. Predictably David believed "spiritual enlightenment" could only be attained with dope, especially LSD, the requisite for "breaking down conscious and unconscious cultural and social barriers within the family." It seemed as if David was the first person anyone met when they came to the ranch, which gave the impression that David was the Ridge's *leader*. The moment newcomers arrived, David "dosed them with acid to gain power over them, and rumor had it that he dealt drugs on the side to help finance his projects. Other income came from new members turning over their savings to the family, along with credit card scams and shoplifting which he rationalized as relieving the store of its bad karma." There was no doubt in Wheeler's mind that David wanted complete control of the ranch and the only obstacle to that design was Wheeler. The majority of the Ridgefolk were convinced that "David's trip was this one person taking all this energy from a whole group of people and becoming very powerful, like Charles Manson, drawing out these people's life forces. You could see in the glazed eyes that they had no will of their own." As far as "Bart" was concerned, David was "psychotic" and had to leave.[55]

By the spring of 1972, the other Ridgefolk had had enough of David's "power-tripping," and led by O.B. Ray, decided to confront David directly and ask him and his family to leave. "Even the most non-political people stiffened in their defense of cherished Open Land freedoms." Indeed, to Wheeler's shock, a group of "vigilantes," led by Ray and all carrying sticks and other implements, went to David and with Ray as their spokesperson told the Manson copy-cat "We'd like to see you gone. You should leave or there'll be violence." Surprised by such "resolve," David, seeing "his ambitions crumpled by the fiber, intent, and direction of the community," decided that perhaps it was indeed in his best interest to leave. To further motivate and hasten David's departure, the Ridgefolk offered the "Oak Grove people" their old school bus. David accepted the community's generosity and on "the day they left the land, all the people stood in a circle, 'oming' and chanting. The skies were all clouded over, but when David's family drove off, the clouds parted and the sun shone and there was a rainbow."[56]

In the meantime, both Gottlieb and Wheeler endured never-ending confrontations with local authorities and their straight neighbors, under pressure to address such issues as sanitation, minimum housing standards (one resident, David Lee Pratt, lived in a tree house he had built for himself), and alleged "lawlessness," ranging from theft, gunfights, harboring of juveniles and criminals, nudity, and obscene behavior, as well as a general disdain for hippies among the surrounding area's straight community. Ed Hochuli, the leader of the crusade to drive the hippies out, told Gottlieb that "We have this regulation. Hippies carry disease and we don't want you around. You grow your hair long and don't take a bath." As one communard noted, to most of the larger community's straight population, hippies were "alien creatures, spacemen from another planet, or untouchables, dirty and diseased." Bill Wheeler put the tension between the two groups in an "historical perspective," believing that the relationship "brought to mind [the] early confrontations between the Europeans and the indigenous inhabitants of this continent. The white men saw only dirty savages who obviously had no right to the land where they had lived for so many generations." However, to both Wheeler and Gottlieb, the immediate issue was economic: their neighbors "were not able to sell their land to the developers for the high prices they wanted because of our presence." Consequently, a "kind of range war" ensued, "the outcome of which would determine whether the land would be used for hundred-thousand dollar homes set in concrete into bulldozed hillsides; or for small biodegradable shacks which blended into the landscape and were infinitely more ecological. Our continued presence would determine whether the land would be protected or exploited." As far as Wheeler was concerned all the building codes he and Gottlieb were accused of violating were "arbitrary laws designed to enrich the building industry. Since only the rich could afford to build under these laws in rural areas, the codes were used to keep poor people in the city ghettoes. The codes were also responsible for the increasing architectural mediocrity that was making America look like a cookie sheet."[57]

Equally important as a land-grab to local straights was their inability to comprehend the concept of Open Land, which "ran so counter to the American private property mania, so totally out of the realm of most people's experience that no one could believe in its viability, especially those persons whose lives and work were based on totally opposite presumptions." Thus, neighbors viewed both Morning Star and Wheeler's Ranch as "cancerous tumors which must be excised from the body politic." For both Gottlieb and Wheeler the local courts became a "second home. We felt like Public Enemies 1 and 2, hippie gangsters. They were after our asses." Indeed, police harassment and raids increased significantly and those arrested were "the most loving and responsible" while the cops left "the winos, speed freaks, and bikers to tear the fragile fabric and drive the good people away." In mid–1968 Sonoma County officials cited Gottlieb for a series of health violations and when he failed to comply jailed him for fifteen days on contempt charges and fined him $1500. By spring 1969 the former Limeliter had had enough "of the constant hassle," and deeded his land to God, announcing that "We belong to the earth, not the earth to us. Who can own the earth? Only God. Who would have the audacity to judge whether He was a qualified grantee?" Unfortunately for Gottlieb, both the local court and the California Court Appeals had the "audacity" to rule that God was *not* a qualified grantee, declaring that "Whatever the nature of the deity, God is neither a natural or artificial person capable of taking title under existing California law." Simply interpreted, God did not have the right to own land in California because he could not sign his name to the deed! The court battles continued for several more years as well as the bulldozing of the residents' makeshift dwellings. Finally, in 1972, Sonoma County authorities succeeded in shutting down Morning Star for good.[58]

The more combative Bill Wheeler hung on a little longer with his Open Land experiment on The Ridge. With the help of two shrewd Berkeley attorneys, Corbin Houchins and Allan Cobb, Wheeler was able to forestall the bulldozing for close to two years by transforming his ranch into a legal, incorporated entity: The Ridge became "The Ahimsa Church," which "exists for the worship of God, our Heavenly Father, and of the earth, our Mother, through the practice and dissemination of the doctrine of harmlessness to the earth and to one's fellow man. Among the primary functions of the corporation is the maintenance of premises of the church as Open Land." Most important Bill Wheeler was no longer the land's legal owner, Ahimsa Church was, and thus he could not be fined or incarcerated for violating any county codes or court injunctions, at least for as long as church existed. Nonetheless, local straights and county officials were as determined to destroy The Ridge as they had been in their obsession to demolish Morning Star. County prosecutors persevered in the courts and the sheriff's department continued their harassment of the Ridge's residents. Despite the unrelenting efforts of Houchins and Cobb to maintain the Ridge as some manifestation of a legitimate entity (even as a campground), the county prevailed, with a judge issuing an injunction on April 10, 1973, declaring that inhabitants had twenty-four hours to vacate the land. Cobb was able to get a "grace period" of ten days from the judge, hoping that the county Health Department would give Wheeler a camping permit if he agreed to build a "kitchen and bath house." The county refused and thus on April 25, 1973, the bulldozers arrived and began the systematic, day-by-day destruction of Wheeler's Ranch, which at that time had a hardcore Openlander population of seventy-five people who must have been "horrified to see those huge monsters lumbering onto the land" charged with a "scorched earth policy." Much to Wheeler's pleasant surprise and joy, some of the bulldozer operators "refused to participate in the carnage," with one man shouting "'Hey, these are people's homes, man! We can't do this! What the fuck's happening, anyway?' He walked away from his machine shaking his head in amazement." Wheeler and some others were so enraged by what they were witnessing that later that evening, after the first day's devastation, with about fifty houses left, they decided that *they* would finish the deed by burning the remaining dwellings themselves, depriving the county of the pleasure of such destruction. "All that night we went from house to house. Burn, baby burn! Hypnotized, we watched with a strange pleasure, a morbid fascination. In a flash of nature's energies, a house disappeared in just five minutes. We turned into insane pyromaniacs. Purification. God power." By morning, when the bulldozers and their sheriff's department escort arrived, the entire Ridge had been razed, thus ending the counterculture's two grandest experiments in open-land communalism.[59]

In some parts of the country, communards took over abandoned towns, as in Georgeville Trading Post, Minnesota; or developed their own villages as in Pandanaram, Indiana. A group of Haight-Ashbury expatriates, led by a former San Francisco State University lecturer and local hip guru, Stephen Gaskin ("Moses in Blue Jeans"), established the Farm in Summertown, Tennessee, in 1971. The Farm became one of the most emblematic, intriguing, and successful hip "collective" endeavors of the era. Gaskin refused to "let anybody call it a commune because people who live in communes are communists. We were a collective, which is scary enough for some people." Gaskin also made it clear although he and his followers had established a collective, they were not Marxists. "I think Marx talked about the problem pretty well but what he said to do about it didn't work very well because almost everybody who's tried it has slid into some kind of dictatorship. He even uses the phrase 'the dictatorship of the proletariat.'" Although Gaskin passed away in July 2014, The Farm remains home for a mix of about 200 diehard old and new "Farmies," and thus Gaskin's vision and legacy has endured, albeit in a modified form. Some would even go so far to claim that the Farm is flourishing, having become in its forty-five year history, not only an influential force in local Tennessee politics but also a font much technological and social innovation, producing the first Doppler fetal pulse detector, a portable ionizing radiation detector, and passive solar-space-heating technology. The Farm has long outlasted the majority of its countercultural peers while fulfilling Gaskin's initial call for his enterprise to serve as a base of operations to "change the world" by spreading good works from Guatemala (where Farmies built 1200 houses for 1976 earthquake victims), to the South Bronx and to Indian reservations (where Farmies provided free ambulance services); to Liberia (an agricultural training program); and to Belize, where Farmies initiated a free lunch program. Farmies were among some of the first responders to arrive in New Orleans after Hurricane Katrina devastated the Big Easy in August 2005. From its inception the Farm was never intended to be just an escape from mainstream culture as Gaskin made social outreach and activism his collective's *raison d'être*. For such endeavors Gaskin and his compatriots formed Plenty International, which won *the other* Nobel Prize in 1980, the Right Livelihood Award, presented by the Swedish Parliament in recognition of the Farmies' charitable efforts in Guatemala, Washington, D.C., and the South Bronx. In addition to its eleemosynary activities, the Farm also has a printing and publishing company, a small electronics firm, a Mayan goods trading company, a woodworking shop, and produces a host of vegetarian food products, most notably one of its first staples, sorghum molasses. Gaskin's fourth wife, Ina May, almost single-handedly put the Farm on the international map for midwifery, and whose book on the subject, *Spiritual Midwifery*, has sold more than 600,000 copies. According to one of the Farm's first communards, Albert Bates, "We're probably the single largest producer of tempeh [a food source made from fermented soybeans] in the world. And of course, there's the Dye Works. Tie-dyes [were] a kind of traditional craft among hippies, and we've carried it to its peak."[60]

The often controversial figure at the center of both the Farm's outstanding successes and equally pronounced failures, was the commune's founder, Stephen Gaskin. Born in Denver, Colorado, in 1935, Gaskin lied about his age (he was seventeen at the time), joined the Marine Corps during the Korean War, and saw combat in that conflict. Mustered out of service at war's end, Gaskin returned to the United States, attended junior college but eventually dropped out, drank heavily, and ran coffee houses in North Beach, San Francisco's Beat enclave. Although embracing much of the Beat ethos and aesthetic, Gaskin nonetheless returned to school, eventually earning a BA and MA in English and Language Arts at San Francisco State University (College during Gaskin's time there), where he became a teaching assistant for the noted linguist and semanticist, S.I. Hayakawa. Upon completing his MA, the university offered Gaskin the position of instructor, teaching not only basic composition and creative writing classes but also the opportunity to present courses on subjects like witchcraft and others with descriptions such as "Einstein, Magic, and God." Heavily influenced by Beat literature and poetry, particularly the Beats' emphasis on stream of consciousness, Gaskin encouraged his rhetoric students to "just write what they felt. Forget about formal stuff like spelling and punctuation." Gaskin's unorthodox approach reflected the trend among many late 1960s college professors who embraced much of the hip ethos, hoping their "sensitivity" would allow them to better understand the "new consciousness" emerging in many of their students, who increasingly were demanding more open, creative, and personal learning environments. No doubt Gaskin's eschewing of academic formalism disturbed many of his more traditional colleagues. However, it was his "Monday Night Class" or "tripping instructions," for which Gaskin gained local and then national notoriety. As one of Gaskin's original followers John Coate noted, "The holy-man scene was a big part of the action in the late sixties, and in San Francisco the guy who worked the local beat was Steve Gaskin." Gaskin's first class held in the fall of 1966 on the SFSU campus, had only six students; by the fall of 1970, as many as 2,000 true believers regularly showed to hear Gaskin "rap" about his brand cosmic spirituality, an interesting amalgam of Buddhism, Christianity, Tantric thought and the psychedelic ruminations of Aldous Huxley, believing in telepathy, loving your enemy, and chanting "om" to cleanse away "bad vibes." Gaskin and his students "talked about what was the most important thing in the world we could talk about right then. We talked about God, we talked about cannabis, love, sex and marriage, death, and religion, non-violence, telepathy, subconscious, and enlightenment." Gaskin's affiliation with SFSU ended in 1967: "I didn't get fired; I just got too weird to get rehired." By that time he was holding his classes at rock entrepreneur Chet Helms' famous dance hall, The Family Dog. For one regular attendee, the Monday Night Class "was *really* about religion and the psychedelic drug-inspired, long-overdue spiritual reawakening which was then just beginning to stretch, come alive, and sweep across our jaded, materialistic, modern world." Gaskin believed his attraction was his "ability to talk intelligently while stoned for longer than most people." For many of his followers, Gaskin was no longer "just the teacher of a class." He had become "a Teacher as in your guru." Gaskin embraced his new accolade, declaring that "I started out teaching people how to trip. Then I found out life was a trip. Then I started teaching people how to live." Perhaps most revealing Gaskin reviled those gurus who charged money for their "wisdom" or "enlightenment," considering such individuals to be "fakirs because spiritual teaching is for free or it ain't real." Interestingly, neither the mainstream nor underground press covered much of Gaskin's Monday Night Class popularity, satisfied to "devote whole pages of their papers to the false prophets of the day: the warped and twisted prophets who said that The Answer was ever more exotic mixtures of reality-altering chemicals."[61]

Gaskin's charismatic youth-appeal got the attention of the progressive American Academy of Religion, who hired him to travel about the country preaching his gospel at local churches and colleges. Joining Gaskin on his fall 1970 speaking junket across forty-two states, were about 250 of his "students," traveling in thirty old buses. Gaskin and company were on the road for four months and as they traveled about "the more people there were who joined the caravan. Pretty soon there were three or four hundred of us and the police were meeting us every time we crossed a state line."[62]

For many hippies Gaskin's emergence represented yet another manifestation of what many referred to as "The Prankster/Millbrook dichotomy." This split in the movement forced many hippies to have to decide which of the two hip trips they would follow: the Ken Kesey/Merry Prankster-Grateful Dead approach to life or the "Tim Leary, Richard Alpert, Stephen [Gaskin], yoga and natural foods" way of being. For John Coate, the Kessey/Prankster/Dead style "was doing acid on the streets and learning to be tough and glib and fast on your feet. Looking for an edge." For Coate, the Dead's music also reflected a similar "wild loose style," as the band "would establish eye contact with individuals and play to them until they got them off. They were doing a lot more than playing music." Most important to Coate, there were "no leaders and teachers." At the other end of the hip spectrum "you have Leary and Alpert tucked away at this huge mansion in Millbrook, NY, tripping, getting quiet and still, everything inner-reaching and working with the whole Eastern religion aspect where you keep yourself high and together with meditation, or stillness, or certain diets or yogas. Structure, organization, method, technique, centering." Gaskin had embraced this approach to life as well as he spoke "about self-discipline and creating good karma, and paying attention to being truthful and correct." By 1970, many hippies, having burned-out from too much acid-tripping à la the Merry Pranksters, but still wanting to personally keep the hip vision alive, were ready to slow down and become more "centered" with a Zen-Buddha purposeful-ness and engagement advocated by gurus such as Gaskin. Equally important was Coate's acceptance of Gaskin's leadership. For John Coate, Gaskin's message "made sense" to him and thus he became one of Gaskin's most devoted disciples and Farmies for several years.[63] Matthew McClure agreed with his fellow Farmie that "the kind of people who started the Farm experiment" had emerged out of their sixties drug experiences with an awareness "of the vibrations and other realms of existence besides the material plain…. We'd had some kind of spiritual realization that we were all One and that peace and love were obvious untried answers to the problems facing our society. Those were the kinds of people who followed Stephen to Tennessee." Walter Rabideau was even more convinced that psychedelic drugs were the key to the Farm's founding and main reason why such an eclectic group of individuals "mixed in together. The reason why they were all there [on the Farm] was that they all took psychedelic drugs. If that hadn't happened, the Farm wouldn't have been there."[64]

Rabideau also believed that he and his fellow Farmies represented that segment of 1960s alienated youth who had "completely lost faith in America, the whole straight society and everything else to do something like the farm." Because "everything was totally fucked" Rabideau believed the Farm reflected starting "absolutely from scratch with a piece of bare dirt and build everything, including your culture, out of whole cloth. And you wouldn't do that unless you just had a totally apocalyptic vision brought on by the war in Vietnam and lots of acid. And that's an unusual combination."[65]

Not only had the majority of future Farmies reached the level of "consciousness" essential for creating an alternative rural lifestyle, but as was true in virtually all rural communes, they were also overwhelming *white*, middle class, and educated, many with college degrees. Nonetheless, true to the hip creed of inclusiveness and egalitarianism, Gaskin welcomed all individuals to the Farm as long as they were willing to work toward the common goal of help-ing to create a self-sustaining rural, agrarian alternative to the mainstream macro capitalist economy. As The Farm's chronicler Douglas Stevenson has observed, "Throughout The Farm community's history, a few people of color have made The Farm their home for some period of time, but for numerous reasons, they have chosen to move on. Consequently the overall population remains a mix of predominantly [white] Western European ethnicities."[66]

Upon their return to San Francisco in January 1971, it became readily apparent to all who had made the pilgrimage of 6000 miles that all wanted to "stay in community." All felt "stronger, more tied together," and that "we could no longer just separate and go back to our separate apartments and our separate lives. So we thought back to the parts of the country we'd especially liked on our tour and Stephen said 'Let's go to Tennessee and get a farm,' and we all said, 'Yeah, let's go to Tennessee and get a farm.'" For Gaskin the decision to go to Ten-nessee was simple: "We can get it on with the dirt."[67] Also motivating Gaskin and his com-patriots was the sad fact that by the early 1970s their beloved Haight-Ashbury, like so many of the hippies' original urban enclaves and the concomitant hip scene that they had so fully embraced, had degenerated into cesspools of crime, hard drugs, and violence. The Haight had "gone decadent," Gaskin recalled years later. "We started seeing guys in long dark over-coats and brimmed hats who were heroin people. We started seeing meth—that was skinny guys sleeping in doorways—you could tell the meth. And we were into natural foods and like that."[68]

Thus in the fall of 1971, some 280 devoted followers, traveling in roughly 80 buses, trucks, and vans trekked to Tennessee. Gaskin's message was simple and direct: he and his followers were OUT TO SAVE THE WORLD, which to Gaskin and his acolytes ultimately meant establishing a spiritually based commune that would become a new "City Upon a Hill"; a shining example of how to live off the land without endangering or destroying nature and wildlife; a much different back-to-the-land refuge than most of its contemporaries. For that purpose Gaskin and his followers purchased 1,700 acres of land for $70 an acre in one of the poorest counties in Tennessee (Lewis), about sixty miles southwest of Nashville. There they established The Farm and became "voluntary peasants." Why the upper South, a region where the majority of citizens hardly possessed warm and fuzzy feelings toward hippies; an area of Tennessee only 35 miles from Pulaski, birthplace of the KKK? According to Gaskin, as he and his parade of disciples sojourned across forty-two states, "We found out a lot of stuff. We found the country was not as crazy in the middle as it was on the edges." The locals became friendlier toward the "tie-dyed Amish" as they were dubbed, after overcoming their fears that "we were the Manson family. Amazingly we found several of the local men helping to cut an opening in the barbed wire and leading a group of longhairs into the trees."[69]

From the moment Gaskin and his companions arrived they knew that "These 60 and 70-year-old farmers" would be "priceless to us. They know how to build everything and fix everything and grow everything." Over time Gaskin and the Farmies "made friends with them and hung around them because we wanted to learn the things they knew. And this really turned them on. They would say 'I didn't know anybody wanted to learn this old stuff anymore.' And we'd say, 'Yeah man. How do you do it?' You can't jive anybody who's teaching you how to run a tractor. It's something to watch a cat who was once a Hell's Angel being taught to run a tractor by an old man and being *respectful* to that old farmer."[70]

One such individual who "took a liking" to the Farmies was Homer Sanders, with whom "we collaborated on a saw mill and other projects." As John Coate further observed, Homer "didn't have any teeth and only half of his tongue. It took real training to be able to understand the jokes he constantly told. He knew how to do everything involved with living on that land. A great guy; a living folk hero and genuine moonshiner who had fought it out with every revenue agent in the area." For several years Sanders was among only a handful of locals who were willing to accept and help "the tie-dyed Amish." Indeed, according to Douglas Stevenson, Homer "became The Farm's most important unofficial ambassador throughout the local area. He spread the word among the rest of the neighbors that the hippies were okay. If Homer heard someone bad-mouthing the hippies, he would set them straight. Homer's early support was an important breakthrough that smoothed the way for The Farm to gain acceptance in the redneck South."[71]

However, for several years the majority of the town's inhabitants remained leery, and thus Farmies "had to hustle to make friends with our neighbors." Coate was certain that if he and his fellow Farmies did not try to cultivate a good rapport with the locals, "they would have shot-gunned us right out of there and burned the place to the ground." Gaskin and his followers believed that the best way to foster a relationship was to try to bond along religious lines, for Farmies considered themselves essentially a "religious group," and thus they "decided to get into religious dialogue with the locals, matching our patchwork eclecticism to their Christian fundamentalism." Gaskin invited members from the Church of Christ to attend the Farmies' "services," which according to Coate, they readily accepted because they "wouldn't turn down the chance to preach to the heathens" and get them to repent their sinful ways, and consequently "they came up in great numbers for these meetings." Much to the chagrin of many local pastors and preachers, Gaskin became a licensed Tennessee cleric, marrying many Farm couples and leading Sunday morning services, which were held either in the huge meadow on the farm or inside the schoolhouse. Regardless of location, Gaskin preached a gospel that he developed from the mystical teachings of various world religions, a synthesis he referred to as "the psychedelic testimony of the saints" or the "totality of the manifestation."[72] Suffice it to say, the moment Gaskin mouthed such esoterica, his message fell on completely deaf ears. Nonetheless, Gaskin and his compatriots were determined to find some sort of accord with their neighbors.

At one of the get-togethers, Gaskin told the story of the Tibetan Yogi Milarepa and how he was similar to "some of the Biblical heavies in the way he had to construct these stone houses and then tear them down, then rebuild them again, each nine times, as a way to become unattached to the fruits of your labor." Apparently Gaskin's "preaching" was beyond the ken of his local audience as the Church of Christ attendees failed to comprehend a single word of his message—rambling—let alone see any analogy to the Bible, and thus one of "the old guys stood up and said, 'excuse me, now I don't about this Miller feller [Milarepa], but I do know that the Bible is the word of God for him too.!'" Suffice it to say there was no meeting of the minds between the Farmies and the local congregation of the Church of Christ. Not to be deterred, the Farmies reached out to the Summertown Covenant Church, which resulted in a righteous harangue courtesy of the main preacher Johnny Prentiss and his wife Betty, in which the Farmies were told "the things you believe in are wrong," and that they were condemning their children "to an afterlife in hell."[73]

After that chastisement, the Farmies decided to abandon reaching out to their neighbors by trying to find religious commonality, an impossibility. They would henceforth pursue a different approach: time; that is "wait it out" and let the town-folk come around to them, which they believed Summertowners would do as they realized that the Farmies were no threat; that Gaskin and his followers were there to stay, and that they were more than willing to become good, participatory citizens in the town's daily life. Most important, Gaskin was certain that his enterprise would eventually become a regional economic boon, and in that anticipation he was correct on a variety of levels.

From its inception, The Farm owed its successes and failures to Gaskin, who was the community's undisputed leader, minister, and "spiritual guide," personally setting policies and procedures for the community based on what he envisioned as The Farm's purpose and philosophy. As former communard Alan Graf remembered, "We had a charismatic leader, Stephen" through whom "most authority went. We weren't a democratic society." Indeed, The Farm defined the concept of an *intentional* commune, in which *everyone* had fairly specific work-related roles or jobs to perform but were allowed or encouraged to choose the kind of work that most appealed to them. Unlike the majority of communes, The Farm was not a place one went to dream their life away in a psychedelic besotted haze. As Albert Bates noted, from the Farm's inception, "it was never intended as some hippie crash pad or beatnik retirement home. It was a platform from which to launch efforts to improve the lot of poor and indigenous peoples, whales, and old growth trees. It was a means, not an end in itself. Stephen was more than a pacifist; he was an activist." According to Ina May Gaskin, "Farmies" were "a special kind of hippie: they worked." Indeed, according to *New York Times* reporter Kate Wenner, these particular "flower children" were "supremely industrious and disciplined. They have dedicated themselves to work in building a totally unselfish and compassionate culture in which others may seek refuge from mainstream civilization. As 'spiritual revolutionaries' these pioneering youth are not so much trying to create a new society as to bring this country back to its early heritage."[74] Gaskin could not have agreed more with Wenner's assessment, telling interviewers from *Mother Earth News* that "If you really want to be spiritual, you don't want to have to sell your soul for eight hours a day in order to have 16 hours in which to eat and sleep and get yourself back together again. You'd like for your work to be seamless with your life and that what you do for a living doesn't' deny everything else you believe in. What we're really into is making a living in a clean way. There ain't nothing devious about it: Right out front, we're trying to build an alternative culture." For Gaskin and his comrades, there was no "cleaner way in making a living than farming. It's just you, the dirt, and God. You can't make friends with an acre of land and expect it to give you an 'A' like some college professor or something. You can't snow [B.S.] that acre of dirt. But if you put the work into it, it'll come back and feed you. It really will."[75]

Gaskin wanted committed people and thus all potential communards had to spend time "soaking"—a trial or probationary period during which "candidates" participated in the communities' various activities, work, and general lifestyle to see if such an experience in alternative living was how they wanted to spend the rest of their lives. At The Farm's entrance, those wanting to enter the commune, were told by the "guards" that "No animal products, no tobacco, no alcohol, no manmade psychedelics [LSD], no sex without commitment, no overt anger, no lying, no private money, no [ownership of] large pieces of private property" were allowed. If after "soaking" a visitor wanted to join the commune, they were required to take a vow of poverty, turning over to the community all cash, credit cards, and possessions, for they were no longer needed by a "Farmie." Most important, initiates had to accept Gaskin as their teacher and guru. According to "Catherine," who visited The Farm in the summer of 1973, looking for friends who had become full-fledged Farmies, "These people behaved as if Stephen Gaskin had some special wisdom that elevated him to the position of a holy man over themselves, people who I knew as well-educated, smart, talented, and formerly free thinking individuals. 'Stephen says' were the buzzwords I heard over and over again."[76] As Kate Wenner aptly observed, it was ironic that "the same people who once stood firmly and loudly against any absolute authority now accept Stephen Gaskin as their unquestioned and unchallenged leader." Communard John Coate recalled, "The catch to living there was 'copping to Stephen.' You had to enter into a student-teacher relationship with him. If you accepted that kind of relationship, all was good with him and everybody else." Wenner agreed, labeling Gaskin as "unabashedly egocentric," which made him simultaneously the Farm's "greatest strength and greatest weakness."[77]

Gaskin consistently downplayed his role as The Farm's leader, telling an interviewer from *The Tennessean* in 1981, that he only used that "terminology" when "copping to that on a national or international level that I am one of the leaders of our movement which is not just the Farm but all the long hairs and pacifists and hippies of the world." Relative to the Farm, Gaskin referred to himself as "the coach," declaring that real authority and "power" was exercised through the Council of Elders, who many disgruntled Farmies claimed was comprised of individuals who "thoroughly copped to Stephen's ideas and way of doing things, no questions asked." John Coate agreed that Gaskin did indeed put yes-people on the Council, that he "was inclined to surround himself with advisors who over time seemed to much prefer advising to nail banging, hoeing, or wrenching. And he sometimes delegated great authority to single individuals, some of whom were utterly unqualified to handle it." As a result, many people "learned to kiss ass to keep their position in Stephen's inner circle. They had to learn what to say and more importantly what not say." The emerging sycophancy coupled with Gaskin's escalating imperiousness and refusal to accept any challenges to his "teachings," had a deleterious impact on the community. As John Seward recalled, Gaskin equated any doubt in his leadership with a lack of faith in The Farm community and its mission. Consequently, "anybody who had doubtful thoughts running through their head was in fairly short order forced to split because you couldn't maintain that feeling and stay there without bringing everybody down. So there was never any big impetus to radically change how things were because anybody who starting thinking that way was just steered out." Walter Rabideau agreed: ""The strange phenomenon that I started to realize was that you couldn't tell the truth to him if it was about him."[78]

Gaskin denied having "this lust for power," and that until the collective reached over 600 people, "we did everything in full meeting and consensus because everybody was there and anyone who wanted to argue could. That part was good at the time, but we got too big for that," and thus according to some, Gaskin's excuse for becoming more high-handed and autocratic. Kathleen Platt, a Farmie for nine years and a member of the Council of Elders, believed the Council was a sham as far as having any real decision-making authority; a ruse designed by Gaskin to create the illusion among his followers that they had a say in Farm affairs. According to Platt, from the group's first meeting, "Gaskin controlled the decisions of the board. Supposedly you had freedom of speech at the Farm but you would be shut down pretty fast if you said something against the flow. I was very excited when I was on the board but I found out it was a joke. We sat there for hours and smoked so much grass that decisions we could come to would all be erased in a couple of days." In fairness to Gaskin, Platt admitted that "we asked for it. That's the crux of it. He couldn't be doing it if all these people did not bow down to him."[79]

Another original Farmie, Wayne Bonser, agreed with Platt, leaving the Farm in 1976, "fed up with Gaskin's authoritarian rule." In Bonser's view, Gaskin believed "he was the second Christ and everybody bought it back then" because "we were all taking a lot of psychedelic drugs back then," and in Bonser's view, Gaskin exploited his "disciples" perpetual hallucinogenic state of mind to dominate them. "No one questioned his authority and you couldn't do anything unless you had his approval. He took whatever women he wanted and nobody questioned it." What happened to those individuals who challenged Gaskin? According to Bonser, they would be visited by Gaskin's "gang of henchmen. If anybody interrupted him at one of his gigs, he sends out one of the guys to remove them." "Removal" meant exiled from the Farm for as long as thirty days, or one was "busted" to a lower status job, such as the crew in charge of picking crops. Interestingly, until his falling out with Gaskin, Bonser was a "big honcho" on the Farm, having some of the operation's plumb jobs such as the Gate security crew, sanitation construction, and the most important one, "the pot crew." Bonser eventually had a major falling-out with Gaskin over child-care issues, especially their diet, which was for quite some time "a kind of soy-bean corn meal mush, three times a day and rarely getting any fruits or vegetables. If your baby cries, Stephen said he's probably on an ego trip. Never mind it's tired, hungry, or thirsty. You should ignore it." So disturbed did Bonser become by Gaskin's imperiousness and callousness, that he believed "There are absolute similarities between the Farm and Jim Jones and Charles Manson."[80]

Another aspect of Gaskin's "tremendous power" over The Farm's "vibrations" that burdened many Farmies was his mantra that The Farm "was the guru for the rest of the world. Everybody on the Farm carried around the idea on their shoulders of being responsible for the whole world. Every act, everything you said, everything you did, the way you lived, the way you dressed, everything was having a vast effect all over the planet." Matthew McClure agreed. "All of us there believed that we were in fact the hope of the world and that if anything happened to this small group of acid heads the world was going to collapse." This was Gaskin's message to his "tribe" every Sunday at their gathering in the meadow; that Farmies "were keeping it together for the entire world because we were a demonstration that people could live together in peace and harmony. Nobody would have gone there if they hadn't believed that." However, having to carry that illusion around in their heads "prevented us from trying a lot of things that would have made the Farm better." Although Gaskin had fully embraced the hip slogan to "question authority," when it came to his own people, "we were institutionally not supposed to think for ourselves in some areas. We weren't allowed to change." John Coate believed that Gaskin unwisely "stifled all that talent and brain power" that surrounded him or tried "to mold it in a narrow fashion. I say Stephen was the luckiest guy in the world to have all that good energy and talent around him. Too bad he didn't see it for what it really could have been."[81]

As with any start-up experiment in alternative living, whether in the early 1970s or now, personality and philosophical clashes of will are inevitably endemic, causing alienation, hostility, and even despair among the individuals or groups involved. Such was the situation at the Farm during its formative years but to accuse Gaskin of being another Jim Jones, or worse, Charles Manson, is extreme in the least. No doubt Gaskin was indeed autocratic, self-serving, and probably on an "ego-trip" at times but as Kathleen Platt admitted "we asked for it." Indeed, virtually all of the individuals who followed Gaskin first on the Caravan and then later to Tennessee, were, in some form or another, some of the more alienated, if not at times, desperate seekers from the 1960s hip-psychedelic scene, yearning for an alternative lifestyle to the mainstream econo-culture of their time. Many believed they had found the answer to their quest in Gaskin's Monday Night Class message, and thus initially were willing to embrace both Gaskin as their undisputed guru and his Farm idea. Although Walter Rabideau believed that Farmies had given Gaskin too much "control over our lives, and that "it was several years before we realized what was happening," Rabideau and his compatriots nonetheless had "agreed to start a community following his [Gaskin's] spiritual teachings."[82]

Moreover, as the Farm grew in population, peaking at around 1500 members in 1979, it was virtually impossible for Gaskin to maintain his initial town-meeting, democratic consensus approach, and thus he, in consultation with a handful of others, increasingly made more and more of the decisions affecting the Farm's daily operation, outreach, and commonwealth. He believed himself personally responsible for the well-being of so many people and in having to constantly exhort them to work toward the common goal, which was based on *his* vision of the Farm's existence and purpose, which he made clear from the outset. Gaskin was a committed, serious seeker, wholeheartedly devoted to making his vision real and his enterprise a success within the context of the hippie ethos and its attendant values and priorities. So were many of his compatriots as confirmed by the fact that The Farm is still in existence and flourishing as testimony to both Gaskin's idea and those individuals who continue to believe in his dream of a completely self-sustaining agricultural alternative to the nation's capitalist techno-industrial macro-economy. Nonetheless, there was pressure from Gaskin and from his more devoted disciples to maintain above all else the community's "good vibes" which required all Farmies to be "into the juice," and that often meant "copping" to Stephen Gaskin's way of being.

Although some had negative experiences at The Farm, for most "Farmies," the place, at least initially "was like a hippie dream—you didn't use any money, there weren't any cops, there weren't even adults. Everybody was your age. For some people that was really what they'd been looking for." Most meaningful was that "A whole bunch of people learned to grow food and build houses, and we learned to live with a bunch of other people.... And doing it together made it so a lot of us could do stuff that we wouldn't have been able to do if we'd done it individually." Perhaps most important for the majority of Farmies, and what kept them on the Farm for more years than they thought possible, was their belief that "we were all one. We believed we were creating a unique reality, controlling our own destiny, and for some years it was true. You can't do that without massive struggle at times. But once again the good feelings are often contained in the way people look into each other's eyes and the silent understanding. It wasn't the brainwash trip by any means. It's a hard thing to quantify." For Peter Else, The Farm provided "an escape from eight to five city living and the chance to form a model society, a chance to be closer to the land. Well, I did escape city living but I ended up working from 6 a.m. to 7 p.m.; I definitely got closer to the land." Moreover, by the early 1970s, large, experimental communities such as the Farm were few and far between and thus for many Farmies, "if you wanted to do something with other people" leaving the Farm "seemed kind of bleak." Consequently, "a lot of people really gave Stephen a certain amount of lip service and 'got with the program' but were really there for the folks rather than being a hardcore [Gaskin] student." For John Coate some of his "finer moments" were fairly elemental but nonetheless uplifting: "When someone would holler 'Joint Break!' across the [car] shop and we would retire to the woods for our communion, I felt that we were living on liberated soil. I could look around at the woods and my buddies and say, 'this is ours.' What could be finer than that?"[83]

As with most start-up communes, there were the "starving times" and such a potential catastrophe visited the farm during the fall 1972–winter 1973, "wheat berry winter," when all Farmies had to eat in any real quantity was boiled wheat berries: "Every night there they were on your plate, beside the blighted potatoes." However, the hard-times did not bring about The Farm's demise; quite the opposite: the true believers persevered even without Gaskin, who had been busted for growing marijuana and incarcerated for a year (1974–75) at the Walls, a penitentiary built in the 1880s in Nashville. Overjoyed by Gaskin's return, upon his release, the Farmies presented him with a grand new residence they had built during his absence; a veritable palace compared to most Farmie's meager abodes. However, to his credit, Gaskin sensed that such ostentation could easily alienate fellow communards and refused to live in his new home, which only enhanced his guru mystique. Nonetheless, Gaskin frequently exploited his followers' love for him, feigning humility by sitting in his chair like a grand potentate, meeting and greeting people with "an attractive woman sitting on either side at his feet, leaning against his legs. The air would be filled with our sacramental herb [marijuana] and the anticipation of his profound teachings." Indeed, in Matthew McClure's view, "Stephen professed to think of himself as a fully enlightened spiritual teacher on a par with Buddha and Christ. The avatar of the Aquarian Age."[84]

By the mid–1970s The Farm had not only turned the corner relative to lasting for more than a few years but also had become "THE place to go, especially in the summertime, when we got all the hitchhiking people, people without homes, the free-lancers, the free spirits. They were all out there and the word started getting out. We were getting 10,000 to 15,000 people a year (ten times our population), coming to visit the Farm, many of them just driving through on Sundays. We had guided tours for local Tennesseans as one of our community obligations." Unlike many communes, Gaskin *did not* have a non-exclusion philosophy or policy, and countless people were turned away after their "soaking" or even at the gate, especially if the gate guards determined they were "real yahoos who were there to see if the ladies really were bare-breasted [as they indeed were at many communes] all the time or something, which they weren't."[85]

However, there were instances when Gaskin felt sorry for a seeker, especially if they were completely lost, mind-blown "blissed-out flower children schizophrenics who just couldn't work but were going to get fed anyway. One of the things Stephen would occasionally advertise was that no matter how crazy you were, if you came to the Farm, he'd make you sane." According to Walter Rabideau sometimes the community could help someone recover from too much psychedelia, but in some instances no amount of group or individual therapy worked and thus "We'd always have at least one psychotic, full-blown, total blissed out freak who would've been in a mental institution if he hadn't been on the Farm. When everybody was ready to thrown them off the Farm, they would go to Stephen and he would get stoned with them and give them another two days [to redeem themselves]." If they were simply unable to "cop" to Farm life after the two-day grace period, whether they were drugged out ex-hippies, a fugitive on the run, or any other form of miscreant unable to embrace the Farm ethos, "We'd buy them plane tickets, bus tickets, whatever, just to get them off the Farm and out of the state." Despite the gatekeepers' vigilance and probing questions, "Some people would know that if you said the right things you could stay. You got to stay for a month before you'd be ask to make a decision to live [on the Farm] or leave. They would stay and get about six weeks of free medical care, a roof over their heads, dope, friendly hippies, and the word was out that this was the place." For Matthew McClure, the Farm's "spirit of compassion" resulted in a "youthful arrogance" among Farmies, certain they could assimilate into Farm life and culture "too broad a spectrum of people." Walter Rabideau and John Seward agreed. "We overloaded ourselves and took on more than we could handle as a result of Stephen's pep talks," Rabideau told Kevin Kelly. Seward concurred, somewhat blaming Gaskin as well for the Farm "taking on all these welfare cases. Stephen would talk on Sunday morning about how you can't close your heart, don't get square, because with good karma, doing good deeds, it'll all balance out and blah blah blah. But it didn't really work that way."[86]

Gaskin's open door-policy was not always as altruistic or humanitarian as was the impression given. The commune's survival was his first priority and thus Gaskin frequently allowed individuals to become Farmies because they represented not only sorely needed labor but often brought with them valuable "assets" in the form of inheritances, vehicles, cash, or other property, all of which had to be relinquished to the community before they could become full-fledged Farmies. No doubt seekers with bounty were a welcome sight especially during the Farm's early years. Relative to the "psychotics" who showed up at the Farm, Gaskin believed he had a moral obligation "not to abandon the casualties of a big psychedelic movement with a free love component. We owed it to the system to take care of these people."[87]

One group of folk who particularly found the Farm to be "the place" to go, were young pregnant women, the majority of whom were unwed. As Walter Rabideau recalled, "Ina May put out the word to the nation at large that 'Hey ladies, don't have an abortion. Come to the Farm and we'll deliver your baby free!'" As result, between the Farm's founding and when the Rabideaus left in the early 1980s, to their recollection, over 1,000 babies were born on the Farm and over half were "from people who didn't live on the Farm. We'd have all these pregnant couples and women come to the Farm six weeks before they were due and at no cost, not even room and board, we would support them for six weeks before birth and sometimes for a month or two after the baby was born." As far as the Gaskins were concerned, "there cannot be too many children living at the commune. 'Farmies' consider them to be their most important crop. They are raised with special care and are Part Two of the Farm's dreams." There was no doubt in Kathryn McClure's mind that the Farm's anti-abortion policy "saved a few babies' lives" but the problem became that all too frequently the child's parent or parents would simply up and leave one day, secure in the knowledge that their child would be taken care of by one of the Farm families. The parents might return for their child but in many instances they did not, abandoning them to the solicitude of Farm families, where they would be fostered out for several years among the community. As Kathryn McClure remembered, "at one point, one-quarter of the kids on the Farm had been dumped there," and consequently it was up to the established Farm families to take them in. Such kindness bred resentment toward the Gaskins, for taking in the wayward children represented a burden; one more mouth to feed, clothe, and care for, while most already had difficulty providing for their own children. As Susan Rabideau observed, "We made the mistake of thinking we could actually take on and help people before we were even helping ourselves, before we had enough for our own families. Our hearts weren't closed; we were just overcrowded and didn't have enough to eat…. You can't be hungry and help somebody else. You have to be together and smart and well fed and know everything in your home is taken care of before you help others." However, according to Gaskin, if one believed their child "was better than anybody else's," that was considered to be "one of the roots of racism. You couldn't think more about your kids than you did about all the kids in the Third World." Rabideau agreed with Gaskin in "consciousness" that "that was how it should be," but such generosity was hard to embrace on a daily basis when "your own kids are right here in front of you and they don't have boots for the winter." Indeed, as famous author and Merry Prankster-acid head Ken Kesey aptly observed, "The commune idea of sharing was great but it all breaks down in the fridge."[88]

Gaskin forbade nudity and as far as sex was concerned, Gaskin decreed that "If you're sleeping together, you're engaged. If you're pregnant, you're married." As *Mother Earth News* remarked at the time, "There's none of this hippie 'free love' monkeying around on The Farm." The Farm was also definitively heterosexual in philosophy and orientation, with great peer pressure placed on singles to "couple-up" as soon as possible, for to Gaskin "the Basic Unit of Mankind was the heterosexual couple." In that context, Farmies were supposed to follow the Tantric sexual path where lovemaking was not only for procreative purposes but as an equally important healing exercise for body and soul. Particularly affected by this philosophy were Farm males, most of whom came from very traditional male-sexual dominant, quasi-misogynistic backgrounds, in which women played a passive/receptive if not subservient role. As John Coate observed at the time, "The early seventies was the time when the feminist movement was on the rise. It was obvious that almost every male in America carried around with him certain inbred attitudes that assumed superiority over females." However, on the Farm, the Gaskins were determined to reverse such "programming" as women now were to be "on top" so-to-speak and as the phrase on the Farm confirmed, "The man steers during the day, and the woman steers at night. This meant for men that all traces of macho had to be eliminated. You had to 'cop to your lady.'" As Cliff Figallo remembered, the new mantra "put sand in the Vaseline! There is nothing that does more to ruin the magic in bed than self-consciousness. The aim of all this, of course, was to enhance the sexual act for women and to extinguish the old stereotype of 'Wham, bam, thank you ma'am." Gaskin and Ina May made Tantric sex part of the Farm's creed and consequently those males who failed in bed to adhere to this doctrine often found themselves publically exposed and ostracized. If they hoped to remain part of the Farm community they had to "purge" themselves by spending time in a special tent Gaskin had constructed called the "The Tumbler" where recalcitrant males "with rough edges could bump up against each other with the idea that they could smooth each other out" by spending hours "ferreting out the subconscious attitudes" that had caused the tension between themselves and their women or with other Farmies, regardless of gender. Individuals would remain in these "sort sessions speaking bluntly to each other without the inhibitions of politeness standing in the way" until they "copped to making visible changes." For Coate and for many others, the Tumbler experience "was like a mental nudist colony. It was a definite flaw in our thinking to imagine that great numbers of people would be interested in that kind of thing." Nonetheless, on the Farm, "a person's inner business became everybody's business."[89]

One of the more absurd "sorting sessions" that occurred in The Tumbler involved a Farm woman who was "not into the juice" of the Farm's "vibes" because she used "big words" such as "averted" and other such "non–Farmese" vocabulary, and for her refusal to use "ain't." The woman had a college degree in English and had published several short stories in *High-lights* magazine, an accomplishment she hid from her Farm peers. According to the woman's daughter, "They wanted her to sound more like them with slow, droned out, stony sayings and using words like 'ain't.' She was very upset and crying in our bus after finding out that people didn't like her using 'big' words. It must have been a long meeting because I don't think she ever copped."[90]

Homosexuality, although not outright condemned was frowned upon by both Gaskin and many communards, leaving "little action for out-of-the-closet gays. There were some gays on the Farm, but there was so little action that they didn't stick around." Gaskin did not believe in "traditional" monogamy, sanctioning a somewhat strange polygamy of spouse-swapping that came to be known as "four marriage"—two couples married together. When asked about this type of "marital arrangement," Gaskin responded by asking the interviewer "What part about being a hippie don't you understand?" Perhaps most interesting, Farmies advocated natural birth control, forbidding all artificial methods that prevented conception. "In their place, we developed the basal temperature/cervical mucus method, which could be very effective if you were *very* disciplined." However, as Cliff Figallo recalled, "Not many of us were at the time, and it took several children for most of us to either catch on to the method, or to cheat and buy rubbers anyway, or to give up lovemaking altogether." By the close of the decade, thanks in large part to the procreation policies, the Farm's population had grown from around 300 to 1500.[91]

Farmies were hardcore vegans, eating soybeans for protein, prepared in as many, different creative ways as possible. According to one communard, the Farmies' devotion to vegetarianism reflected their belief that there would be more food "to go around the world if people ate soybeans instead of cattle." How fanatical of vegans were the Farmies? As one young member recalled, "The adults at 'Seven Nations' (my house) had a meeting because my grandmother sent a gigantic block of Wisconsin cheddar cheese to us. The adults were deciding whether to give the cheese to the neighbors (off the farm), or to just bury it! Meanwhile, the kids, including myself, managed to finish off the entire block of cheese before the issue was resolved." Another young communard remembered "getting really sick of eating so many soybeans in every form," and another not having her first peanut butter and jelly sandwich until she was *nine* after having lived at The Farm all her life. "I was like 'Oh my God, this is the best thing I've ever tasted in my life!'"[92]

As noted earlier one of the Farm's dietary staples, especially for breakfast and lunch was a soybean-cornmeal mush that the children in particular came to loathe. As one Farm child recalled, "the repulsive oatmeal made me gag every morning and every afternoon when we had cold, gloppy leftover oatmeal for lunch. It was agonizingly hard to force through my mouth and down my throat. I would plead, beg even cry, in a desperate attempt to be spared from eating it. It made me choke and vomit with every despicable bite." Some of the other children were allowed "to pour lots of white sugar on theirs but I could not have any sugar on my bowl of torture because to my mom sugar was the root of all evil only for making cakes on peoples birthdays." Dinner was better as long as it "wasn't dumplings, slimy balls of boiled dough just as gag worthy as oatmeal." Fortunately both the kids and adults got a respite at dinnertime because they got to eat "soybean tortillas and that was eating happiness. I wished we could eat happiness for breakfast too." Indeed, "soybeans and soft tortillas—simple, nutritious, and wonderfully satisfying," became the Farm's "national dish."[93]

Parental devotion to an exclusively vegan diet unfortunately deprived communal children of other, much-needed protein sources. So desperate for such nourishment did Farm kids become that they were overjoyed one day when "Archer of the Dogwood Blossom Household scored some cat food, the delicious, little reddish x-shaped treats we weren't supposed to touch or eat." News of Archer's surreptitious acquisition spread like wildfire to the rest of the Farm households, and soon surrounding him were "a growing harem of hungry little vulture children," all of whom would "really love some of that cat food, the thought of its tasty, tasty, gourmet crunch was irresistible." Apparently Archer was in a magnanimous mood that day and shared his treasure, making sure all "got some of the tasty morsels. Cat food is worlds better than slimy, putrid oatmeal. I am so, so happy to have eaten several pieces of forbidden, rare, precious cat food. Thank God we did not get caught by the giant grownups." The Farm's frailer children were somewhat more fortunate than the "normal" kids because they were placed on "the skinny kid's list" and were to receive extra food, sometimes even "exotic foods" such as bananas or oranges, which was "unheard of because we ate nothing that did not come from our own fields." The news of the arrival of such delicacies often caused the older kids to go on clandestine "raids of the food stashes to get some oranges that were reserved for the babies. They weren't bad kids but that's just what they had to do." Indeed, as Marilyn Friedlander confirmed, "We were pretty much a town that ate the same food every night. Sometimes those foods and the events surrounding their appearance were rather weird—the mere mention of them causes simultaneous laughs and moans."[94]

As was true in many communes determined to use only natural or organic substances and ingredients rather than those that had been chemically or artificially adulterated, processed, or man-made, basic hygiene and health care were often neglected in the name of purity and righteousness. On The Farm, both toothpaste and band-aides were not allowed into the compound. As one Farmie recalled, she brushed her teeth every night but could not remember what her mother gave her to use as "toothpaste." However, she remembered vividly the day "we got some toothpaste, it was a treat. A man would use his pocket knife to slice open a completely flattened tube of toothpaste while dozens of people stood around hoping to get a minuscule scraping of its rare, sweet insides." For many Farm kids, "the best thing about getting hurt was possibly getting an incredible band-aide if there was any." Like bananas, band-aides, "out of a rarefied packaged wrapper," were "from the outside, something that wasn't horse poop." Farm kids would often purposely scrape or would themselves in order to "bask in the glory of an extraordinary plastic band-aide. Any kid with a marvelous band-aide displayed it proudly and kept the flesh-colored plastic treat on as long as possible" because one never knew "when you'd be so blessed to get another one instead of a plantain leaf."[95]

Although man-made psychedelics were banned at the farm, marijuana, peyote, and magic mushrooms, all natural substances, were considered to be a holy sacraments essential for enlightenment. Indeed, the majority of Farmies couldn't wait for what they called "hanging out with Uncle Roy," which meant sitting in a big circle, talking and passing around "the doobies." Gaskin believed The Farm grew "the cleanest form of pot" in the country, and it was "lovingly grown" as those Farmies responsible for its cultivation "not only planted it but sat nude and played flute to it." Most important to Gaskin was that "no money ever changed hands." Gaskin's attitude toward drugs was rather unusual for the time: "Don't lose your head to a fad. The idea is that you want to get open so you can experience other folks, not all closed up and off on your own trip. So you shouldn't take speed or smack or coke. You shouldn't take barbiturates or tranquilizers. All that kind of dope really dumbs you out. Don't take anything that makes you dumb. It's hard enough to get smart."[96]

Money was also forbidden and was not needed; everyone picked up their household rations at the Farm Store. If cash was required for an errand to nearby Summertown or Hohenwald, one applied for funds and received the *exact* amount needed from the "Bank ladies." Vehicles were also parceled out in the same fashion; all cars or trucks were procured at the Motor Pool and signed out for a specific time and use.[97]

Gaskin left prison with "big time visions of grandeur" for his particular brand of rural communal alternative living. He was certain that The Farm had become such "a heavy-duty flagship for humanity" that the concept needed to be expanded to as many parts of the country as possible, *now*, while his ideas were still "hot." Gaskin thus began borrowing money to establish "sister farms" in Wisconsin, Missouri, and Florida. Started by "colonizers" from the original Tennessee location, these were intended to become "heavy duty farming operations cranking out cash crops." Unfortunately Gaskin's grand plans never came to fruition; none of the three locations, for a variety of reasons, ever got off the ground, ultimately plunging Gaskin and many of his fellow Farmies into serious financial straits. By 1978, as John Coate succinctly put it, "The Farm from then on had a huge debt as each year went by. We [had] lost our ass."[98] Also by that time increasing numbers of original Farmies were growing weary of their Spartan existence and Gaskin's imperiousness. By 1980 the majority of male Farmies had taken on weekend work in Nashville and the surrounding area, hoping to earn enough money to improve their living conditions, especially their homes. Henry Goodman, for example, wanted to buy linoleum to replace the unfinished plywood in his house "so you could keep it clean and the kids and babies who were crawling around on it wouldn't get grubby or sick." After Goodman and some other men had worked for seven straight Saturdays, for ten-hours a day, they had enough cash to make the repairs on their homes. Gaskin, however, announced that their money "had been earmarked for other purposes." For Goodman and many others, Gaskin's pronouncement proved to be the straw that broke the camel's back. "I remember feeling totally ripped off," Goodman told an interviewer. "The kicker was that as soon as the Saturday work money got collectivized, guess what happened? People quit going out to work on Saturdays. This was a bitter pill for us to swallow, to see that there really was something to the capitalist, free-enterprise philosophy after all." Walter Rabideau agreed, no longer "believing in the system." After waiting several weeks for shoes from the Shoe Lady while his children wore "sneakers with their toes coming out the ends," Rabideau "started buying my kids' shoes on my own. I just avoided the whole system. I'd go out and work Saturday, save the money, and take the kids to K-Mart or someplace on Sunday." Gaskin and the Farm's other true-believers had no choice by the early 1980s but to acquiesce to "capitalist Saturdays," allowing Farmies who got Saturday jobs to keep their money. "At first you could only spend it on houses," John Seward recalled, "but then it got to where you could use it for anything." For several years Seward and his compatriots "didn't have to think about money. This was great. I never touched money, I never had anything to do with money." However, during his last three years on the farm, Seward "never thought about anything but money."[99]

By the early 1980s many adult Farmies worried about their children, most of whom had been living "a Third World Existence in the U.S.A." Although the adults had willingly become "voluntary peasants" their children had taken no such vow of poverty. Concerned for their children's future, increasing numbers of families began leaving the farm, opting to re-enter mainstream society rather than endure more years of deprivation. "Re-entry" for children born and raised on The Farm proved to be quite a psychological, sociological, and emotional adjustment. After her parents divorced, Rena Mundo, along with her sister Nadine and brother Miguel, moved with their mother to Santa Monica, California, where she recalled feeling "like foreigners in our own country. It was really scary. I couldn't tell the difference between a Mercedes and a Corvette. Being from a hippie commune wasn't cool. They [people] were like 'Are you from a cult? Are you a Communist?' So we completely buried it." Zane Kesey, son of legendary acid-head, Merry Prankster, and author Ken Kesey, had similar experiences. "I remember when one of the kids at school called me a hippie. I cried and asked my mom what it meant. She said a hippie is someone who is closer to Jesus." Although extreme in its indictment of communal living, there was perhaps an element of truth to *Newsweek*'s assessment that most of the children in hippie communes at the time were "illiterate, ignored, and unprepared."[100]

In most communes children were raised by all the adults and thus the traditional, exclusive parent-child relationship of the nuclear family had been replaced by an extended family of affectionate adults who all contributed to each child's education and development. As one communard noted, "Nowadays, each child has a special relationship with his own parent (bedtime stories and special cuddling and such), but the casual observer to the farm usually can't tell which child belongs to which adult." According to Kate Wenner, similar to most commune children of the time, "the young Farm hippies enjoy a state not found in the rest of our society. Rather than underling, they are treated on an equal basis by their parents.

Calling them by their first names, the children view their parents more as friends." Such a relationship between communal parents and children, and between adults and children in general in the hip counterculture stemmed largely from the hippie belief in equality, a determination to remain "forever young," a wholesale rejection of all bourgeois convention and values, and as part of their liberation ethos which they extended to children and adolescents, whom they believed were as oppressed as the era's other marginalized affinity groups. Indeed, hippies disdained virtually all aspects or phases of the contemporary notions of white middle class adulthood, and thus as Raymond Mungo declared, hippie males in particular battled daily "the forces attempting to make me grow up, sign contracts, get an agent, be a man. I have seen what happens to men. It is curious how helpless, pathetic, and cowardly is what adults call a Real Man. If that is manhood, no thank you." As another communard declared, "Grownups are dead."[101]

Such contempt for adulthood and veneration of youth naturally led hippie parents to "disavow most of the dominant models of parenthood," since they themselves refused to grow up "to meet middle class standards of maturity and responsibility. These standards are symbolic of what they dropped out of and dropped out for.... Like the little kids who are their children, the big kids who are the children's parents are busy 'seeking their identities.'" In short, on many communes, it became a case of children raising children and consequently children were left to make their own choices and decisions, which in many if not most instances, would be unthinkable today. Nonetheless, as Raymond Mungo made clear, the children in his commune were "fully peers by the time they've learned to eat and eliminate without any help." Consequently, for many communal children "there was something more important than Saturday morning cartoons missing from their formative years—guidance." Communal children were praised by their adult-parent-peers for their displays of self-reliance and "responsibility for taking care of ourselves." However, as one former child communard remembered, for him "it was too much. I was a little kid and I needed to be taken care of. We had too much freedom. I wish my parents would have pushed me a little harder." Another child communard remembered "actually begging my mom for rules. 'Let's have a rule where kids have to go to bed at certain time every night!' I said.... I longed for discipline, for someone to tell me, 'That's quite enough of that young lady.'" However, in hippiedom's heyday, "discipline was out and wild, Dionysian revelry was in."[102]

To their credit, when it came to exposing Farm children to sex and drugs, the Gaskins and Farmies in general, adhered to almost puritanical policies compared to their contemporaries, where marriage and family were eschewed and thus "courtship, coupling, uncoupling, and recoupling [occurred] as frequently and intensely after they are raising children as before." Despite the brief tenure of four-marriage, Gaskin promoted family solidarity and by comparison, a relatively chaste sexual environment, largely because there were so many Farm children around whom Farm parents and Gaskin believed should not be exposed to random sexual practices and discussion. Although devoted to marijuana use, Farm parents did not encourage their children (at least until adolescence) to indulge. Quite the opposite environment existed on most communes, where "Sex was way too much out in the forefront. We knew too much— we were exposed to a lot of talk about sex, a lot of hearing sex, seeing sex, a lot of dirty jokes." As far as drugs were concerned, one child communard recalled being "provided with LSD when I was 13 and told, 'You'll probably experiment, so you might as well have the best.'"[103]

Nonetheless, Matthew and Kathryn McClure agreed with *Newsweek*'s assertion, telling

Kevin Kelly that one of the main reasons why they eventually left the Farm was because of their concern for their children's education, which was overwhelmingly informed by "Third World revolutionary doctrine," propagated not only by Gaskin but then reinforced by Farm teachers from primary school through high school. Missing from Farm classrooms was "a larger global perspective," which unfortunately Gaskin discouraged, wanting Farm children to be "introduced to our lifestyle" rather than to "educate them to some abstract standard," which was not only useless on the Farm but even in the outside world. Indeed, as Gaskin told a gathering at Mount Angel College in Oregon, it wasn't "necessary to either write or talk to become enlightened. Especially not to read or write." To Gaskin and many of his followers, traditional, academic American public education, whether at the secondary or university level, had become sterile, meaningless, void of humanity, and existed only to crank out automaton, mindless, bureaucratic technocrats for the military-industrial complex. In Gaskin's view, "The trouble with universities is that they keep telling you that people can't think. They keep saying that you're not qualified to do anything unless you know how to run a computer and talk gobbledygook and have three degrees after your name. But's that's a big crock and all you have to do to know it's a crock is look back three or four or five hundred years. Folks back then didn't have all this super technology and yet they were quite competent. They weren't all university graduates and yet they built huge bridges and cathedrals and some things we can't build anymore.... Our college educations hadn't taught us a thing about growing our own food or properly disposing of our own wastes. We had pieces of paper which said we were educated but we didn't know any of the basics at all." To Gaskin "most college degrees ain't worth the paper they're printed on. We don't really put the universities down. It's just that we think we've got something going here that's hotter than any university." For the Farm to flourish as an example to the world, its members must be "educated" not only in Farm philosophy but possess the requisite vocational skills essential for the Farm's mission to "save the world"; to be able to share that "knowledge" with the rest of humanity. By 1979 over two hundred children were attending the Farm School, which combined basic academic skills along with equal parts vocational training. Education on the Farm was mandatory but only up until age fourteen, when at that time a child could either choose to continue on in a traditional high school academic environment, à la Farm philosophy, or pursue a specific trade by apprenticing his or herself to one of the Farm's various work crews.[104]

Disturbing the McClures most was the strong sense of anti-intellectualism that pervaded both Farm culture and education, and which Gaskin reinforced with his "teaching to beware of 'conceptual thought' at the expense of real experience." For the first twelve years of their lives, the McClure children "only saw the Farm and hippies," and as a result, "they were seriously culturally deprived—they didn't know how to make change or call information. They were as far from real planetary consciousness as they could be." The McClures were Stanford graduates, had "tripped around Europe," and in their view had a "global perspective and sense of internationalism," which their children presently sorely lacked. The only time they left the area was when they visited their grandparents for vacation. After seeing and experiencing all that they had, "all the intellectual highlights at the time," the McClures chose "to drop out and go be hippies." It became obvious to the McClures "that the education [their children] were getting was inadequate" because of the Farm's anti-academic environment, which sadly most of the other Farmies embraced, to their children's educational detriment, particularly in the area of fundamental literacy. The McClures wanted their children to have the same exposure to the larger world that they had and some of the same experiences, because only then would their children have "the material wherewithal they needed to arrive at a spiritual decision they could live with."[105]

In theory the hippie communard goal was to help each individual to become one with both his immediate community as well as with the New Age and for that to come about, each member had to "leave their ego at the gate," and unite in body and spirit with the larger community. Sacred and respected were individual rights and abilities, but for the commune to realize its higher purpose, it was essential for each person to integrate those talents and subsume personal needs for the good of the community. As one hip writer declared, "Instead of millions of young individuals, what we now have is an entire generation moving headlong into a collective consciousness."[106]

Such an illusion initially produced genuine moments of love, dance, and fraternal feelings, but eventually *real* life obtruded on the euphoria, and hip communards, many of whom were pampered, affluent young white Americans, simply could not deal with the demands and personal sacrifices necessary to live a primitive, tribal existence. As three former Farmies noted, "You'd have no oil, you'd have no margarine, no baking powder sometimes, yet you couldn't complain. You were insufficiently spiritual if you complained about the material plane." Constant deprivation led to hoarding, especially the money Farmies earned doing odd jobs in the local towns, which was supposed to go back into the community. "You'd pocket a little change and go to town and buy something. That's what eventually happened. It was the only way you could provide for your own." According to Kathryn McClure, it was "like changing money on the black market of Czechoslovakia," and to John Seward, it was "Graft and corruption. Capitalism." A group of Guatemalan peasants, whom the Farm was helping through its Plenty Program, visited the Tennessee "mother farm" and upon see its conditions, remarked that "they had vegetables all the time, and decided they had it better down there.... We had to volunteer to have less in order to have a cooperative thing happen," and these sacrifices were simply too tough to overcome for many communards, especially those with children. "It's hard when you start raising kids to face the fact that you've voluntarily lowered your standard of living." The final straw for Kathryn McClure occurred on a Christmas day in the early 1980s when Farmies "splurged" and had "noodles and oranges" for the day's celebratory meal. "While we were eating our daughter Rose said 'I wish we could have noodles sometime besides just for Christmas.' And I thought my God that' really pretty bad. It made me sure we had to leave." For Kathryn McClure, by the late 1970s the grind and difficulty of daily life "was starting to loom larger than any spiritual ideal."[107]

Reflected in the above examples was the individualism inherent in the hip creed and simultaneous yet contradictory devotion to communalism and the embrace of collectivism as mankind's salvation, at least in the United States. To true-believer communards, Americans' survival would only be guaranteed "when everybody is doing for each other." The worship of rugged individualism in the United States was viewed to have led to the evils of privatism, ruthless competition, elitism, selfishness, jealousy, and the territorial imperative as witnessed by the Vietnam War. Although rakish self-expression was to be celebrated, commitment to the group, not the self was paramount. However, after his Farm experience, John Seward believed "Collectives don't work, basically, for all the classical reasons," and the only reason why Farmies referred to their enterprise as a collective was because "Mao was so popular in the counterculture at the time." In Seward's view, the only way for a collective to succeed was if all members "were some tribe in which everybody had been related for 2,000 years. That was one of our mistakes. We called ourselves a tribe, but we weren't. We were all totally unrelated people trying to be a tribe but we weren't." Nonetheless hippie communards believed themselves to be "builders of a New Dawn," certain that once everyone saw by their examples the possibility of living without ego, consumerism, and privatism, a New Age would surely come about. Farmies Cliff Figallo and Matthew McClure certainly embraced such idealism at the time they helped to start The Farm. For Figallo the Farm was "this group of people with these high ideals. One of the reasons for going to Tennessee was to go somewhere where you could actually practice those ideals and really try them out." For McClure the Farm was "a demonstration that there was a possibility we could serve as the seed that might possibly spread so people might get the idea. I thought that if we could be a good and clear enough example we could show people that there was an alternative way of living. And I tried for a good 12 years to put in everything I had to make the world recognize the Farm as such a place."[108]

As reflected in the above comments, the majority of hippies were sincere in their quest for self-fulfillment in small, elemental, intentional communities but most failed to grasp how challenging it would be to create islands of separatism within modern industrial America. Humanity is not perfect and human foibles always seem to obtrude upon the noblest of visions. Nevertheless hippie communards used the education, money, and technological savvy provided by mainstream society in combination with a romanticized view of the American frontier experience, to build communities that not only would serve as sanctuaries from consumer culture but would ultimately save plastic America from itself.

By 1983 over 400 Farm residents, "who just couldn't take it anymore," had left, prompting the remaining 300 to vote, in a series of town-hall meetings, to end the original experiment. They also unanimously agreed that if The Farm was to survive, it had to de-collectivize; to abandon the dream of a cashless communal existence; to rejoin the nation's capitalist system. Gaskin was away when the voting took place, and when asked later how felt about "the changeover," he told interviewers that it "was a coup d'état followed by a downsizing." The die-hards who remained agreed to pay $130 a month in order to bring down the debt, which meant having to get a *real* job nearby, which would require new clothes, haircuts, cars, insurance, income tax—all the mundane stuff essential for existence in mainstream American life. Gaskin, ever the entrepreneur found ways to survive on the Farm, creating with others more than a dozen businesses and nonprofits. Nonetheless, gone from The Farm were all the group homes and group marriages as well as all those individuals who realized they now needed real money to survive. In his campaign statement for the Green Party's presidential nomination in 2000, Gaskin perhaps best summed up who he was as well as who his followers had been since the early 1970s: "I want it to be understood that were are a bunch of tree-huggers and mystics, and beatniks. My main occupations are Hippy, Priest, Spiritual Revolutionary, Cannabis Advocate, shade tree mechanic, cultural engineer, tractor driver, and community leader. I also love science fiction." Gaskin lost the party's nomination that year to perennial favorite Ralph Nader. To the day he died, Gaskin professed to be a "teacher" not "a leader. If you lose your leader, you're leaderless and lost, but if you lose your teacher there's a chance that he taught you something you can navigate on your own." Perhaps no other testimony to his legacy would have pleased Stephen Gaskin more than Margaret Mead's statement that one should "Never doubt that a small group of thoughtful, committed people can change the world. Indeed, it is the only thing that ever has."[109]

Unfortunately for both Gaskin and the Farm's legacy, a very vituperative dispute emerged in 2013 between current Farm board members and Sam Gaskin, Stephen Gaskin's son, and continues to tarnish the Farm's image as a beacon for peace, tolerance, and progress on fronts ranging from midwifery to renewable energy. It was Sam Gaskin's Facebook posts that initially revealed the animosity between the Farm's board of directors and the younger Gaskin. On his posts, Gaskin accused current Farmies of "promoting a philosophy of Jewish supremacy," of "anti–Christian white (men) hating," and of creating a "deviant and decadent drug culture." Gaskin's accusations reflect a wholesale rejection of and hostility toward the Farm's communal ethos that had informed most of his life. So alienated has the younger Gaskin become that he has gravitated toward a completely antithetical philosophy, that of the cult of conspiratorial militant white supremacy and rabid anti–Semitic evangelical fundamentalism (the type of anti-government fanaticism the nation witnessed in rural eastern Oregon in late 2015). On a deeper level Gaskin's bitter disaffection represents a not uncommon sentiment among many former hippie communards, who became restless vagabonds in the post-hip decades, searching for a new community with which they could identify and immerse themselves fully. These individuals desperately hope to find the same feeling of belonging, connection, humanity and spiritual fulfillment they experienced during the heyday of the countercultural quest for alternative lifestyles. Unfortunately many believed they found their new communal nirvana by embracing the authoritarianism of a Jim Jones of Guiana infamy or in the bizarre Christian teachings of the Rev. Sun Myung Moon or of David Koresh of the Branch Davidians. Others such as Sam Gaskin found their new community in the form of the xenophobic, racist, gun-right, anti-government radical libertarianism of the Militia Movement. Regardless of the type of affinity group in which many former hip communards found a new haven, it is the same restlessness and search for the other that drove thousands of seekers in the late 1960s and early 1970s to find such sanctuaries in communities such as The Farm.[110]

In several Facebook rants, Gaskin claimed that The Farm has been taken over by "haters of Christians … my father was downright Christian hostile and his best friends called him their rabbi. It is racial revenge against white men in particular." Even more disturbing to Gaskin than the Farm having been taken over by alleged "Zionists" was that it has supposedly come under the control of "a drug dealing mafia.… The Farm has quite a history of pumping out Jewish drug dealers," and the individual Gaskin most blamed "for this catastrophe of addiction, abuse, and dealing haven it is definitely my father, the acid cult guru." Because Gaskin is determined "to make that place [The Farm] unsafe to the drug dealing mafia that controls it," he is certain he is on some sort of Farm hit-list and thus "You better believe I have a list of names handed out to friends and militia brothers in case I end up mysteriously dead." Gaskin claims that he is "not looking for retribution" but rather "for the true story to be told. We were told that a warrior spirit was wrong and that drugs were spiritual and could be profitable. That has made for a very interesting legacy and a very strange place."[111]

One of Gaskin's more interesting enterprises was to build a retirement village on Farm land, Rocinante, which Gaskin named "after Don Quixote's horse and John Steinbeck's pickup truck so it's a vehicle for an incurable idealist." Rocinante is a Sun City retreat for aging hippies, whom Gaskin was convinced would return to their hipster ways once they were through "selling out" and living in "plastic America." They would want to "turn on, tune in, and drop out" once again and they would have a place to do that on The Farm, courtesy of Stephen Gaskin. Gaskin was confident that many former hippies would find their way back to their true selves and as they did, "collectivity will get interesting again."[112] When asked if the Farm idea would ever emerge in another generation, ex–Farmies John Seward and Matthew McClure were certain that it would, but warned that in order for a new version to succeed its founders must not "follow leaders and don't take on more than you can handle financially. Get enough money together before you start…. It's often not a good idea to start off in poverty." Perhaps most important, "don't have the idea you are somehow responsible for the whole world."[113] Despite the ordeal of daily life and the frequent disappointments and disillusionment, there was no doubt "that the friendships and camaraderie" that developed among Farmies "created a lot of deep and lasting friendships" that would be "treasure[d] for years—there was a very strong bond among those of us who spent all those years trying to make it succeed."[114] Whether or not Rocinante comes to pass, or whether another collective endeavor like the Farm will ever be tried again, there is no denying that out of the thousands of experiments in communal living attempted in a rural environment in the 1960s and 1970s, The Farm remains as testimony writ large to the counterculture's impact on the history of communitarianism in the United States.

One of the more avant-garde rural communes established in the 1960s was the Buckminster Fuller-inspired Drop City, located near the mountains of southern Colorado, a post-industrial village of geodesic domes. Drop City encompassed most of the usual themes informing the hippies' back-to-the-land movement: "anarchy, pacifism, voluntary poverty, sexual freedom, rural isolation," drugs (at least initially), open membership, and hip art, which its founders exuberantly combined with one of the more innovative and intriguing styles of architecture in American history, the "dymaxion," most famously expressed as the geodesic dome. This was the brainchild of one of the nation's most expansive and imaginative 20th century inventors and visionaries, Richard Buckminster "Bucky" Fuller. Drop City's founders, University of Kansas graduates Gene and Jo Bernofsky and Clark Richert, avidly agreed with Fuller that it was time to take an "inventory of the globe's resources." Fuller and his hippie devotees saw "the population explosion, man's myths and antagonisms as foretelling a possible new deluge, " especially if resources were "not utilized to Fuller principles of 'comprehensive design,' and therefore become scarce, men will begin to club each other to death…. Man knows so much but does so little."[115] Inspired by Fuller's ideas, the Bernofskys and Richert were out to prove that at least three human beings were willing to do more than a "little" to preserve the human species. For that purpose they bought for $450 six acres of "rocky and cactus-strewn" land "which normally would not provide for a hungry goat,"[116] near Trinidad, Colorado, and there they built an artists' community that amounted to a veritable new civilization, forged from a "holistic consciousness" of "Materials, Structure, Energy, Man, Magic, and Evolution."[117] In a variety of ways, Drop City became the single outstanding emblem of countercultural communitarianism; a countercultural destination of choice, especially after the mainstream media captured in photographs the spectacular nature of its multi-colored, patchwork structures, set against the background of the Culebra Mountains, pulsating like a psychedelic beacon to those attempting to leave the straight world.[118]

Drop City, probably more than any communal experiment of the time, became the quintessential example of the hippie belief that the United States' post-scarcity economy was so abundant and productive in material output that real deprivation and want were issues of the past; that dropouts could exist on "the leavings" of an affluent but wasteful society. As Dropper Curly Benson told a *Time* reporter, "We're living off the affluence of the country. We scrounge everything we need." Indeed, Droppers took great pride in being labeled as "scroungers, bums, garbage pickers." Those who referred to Droppers as such were "right. Perhaps the most beautiful creation in Drop City is our junk pile, the garbage of the garbage pickers."[119] As Bill Voyd recalled, "We learned how to scrounge materials, tear down abandoned buildings, use the unusable.... Trapped inside a waste economy man finds an identity as a consumer. Once outside the trap he finds enormous resources at his disposal-free. Things have value only in their use. When one stops 'owning' things another can begin to use them. Energy is transformed not lost."[120] As Dropper Peter "Peter Rabbit" Douthit observed, Drop City was "built on the garbage dump of a dying town of 10,000 strung-out coal miners."[121] Contrary to public perception at the time, Droppers did not believe they were poor, at least not "mentally, and no one ever went hungry," according to Clark Richert. "We owned our own land, our buildings, owed no rent, were free of employment, free to create. I felt freer at Drop City than at any other time in my life, I just can't see that as poverty." Jo Ann Bernofsky was equally fond in her memory of her Drop City experience. "It was full of vitality, and it was extremely exciting and wonderful. You had the sense that anything was possible, that the potential was unlimited."[122]

Interestingly, Droppers did not consider themselves "models, hippies, or a commune." Such ascriptions were the "trademarks invented by the establishment media."[123] Like most hippie expressions and "breakthroughs" at the time, the Drop City concept and its inhabitants' artistic creations were "co-opted by the mainstream culture." According to Clark Richert, "It happen[ed] to all of the important art movements. It appears to be inevitable. Forms of idealism eventually reach a large audience and become diluted and corrupted in the process."[124] Droppers viewed their city as an artists' colony, "like a 'happening' but with no distinction between art and life and reality.... It was a very synergetic and creative place."[125] Nonetheless Droppers "shared ownership of the property, ate meals together and agreed upon resolution of issues through consensus."[126] To Bill Voyd, "We [were] immigrants and like all immigrants we banded together to save energy. [We were] like [the] Jews, coming to New York, who banded together in sixes and nines and bought a Brownstone house, for cash. They ate together at a common table. Freed of rent and eating well and easy ... they could turn their pushcarts into million-dollar estates. Today their children get high together."[127] Perhaps most important to Droppers, and contrary to popular myth and mainstream interpretation at the time "the 'Drop' in Drop City did not refer to 'dropping out,'" or to "dropping acid" but rather to the art movement that informed the Droppers aesthetic expressions. "Drop City," as Richert reminds contemporary Americans, was "there before those words were around. It came out of Drop Art, a new genre created by Allan Kaprow, John Cage, Robert Rauschenberg, and Buckminster Fuller at Black Mountain College."[128] Richert and Benofsky also directly contributed to the Drop Art movement by personally dropping objects (painted rocks) from their rooftop loft in Lawrence, Kansas, as means to "explore" the possibilities for a new form of "conceptual artwork."[129]

Although most of the original Droppers had fond memories of their experiment, on a daily, practical basis, life was not as rosy as many would like to remember. Most of the time the Droppers lived hand to mouth and there was absolutely no leadership or structure, often resulting in community members' hostility toward one another, especially toward new arrivals who refused to share in the work. Poverty was a daily, grinding reality for Droppers, yet they embraced it as a creative spur. As Clard Svenson remarked to *Time* reporter Barron Beshoar,

"There are too many mouths to feed," and what "bugged" Svenson the most was "the number of visitors who pour into Drop City," anywhere from 200 to 500 a month. Timothy Leary and Bob Dylan were among some of the era's celebrities who visited, but the majority of "guests" were "hippies or semi-hippies" who came "to stare at the domes appreciatively and always stayed to free-load a few meals."[130] Indeed, as Bill Voyd observed, "The hardest time in a commune, particularly Drop City, is the time after the building gets done. While everyone is working together on actual construction the energy is centered, and there is a fantastic high spirit, everyone knows what he is doing all the time. But after the building is done comes a time of dissolution. There's no focus for the group energy, and most hippies don't have anything to *do* with their individual energy,"[131] but get high, which to most hippie visitors' and free-loaders' disappointment, the Droppers were no longer "into." According to Bill Dodd of the *San Francisco Oracle*, the Droppers had all disavowed psychedelics because "the evolution and development of the Tribe's interpersonal relationships had grown, due to the huge task involved, into such a profound entrustment" that no one in the community wanted to jeopardize "the beauty of such human harmony and sacrifice for the good of the whole."[132] Although in his recollections Voyd conveyed the impression that most Droppers were hardworking individuals, which might have been true on a project-by-project basis, Droppers across the spectrum all shared the beat-hippie disdain for money, material comfort, and work. As Gene Bernofsky recalled, "It's important to be employed; work is important, but we felt that to be gainfully employed was a sucking of the soul and that a part of one of the purposes of the new civilization was to be employed, but not to be gainfully employed, so that each individual would be their own master and we idealistically believed that if we were true to that principle, that if we did nongainful work that the cosmic forces would take note of this and would simply supply us with the necessities of survival."[133]

Although such issues were endemic in most communes, ultimately leading to their demise, Droppers did not seem to be as adversely affected as the other experiments, persevering and creating in the process one of the more unique and "accessible models of what a new America might look like." They produced an array of Drop Art paintings, designs, and sculptures and one of the first underground comic books. Most impressive they built a solar collector to heat a building before most Americans had even remotely contemplated such a possibility. Without question, the Droppers most spectacular accomplishment was the construction of Buckminster Fuller–inspired quasi-geodesic domes from a variety of scrap materials, covering them with the tops of cars and other metals taken from junkyards. After they completed the largest dome on the property, the Cartop Dome, Peter Rabitt proudly announced "that everyone in the world can have a comfortable dwelling unit for less than $1,000. No structure has cost more than $200 to complete (labor not included in this figure since we do everything ourselves.)"[134] Over the course of their eight-year existence (1965–1973), thousands of curiosity-seekers and genuine seekers, as well as the mainstream media, trekked to the barren plains of southern Colorado to see the Droppers' colorful and fantastic creations, the geodesic domes as well as their other fanciful artworks. All were intrigued by the possibility that people could indeed survive, if not flourish (at least artistically and creatively) by using the surplus of "a people of plenty." To Barron Beshoar, the Droppers represented "a new breed of hippies. For all their faults and lapses, perhaps a better breed. They are truly sincere in eschewing drugs and in wanting to be creative.... Perhaps 30-year-old Peter Rabbit told it all in one sentence: 'We are too old to be hippies.'"[135]

The sincerity and perseverance of the Droppers as well as many other communards, reflected the hippie critique of late 20th century American civilization for having devalued honest workmanship, and thus they sought some form of work requiring skill, producing a specific, tangible product. Perhaps most important, they believed their labor could be neither co-opted nor corrupted by submission to the nation's capitalist/military institutions. This explains many hip communards' penchant for the fine arts, artisanship, music, or organic farming. Out-of-the-box thinkers and visionaries such as "Bucky" Fuller found the hippies' disdain for conventional work a hopeful beginning to "doing away with the absolutely specious notion that everybody has to earn a living.... We keep inventing jobs because of this false idea that everybody has to be employed at some kind of drudgery because, according to Mathusian-Darwinian theory, he must justify his right to exist.... The true business of people should be to think about whatever it was they were thinking about before somebody came along and told them they had to earn a living."[136] No wonder so many hippies considered Fuller to be one of their most inspirational gurus.

As liberated and enlightened as communards believed themselves to be, all too often such illumination was not extended to communal women. To their dismay, many hip women found gender roles and sexual expectations in the commune to be as oppressive and resistant to change as those in "normal" society. Many, if not most communal hip males were as chauvinistic, misogynistic, and as sexually driven as their straight counterparts, and this contributed to increasing numbers of hip women gravitating to the then-emerging women's movement. Gender solidarity also often developed among communal women because of their marginalization by their male counterparts. As Kit Leder recalled her communal farm experience, "Even though there was no society-dictated division of labor, even though we had complete freedom to determine the division of labor for ourselves, a well-known pattern emerged immediately. Women did most of the cooking, all of the cleaning up, and of course, the washing. They also worked in the fields all day—so that after the farm work was finished, the men could be found sitting around talking and taking naps while the women prepared supper. In addition to that, one of the women remained in camp every day to cook lunch— it was always a woman who did this, never a man. Of course the women were excused from some of the tasks; for example none of us ever drove a tractor. That was considered too complicated for a woman." Vivian Estellachild, after having lived in two communes, concluded that "the hip commune uses women in a group way the same as the fathers did in a one-to-one way. The communes are too fluid to create any security for a woman. The source of our oppression is *all men*, no exception for bells and beads."[137]

In some communes men and women defined their respective roles within the historical context of an imaginary American frontier, believing themselves to be settlers reminiscent of the pioneer families living on the Western pale of pre-industrial America. Such a down-home environment supposedly caused women in particular to be less anxious or obsessed with gender expectations and identity because such self-absorption would be detrimental to the community, which needed them to perform their traditional roles and employ their particular "skill sets." Such was William Hedgepeth's view of the women at the New Buffalo commune in northern New Mexico. "Without becoming bogged-down in sexual-identity crises and the 'feminine mystique' type traumas that idle females flagellate themselves with back in Suburbia, the New Buffalo girls fulfill themselves naturally not only in sewing, cooking, cleaning or child tending, but also in freely voicing their views and mystical visions, and then acting upon them…. 'We're trying to live a way that's never been lived before,' says Siva [a New Buffalo female communard]. 'There's no double standard here. We'll find out *together* how this works." In reality, even at New Buffalo, traditional gender roles and expectations prevailed; they were simply reframed in a more palatable, expiated form of the frontier fantasy. As one male New Buffalo member told Hedgepeth, "A girl just becomes so, so *womanly* when she's doing something like baking her own bread in a wood stove. I can't explain it. It just turns me on."[138]

Perhaps in no other capacity was the double-standard more readily and visibly apparent in communes than in heterosexual relationships and sexual expectations. Sara Davidson observed in all the communes she visited, "With couples, the double-standard is the unwritten rule: the men can roam but the women must be faithful" and frequently male possessiveness erupted into violent outbursts, as was the situation at Wheeler's Ranch when one male "saw his wife with another man [even though he and his wife were involved in a group marriage between two teen-age girls, a forty-year-old man, and two couples] in the group, pulled a knife, and dragged her off, yelling 'Forget this shit. She belongs to me.'"[139] As far as communes being notorious for their sexual escapades and debauchery, Bill Wheeler believed that although "Tremendous sex myths have been connected to the communal movement in general" with the "hippie chick" becoming "as much a sex symbol for American society as the airline stewardess, there wasn't any more sexual activity" in communes "than anywhere else. It was just that we tried to be more honest and up-front about it than our parents." Indeed, one day communard "Friar Tuck" walked in on a couple "lying on the kitchen table in the '69' position, giving each other head." Tuck embarrassed, apologized for his intrusion but the couple, totally unfazed by Tuck's presence, responded by telling Tuck 'No it's all right. Come on in, we'll be through in a minute. Don't worry about it, sit down and talk a while!' And so between slurps we talked and bullshitted, having a good visit while they sucked each other off. It was my first encounter with good old abject sexuality—just right out front—it blew my mind. I really thought it was hilarious."[140]

In most communes there were more men than women, and thus when a new female arrived, she was "pounced upon, claimed, and made the subject of wide gossip." Yet, many women, having liberated themselves from conventional sexual restraints or "hang-ups" proved just as willing as their male counterparts to engage in random sexual encounters. Such was the attitude of another Morning Star communard, "Corky," who told Sara Davidson that "I love to go around naked. There's so much sexual energy here, it's great. Everybody's turned on to each other's bodies,"[141] which appeared to be quite the understatement at Morning Star and no doubt in many other communes relative to sexual expression and freedom.

Although thousands of hippies lived in rural communes, many more lived in urban equivalents, where, as in the Haight and other hip neighborhoods a genuine counter society emerged. In the metropolitan areas the rural communards' city cousins believed they too could create a more harmonious, less materially obsessed and work-driven society. However, to many hardcore rural communards, urban cooperatives represented only the first step toward becoming *true* "builders of the dawn," which country true-believers felt could only legitimately be created in a pastoral environment, as far away from the corrupt and decaying city as was possible. After all, complete separation from America's oppressive system was nearly impossible as long as one remained in the city; there was no escaping the daily assault of the megalopolis' capitalist system with its bourgeois attractions and distractions. Rural hippies doubted the ability of urban communalists to divorce themselves from the system while they shopped at corporate-owned supermarkets or held *real jobs!*

Nonetheless, communal living flourished in Old Town, Chicago, Peach Street in Atlanta, West Bank in Minneapolis, Pearl Street in Austin, and near Dupont Circle in Washington, D.C. Even more were established in larger state university towns like Ann Arbor (University of Michigan); Boulder (University of Colorado); Eugene (University of Oregon), and of course Madison (University of Wisconsin) and Berkeley. "The frats are dying fast," boasted a Madison hippie, "and some of them have been taken over by collectives—frats turning into communes!"[142] Seekers had little difficulty finding such communities, especially on college campuses, and even in the larger cities, where hip neighborhoods became fairly well-defined enclaves and increasingly popular destinations for both tourists and hipsters. A city's "hippie town" was easily recognized by sight, sound, and smell; STOP signs had WAR painted across their lettering; longhairs were playing Frisbee with each other or their dog; hippies sat on the front porches of brightly painted old Victorian homes, with tie-dyed curtains on the windows. "Amerika" was mocked with the Stars and Stripes prominently displayed over the front door; "rapping" (chatting) could be heard from within, and by the late 1960s, the music of Crosby, Stills, Nash and Young, wafted out to the street along with the smell of musk or grass thick in the air.[143]

Urban communes tended to be more transient and varietal in purpose, philosophy, and composition of members than their rural counterparts, and thus had to employ a variety of creative approaches and philosophies to sustain themselves to survive longer than a few months. In many ways urban communes faced many more challenges to their existence. For one, more vagrants and drifters passed through urban communities, and constant visitors created constant disturbances. Also, it was next to impossible for urban communes to sustain themselves economically, given that they could not grow enough of their own food in meager backyard plots. City cops were far tougher in enforcing anti-drug laws than those of their rural comrades. As a result of these dynamics, many urban communal experiments degenerated into dens of iniquity; "crash-pads" for misfits and miscreants. Or worse, cults led by Manson-esque individuals, using communal members for debauched or sinister purposes. There was Kerista of Greenwich Village, founded by Jud the Prophet (ex–Air Force officer John Presmont), and the "Lyman Family" founded by Mel Lyman, who claimed in his book *The Autobiography of a World Savior*, to have come from another planet and had been sent to earth to restore humanity to its original "balance." There were various Jesus-freak collectives, many of which, according to William Hedgepath, "tended toward a sort of space-age religious zealotry, complete with their own built-in avatars, fanatical-eyed young followers and well-ordered sets of loony notions about how to avoid the Apocalypse." Although perhaps true for the Lyman Family's Fort Hill commune or that of the Keristans, such a generalization could not be applied to all urban communes. Most urban communes consisted of an apartment or house where a steady stream of all manner of seekers and dropouts lived together in a loosely cooperative arrangement before "either (a) going back home; or (b) contracting some disease (and going back home); or (c) pushing onward to a more stable commune" usually in the country.[144] Regardless of location—rural or city—philosophy and purpose, communal living represented for many hippies the next, most logical step toward breaking free from an Establishment they viewed as corrupt, broken-down, and past its prime.

Whether they lived in the country or the city, hippie communards attempted to establish a collective lifestyle by combining two ultimately irreconcilable desires: "doing one's own thing" while simultaneously trying to function as a community of equals. In a historically long line of utopias, hippies believed that they could indulge in unrestrained individualism yet escape its social consequences because all in the community would respect each other's need for such self-discovery. They would be willing to cooperate with each other in dealing with the realities of everyday life (communal chores and responsibilities). Unfortunately these beliefs were never realized in the majority of communal experiments, causing them to fail within a year or two of their existence. In addition to their own internal conflicts, violent outbursts against hippies, especially in rural areas, increased significantly as both the hippie population and communes proliferated in certain regions of the country. Surprisingly, in usually "laid-back" New Mexico, some of the worse attacks on hippies occurred in the Taos area. Despite being beautiful but not "political," hippies became targets for community rancor. The town's Mexican-American population, at the time suffering a 25 percent unemployment rate, resented "the white middle class hippies obvious flouting of the American ideal." School principal Francis Quintana told *Time* that Taosenos believed the hippies were "'making fun of our poverty and our fight for survival.'" Indeed, as a Chicano member of New Mexico's Reality Construction Company commune told a visiting reporter, "Every time a white hippie comes in and buys a Chicano's land to escape the fuckin' city, he sends that Chicano *to* the city to go through what he's trying to escape *from*, can you dig it? What can you do without that bread out here, man? Nothing. Then when that money's gone, see the Chicano has to *stay* in the city, cause now he ain't got no land to come back to. He's stuck and the hippie's free. That's why they don't dig the fuckin' hippies, man."[145]

Local entrepreneurs also hated the hippies' presence because many, such as Mrs. Beverly Gonzales, wife of a local merchant, believed that they were hurting the town's main source of income: tourism. According to Gonzales, "'Tourists don't want to come and share the venereal disease and hepatitis with us.'" As a result of such hostility, "Hippies have been beaten. Their homes and 'free stores' have been vandalized. Last month [May 1969] a hippie girl was gang-raped.... The prospect of a spring and summer invasion of new hippies has prompted local residents to form vigilante groups" and for many straight New Mexicans, "The only good hippie" was "a dead hippie. Kill." In August 1970, Michael Press of the Kingdom of Heaven commune was found dead, victim of an obvious homicide. The perpetrators were given light sentences on a reduced charge, further illustrating how deep local antipathy for the hippie invasion had become. Interestingly, contrary to public denunciations that the hippies' presence had hurt the local economy, the opposite proved to be true: the hippies had stimulated an "economic boomlet" for Taos, "by injecting nearly a half million dollars in the local economy with their land purchases alone." Despite their positive impact on the Taos economy, many hippie communes began "slamming doors on newcomers," for fear of further antagonizing locals. "When a transient arrives looking for a place to crash, we send him to a motel" declared one communard. "'We'll be the straights. We'll throw them out.'"[146] Unfortunately for seekers of the New Age, by the early 1970s many once open-door communes had no choice if they hoped to survive local wrath, but to close their doors, which over time caused many communes to disappear entirely.

Even more fatal to communes' survival than straight harassment of hippie communards, was the internal strife among communards over a variety of issues, many of which in retrospect seemed petty but at the time loomed large enough to cause bitter dissension and rancor among members and in many instances, the end of the commune. Such was the fate of the Freefolk community, a small rural anarchistic commune in Pennington, Minnesota that lasted two years, 1968–1970. According to one of its founding members, Patsy Sun, what caused her commune to "flop" was not "economic hassles or pressure from the outside," but rather something much simpler: too much togetherness and not enough "appreciation for separateness. It was really difficult for us to admit that we were uptight, needed more room, more time to ourselves or really didn't care that much for each other sometimes…. We became strangers living in the same house." Freefolkers also bickered over "whether we should eat all our honey in the fall or ration it through the winter; whether we should tie the cow or let her move around the barn; whether we should fence the garden around front or back; whether we should restrain the kids or let them clobber each other…. It was the small things that caused friction." Indeed, after a year-and-a-half, the "small things" ended up causing so much internal division that "Bitterness grew and silence grew until it filled up the clearing and now we're all gone except for the winter birds and the rabbits."[147]

Communards had convinced themselves that they had escaped "the system"; that their fledgling commune was an island of ecological and social righteousness free of the bourgeois consumerism that surrounded them as well as from the socio-political and economic problems tearing the nation apart, soon to cause its implosion. The unfortunate reality, however, was that, in conjunction with money from affluent middle class parents, most communes would not have lasted very long without Uncle Sam's largesse—welfare, unemployment compensation, government surplus foods, and food stamps. Government also provided for hippies in other, more subtle ways. As one communard wrote, "Maybe we're cheating. It's easy for us. No matter what we say or do, the hospital in Norton goes right on existing. I've often walked past a hospital and thought, 'They'll never get me sucked into their operations…. But when Allan was in a coma after his car accident I found myself praying that the hospital would save him."[148] To this particular communard, hospitals became one more symbol of many communes' dependence upon the very society and government they disdained—the government that also subsidized hippies' desire for clean rivers, roads, and local libraries, all niceties, services, and institutions heavily used by hippie communities.

The truth was the children of a technological age were totally ill-equipped—experientially, morally, emotionally, and even spiritually—to regress into tribal primitivism, except as a short-lived lark. As one individual observer of communes at the time opined, the factors leading to the countercultural revolt and formation of communes were "not enough to motivate an individual to throw away the security of the bourgeois life-style. Middle-aged Americans watch communal ventures with a jaundiced eye. They know [that joining] a commune may be nothing more than a pleasant interlude in the life of a post-high school nineteen-year-old."[149] Nonetheless, today, in pockets of the American economy, there remain farmers and woodworkers, programmers, and musicians, who give continuing meaning to the idea of Woodstock Nation, reflecting in their lifestyles and temperament the legacy of the hippie communes of the late 1960s and early 1970s. Regardless of what drove hippies to establish rural communes, they were media attention-grabbers, with photo opportunities galore and plentiful stories of all manner of extravagant behavior, courtesy of the strangest, most outrageous-looking human beings most Americans had ever seen. Press coverage was intense from about 1969 through 1972 and no doubt many aspiring mainstream journalists earned their first accolades covering the hippie communes. Those communes that have survived to the present represent a very visible, tangible legacy of the hippie world of the late 1960s and early 1970s.

11

The Emergence of the Yippies and the 1968 Chicago Democratic Convention: The Beginning of the End for the 1960s Counterculture

"A yippee is a stoned idealist, moved by a vision of a future utopia. He is a romantic. It is not fear which moves the yippee; it is faith and hope."—"Notes from a Yippizolean Era," *East Village Other*, February 16–22, 1968, 8.

As introduced in Chapter 7, on New Year's Eve 1967, during a euphoric and clairvoyant moment of "reefer-madness," Jerry Rubin, Abbie Hoffman, and Paul Krassner conceived of a new, theatrically inspired, "street-action-oriented," aggressively provocative manifestation of hip; a fusion of hippie "flower power" and New Left political activism; a new brand of hipster whose agenda and ideology reflected the composite of all current countercultural ethos and activity. They believed that they could attract the apolitical hippies to their movement if they made political engagement fun by promoting and incorporating into their activities dope, rock music, and the general saturnalia of the hip scene. To Yippie co-founder Paul Krassner, Yippie "became a label for a phenomenon that already existed, [the] organic coalition of psychedelic hippies and political activists."[1] Intrigued by all the "creativity that was coming out of the hippie movement"—the Diggers "free food in the streets" as well as their "theater of the streets"—and by the vitality "coming out of the political movement," Rubin recalled those counterculturists who joined YIP reflected "the merger forged of the political radical and the hippie, and it [the term] describe[d] that restless youth tying into a political movement.... If one could combine the new culture of the young people [that of the hippies] with the frame of reference of politics, one would have an explosive combination that would challenge America to its foundations. It would steal the children of America. The young people would choose us because we had excitement and they had boredom."[2] Indeed, Yippie leaders believed the turned-on baby boom generation represented the revolution in embryo, and what the mainstream media called the "hippie lifestyle" was actually those individuals who had already committed themselves to the impending youth insurrection against the Establishment. Although such a projection turned out to be wrong on several levels, at the moment, 1968, the Yippies were determined to make their assertion come true.

The Yippies condemned both the old and New Left, for being "romantics" who still believed the nation's working class to be the revolutionary vanguard (such as the Communists or the Progressive Labor party), or the New Left who endlessly debated on how to bring about the revolution. To Rubin, New Leftists were "dogmatic Puritans" who stood for sacrifice not fun and thus they turned people off, especially at their mind-numbingly boring, tedious meetings or with their bombastic ideological pronouncements and "position papers." For Rubin and his Yippie compatriots, "Impulse—not theory—makes the great leap forward. Ideology is a brain disease." To the Yippies, the New Leftists were not revolutionaries, for how could they be when their movement was "made up of part-time people whose lifestyle mocks their rhetoric…. How can you be a revolutionary going to school during the day and attending meetings at night?" Yippies, by contrast, lived the seamless life of the committed insurrectionist because "doing it," *action now*, defined their creed. Yet, according to Rubin, the Yippies considered themselves Marxists, who "follow in the revolutionary tradition of Groucho, Chico, Harpo, and Karl. What the yippies learned from Karl Marx—history's most infamous, bearded, longhaired, hippie commie freak-agitator—is that we must create the spectacular myth of revolution. Karl wrote and sang his own rock album called 'The Communist Manifesto.' 'The Communist Manifesto' is a song that has overthrown governments."[3] Thus for the Yippies, activism meant aggressive, provocative civil disobedience not just resistance and rhetorical criticism of what was wrong with 1960s American culture, society, and liberal politics. Effective political energy also required outrageous, agitating, poignant, yet fanciful street theater—pranksterism— in its most refined, creative, impassioned, and grandiose form—designed to disrupt the status quo; shock and shake Americans out of their apathy and liberate them from their bourgeois obsessions.

As "guerrilla fighters" on the nation's city streets, the Yippies' hit and run tactics, their spontaneity, allowed them to choose, on their own time, the "battlefields" on which to confront their enemies. They refused to wait around for Establishment-approved permits, to deliver their message of revolt, such as the right to hold a weekend rally in an assigned parking lot, which New Left, antiwar organizations did constantly, complete with bombastic speeches, esoteric handouts, manifestoes, trite, clichéd slogans, sappy folk songs; in effect, a peaceful, hand-holding Kumbaya experience with *no action!* Instead, the Yippies confronted the system in "sneak attacks." By moving fast like guerrilla insurgents and by continually changing their theatrical antics, the Yippies avoided permit limitations. They were master improvisers and their ability to strike fast and adapt their tactics on the run allowed them to elude and baffle authorities, who rarely, if ever knew when or where the next Yippie strike would occur. As Abbie Hoffman advised his fellow Yippies when engaging the Establishment, "Don't rely on words. Words are the absolute in horseshit. Rely on doing—go all the way every time. Move fast. If you spend too long in one play [action] it becomes boring to you and the audience. When they get bored, they are turned off. They are not receiving information. Get their attention, leave a few clues and vanish. Change your costume, use the props around you."[4]

Suffice it to say New Leftists did not take the Yippies' criticism kindly, responding with their own condemnations of the Yippie ethos and agenda. SDS felt especially aggrieved and published a long anti–Yippie essay in their journal, *New Left Notes*, entitled "Don't Take Your Guns to Town," in which SDS leaders accused the Yippies of "using talk of rock and pot as lures to put kids 'up against the bayonets.'" Indeed, the most divisive issue between New Leftists and the Yippies was the latter's association with and embracing of the hippie drug culture, which hard-core New Leftists simply could not accept as a legitimate revolutionary component. They thus condemned with much verbal venom the Yippies use of drugs. To New Left zealots, dope was "basically a diversion, a distraction, an irrelevance, an impertinence, a conceit, a siphoning off of energies desperately needed elsewhere, a way of opting out of what is heartlessly unfair to those who are left, a way of saying to those others, 'My pleasure is more important than your misery.'"[5] In effect, many New Leftists saw both the hippies and Yippies in the same light: as petty, bourgeois, and self-indulgent. However, not all traditional Leftists castigated the Yippies; some were even very supportive of the Yippie vision such as Julius Lester of the *Guardian*, one of the few African American writers in the underground press. Lester believed the Yippies had indeed been instrumental in politicizing the hippies and that unlike the New Left, whom he claimed was too focused on the politics, the Yippies rightly concentrated their efforts "at the youth ... on strike against the way of life America was presenting them.... Once you're in a liberated zone, you'll fight to keep it from being reclaimed. The Yippies are a liberated zone."[6]

The Yippie goal was to create a decentralized, anarchistic new nation based on the communalism and liberation ethos of the hippie counterculture. As Abbie Hoffman declared, "We want everyone to control their own life and to care for one another.... We cannot tolerate attitudes, institutions and machines whose purpose is the destruction of life, the accumulation of profit. We shall not defeat Amerika by organizing a political party. We shall do it by building a new nation—a nation as rugged as the marijuana leaf."[7] To the Yippies, 1968 America had become "a nation of alienated young people ... presently held captive in the penitentiaries of a decaying system.... It seems America has lost her children."[8]

Looking back, anyone listening or reading these manifestoes or about Yippie activities, would laugh at their absurdity; most if not all the Yippie declarations were typical Rubin-Hoffman put-ons and pranks. Nonetheless, in the minds of the older generation and straight Americans in general, the Yippie platform represented what they had long suspected and feared about the hippie counterculture: that lurking beneath that "peace and love" façade and supposed detachment from and contempt for mainstream America was a sinister, drug-crazed revolutionary anarchist who had cleverly disguised himself as Jesus when in reality, his ultimate purpose was to destroy the American way of life. Such a perception of the counterculture by straight Americans could not have made Rubin more ecstatic, for that was the exact image he hoped to project to the public of the Yippie: a "Marxist acidhead, [a] psychedelic Bolshevik," who "didn't feel at home in SDS, and he wasn't a flower-power hippie or a campus intellectual." He or she was "a stoned politico.... A street-fighting freek [sic], a dropout, who carries a gun at his hip. So ugly that middle class society is frightened by how he looks. A long-haired, bearded, hairy, crazy motherfucker whose life is theater, every moment creating the new society as he destroys the old."[9] Yippie slogans such as "We will burn Chicago to the ground!" "We will fuck on the beaches!" "We demand the politics of Ecstasy!" and "Acid for all!"[10] only further incensed and fanned the flames of fear and hostility toward hippies in general already in the hearts and minds of the majority of straight Americans.

The press loved the Yippies and Rubin and Hoffman delighted in the media attention; the more the press took their wild pranks literally and spread that information to as many Establishment authorities as would listen, the greater the myth of Yippie power and presence became. Indeed, from that stoned moment when Hoffman, Rubin, and company conceived of their movement, they knew that the media would be their message, putting forth great energy to create what they termed the "Yippie myth," an advertising campaign contrived to

By 1968, the antiwar movement was reaching its crescendo, and during the spring of that year draft-card burning days in front of induction centers exploded throughout the nation. One such instance occurred outside the Federal Building in Berkeley, California, in April (photograph by Michelle Vignes, courtesy Bancroft Library, University of California, Berkeley).

build the image of a do-anything, say-anything revolutionary Yippie insurrection that no newspaper or media outlet could ignore. The more the Yippies appeared in the popular and the underground media, the more fascinating, appealing, and menacing they became; the precise image Yippie leaders hoped to project, cultivate, and inculcate in the public mind, especially among young people and ironically, among Establishment authority figures as well, whether they were the cops, city officials, or national politicians. As Abbie Hoffman declared, "We tear through the streets. Kids love it. They understand it on an internal level. We are living TV ads, movies, Yippie!" Hoffman and his comrades wanted to fabricate "a vast myth, for through the notion of myth large numbers of people could get turned on and, in the process of getting turned on, begin to participate in Yippie!"[11]

The myth the Yippies hoped to propagate through their antics was that the United States government, the Johnson administration, had lost its ability to govern the nation while simultaneously involving the U.S. in a war of alleged imperialist-capitalist aggression. Rubin and company believed that if they acted or created the illusion through their words and deeds that the government was collapsing it would indeed fall in the minds of young people everywhere. To Rubin the myth was real because he and his compatriots had built the "stage for people to play out their own dreams and fantasies.... We'd steal the media away from the Establishment and create the specter of 'yippies' overthrowing Amerika."[12] In short, the Yippies believed that by manipulating the media through a series of events—"street theatrics"—the Establishment response would guarantee the publicity they needed to graphically demonstrate the flaws of liberal-capitalist institutions. Modern revolutionaries, Hoffman argued, had to "learn to manipulate the tools of mass communication and the symbols of mass society," if they hoped "to bring down the modern warfare state."[13] Yet, according to Rubin, "It was mutual manipulation. To interest the media I needed to express my politics frivolously.... If I had given a sober lecture on the history of Vietnam, the media camera would have turned off."[14]

As was true with most everything the counterculture did during the 1960s, the mainstream media quickly latched onto the Yippie myth, with many asserting that the Yippies were simply transformed hippies who had adopted a more public personae of contempt and rage against the status quo; the logical next iteration or evolution of the hip counterculture. The press' obsession with the Yippies delighted Hoffman and his comrades because "we never had to pay for ads. The papers and the electronic media provided us with free coverage. We stole thousands upon thousands of dollars' worth of free publicity using gimmickry."[15] Indeed, by the summer of 1968 Hoffman and Rubin had successfully created the *reality* of the Yippie myth in the mainstream media, which had swallowed all of the Dynamic Duo's "risk, drama, excitement, and bullshit," hook, line, and sinker.[16]

In February 1968 Jerry Rubin wrote his friend Allen Cohen, editor of the *San Francisco Oracle*, revealing Yippie plans for the August Chicago Democratic National Convention. "Our idea is to create a cultural, living alternative to the Convention. It could be the largest gathering of young people ever: in the middle of the country at the end of summer. We want all the rock bands, all the underground papers, all the free spirits; all the theater groups—all the energies that have contributed to the new youth culture—all the tribes—to come to Chicago and for six days [August 23–28] we will live together in the park [Grant Park], sharing, learning, free food, free music, a regeneration of spirit and energy. In a sense, it is like creating a SF–Berkeley spirit for a brief period in the Midwest. We want to break people out of their isolation and to help spread the revolution. The existence of the Convention at the same time gives us a stage, a platform, an opportunity to do our own thing, to go beyond protest into creative cultural alternative."[17]

In an interview with another underground paper, the *Chicago Seed*, Rubin

A despondent draftee with his one-way ticket to Vietnam in his pocket (photograph by Michelle Vignes, courtesy Bancroft Library, University of California, Berkeley).

revealed how he and his compatriots hoped to turn their "Festival of Life" into a media spectacle. "In Chicago in August, every media [outlet] in the world is going to be there, and we're going to be the news and everything we do is going to be sent out to living rooms from India to the Soviet Union to every small town in America. It is a real opportunity to make clear the two Americas. At the same time we're *confronting* them, we're offering our alternative and it's not just a narrow, political alternative, it's an alternative way of life." The key word in Rubin's press statement was "confronting"; both he and Hoffman knew that Chicago mayor Richard Daley would not tolerate their presence and would brutally unleash upon them the forces of law and order.[18] Rubin and Hoffman hoped their party would galvanize a groundswell of support for their cause; that they could politicize hippies, especially if their assault on the Establishment was as much cultural as it was political.

Prompting the Yippies to believe that they could attract the hippies to their cause was the fairly substantial hip participation in the October 1967 March on the Pentagon, organized by the National Mobilization Committee to End the War in Vietnam, popularly known as Mobe. In the spring of that year representatives from various New Left and antiwar associations had met in Washington and decided to officially combine their efforts and unite their agendas under the Mobe banner, which all the various coalitions believed would be a much more effective way to protest the most recent U.S. troop escalation in Vietnam, which had reached 400,000 in the fall of 1966. The Mobe then proceeded to schedule a major civil disobedience action to take place in the nation's capital in late October. Veteran pacifist and editor of *Liberation* magazine David Dellinger was elected chairman of the new organization. Soon after his election Dellinger asked Jerry Rubin, who had been immersed the past two years in the Haight-Ashbury scene and now saw the world through a hallucinogenic fog of pot and LSD, to come east to direct the Washington action. No sooner did Rubin take charge of the forthcoming demonstration than he insisted that the target be the Pentagon. Peyote-using Indians considered five-sided figures symbols of evil and an "exorcism" of the Pentagon, with the result of having the most famous structural manifestation of power in the world levitate 300 feet off the ground. Once in the air, the edifice would turn orange and vibrate until all evil emissions had fled and the war would end forthwith. Such a spectacle would inspire Movement members as well as the general public, so hoped Rubin. Indeed, Rubin and company were determined that this particular event would be both memorable and different from all previous demonstrations. What would be the point of such a massive gathering of humanity if all they were going to do was listen to boring speeches, and then march in silence with placards? If the Movement had come to Washington to protest the war, then it was time to aggressively "go after it" by directly assaulting the beating heart of the war machine—the Pentagon.[19]

Many Mobe leaders questioned Dellinger's judgment in appointing Rubin as the event's coordinator, rightly worrying that Rubin, Hoffman, and friends would turn the Pentagon march not only into a freak show but confrontation as well with law enforcement. As Jerry Rubin told reporters, the Yippies and their followers were "now in the business of wholesale disruption and widespread resistance and dislocation of American society."[20] Matters got even hairier a few days later when one of Hoffman's Yippie buddies, Keith Lampe, published an article in the *Mobilizer*, the Mobe's official publication, outlining the forthcoming agenda and activities once the protesters arrived in Washington. "On Making a Perfect Mess," promised zonked-out-of-the-head chaos for the nation's capital: "A thousand children will stage Loot-ins at department stores to strike at the property fetish that underlies genocidal wars.

Hey, who defoliated the White House lawns? Hey, who kidnapped the guard at the Tomb of the Unknown Soldier? During a block party in the front of the White House a lad of nine will climb the fence and piss, piss, piss."[21]

Although the peaceful march degenerated into bloody, civil disobedience, all while the Pentagon remained stubbornly earth-bound, the Yippies' zany antics succeeded in attracting sufficient numbers of hippies to the march, enough to prompt novelist Norman Mailer to write in his now-classic *Armies of the Night*, which was about his personal experiences and observations of the Pentagon March, that the hippies looked "like the legions of Sgt. Pepper's Band." To Mailer, the hippies in conjunction with all the other protesters seemed to be the composite of humanity "assembled from all the intersections between history and the comic books, between legend and television, the Biblical archetypes and the movies."[22] Mobe leaders had organized the demonstrators according to their respective affinity groups with the self-identified hippies designated with the letter F for "flower children." It was the hippies who picked flowers from the public gardens (many of which eventually ended up in the gun barrels of Army troops) and pretty much slept during all the political speeches while discussing all the "uptight" people at the Pentagon they would exhort to embrace peace by shouting "love" at the Pentagon windows. To counter the prospect of being sprayed by Mace, the hippies concocted their own defensive potion, which they called LACE (lysergic acid crypto ethylene), a purplish aphrodisiac brewed by none other than hippiedom's pharmacist Owsley. According to the hippies assembled LACE would "make you want to take off your clothes, kiss people, and make love." The hippie contingent also declared that they would assault the Pentagon "with noisemakers, water pistols, marbles, bubble-gum wrappers and bazookas," along with "sorcerers, swamis, priests, warlocks, rabbis, gurus, witches, alchemists, speed freaks, and other holy men."[23] Despite their obvious apolitical disinterest and continued ethereal devotion to their peace and love ethos, the presence of so many hippies delighted Yippie leaders; their plan to "potliticize" the hippies seemed to be working and such a transformation would hopefully take place in time for Chicago. Indeed as *Time* observed in the aftermath of the March on the Pentagon, "Unsophisticated pacifists or anti-draft outfits and digger do-gooders from the hippie subculture are frequently suckered into the hardline camp and end up unwittingly propagandizing as activists." For Jerry Rubin the March on the Pentagon made him feel as if he and his compatriots "were making history. We were at the center of action. Our lives were *relevant*." He was confident that along with the forthcoming Chicago demonstrations, the March on the Pentagon would help Americans "come to [their] senses and get out of Vietnam. We hadn't physically levitated the Pentagon, but we had spiritually levitated it. The government would have been smarter if they had just ignored us.... All the kids who were in high school at the time of the Pentagon demonstration watched it on TV and said 'I'm going to do that.' *We'd become role models*."[24]

However, the majority of hippies wanted nothing to do with the Yippies' zaniness or with their confrontational style, believing rightly that motivating Hoffman, Rubin and other Yippies to "take it to the streets" was their greater individual desire to be featured on the nightly news or to have their faces plastered on the cover of *Time* or *Newsweek*. What Hoffman and Rubin failed to realize was that the majority of hippies had chosen to be apolitical and were steadfastly determined to preserve that integrity. They had divorced themselves from all collective political and cultural activism and thus were not about to engage in any of the confrontational antics or marches or protests devised by either the Yippies or their New Left counterparts, who also showed up in Chicago in alliance with the Yippies in demonstrations against the Democrats' "death convention." In short, hippies distanced themselves as much as they possibly could from either radical group. The lion's share of hippies had long concluded that 1960s mainstream, hegemonic bourgeois American society and culture were beyond redemption; that's why they had dropped out in the first place, and thus no amount of showmanship or theatrics or other physical displays of cultural radicalism or exhortations to get involved was going to convince them to disavow their commitment.

Rubin, Hoffman, and their Yippie followers hoped to turn the 1968 Chicago Democratic Convention into the greatest countercultural protest spectacle to date, and in the process, so disrupt, discredit, and ultimately bring down the Democratic liberal establishment. To the Yippies, 1968 would thus be the climatic year, in which "all the energies of the youth culture" would coalesce at Chicago, and at the end of six days of youth inspired bedlam, the Age of Aquarius would begin its ascendancy. To *New York Times* journalist J. Anthony Lukas, Chicago was "the perfect city for the elemental clash."[25]

Lured by the promise of showcasing the nation's greatest rock bands, Hoffman and Rubin were confident that hundreds of thousands of long-haired, pot-smoking, cop-hating, peace freaks would stream into the Windy City. Once there the Dynamic Duo, would further politicize them into cultural revolutionaries who would then take to the city's streets their new consciousness, engaging in all manner of activities ranging from meaningful, legitimate demonstrations and protests against the war and the Johnson administration, to typical Yippie antics of the absurd and the outright crazy, all designed to "make clear there are two Amerikas."[26] Yippie leaders also hoped their theatrics would be sufficiently antagonistic to provoke the Establishment into confrontation. Mayor Richard Daley and the Chicago police were already paranoid and volatile, a disposition resulting from the riots than had ensued in Chicago's black ghettoes in the aftermath of Martin Luther King, Jr.'s assassination in early April 1968. Many counterculture critics suspected a police riot was *exactly* the Yippie objective from the outset, with the hope of plunging both Chicago and the convention into chaos. "We spent a year-and-a-half organizing for the Chicago demonstration," Rubin recalled, "and I think we saw them as a cataclysmic event that was going to be a historical trial of America in the streets."[27] Rubin was so confident of Yippie revolutionary prowess that he was certain that after Chicago there would be "Total instability, every day a minor revolution, wave upon wave of mass action, the break-up of institutions, a lot of friends in jail, angry, bloody demonstrations, fierce confrontations for power between right and left wing forces, mass disruption of high schools and colleges."[28]

Besides covertly planning activities and pranks guaranteed to incite the Chicago police, the Yippies' festival agenda also included other fun and games as well: rock concerts, poetry readings, workshops on LSD and draft resistance, films, marches, and light shows, all to be held in Chicago's two main city parks, Lincoln and Grant. Other high jinks called for "battalions of super-potent hippie males," dressed as bell-boys to "seduce female convention-goers," especially delegates' wives, while phony Yippie-manned taxis would pick up Democratic delegates at their hotels and drop them off miles away in Wisconsin. The Yippies also threatened to float 100,000 nude bodies in Lake Michigan during the day and at night burn draft cards in unison creating a bonfire that would spell BEAT ARMY. They would wear Vietcong pajamas and give out free rice in the streets. They told reporters they intended to take over the Chicago office of the National Biscuit Company and distribute bread and cookies to the masses. They labeled their flyers "secret" and then handed out New York Mets score-cards to journalists. Finally they circulated the rumor that they planned to spike the city's water supply with LSD. Unfortunately there is no public record, police or otherwise, of Abbie Hoffman's threat to pull down Vice President Hubert Humphrey's pants! The Yippies' plat-form advocated peace, freedom, free birth control and abortion, legalization of marijuana and psychedelics, police disarmament, and that "people should fuck all the time, anytime, whomever they wish," and that the government should abolish money and pay toilets. "Write your own slogan. Protest your own issues. Each man his own Yippie." The final demand blank: "you can fill in what you want."[29]

By the time the convention officially began at the city's International Amphitheater (next to the Union Stockyards) on Monday, August 25, 1968, only about 5,000 Yippie/New Left/politico activist out-of-town protesters were in Chicago and at no time during the week were there more than 10,000 total—not quite the hundreds of thousands Yippie leaders had proclaimed would be there ready to ignite the revolution. In truth, most of the demonstrators had no Yippie affiliation whatsoever, such as the hundreds of Chicago street kids—the "Park People" as the activist politicos called them—white and black juveniles (some as young as fourteen), who piled on when the action got hot and heavy. The Park People were "greasers," motorcycle toughs, and street-hardened working-class teenagers from some of the city's roughest, blue-collar ethnic neighborhoods; white kids but estranged from and even hostile toward the Yippies and the other "peacenik" demonstrators whom many greasers regarded as pampered, "pussy white boys" from suburbia. Indeed, many of these non-affinity toughs had as much contempt for the Yippies and hippies as they did for the cops. Nonetheless, the activists welcomed the Park People's participation in the protests and ensuing melees, believ-ing their presence was a sign that the Movement was at last attracting "the urban proletariat," which was delusional. The Park People's politics was mostly the politics of neighborhood; anyone who wanted to take their turf away or entered their "hood" unwanted or uninvited was in trouble. The Park People embraced their identity as juvenile delinquent freaks; a com-posite of the Beats, James Dean, and the Hell's Angels to whom the ideas of the New Left, of the Movement in general, were not only laughably irrelevant but far beyond their working-class ken. Nonetheless the Yippies and other activist groups romanticized the Park People as the emergence of the symbolic proletariat, who had joined with their intellectual/radical counterparts, much in the same way such individuals had joined the Bolsheviks in Petrograd and Moscow in 1917, to engage the cops/the czar's Cossacks, on the city's streets when they attacked the demonstrators. Interestingly, the majority of the protestors caught on the tele-vision cameras battling the police with all manner of projectiles—rocks, beer cans, balloons filled with urine and other human detritus—stopping cars, running through traffic, throwing up the barricades; busting police car windows with bricks and rocks; rocking police cars and paddy wagons and trying to overturn them, and even pounding on an isolated cop when they could, were the Park People. To be sure some of the Yippies and other affinity-groups such as the New York Motherfuckers joined in the fracas' but rarely, if ever led or initiated such action. Jerry Rubin became so enamored with the Park People that he hired a leather-vested biker named "Big Bob," to be his body-guard. Rubin was surely shocked when his "brother" showed up at his conspiracy trial to testify against him, for his romantic hero had been an undercover cop (Robert Pierson), one of hundreds who posed as street toughs or hippies in order to infiltrate the various radical groups. As participant, first-hand observer Todd Gitlin noted at the time "undercover cops could play greasers better than they could play Movement intellectuals." Indeed, for every six activists during the convention there was one undercover agent.[30]

Rubin and Hoffman had also promised to deliver a dozen famous rock bands for the festival, including the Beatles, the Rolling Stones, the Grateful Dead, the Jefferson Airplane and others. Only John Sinclair's MC5 showed up. Far more important was that Saturday, August 24, was to be the day when hundreds of thousands of the young protestors were supposed to arrive, at least according to previous Yippie declarations. However, as ex–SDS leader Tom Hayden, who had come to Chicago to participate in the "festivities," quickly surmised, "My God, there's nobody here!"[31] Indeed, it had become apparent that all the Yippie ballyhoo that their massive "do-in" would mark "the death of the Establishment," and that Chicago would "burn" in the process, was nothing more than typical Hoffman-Rubin bluster and bravado and posturing for the media. The majority of American youth, even if they opposed the war (the draft), and were disgusted by racism and despaired of the nation's other ills, were not about to come to the Windy City, throw up the barricades, and engage in urban guerrilla warfare with the Chicago police and the National Guard. They simply were not made of such "revolutionary stuff." They were, after all, the secure, well-educated sons and daughters of the most affluent citizens in the world, who quickly realized how much they had to lose. Consequently they decided that in the end, a bloody skull or fractured rib was not worth the cause or the crusade. Writing in the aftermath of the Chicago melee, music critic Robert Christgau opined that henceforth "almost all kids" would be "very chary of revolution. The reason is simple: Real revolutions are unpleasant, not groovy. You can get killed and everything. And so caution is more than justified, especially in the face of overwhelming odds.... All revolutions are unpleasant, but the ones you lose are really for shit."[32] Nonetheless, as columnist Mike Royko of the Chicago *Sun-Times* observed, "Never before had so many feared so much from so few."[33]

The highpoint of the Yippies' Festival of Life (Friday, August 23, three days before the convention officially began) was the nomination of a 145-pound black and white pig ("Pigasus") for president and running him on the slogan "They [the Democrats] nominate a president and he eats the people. We nominate a president and the people eat him." Naturally Rubin and Hoffman called a press conference for the announcement of their "nominee," which of course attracted several hundred people, including cops keen to suppress any trouble. *Washington Post* reporter Nicholas Von Hoffman caustically observed that showing up for the Yippie convention "were 600 newsmen, 300 cops, and 7 scraggly hippies and four old ladies on their way to a morning's shopping at Marshall Field's."[34] No sooner did the old station wagon carrying "Pigasus" open its door to let the animal out than the police caught the creature and threw him in the back of a paddy wagon. Meanwhile the Yippies had told reporters that they had telegrammed President Johnson asking for the same Secret Service protection for Pigasus that the other candidates received. Pigasus' new White House became the Chicago Humane Society while Rubin and four of his comrades were hauled off to police headquarters and would remain there until their $25 bonds had been posted, which they were by the next day. In a week that would become one of the most watched mayhems in post-war American history, a brief moment of levity occurred between the Yippies and the Chicago police. As Rubin and his compatriots were being "booked, one of the policemen came in and shouted out all our names and then said, 'You guys are all going to jail for the rest of your lives—the pig squealed on you.'"[35] Even though the Yippie put-on was over in minutes, Rubin, Hoffman, and comrades deemed their convention a success: they got the national media attention they wanted, mocked the presidential nominating process, and all while having the time of their lives.

Although much of what Rubin, Hoffman, and company proposed were nothing more than Marx Brothers–style pranks and high jinks, their intentions must not be taken lightly as there is no doubt that the Yippies had come to Chicago for the purpose of making a farce of one of the nation's most sacred rituals, and in the process, create enough bedlam to guarantee a violent response from city authorities. Former SDS president Carl Ogelsby believed confrontation was "unavoidable because the police wanted it, convinced it was time for a showdown. Mayor Daley wanted it, ready to show that his was the fist that ran Chicago. FBI director Hoover wanted it, tired of playing games with these crypto Commies.... And the media people smelled hot copy."[36] Perhaps the most important factor guaranteeing violence between the Chicago cops and the Yippies was that by 1968, "The Movement [had begun] to turn violent," according to Jerry Rubin, largely because "of boredom. I mean you're sitting in. 'Well, what else is new since you sat in last week? You're not on page one anymore, you're on page ten.' Okay then we'll block the dean's office.' So you get headlines for blocking the dean's office, but next week you don't get headlines for that, so now you have to blow up the dean's office at three A.M.... The Movement had to produce more and more stimulation for society out there to keep the Movement going."[37]

The Yippie plan from the beginning was to send the public's circuits into overload, which they knew would not be difficult. Mayor Richard Daley had already made it clear in April with his "shoot to kill order" against arsonists and "shoot to maim looters" during the Martin Luther King riots, that he would do the same to demonstrators if "they got out of hand." Indeed, on April 27, 1968, Daley made clear his position on protesters when he unleashed the city's police, who viciously clubbed and maced 6,500 peaceful fellow Chicagoan antiwar marchers, who were shocked by such a heavy-handed response to their placid vigil. Even many of the cops that day were taken aback by the order to "wade-in" on the crowd with their riot batons. "Each one of us was told that we had to make an arrest. I couldn't believe it. There was nobody bad there." By August Daley was even more loaded for bear relative to crushing any displays of lawlessness, no matter how small the transgression or "disturbance"; nobody was going to make a shambles of *his* convention, destroy *his* city, nor defile his reputation; the Democratic National Convention would come off without a hitch, come what may.[38]

To the Yippies' chagrin but to Daley's delight, black Chicagoans wanted nothing to do with the demonstrations, especially any affiliation with the Yippies and their antics. Indeed, black leaders such as Dick Gregory and Jesse Jackson, both of whom attended the convention, nonetheless urged black folk to stay away from the Windy City for that week. Both men "sensed" the trouble and violence that was coming to the city's streets. Jackson, who had had run-ins with the Chicago police, told Rennie Davis, "Probably Blacks shouldn't participate.... If Blacks got whipped nobody would pay attention. It would just be history. But if whites got whipped, it would make the newspapers."[39] Calvin Lockeridge, leader of the Black Consortium, an organization comprised of thirty-nine national and local African American associations, was even more direct in his message that the majority of black Americans considered both the convention and the protests as "a white folks' thing," and thus would not become involved.[40]

By the 1960s Richard Daley had become one of the most powerful Democratic politicos in the country; a "maker and breaker" of presidents (he had helped deliver the Oval Office to John Kennedy in 1960); the epitome of the old-time big-city boss of the late 19th and early 20th centuries. Indeed, Daley seemed to define the quintessence of American bossism and probably was the last of such a notorious breed of American politicians, who ruled their metropolitan fiefdoms with unlimited sovereignty for as long as they wanted. Indeed, according to *Time*, "he has ruled his province [Chicago] like a Chinese warlord.... Chicago is Mayor Richard Daley's satrapy." Yet, Daley had been "a creative autocrat, lacing his megalopolis with freeways and pulling in millions in federal spending.... His understanding of Chicago's muscles and nerves is deeply intuitive." Few, if any big-city mayors since his death have wielded such power, especially at the national level. "King Richard is one of the most assiduously courted Democratic politicians in the country." As Robert Kennedy observed, no doubt remembering how crucial Daley's support was for his brother's 1960 election victory, "'Dick Daley means the ball game.'"[41] Interestingly, by the time of the convention, Daley had lost enthusiasm for the war effort mainly because he believed the United States could not win. Nonetheless, Chicago was *his* town and like most white, working-class ethnic Americans (Daley was Irish Catholic), the mayor hated hippies, and had a "loathing for young white radicals." Daley reflected the complex feelings of many who joined the backlash of the late 1960s. Indeed, Daley knew that if push came to shove, the great mass of white Chicagoans who were flag-waving true-believers in the American way, would back him without hesitation, just as they had supported his "shoot to kill order" during the black riots in April.[42]

Even white adolescent Chicagoans shared the mayor's hostility toward Yippies/hippies. "They better not come here" a thirteen-year-old boy told a *New York Times* reporter, or "We'll get scissors and cut all their hair off." A ten-year-old was even more disdainful, declaring "We'll take their hippie chains and strangle them." A woman from Daley's neighborhood believed there would "be slaughter. Just slaughter on both sides. They better not come where they're not wanted." Another individual from the mayor's neighborhood was confident the police would be able to handle the demonstrators—"people who sympathize with the Communists"—and thus "most people will just sit on their porch and watch" the bloodbath about to unfold.[43]

Moreover, Daley relished his role as the arbiter of law and order, shrewdly putting his forces into place: 11,500 policemen, 5,600 Illinois National Guardsmen, 1,000 federal agents, and a reserve of 7,500 specially trained (in riot control) U.S. Army troops stationed at Fort Hood, Texas, which he could summon to Chicago on a moment's notice if he needed reinforcements. In effect, Daley had transformed Chicago into a police state and the Amphitheater into fortress America surrounded by a seven-foot barbed-wire fence with bullet-proof panels protecting the building entrance. Manhole covers outside were sealed with tar to stop possible saboteurs. Fifteen hundred policemen constantly patrolled the area around the building as well as the neighborhood. Sharp-shooters were stationed on nearby rooftops while others were in helicopters hovering overhead. Daley was prepared to meet protest with undisguised repression. The Amphitheater was too small to comfortably accommodate 6,511 delegates and alternates and was so close to the malodorous stockyards that attendees could be seen walking about with perpetually grimaced faces and flared nostrils of disgust. French playwright, novelist, and countercultural *provocateur* Jean Genet was in Chicago at the time of the convention and witnessed first- hand many of the bloody encounters between demon-strators and police. Legendary for his ironic prose, Genet had this to say about the Amphithe-ater and the Democratic convention. "What your television fails to bring you is the odor. No: the Odor, which may have a certain connection with order? The reason is that the Dem-ocratic Convention is being held right next to the stockyards and I keep asking myself whether the air is being befouled by the decomposition of Eisenhower or by the decomposition of all America."[44] Even Chicago's weather helped to contribute to the already heated relations between Daley and the demonstrators. According to Abe Peck, editor of the underground *Chicago Seed*, "It was one of those Summer Specials Chicago seems to import from Equatorial Africa, muggy enough to send the mosquitoes out on strike."[45]

Many in the mainstream media also questioned the Democrats' wisdom of having their nominating convention in a city filled with such tension and hostility toward the press, "out-side agitators," virtually anyone Richard Daley deemed a threat to the security and stability of *his* city, and whose views and policies the majority of white Chicagoans agreed with. Indeed, to Daley the popular press was as much of a threat to the "good people of Chicago" as the Yippies, and thus he made it clear to reporters that "We don't anticipate or expect [trouble] unless certain commentators and columnists cause trouble."[46] As NBC's Tom Brokaw observed at the time, "Mayor Daley had put the Chicago police department on full alert. Streets were cordoned off. Cops were on every corner, watching as long-haired kids carrying backpacks and shouting 'Peace now!' mingled with earnest middle-class couples who had come to show their solidarity with the antiwar movement. At first it was all relatively festive, a movable feast of political theatre ... in the heart of one of America's great cities. But the climate very quickly took an ugly turn."[47]

The thoroughness of Daley's security precautions caused many once enthusiastic radicals and antiwar people to have second thoughts about coming to Chicago. It had become clear that Daley's cops were going to bloody heads; there would be a massacre, for the police were poised to unleash their wrath on the demonstrators at the slightest provocation. Indeed, the cops would be looking for any excuse to unload their fury. The majority of the city's police force viewed all longhairs as the same, regardless of the affinity group to which that *hippie* belonged. To patrolman Len Colsky, "it was hard to distinguish the hippies from the criminals; they all looked the same. And the ones who were causing trouble and promising to do damage looked and dressed like hippies." As cop Ernie Bellows recalled, "I'm not sure how people think that we should have been able to tell these people apart; they didn't look any different, they didn't speak any different, dress any different, their signs said the same thing; they were trouble—we read about them, and they spoke of causing trouble in our city for the convention. Poisoning things, having sex on the streets, and hurting delegates." Former policeman Mel Latanzio agreed with his partners that there was "no distinguishing hippies, Yippies, Diggies [ers], SDSers, and all those radical groups.... I think they were pretending that they were different at times, but that was just a ploy because when they got on the street, they all behaved the same way." As far as the Chicago police were concerned, the once innocent "flower chil-dren" had metamorphosed into menacing, violent street thugs called Yippies, whose planned activities perplexed and disquieted the city's cops because "we didn't know what or where the hit was going to come from. We worried about the delegates, we worried about the infra-structure, the power, the water—we didn't know what was going to happen, and there was fear, all right, as silly as some of that fear may seem now." At the time there was no doubt in former cop Norm Nelson's mind that hippies had transformed into confrontational, dangerous Yippies, who, by 1968, if not earlier, had abandoned all pretense of flower power and peace. Such a disposition had always been a "myth" according to Nelson, with "war" coming to the nation's streets "from '67 on.... It was a battle, and they [the hippies] were showing their true colors in the weeks and months leading up to the convention in our city.... Let's put it this way, we were ready for those SOBs."[48]

Such an ominous portent prompted many counterculture leaders to urge the Yippies and other groups to call off their Festival of Life, which Abe Peck believed would become "a Festival of Blood, a Death Gala" for the protesters. As Peck reflected years later, "Obviously we'd been totally naïve to think we could pull off a peaceful counter-event in this environment." The *Seed* thus issued a special broadside, warning potential demonstrators, "If you're coming to Chicago be sure to wear some armor in your hair. Don't come to Chicago if you expect a five-day Festival of Life, music, and love. The word is out. Chicago may host a Festival of Blood."[49]

Even more disturbed by what would inevitably happen in Chicago, and disparaging of the two men he believed responsible for the bloodbath about to visit the 10,000 demonstrators—Jerry Rubin and Abbie Hoffman—was Jann Wenner, the twenty-one-year-old former UC Berkeley student who had just started *Rolling Stone* magazine in San Francisco a year earlier. By the time the magazine's first issue rolled off the press in November 1967, Wenner had become so thoroughly disillusioned with the nation's general political climate that he completely disassociated himself from both radical and mainstream politics, finding solace for his disenchantment in rock and roll music and thus the birth of *Rolling Stone*, which from the beginning Wenner wanted to be "professional-looking, with professional standards, and primarily about rock and roll." Wenner believed "both sides" (the Right and the Left) to be "bankrupt" and that the only "way out" was "rock 'n' roll, the *only* way in which the vast but formless power of youth is structured." Wenner had never been a New Leftist and thus his magazine rarely advocated demonstrations and never confrontation; *Rolling Stone* was a for-profit enterprise.[50]

In a no-holds-barred editorial titled "Musicians Reject New Political Exploiters," Wenner unleashed one of the most scathing indictments of the Yippie movement, especially of its leadership, Jerry Rubin and Abbie Hoffman, whom Wenner labeled as "'reckless, out-of-it media trippers'" and "'a self-appointed coterie of political "radicals" without a legitimate constituency.'" To Wenner the forthcoming Yippie Festival of Life in Chicago was "'as corrupt as the political machine it hopes to disrupt.'" Although at times hyperbolic and non-committal about the war, Wenner's editorial nonetheless reflected the ideas of the majority of the nation's young people: that the rock and roll music pouring out of stereos was what was changing youth culture; that politics of any stripe was by nature corrupt; that Leftist ideas were unrealistic and thus would never be realized; and that "'progressive violence'" was not "righteous" and thus no better than "'official violence.'"[51]

Wenner also asserted that the Chicago newspapers "'were so dumb'" to believe the Yippies represented "'some big movement'" when in reality, "there were only three Yippies"— Jerry Rubin, Abbie Hoffman, and Paul Krassner. Wenner correctly contended that the Yippies "'whole existence depended on the coverage they were getting. The only way they were going to get people to Chicago for the Convention was to claim it was a rock 'n' roll event," which, according to Wenner greatly angered many bands who told the publisher that "'We're not coming; someone's using our name without permission so we took the lead in calling the bullshit.'" In Wenner's view, Rubin and Hoffman acted "selfishly and recklessly" by encouraging "all these people to come thinking it was gonna be a Festival of Life, this harmless thing. I thought Abbie and Rubin's activities were extremely destructive, and I was right." Suffice it to say, neither Hoffman nor Rubin took kindly Wenner's indictment of their movement; Hoffman considered Jann Wenner to be "The Benedict Arnold of the sixties."[52]

Robert Christgau agreed with Wenner's assessment of "rock and revolution," reminding his readers that "musicians have never tried to be in the political vanguard—whatever their metaphorical proclivities, artists usually like peace and quiet as much as, if not more, than anyone else. The musicians never called for revolution in the first place, only certain of their fans." Sadly, thanks to the mainstream media, by 1968, the word "revolution," like everything else related to the counterculture, had evolved from simply being an idea bantered about among "humorless politniks to a hip password promulgated free ... and made more dangerous." The result: a "hype" that caused cultural radicals such as the Yippies to emerge and become a "movement infatuated with itself." Like Wenner, Christgau believed that "The political value of rock is a function of how many people it reaches" and if rock became "more political" it would "reach fewer people."[53]

Despite the warnings and admonishments of fellow counterculturists, Rubin and Hoffman were determined in their mission to make a mockery of everything Daley and the Democratic Party stood for even if it meant getting their heads bashed by crazed, free-wheeling Chicago cops. As Jerry Rubin confessed years later to Abe Peck, "We were not just innocent people who were victimized by the police. We came to plan a confrontation, to make Chicago a moral center of antiwar protest for the world. I wanted to embarrass America internationally because of what America was doing in Vietnam. I felt that America had to have on national TV a violent purge in which it came to terms with its own violence. It didn't understand dropping bombs on the Vietnamese because war is accepted violence. But somehow police beating up kids in the streets; hitting sixteen-year-olds over the head, now that was something guaranteed to get people's attention."[54] Daniel Walker, head of the commission which investigated the violence at the Chicago convention, agreed with Rubin because Rubin and Hoffman did an incredible job of convincing the FBI of "all of [their] wild hippie claims that they would parade naked girls on the beach to distract conventioneers ... that they would poison the water supply. All of those were taken as gospel ... although it was just great drama to Abbie Hoffman and Jerry Rubin. They wanted to drive the police up the wall and they succeeded."[55]

Rubin and Hoffman and their Yippie followers were not the only dissidents to descend on Chicago that summer. Radical leaders, like their Yippie counterparts, envisioned hundreds of thousands of angry citizens storming the convention hall to denounce the war and the renomination of Lyndon Johnson for president. However, by 1968, the Left had become a "many splendored/splintered thing" and thus those who came to Chicago represented a coalition of various New Left factions and émigrés, some of whom were as committed as the Yippies to provoking violence in order to advance their cause. Such were the sentiments of one of the coalition's leaders, ex–SDS president Tom Hayden who had long since abandoned his pacifist principles. As early as January 1968, Hayden had begun to agitate for the use of violence if and when necessary at forthcoming demonstrations. "We should have people organized who can fight the police, people who are willing to get arrested.... My thinking is not to leave the initiative to the police; don't want to get into the trap of violence vs. passive action."[56] Although factionalized, the New Left's primary issues remained the war and racism; that there must be purity at home first, that the United States must heal its own sick society before it can presume to treat others. To liberals such as Irving Howe, New Leftist rhetoric displayed "an unconsidered enmity toward something vaguely called the Establishment, an equally unreflective belief in the 'decline of the West,' and a crude, unqualified anti–Americanism drawn from every source." For Old Leftists, their new counterparts' protests were "mostly cries of rage" with no agenda for the future other than rejecting affluence, of having a mystical faith in the integrity and wisdom of the poor, and of condemning an American "foreign policy that is no more sophisticated than rape." In Daniel Bell's view, the New Left was "at best all heart" and "at worst it has no mind."[57]

Emboldening Richard Daley to use force if necessary against the same "subversive-criminal-hoodlums" whom F.B.I Director J. Edgar Hoover believed had made up the bulk of the Pentagon marchers, and were about to "infiltrate" Chicago, was the public support the Johnson administration received for their handling of the protesters from both the mainstream press and the general populace at the time of the March on the Pentagon. Even some of the allegedly more liberal publications such as the *New York Times*, were outright vicious in their condemnations of the demonstrators. Such was the view of James Reston, who blamed the confrontations that occurred on "the ugly and vulgar provocation of many of the militants." Also appalling Reston was the protesters' barrage of obscenities and insults leveled at the president, members of his cabinet, and of course at the various law enforcement agencies called out to protect "the sanctity of property"—the Pentagon. Reston of course lambasted the "theatrical performances put on by the hippies." It was apparent that despite increasing protests and escalating resistance and confrontation between Establishment authorities and activists, the popular press still supported the Johnson administration's policies in Vietnam and thus were unwilling to entertain the idea that perhaps what the marchers were questioning had any legitimacy whatsoever; that the United States might indeed be involved in an "obscene" foreign conflict that was costing billions of dollars while wasting the lives of so many young citizens, let alone countless numbers of the Vietnamese people. Rather, as Norman Mailer observed, the press focused on the minutia of "every rock thrown," and "of windows broken" of which "there were only a few."[58]

Daley hoped that if he refused to issue parade and camping permits to the various Mobe factions they would simply go home, for without permits their presence would be meaningless, for they would have no venues from which to launch their planned operations. Many radicals wondered why a citizen would need such permission while the United States government engaged in an illegal war, of having a "license to kill," without the people's consent. The ever-optimistic Mobe leader, David Dellinger, believed Daley would "reconsider his decision, that perhaps he will understand the best way to deal with a situation like this might be to accommodate it ... not defy it."[59] According to Tom Brokaw, "Some of the elders of the antiwar leadership such as David Dellinger had counseled the young people to protest with dignity, but that message was overwhelmed by the steadily rising tension between working-class Chicago cops and the younger demonstrators, most of who came from college campuses." However, as Brokaw also observed, constantly chiding and undermining Dellinger and others' attempts to maintain the peace were "the provocateurs such as the yippies, led by that cunning master of public theater, Abbie Hoffman, and his sidekick Jerry Rubin."[60] Indeed, initially neither SDS nor Mobe wanted to be associated with the "childish antics" promised by the "crazies" and the "freaks" that Hoffman and Rubin were bringing to Chicago, yet, at the same time, Dellinger suspected that neither Tom Hayden nor his comrade Rennie Davis were earnest about keeping the protests "nonviolent and legal"; that both SDS'ers had already "gone to the dark side" of endorsing the Yippie plan for provoking confrontation. No doubt Tom Hayden's statement to the press in which he announced that "'We are coming to Chicago to vomit on the politics of joy, to expose the secret decisions, upset the nightclub orgies, and face the Democratic Party with its illegitimacy and criminality," greatly alarmed pacifists such as Dellinger.[61] Tragically, Dellinger's and others' entreaties to Daley fell on deaf ears. The mayor's refusal to grant permits and subsequent brutal suppression of peaceful protesters forced SDS, Mobe, and other peace factions to embrace the resistance position of the crazy Yippies and the other advocates of fighting back. Consequently, many liberals agreed with Eugene McCarthy aide Allard Lowenstein, who concluded that Daley and his Chicago police "seem determined to have a confrontation that can only produce violence and bloodshed."[62]

What Daley failed to reckon with was that although only 10,000 protesters had shown up in Chicago, of that number, a good percentage, in proportion to the total number, were ready, willing, and able to engage his police force in open street fighting; that they would not "turn tail" and run. As Abbie Hoffman declared, "we knew the bravest of our generation would answer the call.... This is the United States 1968.... If you are afraid of violence you shouldn't have crossed the border."[63] Other affinity groups hoped to keep the festival peaceful and "life affirming." Todd Gitlin knew that once the police "bared their teeth" there would be no stopping the confrontations because the hardcore Yippies and the Park People were just as determined as the cops for a clash. "Part of the New Left wanted a riot, then, but the street-fighters could not by themselves have brought it about. For that they needed the police."[64] Moreover, unlike previous demonstrations in which the male-female ratio was usually about fifty-fifty, in Chicago men out-numbered women in the street actions by eight or ten to one, thus increasing the likelihood of violent confrontations between the police and protesters as male *enrages* were more likely to clash with the police in street fighting than their female counterparts. By the time of the convention's first night, Mobe leaders and their Yippie allies together with city officials had set the stage for the play that was about to unfold called "The Battle of Chicago." However, the playwrights were no longer Jerry Rubin and Abbie Hoffman, or even Tom Hayden or Rennie Davis; Mayor Richard Daley was now writing the script.[65]

What exploded in Chicago the week of August 25–30 was the climax of unrelenting socio-cultural and political pressures that had been accelerating in intensity for almost the entire decade: the unraveling of the liberal consensus, the increasing hostility and oppression by authorities, especially of African Americans and the counterculture, the resolve and recklessness of the counterculture and the New Left, the increasing polarization caused by the Vietnam War, and largely the result of the war's divisiveness, the demise of the Democratic party as the progenitor and bastion of positive government. At Chicago these dynamics coalesced in a cauldron of fury, rage, and wanton violence of citizen upon citizen, the likes of which had yet to be seen on American city streets. Most devastating to the nation's image, television cameras captured every melee "live and in living color," for the whole world to watch. From that week on, all of the decade's hopes and fears became actual and real. The Movement splintered into several factions, with some emerging more committed than ever to violent revolution; the Right emerged determined to bring about a counterrevolution of repression, and liberals continued their slide into persona non grata with the American electorate, who saw them as being unable to control the excesses of the welfare state they had brought about, let alone govern the nation. The "Days of Rage" eliminated the last vestiges of hope that the counterculture and the mainstream could somehow work out a rapprochement and find a way to accept each other's presence as part of an ever-evolving, pluralistic society and culture and peacefully co-exist in the same nation as had previous antithetical groups of Americans. Sadly, after Chicago, their antagonisms would play themselves out to a bitter end with the counterculture ultimately disappearing into the historical woodwork. Over four decades later, the polarizations of the 1960s continue, at a variety of levels, to affect the American socio-cultural consciousness, which in turn reverberates through the nation's politics.

Trouble began as early as Sunday, August 25, the eve of the convention, when about 1,000 Yippies refused to leave Lincoln Park where they had been denied a camping permit. When the 11:00 p.m. curfew passed, the cops arrived and ordered them to leave. The Yippies refused and many started taunting the police, chanting "Pig, pig, fascist pig," and "Pigs eat shit!" After a few such choruses, the cops, who came dressed in street battle/riot gear, did not hesitate to unleash their fury, first launching tear gas and then charging into the park, unloading their clubs on every "hippie" they came across, even chasing them through the streets, clubbing them as they fled the park. The cops not only chased the kids through the streets of Old Town, Chicago's hip neighborhood, but along the way, whacked virtually anyone in the area they came across, including innocent, straight bystanders, people going to dinner, and two dozen reporters and cameramen. To John Schultz, the beating frenzy was "mass cop violence of unmitigated fury.... No status or manner of appearance or attitude made one less likely to be clubbed.... A few upper middleclass white men said they now had some idea of what it meant to be on the other end of the law in the ghetto."[66] A medical student from Northwestern University, serving as a "demonstration medic," told the Walker commission that when a protester fell, "three or four cops would start beating them. One kid was beaten so badly he couldn't get up. He was bleeding profusely from the head."[67] As journalist Nicholas Von Hoffman of the *Washington Post* remembered, the police had "taken off their badges, their nameplates, even the unit patches on their shoulders to become a mob of identical, unidentifiable club swingers." As Von Hoffman's sponsoring newspaper wrote at the time, "The Chicago police force understands very little about civil liberties and apparently cares even less."[68] The battle at Lincoln Park continued sporadically and violently for the next two nights.

At the same time, at Grant Park, across the street from the downtown Conrad Hilton Hotel where the delegates stayed, Movement faithful gathered every night and chanted "Fuck you, LBJ," "Dump the Hump" (Vice President Hubert H. Humphrey, the Democratic heir apparent who had LBJ's support), "Sieg Heil," and "Disarm the Pigs." Cadres of Mobe and even Yippie leaders, including Rubin and Hoffman, tried to get the agitators to disengage but to no avail as the Park People greeted them with "Fuck the marshals!" and "Marshals are pigs!" About the only people who paid attention to the peaceniks were the cops who clubbed them out of action. The name-calling and insults naturally brought out the police and minor confrontations occurred but they would all pale in comparison to the blood-letting that occurred on Wednesday evening, August 28, when the week's most vicious, out-of-control struggles ravaged the city.[69]

Wednesday evening, August 28, the convention was to nominate the Democratic candidate for president. Earlier that day party regulars had voted down a peace platform (1567 to 1041) that had been put forth by the Eugene McCarthy—Robert Kennedy supporters. Apparently the delegates remained unaffected by the fact that 80 percent of the primary voters had voted for antiwar candidates. With Johnson, Dailey and other behind-the-scenes operators pulling the convention strings, and with party hacks overrepresented, it was a foregone conclusion Hubert Humphrey would be nominated that evening. While delegates voted down the peace plank, Eugene McCarthy was telling an African American audience in the city's South Side that powerful party bosses such as the Mayor of Chicago, made it impossible for individuals like himself to challenge incumbents. His party was "afraid to change the system. We tried to change it and whether we changed it or not we gave it one or two shakes and kept it alive." McCarthy then told the crowd that if his party chose Humphrey as their standard-bearer to run against Republican nominee Richard Nixon, Americans will be choosing "between two echoes."[70]

In fairness to Humphrey, let it be said he had tried mightily for days to work out a compromise that would placate both the McCarthy-Kennedy (both Bobby and his brother Ted, who had taken up his fallen brother's mantle) peace faction and the president and his advisor's (most notably the hard-line position of his national security advisor, Walt Rostow, who had replaced Robert McNamara as LBJ's most trusted confidant relative to the war), more hawkish position. Unfortunately, the president's militant policy prevailed. As LBJ told a doleful Humphrey, the vice president's peace agenda "just undercuts our whole policy and by God, the Democratic party ought not to be doing that to me." Rather than incur LBJ's ire and thus lose the nomination, Humphrey relented, although years later he regretted his capitulation: "I should have stood my ground."[71] During the three hour debate over Vietnam, Congressmen Wayne Hayes of Ohio accused the peace advocates of pandering to the antiwar demonstrators; that they were substituting "beards for brains, license for liberty, pot [for] patriotism, sideburns [for] solutions, [and] riots for reason."[72] When the tally ended, McCarthy delegates tied black bands around their arms, and led by folksinger Theodore Bikel, New York delegates sang, "We Shall Overcome."[73]

Outside the convention hall 10,000 antiwar protesters assembled at Grant Park for the only peace rally Daley had approved. No sooner had the demonstrators gathered at the park's band shell than a hundred cops marched up in formation and within a matter of minutes, skirmishes between the protesters and the police quickly turned the peace rally into a battlefield. Suddenly everyone noticed that a youngster had climbed the flagpole near the band shell and began lowering the American flag. The police immediately swooped in clubbing and arrested the boy. A group of men stepped out of the crowd, finished taking down Old Glory, and raised some kind of red cloth in its place. CBS later reported that some 200 undercover agents were in the crowd, and at least one of them was part of the group who took down the flag. Mobe and Yippie leaders were convinced that the whole flag episode, sans the original young man who had climbed the pole, was the work of agent provocateurs, for no sooner did the red cloth go up the pole than the police formed a wedge and charged. Some reports, however, had the protesters initiating the ensuing bedlam, screaming "Pigs, Pigs, Kill the Pigs!" while pelting the cops with everything from eggs and chunks of concrete to balloons filled with paint and urine when they came to arrest the flag pole climber. The police responded with billy clubs, mace, and tear gas. As the police charged loaded for bear, Rennie Davis intervened between the two groups trying to cool things down but it was too late for such a gesture and the cops clubbed him senseless. All the while the chanting continued: "Pigs are whores"; "Pigs eat shit!" and so did the police attacks on the crowd. As the protesters tried to find a safe exit out of the park, a shaken but enraged Tom Hayden, who had just finished giving aid to an unconscious, bloody-faced Rennie Davis, grabbed the microphone and shouted, "The city and the military machinery it has aimed at us won't permit us to protest in an organized fashion. Therefore, we must move out of this park in groups throughout the city, and turn this overheated military machine against itself. Let us make sure if blood flows, it flows all over the city. If they use gas against us, let us make sure they use gas against their own citizens." Allen Ginsberg, ever the devoted peacenik, tried to calm the crowd by exhorting them to chant "OM," which he declared would "quell the fluttering of butterflies in the belly." As the *New York Times* reported, as the astonished policemen peered through their Plexiglas face shields, "the huge crowd chanted 'om, om,' sending deep mystic reverberations off the glass office towers along Michigan Avenue."[74]

Even greater violence and carnage occurred near Grant Park at the Conrad Hilton Hotel, where the McCarthy, Kennedy, and George McGovern people had their headquarters. As the nomination process began inside the Amphitheater, thousands of angry protesters who had assembled in front of the Hilton were viciously attacked by the police backed up by 600 Illinois National Guardsmen. They scythed into the crowd, smashing heads, limbs, and crotches, beating people and spraying mace indiscriminately: bystanders, demonstrators, medics, reporters, and photographers, all became targets. They exploded with rage to provocations such as "Fuck the pigs"; "Who's fucking your wife this afternoon, pig;?" "Mother Fuckers"; "Shit-heads"; "Ho Ho Ho Chi Minh," and "Pig, pig, oink, sooo-ee." All the while the cops could be heard yelling "Kill, kill, kill," "Get the Bastards," and "Kill the commies." The police pressed the trapped crowd so hard that the window of the Haymarket Lounge of the Hilton Hotel shattered and people were shoved through, many of them cut badly by the glass, only to be chased inside the hotel lobby and then clubbed and battered again by police screaming, "Get out of here you cocksuckers."[75] Looking down on the street violence from his 15th floor campaign suite, Eugene McCarthy likened the scene to something out of Nazi Germany when Hitler would send such goon squads through certain anti–Nazi neighborhoods inflicting terror and brutality on anyone they came across. To Daley's "storm troopers" the protesters were hippies gone wild. "It was scary to get close to these kids," one cop remarked after, "their faces were flushed; their eyes were glassy. They looked at you but it was if they were looking right through you—and up close you could smell the dope on them."[76] Surprisingly, not all the cops reveled in the blood-lust or in the brutality and pain they inflicted. Years later, a Chicago cop involved in the street battles told Abe Peck how he and many other cops viewed "The Battle of Michigan Avenue." "Each one of us was told that we had to make an arrest. I couldn't believe it. There was nobody bad there. When things got really heavy, I grabbed this shrimpy little kid from the U of C [University of Chicago]. He started to yell, but I yelled louder, right in his ear: 'Don't worry, I won't come to court.' Some of the coppers were tossing people *up* into the squadrols [trucks] so their heads banged off the door lintels. I managed to get my kid in without him getting smashed. Fuck, *I* got hit on the shoulder. I quit pretty soon after that. That was it for me."[77] Sadly few cops shared such remorse. According to Terry Southern, the overwhelming majority of police mercilessly beat even those demonstrators who did not resist arrest or who voluntarily surrendered. All were eventually taken into custody but not after "they [the cops] beat the hell out of them with nightsticks or the butts of shotguns. They clubbed them until they got up and ran, or until they started crawling away (the ones who were able) and then they continued to hit them as long as they could with what was obviously mounting fury. And this was a phenomenon we were to observe consistently throughout the days of violence; that rage seemed to engender rage; the bloodier and the more brutal the cops were, the more their fury increased."[78]

McCarthy aide Jeremy Larner was aghast at what he witnessed from the hotel's 15th floor. "It was worse than anything I later saw on television.... A man tried to carry a bleeding woman into the hotel and they were both clubbed and thrown into the wagon. People ran up to plead with cops beating kids on the ground and the cops turned around and clubbed them. They clubbed men in white who knelt to carry off the fallen and clubbed anyone with a camera on his neck.... Very few were fighting back; I saw none with weapons. What I saw was blue helmets surging forward in waves, clubbing and clubbing, and clubbing. You could hear the sodden *thuck* of the club on skull clear up to the 15th floor."[79]

Time's Lance Morrow, who was a twenty-eight-year-old reporter for the magazine at that moment, agreed with Southern about the cops' fury, contending that often intensifying the cops' pummeling frenzies were "unarticulated class antagonisms"; the majority of the protesters were college kids from affluent homes while the majority of the police were from the city's or surrounding area's blue-collar and ethnic neighborhoods. "The adrenaline of that difference gave the clubs more force when the cops at last cut loose and went after the kids' ribs and skulls." Regardless of location, when the cops attacked, they did so "with surprising speed, nimble fury, and methodical ferocity." Most disturbing to Morrow and many other eye-witnesses, was the impression that these "blue rhinos" of "immovable heft" displayed "a certain professional satisfaction of the kind a hitter feels sometimes" when they found the "ghastly sweet spots" for their riot batons when they cracked a protester's skull. When Morrow saw or heard "the thunk" of their clubs on "a human skull—in earnest—it awakens in the hearer a sickened, fearful amazement."[80]

The melee spilled into the surrounding streets for hours but it was the beating frenzy that took place in front of the Hilton that shocked the nation for it was concentrated and took place under the TV lights, seventeen minutes *live* with the crowd chanting "The whole world is watching." The world was indeed watching, or at least an estimated 89 million horrified Americans. They saw CBS News reporter Mike Wallace get punched in the face and twenty other reporters assaulted. NBC news commentator, the venerable Chet Huntley, declared to his viewers that the "news profession in this city [Chicago] is now under assault by the Chicago police." Those who did not watch the bedlam on their televisions read in the newspapers that even "elderly bystanders were caught in the onslaught." "Some tried to surrender by putting their hands on their heads," wrote a journalist, "but as they marched to vans to be arrested, they were rapped in the genitals by the cops swinging billies." As the crowd scattered down side streets with police in pursuit, the journalist Theodore White scribbled in his notebook, "The Democrats are finished."[81]

The television networks repeatedly showed out-of-control cops charging protesters without any tangible provocation, other than the name-calling. NBC news put together a particularly chilling montage juxtaposing the violent Chicago police actions with Soviet tanks rolling into Prague putting down the peaceful democratic government of Alexander Dubcek.

Other images showed a smiling Richard Daley on the convention floor juxtaposed against Chicago cops clubbing young protesters, giving viewers the impression that Daley relished the "law and order" his cops were meting out to "commies and anarchists." *Newsweek* reported that the police "went on a sustained rampage unprecedented outside the most unreconstructed boondocks of Dixie." *Time* echoed a similar assessment, asserting that the Chicago police caused "sanctioned mayhem," blatantly contravening "every acceptable code of professional police discipline," while violating "the civil rights of countless innocent citizens.... Ironically—and perhaps significantly—the demonstrators' most effective allies were the police, without whose brutal aid the protest would not have been so striking." The mainstream media, both print and television, sided with the protesters, depicting them as young, courageous idealists, as "our children" who had come to Chicago to engage in peaceful, democratic protest "as is their Constitutional right, free from any sort of suppression of that guaranteed liberty." Tom Wicker of the *New York Times* wrote that "these were our children in the streets and the Chicago police beat them up." Violence even occurred inside the convention hall over the issues of race and war, as Southern black and white delegates engaged in fisticuffs on more than one occasion, and in one particular confrontation CBS news reporter Dan Rather was slugged and knocked to the floor by a policeman serving in a security capacity as he tried to break-up a potential fight between two delegates. An astonished CBS anchorman Walter Cronkite labeled Daley's police "a bunch of thugs."[82]

Throughout convention week, the Chicago police not only made the hippies and Yippies their targets, but were equally keen on attacking the press corps, who Daley and the police blamed "for attracting the yippies and giving them publicity." Whether it was print journalists, television news people, reporters, photographers, or cameramen, all became fair game for the cops and their rage. Indeed, on the convention's first night, "some 20 newsmen were beaten up and three hospitalized." The media not only blamed Daley for such oppression and attempted censorship—"the chief villain"—but also the power-brokers of the Democratic Party, who, according to David Brinkley, "did not want reported what was happening." Daley of course justified his heavy-handedness by declaring that "If the police ask a newsman and a photographer to move, they should move as well as anyone else." It was obvious to columnist Max Lerner that Daley's attempt to suppress the media reflected not only the mayor's "unflinching resolve" not "to show what America is really like," but those as well within the Democratic Party who shared Daley's mentality.[83]

Conditions inside the convention hall were not much better. Delegates were stunned when they saw the violent images on various television screens of the bloody mayhem taking place outside. Connecticut peace senator Abraham Ribicoff took the podium in an attempt to trump the pro-war plank LBJ had railroaded through with Hubert Humphrey's approval, which secured for Humphrey a first-ballot nomination. Humphrey's ordination prompted Jean Genet to wonder "in what drunken bar did a handful of democrats make their decision?"[84] After denouncing the party's pro-war platform, Ribicoff then tried to nominate fellow dove Senator George McGovern of South Dakota, who, along with Ribicoff, had been Bobby Kennedy supporters. As he spoke of McGovern's credentials, Ribicoff, who despised old bosses like Daley and was greatly disturbed by the police violence against the demonstrators outside, decided to take Daley to task for his vicious suppression. Staring directly at the mayor, Ribicoff exclaimed "With George McGovern we wouldn't have Gestapo tactics on the streets of Chicago." Infuriated Illinois delegates jumped out of their seats and started waving their fists and shouting angrily, many swearing at Ribicoff for his remark. However, no Illinoisian was as apoplectic with rage as Daley who shouted back with words that could not be heard because of the bedlam but were lip-read by many in the national television audience: "Fuck you, you Jew son of a bitch, you lousy motherfucker, go home." Ribicoff replied with a smile, "How hard it is to accept the truth. How hard it is."[85] The Ribicoff-Daley exchange along with all the other fracases that took place in the convention hall, including the defeat of the peace platform and Humphrey's contrived "slam-dunk" first ballot nomination, caused a dispirited Allard Lowenstein to lament that "this convention just elected Richard Nixon President of the United States."[86] Veteran newsman Eric Sevareid called what was taking place inside the convention and outside on Chicago's streets "the most disgraceful spectacle in the history of American politics."[87] After witnessing the bloody furor, Jean Genet concluded that "it would be good, for America and for the world, for it [the United States] to be demolished, for it [the US] to be reduced to powder."[88]

Lance Morrow of *Time* cogently summed up the extreme polarizations he saw come to the fore in Chicago. "In front of the Hilton, on Michigan Avenue, two sides of America ground against each other like tectonic plates. Each side cartooned and ridiculed the other so brutally that by now the two seemed to belong to two different species. The 60s had a genius for excess and caricature, on one side the love-it-or-leave it proud Middle American. On the other side, the countercultural young, either flower children or revolutionaries, and their fellow-traveling adult allies in the antiwar movement, the Eugene McCarthy uprising against the LBJ people whose hatred of the war in Vietnam led them into ever greater alienation from society and its figures of authority."[89]

All during the shocking confrontations the Johnson-Humphrey forces remained unrepentant. Senator Edmund Muskie of Maine, chosen to be Humphrey's vice presidential running mate, publicly defended Daley and his police force. The mayor, he said, had done nothing wrong: "The obscenity [of the demonstrators], the profanity, the filth that was uttered night after night in front of hotels was an insult to every woman, every daughter, indeed, every human being.... You'd put anybody in jail for that kind of talk.... Is it any wonder that the police had to take action?"[90] Nominee Hubert Humphrey was equally oblivious and oblique in his post-convention assessment of what had caused the riots, and like Muskie, defended Daley's and the cops' actions, focusing not on what motivated the protesters to come to Chicago in the first place—the war—but rather obsessing on their foul language, which perhaps to the Old Guard was symptomatic of their alleged general moral dissipation; as if crude name-calling of government officials and their policies were enough to justify such brutal reprisals. It seemed that both Muskie and Humphrey had momentarily forgotten about the Bill of Rights. "Goodness me, anybody who sees this sort of thing is sick at heart and I was. But I think the blame ought to be put where it belongs. I think we ought to quit pretending that Mayor Daley did anything wrong. He didn't.... I know what caused these demonstrations. They were planned, premeditated by certain people in this country that feel all they have to do is riot and they'll get their way."[91]

Many Americans did wonder, believing Daley's fears that the Yippies and Mobe represented the majority sentiment of American youth toward established authority, were way overblown, especially given the activists' modest numbers at Chicago. The mayor made a dreadful error in judgment by ordering curfews and refusing to grant permits to the protestors to sleep in the city's parks. Many asked, what harm would have been caused by a few thousand kids sleeping in a public park? Daley could have been more generous in setting guidelines for marches and demonstrations. By taking such a hard line on these issues, Daley only fueled the dissidents' already passionate resentment toward Establishment authoritarianism thus their casus belli. Daley could surely have restrained his police. Instead, he encouraged them to run amok. Indeed, Attorney General Ramsey Clark believed "that crowds of [demonstrators] can be controlled without denying rights of speech and assembly. Above all such crowds can be controlled without excessive force and violence by police. Of all violence, police violence in excess of authority is the most dangerous." Democratic Illinois State Treasurer Adlai Stevenson III, agreed with Clark, that the bloody nightmare Chicago became could have been avoided had the "Doors to legitimate dissent and peaceable assembly" been open to the demonstrators. According to Stevenson, the protesters should "have been welcomed to Chicago—the parks opened, the parade routes and television coverage arranged." If Daley had wisely made those gestures, Stevenson was certain "the agitators would have had no reason to provoke disorder." By "clubbing them" the "system became their unwitting ally." One Johnson administration official was more direct in his assessment of what caused the Chicago disaster: "Daley went crazy."[92]

In "going crazy" Daley played into the hands of Hoffman, Rubin, and the other radical activists. As *Time* opined in Chicago's aftermath, "They [the Yippies and their New Left allies] left Chicago more as victors than as victims." Even though "they stood no chance of influencing the political outcome or reforming 'the system,'" they nonetheless succeeded in "irritating the police and the party bosses so intensely that their reactions would look like those of mindless brutes and skull busters. After all the blood, sweat, and tear gas, the dissidents had pretty well succeeded in doing just that." Jerry Rubin agreed, years later confessing that, "We wanted exactly what happened. We wanted the tear gas to get so heavy that the reality was tear gas. We wanted to create a situation in which the Daley administration and the Chicago police and the federal government of the United States would self-destruct. We wanted to show that America wasn't a democracy, that the convention wasn't politics. The message of the week was of an America ruled by force. This was a big victory."[93] Despite the bloodshed, Jean Genet believed Chicago had been a "Fabulous happening"; that "At long last America is moving because the hippies have shaken their shoulders"; and that those who participated, "the Hippies! Glorious Hippies," should continue their struggle "to fuck all the old bastards who are giving you a hard time." However, if the hippies were going to "win" their war against "all the old bastards" they must remain united and steadfast in their commitment to bring about the new consciousness. "I address my final appeal to you: children, flower children in every country, unite, go underground if necessary in order to join the burned children of Vietnam."[94]

The blue ribbon commission that later investigated the causes of "The Battle of Chicago," the Walker Commission (headed by progressive corporate lawyer, Daniel Walker, general counsel for the retail giant, Montgomery Ward), compiled volumes of information from thousands of eyewitnesses (3,437), along with 180 hours of relevant film taken by the major networks and local television stations, all of which confirmed the commission's conclusion that what happened in Chicago during the week of August 25–29 was a "police riot"; that "There is no question that many officers acted without restraint and exerted force beyond that necessary under the circumstances." Many witnesses also noted that if a "hippie" the cops were chasing got away, they "would simply club whoever else was handy." Particularly out of control were the cops in front of the Conrad Hilton Hotel, who went "berserk," and whom the deputy superintendent in charge had to pull off of pummeled and bloodied demonstrators, shouting at the cops to "Stop, damn it, stop! For Christ's sake, stop it!" The Walker Report also criticized the police for venting their rage at the press corps, who contended that the cops intentionally attacked them, destroying their equipment in the process and thus preventing their coverage of the brutality. However, the report did rebuke the protesters for provoking *individual* cops "to get out of line" with their incessant verbal harassment and their chanting of such threatening and nasty taunts as "Kill the pigs" and "Your wife sucks cock" and other such phrases. However, the myth lives on within Right wing circles that the cops, besieged by bags of urine and excrement, and by the offensive, menacing vile language (which they presumably had never heard before), acted with justification. As far as the use of foul language, the cops gave as good as they got: "You'd better get your fucking ass off that grass or I'll put a beautiful goddamn crease in your fucking queer head"; "Move, I said, move god dammit! Move you bastards!"; "Get the hell out of here; Get the fuck out of here; Move your fucking ass!" To expect a Chicago cop, many of whom came from some of the roughest working class/ethnic neighborhoods in the city, to refrain from the use of obscenities when "doing their job," is naïve if not delusional thinking. Nonetheless, as many subsequent books on the Chicago fiasco have revealed in a number of crucial instances it wasn't a matter of wanton individual cops unloading on the demonstrators and innocent bystanders; the Walker Report provided ample evidence that in most of their confrontations with the protesters, the cops had been *ordered* to assault the crowds.[95]

Despite the cracked and bloodied skulls, battered and bruised bodies, and 668 arrests, the Left remained sanguine that their cause would go on and in fact, claimed Chicago to have been a success. Indeed, Rennie Davis prophesied that "there'll be Chicagos everywhere the candidates go. People will be out to challenge and confront them."[96] After the Battle of Michigan Avenue, the Yippies were particularly buoyant because they believed that they had accomplished their number one objective: that from Chicago forward, television screens across the nation would beam shocking physical and emotional violence into white, affluent, middle-class suburban homes, bombarding such individuals with daily reminders of the fragility of civil order and the potential for violence lurking beneath the United States' democratic ideals. The Battle of Michigan Avenue had helped the Yippies to "turn on" America, or as Yippie Stew Albert more profanely but succinctly declared, Chicago was "a revolutionary wet dream come true."[97]

To the dismay of many liberals and certainly to those young folk who marched and battled the cops in Chicago, subsequent polls revealed that the majority of the American people defended the riotous behavior of the Chicago police under the circumstances. Indeed, the Johnson White House received a flood of letters from citizens defending Daley, the Chicago police, and telling the president that the Yippies got what they deserved. Many white Americans believed the Yippies to have been "traitors" for flying the Viet Cong flag and for demanding the repeal of drug laws and the draft. Such were the sentiments of Walker Paine of Texas who told LBJ that he "should give the policeman [sic] the power to kick the teeth out of the Hippies." Romney S. Philpott of Oklahoma agreed with Paine, asserting that the demonstrators' actions warranted the beating the cops gave them. "Please say that those who fly the Viet Cong flag are traitors and deserve much worse than a rap with a policeman's stick. Please explain that the police were protecting the lives of all the delegates, even those silly asses who complained about 'Police State' [sic]." A Mrs. C.R. Gardner perhaps best reflected many white, particularly working-class/middle class Americans' indignation at what took place in Chicago while professing an unflinching patriotism. "I'm an American. I love my country and I respect my flag. I work hard for my money. I pay taxes on my salary. I resent these few persons being made [by the media] the misfortunate, misunderstood peoples with a cause. The only cause they have is to divide and disrupt the peace of this nation. How dare they upset the order of a city! How dare any public official condone that disruption!"[98]

Such reactions came as a particular shock to the dean of the Establishment press, CBS' Walter Cronkite, when the network received a torrent of letters revealing that the senders, 11 to 1 supported the police. *The New York Times* admitted a similar overwhelming support for the police in their polls. As one Chicagoan opined, "If other mayors followed Daley's action then we'd have a much better society." Far-right independent candidate for president in 1968, the legendary governor of Alabama George Wallace, declared that the Chicago police "probably showed too much restraint." Many of Wallace's fellow state stewards shared similar views, such as New Mexico Republican governor David Fargo who advocated expelling all freaks from the Land of Enchantment, while his conservative Democratic counterpart, Buford Ellington of Tennessee declared "It is war. We want every longhair in jail or out of the state."[99]

Like so many events in 1968, Chicago further polarized an already bitterly divided American people while obliterating the political center in the process. Activists and students felt betrayed by both the liberal establishment and the Democratic Party, now considering both to be part of a corrupt machine of war and racism. Increasing numbers of youth became so alienated in Chicago's aftermath that they believed that democracy was a sham and that the United States government had become an illegitimate entity led by "war criminals" and sustained and protected by "pigs." Many young people believed the nation had become a Steppenwolf, an enraged monster, a cruel society that murdered peasants abroad while using brute force at home on its own citizens because they dared to be different—the hippies—or were unwilling to accept the status quo—minorities and dissidents. Interestingly, actual hippie participation in the Chicago protests was virtually non-existent compared to their numbers at the October March on the Pentagon. But thanks to the Yippies' clever press manipulation and hippie garb costuming, mainstream Americans, having already lumped the general counterculture into one easily identifiable package called hippies, were convinced that the hippies had finally shown their true colors: from their inception on the streets of the Haight-Ashbury two years earlier, their *raison d'être* had been to subvert the American way of life, with violence if necessary; from the beginning their peace and love ethos had been a ruse contrived to win followers and dupe Americans into believing that they were sincere in their quest to bring about a new consciousness of humanity and the brotherhood of all mankind. They believed Chicago revealed that the hippies were actually violent revolutionaries determined to overthrow the American government. This, of course, could not have been further from the truth, although unfortunately, the Chicago "days of rage" cemented that impression in the minds of the majority of straight Americans. The overwhelming majority of hippies had distanced themselves from the politicos long before Chicago, and many in the aftermath continued their disassociation publicly, but still, in the facile minds of Middle Americans they remained guilty by alleged association.

Nonetheless, Chicago's aftermath saw more kids gravitate to the counterculture or to radicalism than ever before; Chicago did more to rally youth to challenge authority and embrace alternative lifestyles and values than all the pamphlets and books and speeches by the New Left had ever accomplished. Repression did not suppress the counterculture; on the contrary, the behavior of the dominant culture boosted the counterculture. Indeed, as Tom Hayden noted "We would hardly have been notorious characters if they left us alone on the streets of Chicago [but instead] we became the architects, the masterminds, and the geniuses of a conspiracy to overthrow the government—we were invented."[100] However, in reality, over the course of the next two years, as the backlash went into full force under the Nixon administration's law and order banner, meting out at times even more vicious and deathly reprisals than that witnessed at Chicago, the hippie/Yippie dream that there would be a countercultural revolution in America was actually beaten into oblivion in Chicago. Subsequent events would only accelerate the hippies' inevitable demise as a visible, cultural force for change in American society.

12

Woodstock, August 1969: A Brief Ray of Hope for the Hip Counterculture's Survival

"If these are the kids that are going to inherit the world, then I don't fear for it."—Max Yasgur, owner of the dairy farm on whose land Woodstock was held.

By 1969 hippies and straights had gathered at numerous rock festivals throughout the nation, from Monterey to Miami, from Seattle to New Orleans. On July Fourth weekend of that year over 100,000 braved 100 degree heat in Atlanta to hear such rock legends as Credence Clearwater Revival, Johnny Winter, Janis Joplin, Blood, Sweat & Tears, and Led Zeppelin as well as a host of other up and coming bands such as Grand Funk Railroad. The three-day event saw few problems other than those related to the heat, which local fire departments helped to ameliorate by using fire hoses to create "sprinklers" for the crowd to play in and cool off. Two weeks before Woodstock (August 1, 2, and 3, 1969), another tribal gathering of over 100,000 took place at the Atlantic City Pop festival where attendees "grooved" to the music provided by the likes of Crosby, Stills, and Nash, CCR, Three Dog Night, Joni Mitchell, the Byrds, Chicago, and Little Richard to name but a handful of the 33 performers who appeared at the Atlantic City race track. Again, minimal problems occurred, other than a few drug overdoses and people jumping into the infield lake to cool off. In all cases, festival organizers did a remarkable job of planning and preparation, ensuring the festivals were both peaceful and profitable for its promoters.[1]

Although Atlanta and Atlantic City set records for attendance, it was Woodstock that was destined to become not only the era's most famous festival but one of the most mythologized events in the history of the 1960s counterculture. "The happening" at Woodstock created a generational legend that shows no sign of fading. Although much of Woodstock's mystique resides in the romantic minds of that generation, it nonetheless can be considered a critical encounter in the socio-cultural history of post–World War II America, similar to the January 1967 Be-In in San Francisco that launched the hippie impulse. Woodstock was a defining moment in that it represented the counterculture's crescendo as a movement, creating the belief among many hippies that their demonstration of peace and love at Woodstock marked the beginning of their crusade's ascendancy to change American culture.

Post-Woodstock hippies saw themselves as the *avant-couriers* of the next evolutionary step on the way toward planetary peace and love.

Although identified as the quintessential hippie gathering, this impression of Woodstock is not entirely accurate. The majority of the 400,000 plus young people at the festival *were not bona fide hippies* but rather, they represented the coalescence of the various ideals of the general countercultural movement that had come to affect the lion's share of American youth by the late 1960s. By that time, the hippie movement in particular and its attendant values and attitudes appeared to have had great impact on American youth as manifested at the Woodstock jamboree. Contrary to the popular stereotypes propagated by the mainstream media and embraced by straight America, Woodstock was not simply the grandest of all the hippie spectacles, but rather a unique moment in the history of American youth, when all of the various dynamics that had come to inform the countercultural rebellion of the 1960s came together. For three joyous days of music, peace, and dope hippie ideals were celebrated among several hundred thousand of the nation's young people, reflecting that the hippie ethos had indeed become one of the most popular bohemian and dissident impulses in the nation's history.

Woodstock began as a commercial enterprise, the collaborative efforts of four motley individuals: John Roberts, Joel Rosenman, Artie Kornfeld, and Michael Lang. Roberts, 26 was the money man, heir to a drugstore (Block Drug) and toothpaste manufacturing fortune. Roberts had a multimillion-dollar trust fund, a University of Pennsylvania degree, a lieutenant's commission in the Army and had seen only one live rock concert, the Beach Boys in 1965. Joel Rosenman, 24, Roberts' slightly hipper friend, was the son of a Long Island orthodontist who had just graduated from Yale Law School when he met Roberts on a golf course. At the time Rosenman was not practicing law but earning a livelihood by playing guitar for a lounge band in motels across the country. At the time of his meeting Roberts and Rosenman, Kornfeld, 27, was a vice-president at Capitol Records and had written about 30 hit singles, including Jan and Dean's "Dead Man's Curve." The fourth member of the consortium was Michael Lang, the only real hippie in the group. Long-haired and barefoot, Lang, 23, owned a head shop in Miami and a year earlier helped to produce the two-day Miami Pop Festival which drew 40,000 people.[2]

The four met in February 1969 and after their third meeting formed a company called Woodstock Ventures for the purpose of producing the largest music festival ever held in the United States. They had the money (Roberts), the expertise (Lang), the chutzpah (Rosenman), and the connections to rock and roll bands (Kornfeld) to put on such an extravaganza. All they needed now was a site big enough to hold what they hoped would be 100,000 people. They eventually found such a place, a 600-acre dairy farm in upstate New York near the town of Bethel in the Catskills, owned by Max Yasgur, to whom the four producers offered $50,000 for the use of his land and an additional $75,000 to be held in escrow for any damages to his property. Lang was euphoric with the layout of Yasgur's farm. "It was magic. It was perfect. The sloping bowl, a little rise for the stage. A lake in the background. The deal was sealed right there in the field." The 600 acres Yasgur leased to Woodstock Ventures was only part of his 1,000-acre dairy farm, which at the time of the Woodstock festival had allowed Yasgur to become the largest milk producer in Sullivan County. As one Woodstock attendee later hypothesized, "Max wasn't particularly pro-or-con all this fuss, but in the great American tradition of tolerance, probably figured 'What the hell, for that much money they can trash my corn field.'" Other locals as well saw the potential for financial gain Woodstock represented. A Bethel businessman was certain that the influx of tens of thousands of "these children" would "bring an economic boost to the County, without it costing the taxpayer a cent."[3]

Interestingly, Woodstock's original site was to have been in the town of Wallkill in Orange County, New York, at the 300-acre Mills Industrial Park but disputes between Woodstock Ventures and city officials over zoning issues eventually forced Lang and company to find another location. Although initially miffed by the town's rejection, Roberts believed that from the very beginning of negotiations, "The vibes weren't right there. It was an industrial park." By the end tensions between Woodstock Ventures and the town's Zoning Board had become so strained that Lang feared that even if they prevailed over the zoning controversy, "It wouldn't have worked. I didn't want cops in gas masks showing up and that was the atmosphere there." Another Woodstock Ventures member Lee Blumer remembered hearing locals declare that "They were going to shoot the first hippie that walked into town."[4] Wallkill's rejection proved a blessing in disguise not only for Woodstock Ventures but for the eventual 400,000 young people who attended the penultimate gathering of the tribes.

By the time the deal was finalized, Woodstock Ventures had only three weeks to get the site ready. The promoters had already sold 186,000 advance tickets at $18 a head (the equivalent of $114.65 in 2014) which was good for three days of non-stop rock and roll music and participation in all manner of individual and collective revelry. Attendees could also buy tickets at the gate for $24 ($152.87 in 2014). Thanks in large part to Kornfeld's music industry connections the company was able to sign some of the biggest rock and roll bands of the late 1960s. From the outset the partners knew that if their festival was going to be the success they hoped, they had to book, according to Lang, "three major acts, and I told them [his partners] I didn't care what it cost. If they [the prospective bands] were asking $5,000, I'd say pay 'em $10,000." Although willing to open their wallets, Woodstock Ventures knew that the big-name bands they were seeking would be reluctant to sign with a novice outfit that might not be able to deliver. To Rosenman it was simple: "To get the contracts [sign the bands] we had to have credibility, and to get the credibility, we had to have the contracts, so we solved the problem by promising paychecks unheard of in 1969," and they did. Their first big coup occurred with the signing of the top psychedelic band of the day, The Jefferson Airplane, for the incredible sum at the time of $12,000 (the band usually accepted between $5–6,000 for gigs), the equivalent in 2014 dollars of approximately $76,433; not bad remuneration for roughly two hours of work! News of the Airplane's lucrative deal spread quickly throughout the rock and roll community, enticing other big name bands to sign on such as Credence Clearwater Revival, who agreed to play for $11,500, and The Who, who were paid $12,500. In all, Ventures spent $180,000 (in 1969 dollars; $1,146,496.82 in 2014) on talent. The signing of The Jefferson Airplane, CC&R, and the Who proved to be the turning point relative to attracting other acts, for as Lang reflected "they gave us instant credibility." Indeed, by the festival's opening day, the partners had signed over two dozen performers, including Jimi Hendrix (for the unheard of price of $32,000; $203,821 in 2014), Janis Joplin, The Grateful Dead, Country Joe and the Fish, and Crosby, Stills, Nash, and Young; a veritable who's who of the biggest names in late 1960s rock and roll, sans the Beatles and Rolling Stones; the former on their way to splitting up while the latter was getting ready to embark on their own soon to be infamous U.S. tour.[5]

Initially most of Max Yasgur's neighbors and fellow town folk were not too happy about his having leased such a sizeable portion of his land to hippies. Indeed as news of the impending tidal wave of youth about to hit Yasgur's farm spread throughout the surrounding townships, the more upset locals became with Yasgur and the more fearful if not paranoid they became about the tens of thousands of these strange human beings called hippies about to inundate their communities, destroying like locusts their bucolic way of life. Anonymous signs began appearing in and around Bethel, and on Yasgur's property, protesting the town council's granting of permits to Woodstock Ventures to hold their festival on Yasgur's land and chastising Yasgur personally for having "sold out" his own community by "selfishly" leasing his land to "a bunch of scruffy, drug-crazed Hippies." Most of the resistance came from an ad hoc group of about 2,000 members spread throughout several counties, called the Concerned Citizens Committee. However, plenty of individuals took it upon themselves to show their displeasure with Yasgur, with one anonymous party erecting a large sign that read "Local People Speak Out / Stop Max's Music Festival / No 150,000 Hippies Here / Buy No Milk." The last declaration was meant to intimidate Yasgur into retracting his agreement with Woodstock Ventures by threatening a town boycott of his dairy, his livelihood.[6]

Yagur also received anonymous, threatening phone calls. The police were called but the culprits were never identified much less caught. One of Michael Lang's associates, Stan Goldstein, who was in charge of the campgrounds, such as they were, remembered seeing people approach Yasgur on the street "with red faces and tempers flaring. People driven by fear do very strange things. They raise their voices and say stupid things they would never ordinarily say, like threatening to blow up his [Yasgur's] house." To the day he died in 1973 at the age of 53 from a heart attack, Yasgur refused to discuss how his neighbors turned against him in 1969. "I know that it is a part of history, but I don't want to bother about it" was the response he always gave to those asking. Another of the festival's town supporters, White Lake resort owner Elliot Tiber, also received menacing phone calls and threats. "They'd say that it'll never happen, that we will break your legs. There was terrible name-calling. It was anti–Semitic and anti-hippies. It was dirty and filthy."[7] Rolling Stone honored Yasgur for his historic contribution with a full page obituary, making Yasgur one of the few non-musicians to be so recognized by the magazine.[8] Much to the relief of both Woodstock Ventures and to the eventual 400,000 plus young people about to inhabit his farmland for three days, Yasgur did not buckle to community pressure, honoring his contract with Woodstock Ventures.

From the beginning, Woodstock was not a matter of building stages, signing acts or even selling tickets and making a profit. Even for all four promoters, the festival was always a state of mind, a happening that would be testimony writ large of their generation's commitment to peace and love; of bringing greater enlightenment to the nation through the ideals of its youth, displayed within what had become the most important "set and setting" for the majority of young Americans: the sound of rock and roll music. Initially, the festival was to be promoted as an "Aquarian Exposition" but after some deliberation, it was agreed that such a billing was too esoteric or conceptual for the average 1960s teenage mind to grasp, so the group settled on a much simpler, more mundane slogan, "Woodstock Music and Art Fair: Three Days of Peace and Music."[9] "Peace" was the key word, for the promoters wanted to link their rock concert to the still strong antiwar sentiment/movement in the country as well to be a reminder to all who gathered that their generation was all about peace and humanity, and thus they were expected to behave accordingly.

To the eventual shock of millions of other Americans, certain Woodstock would degenerate into complete bedlam within hours of the arrival of thousands of kids, nothing close to mayhem occurred at any time over the course of the three-day event. In fact, quite the opposite, beginning with the greatest traffic jam in New York state history, which shut down every roadway to Yasgur's farm for a 20 mile radius, instantly creating on New York's country roads the third largest city in the state! So clogged had all the roads leading to Woodstock become, that what normally was a two-hour trip from New York City was now taking five to eight hours. Even Woodstock officials began sending out messages to radio and television stations urging people not to come. "Due to the overwhelming response highways are impassable. We therefore request and urge everyone coming to the Woodstock Pop Festival to turn back." Wes Pomeroy, the festival's security director told the press that "Anybody who tries to come here is crazy. Sullivan County is a great big parking lot." Indeed, in some places four to five columns of vehicles were splayed across the two-lane turnpike.[10] Clearly few people heeded the warnings; they wanted to be a part of history. Despite the mass of humanity, to twenty-three-year-old Peter Franklin, an actor from La Mama Theater in New York, Woodstock was a must-attend event, for "The cream of the underground will be there. Everybody's coming from all over the country. There'll be drugs and psychedelics and music and riots." Not all attendees were as euphoric about the possibilities for drugs and riots as Franklin. Especially bemused were teenagers such as a sixteen-year-old girl from Westbury, New York, whose parents "didn't want me to come. I know there'll be drugs everywhere and I wonder what it will all be like. I've never been away from home before. I wonder what will happen to all of us."[11]

Local cops, townsfolk, and the rest of America waited for the melee to begin, but to their surprise, "there wasn't even much honking of horns"; it was, according to *Washington Post* reporter, B.J. Phillips, "the most patient traffic jam perhaps ever in the history of American automobile travel. There was nothing to do about it, except perhaps park and walk [which many did, abandoning their cars right where they were in the traffic jam and setting off for the festival site on foot], so they [the festival goers] broke out guitars and drums and tambourines, sat on the hoods, trunks, and roofs, and tried to make the best of it. They played songs, shared food, drinks, and joints, waiting patiently until they could enter the field." According to Phillips what kept the peace during the traffic jam was the anticipation that sooner or later all would be on the meadow, grooving to the music that defined their generation. "What brought them to Bethel is rock music—their common denominator, the distillation of the finest, the worst, the angriest, the most gentle, the happiest, the saddest thing that youth believes in, in their lives."[12]

Jason Zapator of New Jersey, who turned nineteen on the festival's first day, seconded Phillips' assessment of "the parking lot scene," which in many ways set the tone for the rest of the weekend, reflecting the incredible peace and harmony that would prevail over the course of the next three days among the eventual 400,000 attendees. "There was a camaraderie even with the state troopers who were directing traffic that was amazing. People were smoking marijuana and doing things like that, and the state troopers weren't batting an eye. I had never seen anything like it."[13] Indeed, local law enforcement people were as impressed with the "kids' behavior" as were the young folk stuck in the traffic jam. As a state police lieutenant told *New York Times* reporter Barnard Collier, "There hasn't been anybody yelling 'pig' at the cops and when they asked directions they are polite and none of them has really given us any trouble yet."[14] Some festival goers believed that "If traffic congestion had not been a problem the number of attendees would have exceeded one million!"[15]

Another potential disaster loomed as well: controlling access to the concert site, which the promoters had failed to secure because they did not have enough time to finish putting up the fences. By late Friday afternoon, August 15, some 50,000 people had already arrived, many with tickets but most hoping to buy them at the gate, such as it was. Ticket or no ticket the crowd thronged onto the field and as the flood of humanity began settling in, pitching tents and tepees ready to have the time of their lives, Woodstock Ventures realized the utter futility of trying to clear the meadow and have those early arrivals show their tickets at what was becoming an illusionary gate. In the meantime, hordes of gate-crashers busily dismantled what was left of the fences and they too poured into the pasture. It was decision time for the promoters: try to force the 50,000 or more out of the area or accept reality and simply declare that henceforth Woodstock would be a *free* festival. They wisely chose the latter course of action even though they knew they would lose tens of thousands of dollars, if not millions, on their venture. As Roberts told the *New York Times* in a post-festival interview, "Something had to give and the first thing that gave was the money and ticket collection. Our security men were needed elsewhere so we had nobody to guard the gates and the people just came on in.... If we had any inkling that there was going to be this kind of attendance, we certainly would not have gone ahead." Roberts and company's only compensation for their unanticipated generosity was the hope that revenue from the eventual release of Michael Wadleigh's documentary *Woodstock* along with audio recordings would help them recoup their losses, both of which over a decade later provided rather handsome remuneration. It has been estimated that over a million and a half people arrived at the chaotic crossroads but only 400,000 or so remained for their three days of peace and music, and less than a quarter of those were bona fide ticket holders.[16]

The filming of the Woodstock phenomenon was an idea Artie Kornfeld wanted to implement from the very beginning. According to Elliot Tiber, Kornfeld made Warner Bros. "an offer it couldn't refuse": all Kornfeld and Wadleigh wanted was money: $100,000 to pay for film; all the crew and staff involved would be paid later, double their regular pay if the picture was a success but nothing if the film was a bust other than front-row seats to the greatest outdoor musical event and gathering in the history of American youth culture. Wadleigh and Kornfeld believed there was no need for any other expenses because "the concert would take care of the acting, the lighting, the dialogue and the plot." Kornfeld was honest with the movie conglomerate, telling its representative Ted Ashley that he could not predict the outcome but that his studio really had nothing to lose: "Spend $100,000 and you might make millions. If it turns out to be a riot, then you'll have one of the best documentaries made." As far as Wadleigh's artistic vision was concerned, he wanted his movie to be "a modern-day Canterbury Tale, a pilgrimage back to the land." It was to be a film that focused on the nation's counterculture as much as the era's music. "He wanted the stories of the young people, their feelings about the Vietnam War, about the times. The stories of the townspeople. These would make the film, not just the music." That Wadleigh succeeded in his goal became evident in 1970 when *Woodstock* received that year's Academy Award for best documentary.[17]

Much to everyone's delighted surprise, despite the massive traffic jam, the concert scheduled to start at 3:00 p.m., began just over two hours later, when African American folk singer and guitarist Richie Havens took the stage amid deafening cheers, officially signaling the beginning of the greatest rock festival in American history and the largest assemblage of citizens in one place for one simple purpose: to enjoy rock and roll music and human fellowship.

Prior to Havens' performance, the promoters kept the crowd of 100,000 entertained with all manner of non-music acts, including a series of yoga exercises provided by Tom Law, a member of a New Mexico hippie commune, the Hog Farm. No doubt the crowd wanted the music to begin but appeared to understand with incredible patience the logistical problems the traffic jam had caused in getting the bands to the festival site. Indeed, Havens was not the scheduled first performer; an up and coming band named Sweetwater was to open Woodstock but the group was mired in traffic with all of its equipment. Festival officials dispatched a helicopter to find them. The only other performer who had arrived was Tim Hardin ("If I Were a Carpenter"), but he was so stoned he could barely stand up let alone play guitar and sing. As the crowd started chanting for the music to begin, Lang and Kornfeld approached Havens, who was not to appear until the event's second day, and told the singer, "You are the only one who can save us!" Havens apparently grasped the urgency of the situation and agreed to go on, proclaiming to the audience, "We've finally made it! We did it this time—they'll never be able to hide us again!" Lang and Kornfeld also exhorted Havens to perform as long as he possibly could (which ended up being for three hours) because most of the other bands and artists were still having difficulty getting to Woodstock. Havens agreed and his Woodstock appearance proved to be a pivotal turning point in his career, catapulting him to the forefront of desired concert performers. Interestingly, by his unprecedented seventh encore Havens had run out of tunes to play and thus had to improvise, choosing an old Negro spiritual, "Motherless Child," transforming it into his most memorable Woodstock song, "Freedom."[18]

Right before Havens appeared, Michael Lang's voice boomed out of the loud-speakers, enjoining the crowd "to help each other work this out, because we're taxing the systems that we've set up. We're going to be bringing the food in. But the one major thing you have to remember tonight is that the man next to you is your brother and you need to share with him what you have because he may not have anything and we don't want that to be the case for anyone who has come to this celebration to find peace and love. We want all to find and have those beautiful things."[19] For many attendees the fellowship displayed at Woodstock transformed the event from a mega rock concert into a seminal countercultural experience. As one participant recollected, "Everyone needed other people's help, and everyone was ready to share what he has as many ways as it could be split up. Everyone could feel the good vibrations." Such spirit of cooperation prompted one festival-goer to recall feeling "exhilarated. We felt as though we were in a liberated territory."[20] Indeed, in many ways the crowd was in such nirvana because their sheer numbers made busting kids for nudity or drug use an exercise in complete futility for local law enforcement. Woodstock thus became the decade's greatest mass expression of countercultural values. As Janis Joplin declared, "We used to think of ourselves [hippies] as little clumps of weirdos. But now we're a whole new minority group."[21] *Time* magazine agreed with Joplin's assessment, proclaiming Woodstock to be "the moment when the special culture of U.S. youth of the '60s openly displayed its strength, appeal, and power; it may well rank as one of the significant political and sociological events of the age. Thousands of young people, who had previously thought of themselves as part of an isolated minority, experienced the euphoric sense of discovering, that they are, as the saying goes, 'what's happening.'" For many of the performers Woodstock was "a special place, a moment when we all felt we were at the exact center of freedom. We were there to look at each other, meet each other, identify our support for each other. We were there to celebrate."[22] If sex, drugs, rock, and granola could transform the children of consumer-driven, careerist, materialistic parents into Zen saints, Woodstock was the moment. The festival represented the momentary triumph of an idealistic young America.

Another impromptu act followed Havens; that of Country Joe McDonald, who also agreed to appear out of turn because Sweetwater had yet to arrive. McDonald, performing without his band, ignited the crowd with his famous "Fish Cheer," in which he shouted to the audience, "Gimme an F!" and the crowd now numbering 250,000, enthusiastically roared back "F!" "Gimme a U!" and so on until the call and response ended with what has become the loudest uttering of an obscenity ever. After completing the Fish Cheer, McDonald then launched into what had become his signature song, "I-Feel-Like-I'm-Fixing-to-Die Rag," with McDonald shouting to the crowd to sing along with him, which of course they did, all 250,000 standing and singing along with Country Joe during the last two stanzas. Following McDonald were John Sebastian, the Incredible String Band, Tim Hardin, and Joan Baez, all of whom gave outstanding performances but especially captivating was the legendary Baez. The closing song to her set, "Joe Hill," was a tribute to her imprisoned husband, David Harris, in jail for having publicly burned his draft card as an antiwar statement, electrified the crowd. Although giving a bravura performance, in many ways Baez, her acoustic guitar, the overtly political songs she sang (such as "Joe Hill"), and her famously pure voice, all seemed to be an anachronistic legacy of an earlier time. The majority of the bands played an apolitical form of blues rock with only a few solo artists such as Country Joe, Richie Havens, and Arlo Guthrie making any sort of socio-political statements and singing ballads with political messages. Nonetheless, Joan Baez's "Joe Hill," Havens' "Freedom," and Country Joe's "I-Feel-Like-I'm-Fixin'-to-Die Rag," remain Woodstock classics.[23]

The weekend's first major thunderstorm and downpour occurred during Ravi Shankar's performance, forcing the sitarist and his accompanists to leave the stage. Indeed, the rains came and came, turning much of the pasture into ankle-deep muddy quagmires, especially the area in front of the main stage. The inclement conditions did not dampen the crowd's general élan; most made the best of it, with many frolicking in the mud and viewing the poor weather as an opportunity to demonstrate the power of hippie collective thought; thousands chanted "No rain, no rain," as though even the elements could be pacified by the will of a united community.[24]

The bands played on as well, and those attendees brave enough to endure the interspersed thunder, lightning, and heavy rain, saw stellar performances given by the Who, Santana, the Grateful Dead, Jefferson Airplane, Blood, Sweat, and Tears, Johnny Winter, Creedence Clearwater Revival, and Sha Na Na. As John Fogerty of CCR recalled, "We were ready to rock and we waited and waited and finally it was our turn. It was 3 a.m. and by that time there were a half million people asleep. These people were out. It was sort of like a painting of a Dante scene, just bodies from hell, all intertwined and asleep, covered with mud. And this is the moment I will never forget as long as I live: a quarter mile away in the darkness, on the other edge of this bowl, there was some guy flicking his Bic [lighter], and in the night I hear 'Don't worry about it John, we're with you.' I played the rest of the show for that guy."[25]

Without question, one of the most memorable performances of the entire festival was that of headliner Jimi Hendrix. Hendrix was one of the few musicians of color playing for an adoring but overwhelmingly white audience. Indeed, besides Hendrix, the only other African American performers of note were Richie Havens and Sly and the Family Stone. Even more revealing was the paucity of black faces "in that massive come-together." As *New York Times* writer Craig McGregor observed, white hip and white rock and roll had been "liberated, primarily, by the black race" from whom white youth had borrowed their "music, dance, language, style and much of its sense of brotherhood." However, to McGregor, Woodstock rightly represented a racial paradox: that the hundreds of thousands of supposedly racially enlightened white youth had "so far done little to free those who had freed them." McGregor believed that if the Woodstock "ethic was to survive," it was imperative that "young white America" leave Yasgur's farm with a renewed sense of determination to make good the ideals they displayed and celebrated for three days at Woodstock and continue the crusade "to free black America." Otherwise, as Norman Mailer and Eldridge Cleaver had warned, "'There's a hurricane in the wind.'"[26]

Pundits were not the only Americans concerned about the dearth of black youth at Woodstock; many in the general public were equally "aware." In a letter to the *New York Times*, Ralph Marvin Abee of Santa Monica, California, reflected the same sense of foreboding about the paradox of the white counterculture ethos, if not its hypocrisy, relative to race, as McGregor. "It is curious in your extensive coverage of the Woodstock Festival no mention is made of the fact that at that fantastic outpouring there was almost a total absence of Negro youth. This is remarkable in view of common rhetoric and popular myth." To Abee, as to McGregor, the obvious scarcity of African American young people at Woodstock reflected a "latent racism in the [white] 'youth' scene of which the elders are accused."[27] Although both Abee and McGregor were right to raise the issue of race relative to the counterculture, especially at such a massive gathering of supposedly liberated young white people, to what degree the majority were latent or even closet racists, is questionable. In reality, the lion's share of those young white Americans who gathered at Woodstock or identified themselves as hippies, sadly were often too self-absorbed in their own search to find themselves to worry about the plight of others, even though they proclaimed to want such freedom for *all* their fellow human beings. Moreover, no matter how welcoming to their cause or crusade white hip youth might have been of their non-white counterparts, to the majority of "minority" young people at the time, the overwhelming white, affluent counterculture had little appeal for a variety of reasons, the most important of which was the lack of common experience in a socio-cultural and economic context. Although to be taken lightly, there is a degree of accuracy to conservative activist Herbert London's observation that the majority of attendees "weren't poor kids trapped in the inner city of marginal schools and insufficient jobs. They [the Woodstockers] were the progeny of privilege acting out in a town far from home with kindred souls who found the liberating effects of drugs."[28] It would be difficult, to say the least, for a late 1960s inner-city young African American, Hispanic, or even an Asian American person, striving to break out of poverty, to identify with their materially secure, insulated, white suburban cohorts. They could ill-afford either financially or leisurely, to attend for three days an event as "frivolous" as Woodstock. Indeed, minority kids, if they had a job, more than likely had to work on those three days in August 1969.

Of all the songs Hendrix played during his dawn appearance, it was his astonishing rendition of the "Star-Spangled Banner" that lives on in rock history. By default, Hendrix's interpretation of the national anthem also became a fitting close for a tumultuous decade. Hendrix originally had been scheduled to close the three-day extravaganza the night before (Sunday, August 17), but because of the bad weather, which waylaid all acts, Hendrix became the finale instead, performing at sunrise on Monday before an audience of only about 30,000 diehard fans who remained out of the 400,000 who had originally gathered at Max Yasgur's farm to create in three days the myth of the "Woodstock Nation." The comparatively sparse crowd did not affect Hendrix, who probably had difficulty distinguishing between people and the debris left by the masses that already had departed. Indeed, Hendrix played his music while volunteers attempted to clean up the mountains of garbage left by a counterculture that allegedly abhorred such environmental despoliation; a rather blatant complicity with a waste culture hippies claimed to oppose. Festival officials told the media that clean-up "would take at least two weeks."[29]

The Jimi Hendrix who played that early morning was the antithesis of the rocker who burst on the scene a mere two years earlier at Monterey. Although dressed elegantly outlandish as always, wearing an Indian-fringed suede jacket, blue velvet bell bottom pants, boots, beads, and silver earrings in both ears, and still sporting his signature Afro, other than looking like the "old" Jimi, the Jimi of Monterey and Fillmore East fame was no more. Gone completely from his act, other than a few token tongue flicks at his guitar, were all the erotic and phallic gestures and allusions that had marked his previous performances and for which he had been lambasted in the rock press. Instead, a physically subdued Hendrix appeared whose only body parts in constant motion were his hands, punctuated by a face of intense concentration, reflecting the combination of passion and skill required to convey a complex message. In essence, Hendrix wanted his Woodstock performance to be remembered not for "the Show" he presented but rather for providing his audience with a guitar virtuoso that they would remember forever. In retrospect Hendrix's "Star-Spangled Banner," which the 1970 film *Woodstock* used as its closing scene, made Hendrix a countercultural icon and his rendering symbolic of countercultural values and *raison d'être*. Interestingly, Hendrix first played his version at a concert at the Los Angeles Forum five months earlier, prefacing his interpretation with the statement, "Here's a song that we was all brainwashed with." Rock historian Lauren Onkey's description of Hendrix's performance captures much of what Hendrix hoped to convey with his unique playing of the national anthem: "Hendrix began his instrumental version of the song by flashing a peace sign to the audience. Then accompanied only by Mitch Mitchell's psychedelic jazz drumming, he played the first verses of the song, adhering closely to its familiar form. When he got to the line 'and the rockets' red glare,' Hendrix let loose with a carefully orchestrated sonic assault on the audience in which his shrieking, howling guitar riffs, modulated and distorted with feverish feedback, attained the aural equivalent of Armageddon. The bombs bursting in air and ear transformed Yasgur's placid cow pasture into the napalmed and shrapnel-battered jungles of Vietnam. As the song drew to a close, Hendrix solemnly intoned a few notes of 'Taps,' memorializing not just the slain but perhaps his own former pro-war stance that dated back a few years to his hitch in the army."[30]

Those who might have been in a sleepy haze when Hendrix started playing his "bravura deconstruction" of the national anthem were now not only fully awake, but simultaneously charged and awe-struck by what they had just heard. With only his guitar, Hendrix managed to evoke both "chauvinistic pride for and unbridled rage against the American way of life." Many rock pundits wondered why Hendrix chose to play the song at, of all places, Woodstock, promoted as "Three Days of Peace & Music." Hendrix responded, "Because we are all Americans. When it was written it was very nice and beautifully inspiring. Your heart throbs and you say, 'Great, I'm American.' Nowadays we don't play it to take away all the greatness that America is supposed to have. We play it the way the air is in America today and that air is slightly static."[31] In retrospect there was no better closing song and performance for the largest, most peaceful and cooperative gathering of the tribes than Jimi Hendrix's playing of the "Star-Spangled Banner," which has come to reflect the proud and revolutionary music, voice, and spirit of one of the counterculture's most revered icons.

By the close of the second day, over 400,000 human beings occupied Yasgur's farmland, and as far as one could see there were young people "walking, lying down, drinking, eating, reading, and singing. Kids were sleeping, making love, wading in the marshes, trying to milk the local cows and trying to cook the local corn."[32] The sheer numbers of humanity was fast turning the event into a disaster area. Indeed, Sullivan County officials declared a state of emergency, urging Governor Nelson Rockefeller to send 10,000 New York State National Guard troops to the area. Rockefeller called the promoters, insisting that they needed such "assistance," but Roberts dissuaded the governor from taking such action, convincing him that to do so could cause the crowd "to react in a negative way," for many would believe the troops had come not to help out but to shut the festival down. Rockefeller heeded Roberts' advice and refrained from "sending in the Guard." Troops or no troops, the myriad problems, it seemed, escalated by the hour. Sanitation facilities—portable toilets—were woefully inadequate in number (Woodstock Ventures had the greatest difficulty procuring a sufficient number because no one company could provide all their needs and so they had to obtain the privies from several companies, many of whom failed to deliver even one!), causing thousands of festival goers to line up for over an hour to relieve themselves. Many simply gave up and used the great outdoors. Those toilets available overflowed constantly from such perpetual use, causing all manner of hygienic problems. The hungry crowd consumed a half million hamburgers and hot dogs on the first day and food ran out as did almost all drinkable water. Those folk who brought sufficient food and water shared what they had with those less fortunate and that spirit of generosity came to be one of the festival's hallmarks.[33]

It would be naïve and delusional however, to think that *no one* took advantage of the desperate situation. Although the organizers mouthed hippie platitudes about the dollar being less important than welfare and music, there was noticeable exploitation, with some hippies selling not just dope but food and water for exorbitant if not extortive prices—LSD tabs for $6 a pop (they usually sold for no more than $2 a pill), a "lid" of marijuana for $30 (usually sold for $10); water for a $1 a quart, 25 cents for a glass, and peanut butter and jelly sandwiches for as much as $2 a sandwich. As one Woodstock attendee stated, two one-day tickets at $7 each would "get you a peach or a half a sandwich."[34] Suffice it to say some of the "love crowd" left their compassion at the gate and brought instead into Max Yasgur's pasture the self-serving consumer/capitalist mentality of their white bourgeois suburban upbringing, which they professed to disdain and had long since supposedly eschewed. The black market activities of many tribal members at Woodstock revealed otherwise to have been true, as many hippies profited from their compatriots' misfortunes.

However, such shady activity did not last very long, allowing Woodstock to retain its aura of solicitude and generosity which was more prevalent than not. News of opportunism circulated rapidly among the crowd and pressure from the masses, Woodstock officials, and the Hog Farm communards, who manfully fed thousands of people every day *for free*, to stop such abuse prevailed. Indeed, as Hugh Romney, aka "Wavy Gravy" announced one morning, his fellow Hog Farm communards planned to provide "breakfast in bed for 400,000. Now it's not gonna be steak and eggs or anything. But it's gonna be good food and we're gonna get it to you."[35] "The concessionaires—hot dog stands and so on—started out with prohibitive prices and the kids complained to the management. All day there were announcements that the concessionaires had knocked their prices down to cost."[36] As the *Quicksilver Times* noted, "In spite of the schemes of hippie capitalists, good things happened at Woodstock." The "aura of Woodstock" was that of "Elysium Fields of peacefulness, of harmony with other souls, and with nature, of the freeing of the hung-up mind."[37] The exploitation that momentarily visited Woodstock paled in comparison with the profiteering that occurred at subsequent rock festivals, most ironically at the attempts to recreate the "spirit of '69" at Woodstock 1994 and most dramatically and violently, at Woodstock 1999.

The popular media naturally jumped on the opportunity to condemn Woodstock, with the *New York Times* leading the way, referring to the festival as the "Nightmare in the Catskills." "The sponsors of this event, who apparently had not the slightest concern for the turmoil it would cause, should be made to account for their mismanagement. To try to cram several hundred thousand people into a 600-acre farm with only a few hastily installed sanitary facilities shows a complete lack of responsibility." The spectacle of a big mud pile filled with romping, smiling, disheveled young people, prompted the *Times* to ask "What kind of culture is it that can produce so colossal a mess?" The editorial compared the Bethel pilgrimage as having "little more sanity than the impulses that drive lemmings to march to their deaths in the sea."[38]

Security was also another potential catastrophe, as the individual hired to procure 346 off-duty New York City police officers to serve as "ushers" could not deliver because the city's police commissioner issued an edict forbidding anyone from the force from "moonlighting" outside of the department in a security capacity. Commissioner Howard R. Leary issued his prohibition one day before the festival was to begin. Suffice it to say Woodstock Ventures officials were a bit anxious. As the head of security for the company, former Johnson administration Justice Department special assistant Wesley Pomeroy told the media, "Now I don't have any security people at all. I've been struck. We're having the biggest collection of people there's ever been in this country without any police protection."[39]

The promoters scurried to find someone willing to provide such a service, finally cajoling members of the Hog Farm to be the event's "Please Force." Hugh Romney agreed to organize the squad. Suffice it say, many were suspect about such individuals providing security, with journalists' peppering Romney with questions about his "qualifications" for such a crucial undertaking. Romney responded to the reporters' queries by asking "Do you feel secure?" When one of the news people replied yes he did, Romney quipped, "It seems to be working!"[40] To augment the Hog Farm's "Please Force" Pomeroy also hired another 200 men as a "peace security force," consisting of off-duty New York policemen willing to moonlight regardless of the edict against such activity, local cops, sheriff's deputies, constables, and state troopers. As far as the off-duty New York cops were concerned, Pomeroy told the press "I don't ask if they're from New York." The promoters initially interviewed over 800 law enforcement people for their peace security force, asking them such questions as "'What would you do if a kid walked up and blew marijuana smoke in your face?' Incorrect answer: 'Bust him.' Correct Answer: 'Inhale deeply and smile.'" Those ultimately selected wore a uniform of red Day-Glo shirts emblazoned with the peace symbol. They could not arrest people or use force; they were merely to be present to direct traffic and assist in other emergencies; the real work of maintaining law and order became the responsibility of the Hog Farm's "Please Force."[41]

Because dope was plentiful—sold and given away openly—many consumed too much;

about 800, according to Dr. William Abruzzi, Festival Medical Director, were treated for "adverse recreational drug reactions." The *New York Times* estimated that 99 percent of the festival goers smoked marijuana brazenly, prompting a state police sergeant to comment that, "As far as I know, the narcotics guys are not arresting anybody for grass. If we did, there wouldn't be enough spaces in Sullivan County or the next three counties to put them in." As one young attendee observed, "There was so much grass being smoked last night that you could get stoned just sitting there breathing. It got so you didn't even want another drag of anything."[42] According to Andrew Kopkind, since *real*, uniformed cops had been forbidden inside the campgrounds, "word went out that there would be no busts for ordinary tripping, although big dealers were discouraged." Consequently, "Dope became plentiful and entirely legitimate" as "portable head-shops" appeared out of nowhere and everywhere while dealers meandered through the crowd shouting "Acid, mesc, psilocybin, hash" for sale like vendors at a ball game. It was virtually impossible at times *not to be stoned* on something as "joints were passed from blanket to blanket, lumps of hashish materialized like manna, and there was Blue Cheer, Sunshine acid, and pink mescaline to spare."[43]

As *Time* observed in a post–Woodstock essay, "The all but universal acceptance of marijuana, at least among the young, raises the question of how long the nation's present laws against its use can remain in force without seeming as absurd and hypocritical as Prohibition."[44] Despite rumors about "bad brown acid" being circulated and ingested, there was only one death reported from drug use and that was the result of a heroin overdose rather than a bad acid trip. The only other fatality of the entire three-day jamboree occurred when a tractor driver accidently ran over an attendee he did not see asleep in a sleeping bag as he tended his hayfield. Moreover, there were no rapes, assaults, robberies, and as far as anyone could recall, not one single fight, which, *Time* noted, "is more than can be said for most sporting events held in New York City." Indeed, as Dr. Abruzzi noted "We didn't treat one single knife wound or black eye or a laceration that was inflicted by another human being."[45]

Given the size of the crowd, that only 800 individuals (or 2 percent, a minuscule figure in proportion to the number of human beings) had to be treated for taking too much dope, was rather miraculous. Such a revelation prompted many post–Woodstock commentators to make the rather ludicrous claim that not only the lack of drug deaths but also the general bonhomie that marked the festival, were the result of the prevalent use of psychotropic substances! Moreover, because of the absence of such hard drugs as methedrine, heroin, cocaine, and even alcohol, the outbreaks of violence and rioting that marred subsequent concerts, did not occur at Woodstock. Perhaps there is some truth to the latter contention and even some credence could be given to the first assertion, but Woodstock's overall "uniqueness" cannot be explained by such simplistic notions; many of the reasons that it genuinely became three days of "Music and Peace" were much deeper and had little, if anything, to do with the dope scene.

First of all, the "good vibrations" felt by festival-goers also affected many of the older generation and local non-hippie youth, especially those living in Bethel. Both young and old town folk interacted with the hippies, and after such engagement, many locals, such as Sullivan County Sheriff Louis Ratner concluded that, "This was the nicest bunch of kids I've ever dealt with," while Monticello police chief Lou Yank, told the *New York Times* that, "Notwithstanding their personality, their dress, and their ideas, they were and they are the most courteous, considerate, and well-behaved group of kids I have ever been in contact with in my 24 years of police work." Even the usually stoned faced, "cut-no-slack" state troopers "smiled broadly as they waved cars on [as the diehards left the festival site on the last day] with their fingers extended in the 'V' peace sign."[46] Such positive exchanges inspired many local farmers and residents to transform their homes into soup and sandwich kitchens as well as allowing the kids free access to their garden hoses for drinking and bathing. It should also be remembered that helping to prevent Woodstock from devolving into possible violent anarchy was the help of countless other members of the "adult Establishment"—policemen, electricians, food suppliers, and medical professionals. Even the United States Army pitched in with 50 doctors, several nurses and medical supplies and dispatching helicopters for those in need of serious medical attention when the massive traffic jam prevented emergency vehicles from getting to the festival site.[47] Woodstock's potential for disaster, interestingly, made things cohere. As an op-ed in Houston's underground paper, *The Space City News* noted "When a natural disaster strikes, people pull together in a rare way that they all remember with amazement years later."[48] If any U.S. citizenry would know about natural disasters and the necessity of "pulling together," it would be Houstonians, living from June to November in fear of being hammered by a hurricane. Or, as Wavy Gravy, succinctly put it, "There's always a little bit of heaven in a disaster area."[49] Even some of the Establishment press lauded the hippies at Woodstock, with *Life* magazine exulting that despite "nearly half a million people" living "elbow to elbow in the most exposed, crowded, and rain-drenched, uncomfortable kind of community, there wasn't so much as a fist fight."[50] Even the *New York Times* changed its perception in Woodstock's aftermath, declaring the festival "essentially a phenomenon of innocence.... They came, it seems, to enjoy their own society, free to exult in the life style that is its own declaration of independence. To such a purpose a little hardship could only be an added attraction.... The great bulk of the freakish-looking intruders behaved astonishingly well, considering the disappointments and discomforts they encountered. They showed that there is real good under their fantastic exteriors." The *Times* became even more rhapsodic in its assessment of the Woodstock "phenomenon" in the weeks that followed. In an article for the *Sunday Times*, Patrick Lydon asserted that "Hippies have never been so successful together, never before had they so impressed the world that watched.... What began as a symbolic protest against American society ended as a joyful confirmation that good things *can* happen here, that Army men can raise a 'V' sign, that country people can welcome city hippies.... Yes, most everything happened up on the farm."[51]

Also contributing to Woodstock's success was the actual physical setting, which according to Sixties historian Maurice Isserman, who was at Woodstock, helped maintain the overall bonhomie among the 400,000 attendees. "You were on Max Yagur's farm, these 600 acres. And you were surrounded by this beautiful Catskills countryside. It was in the woods, and the lake, and the cows, and Max Yasgur coming out and talking to the crowd. It had a very calming effect. There was a real anti-modernism in the '60s counterculture, a desire to sort of get back to the garden." Hippies embraced the natural serenity and beauty that enveloped them on Yasgur's farm, and did their best not to despoil such an idyllic landscape. Isserman also believes that because Woodstock appeared to be so haphazardly thrown together, there was a "desire" among attendees "to make it work. There was a homemade quality to it. It was like Judy Garland and Mickey Rooney in one of those '30s movies saying 'Let's put on a show, kids,'" and 400,000 kids put on quite a show indeed. David Fricke of *Rolling Stone*, who also attended the festival, agreed with Isserman's assessment. "Hardly utopia and not quite a calamity, Woodstock was a profit-motivated mega-gig that kicked into tornado over-drive and then, somehow, went incredibly and wonderfully right…. The original, for all its undeniable headaches and screwups, was a one-time model of synchronicity and modest ambition—the right people in the same place at a critical time, faced with imminent disaster but grounded enough to just ride the music out of the bullshit. At the time it didn't seem that hard to do."[52]

Although many adults and straights regarded Woodstock as "a squalid freakout, a monstrous Dionysian revel, where a mob of crazies gathered to drop acid and groove to hours of amplified cacophony,"[53] the hippies found in Woodstock a consummate gathering of the tribes, encompassing and reflecting virtually every manifestation of their ethos, hopes, and dreams. As Max Lerner told *Rolling Stone* magazine a month after the event, "The historians will have to reckon with it. These young revolutionaries are on their way to slough away the lifestyle that isn't theirs and find one that is." Greil Marcus echoed Lerner's sentiments, telling the same magazine that Woodstock was "a confused, chaotic founding of something new, something our world must now find a way to deal with. The limits have changed now, they've been pushed out, the priorities have been rearranged, and new 'impractical' ideas must be taken seriously. The mind boggles."[54] Even *Time*, which had cast a jaundiced eye on the hippie movement in most of its previous essays had a noticeable change of heart and mind about the counterculture in Woodstock's aftermath, proclaiming the event to have been one of "the great groundswells of popular movements that affect the minds and values of a generation or more, not all of which can be neatly tied to time and place. Looking back upon America in the '60s, future historians may well search for the meaning of one such movement." For the article's writers, "What took place at Bethel" was "much more than an 'Aquarian Exposition' of music and peace." Woodstock became "history's largest demonstration to the adult world that young people could create a kind of peace in a situation where none should have existed, and that they followed a mysterious inner code of law and order." Psychoanalyst Rollo May described Woodstock as "'a symptomatic event of our time that showed the tremendous hunger, need, and yearning for community on the part of youth.'"[55]

Even though Woodstock became, "the stuff of which legends are made," it was never to be duplicated; it was truly a-once-in-a-lifetime, generational event. Although two commemorative Woodstock events took place in the 1990s, one in 1994 and then another five years later in 1999, both festivals not only failed to replicate the original Woodstock in spirit, sound, and élan, but Woodstock 1999 degenerated rapidly into a violent melee, with scores of sexual assaults, theft, the pillaging of vendor booths, and the destruction of property such as the stage, portable toilets, and whatever else the revelers could get their hands on to burn in the huge bonfires they started in the middle of the dance area in front of the stage. As *Rolling Stone's* Rob Sheffield observed, "trouble was brewing long before the looting and burning. The promoters were outrageously clueless the physical toll the [setting] would take on the kids…. And the fans were ridiculously clueless about the laws of self-preservation, skimping on sunscreen and earplugs while accepting lethal drugs from strangers. The sheep mentality inspired routine mob violence…. Woodstock [1999] was the triumph of the bullies, with fighters winning out over lovers." New York state troopers, local police, and other law enforcement agencies arrived, dressed in riot gear and proceeded in 1960s battle line formation to "push" the crowd out of the main performance area where the bonfires had been set and the damage done. Only a few in the crowd resisted, while the rest of the thousands who had participated in the mischief fled pell-mell back to the campground at the other end of the field or out the main entrance.[56]

MTV host Kurt Loder described the scene for a July 27, 1999, *USA Today* issue: "It was dangerous to be around. The whole scene was scary. There were just waves of hatred bouncing around the place. It was clear we had to get out of there. It was like a concentration camp. To get in you get frisked to make sure you are not bringing in any food or water that would prevent you from buying from their outrageously priced booths [a slice of pizza sold for $12 while a US 20 fl. oz. (590 ml) bottle of water or a 12 oz. can of soda for $4]. You wallow around in garbage and human waste. There was a palpable mood of anger."[57] What a stark contrast to the "set and setting" of the original Woodstock, and more important and telling, the peaceful co-habitation, cooperation, and general good-will toward their fellow man that pervaded *the Woodstock* festival was sorely missing from those who tried to emulate the "good vibrations" from 25 to 30 years ago. No doubt, many of the "Woodstock Nation" still around (alive) in 1994 and 1999, were sorely disappointed if not appalled by what took place at those two events, especially by the madness that engulfed Woodstock 1999.

As Maurice Isserman has rightly observed, it is impossible to recreate Woodstock "because you'll never get back there; there will never be an event again—under that name— that has such a dramatic impact or creates such a durable myth.... Every generation should create its own mythology and have its own transcendent experience."[58] As John Hilgardt who had attended Woodstock 1969 wrote in the *East Village Other* in the festival's euphoric after-math, he was certain that "Maybe, just maybe, it will be a new beginning for us despite our walking away from the most beautiful experience many ever had. We know we can live together as we had done only previously in our fantasies. No one will leave here the same person that existed before. For a few days we were all in a beautiful place. Can we do it again? All I know is I don't want to leave here. I feel like I've come home."[59] Even Max Yasgur got caught up in the post–Woodstock jubilation and mystique, proclaiming that "if we join them [the coun-terculture], we can turn those adversities that are the problems of America today into a hope for a brighter and more peaceful future. If these are the kids that are going to inherit the world, then I don't fear for it. What happened at Bethel this past weekend was that these young people together with our local residents turned the Aquarian festival to a dramatic victory for the spirit of peace, goodwill, and human kindness."[60]

Not *everyone* who attended Woodstock left on a "high" or with any expectation that the event marked the beginning of the Aquarian Age or that a new culture of compassion, fel-lowship, and peace would soon emerge. Some attendees walked away with "negative" rather than "positive vibes." Such was the view of David Malcolm who saw the festival as "a lot of shit. It was three days in a muddy cow pasture with the toilets blocked up.... I did drugs and I smoked grass and I wore my hair a lot longer than I wear it now but I was not a hippie by any means.... I never adopted that sort of wide-eyed naïve ethic of the hippies.... I did not admire the generation of the Sixties much, or anyone who was stupid enough to think that Woodstock was a blueprint for modern society." For Malcolm, Woodstock boiled down to a "bunch of sick people wallowing in the mud" for three days. Herbert London would agree. [Woodstock] is the story of wild orgies, drug-fueled memories, and filthy port-o-potties that didn't work, mounds of vomit and excrement that was ground into the soil as fertilizer."[61] Another less than elated individual was Gene Katz, who saw Woodstock as the most "woefully understaffed and poorly planned extravaganza" that will be "remembered as the most suc-cessful fiasco in history of entertainment. The Woodstock festival was never intended to be the monstrosity it became." According to Katz even some of the bands noticed what an overall disaster on many levels Woodstock supposedly was. "It was chaos, wasn't it?" Pete Townshend of The Who opined. "What was going on off the stage was just beyond comprehension— stretchers and dead bodies, and people throwing up, and people having bad trips.... I thought the whole of America had gone mad." Although Townshend's perception is overblown, many people who arrived did indeed find the prospect of living for three days in an "immense pit of mud and sheep manure" not that inviting, and regardless of the great music and human bonding and generosity that prevailed, tried to leave if they could.[62]

In a September 1969 article in the *Saturday Review* Ellen Sander perhaps best captured Woodstock's immediate significance for the 60s' generation. "No longer can the magical multicolored phenomenon of pop culture be overlooked or underrated. It's happening everywhere, but now it has happened in one place at one time so hugely that it was indeed historic [and] the audience proved to be a much bigger story than the groups. What happened was that the largest number of people ever assembled for any event other than a war [Sander was mistaken in her exaltation; five million Hindus gathered at the Ganges River in 1966 for a three-week religious revival] lived together, intimately and meaningfully and with such natural good cheer that they turned on not only everyone surrounding them but the mass media, and by extension, millions of others, young and old, particularly elements hostile to the manifestations and ignorant of the pop culture."[63] Rock critic Ellen Willis agreed with Sander's assessment, that although "rock was the only thing that could have drawn such a crowd," the music was of secondary importance at Woodstock; "the mass presence of the hip community was the focal point," with the music providing "a pleasant background" to the mega-celebration of hippiedom.[64]

Both Monterey and Woodstock played key roles in transforming the way in which popular music was seen and heard. Monterey provided the template while Woodstock established the belief that massive outdoor concerts could be both appealing and profitable if they were effectively organized, with particular attention paid to controlling ticket sales at the gate and even those sold beforehand. Future promoters also learned from Woodstock the imperative of providing more than adequate sanitation systems, concessions, and protection from inclement weather. However, after the December 1969 Altamont disaster (to be discussed in detail in the next chapter), pop paladins rethought the future feasibility and their remuneration with continuing the outdoor festivals featuring multiple performers playing a variety of rock and roll genres. Beginning in the mid–1970s and for the next two decades rock concerts went back indoors but not to the dancehall venue of the mid to late 1960s but to a new "set and setting" of sports stadiums and convention halls, the perfect environment for seeing and hearing post–1960s rock and roll which the heavy metal and punk rock scenes dominated for a few years in the mid to late 1970s. Shows were now not only performed in a confined space, complete with fixed and segregated seating based on the amount paid for the ticket (the higher the price of admission the closer one got to the stage), but also the acts were limited to a single day or evening with attendees seeing and hearing a limited number of rock bands performing one or two of the latest, most popular sounds. Gone until recently were the jamborees (such as the Coachella Valley Music and Arts Festival held on the outskirts of California's Mohave Desert) featuring multiple bands of varied musical expressions, lasting several days in the great outdoors. The advent of "arena rock" marked the end of both the dancehall concept as well as the pastoral, festival experience of Woodstock, where fans from all walks of life bonded for a brief moment in an egalitarian community of rock and roll compatriots. Woodstock is considered by many to have been the quintessence of such bucolic bonhomie.[65]

For all the fond memories *the Woodstock* continues to generate, the "Three Days of Peace and Music" unfortunately set in motion less than "groovy" impulses, the most important of which became corporate capitalism's realization that the gathering's largely left-of-center, overwhelmingly affluent white crowd, including the apolitical full-fledged LSD-popping hippies, represented a legion of potential consumers that mainstream businesses would not underestimate again; that there was more to sell them than Zig-Zag Man rolling papers and LP's.[66] Indeed, after the buzz wore off, the utopian communal aura of Woodstock Nation quickly degenerated into the reality of a Woodstock Market; a demographic target group that would soon see its idealism and radicalism transmogrified into profitable commodities by the very capitalist system which many manfully resisted or outright rejected for many years but which proved too powerfully overwhelming to continue the fight. Thus, in the end, many if not most ultimately succumbed to system's lucrative wiles.

Prior to Woodstock, the hippie subculture was still largely self-invented and isolated; there were pockets of freaks in cities and handfuls in smaller towns. Regardless of locale, nearly all felt like outsiders. Thus for many if not for most of the young folk at Woodstock, no matter whether they were genuine hippies, pseudo-hippies, "weekend plastics," or straights with long hair, just seeing and joining that large of a crowd was more of a revelation than anything that happened onstage. It proved that "young America," but particularly the counterculture in all its variations and commitments, was not some negligible minority but a *real* youth culture or "counterculture." In short, Woodstock legitimized the existence of an authentic counterculture in 1960s America; the largest, most visible, and active in the nation's history. In many ways hippiedom reached its crescendo at Woodstock while simultaneously opening "itself to imitation and trivialization—one more glimmer of rebellion to become commodified into a style statement."[67] Nonetheless Woodstock proved something to the rest of the world: that at least for one weekend hippies meant what they said about peace and love. Woodstock was not an historical event that shaped the nation's future nor was it a phenomenon that faded quickly into oblivion. Woodstock somehow has bridged the gap between significance and obscurity and thus nearly 50 years later the sensation endures.

13

The Manson Murders and the December 1969 Altamont Calamity: The Roads to Hippie Perdition

"Of course some people wanted to say Altamont was the end of an era. People like that are fashion writers. Perhaps it was the end of *their* era, the end of their naiveté. I would have thought it ended long before Altamont."—Mick Jagger

Altamont did not represent the first unmasking of the hippie counterculture's penchant for self-destruction. Five months earlier, in August 1969, only a few weeks before Woodstock, this predilection appeared in the person of one of the most notorious serial murderers in American history, Charles Manson. Manson was a former Summer of Love transient and Haight-Ashbury resident. Struggling to become a songwriter/musician, Manson, like many other misfits who came to San Francisco during the summer of 1967, immersed himself in the drug scene, not only ingesting LSD but shooting heroin and speed as well on a regular basis. Before drifting into the Haight, Manson had spent 20 of his 35 years on the planet in and out of foster homes, juvenile detention centers, or in prison. His mother was a prostitute and he never knew his father. As one acquaintance told *New York Times Magazine* reporter Steven Roberts, "If Charlie has any roots they're in the penal system."[1]

Although reported by only a few journalists at the time of the Manson Family's killing spree, Manson was insane; certified by a state psychiatrist who diagnosed Manson at the age of 20 as sociopathic, if not psychotic. Despite the standard interpretation of Manson and his murderous minions, Manson *was not* a satanic incarnation of the darkest impulses and excesses unleashed by the hippie counterculture. Rather, Manson was your garden-variety sociopath with above-average social skills learned and honed while incarcerated, and a lifelong predator whose childhood and adolescent history reveals the typical profile of a small-time criminal.[2] As Manson later told interviewers, he "didn't really want to come out of jail—I was frightened and didn't know where to go.... I can't go outside there, I knew I couldn't adjust to that world, not after all my life had been spent locked up and where my mind was free. I was content to stay in the penitentiary, just to take my walks around the yard in the sunshine and play my guitar."[3] Unfortunately prison officials ignored Manson's desire to remain on the inside and released him to the outside world again, where he would become in two years' time, the mastermind of some of the most blood-curdling murders in American history.

No sooner was Manson paroled than he headed for San Francisco and the Haight-Ashbury, just as the hippie movement was cresting in the City with the impending Summer of Love. For survival, Manson, along with countless other hippies that summer, panhandled and sold dope, eventually finding someone to take care of him in the person of Mary Bruner, a recent graduate of the University of Wisconsin–Madison and an assistant librarian at UC Berkeley. Soon after moving in with Bruner Manson started his "Family," convincing Bruner of his messianic need to do so while using sex and drugs to recruit other women to live with them. By the end of the Summer of Love, eighteen women had become part of the Family, "nesting" together in a two-story building at 636 Cole Street.[4]

In reality Manson loathed the hippies, considering them to be nothing more than pathetic "play-acting" people and being called a hippie sent him into a rage of denial. Yet he himself did a masterful job of passing as a hippie and used the hippie scene for his own debauched and sinister purposes; the 1967–68 Haight-Ashbury provided him with the perfect environment in which his particular mode of sociopathic behavior thrived. By the late 1960s as the hippie movement began to wind down, the counterculture's once vibrant haunts deteriorated as well, becoming "a new sort of refuge for criminals and ex-cons," who "grow hair, assume beads and sandals, and sink—carnivores moving with vegetarians—into the life of hippie colonies from the East Village to Big Sur." Manson had found the Haight to be a particularly inviting haven: "with an exquisite sort of diplomatic skill, [he] adopted the local coloration as a means of controlling, utilizing, and dominating the impulse-ridden, alienated, drug-directed kids he discovered there."[5] According to Dr. Roger Smith, Manson's parole officer and research criminologist, upon arriving in the Haight, "[Manson] was really sort of shaken by it all—by the fact that people were friendly, open, and willing to do things with him. The first night he was in the Haight, the chicks were willing to go to bed with him. They didn't care whether he had just gotten out of the joint. That was a real shocker for him." Smith also believed that it did not take Manson very long to realize just how perfect the Haight was for his predatory nature. "You have a very transient, mobile delinquent population, and many of them end up in scenes [the Haight] like this. They pick up the rhetoric and sort of blend in and exploit and manipulate the scene. I think that's where Charlie fit in."[6]

It was from the many desperate, abused, broken, and outright ruined young people—mostly unstable teenage runaways—that Manson found some of his most devoted female followers, such as Lynette "Squeaky" Fromme and Susan Atkins, both of whom worshipped Manson and were involved in the 1969 bloodbaths in southern California. Indeed, Atkins became Manson's "right-hand man," and Fromme his "main lady," and "chief cheerleader of the Manson cause"; one of his "shrewdest, toughest, most slavishly obedient followers."[7] *New York Times* reporter, Steven Roberts, who spent hours interviewing many of the Manson women in the immediate aftermath of their murderous rampage, concluded that Manson was an incredibly "shrewd recruiter and seducer." He found the women to be especially "empty vessels. There was a hole in each of their lives—a lack of confidence, a lack of accomplishment, a lack of identity."[8] A San Francisco psychiatrist agreed, opining that most of "Charlie's girls" were "hysterics, wishful thinkers, seekers after some absolute" who saw Manson as an "all-powerful, all-knowing high priest."[9]

Dr. David Smith of the Haight-Ashbury Free Clinic, who treated the Manson girls for their various venereal diseases, described "the Manson process": "Charlie's group was unlike any other commune I've known. They called themselves a family, but most family communes are monogamous sexually. The members pair off and don't indiscriminately change partners. A new girl in Charlie's family would bring with her a certain middle-class morality. The first thing that Charlie did was to see that all this was torn down. The major way he broke through was sex. The girls were expected to have sex with any men around. If they had hang-ups about it, then they should feel guilty. That way he was able to eliminate controls that normally govern our lives. Sex, not drugs, was the common denominator."[10] One of Manson's devoted male followers, Tex Watson confirmed Smith's assessment: "Sex was an important tool in Charlie's deprogramming, and he did tell us that as long as we had any inhibitions we still weren't dead, we were still playing back what our parents had programmed into us."[11] Did Manson feel any genuine "tenderness" toward his female followers? According to Dr. Roger Smith, "not a damn bit. I never sensed he had any real warmth toward the girls. They were his possessions." Indeed, even Manson's orchestrated group sex was to make sure there were no lasting attachments to anyone but him.[12]

As important as sex was in Manson's deprogramming of his disciples, Tex Watson believed that dope played an even greater role in the process. "I think acid was the key, not just to the women but to all of us; it combined with Charlie's diabolically forceful personality and his joint-nurtured insight to turn rebellious American kids into pliant slaves ... through the acid we became his creation, his true believers, finally his slaves. Charlie never gave up using the acid for his teaching to break down our egos and completely dominate us."[13] In her memoirs, "Squeaky" Fromme believed that through drugs and sex, "Charlie tricked us. He tricked all us girls, and then tricked some guys. They say he's a con man, a devil. And that he was."[14] By the spring of 1968 Manson had grown weary of the Haight—it had become "ugly and mean"—and was ready to move on with his Family. He traded a grand piano he had acquired in the Haight for a dilapidated school bus which he refurbished as a hippie-mobile à la the Merry Pranksters, and headed for Los Angeles.[15] By the time Manson moved to southern California his family consisted of ten women and three men—Charles "Tex" Watson, Bobby Beausoliel, and Steve "Clem" Grogan.

The Manson Family moved to southern California in 1968, ultimately taking up residence in an abandoned movie studio, the Spahn Ranch in San Bernardino. It was at this time that Manson came to believe that an apocalyptic race war was about to descend upon the United States, led by the Black Panthers and that it was his God-ordained destiny to save the white race from extinction. As Tex Watson remembered, "Charlie rapped about a bloody conflict between blacks and whites.... Now 'Helter Skelter' was coming down fast was the main theme of everything he said.... All the centuries of oppression and exploitation of blackie were over, his karma had turned, and it was time for him to rise and to win and blacks would end up on top as the establishment," but only for a while because "blacks were less evolved than whites and therefore fit to be their slaves." "As the Beatles sang, this was not some event in the distant future; it was 'coming down fast.' We were living in the last few months, weeks, perhaps days, of the old order."[16]

For months Manson had been preparing for and predicting this "day of reckoning," convinced Armageddon was imminent. He believed this to have been the whole purpose of the Beatles' *White Album*, declaring to his followers on New Year's Eve 1968: "Are you hip to what the Beatles are saying? Dig it.... They know what's happening in the city, blackie is getting ready. They put the revolution to music; it's Helter Skelter.' Helter Skelter is coming down.... From across the Atlantic the hottest music group in the world substantiates Charlie with an album which is almost blood-curdling in its depiction of violence. It was uncanny.... At that point Charlie's credibility seemed indisputable. Charlie believed in the Beatles and we believed in Charlie."[17] Here was not only Ralph Gleason's earlier foreboding that rock music possessed the power "for evil," but also Ken Kesey's lament that the earlier Beatles had failed to exploit their popularity "to snap" kids into a new consciousness. Much to the Beatles' subsequent horror, their music did indeed snap someone, a psychopathic killer names Charles Manson.

Manson first heard the *White Album* within a month or so of its November 1968 release. According to Catherine Share, a Manson family member, the moment the album came out Manson became obsessed, "listening to it over and over and over again. He was quite certain that the Beatles had tapped into his spirit, the truth—that everything was gonna come down and the black man was going to rise. It wasn't that Charlie listened to the *White Album* and started following what he thought the Beatles were saying. It was the other way around. He thought that the Beatles were talking about what he had been expounding for years. Every song on the *White Album* he felt that they were singing about us. The song 'Helter Skelter'—he was interpreting that to mean blacks were gonna go up and the whites were gonna go down."[18]

Manson believed his first mission was to eliminate those white people he believed were collaborating with black subversives, as well as anyone who could possibly threaten his purpose. Certain that it was his calling to precipitate the race war, Manson began by exhorting the "young love" (America's young white female youth) to join his Family. Recruits were to be found among white female hippies who had inundated the Haight during the Summer of Love. Manson's plan was to remove them from the neighborhood in order to deprive black men of the white women allegedly sexually available to black men because of the civil rights movement. "Dig it man, that's why blackie has been so pacified; he still got a handle on whitey's women. He's up in the Haight Ashbury right now raping the young love, expending all his energy." However, these young girls were now "starting to split" from the Haight, and of course were headed for the Spahn Ranch to join Manson's Family. This female exodus from the Haight was "gonna cause blackie to get real frustrated and that's when he's gonna blow it."[19]

Enraged, sexually frustrated black men would unleash their wrath on whites, "in the establishment, pig neighborhoods like Beverly Hills or Bel Air, where they would perform murders so hideous—stabbing, mutilation, messages written on walls in the victim's blood—that the white establishment would be thrown into mass paranoia."[20] This would lead to a murderous retaliatory rampage by whites against black and non-racist whites. The majority of African Americans slaughtered in the white furor would supposedly be the "Uncle Toms" because Manson believed "the smart ones"—the Black Muslims and the Black Panthers—would be "hiding in their basements with all kinds of weapons and strategies while the shit's comin' down, and when the time is right they'll come out and finish off what's left of whitey" who had become polarized during the conflict. According to Manson's foretelling, eventually an internecine, fratricidal war would emerge between racist and non-racist whites, "between hippies and liberals on one side and conservatives on the other," over African American's treatment. A white conflagration so vicious and all-encompassing that, "families would divide, with parents shooting their own children and children slitting the throats of their parents." As whites battled each other, militant blacks would finish off the rest of the white population; indeed they would kill off all non-blacks.[21]

Throughout the holocaust, Manson and his followers would have little to fear; sheltered in a secret city underneath Death Valley. As the only surviving whites, Manson envisioned that they would wait until the now-satisfied blacks tried to govern the world but "Blackie would realize he couldn't run the world, realize he wasn't good for anything but serving whitey and copying what he did. So, the blacks would turn to the only white man left with the smarts to help them; they would turn to Charlie, to Jesus Christ, who would lead the chosen people out of the pit to rule the world forever."[22] Manson announced to his family that his race war would be "ready to happen" in the summer of 1969, for by then "blackie would be ready" because "he never did anything without whitey showin' him. We're gonna show blackie how to do it.... Blackie was so stupid that somebody would have to show him how to start Helter Skelter."[23]

From their commune at the Spahn Ranch, Manson, in late July and early August 1969, sent out certain family members on ritualistic killing sprees into the tonier neighborhoods of the Los Angeles area that ended in the vicious slaying of eight people—actress Sharon Tate, eight-month pregnant wife of genius film sorcerer Roman Polanski, and considered one of Hollywood's more promising young stars; Jay Sebring, Tate's ex-fiancé, who was in the process of revolutionizing the fashion industry by introducing hair-styling for men; Wocjech Frykowski, Polanski's boyhood friend, who had aspirations of emulating Polanski but by the time of his murder, he had been directing "home movies" (industry code for pornographic films) and had become a dope fiend; Abigail Folger, heiress to the Folger's Coffee millions and Frykowski's girlfriend; Steve Parent, an eighteen-year-old from the L.A. suburb of El Monte, a friend-of-a-friend, an innocent nobody who just happened to be at the Tate house when Manson and his followers showed up to perform their "ritual"; Leno La Bianca, owner of a grocery chain and his wife, Rosemary. The La Biancas knew nothing of Sharon Tate and her friends living miles away in different neighborhoods and different worlds; and Gary Hinman, music teacher, bagpipe player, and one-time Manson friend. In the course of the family's rampage, Manson personally murdered none of the victims; he simply instructed his minions in the performance of the executions.[24]

No sooner did the public become aware of the murders than the news media, like the Santa Ana winds whipping wildfires through southern California arroyos, fanned fears of near hysteria, especially about the hippies. Overnight "those gentle children with flowers in their hair and tabs of acid in their pockets would suddenly seem menacing and dangerous. The Beverly Hills–Hollywood circuit would snap shut like a trap."[25] Vincent Bugliosi agreed that before the Manson slayings, "no one associated hippies with violence and murder, just drugs, peace, free love, etc. Then the Manson Family comes along, looking like hippies, but what they were all about was murder. That was their religion, their credo. That shocked a lot of people and definitely hurt the counterculture movement."[26]

The Manson Family killing spree outraged and horrified the overwhelming majority of hippies. They loathed Manson, for giving longhairs "a bad name." As one freak claimed, he represented a "social category, a demon hippie, a symbol of 'What can happen to your son or daughter.'"[27] Indeed, thousands of parents genuinely feared that their long-haired, rock-music listening kids would turn into hippies, ending up victims of cults and drugs. It seemed that an "acid fascism" had emerged within the counterculture, led by charismatic, demonic sick wackos such as Charles Manson, their sole purpose to regularly get people so high that they came to possess their devoted followers. These freaked-out zombies would do whatever the leader commanded them to do, from engaging in all manner of sordid sexual escapades and even murder. Manson not only further aroused the straight world's already heightened sensibilities about hippies in general, but now, hippies with guns and knives, wantonly killing innocent people. Such revelations proved to be the tipping point for many straights; all that talk about hippie peace and love, nonsense; all had been a ruse to conceal that hippies were inherently evil; that hippie narcissism and hedonism had finally transformed longhairs into advocates of violence and death. For most straight Americans, the Manson slayings became the ultimate "I told you so" to those who had embraced the hip lifestyle. Yet, for some, the murders were also perplexing, for as *Time* noted in the aftermath, "how could children who had dropped out for the sake of kindness and sharing, love and beauty, be enjoined to kill?"[28]

According to sociologist and criminologist, Dr. Lewis Yablonsky, who had become "a close student of the [hippie] phenomenon," the Manson murders should not have shocked so many people, because for some time, "criminals and psychotics" had been "infiltrating the scene. They were rapidly accepted, as anyone could be who is willing to let his hair grow and don a few beads; they found, just as do runaway teenagers, that it is a good world in which they can disappear from law and society. Hippiedom became a magnet for severely emotionally disturbed people." Some crazed individuals like Manson, found other advantages to becoming a hippie, especially because "The true gentle folk were relatively defenseless. Leaderless, they responded readily to strong leaders [such as Manson]." In short, Yablonsky believed that after two years of "intense study of the hippie phenomenon," the majority of hippies were "actually lonely, alienated people; they can be totally devoid of true compassion. That is the reason why they can kill so matter-of-factly." Yablonsky believed his research verified and the Manson murders confirmed, that there had "always been a potential for murder" within the hippie movement.[29] Although the overwhelming majority of hippies passionately condemned all such cult leaders and their actions, unfortunately, in the aftermath of the Manson murders "guilt by association" became the order of the day for hippies.

Despite hippie denunciation, the mainstream media predictably had a field day with the Manson murders, bombarding the public with sensationalized, shocking portraits of the hippie community as one that no longer promoted peace, love, and gentleness but rather one that was full of rage, perversion, and outright savagery. The fall-out was swift and all-encompassing. Who could forget the Manson black-and-white mug shot on *Life*'s cover, his demonic stare with those off-kilter eyes, the left slightly higher than the right, projecting the maximum psycho-killer affect? Thanks to the media exploitation of the Manson episode, in the public mind, hippies almost overnight became sex-crazed, blood-thirsty beings living in spaced-out communes. Karlene Faith assessed that straight culture and the mainstream media were "in cahoots," waiting for just such an event as "proof" writ large "that the hippie movement was no good.... They latched on to people's worst fears about hippies and the antiwar movement.... The antagonism between hippies and straight society was based on their antithetical values. In the context of social disruptions the Manson murders were a convenient excuse for a backlash. Parents were warning their hippie kids, 'See what could happen to you?'"[30] LSD, of course, fueled hippies to commit acts of violence, and in the wake of the Manson murders, other alleged "hippie killings" took place around the country, with each becoming more sensationalized than the last, blaming the murders on hippies and their mindless passion for psychedelic drugs. According to Manson family attorney Paul Fitzgerald, the Tate–La Bianca homicides would be remembered "as the first acid murders. We're on the brink of a whole new concept of violence against society by people who have reached a different plateau of reality through LSD."[31]

Almost as disturbing to hippies as the actual murders were Manson's notorious sexual perversions and orgies, legendarily having sex with his "young loves" sometimes three a day. "Hippie sex" became in the straight mind yet another stereotypical ingredient, if not staple of the hip lifestyle. As one social scientist observed, "The idea that communal life is a sexual smorgasbord is a myth created and sustained by the media." Much of the media's sensational coverage and out-of-proportion fascination with the Manson case reflected that "Manson and his covey of willing women can be explained by the fact that he personally staged many men's fondest sexual fantasies." This assertion was confirmed by an undercover investigative reporter who disguised himself as a hippie in order to learn more about this particular counterculture group. Almost daily, straights, especially businessmen approached him and inquired about his "sexual habits. These guys just seemed to assume that because I was hairy I was some kind of incredible stud getting laid constantly." Contemporary Establishment columnist and essayist Richard Atcheson, who was "more favorably disposed" toward hippies, contended that most straights hated hippies because "They are presumed to be sexually free, and they have to be hated for that." The Manson murders according to San Francisco's underground *Express Times*, created "a public frenzy of hate and fear not only against Manson but also against communes and longhairs in general."[32]

Unfortunately but predictably, there were some counterculturists at the time of the Manson episode who helped fuel the fires of straight hostility toward hippies by celebrating Manson as a countercultural *hero* in many of their underground publications. Some of the most outrageously inflammatory came from the radical Weathermen, who proclaimed Manson their idol on the assumption that he was *guilty*. The organization praised Manson for having "offed some rich honky pigs." The Weathermen produced thousands of bumper stickers that read, "MANSON POWER—THE YEAR OF THE FORK!" The supposed pro–Black Panther, fanatically egalitarian group, apparently forgot about Manson's intense racism toward blacks, his treating of women as sex objects and brood sows, of an individual void of all human decency, saluted their new partners (the Manson Family) in "revolution." Weather-leader Bernadine Dohrn declared that "Offing those rich pigs [in this instance she was specifically referring to the La Bianca's] with their own forks and knives, and then eating a meal in the same room—far out!" So inspired by Manson's insanity, the Weathermen adopted a new hand greeting: four fingers held up, slightly spread, a fork. One of Los Angeles' underground papers, *Tuesday's Child*, plastered Manson's photo on the front page of one of their editions, proclaiming Manson their "MAN OF THE YEAR"; next issue depicted him as a crucified hippie. Manson's face made the cover of *Rolling Stone* for being "The Most Dangerous Man Alive." Even that more even-handed, if not staid publication momentarily got on the Manson bandwagon, opining that perhaps Manson was a scapegoat, for "the relentless gloating of the cops who, after a five-year search [since hippiedom began] finally found a longhaired devil you could love to hate." The magazine then asked the question, "Is Manson a hippie?"[33] Journalist David Dalton believed so, certain Manson had been "railroaded" by the Establishment because "he looked just like one of us. He had long hair and a beard and although skinnier, resembled Jim Morrison or maybe Jerry Garcia. We knew anybody who looked like that could never have done these horrible things they were saying he did. It was just the pig picking on some poor hippie guru.... It was surely some drug deal gone bad or revenge by an outraged lover for some kinky sex scene."[34]

Dalton initially believed Manson was innocent because he viewed the whole Manson episode as an assault on the hippie counterculture. "We need to tell our side of the story. I saw the Manson case as a fight for life of the counterculture itself—one of our own was being martyred, our most cherished beliefs were being trashed by the cynical establishment and their lackies, the LAPD. I was not alone in this delusion." However, after Bugliosi's assistant showed him the police photos of both night's slayings, Dalton had second thoughts about Manson's being innocent. The clincher for Dalton was seeing HELTER SKELTER written in Leno La Bianca's blood on the refrigerator. "I may have thought the LAPD storm troopers were capable of almost any kind of sleazy frame-up but daubing Beatles lyrics in blood on a refrigerator was a little beyond imagination." By the end of his interviews with Manson and later with some of his "young loves" and others at Spahn Ranch, Dalton left shaken and scared from having escaped with his life "from the Isle of Mutants [the Spahn Ranch Mansonites still there] in a small dinghy as a pack of zombies wailed their anguished cries from the dock; from Dr. Manson's fiendish experiments just in the nick of time." He was certain he had fled from "a demon of the zeitgeist immaculate in his terror and confusion. Appearing with almost supernatural precision in the last months of the sixties, he seemed to call into question everything about the [hippie] counterculture."[35]

Long-time East Village hipster Ed Sanders found his own grisly answer about whether Manson had been framed because he was a hippie. One year after the murders had taken place, Sanders was furiously writing *The Family*, which he hoped would become the definitive freak's history of Manson, his followers, and the reason for the murders—an apologia of sorts that would be competing with prosecutor Vincent Bugliosi's much more famous *Helter Skelter*. Sanders contended that Manson's actions reflected a seriously flawed national penal system that if not reformed, would produce more Mansons to stalk American communities. Sanders also rightly argued that the overall hippie lifestyle should not be indicted along with a few werewolves. However, one night a source slapped a photograph down on the bar where Sanders was having a drink, causing the hipster to throw-up his vodka tonic; it was a picture of the once-lovely Sharon Tate, "eyes open, belly sliced, and a rope around her neck." The horrific photo completely changed Sanders perception of Manson and his followers. "It was beyond the worst visual experience for me in my life," Sanders recalled. "I realized that anything that supported that type of behavior was something I was totally opposed to with all my moral being."[36] Even the most hip of hipsters could not condone or make excuses for such a heinous act of violence. Although continuing in his support of the counterculture and personally remaining a hippie, the Manson murders forced Sanders and many others to readjust their once-roseate lens through which they subsequently viewed the hippie movement.

Sadly, Jerry Rubin, continued to play the fool, and by doing so relative to Manson, deservedly lost much of his credibility within countercultural circles. Indeed, many hippies and other Leftists wholesale rejected Rubin as any kind of leader or spokesperson for their causes, dismissing him not only as an easily duped buffoon but as a completely self-absorbed, vapid, callous "media junkie." After his jailhouse visit with Manson in 1970, Rubin described his encounter: "I fell in love with Charlie Manson the first time I saw his cherub face and sparkling eyes on TV. We met Gypsy and Squeaky, two of the Manson family not in jail, and they were outasight. Squeaky is tiny with a squeaky voice, blond hair, blue eyes, and a face and smile you'd trust. She's supposed to have offed a couple of people but I don't believe it. Squeaky? No! Charlie entered. I tried to shake hands or embrace but he backed away. His words and courage inspired me and I felt great the rest of the day, overwhelmed by the depth of the experience of touching Manson's soul. He said he was innocent of the Tate murders and was being prosecuted by the pigs because of his lifestyle." Then in typical Rubin flip shallowness and juvenile naivety, he asked "What is innocence and what is guilt?"[37]

Unfortunately, no matter how vociferous hippies were in their condemnation of the Manson Family and their heinous acts of violence, the murders only further intensified anti-hippie sentiment among an already hostile mainstream America. Indeed, by 1969 straight Americans had come to associate and define all long-hairs and freaks of any stripe, as hippies, and consequently when an individual such as Manson emerged, wrapping himself in the hippie mantle and mouthing the hippie mantra, and then ordering the brutal slaying of eventually nine people (in late August 1969, Manson ordered the killing of Spahn ranch-hand Donald "Shorty" Shea), that was the end of any patience, understanding or empathy mainstream Americans might have had for the hippie movement. The December 1969 Altamont concert fiasco put the final nail in the hippie coffin. Perhaps the *real* hippie did indeed die in October 1967.

Not to be outdone by their Northeastern Woodstock counterparts, West Coast hipsters in early December 1969 planned yet another massive festival featuring the rock band that had come to epitomize in lyrics and on-stage performance, the darker side of counterculture rock and roll, the Rolling Stones. The Stones most recent hits, "Street Fighting Man," and "Sympathy for the Devil," reflected the growing violence of the culture in which they had

"The day the music died" at the hands of the Hell's Angels, foolishly hired by the Rolling Stones to provide security at the Altamont Rock Festival, December 1969 (photograph by Michelle Vignes, courtesy Bancroft Library, University of California, Berkeley).

become superstars. Mick Jagger and Keith Richards consciously postured themselves as social outlaws, heaping contempt on mainstream society by mocking its most cherished values in many of the songs they recorded, including the ones that became their biggest hits, such as "I Can't Get No) Satisfaction" (1965) and "Get Off of My Cloud" (1965). According to 1960s music critic Robert Christgau, "Above all the Stones were rebels, by commitment as well as by necessity. They flaunted their clothes and hair, their collective sneer, and their music itself.... The Stones were always anti-utopian. They never idealized, and they never expected to be pure." Better than any other band of that time, the Stones "voiced the enthusiastic hostility of the new mass bohemianism," while the majority of the other bands "muted their hostility because they were too busy just surviving to pursue hopeless battles." Lewd, sneering, and surly, they wanted to differentiate themselves from that "other" British band, the Beatles, whose music was "basically optimistic and rooted in American pop," while the Stones' sound "came from a darker, angrier place." The individual most responsible for crafting the Stones' anti-wholesome, "bad boy" image was their savvy second manager (Giorgio Gomelsky was their first), Andrew Loog Oldham, who wanted his "lads" to appear and perform as the complete opposite of the neat, smiling Beatles. "The overall hustle I invented for the Stones was to establish them as a raunchy, gamy, unpredictable bunch of undesirables. I decided that since the Beatles had already usurped the clean-cut choir boy image with synchronized jackets, I should take the Stones down the opposite road. I wanted to establish that the Stones were threatening, uncouth, and animalistic," which he was confident the press would find most alluring. Indeed, when giving interviews, Oldham encouraged the Stones to be as flip and

Enjoying a peaceful moment at Altamont, December 1969 (photograph by Michelle Vignes, courtesy Bancroft Library, University of California, Berkeley).

insulting in their responses as possible to journalists' queries. Oldham believed that after such encounters the media would "plaster" the Stones photos all over magazine and newspaper covers with captions or headlines declaring the band "Those dirty Rolling Stones. The opposite of these nice little chaps, the Beatles.... I'm gonna make you famous." By 1965, Olham's revamping of the Stones had come to fruition, at least according to Beatle George Harrison, who believed that "the real hip kids—or the kids who think they are—have gone off us. The in thing for those kids now is to be a Stones fan, because their parents can't stand the Rolling Stones."[38] Other band members included blues guitarist Brian Jones, bassist Bill Wyman, and drummer Charlie Watts.

Presenting themselves as the complete opposite of the comparatively wholesome Beatles, the Stones quickly gained a reputation for presenting a sound that was grittier and of greater intensity, depth, and complexity than that of the Beatles. As Christgau observed, "Their insistence on beat and volume was so aggressive and single-minded that they drove off the tender-minded altogether,

A brief moment of joy and celebration for at least one Altamont attendee in an otherwise completely calamitous day for rock and roll fans, December 6, 1969 (photograph by Michelle Vignes, courtesy Bancroft Library, University of California, Berkeley).

which was the whole idea." In Christgau's view, the Stones' music was signature "black-oriented rhythm and blues. [They] were wise enough to intuit that the Afro-American source would be a necessary and authentic part of whatever they did." The Stones, better than any other British or American white band, had mastered rock and roll's black origins, producing a sound that was not only more unique than any of their contemporaries, but one that also surged "with America's increasingly violent energy." Wyman and Watts provided the background beat while Jones and Richards the middle ground, allowing Mick Jagger to establish himself as one of rock and roll's most vibrant, erotic, and profane lead singers of any rock and roll band of the era. Jagger screamed out lyrics in a style that alternated between ecstatic self-love and willful defiance. "Like so many extraordinary voices, Jagger's defied description.... It was liquescent and nasal, full-throated and whiny. It was the voice of a white boy who loved the way black men sang."[39]

Nothing was sacred to the Stones, no social taboo safe from mocking ridicule. With his large lips pouting, or pursing, or curling, and tongue rolling about and out of his mouth, either licking those lips or pretending to lick something else, Jagger strutted the stage like a bantam rooster, exuding sensuality with his every stride, for the Stones delighted in lacing their songs with sexually suggestive language, which Jagger loved to play out on stage. Yet, according to Christgau, Jagger "wasn't even male in the usual sense. The most sexually exciting man in rock had always been the most androgynous, deliberately counter-posing his almost girlish demeanor to Keith's [Richards'] droogy leer."[40] Like all 1960s rock bands, the Stones wanted to "strut their stuff" on American television, and of course, the premier series for such a display remained *The Ed Sullivan Show*. Even as late as 1967, Sullivan and CBS still censored many of the rock and rollers who appeared on the show and the Stones were no exception. One of the band's big hits for that year was titled "Let's Spend the Night Together," which Sullivan insisted they must change to "Let's Spend *Some Time Together*" if they wanted to appear on his show. The Stones changed the lyrics "for whatever material benefits might accrue" from their performances and record sales, and[41] appeared a record six times on the show during the decade, beginning in October 1964. Their final appearance in November

1969 kicked off their first full U.S. tour in three years and climaxed a month later in the violent and bloody Altamont disaster.

Although donning counterculture attire and engaging fully in the hip drug scene, the Stones' music remained essentially rock and roll. None of their songs reflected the influence of the San Francisco acid rock sound or any of the Beatles' psychedelic musical meanderings or bizarre studio experiments with instruments. Although many of their songs were infused with drug references, none spoke directly of the "beauty" of acid trips or of love or finding truth within. As the 1960s progressed, the Stones' music took on a darker hue, evoking troubling images of ghosts and demons in "Paint it Black," "Let It Bleed," and "Sympathy for the Devil." These were dark rhapsodies of lost innocence, loneliness, despair, and death. The great bands of the decade all had their own "karmic aura"; the Grateful

As was true at Woodstock, there was plenty of dope available for Altamont festivalgoers as well. It appears as if these four attendees momentarily escaped the bedlam on the stage by finding a peaceful sanctuary behind the scenes and cooling out with a "doobie," December 6, 1969 (photograph by Michelle Vignes, courtesy Bancroft Library, University of California, Berkeley).

Dead and Jefferson Airplane, for instance, exuded such "positive vibes" that the souls of even the era's most savage beasts, the Hell's Angels, were soothed. However, the Stones' music cultivated a different affect and image, as Jagger "became the midnight rambler jumping your garden wall," and was "in character when he screamed 'I'll put a knife down your throat, baby, and it hurts!' He was a sinuous East End actor with a stage dagger and a crimson cape." Although Jagger considered the songs he sang and the antics he performed were all "for show"; many in his American audiences interpreted the Stones' music and lyrics as subliminal messages propagating violence and mayhem. Jagger "had no idea what he was conjuring."[42]

By 1969 not only had the Stones' music and lyrics changed dramatically along with their stage personae, but so had their fan base, which had become older and angrier, even outright hostile at times and thus potentially violent; consequently the appeal of such songs as "Street Fighting Man" and "Sympathy for the Devil." Their flirtation with the "love ethos" of the hippie movement, reflected in such songs as "Ruby Tuesday" and "As Tears Go By" had been brief and not at all indicative of whom the Stones *really were:* rock's true "bad boys" since their inception in 1962. A variety of factors had caused such an abrupt mood change among Stones aficionados: the increased use of hard drugs among attendees; increasing exposure to violence on television whether at home on city streets or in the jungles of Southeast Asia; and for many a desire for more daring and self-destructive kicks. Whether intentional or unwitting, Stones' performances seemed to fuel such behavior; they appeared as the incarnation of a foreboding that seemed to be fast engulfing the hippie movement by 1969.

As Stones chronicler Stanley Booth remembered, "Up until then [1969] their performances in the U.S. had been brief, incandescent explosions of desecration, attended almost exclusively by shrieking adolescent girls." However, by 1969, the teeny-bopper girls had disappeared from the rock concert scene, and the counterculture temperament became more desperate, jaded, and hostile, fueled by hard-drug use, the Stones attracted increasing numbers of fans who reflected that shift in disposition. In retrospect, there were indications that Altamont would be different than Woodstock because of the type of crowd the Stones' attracted. According to Booth, just one week before the Altamont disaster, a throng attending a Stones concert at Madison Square Garden became "a phenomenal crush. It started with a crush toward the front of the stage that you would have normally expected near the end of a concert, and then it simply grew from that." To Keith Richards, late 1969 concert goers were so raucously omnipresent and oblivious to space and any semblance of order, that "one got the feeling they really wanted to suck you out."[43] Given such preoccupations with nihilistic moods as well the changing face of the counterculture, it is not surprising that trouble shadowed the band wherever they went. Nonetheless, by the time of their 1969 U.S. tour, many critics considered the Stones to be the greatest rock and roll band in the world; in Robert Christgau's view, the Stones had embarked on "history's first mythic rock and roll tour."[44]

For all their outlaw posturing, on-stage lewdness, and general roguish behavior, the Stones were not by a long-shot the most nihilistic, self-absorbed, and destructive band of the late sixties. That acclaim went to the West Coast/Los Angeles area group the Doors, led by its deeply disturbed lead singer Jim Morrison who fancied himself a poet in the vein of Blake and whose blatantly obscene live performances made even Jagger's most rakish antics pale in comparison. For his outrageous, profane behavior, Morrison became the first rock artist ever to be arrested (New Haven, Connecticut, December 9, 1967) on stage during a concert performance. Morrison saw the Doors as "erotic politicians; our power is sexual. We make concerts sexual politics. The sex starts out with me, then moves out to include the charmed circle of musicians on stage and then to the audience and over the course of the concert becomes one big ball of fire" with Morrison eventually consumed by that sexual flame as he "writhes against the microphone stand, leaping from eyes-closed passivity into shrieking aggression, and moaning sweet pain like a modern St. Sebastian pierced by the arrows of angst and revelation."[45]

The Doors' more apocalyptic songs and concerts were far darker and more menacing than anything the Stones produced or performed, prompting one critic to declare that they "specialized in shocking their audiences, giving them the psychological equivalent of the guillotine."[46] The band took their name from one of Morrison's poems, "There are things that are known and things that are unknown; in between are doors," inspired by the poet William Blake's belief that individuals possessed certain visionary powers (enhanced of course by the use of hallucinogenic drugs), that could open "the doors of perception," allowing people to discover an infinite, enlightened, and purer reality. But the Doors saw the cosmos as a place of violence, sexual perversity, nihilism, and death, and these became the central themes of many of their songs. As Morrison told *Time*, "I'm interested in anything about revolt, disorder, chaos, especially activity that has no meaning. It seems to me to be the road to freedom." Thus the Doors developed a sound "at once more plaintive and dramatic" than their SF counterparts, that "startles and bemuses with a uniquely mournful and moody tone."[47]

The Doors' music was a fusion of rhythm and blues, acid rock, and thanks to the musical talents of keyboardist Ray Manzarek, a unique blend of rock and roll and psychedelic rock, producing such hits as "Break on Through (To the Other Side)," "Light My Fire," and "Hello, I Love You." The last two songs were number one singles, with many pop charts rating "Light My Fire" as 1967's number one song. If any southern California band came close to developing a unique "LA sound" it was the Doors. Morrison believed the band's music and lyrics reflected the LA scene. "We're into LA. Here, the kids live more freely and more powerfully than anywhere else, but it's also where old people come to die. Kids know both and we express both.... This city is looking for a ritual to join its fragments" and Morrison believed the Doors music and lyrics would be the "electric wedding" that would bring everything together in the City of Angels.[48]

By far, the Doors' most controversial and disturbing song (and the one that interestingly and unfortunately came to define the band more than any other of their songs, including their number one hits) was the 11-minute long Oedipal-laced "The End," in which a psychotic son murders his sister, brother, and father and then rapes his mother. Morrison sings the narration of events, from driving to the killer's parent's house to the actual murder of his siblings and father and rape/incest with his mother. Despite the song's gruesome images and unsettling lyrics, some critics hailed the song as "truly revolutionary" while declaring the Doors "the finest performing musicians on the contemporary scene." In the same essay Albert Goldman credited rock and roll music with having elevated popular tastes to "the summit of popular culture."[49] No doubt many Americans were taken aback by Goldman's exaltation of those rock and roll bands such as the Doors who sang about incest and patricide. Despite the often prurient and malevolent message of many of their songs, the majority of contemporary critics agreed with Goldman that the Doors, "When they're good," were "simply unbeatable," producing albums such as the 1970 *Morrison Hotel*, hailed by many rock pundits as being "one of the best albums of the decade."[50]

Unfortunately for the Doors, Morrison was a notorious profligate, who frequently showed up for both recording sessions and for live concerts either stoned out of his mind or completely inebriated. Because of Morrison's inability to stay sober, the Doors played their last live performance in December 1970 in New Orleans. Midway through the band's first set Morrison broke down on stage, falling to his knees and then pounding the microphone as hard as he could on the stage floor until the platform underneath was destroyed. He then sat down on the stage in a quasi-catatonic state and refused to continue to perform. The show was over and his fellow band members—John Densmore (drummer), Robby Krieger, lead guitar, and Ray Manzarek decided then and there they were through touring and that it was time to look for a new lead singer.[51] Morrison stayed clean long enough for the Doors to produce one more album, *L.A. Woman,* which received critical acclaim, resurrecting the Door's image after the Morrison debacle in New Orleans. Soon after the album's release in March 1971, Morrison took a "leave of absence" from the band and moved to Paris, France, with his long-time girlfriend, Pamela Courson. Unfortunately Morrison could not stay off the booze and drugs and finally succumbed to an overdose in early July 1971 at the age of 27. Courson found Morrison dead in the bathtub of their Paris apartment. Morrison was buried in the "Poet's Corner" of Père Lechaise Cemetery in Paris and inscribed on his headstone in Greek is KATA TON ΔAIMONA EAYTOY, which translates to "According to his own demons."[52] Courson fought her own addiction, following Morrison to an early death a few years later. Despite the band's often disturbing and menacing music and lyrics and Jim Morrison's schizophrenic behavior, the Doors remain popular and are considered one of the late 1960s more innovative rock and rollers, producing a sound and songs different from any other of their contemporaries. *Rolling Stone* magazine ranked the Doors number 41 on their list of 100 Greatest Artists of all time.

Having missed the Woodstock extravaganza, the Stones wanted the climax of their first U.S. appearance in three years to be a free concert. By this time in their career, the Stones had an image among many in the counterculture as profiteering rip-off artists, who had been charging their adoring fans $8.50 a head on their U.S. tour (the equivalent of $54.17 in 2015). Consequently, many in the Bay Area's hip communities believed the "festival" would be "one more shuck."[53] However, the band's tour manager, Sam Cutler, asserted that although the Stones "were broke when they did that tour," and that "they needed the money, I don't think the Rolling Stones could ever be accused of only playing for money. The Rolling Stones love to play. They give really great value for the money—they play for two or three hours always, when they do shows…. You can't do things that long and with that intensity without loving, it man."[54]

By the close of the 1960s, rock and roll had become big business; one of the most lucrative if not *the most* profitable enterprises to emerge out of the 1960s youth rebellion. Outdoor rock festivals had become stylized, expensive showcases of the most commercialized rock bands and individuals in the business. Disappearing from the rock scene were the altruistic charity gigs such as Monterey, and along with those concerts, the fan-band connection that had been the hallmark of the great dancehalls such as the Fillmore or Avalon Ballroom. Ultimately, the fans simply became an "audience" and performers became detached celebrities; rock and roll, like much of everything else in the counterculture, had been appropriated by corporate America in the name of profit. In the process most bands as well as individual rockers became as mercenary and as opportunistic as the record companies and concert promoters who competed for the artists' talents and commercial appeal.

The Stones Bay Area performance was also to be the climax of the documentary film of their complete tour by filmmakers Albert and David Maysles. The concert originally was to be held in one of San Jose State's large football practice fields, which just a few weeks prior hosted a huge outdoor free festival featuring 52 local bands and attended by some 80,000 people over the course of three days. However, San Jose city officials were not in the mood for another jamboree and denied the permit. Dirt Cheap Productions, hired by the Stones to procure a site, tried then to secure Kezar Stadium in Golden Gate Park, home of the NFL San Francisco 49'ers, but that venue was unavailable because the team had a Saturday game scheduled with the Chicago Bears. In any case, by 1969, the Haight had become a refuge for all manner of dissipated and desperate people: teenage runaways, strung-out Vietnam vets and draft-dodgers, hardcore drug pushers and criminal gangs. The City was no longer a sanctuary for the nation's restless seekers but rather for its wrecked and ruined. When Moby Grape guitarist Peter Lewis heard about "how beautiful" the Summer of Love was, he observed "'Where was that?' It was there but always lurking below was this seething rage and fear from Vietnam and the Cold War. There was always a feeling that we were going to die." Not only the Haight but San Francisco in general, "was descending into its Season of the Witch."[55] It should come as no surprise then, that city officials would not allow another tribal gathering of alleged drug-crazed, self-destructive wastrels, especially with a headliner band notorious for its sinister and misogynistic message and deviant behavior: the Rolling Stones. The last thing the City of Saint Francis needed as the turbulent decade of the 1960s was about to end, was a potentially violent explosion of youthful mayhem in one of its most beautiful and iconic public spaces.

After being rejected by San Francisco authorities, the promoters had only three days to find another venue. On Wednesday, December 3, the director of Sears Point Raceway offered his grounds free of charge, but the actual owners of the racetrack, Hollywood-based Filmways Corporation, smelled a huge profit-making possibility and demanded film distribution rights in lieu of a fee. The Stones' manager Sam Cutler and the Grateful Dead's manager Rock Scully, refused the deal, prompting Filmways to counter-offer with a fee of $100,000 to lease Sears Point for the day and another 100k to be put in escrow for "damages to property" as well as for post-concert clean-up. Needless to say Cutler and Scully, as well as the Stones rejected the latest negotiation. Meanwhile, tons of equipment for the concert had been set up at the drag strip. As Michael Lydon noted, it was becoming apparent that because "it was a Stones concert, free or not, everybody wanted a piece of the action. Hustlers of every stripe swarmed to the new scene like piranhas to the scent of blood."[56] At this juncture it looked as if the concert would be cancelled. Jagger, however, was not to be deterred from the venture: "'Well, man, we'll play in the streets if we have to.'" According to Rolling Stone, "He [Jagger] was almost prepared to pick a street corner in downtown Market Street in San Francisco and play there."[57]

Coming to the rescue was Dick Carter, owner of yet another race track, Altamont Raceway located on the outskirts of Livermore, California, 46 miles east of San Francisco between the working class towns of Tracy and Livermore. Carter offered his place for free, raising a lot of eyebrows because he was "totally without experience in the rock and roll game." But his motives were simple: he wanted the publicity because he hoped to use the event as a way to "rehabilitate" the track's image and believed sponsoring a massive "youth concert" would go far toward the resurrection. Carter spoke and looked more like a used car salesman than a hip rock and roll promoter, with his thin mustache and black and white checkered sport coat and white shoes. He confided to a *Rolling Stone* reporter, "By the way young fella we're trying to give this place a kinda new image, if you know what I mean. The old management hasn't been so good, so we want to identify it a little more differently. So when you write about the place, I'd appreciate it if you called it *Dick Carter's* Altamont Raceway."[58] By the end of Altamont his race track would become infamous rather than famous; identified for having sponsored one of the most violent outdoor rock concerts in the nation's socio-cultural history.

The raceway, which no longer attracted real motor races but rather third-rate stock car challenges and demolition derbies, had become a dilapidated track surrounded by equally unkempt grounds that at best could accommodate a crowd of 20,000 people; not the eventual 300,000 who showed on a site about one-sixth the size of Yasgur's Woodstock farm. Compared to attendees at Woodstock's bucolic green, those who came to Altamont found themselves packed in a dust bowl encircled by brown, scrub-covered hills; a landscape so bleak and desolate of vegetation that the environs looked "apocalyptic" and "unimaginably appalling, a mini [defoliated] Vietnam of garbage and old car wrecks." To Spencer Dryden of the Jefferson Airplane, the area "was just a horrible, pink-sky Hieronymus Bosch dustbin, not a tree in sight, just a hellhole." Stones' tour photographer Ethan Russell agreed: "It was a dull, lifeless landscape.... When we arrived there was no palpable feeling of joy or even happiness. It slowly dawned on me that this concert might not turn out to be what I expected."[59] According to *Rolling Stone* Altamont Raceway "was just a patch of land, covered with bleached-out long grass and sticker burrs," and thus "the physical atmosphere was singularly ominous and depressing.... And the later it got, the worse the air became—filled with a rancid combination of fog, dust, smoke, and glare." By nightfall Altamont had become "an instant city" of 300,000 human beings, "a decaying urban slum complete with its own air pollution" caused by the "dozens of garbage fires [that] had been set all over the place.... The stench of the smoke from tens of thousands of potato chip packages and half-eaten sandwiches brought vomiting to many."[60] To Dryden, so awful was Altamont's natural "set and setting" that it came as no surprise that the concert would mark "not the beginning of the end" but "*the end*" of the counterculture.[61] The *San Francisco Chronicle*'s veteran music critic Ralph Gleason agreed with Dryden, opining that "If the name of 'Woodstock' has come to denote the flowering of one phase of the youth culture, 'Altamont' has come to mean the end of it."[62]

In the planning stages the Stones believed that the best Bay Area folk to consult about how to go about organizing a free concert were the Grateful Dead and the Diggers: individuals legendary for all things free. Despite their growing national acclaim, the Grateful Dead still considered themselves a City/Haight-Ashbury band, whose concept of a free gig was spontaneous simplicity: "You want to hear music? Okay, do it! Get a place, a source of power, a few flatbed trucks or a stage, a few bands, spread the word, trust to God, and have the thing."[63] Wherever the physical venue might be, Grateful Dead free concerts were by and large wonderful occasions, marked by a sense of shared identity and community. According to Rock Scully, the band's manager for twenty years, The Dead considered their free gigs as a form of "social work. For us it seemed really important to get kids off the street and into the park [Golden Gate]"or anywhere in the Haight neighborhood they could find electricity. "Sometimes that took the form of a generator, sometimes it took the form of an extension cord from someone's washing machine outlet from an apartment across the street, dropped down from the trees to amplifiers."[64] But Sam Cutler saw the Dead's quaint "naturalness" as naïve relative to the changed outdoor concert scene, and thus the Dead "didn't have a clue" about organizing a rock festival the magnitude of Woodstock, featuring the Rolling Stones. "I mean, the Grateful Dead couldn't organize a piss-up in a brewery in those days. And everybody else [the SF/Bay Area hip community], they were on this trip and it was chaos."[65] Even the optimistic Diggers got cold feet as one venue after another fell through. As Peter Coyote remembered "We tried to warn the Stones before Altamont but they were too rich, too powerful, and there was too much flow of multinational capital to listen to us. We warned the Dead too. They should've known better. We were the experts at bringing thousands of people together with no violence. But mainly I blame the Stones, who were planning to make a fortune off the movie rights, for trying to put on a phony free concert.... And I blame Mick Jagger for fucking with black magic. They reaped what they sowed. So you want to go strolling on the dark side, boys? This is what it fucking looks like."[66]

There were other logistical problems as well: a lack of facilities such as portable toilets and medical tents along with woefully inadequate parking and supplies of food and water. Perhaps the most serious problem was the stage, which was only 39 inches above the ground, making it very accessible to the throngs of humanity about to descend on Altamont.[67] The organizers, however, made short shrift of such concerns, confident all would go well because after all this event was to be "Woodstock West," where the same spirit of togetherness, that had defined "Woodstock East," would be as bountifully present at Altamont as well. In Woodstock's euphoric aftermath, regardless of how severe the logistical problems (for Woodstock allegedly had proved that hippies could make do even in the most deprived circumstances), countercultural faithful were certain that every subsequent rock festival would further the reality of the Age of Aquarius and planetary peace and love. Unfortunately to hippies' horrible dismay, Altamont had the complete opposite effect. As *Rolling Stone* observed the concert marked "the death of rock culture" for it "ended certain notions about how groovy everything was, and how everything was going to take care of itself." To the authors, Altamont reflected everything that had gone wrong with the counterculture, which they believed had succumbed to greed, carelessness, and violence. "Altamont was the product of diabolical egotism, hype, ineptitude, money manipulation, and, at base, a fundamental lack of concern for humanity.... It was such a bad trip that it was almost perfect. All it lacked was mass rioting and the murder of one or more *musicians*. These things *could* have happened, with just a little more bad luck. It was as if Altamont's organizers had worked out a blueprint for disaster."[68]

As important to many attendees as recreating the Woodstock myth, was the equally desperate hope that the Stones would create a *new* kind of theater. However, what these individuals failed to realize was that the Stones' had a naïve, if not delusional image of America and thus their theatrics were simply caricatures of the American hip counterculture. However, Altamont would shatter the band's illusions, unnerve them emotionally, and simultaneously expose the artifice of their bad-boy image.

Perhaps the most tell-tale sign that Altamont *would not be* another Woodstock was reflected in the crowd's overall composition and its general demeanor. One of the keenest observers of such events was Michael Lydon, who had attended and had written about virtually every rock festival of the decade, beginning with Monterey. He of course did not miss Altamont. In retrospect he probably wished he had because as he quickly discerned, although there were "the dancing beaded girls, the Christ-like young men, and smiling babies familiar from countless stories on the 'Love Generation,'" there appeared to be a greater preponderance of "weirdos, whose perverse and penetrating intensity no camera ever captures. Speed freaks with hollow eyes and missing teeth, dead-faced acid heads burned out by countless flashes, old beatniks clutching gallons of red wine.... There were people who were damaged, or people who had been in prison for drugs. [People] that you knew were just unbalanced. People adrift, homeless, spaced, and so ill-educated that they didn't have any defense against culty-type vibes.... Face by face, body by body, the crowd is recognizable, comprehensible. As ugly beautiful mass, it is bewilderingly unfamiliar—a timeless lake of humanity climbing together through the first swirling, buzzing, euphoric-demonic hours of acid." As the day progressed and the crowd became more dissipated and unruly, Lydon observed "large segments of the crowd shar[ing] a dangerous desire to tighten up that festival idea a few notches, to move to a new level—just how weird can you stand it brother before you will crack." As he watched the day unravel into bedlam, Lydon wondered where the counterculture was headed; if it was "going anywhere" at all, or would it simply die in that "junkyard-graveyard" called Altamont; perhaps a fitting burial ground for a movement that appeared to be fast degenerating into anarchy and violence, of "aggressive paranoid frequencies that demand self-justification.... One third of a million post-war boom babies gathered in a Demolition Derby junkyard by a California freeway to get stoned and listen to rock 'n' roll—is that what it's all been about? Are we lost or found? Who are we? ... Community? It just doesn't feel like that anymore."[69] Grace Slick of the Jefferson Airplane agreed with Lydon, noting that the moment she arrived at Altamont, "The vibes were bad. Something was very peculiar, not particularly bad just real peculiar. It was that kind of hazy, abrasive, and unsure day. I had expected the loving vibes of Woodstock but that wasn't coming at me. This was a whole different thing."[70] Little did Grace Slick know just how "bad the vibes" would be at Altamont that day, especially for one of her fellow band members.

Some of the more intriguing summations of the Altamont crowd came from the Stones themselves. To guitarists Keith Richards and Mick Taylor the Altamont disaster reflected the inherently profound socio-cultural differences between American and British "civilization" by the late 1960s, especially among the nations' respective youth and the issue of violence. As Richards told the British press in the festival's aftermath, nothing like what occurred at Altamont would ever happen in the United Kingdom because, "You can put half a million young English people together and they won't start killing each other. That's the difference."[71] Taylor believed that by the late 1960s Americans in general had become so inured to violence that what happened at Altamont, though personally shocking, was to be expected from a people "so used to it [violence] over there, it's a commonplace thing. They find it easier to accept. I've just never seen anything like that before. I had expected a nice sort of peaceful concert. I didn't expect anything like that in San Francisco because they are so used to having nice things there."[72] While Richards and Taylor mollified the British press with their naïve and self-serving views of American society and culture, four people laid dead, one of whom was murdered largely because of their short-sighted hubris and artlessness.

Joining the Stones were Bay Area notables Santana, the Jefferson Airplane, the Flying Burrito Brothers and The Grateful Dead. Also appearing was the new but already nationally famous consortium of Crosby, Stills, Nash, and Young, fresh from their successful first appearance at Woodstock. All were former members of prominent rock and roll bands of the mid–1960s such as the Byrds (David Crosby); the Hollies (Graham Nash); and Buffalo Springfield

(Stephen Stills and Neil Young). No sooner did the crowd of 300,000 gather than all of Altamont's shortcomings became readily apparent. Sanitary facilities were wholly inadequate; the sound system was terrible which caused participants to crush closer and closer to the stage so they could hear the music; all compounded by such a cheerless "set and setting; " no peaceful, bucolic pastures and meadows here which might have gone far toward creating a more tranquil environment for attendees. Dope peddlers were as openly plentiful and as ubiquitous as they were at Woodstock, although "bad dope" seemed more prevalent; lots of bad dope, including inferior acid spiked with speed, circulated through the crowd, causing all manner of "freak-outs" and seriously bad trips, which harried medics had a hard time keeping up with, especially as the Thorazine temporarily ran out with which to treat the epidemic. According to Richard Fine, chairman of the Medical Committee for Human Rights, "We had one day to mobilize medical personnel and supplies. We got shitty support from the people running the thing who didn't realize what was crucial from a medical standpoint.... It was just piss-poor planning. A lot of the bad trips were violent because there was so much violence in the air.... We felt that we, as well as everyone else in the crowd, were exploited by the promoters." Most appalling to Fine was the refusal by the "Stones people" to turn on the backstage lights when it got dark so the medics could treat the dozens of people who lay injured in the triage area. Cutler had ordered the stage crew not turn on the lights until the Stones came out to play. "To turn them on before might rob some impact from the Stones entry," management told Fine. "People were injured? Well, tough shit, the Stones were more important."[73]

Management callousness did not stop with caring for the already injured; throughout the entire day and night, regardless of how potentially dangerous or life-threatening the situation might be, the individuals in charge refused to help out. Such was the reality confronting a young man desperately searching for the father of a toddler who had been stepped on by a Hell's Angel (by accident) during one of the many melees, and who many believed was dead. Cutler not only prohibited the young man from making an announcement for help in locating the father, but also personally refused to put out a call for assistance. "We're not making any personal announcements; we've told people where lost and found is, we've told people where Red Cross is. There will be no personal announcements. I don't care if you die; there's not going to be an announcement." Fortunately the baby was fine, a few minor bruises but alive.[74]

How "out of it" were many of the Altamont festival goers? According to ex–CIA operative and former cop turned millionaire drug-manufacturer-pusher, Lyle T. Dodge, who sold dope at both Woodstock and Altamont, "Folks were so stoned that you'd shit on someone's head and they'd smile, give you the peace sign and say 'far out man, like *dig* this gooey warm brown stuff.' Of course, everyone else was on a bummer. At Woodstock you had your acid, pot, 'shrooms and peyote, you know—soft fuzzy stuff. But Altamont demanded a ruder approach." As far as Carlos Santana was concerned, causing "the whole fucking mess" were the copious amount of "reds (barbiturates, "downers,") and liquor" consumed by the audience as well as by the Hell's Angels. "People just got fucked up and wanted to fuck up everybody. You lose control of and respect for yourself, and you lose control and respect for everybody else. That's what happened—reds and liquor did it."[75]

Unfortunately for Altamont attendees who had taken bad dope, there was no Chip Monck who came on the Woodstock P.A. system to gently warn people about the "bad brown acid" circulating through the crowd; an address that has become as famous as the festival itself. Sadly, no such similar alert came from Sam Cutler, who assumed the MC duties at Altamont. Monck was also at Altamont, but after setting up all the sound equipment and the stage he found himself marginalized by "the Stones' people." When told about all the people "really freaking out" on bad dope, Cutler's response was "Tough shit," demonstrating "his little regard for the audience's welfare." Blaming Cutler for the whole Altamont fiasco, Monck believed the root cause of the disaster was ego, for what else would prompt Cutler to announce the Stones as "The Greatest rock 'n' roll band in the world?" In Monck's view, nothing else mattered to Cutler and his crew, including "the safety and caring of the people and the arrangement of everything else," such as security. Indeed, when approached about the problems with the Angels and "crowd control," Cutler's response was "We don't give a fuck; just keep these people away."[76] Bad trips were not the only problems for the medics as they treated almost as many victims of the increasing random violence that seemed to permeate the crowd and escalate as the concert progressed.

Responsible for most of the violence that day were the Hell's Angels, whom the Stones and promoters had foolishly agreed to hire to keep the peace for $500 worth of beer. Ever since Ken Kesey had invited the Angels to his commune in La Honda to participate in his Acid Tests, the Angels and the hippies had developed an interesting rapport; "a sentimental romance," with the former considered by hippies to be "outlaw brothers of the counterculture" while the Angels became the hippies' "guardian Angels" against all those who "hassled" them; "they're so bad they're good went the line." Since the famous 1967 January Be-in the Angels had provided "security" for many of the local hippie bands when they gave public concerts, most routinely for the Grateful Dead. It was on the Dead's advice that the Stones hired the Angels to guard the stage.[77]

It is hard to pinpoint what prompted the Stones to make such a colossally bad decision to employ the Hell's Angels as the concert's security force. A variety of factors reflected the overweening, delusional desire of the Stones, concert promoters, and the fans to replicate Woodstock à la West Coast. They were determined *to have* the festival regardless of the warning signals that foretold a perfect storm for disaster. Once the concert had been announced, it *had* to happen, even if there remained a few details such as security and having to move the entire site to a horrible environment just twenty hours before the first performance. In some fairness to the Stones, the possibility of hiring on such short notice a professional security force or even a slew of local off-duty cops to provide such services was logistically impossible. The Hell's Angels were immediately available, cheap, and had experience as a police force since the January Be-In of protecting the SF bands tech equipment, generators, and even the stage from potentially raucous fans. Prior to Altamont, the Angels had done a decent, respectable job of maintaining the peace at Bay Area concerts, with minimal to no violence involved. However, it must be remembered that the Angels were guarding bands and people they knew fairly intimately, the trippy jam bands such as the Grateful Dead, Jefferson Airplane, and The Quicksilver Messenger Service; music and individuals they had "grown up with" in the Haight-Ashbury. Even though the Dead, the Airplane, and Santana were on the Altamont bill, the concert was nonetheless a *Rolling Stones* gig, and they had brought a distinctly different vibe to the United States in 1969; a karma not at all trippy but dark and sinister; in many ways an aura and sound that fueled the inherently violent nature of the Hell's Angels ethos and individual temperament.

To what degree were the Stones aware of the Angels *true* reputation? According to Cutler, "The idea that the Stones were this kind of naïve bunch of English fuckwits is actually insulting. I never had any illusions about who the Hells Angels were. I've always thought of them as being really heavy, really scary guys that you definitely didn't want to piss off in any way, shape, or form." But desperate times called for desperate measures; the Stones had little time and there was, after all, the Grateful Dead's "seal of approval" that the bikers would be just fine in a "security capacity." Thus a simple deal was made: the Angels would hang around the generators and safeguard the other tech equipment, and keep the stage clear of crazed people; all duties they had performed for the SF bands, in exchange for $500 worth of beer. "They'd just hang out and no one would fuck with them, so the power supply was secure," Cutler noted later. "The bands—all of the bands—were supposed to pay that money. The person who paid it was me, and I never got it back, to this fucking day."[78]

Grateful Dead manager Rock Scully contended that having the Hell's Angels involved in the concert was part of a larger, altruistic, "socially-conscious" effort "to bring all kinds of different people together over music. What we were trying to do was not just notify the Hell's Angels about having beer, we were talking about getting the Latino gangs to come out and provide ethnic food, and same with the Chinese gangs, who were warring in the northeast area of San Francisco."[79] Indeed, by 1969 ethnic and biker gangs were engaged in vicious turf wars all across the City, bringing to San Francisco an unprecedented wave of gang violence the likes of which residents had not witnessed in decades. As founding editor of *Rolling Stone* David Dalton further opined, Scully and others believed a "big powwow" a "gathering of the tribes would be just the thing. Get a budget from the Stones for beer, briquettes, beans, rice, burritos, and so on" and all the gangs would show up and a peace would be brokered by the local hipoisie. However, the Altamont location made such a tribal gathering impossible, for as Dalton reminded his readers, "How were the Chicanos, blacks, Chinese expected to get the hell *out* there? Take the non-existent bus?"[80] In 1967, at the height of the hippie movement, the "love and peace" flowing out of the Haight's hip residents might have been able to bring about such a rapprochement; in 1969 such a prospect was fanciful thinking. Indeed, as Scully admitted, he and his compatriots "were still young and idealistic."[81]

In a post–Altamont interview, Keith Richards admitted hiring the Angels was "not a good idea but we had them at the suggestion of the Grateful Dead. The trouble [was] a problem for us either way. If you don't have them to work for you as stewards, they come anyway and cause trouble."[82] Richards was correct; the Angels would have undoubtedly shown up at Altamont regardless of their "employment status," for as Michael Lydon confirmed, they would have "come, of course, as they always [did], but we hoped as friends."[83] It must also be remembered that according to the majority of post–Altamont analyses, the Angels wreaking the most havoc and violence were allegedly "prospects"; individuals aspiring to become gang members but who needed to prove themselves worthy of admission; that they were tough enough, mean enough, and ready to rumble at the slightest insult or provocation or threat to their manhood, or pack or bike. Altamont provided the perfect venue for their initiation rites. These were the toughs responsible for the first wave of violence that occurred during Santana's performance, the first band to play. To Lyle Dodge, these "novitiates" were the "Brownshirts ... hired to soften up the crowd for the Gestapo." By contrast, Woodstock invited "Mr. Rogers to gently monitor their festival." It was not until later in the day, almost dusk, at the close of Crosby, Stills, Nash, and Young's set, that the *real* Angels showed up, just in time to "protect" the Stones. For most of the day, the hardcore Angels had been in Oakland discussing the turf wars and which particular gang was the greatest threat to their hegemony.[84]

Also perhaps prompting the Stones to hire the Hell's Angels as security was their earlier experience with a British version of the biker gang, whom they employed as bodyguards for a concert they gave in Hyde Park in July. Compared to Altamont's "set and setting," Hyde Park was a veritable paradise and the weather that day (July 5) was perfect, the massive crowd—estimated at between 250,000 and 500,000—peaceful, and thousands remained after the show to help pick up the garbage. The Stones filmed the concert—*Stones in the Park*—and from the footage, the crowd, the overall "vibe," appeared Woodstockesque—relaxed and peaceful, with stoned, smiling faces everywhere. Most important, by the stage, "protecting" the Stones from frantic females wanting to get close to Jagger, were a "bunch of risible wannabe bikers" who called themselves the Hell's Angels, and who even had the real gang's insignia hand-embroidered on their jackets. As David Dalton noted, they were "East End yobs playing at being in a motorcycle 'club'" who helped to reinforce the Stones image as rock's "bad asses"; "fun and decorative pantomime violence with that bit of *Clockwork Orange* frisson" the Stones loved to project. Given the attendees overall "mellowness," the ersatz Angels had little to do but enjoy the show while sipping cups of free tea! Rock Scully attended the Hyde Park concert, warning the Stones that the *real* Hell's Angels were nothing like these "posers," and that these California Visigoths *were not* guys you would want to hire to do security. As Stanley Booth told Cutler and the Stones, contrary to hippie hype and delusion, the Hell's Angels were not "righteous dudes" who carried "themselves with honor and dignity. That was Bullshit! Any one of them would just as soon kill you as look at you." Or as David Dalton more graphically summed up the Angels persona, "These guys are red-and-white-and blue, real-time, Death's Head Angels. They went to Korea! Vietnam! They're fuckin' *killers*."[85]

According to Scully, the impression that the Stones and others had was that the SF bands were "tight" with the Angels, which was a myth; they were only friends with or knew well and trusted a handful of the gang's veteran leaders such as Chocolate George, Pete Knell, and some others and it was those particular individuals the hippie bands would hire as security at concerts, and that "was why not even a punch had ever been thrown."[86] Contrary to subsequent denials, Cutler and Jagger were both "smitten" by the idea of the Hell's Angels as bodyguards; Jagger was especially infatuated with the Angel's heraldry and sure the bikers would jump at the chance to serve as *his* and his band mates Praetorian Guard. In short, the image of the Hell's Angels, like the black knights of the Round Table, surrounding their Satanic Majesties on stage was simply too enticing for the Stones to resist.

Even before the Stones took the stage the tribal gathering at Altamont had degenerated into a violent and bloody melee in which scores had been beaten indiscriminately by Hell's Angels with loaded pool cues sawed off to the length of billy clubs for getting too close to the performers. According to Angel Pete Knell, Cutler had given his gang very little specific instruction for stage security other than telling them "just to keep people off the stage" and this was interpreted as carte blanche to do whatever they deemed necessary to earn their $500 worth of beer. As Knell told the press, "If we say we're going to do something, we do it. If we decide to do it, it's done. No matter what, nor how far we have to go to do it." Apparently the Angels believed that they had to go as far clubbing people for offenses real or imagined. Interestingly, it has been revealed that there were scores of professional, plainclothes security guards secretly hired by Dick Carter to protect his *property*, rather than for the safety and well-being of the concert-goers. There were also uniformed police at Altamont but only a handful on or near the stage as most had been assigned traffic duty to try to keep the highway clear for emergency vehicles, which ironically, were in great demand that day. As the stage area descended into violent anarchy, various individuals approached the cops for help in dealing with the Hell's Angels running amok. One of the cops told Cutler that he had been calling for back-up all day but no response, and that "We don't have enough manpower to deal with these punks. These guys are psychos." The cop further told Cutler and others that he and his few fellow officers were not about to risk their lives attempting to arrest "those crazy biker dudes."[87]

The overall lack of concern by local law enforcement raised the question about whether such disinterest in keeping the peace at Altamont was by design. Perhaps the local authorities' detachment from the violent melee happening at Altamont reflected the feeling among many "normal" Americans by 1969, that the best way to rid the nation of the counterculture was to allow it self-destruct, and if that process could conclude more rapidly by letting them kill each other, then so be it. Tragically, that appeared to be the prevailing mentality among Livermore and Tracey police as well as the county sheriff's office, all of whom had grown sick and tired of the hippies and all their excesses. The innocent were just the collateral damage and that was a sad commentary on 1969 America across the board.

Legendary rock promoter Bill Graham contended that concerned law enforcement, or lack of, was the biggest culprit of all responsible for the Altamont disaster. "The law had the greatest power to avert this. The law is the most responsible whenever there's a danger and they don't stop it. To me, anytime the law sees anything like this coming, which is a holocaust, when the law realizes the citizenry of an area is in danger, they can stop anything at any time. You can block a highway, you could force them by injunction, or by force—sometimes force is valid.... My point is the law *knew* what was coming" but irresponsibly and callously did nothing to prevent the impending calamity or intervene once the bloodletting started. In the ensuing days, several sheriff's officers began coming forward, expressing feelings of guilt or responsibility for what happened at Altamont, "that they should have prevented the Angels from taking over. Whether or not the *Stones* wanted cops to handle security for the concert, the decision ultimately rested with the cops themselves" but at the time the majority of deputies were "too busy" with other "problems."[88]

According to attendee Frank Wise, who had dropped out from his job as a college professor in New York and became a devoted Learyite, the entire Altamont calamity was "a government plot to demonize the hippies" and that the Hell's Angels were *not* hired by the Stones but rather by the CIA and FBI to inflict as much damage on the hippies as possible and to motivate them to do so, both agencies "fed downers to the Hell's Angels and lots of alcohol, which made them wild and crazy and violent." Even the Maysles brothers were part of the "conspiracy," paid by the CIA to film the counterculture's self-destruction. Even the injured "were actors" according to Wise. "They tried to make Altamont as near to HELL as they could, in order to demonize hippie-ism" in the minds of Americans.[89] Although far-fetched, Wise's outlandish assertion reflected the impact the uncontrollable violence had on individuals and their desperate attempts to try to explain the horror they witnessed at Altamont. They simply could not square the calamity in their heads with Woodstock's euphoric aftermath, where, just four months earlier, not even a fist-fight occurred.

As the villains of Altamont the Hells' Angels were the perfect scapegoats for the Establishment's secret desires to crush the counterculture. In many ways Altamont was a "culture clash" with the Angels representing the forces of brutal reactionary oppression. The majority of Angels, contrary to hippie mythology, despised the freaks. As Sonny Barger, president of the Oakland chapter made clear, he and his gang "ain't no peace creeps." Indeed, in 1965, Barger and company, with the approval of the Oakland police, viciously assaulted anti–Vietnam War demonstrators, while the Berkeley cops tried to shield the protestors from the Angels' fury. As an observer concluded, there were no cops at Altamont because "they were smart.... Let the Hell's Angels kill the hippies, what the fuck do we [straight Americans] care?"[90]

Vibrations of fear and paranoia spread from Angels outward through the crowd. Indeed, the Angels were not the only ones shredding the Woodstock image. Fueled by alcohol, LSD, and amphetamines, the crowd had also become increasingly antagonistic and unpredictable, attacking each other, the Angels, and the performers. As Tim Cahill, a writer for *Rolling Stone* observed, "There was this big fat guy in Bermuda shorts, real woozy who sat on a guy and grabbed his girl's tits. Nobody in this place where we were all mellow said anything—including, I'm afraid, me." Six months pregnant Denise Jewkes of the local San Francisco rock band, the Ace of Cups, was hit in the head by full beer cans thrown either from the crowd or by the Angels, suffering a skull fracture. Sadly, pathetically, the hippies did nothing but hold up the peace sign when confronted by the Angels' brutality, as if that was all they needed to do to remind the Angels that their violence was defiling the counterculture ethos of "peace and love," and that the bikers were fast destroying their dream of "Woodstock West."[91]

Sadly, only a handful of individuals had the courage to try to stop the vicious assaults; the other 299,000 either did nothing, or could not see the mayhem or simply were too scared to confront such brutal bullies. Indeed, one of the most revealing realities about the late 1960s counterculture was how feebly they responded to a crisis *without* those very guardians of white middle class society that hippies had railed against so vociferously. There's never a "pig" when you need one! All the while the Angels poured down the beer or wine, the latter gifts from the crowd who were trying to appease the progressively intoxicated, agitated, and violent Angels, who were determined to drive the crowd further back from the stage. As photographer Michael Zagaris noted, "You could tell everyone hated them. As stoned as I was, I was thinking 'This is like Poland when the Nazis marched in.' Everyone hated them but felt they couldn't do anything.... I used to hear all the time in the Haight, 'Hey the Angels are our brothers,' but I thought most of these guys are killers.... How the fuck are these guys our brothers?"[92]

Yet, strangely, when the Jefferson Airplane performed their set, they summoned the Angels to join them on the stage to pay them homage, "with all the grandeur of Bert Parks inviting last year's Miss America to step forward." By the time of Altamont, the Airplane was no longer just a hippie band singing acid rock; they had changed their sound with the times as their music now reflected the increasing anarchic rage that appeared to be consuming the counterculture. The song they sang to the Angels was "We Can Be Together." Within a few minutes of singing the Angel's praises, the Airplane's lead singer Marty Balin was knocked out cold by an Angel as Balin attempted to stop several Angels from beating yet another fan, "a black man getting swallowed up by the forces of chaos and anarchy, half a dozen of whom were thumping the shit out of him" with their pool cues. As Balin remembered, "I saw the whole crowd, this mass, just back up and allow it to happen. I said 'To hell with the song, this guy needs help. So I went down there and started fighting, helping this guy out. When

I woke up, I had all these boot marks tattooed all over me." Later, when the Angel "Animal," who had cold-cocked Balin came back stage to "apologize" a still-enraged Balin said "Fuck you" and the biker knocked him out again. As Peter Coyote noted Balin was one of the few "stand-up" guys at Altamont. As the rest of the band watched their founder get pummeled, Grace Slick, shocked and terrified, shouted "What the fuck is going on?" and then pleaded in vain, "Everybody please cool out." Perhaps most disturbing, after the Balin incident, it had become clear to most reporters that the Hell's Angels "were in charge of the stage. It was *theirs*, musicians or no musicians," and thus the concert had become in the view of the *Rolling Stone* contingent, "a Hell's Angel Festival."[93]

Miraculously, and to everyone's elated relief, nothing violent happened; not one Angel fist or pool cue landed on anyone's face or head during the Flying Burrito Brothers perform-ance and for a brief moment there were smiles, balloons rose in the air, people were dancing and blowing bubbles. It appeared as if the band's countrified electric music had momentarily soothed the savage beasts. No sooner did the Flying Burrito Brothers finish playing than the pool cues reappeared and the beatings resumed.[94] Indeed, by the time Crosby, Stills, Nash and Young had finished their "desultory performance," the Angels had racked up quite the carnage after they had charged into the crowd with "pool cues flailing [at] whoever got in their way. Several stretchers were sent into the audience and bodies were passed overhead and across the stage to the Red Cross area. Those who were carried out and those who departed under their own steam were quickly replaced, as it became obvious the next set was going to be the Stones."[95]

All the while, the Grateful Dead, who were actually to perform before the Stones, had been watching the melee outside through their old school bus' windows, scared to death by what they were witnessing. Periodically, one of the band members had the courage to venture outside to the stage area and witness first-hand the "slaughter" and report back to his band mates. Pigpen never left the bus, too terrified to do so and "Jerry [Garcia] was shaking and huddling with Mountain Girl [Garcia's wife] on the floor of the bus through the worst fight-ing," and although they had arrived loaded to the gills on opium and mescaline, even in such an anesthetized state, "all the dope in the world wasn't going to help a bummer like this." Meanwhile Phil Lesh gave a running commentary on the savagery taking place outside. "Jesus Christ, there's this three-hundred-pound naked guy, and—oh-God!—the Angels are beating him to a pulp." The rest of the band members were hiding in the back of the bus "too numb to react." Garcia finally mustered enough courage to go out of the bus to watch the Jefferson Airplane perform, arriving in time to watch Marty Balin get cold-cocked by "Animal." Wit-nessing a fellow Haight-Ashbury guy and friend get blasted by a Hell's Angel was too much for Garcia, who fled back to the bus completely undone by what he had just experienced. His face ashen, his body shaking, he announced "Oh maa—aan, there is no way we're doing this. There is absolutely no way." The Dead powwowed and agreed that the Stones needed to play sooner than later and consequently they would forego their appearance for the sake of hope-fully ending the violence. After all, it was the Stones, not the Dead, 300,000 people had come to see! It was time "to find a way out of this godforsaken place; this demonic gully." Moreover, as Phil Lesh aptly assessed "the scene," ending any further the debate about whether or not the Dead should play, "Let the Stones go on, this is *their madness*." And the Grateful Dead did precisely that as they escaped Altamont while the Stones were playing, beyond relief at having "gotten the last helicopter out of Saigon."[96]

At nightfall, after keeping the crowd waiting in the cold for more than an hour, allowing the attendees even more time to become intoxicated or high, rowdier or outright hostile, the Rolling Stones came on stage, but not for very long. As soon as the Stones left their trailer a crazed freak, high on reds and cheap Red Mountain wine broke through the Angel's escort, screaming "I hate you, I hate you," and punched Jagger smack in the chops; a portent of what was to come very soon. Jagger was wearing yellow crushed velvet pants, a red silk shirt, and leather cape; attire that symbolically represented the dark, sinister nature of their music and stage persona. By the beginning of their third song "Sympathy for the Devil" the atmosphere was tense and eerie; violence permeated the air. Jagger, visibly appalled and intimidated by the mayhem, urged everyone "to just be cool down in front there, don't push around." At that moment, a drugged-out-of-her-mind, bare-breasted girl kept trying to climb on the stage to get at Jagger and the Angels quickly intervened, roughly manhandling the woman. Richards, obviously disturbed by the bikers' needlessly harsh treatment, leaned into Barger's face, and said, "Man, I'm sure it doesn't take three or four great big Hell's Angels to get that bird off the stage." Barger agreed, told the other guys to leave the girl alone and then walked over to the edge of the stage where the woman was sprawled and kicked her in the head; she rolled off the stage, onto the ground, unconscious. "How's that?" he asked Richards, as the rest of the band watched in horror.[97]

As the Angels were roughing-up the young woman, one of the Maysles brothers, David, caught one of their cameramen shooting the whole scene. Maysles did not want such "ugliness" on film and told the cameraman to stop shooting because "We only want beautiful things" in the movie. The cameraman quickly responded, rather incredulously "How can you possibly say that? Everything here is so ugly." A few minutes later Richards approached Barger again because the Angels had unleashed yet another barrage of attacks on the fans, and told the Huns' leader that "Either these cats cool it, man, or we don't play." It was at this juncture that Barger's and his fellow Angels' contempt for the "prissy" Stones became apparent; the band's fame had no traction in this mad abyss. Barger stuck a gun in Richards' chest and told the guitarist to start playing or he was a dead man! According to Barger's later account, after his "words" with the guitarist, Richards "played like a motherfucker."[98]

Nonetheless, there was Jagger, reveling in his image as rock's "prince of evil" prancing on the stage while the Angels continued to flail away with their pool cues as well as with chains, anyone who got too close to the stage. The violence was even too much for Jagger who stopped the music more than once to plead for order but to no avail, leaving him no choice but to sing on. Jagger's meek attempts at trying to stop the madness disappointed Ethan Russell, who believed naively that Jagger "had the power and [I] was disappointed he seemed so timid; Keith Richards [had been] much bolder" in confronting the Angels. The band had almost finished "Under My Thumb" when the most gruesome incident of the entire Altamont debacle occurred just a few feet in front of the stage in Jagger's full view: the knifing to death of an eighteen-year-old black man named Meredith Hunter by the Hell's Angel Alan Passaro. Subsequent evidence revealed that Hunter was not a completely innocent victim of the Angel's wanton violence that day. Before the knifing, Hunter had scuffled with some Angels when he tried to get onstage with other fans. He was punched in the head and thrown back into the crowd. According to Rock Scully, who witnessed the entire fracas from the top of a truck by the stage, Hunter, enraged, "was crazy, he was on drugs and that he had murderous intent. There was no doubt in my mind that he intended to do terrible harm to Mick or somebody in the Rolling Stones, or somebody on that stage." Footage from the Maysles brothers' documentary *Gimme Shelter* shows Hunter (seen in the film in a bright lime-green suit) brandishing a long-barreled revolver and the moment the gun was revealed Passaro attacked Hunter, knocking the gun from his hand and stabbing him five times. The moment Hunter fell to the ground witnesses saw other Angels stomping on him, kicking in his face. Horrified and stunned the crowd did nothing. Hunter died in a pool of blood. The entire brutal spectacle was captured on film, becoming the "highlight" of the movie *Gimme Shelter*.[99]

The gun was recovered and turned over to the police. Hunter's autopsy revealed he was indeed high on methamphetamine when he died. Passaro was arrested and tried for murder in the summer of 1971 but thanks to those few seconds of movie footage of the concert that captured the whole incident, the jury acquitted Passaro on the basis of self-defense. All through the mayhem Jagger pleaded to stop the violence but his entreaties fell on deaf ears as the Angels, now in a wild frenzy, beat people at will. Wanting to prevent a wholesale riot, the Stones, after several interruptions, decided to play on and after finishing their set's last song, another potentially unwise choice, "Street Fighting Man," quickly departed by helicopter. After they had returned to the safety their hotel room, the Stones tried to come to grips with the murder and mayhem they had just witnessed. In their attempts to express their feelings to a San Francisco radio station, they came across as stumbling, bumbling, inarticulate, stupefied English dandies who had found themselves in some forsaken, barbaric outpost of the British Empire. When Jagger spoke, it sounded as if he was about to sob: "I thought the scene here was supposed to be so groovy. I don't know what happened. If Jesus had been there, he would have been crucified." Keith Richards, less emotional but equally fatuous believed something like Altamont "could only happen to the Stones, man. Let's face it. It wouldn't happen to the Bee Gees, and it wouldn't happen to Crosby, Stills, and Nash." Nonetheless, Richards was perhaps more accurate in his appraisal than not; had the Stones not been the headliners, promising a free concert, and had they not hired the Hell's Angels as security, then Altamont probably would not have become rock's most infamous day.[100]

No sooner was Altamont mercifully over and Meredith Hunter lay on a slab in some East Bay morgue, than the finger-pointing began. As predicted, *no one*, not any of the individuals or groups involved in putting the show together, willingly came forward and admitted or assumed any responsibility for the worst day in rock and roll's history. The post-mortem days of Altamont witnessed buck-passing par excellence, as all the people involved, from promoters and organizers to management to musicians, all blamed someone else for the disaster. Some individuals even dismissed the whole tragedy as simply "collateral damage"; a calamity to be expected when there was "a mix of ecstasy and depravity," which according to the quintessential "cosmic cowboy," Stewart Brand, had been part of the countercultural ethos since its inception. Priding himself on being "un-shockable," Brand was not at all surprised by what happened at Altamont. Indeed given the heady witches brew of such countercultural excesses present, the violence and general mayhem was to be anticipated and thus Brand thought the concert "was terrific.... It seemed entirely appropriate that there'd be people beating each other to death in the midst of all that. Dionysus leads people to being shredded and eaten. Those were the death-defying leaps we were about in those days, and some people die in the process."[101]

Hip's perennial optimist, Timothy Leary, loaded as usual on LSD, had the same take as

Brand on Altamont and believed he had to remind people "that there were three or four hundred thousand people who did sit peacefully and get high and watch the sun and the clouds and the stars and listen to the music and were not at all involved in the violence.... There were less than fifty violent people there in a throng of 400,000 [actually 300,000]. In a sense Altamont is a Microcosm of the overall political situation. 99 percent of everybody wants to get high, and groove and love...." Even more dismissive of the murder and violence was an op-ed in *The Berkeley Barb* that blithely if not callously declared, "Four babies are born and four people die. An even exchange of souls."[102]

Although some hipsters such as Brand and Leary tried to spin Altamont as positively as they possibly could, the overwhelming majority of hippies, the bands who performed, and their straight supporters in the music/youth business world, condemned the Altamont bedlam vigorously and at times most venomously, roundly blaming the Hell's Angels, the Stones, and particularly the Stones' management, and even the crowd for the fiasco. For Carlos Santana "There was bad vibes from the beginning. The fights started because the Hell's Angels were pushing people around. There was no provocation; the Angels started the whole violence thing and there's no fucking doubt about that." As far as the audience was concerned, "There was no energy there. The vibrations were really strange. Everybody was trying to have a good time but there just wasn't any energy from them. It was all a big ego thing. They wanted to have another Woodstock, but they didn't want to make one, they wanted it to just happen to them."[103] As Michael Lydon aptly discerned, "Woodstock was a three-day encampment at which cooperation was necessary for survival; it was an event only because it became an event. The Altamont crowd is *demanding* that an event come to pass, be delivered in a single day; should it go bad—well, it'll be over by evening.... At Altamont, the dark side snarled its ugly answer to Woodstock's August joy."[104]

David Crosby also believed the Hell's Angels were not only completely out of control but should not have been there in the first place, because Crosby believed "that security isn't part of anybody's concert anywhere anymore. I mean our road managers could have covered it. The mistake that was made was in thinking security was needed, and that the Angels should do it. That's not real and they [the Stones] just found out the reality of it.... In their [the Angels] mind, guard a stage means you guard it. That means if anyone comes near it, you do them in, and in the Angels' style if you do them in, *you do them in*.... They are pure unadulterated danger. Don't mess with them but I don't think they were the major mistake. I think they were just the most obvious mistake. Unfortunately we all had to pay some dues for that."[105]

Bottom line for Crosby: the Stones were largely to blame because they were "into an ego game and a star trip, and who qualify in my book as snobs. I don't like them and they have an exaggerated view of their own importance; I think they're on a grotesque ego trip," which Crosby believed was "intensely negative [dark and sinister]," and which their "two leaders"—Jagger and Richards—exuded both on and off-stage. Another SF musician, whose identity Crosby refused to reveal, believed Jagger was solely to blame because of "the ego trip he is on," and that "If I ever get that asshole up against the wall, he ain't ever gonna walk away."[106]

Twenty-seven-year-old attendee John Peters agreed with Crosby, expressing his views in the underground SF *Good Times* letters section. Peters also cogently summed up what forces were causing the counterculture's "darkening mood" and thus its impending, inevitable demise. "What made Mick and the boys rich and famous and great is their whole fantastic trip of power and violence, and it's a very American trip by the way.... For [the Rolling Stones], power and violence is fantasy, something close to pornographic literature. But Americans just ain't like that. The real Americans want to get their hands and faces in the mud and blood and the beer. The Love Generation never made it, except for a few communes off by themselves, because it had no roots.... The Angels and tough blacks, whatever their differences, they all have roots. Put any of them in a frontier town and they'd be running around with the worst motherfuckers within a week. Their power and violence isn't a fantasy."[107]

The respected veteran pundit of the Bay Area's music scene, Ralph Gleason, took virtually everyone to task for the debacle—the Stones, Sam Cutler, Rock Scully, the Grateful Dead, Emmett Grogan, and Chet Helms—all of whom he believed were " as guilty of that black man's [Meredith Hunter] death as the Hell's Angels." Gleason was especially upset with "the locals"—Helms, Scully, the Dead—who not only should have known better than to allow the Stones to hire the Hell's Angels, but because of all their experience in presenting free concerts, they should have been aware that a one-day, massive preparation for 300,000 people was doomed to failure it not outright catastrophe from the start. "How could they have gone along with such a ridiculous idea?" Their short-sightedness, arrogance, and greed, caused Altamont to end "in murder. And that was murder, not just a 'death' like the drowning, or the hit-and-run victims. Somebody stabbed that man five times in the back.... Is this the new community? Is this what Woodstock promised? Gathered together as a tribe, what happened? Brutality, murder, despoliation, you name it.... There was no love, no joy at Altamont. It wasn't just the Angels. It was everybody. In twenty-four hours, we created all the problems of our society in one confined area—congestion, violence, dehumanization." Altamont convinced Gleason that by 1969 rock and roll had become corrupted by "money, power, and ego, and money is first, and it brings power." In Gleason's view, the Stones were just one in a long list of many bands who had succumbed to fame and fortune, and if anyone still believed that the Stones did Altamont for free, they were delusional. "They did it for the money, only the tab was paid in a different way."[108]

As disappointed and angry as Gleason with the Altamont calamity was the legendary rock promoter Bill Graham, who, like Gleason had been one of the counterculture's staunchest supporters and apologists. Like Gleason, Graham felt duped and betrayed by what had happened at Altamont and thus blasted all those he felt were responsible for the nightmare. He was especially "pissed-off" by the "stupidity" of "certain locals in agreeing to this; they *certainly* should have known better. Without realizing it, they were accessories to the crime." Graham however, reserved the most verbal venom for Mick Jagger and his band, viewing them as locusts, sweeping across the United States, "devouring young people," and then leaving "this country with $1.2 million. What did he leave behind throughout the country? Every gig he was late. Every fucking gig he made the promoter and the people bleed. What right does this god have to descend on this country in this way? What right did you have, Mr. Jagger, to walk out on stage every night with your Uncle Sam hat, throw it down with complete disdain and then leave this country with so much money, it makes me sick to think about it." Graham believed or hoped that something good would in the end, come out of Altamont, and that was the end of giant outdoor festivals, for which Graham had never been a fan. "The strange thing that went on this past weekend is that in the long run, it [Altamont] may help to eliminate festivals, which I think is one of the best things that can happen to rock and roll." Graham readily acknowledged how incredible Woodstock had been, "a miracle," but at the same time he also believed that "the reality" of future festivals would be similar if not worse than Altamont because "you just can't put that many stoned-out people together with that kind of music, and expect nothing to happen. People come expecting too much and when what they believe *should* happen, doesn't happen, you will have trouble; violence for sure and maybe even death. You just can't contain that many people and expect good vibes and peace throughout the whole thing."[109] *The Berkeley Tribe* seconded Graham's assertion, opining that "Bringing a lot of people together used to be cool. But at Altamont ... the locust generation came to consume the crumbs from the hands of an entertainment industry we helped to create.... Everybody grooved on fear. Our one day micro-society was bound to the death-throes of capitalist greed."[110] In short, as far as Graham was concerned, Altamont made the countercultural idea of massive outdoor music festivals as the progenitors of a "new community" look as naïve as it patently was.

Conspicuously absent, or at best mentioned in passing in most post–Altamont assessments, was the fact that Hunter was African American and his girlfriend, Patti Bredahoff, *white*. It was if none of the Monday-morning rock/youth quarterbacks dared suggest that Hunter's murder was racially motivated, for to do so would be to admit the reality that 1969 America was still a racist society and culture and that despite the advances of the civil rights movement, little progress had been made in changing white hearts and minds relative to race. When it came right down to it, a high percentage of hippies feared and loathed blacks, reflecting that many, if not most, carried with them from their white suburbs, racial fear, stereotypes and prejudices. In the post–Altamont finger-pointing, it seemed no one, not even the *Rolling Stone* reporters, wanted to delve too deeply into Hunter's brutal murder.

The question that needs to be asked was why *no one*—not a single white person in the crowd or any of the plainclothes off-duty cops on the stage (who were also all white), "protecting" the Stones, tried to stop the murder. *Rolling Stone* rather gingerly, did ask that question: "It is authoritatively reported (by an intimate of the higher echelons of the Sheriff's Department) that there were four, possibly five, plainclothesmen from the department near the stage, close to the action, on duty—which means that they were carrying their firearms. Their exact instructions are unknown, but generally, it is a law enforcement officer's duty to stop any crime he sees being committed, especially murder. (In fairness, it is not certain they were present during the Hunter murder)."[111] Why did no one in the crowd, which could have easily massed together, swarm the Angels, overpower them, and prevent the murder? Were they too high to think of such an organized move, or simply too scared of the Angels? Was it the shock of his gun, or was it because Hunter was black? Had Hunter been white would the crowd have been more willing to intervene and try to stop the killing? Hunter's death will always resonate with poignant racial overtones.

Altamont obliterated the myth of the power of rock music to change consciousness for the good. Rock music had been the 1960s youth rebellion's soundtrack; music was going to change the world. At Altamont, however, the music was useless in the face of the Angels' wanton, brutal violence and eventual killing spree; as ineffective in bringing calm to the concert as the peace signs flashed at the Angels by the terrified and pitilessly quiescent audience in hopes of soothing the biker thugs. Music, especially that of the Stones, had helped create the problem.

Altamont made it graphically clear to hopeful hippies that the Age of Aquarius, of planetary peace and love, would not be realized through rock festivals; that Woodstock indeed had been a once-in-a-lifetime, almost miraculous, tribal gathering. Little if any of the generosity of deed and spirit, of general kindness and bonhomie that pervaded Woodstock, was witnessed or experienced at Altamont, an event that disgusted hippies, with many calling the disaster "The Failure of the Counter Culture," and the "Pearl Harbor to the Woodstock Nation." One hip attendee lamented that "It made you want to go home. It made you want to puke."[112] As the Berkeley *Barb* declared, hippie "Love and peace were fucked by the Hell's Angels in front of hundreds of thousands of people who did nothing. The brothers and sisters could have cooled the Angels and any other violence-spuming toughs, but they just let hate happen."[113] Contemporary behavioral scientists were not all that surprised by the Altamont violence, asserting that since many hippies were "socially almost dead inside," they "require[d] massive emotions to feel anything. They need bizarre, intensive acts to feel alive—sexual acts, acts of violence, nudity, every kind of Dionysian thrill."[114] In Altamont's aftermath, *Business Week* proclaimed that "Middle America has come to view festivals as harbingers of dope, debauchery, and destruction."[115]

Perhaps journalist David Dalton best summed up Altamont's impact on the hip counterculture and its future. "As we all drifted away from Altamont that night, everyone who was there knew it was the end of that kind of event forever. We could no longer afford apocalypses. We had used up all the unreasonable cosmic-radical anticipations for another hundred years." Altamont was "guns, drugs, and the end of the [countercultural] world."[116] From Woodstock to Altamont: the heights and depths of a generational movement all in one four-month period. As rock historian Ed Ward observed, "Meredith Hunter died at Altamont but a generation's faith in itself was mortally wounded."[117] Todd Gitlin could not have agreed more. In a post–Altamont article for the Liberation News Service, a disillusioned Gitlin criticized the hippie movement for its failure to confront the havoc of drugs, which he believed was causing "a generation to strip itself naked. Center stage turned out be another drug. The suburban fans who blithely blocked one another's views and turned their backs on the bad-trippers were not cultural revolutionaries. Why doesn't this contaminated culture, many of whose claims are based on the virtues of drugs, help its own brothers and sisters? Who could any longer harbor the illusion that these hundreds of thousands spoiled star-hungry children of the Lonely Crowd were the harbingers of a good society?" Also disgusting Gitlin was how powerful and rich hippies, youth in general, had made rock stars such as the Rolling Stones, whom he labeled as "messiahs on the cheap." If, as hippies claimed, their venerated rock bands such as the Stones were "part of the family," then Gitlin asked, "Why don't they turn back their profits into family enterprises?" Since none of the bands were about to do that in any capacity, Gitlin concluded that in the end, the only "thing" the youth culture of the 1960s would "leave behind" was "a market." Upon deeper reflection years later, Gitlin contended that "The revolutionary mood had been fueled by the blindingly bright illusion that human history was beginning afresh because a graced generation had willed it so. Now there wasn't enough life left to mobilize against all the death raining down. We witnessed the famous collectivity of a generation cracking down into thousands of chards."[118]

14

The Counterrevolution to the Counterculture: The Middle Class Backlash to a Decade of Excess

"America wasn't made to have these pansy-assed creeps running around wild."—Anonymous New York blue collar worker's condemnation of hippies and the antiwar movement

The Chicago riots, the Manson murders and the Altamont calamity greatly discredited the hippie movement, even though actual hippie presence and participation in the events at Chicago and Altamont was minimal. Suffice it to say, hippies had nothing to do with the Manson episode. Nonetheless, all three incidents were seen by straight Americans to have been the handiwork of the hippies; the blanket term mainstream Americans used to identify all 1960s counterculture affinity groups. Ironically, from the beginning of the 1960s youth rebellion, the hippies had tried to be the least offensive in their behavior, hoping that their ethos of love and peace would be embraced as representing an alternative to the acquisitive materialism, ruthless competition, and mass conformity that had come to define 1960s bourgeois culture, along with widespread street violence and a disastrous foreign war, all of which, to the hippies portended of a nation in socio-cultural decline. Hippies saw themselves as the harbingers of a new way of being, who would bring about a regeneration of American society and culture, based upon the hip creed of compassion, understanding, cooperation, and the brotherhood of all mankind. Unfortunately, the hippie's Age of Aquarian message fell on deaf ears, as mainstream Americans had had enough of the hippies' perceived excesses as well as those of the decade's general youth insurrection.

Even before these unfortunate events, the majority of mainstream Americans doubted the sincerity of the hippie mantra. Many believed the hippies' search for greater personal awareness and freedom through the use of conscious altering drugs such as LSD to be nothing more than self-indulgent rhetoric, and an excuse to become shiftless, indolent vagabonds, drifters, and drug addicts. In the minds of many straight Americans, it was only a matter of time before the decade's youthful intemperance unleashed violence, mayhem and murder. Historian Robert Nisbet believes one would be hard pressed to find "a single decade of Western culture when so much barbarism—so much calculated onslaught against culture and convention in any form, and so much degradation of culture and the individual—passed into print, into music, into art, and onto the American stage as the decade of the Nineteen Sixties."[1] To be sure Nisbet's assessment contains some elements of validity. However, what Nisbet failed to incorporate in his retrospective was the *crucial* role the mainstream media played in sensationalizing and distorting the hippie image; to manipulate the public mind to see only barbarism and degradation. The majority of hippies were not Charles Mansons, nor Molotov-cocktail throwing Yippies, nor even those responsible for such debacles as Altamont; hippies were disgusted and appalled by such individuals and events, for all ran completely counter to the hippie ethos, to which the majority of hippies remained true for as long as they possibly could.

Nonetheless, the Manson killings, the Chicago melee, and the Altamont disaster only intensified the animosity of if not outright hatred of hippies and other perceived white radicals and student activists (as well as toward blacks) by an increasingly anti-liberal/anti-progressive working-class or blue collar America, that was fast galvanizing into the backbone of one of the most profound ideological backlashes in American history. In the late sixties, the nation "awoke" one morning to an angry yet somewhat amorphous white working class claiming to be fed up with the hippies' defamation of all they believed about American greatness and exceptionalism. The mainstream media and right-wing politicians referred to these disgruntled citizens as the Silent Majority, the Troubled Americans, and the Middle Americans. The first indication that such individuals had become alienated and hostile toward a variety of the decade's excesses was in the aftermath of the disastrous 1968 Democratic convention in Chicago, when polls revealed that 56 percent of Americans supported the police in their violent repression of both the press and demonstrators. Predictably the mainstream media ran with such a revelation, and almost overnight, an alleged full-blown white backlash had emerged in the country, ready to embrace the type of law and order meted out in Chicago. According to Barbara Ehrenreich, these "troubled Americans" began showing "scattered signs of discontent that became, in the media, a full-scale backlash: against the civil rights movement, the antiwar movement, and apparently against middle class liberalism in general.... As the news media presented it, a blue-collar vanguard was leading Middle America in its shift to the right." However, the media failed to reveal "the working class that was—in the late sixties and early seventies—caught up in the greatest wave of labor militancy since World War II," as confirmed by massive strikes and walk-offs in the first nine months of 1970. Rather than focusing on this blue-collar reality, the media opted instead to play up the "dumb, reactionary, and bigoted" image of the working classes.[2] Such a portrayal was guaranteed to exacerbate further the animosity that already existed between these Americans and the hip counterculture.

Very few hippies came from working class homes, having grown-up instead in the affluent suburbs. Working class Americans, as well as many of their progeny, came to resent these upscale families and their prosperity for creating such a pampered class of young people who used their freedom from want to create a visibly dissipated, narcissistic antithetical youth culture. Lower class youth must have been baffled to see hippies, "the children of our new affluence dressing themselves in rags and tatters and taking to the streets as panhandlers." To less affluent young people, the hippies playing at being poor represented a spoiled temper tantrum, a "neurotic discontent of those who cannot settle down gratefully to the responsibilities of life in an advanced industrial order."[3] Jay Stevens believes there were good reasons

As the 1960s progressed, the hippie appeal seemed to attract ever younger hearts and minds, no doubt causing great anxiety among many white middle class parents. Photograph taken in 1967 (Dennis L. Maness Summer of Love Photograph Collection (SFP51), San Francisco History Center, San Francisco Public Library).

for hippie defiance of conventional norms, for "Everything about them [the hippies] their hair, their music, their clothes, the way they talked, their heroes, their dreams, all were considered illegitimate by a generation which couldn't stop patting himself on the back over how democratic and liberal it was."[4] However, this post–World War II "greatest generation" was only willing to extend their supposed magnanimity to those individuals willing to accept their standards, their criteria of what constituted the right behavior and attitudes essential in the pursuit of *their* concept of the American Dream.

The hippie rejection of conventional middle class lifestyles and ethos, writ large with the open use of drugs, and ongoing flagrant displays of sexual liberation, presented middle class Americans with noisy and discordant challenges the likes of which they never saw coming and few could understand, let alone condone. They feared they were not only losing their grip on the country but their status as well to liberals, radicals, and the defiant young. No one venerated them; intellectuals dismissed their beloved lore as banality; pornography, drugs, and dissent seemed everywhere, even permeating once impregnable communities where family, tradition, duty, patriotism, and decency defined a way of life. Now, many of their progeny had turned against their ethos, and to their horrible dismay, embraced instead countercultural values. "We are becoming cannibalized," bemoaned a working class Italian American from Brooklyn. "We didn't sass the policeman when he told us to move. Now in school they call the teachers 'motherfucker.' ... This sexual permissiveness is disgraceful; it's like dogs in the street. The way of living today, there are no values."[5] It was profoundly perplexing to this generation why anyone would want to destroy "the greatest country in the world." Such sentimentality represented a state of mind, a morality, a construct of values and prejudices, and above all, a complex of fears and anxieties that American society, culture, and ideology no longer reflected the ethics of the Depression and World War II. The difficulties and want of that era had inculcated the wisdom of accumulation and the dread of joblessness; a 1950s civics-book sense of virtue, and comprehension of what an education could do and what it meant. Unfortunately for the hip counterculture some of their compatriots, such as the editors of the *Berkeley Barb*, helped to fuel the fires of Middle America's disdain for hippies by proudly proclaiming "We defy law and order with our bricks bottles garbage long hair filth obscenity drugs games guns bikes fire fun & fucking—the future of our struggle is the future of crime in the streets."[6] Unsurprisingly, the rise of the hippie counterculture further polarized an American society already divided on the issues of race and war and now increasingly alienated along class, generational, and ideological lines as well.

Though largely disdained by mainstream culture, interestingly, long-haired hippies aroused less middle class ire than their student activist/radical counterparts, who had made the issues of race and war their *raison d'être* rather than the drugs, sex, and rock and roll lifestyle the hippies had chosen. Although by 1968–69 it seemed to conservative Americans that hippies were everywhere, in reality, they were not nearly as ubiquitous as middle class Americans believed. Far more present, actively visible, strident, and as Chicago proved, threatening to the status quo, were the young radicals. Middle class stalwarts interpreted draft resistance while protesting the Vietnam War as direct challenges to U.S. Cold War/anti-communist foreign policy and thus an affront to American patriotism. Even though many had tired of the war, they nonetheless remained passionately patriotic and class conscious and deeply resented those spoiled, rich-kid hippies defiling all they still held sacred, especially respect for country. These sentiments were particularly strong among those who had served in the armed services during World War II, the most righteous and just cause in which the nation had ever engaged, and they carried heroic pride for the part they played in this most moral endeavor. Many perceived the struggle in Vietnam against the advance of communism in a similar context. Their unshakeable view held that when the country is threatened and duty calls, a *real man* does not protest nor shirk his responsibility to serve his country by running away, but "bucks-up" and does his part. Neither the hippie message of peace and love nor the activists' demonstrations against an immoral war or their propagation of anti–American in general, sat well with these Americans. As one mother and father of such background articulated, "The college types, the professors, they go to Washington and tell the government what to do. Do this, they say; do that. But their sons, they don't end up in the swamps over there, in Vietnam. No sir, I think we ought to win that war or pull out. I hate those peace demonstrators. The sooner we get out of there the better." His wife added, "I'm against this war too—the way a mother is, whose sons are in the army, who has lost a son fighting it. The world hears those demonstrators make noise. The world doesn't hear me."[7] Paul M. Deac, who in 1970 was executive vice president of the National Confederation of American Ethnic Groups, representing 18 million former immigrants (primarily European), expressed similar outrage, blaming the "professional liberals" for letting "the genie out of the bottle—racial hatred and lawlessness," which Deac defined as white middle class opposition to black militancy and white intellectuals. "Our families don't have long-haired brats—they'd tear the hair off them. Our boys don't smoke pot or raise hell or seek deferments. Our people are too busy making a living and trying to be good Americans."[8]

Hippie women celebrating their bodies, hoping to get a rise out of a straight member of the older generation determined to ignore their alluring frolicking in Golden Gate Park, circa 1968–69 (photograph by Larry Keenan, courtesy Bancroft Library, University of California, Berkeley. © 1997 Larry Keenan. All rights reserved).

By the late 1960s universities and colleges were seen by increasing numbers of traditional Americans to be the breeding-grounds and havens for countercultural activity, whether insurrection against the status quo presented in the form of antiwar protest, student radicalism, or as incubators for the hippie revolt; they had allegedly become "rallying points for a revolution in sensibility, a revolution that brought together radical politics, drug abuse, sexual libertinage, an obsession with rock music, exotic forms of spiritual titillation, a generalized anti-bourgeois animus and an attack on the intellectual and moral foundations of the entire humanistic enterprise."[9] Reared to cherish education, especially a college degree with a reverence that bordered on the sacred, Middle America resented the student unrest on college campuses, even those protests that rightly challenged the impersonal, bureaucratic, and oppressive policies and procedures of the "multiversity." Anti-counterculture, working class philosopher Eric Hoffer, who dismissed the hippie movement as a fleeting attempt by spoiled, bored, and disgruntled affluent white youth to "extend adolescence," believed American colleges and universities were "being destroyed by a bunch of crummy punks. Who the hell would have dreamt that a thing like this was possible? Ignorant, bedraggled, illiterate punks! Our institutions are tremendously vulnerable. What are we afraid of? Of the Government? Of the police? Of Congress? No, for God's sakes, we're afraid of the individual, of the beast masquerading as a man." Historian Daniel Boorstin agreed with Hoffer, declaring at the time that the nation was "witnessing the explosive rebellion of small groups [the hippies and the student activists/radicals], who reject the American past, deny their relation to the community. This atavism, this new barbarism, cannot last if the nation is to survive." To a certain degree they were correct: many in the counterculture had a limited understanding of the country's history, as an anecdote about the Chicago Democratic convention nightmare somewhat confirmed. As a young protester was being apprehended by a cop, he shouted "Long live the proletariat!" Before the cop unloaded on him with his nightstick, he reminded the young man that he *was* the proletariat! Whack![10]

Yet, as other observers of the 1960s youth uprising have noted, most of the institutions of higher learning remained closely allied with the military-industrial complex, and continued to produce young, new technocrats for such enterprises and entities. "The American higher education system geared up to perpetuate the new technocracy by educating young citizens, particularly white middle-class males, for compliantly assuming their rightful place in the corporate hierarchy."[11] University administrators, such as the powerful president of the entire University of California system, Clark Kerr, made it publicly very clear that in his opinion the most important purpose of higher education was indeed to provide educated technocrats either for government service or as managers and future CEO's for the private sector. "The university is being called upon to respond to the expanding claims of national service; to merge its activity with industry as never before; to adapt and re-channel new intellectual currents."[12] It was precisely this type of "re-channeling" that hippies and other anti-technocracy groups chafed against, refusing to become the institutionalized products of such impersonal bureaucratic organizations. One of the hippies' few accepted intellectual gurus, Charles Reich, supported the hippie view that if one succumbed to the new "technocratic totalitarianism" he would be "stripped of his imagination, his creativity, his heritage, dreams, and personal uniqueness, in order to style him into a productive unit for a mass, technological society."[13] For the majority of hippies, the modern world was a meaningless, menacing place; an environment in which it was impossible to find peace, humanity, and spirituality. There was an alternative however; individual salvation from the rat-race was possible if one chose to embrace the hippie ethos of dropping out altogether and pursue the countercultural lifestyle in which one could reclaim the true self.

Reflected in many blue-collar parent's feelings about Vietnam, was their belief that the conflict had become a "rich man's war" but a "poor man's fight" as demographic and other statistics have clearly revealed. Indeed, as the nation absorbed Vietnam into itself, one of the conflict's most important ramifications was that it brought to the surface the often brutal disparities of social class in the United States that Americans have always tried to hide. Vietnam became for the country essentially a class war as the majority of those sent off to the jungles to fight and die were from the nation's poor and lower middle or working class. The children of the privileged frequently received deferments to go to college (or take a hiatus and become a hippie for awhile), or exemptions fabricated by family doctors certifying that this particular young white male was psychologically or physically unfit for duty. Most hippies were from such socio-economic backgrounds and engaged in all manner of artifice to avoid the draft. Thus it should not be surprising that blue collar Americans in particular came to despise *all* longhairs—hippies, activists, students—anyone who looked the part. Frustrated and disillusioned, they cast all such youth as spoiled, selfish, lazy, and hedonistic cowards and sissies, pretending to be righteous crusaders against the world's injustices; or worse, outright losers, drop-outs disguising themselves as members of a "love generation" that preached peace and brotherhood while living the life a privileged slacker. Meanwhile their sons and daughters continued to work hard to rise above their comparatively meager upbringing or served their country and died in the process. It was these "silent majority" Americans who found Richard Nixon most appealing in 1968, especially his call for law and order.[14]

Nixon's narrow margin of victory in 1968 was the result of the widespread disaffection among many white working class Democrats, who displayed their discontent by voting Republican, many for the first time in their adult lives. Indeed, until 1968 the working class had been one of the Democratic Party's most vital constituencies, steadfastly loyal to the party and to the fundamentals of the liberal ethos since the days of FDR. But by 1968, they felt betrayed by the party they had faithfully supported for decades. Nixon and his campaign strategists devised a brilliant politics of polarization plan to exploit the alienation among blue collar Democrats as well as all other Middle Americans as outraged by the decade's liberal exorbitance and perceived profligacy. Causing the alienation was the perception that the liberalism they once embraced had been high-jacked and perverted by Ivy League educated technocrats, social engineers, and "limousine liberals"—the privileged classes who lived in lily white suburbs and indulged their kids to the extent that they became narcissistic dope fiends and libertines—hippies. They simultaneously and disingenuously preached integration and welfare assistance while condemning as callous racists anyone who did not support their policies or try to "understand the younger generation." The very rebels they helped to create by their pampering were now trying to rip apart the seams not only of liberalism but of the very fabric of American society. Working class Democrats felt duped by the American Dream that had been sold to them since the advent of television, advertising the very products factory workers cranked out—most of which they could not afford to buy on their weekly wages. They came to believe they were now working only to make more "things" for those fellow Americans who lived in the alien world of white collar suburbia. According to Floyd Smith, who in 1970 was the president of the International Association of Machinists,

"In the land of the media, whether it is movies, magazines, or TV, Daddy always goes to the office, not to the factory and he brings home plenty of money without appearing to sweat hard for it."[15]

The white backlash of the late 1960s of course raged against more than just the hippies, the student activists and the antiwar demonstrators. Conservative white Americans felt equally outraged by the excesses, abuses, and the pandering to special groups by the welfare state, crime, black militants, and the government programs that favored minorities and elite special interests: In short, all the manifestations of what they considered to be a perverted liberalism run amok. To working class Americans, especially to ethnics of such status, all such recipients of government largesse were "leeches," "cheaters" and "welfare bums." They were incensed by African Americans and other "loafers on the dole." As one Italian-American city worker railed, "These welfare people get as much as I do and I work my ass off and come home dead tired. They get up late and they can shack up all day long and watch the tube.... I go shopping with my wife and I see them with their forty dollars of food stamps in the supermarket, living and eating better than me.... Let them tighten their belts like we do." Worrying many such individuals was the prospect that their own children would become hippies with the same degraded values and become the same sort of "leeches." The perceived demand by sixties youth for instant gratification as well as apparent lack of appreciation or understanding for the sacrifices their parents had made for them to have such abundance, caused many in the older generation to fear that their children had lost all sense of a work ethic. A Jewish businessman recalled his "old man" giving him a "hand-truck when I was nine, down in the garment district. He said to me, 'Here go to work!'" Not so with 1960s youth, he complained, "nobody wants to work or wait for anything."[16]

They even blamed liberalism for the break-up of the nuclear family and illegitimacy. In many instances backlash fear and anger was overblown. Nonetheless, many of the nation's most sacred and entrenched institutions and assumptions about American life were under assault and some rightly needed to be challenged. Statistics at the time revealed that the overall crime rate, particularly for many inner-city urban Americans, regardless of race, had risen. Serious felonies such as murder, rape, robbery, and auto theft, all had increased substantially by the late 1960s after having steadily declined since World War II.[17] The media of course helped fuel the image of American cities as places rife with murder and mayhem, sensationalizing events to appear far more ominous and common place than they really were. The hippies and alleged un–American misfits creating problems in the country represented a minority population, especially the actual number who became full-fledged hippies or yippies, or fanatical student radicals. In fact, the overwhelming majority of American white youth during the decade remained largely straight; that is they may have dipped a toe or even one foot in the hippie pool and let their hair grow a bit longer, worn some form of hip attire, maybe marched a time or two against the war, smoked a little dope, engaged in premarital sex, played hippie for a weekend. But they never strayed too far from the comforts, security, and stability of their mainstream middle class existence. Indeed, according to Daniel Yankelovich, "Almost every public opinion poll taken during the war showed that youth, in the aggregate, proportionately *supported* the war. (Surprisingly the most 'dovish' age group turned out to be people over fifty-five)."[18]

Contributing to the hippies' demise was the economic recession of the 1970s, and interestingly the Vietnam War, which had done so much in the late 1960s to discredit authority and galvanize the hippie movement. By 1967 the war loomed heavy in most male minds ages 18–25, but especially in the counterculture view as testimony of Americans' inherent blood-lust. By 1968, the war, "more than any other force" in American society at that time had "alien-ated the American young from their elders—and, in equally tragic ways, from one another. The war was the dark hallucination, the black magic that would come and take the young and bear them off to the other side of the world and destroy them, for reasons progressively more obscure."[19] Consequently, hippies expended a lot energy disassociating from being American. Both the Johnson and Nixon administration sensed that public support for the war was perfunctory at best, and would evaporate completely if the conflict ever demanded home front sacrifices à la World War II rationing.

By 1969 the Nixon administration's de-escalation policies—"Vietnamization"—took from the counterculture much of its *raison d'être*. Nixon's policy ("peace with honor") was to withdraw as quickly as possible the number of U.S. ground troops in South Vietnam (which had reached 545,000 by the time Nixon entered the Oval Office). Nixon hoped this approach would help silence the antiwar movement, which had been using the increasing American death toll to rally supporters.[20] Interestingly, at this juncture in the war, all but the radical fringes in an increasingly factionalized peace/New Left movement were willing to give Nixon time to make good his promise to extricate the United States from Vietnam, and thus momen-tarily supported his agenda. Indeed, during the 1968 presidential campaign, Nixon declared that "We must listen to the voices of dissent because the protester may have something to say worth listening to. If we dismiss dissent as coming from 'rebels without a cause,' we will soon find ourselves becoming leaders without an effect." Nixon then accused the Johnson administration of having caused the present "unprecedented chasm in our society," the result of Johnson's "insensitivity and arrogance" relative to the "voices of dissent." By 1970, the term New Left or the Movement, had become a general label and an umbrella of sorts under which gathered left-leaning liberals, socialists, "old-time" New Leftists and a cacophony of other identity-driven organizations and their often oddball politics. The centrality of Vietnam to the Movement's cause belied the philosophical disunity and ambiguity that had taken over much of the New Left debate.[21]

Part of Nixon's plan was to turn the ground fighting back over to the U.S.-trained ARVN (Army of the Republic of Vietnam), in accordance with the United States' original intention since 1956 when Vietnam was permanently divided during the Eisenhower administration, at which time Nixon was vice-president. Unfortunately, by this point in the war, ARVN had become so demoralized and corrupt, partially the result of American arrogance and racist disdain, that the army no longer had the will or motivation to be an effective force in the field. Nonetheless, Nixon had been true to his word, bringing home 25,000 U.S. troops in the summer of 1969 and by the end of 1971 Nixon had reduced the number of American sol-diers to 140,000, half of whom served in a non-combatant capacity. Although impressive in rhetoric and on paper, critics lambasted Vietnamization as simply "changing the color of the corpses."[22]

As the war dragged on, Nixon's campaign pledge that he would end the war if elected rang hollow, especially with the antiwar movement, which revitalized as youthful alienation deepened. Hundreds of thousands of young Americans, increasingly joined by their older counterparts, hit the streets in protest once again throughout the nation, climaxing in another massive March on Washington in November 1969. Nixon blithely dismissed the protestors that weekend, announcing that he spent Saturday afternoon watching college and professional football while from 250,000 to 800,000 gathered at the Mall to decry the war. His nonchalance belied his real feelings about the demonstrators; he seethed with rage at their presence and wanted to crush them forever; he was simply waiting for the opportune time to finish off "all the hippies" while simultaneously making good his promise to the silent majority that he was their law and order guy. That moment came in late April and early May 1970 when Nixon announced that in conjunction with ARVN forces, U.S. troops would invade Cambodia to destroy the NVA bases in that country. Nixon told the American public that if his efforts failed in Vietnam to secure "peace with honor," the United States would become a "pitiful, helpless giant" respected by no one. According to Henry Kissinger, of all the 1968 presidential candidates, Nixon was the *least likely* to pursue an honest peace initiative. "Seeing himself in any case as the target of a liberal conspiracy to destroy him, he could never bring himself to regard the upheaval caused by the Vietnam War as anything other than a continuation of the long-lived assault on his political existence.... In the process he accelerated and compounded" the already deeply divided and bitter American people.[23]

The Cambodian invasion further invigorated and enraged the antiwar crusade, energizing its supporters to take to the streets once again in a protest that proved to be their last hurrah. Within days of Nixon's speech announcing the incursion, classes were canceled at over a third of the nation's colleges and universities, as students, joined by many of their professors protested against what they perceived to be Nixon's widening of the war rather than ending it. One such campus was Kent State University in Ohio, where only a few weeks before a group of radicals belonging to the violence-oriented Weathermen, burned the ROTC building. Ironically, Kent State was a "blue collar" university, whose 20,000 students were mostly from working class-lower middle income homes, most of whose parents were the backbone of Nixon's "silent majority." The majority of the students were not at all interested in activism of any kind; they were there for a college education which they hoped would be their ticket out of their present socio-economic status.[24]

Looking for an excuse to send in the National Guard, Ohio Republican governor, Jim Rhodes, elected on a law and order platform, and seeking his party's nomination for the Senate, told Nixon that the Guard's presence was necessary to preserve peace on the campus (code for the use of force to crush the demonstrators). Rhodes considered the student protesters to be "worse than the brown shirts and the Communist elements; the worst type of people we harbor in America and we are going to eradicate this problem." This was the moment Nixon had been waiting for to demonstrate his resolve to destroy the counterculture, and he approved the governor's request to "send in the Guard." On May 4, nervous guardsmen in gas masks (most of whom were recently activated pharmacists, accountants, and salesmen, as well as some who had evaded the draft by joining the Guard), opened fire with their M-1 rifles, and when the smoke cleared 4 students—two young men and two young women (Sandy Scheuer, Jeff Miller, Allison Krause, and Bill Schroeder)—lay dead while eleven others were wounded. The two girls killed in the fusillade were simply walking to class. A fifth victim, Dean Kahler, was permanently paralyzed from the waist down by a Guard bullet. Defenders of the shooting claimed that the students had violently menaced the troops, threatening to kill them, but insults and a few rocks and other debris thrown hardly justified the murderous barrage. Ten days later a similar scenario occurred at Jackson State University in Mississippi, where state troopers opened up on a dormitory with 28 seconds of continuous gunfire, killing two women and wounding twelve other students. The Jackson State student "riot" was not directly related to the antiwar movement although it was one of the student protesters' issues. It must be remembered that in proportion to their percentage of the overall U.S. population at the time, the number of black soldiers in Vietnam was higher than that of their white counterparts. Nixon's callous, offhand response to the killings: "When dissent turns to violence it invites tragedy." Even more shocking was the public's response to the incidents. Polls revealed that the majority of Americans supported the Cambodian invasion and even greater numbers believed "radical, hippie" students, not the Guardsmen, provoked "the mayhem"; that the Guardsmen were only protecting themselves from the students' "violent onslaught." Indeed, a mother whose son attended Kent State declared that "It would have been a good thing if all those students had been shot." The astonished son reminded his mother that, "Hey, that's me you're talking about" but the mom didn't care, insisting that "It would have been better for the country if you had all been mowed down."[25]

The majority of students attended Kent State for an education, and on the day of the shootings they went about their business as usual. They nonetheless resented the Guard's presence. For some time the forces on the Right had been using the convenient term "outside agitators" to describe a cabal of supposed professional radicals who toured college and university campuses as "agents provocateurs" to incite normally "good" students to protest and resistance. Rarely, if ever was that the case, and as one Kent State student remarked "we never gave much credence to that. If anyone was an outsider, it was these guys who came to our campus with rifles and bayonets. We looked upon them as an occupation army that had invaded our campus and we wanted them gone."[26]

By the late 1960s, for the majority of college students, the university and all it represented to them—enlightenment, knowledge, research, opportunity, career, athletics, camaraderie, fun—had become sacred ground; a safe, noble, and revered sanctuary, where for a few hours a day, they escaped to a world that was of their own making. There they were center-stage, and told repeatedly that they represented "the best" of America; the nation's future was in their hands. Young people, especially from working class families, the majority of whom represented first-generation college students, took this charge very seriously and believed it was their duty to safeguard the sanctity of the university, especially from unwanted invaders such as the National Guard, sent there to crush their *right* to free speech, to assemble, and to question wrongful authority, oppression, and other harmful and reactionary ideas. Ironically, such notions had been inculcated in the classroom and now they were taking what they had learned into action, for wasn't that the purpose of an education? To increasing numbers of college students nationwide the Vietnam War represented all that had gone wrong in America and many felt it was their duty to challenge and change this disastrous course of history. Unfortunately by the late sixties and into the early seventies, the Establishment, including university administrators, recoiled from what their schools had wrought: students no longer willing to sit passively and accept what they were told; the universities had unwittingly created thinking students rather than churning out products for IBM or the military. In many ways this was what Kent State and other student uprisings at the time were all about, and neither the university administration, nor the governor of Ohio, or the president of the United States could or would accept such questioning, and thus occurred the horrible tragedy at Kent State.

Federal indictments against the Guardsmen were eventually handed down but the judge ruled that the Justice Department did not have sufficient evidence to prove that the

Guardsmen conspired to violate the students' civil rights and thus case dismissed without ever being sent to the jury. In the end, the Guardsmen received what amounted to "a slap on the wrist" by both the presidential commission as well as the FBI, who "condemned" the rifle fire as "unnecessary, unwarranted, and inexcusable.... Even if the Guard had authority to prohibit a peaceful gathering—a question that is at least debatable—the timing and manner of dispersal was disastrous.... The rally was peaceful and there was no impending violence." Indeed, as students told reporters and investigators in the tragedy's aftermath, "Whenever the Guard came near us we backed away.... The Guard had already stabbed people with bayonets, and nobody was foolish enough to stand there."[27]

The Nixon administration was not through finishing off the counterculture. On May 8, 1970, four days after the Kent State incident, 200 construction workers at the New York World Trade Center viciously attacked an antiwar march, shouting "Kill the Commie bastards" as they weighed into the demonstrators flailing fists, hammers, and lead pipes, injuring seventy, as they "chase[d] youths through the canyons of the financial district in a wild noontime melee." As The New York Times further opined, "The hardhats, long scornful of excesses by privileged longhairs on campus, were obviously delighted at the opportunity to pour out their hatred on the students and any who dare to raise a voice in their defense." A young female city official from the mayor's office, Susan Harman, who tried to stop three construction workers from pummeling a student protestor, encountered a resentment and rage that knew no boundaries as the three men assaulted her as well, breaking her glasses and bruising her ribs so badly that she had to be taken to the hospital. Before they began punching her, one of the workers shouted "Get off me bitch. If you want to be treated like an equal, we'll treat you like one." New York police, who had been called out to keep the march peaceful and orderly, looked the other way as the workers attacked the marchers. According to one observer, the hard-hatters "went through those demonstrators like Sherman went through Atlanta." Such was the observation of stockbroker Edward Shufro of the firm Rose and Ehrman, who watched the entire spectacle through binoculars from his office window. He also told reporters that he saw several "men in grey suits directing the workers as if they were generals commanding troops in a battle." Such white-collar complicity should not be surprising; many in that socio-economic status were as hostile toward the counterculture as the hard-hatters, and were willing to allow these new working class "sons of liberty" thugs to do their dirty work while they remained "clean." Inspired by their New York brethren, a group of St. Louis construction workers unleashed a similar reign of terror on antiwar demonstrators in that city as well. Expressing the sentiments of "hard-hatters" (Nixon's silent majority and conservatives in general) throughout America, a New York blue-collar worker declared that "I am an American and America wasn't made to have these pansy-assed creeps running around wild. I don't mind people demonstrating but these brats rip, spit on and chew up the flag, what are we supposed to do, stand around and kiss them?" Dolores Fanale, a longshoremen's wife agreed: "We wanted to tell those kids off. They have too much."[28]

Working class confrontations with student protestors was not confined to construction sites; such encounters even occurred on university campuses such as Northwestern University, where a campus worker confronted a group of students who were waving the American flag upside down, shouting at them for denigrating the symbol of his patriotism. "That's my flag! I fought for it! You have no right to it!" The students began arguing with him and the man responded, "There are millions of people like me. We're fed up with your movement. You're forcing us into it. We'll have to kill you. All I can see is a lot of kids blowing a chance I never had." A Chicago white collar advertising salesman agreed with his blue-collar compatriot: "I'm getting to feel like I'd actually enjoy going out and shooting some of these people. I'm just so goddamned mad. They're trying to destroy everything I've worked for—for myself, my wife, and my children." Such declarations of rage were hardly isolated sentiments in the spring of 1970.[29]

Workers were shocked when their actions received much rebuke, particularly from the city's major newspapers and even from many union members, such as Lawrence Eliot of the Building and Construction Trades Council, who felt aggrieved and embarrassed "That the attackers should be members of a union is only sad evidence of how far we have slipped from the time when unionism meant striving for human decency and social justice."[30] *The New York Times* was especially harsh in its criticism, referring to the incident as an example when "right-wing vigilantism finds left-wing extremism an excuse for pushing aside constituted authority and enforcing its own brutal form of injustice." The riot even disturbed the more conservative *New York Post*, which called the hard-hatters "cold-blooded bullies" and "hard-hat rightist brutalitarians." Columnist Peter Hamill labeled the workers "cowards" and "the sour children of right-wing frustration." *The Nation* feared that such wanton violence inflicted on peaceful demonstrators reflected "a pattern that contains the classic elements of Hitlerian street tactics."[31]

A week after the New York melee, 100,000 New Yorkers, mostly blue collar workers, staged a pro-war march, waving flags and singing "God Bless America." New York mayor, liberal Republican John Lindsay (whom Nixon despised as a turncoat and who would later become a Democrat) had also become a target of hardhat rage. Lindsay had wanted to fly the flag at half-mast in the aftermath of the Kent State killings to honor the dead students, which outraged the hard-hatters, who carried insulting and scurrilous placards that read "Lindsay Drops the Flag More Times Than a Whore Drops Her Pants." Soon after the hard hat rally, Nixon invited Peter Brennan, head of the New York Building and Construction Trades Council, to the White House where, in a quasi-official photographed ceremony, Brennan gave Nixon a hard-hat, symbolizing the president's solidarity with the silent majority and his approval for their support on his war on the counterculture. Indeed, Nixon's silent majority had a last found its voice and it was a howl of rage against the hippies, for in the blue collar/conservative American mind, any young male in long hair who dared criticize or vilify the United States in any capacity, was a "pansy-assed" hippie.[32]

"Bloody Friday" in New York and other student-construction worker confrontations throughout the country reflected not so much blue collar support for the war, but rather a built-up rage toward white upper-middle class privilege and affluence, which student demonstrators and hippies had come to symbolize. Labor historian Jefferson Cowie contends that by 1969–70, for a variety of reasons, the majority of blue collar workers "were more opposed to the war and more in favor of withdrawal than the college educated." Workers' alleged pro-war position was a media and right-wing contrivance designed to bolster support for the Nixon administration's distorted escalation policies. Thus what Americans witnessed on May 8, 1970, was the "workers' class resentments toward the protestor's methods, privilege, and apparently non-existent sense of duty."[33] Because of their status and education, students and hippies did not have to do manual labor all day long in the hot summer or in the dark, cold days of winter as the hardhats did, living from weekly paycheck to weekly paycheck, and who increasingly saw their wives go off to work as well in comparatively menial occupations in order to make ends meet. As one World War II veteran appraised his career, "Sure it was a rotten job, but what the hell. I made a good living. I took care of my wife and kids. What more do you expect?"[34] Those were hard-scrabble values expressed during economically trying times.

In the hardhat world, these "rich kids" were using their entitlement to become draft dodgers; effete, pampered shirkers, while many of the workers had sons in Vietnam fighting and dying for their country. "Here were these kids, rich kids, who could go to college, who didn't have to fight, they are telling you your son died in vain. It makes you feel your whole life is shit, just nothing."[35] Fueling the violent encounters was a combination of class grievances, threats to manliness, and status anxiety at having lost position in popular culture, political discourse, and even in advertising, as the heart and soul of post–World War II middle class America. As Assistant Secretary of Labor Jerome Rosow told *Time* in 1970, "All blue collar workers, skilled or not, have been denigrated so badly, so harshly, that their jobs have become a last resort instead of decent, respected careers. Fathers hesitate—and even apologize—for their occupation instead of holding it up as an aspiration for their own sons." Compounding working class domestic woes was the beginning of "outsourcing" by increasing numbers of major U.S. corporations to developing countries, their nastiest, loneliest, most arduous jobs. Thus the American economy during the 1970s required fewer longshoremen breaking their backs moving crates onto piers; fewer butchers holding frozen slabs of meat inches away from whirring blades; fewer tannery workers stinking of acid; and fewer merchant sailors thousands of miles from home. Blue collar workers' sense of loss and consequently their alienation, gave rise to an antagonism especially towards those perceived to have everything but had done very little, if anything, to earn it. Public displays of solidarity manifested in assaults on the demonstrators became one way for hardhat workers to reclaim their stake in American culture and society; to become visible again rather than "feeling cheated by the affluent society" and of "having a sense of loss and neglect."[36]

As the 1970s progressed, students everywhere appeared to have had enough with protest and trying to change the world; the activist, reformist zeal of the sixties was fast burning itself out. Much to the relief of parents, college administrators, local and state officials, and the Nixon administration, students across the land were now simply going to school or work or both. "Normalcy" had finally returned to American universities and colleges, and students had apparently reclaimed their sensibilities. As one Kent State student observed three years after that horrible day, "Kent State is now a household word. But Kent State as a symbol is more important to other universities than it is to itself." Even those who were on the front lines that day had become disillusioned and disengaged; "it was over"; the Establishment had prevailed and now it was time to get back to business as usual. Such were the sentiments of one of the "Kent 25," Bill Arthrell. "You can't maintain your outrage forever. Now everyone has their own trip; dope, work, or the counterculture." Sociology professor Jerry Lewis agreed: "As much as we want justice, we're all tired. Many of us are just trying to go to school."[37]

Indeed, all the previous years of student unrest and general youth roiling seemed part of a distant past as an unexpected but joyously welcomed (especially by university administrators) calm had returned to most college campuses. Rarely could be heard the abrasive cant of radicals or the sound of acid rock emanating from dorm rooms or the student center. Rather, one heard students discussing the weeks' lecture in History 1301 in the commons while in the background could be heard the soft ballads of Neil Young, Gordon Lightfoot, Carole King, and James Taylor. Yale president Kingman Brewster referred to this new quiescence as an "eerie tranquility." What accounted for this rather abrupt change in student outlook, campus life, and general youth behavior? According to Stanford's Dean of Humanities and Sciences, Albert Hastorf, "People got scared. In 'the feel-not-think' philosophy they saw their world coming to an end. This fall the point of many lectures has been that thinking is not necessarily an ally of fascism."[38]

In retrospect, the Manson slayings and the murders at Kent State and Altamont marked the symbolic and metaphysical deconstruction of the hippie movement. Altamont and Kent State in particular shattered the hippie illusion that if enough youthful minds trusted the inherent power of love, community, rock and roll music, the arts, and dope, especially LSD, all the ills of late 1960s liberal/bourgeois American culture and society would be rectified, or at the very least significantly ameliorated. However, such was not to become the new reality. In fact, according to Bruce Pollock, the Kent State tragedy, which occurred only five months after the Altamont debacle, marked the beginning of the end of the hippie's hopeful dream; by the close of the 1970s hippies had all but disappeared from the nation's sociocultural landscape. "It [the year 1970] was the end of the Beatles, the end of Woodstock Nation, the end of the Greenwich Village folk scene. 'The Bus' went into the shop permanently. In San Francisco, Bill Graham got out of the Fillmore business, the Airplane became the Starship, the Dead incorporated. Jimi Hendrix, Janis Joplin, and Jim Morrison reached the end of the road. As Dave Von Ronk told me, 'The check was not in the mail.' As Tom Wolfe quoted Ken Kesey as saying, 'We blew it.' And as Monkee Peter Tork said, 'When they shot them down at Kent State that was the end of the Flower Power era. That was it. You just throw your flowers and rocks at us, man, and we'll pull the guns on you. Essentially, the revolution, which was sort of tolerated as long as it wasn't a significant material threat, was not tolerated any more. And everybody went 'oops' and scurried for cover and licked their wounds. They became isolated, which was the point of it all. Because the less togetherness there is, the more room there is for exploitation.'"[39]

As student activists, radicals, Yippies, and even some hippies, grew weary of the tear gas and nightsticks, they concluded that mass demonstrations as a tactic to bring about sociocultural and political change had failed; interestingly a form of protest against the status quo that many of hippies had warned their counterculture compatriots would not work. Hippies counseled that the best approach was to simply opt out of the straight world and all its "messiness." The majority of Americans were on the side of law and order and even within the students' own ranks, few were committed to maintaining the resistance as Establishment reprisals became increasingly more oppressive and violent. Nonetheless, the counterculture in general and the hippies in particular, got the attention of America for good or bad, exposing in the process the inequities, the discrimination, American's obsession with material aggrandizement, the hypocrisy, and a hidebound educational establishment, to name but a few of the legitimate targets of protest and causes for alienation. Neither the hippies nor the student protesters could be dismissed as aberrations. The memory of the decade's violence and youth insurrection has endured and so has the existence of the student activists and their hippie counterparts as a once and future conscience and collective voice of national concern.

Epilogue and Legacy

One must be careful not to bury the hippies too precipitously in the aftermath of events such as Chicago, the Manson murders, Altamont, and Kent State. Although those episodes helped to further discredit the hip counterculture in the eyes of straight Americans and accelerate the hippies' demise, they were not necessarily the *final* nails in the hippie coffin. As far as one historian is concerned, Altamont in particular "was only the end of a shitty California answer to Woodstock, certainly not the end of the counterculture. In the rest of the nation, no one cared about Altamont."[1] Although such an observation is probably true in the larger countercultural picture, the shock of the campus killings, the Manson horror, and the debacle at Altamont along with the hard hat demonstrations and assaults, it was clear that the counterrevolutionary backlash was at full throttle, determined to crush the last hippie vestiges and the counterculture in general. Assisting these reactionary forces was the mainstream press, which continued to hammer the hippies as the harbingers of dope, debauchery, and destruction. As reprisals became more draconian and violent, many hippies opted to drop back into mainstream society in one form or another. Thus, for many hippies, who never were willing to commit themselves to anything more than a transitory, self-gratifying hedonism, perhaps it was time to "get back to their suburban gardens"; that is to the safety of their rarefied middle class enclaves; free from the fear of being harassed by the cops or by hard hats for their appearance and lifestyle, or worse, beaten or killed by a straight America whose denizens seemed to be waiting in line to help obliterate the hip counterculture.

Terrorized by the influx of debilitating drugs, diluted by plastic hippies, the movement limped through the early 1970s a paranoid, fragmented version of its former self. No longer buoyed by hope of a gradual takeover of the System and the prospect of eroding away the Establishment with "love," many hippies concluded that their "flower power" ethos was not going to make General Motors or Dow Chemical go away, and thus some accommodation would have to be made with the larger society. As the *New York Times* observed in a 40-year restrospective essay on the Summer of Love, "We discovered that love was never all you needed; in the 1960s, in fact, it was barely there, unless by love you mean sex, which was plentiful as it tends to be in youth movements. Young people are by definition narcissistic, all clammy ego. They want what they want. There is no past that matters; the future isn't yet real."[2] In other words, the hippie movement was experienced almost entirely in the present; no wonder it seemed so monumental at the time but now seems so strangely anticlimactic to many boomers.

351

Also taking the wind out of the hippies' sails ironically was, Nixon's Vietnamization policy, which saw U.S. combat deaths fall from nearly 200 per week in 1969 to 35 by early 1971.
Congress' March 1969 bill limited the draft to nineteen-year-olds to be chosen by lottery
and therefore males twenty and older no longer needed to worry about "coming home in a
box." In January 1972, Congress ended the draft entirely. The economic downturn of the
early 1970s also contributed to hippiedom's demise, as many young people became less cav-
alier about their affluence, inducing a more cautionary frugality and material insecurity, resulting in their return home to middle class comforts from which they had merely taken a brief
hiatus. Finally, a more insidious dynamic was at work undermining hippie perpetuity: time.
With each passing year more hippies wandered back to "normalcy"; that is they started families, began professional training or went back to school to finish a degree, and entered the
job market. In short, they "grew up," becoming full-fledged responsible adults. As Todd Gitlin
has observed, "Those who had dropped out of professional careers found that they still cared
about excellence along with freedom. The fugitives from meritocracy rediscovered merit.
Middle class dropouts looked for ways to drop partway back in, recognizing that right action
is not accomplished by hostility to authority alone...."[3]

Some dropped back in even more than partway: by the 1980s, many former hippies had
metamorphosed into some of the most acquisitive, status-seeking, materialistic conservative
suburbanites in American history: young urban professional—"yuppies." Many ex-hippies
believed, however naively, that they would remain forever young, living their lives in a revo-
lutionized, greened America, a Woodstock Nation of peace, love, and pleasure. Many of these
illusions rested on monthly subsidies from all-too-bourgeois parents. Once such support
ended and the hard realities of the marketplace hit, many former hippies "chilled out" during
the 1970s, compromised, and began their evolution into yuppiedom.[4] It must also be remembered that the majority of the affluent, college-educated Sixties generation who transformed
into 1980s yuppies never were or were only barely affected by the antiwar movement and
protest, civil rights or the rights revolution in general, environmental concerns, and sex,
drugs, and rock and roll. Nonetheless, according to Ken Gofman and Dan Joy, the lion's share
of hippies had withdrawn from the counterculture as early as 1972, and in their view, it had
become "clear that the hippest generation was mostly made up of ordinary, selfish, unimaginative human beings ready to make accommodations with the particulars of capitalism and
the customary requirements of adulthood—ready to drop back in and compromise with the
system."[5] As far as Roger Kimball is concerned, ex-counterculturists drive much of the present
consumer culture, or "Dionysius with a credit card and a college education," and in his somewhat cynical view, hippies were never as anti-capitalist as their rhetoric declared but rather
were "the toxic by-products of capitalism's success."[6]

According to journalist Tom Wolf, by 1976, many a former hippie and sixties rebel/
activist had joined the ranks of the "me generation," which ironically the counterculture had
helped to foster during the sixties with its emphasis on personal freedom and self-expression.
Now such introspection and focus on developing the "inner self" had morphed into self-
absorption, as increasing numbers of Americans, regardless of former affiliation, slavishly
pursued the liberation ideology of the 1960s. The new hip mantra of the 1970s became "Let's
talk about me," and "Only *you* can decide what's right for *you*." By 1979, 39 percent of all
Americans and close to 60 percent of educated young Americans, agreed that "people should
be free to look, dress, and live the way they want, whether others like it or not."[7] The old

ethic of social responsibility, of sacrifice for the community, was giving way to a new ethos of self-indulgence on a grand scale, which made the hippies' quest for self-gratification pale in comparison. "Doing one's own thing" appeared to have become the new national creed, which few hippies believed in 1967 would be the end result of their individual pursuits for greater enlightenment. Indeed, Americans would *live for themselves*, regardless of how such behavior, attitude, or words affected others. As the author of *Looking Out for Number One*, Robert Ringer declared, "Clear your mind. Forget foundationless traditions, forget the 'moral' standards others may have tried to cram down your throat, forget the beliefs people may have tried to intimidate you into accepting as 'right.'" Another 1970s best seller exhorted, "When you say 'I should do this' or 'I shouldn't do that,' you are also in many cases allowing yourself to be trapped by the past, following rules set down by parents, teachers, and other mentors that may no longer have real meaning for you in our crisis culture."[8]

According to Christopher Lasch, the hippies' personal liberation ideology had engendered a "culture of narcissism" by the late 1970s, which "after the political turmoil of the sixties," caused Americans to retreat "to purely personal preoccupations ... getting in touch with their feelings, eating health food, taking lessons in ballet or belly-dancing, immersing themselves in the wisdom of the East, jogging, learning how to relate, overcoming the fear of pleasure."[9] Indeed, during the 1970s running became one of the most popular crazes of the post–World War II era, and like most any other activity of the decade, one ran *for oneself*. For its more fanatical participants running became a spiritual act like mediation. As the runners' guru Jim Fixx wrote, if one ran long enough and hard enough, one would experience a "trance-like state, a mental plateau where they feel miraculously purified and at peace with themselves and the world." Even if a runner did not reach Fixx's sublime state, the individual nonetheless had attained a degree of elevated consciousness. Rigorous exercise (particularly running or biking, which became the second most popular form of physical activity in the 1970s and beyond) became one of the most important sacraments in the new religion of the self. Indeed, according to Fixx, "Having lost faith in much of our society—government, business, marriage, the church, and so on—we seem to have turned to ourselves, putting what faith we can muster in our own minds and bodies."[10] For many ex-hippies running became the new psychedelic experience, sans dope, and for straights who had not indulged in the hip lifestyle and its many excesses during the previous decade, running provided a momentary hallucinogenic high. Lasch also maintained that many former hippies had become some of the most avid bourgeois consumers—the very type of individual they once scorned. "The propaganda of commodities serves a double function. First it upholds consumption as an alternative to protest or rebellion.... In the second place, the propaganda of consumption turns alienation itself into a commodity. It addresses itself to the spiritual desolation of modern life and proposes consumption as the cure."[11] Too often, it seemed, the hippies mirrored the society they were attacking.

Although far less in numbers than the media portrayed (perhaps no more than four million by the mid-eighties), the college-educated, professional, high-income yuppie social type was nonetheless sufficiently present and financially successful to sustain thousands of high-end restaurants and chic boutiques and shops, state-of-the-art exercise clubs, therapy centers, and a growing organic foods industry. Comparatively few 1960s rebels-turned-Yuppie were the vacuous, greedy, cocaine-using generation unleashed upon the stock markets by Ronald Reagan's deregulatory agenda, becoming Republicans in the process. Rather, the majority continued to adhere to the fundamentals of their 1960s hip ethos by reframing their previous notions about money and wealth, with many concluding that money-making was not antithetical to meaningful social change but absolutely essential to bring about a larger good. Even as outrageous a character as Jerry Rubin succumbed to the reality of American life, becoming a successful multi-level marketer of health foods and nutritional supplements as well as an early investor in Apple Computers. Rubin no doubt shocked quite a number of people, but especially his Sixties contemporaries who were still around and still clinging to "the dream," when he publicly declared in the 1980s that the counterculture's abuse of drugs, sex, and destruction of private property during that tumultuous decade had created "a scary society in itself; a culture of materialism and dehumanization." He also announced that "wealth creation is the real American revolution. Money is power. What we need is an infusion of capital into the depressed areas of the country.... I know that I can be more effective today wearing a suit and tie and working on Wall Street that I can be dancing outside the walls of power.... Welcome, Wall Street, here I come! Let's make millions of dollars together. " As one pundit aptly remarked Rubin had come to accept the reality of the American capitalist system that "the individual who signs the check has the ultimate power." For Rubin and for many other transformed Sixties radicals and hippies, embracing the idea that socially conscious entrepreneurship was the best way to help people and the best alternative to the bureaucratic, academic welfarism of Great Society liberalism that Rubin and his compatriots had denounced most vociferously during the 1960s. Jerry Rubin died rather unceremoniously at the age of 56 in 1994 from injuries sustained after being hit by a car as he jaywalked across heavily trafficked Wilshire Boulevard in Los Angeles.[12]

Rubin's sidekick, Abbie Hoffman, however, remained true to his countercultural roots to the day he died in 1989 at the age 52. Cause of death: suicide from ingesting 150 phenobarbital tablets which he washed down with hard liquor. Nine years earlier he had been diagnosed as bipolar. Despite having taken two completely different paths by the late 1970s, Rubin and Hoffman had remained close friends; Rubin believed his 1960s comrade-in-arms had "died of a broken heart. At one level he fell victim to brain chemistry but he saw all the pain in the world and he saw [that] no one cares and that in many ways was what killed him." Yet, for all his personal flaws, Hoffman never sold out, allowing himself or his ideals to be co-opted by mainstream culture; he remained an activist rebel until his death. As iconoclast professional basketball player Bill Walton observed at Hoffman's memorial service, "calling Abbie a fugitive from justice is funny. As I see it, justice was always a fugitive from Abbie." To Mary Schultz, who had marched with Hoffman on several occasions against the war and other issues, Abbie "was a hero who tried to be a clown. Today, there are clowns trying to be heroes." Perhaps the most apt defining of Hoffman's activist life came from Temple Emanuel's Rabbi Norman Mendell, who believed that although Hoffman's long history of protest was often more put-on than substantive, Hoffman nonetheless remained true to the "Jewish prophetic tradition, which is to comfort the afflicted and afflict the comfortable," and in that capacity both Abbie Hoffman and Jerry Rubin had great success.[13] In the end, few hippies succeeded in seceding from mainstream American life, and those who did, such as Hoffman, were marginalized by the dominant corporate culture.

Baby boomers now control conventional society; a society and ethos they once condemned proved far more tolerant and amenable (and resilient) than former radicals were willing to admit during their days of protest and rejection. Hippies contended that the United

States had become such a "people of plenty," of such limitless bounty for all, that post-scarcity was a permanent situation. Thus many hippies believed "that it would be easier to transcend capitalism than destroy it. Time was on their side, they maintained, because the coming leisure society would likely erode most strictures associated with capitalism." Unfortunately for the counterculture, "the huge leisure society" many hippies predicted never materialized.[14] Indeed, by the end of the decade post-scarcity had become a myth as the United States government announced that the nation could no longer feed the world. Thus as the 1970s began, gone from hip discussion was the development of a New Man to live in the Post-Scarcity Age; rather the conversation was about disastrous world overpopulation and a dark future of chronic shortages.

Even though the hippies erred that a leisure ethic would come to inform the American work place and societal values in general, they correctly forecast that the old hard-grinding work ethos would fade away as the nation's need for such labor diminished. Replacing the traditional work mentality beginning in the 1970s was the increasing desire among individuals, especially those who had been affected by the hip creed in some form or another, to work for oneself rather than to support others; the priority of doing work that was self-fulfilling and self-expressive. Indeed, only 28 percent of college graduates in the job market considered "prestige" and "money" important considerations in their prospective careers, while the ability to "express oneself" and to have a position that provided them with a "quality of life" were at the top of their lists of job preferences.[15]

One of the great ironies of hippie disdain for American capitalism was that their lifestyle showed the way to create even more commodities from which corporate America could profit. Of all the invidious forces arrayed against the hippies, in the end one of the most powerful proved to be good, old-fashioned American corporate capitalism, which from the movement's inception set its sights on defining, popularizing, and ultimately helping to destroy the hip counterculture by absorbing hippiedom into mainstream consumer culture. From drug dealers to record companies to Fifth Avenue Fashion designers and myriad other consumer goods manufacturers and human opportunists, all discovered there was plenty to be made from the most popular bohemian movement in American history. As the 1960s progressed, the hippie movement proved too profitable for the nation's business establishment to entirely subvert as co-optation proved just as effective and certainly more remunerative. As corporate America increasingly commodified hippiedom, hippies came to be defined in terms of their lifestyle accessories and excesses. The rapid seizure and commercialization of the hip experience by the mainstream business culture quickly destroyed the authenticity that had characterized the original community, as not only capitalist enterprises co-opted the counterculture but young people as well who wanted to *play* hippie rather than *be* hippies, bought all the appropriate attire and accouterments to become "cool" as long as it was popular or faddish to do so, just as their parents were snapping up the latest new gadget or token of affluence in their rarefied suburban world for essentially the same reasons. By the beginning of the 1970s, growing long hair and wearing bell-bottoms had become more a matter of fashion than reflection of a revolutionary attitude or change in consciousness; for most merely a shift in superficial values. In the process the capitalist establishment succeeded in transforming non-conformity into profitable conformity, thus sadly turning hippies into parodies of themselves.[16]

The warning signals of hippiedom's inevitable commodification and commercialization appeared very early in the movement's brief history. It was apparent by close of the Summer of Love, according to Dan Evans and his wife, Theresa Gray, who had moved together to LA from Indiana. "The hippie scene was already becoming big business, with everyone in the straight culture picking up and capitalizing on the hippies. We would see old movie stars wearing love beads, hippie clothes and long hair. Computer techs were showing up at work with beards and moustaches. Rich Beverly Hills people bought grass like there was no tomorrow and served it with their after-dinner drinks at their fancy dinner parties. Expensive department stores began selling faded jeans and India-print dresses at their usual high prices while white middle-class, middle-aged people went to see professional hippies take off their clothes in *Hair*. A movement that had seen itself as a radical rejection of the whole materialistic, business-governed American bag had become just another tool of the corporate machine, another way to make a buck." On the "brighter side" both Dan and Theresa welcomed "the sexual freedom and the drugs that became a permanent part of the lifestyle of American young people. Both these changes were all right with us."[17]

It was inevitable that corporate capitalism would co-opt hip culture, profiting by making hip faddish and chic. As seen with Jerry Rubin, the Gap, and many other ex-hippie current enterprises, the 1960s countercultural rebellion has turned out to be one of the driving forces of entrepreneurial capitalism in the United States over the last thirty years. Quite a number of countercultural rebels became avid producers and consumers of New Age merchandise and services—from 1960s and 1970s "vintage" clothing boutiques to homeopathic medicines and numerous alternative psychological therapies. Many of the accessories, styles, values, and attitudes of the 1960s counterculture have become mainstream "cool" and profitable for its purveyors, many of whom were and are ex-hippies. According to Joseph Heath and Andrew Potter, many 1960s countercultural values have become "the very lifeblood of capitalism. Cool people like to see themselves as radicals, subversives, who refuse to conform to accepted ways of doing things. And this is exactly what drives capitalism."[18] Consequently, in those metropolitan areas that had hip communities during the counterculture's heydays in the mid to late 1960s, there has emerged a post-hippie hip scene in the very same neighborhoods where the original hippies had resided. One can easily take a walk down memory lane in many of those cities and in some instances the original hip store or restaurant might still be there. If not, the ex-hippie entrepreneurs or their younger variations who have taken over the area, gentrified it in the process to attract more upscale consumers, will provide visitors and tourists with nostalgic memorabilia from funky, psychedelic-looking cafes, vegetarian restaurants, vibrant musical scenes, New Age specialty shops and a variety of other cool venues and sights. Even the more amorphous New Age phenomenon (a more apt descriptive than *movement* for this most recent quest for alternative living and consciousness) that emerged in the 1990s, owes much to the hippies.

For the mainstream press the intent from the beginning seemed to be a desire to discredit the movement as much as was possible with their coverage, which was superficial at best and mostly negative. Few news agencies had their reporters spend much time in the various hippie enclaves that had emerged by the late 1960s throughout the country's metropolitan areas, usually no more than a few days, which was hardly enough time to make sense of this latest bohemian phenomenon, the likes of which had never occurred in American history. Consequently the hippies became incomprehensible roiling mobs of weirdos; menaces to the nation's youth with their passion for indolence, promiscuous sex, and drugs, which turned them all into madmen. Few mainstream journalists had any interest or sufficient imagination, intellectual curiosity, or patience to drill down deeper into the community's philosophy, daily life, or creativity, both in an aesthetic and spiritual context. On individual who did immerse himself in "the scene" for several weeks was *Look* magazine writer William Hedgepeth who "crashed" in the Haight-Ashbury long enough to be affectively impressed by what he saw and experienced. Upon returning to New York, Hedgepeth "never wore a suit and tie again. Consciousness is irreversible. It changed my life."[19]

These were not the "positive vibes" *Washington Post* journalist Nicholas Von Hoffman got from the Haight, even though he stayed in the neighborhood almost the entire Summer of Love. After countless interviews with scores of individuals, ranging from Dr. David Smith of the Free Clinic to hardcore drug dealers, to teenage runaways, Von Hoffman's take away was that the hippie scene was "appalling," which unfortunately was the same conclusion the majority of Von Hoffman's peers had of the hippie movement and which they constantly broadcast to the public. To Von Hoffman, "this mass of young people had no political knowledge, were not particularly well educated, but the thing you could get them to do was sex, drugs, and rock 'n' roll." Even though Von Hoffman probably stayed longer in a hippie community than any of his compatriots and thus his coverage was more thorough than most, he nonetheless in the end proved no different than his colleagues in reducing the hippie movement down to its alleged "essence": the three trite, universally applicable clichés of sex, drugs, and rock and roll. Taken aback by what he saw, Von Hoffman persuaded the *Post*'s managing editor Ben Bradlee to come to the City and see for himself America's degenerated youth, "to see all the shit" that was happening to the nation's young. Bradlee arrived in early August 1967, just as the Summer of Love started to deteriorate into much of what Von Hoffman later described in his book noted in Chapter 7. By then the Haight had become so "full of hate" and hard drugs, rapes, beatings, and even murder, that "if a tour bus' air-conditioning broke down, the tourists would be afraid to get out, even in 95-degree heat." For Bradlee's tour finale, Von Hoffman took his editor to a meth lab and the next day "Ben flew back still in a state of shock" with Von Hoffman following him, equally disgusted by and disdainful of the hippie movement.[20]

Unfortunately, community members, attempting to ingratiate themselves with the reporters were not very effective in convincing the press that there was much more to the hip ethos and their lifestyle than sex, drugs, and rock and roll. Those neighborhood leaders who should have spoken to the press either did not because they knew it would not make any difference what they said since the press had already made up its mind about the hippies; or those who did, rambled on clumsily, incoherently, as if they were on some kind of high about "flower power" or the virtues of psychedelics, or communal living, or their liberated ideas about sex; all such meandering only confirming in the public mind that hippies were drugged-out vagabonds searching for their next thrill, whether it came in the form of acid, sex, or a trips' festival at the Fillmore. As one Hashbury resident told an interviewer, "Our secret formula for who we are, is grass, LSD, meditation, hot music, consolidation, and a joyous sexuality."[21] Unfortunately, the press' exposure of the nation's hip communities proved to be great "PR" for the hippie movement, but not necessarily the kind of advertisement *real* hippies welcomed in the end. The mainstream media's constant talk of how debauched the hippies were and how their love ethos had made their communities' open to everyone, naturally attracted all manner of miscreants, crazies, and outcasts, all of whom eventually overwhelmed the neighborhood's original hippie denizens. They simply could not keep such individuals at bay and the hippie dream of an urban utopia of alternative lifestyles disinte-grated, destroyed not by visionaries and seekers but by a wild kid from suburbia attracted to the thrills of bohemia and its freedom from white middle-class morality. All the while the press hammered away at the hippies while corporate capitalism pursued its profitable co-opting subversion.

Despite the external forces arrayed against the counterculture, many of hippiedom's fun-damental ideals and ethos actually expanded in the Seventies and beyond, cultivating over the subsequent decades the acceptance if not normalization of a less formal, more open, free-wheeling way of life. In effect, a "Sixties culture" emerged in the post-counterculture era, a combination of former hippies, activists, minorities, and feminists, who collectively (although they never formally united or organized into a mass movement) helped to galvanize and sus-tain the "rights revolutions" of the 1970s and 1980s. Together they transformed the Movement of the 1960s from socio-political activism focused on civil rights, university campus issues, and war to a counterculture that persisted to challenge the values and priorities of mainstream culture. These new hip activists also continued to pursue greater individual liberation from cultural restraints and taboos as well as simultaneously advocating for the empowerment of previously disenfranchised and alienated groups. In effect, by the late 1970s, with the Vietnam War rejected, a president discredited and driven from office, and marijuana decriminalized in a number of states, Grateful Dead manager Rock Scully found it obvious "America [had] joined the hippies."[22]

It was their parents' faith in rationality, central planning, and control that hippies rejected. Consciously created order looked beautiful in the plans and blueprints but to hippies such regimentation, homogenization, and conformity in daily life was brutal, alienating, and inhuman. Hippies rebelled not only against regularity and conventional deportment of every kind but also against the cool, methodical habits of mind that undergirded those institutions that promoted and sustained the Establishment's suppression of the free spirit. Resentment against the crimping and cramping of the individual personality not only became the *raison d'être* of the hippies but for the 1960s counterculture in general.

However, the hippies' efforts to ignite a cultural revolution, of creating a viable alternative way of life, failed or became diluted. Communes drifted apart; underground publications mainstreamed (*Rolling Stone*), or closed down all together; free clinics applied for government funding. Nonetheless the hippies were not just a bunch of people getting stoned. Although they failed to put into effect many of their ideals and even found that certain of their concerns were phantoms, as a human endeavor, their actions were noteworthy. They were the first post-war generation to question the reasons for war, the sanctity of technology, and human nature in general at both an intellectual and spiritual level. Their hearts were often in the right place but unfortunately just as frequently their heads were not.

As the 1970s progressed the mainstream media loss interest in the hippies, confirming their assertions all along that young America's enchantment with the counterculture was just another fanciful, momentary fascination that in the end represented nothing more than yet another fad. Such an assessment could not have been more shortsighted or dismissive. As one astute observer of the hippies has noted, "Often we are victimized by our own naiveté at accepting the trivializing vision of the media which define and dismiss revolution as an event rather than seeing it as a long and incremental process."[23]

Thanks to the hippies, pleasure and play are no longer considered "demonic" but rather an essential ingredient of the holistic free and meaningful life. Until recently mindless exploitation of the planet was the order of the day for most Americans, but now, thanks to the hippies who argued that the earth needed to be protected not abused, the majority of Americans have become more interested in ecology and the environment, preserving rather than conquering nature as increasing numbers of citizens are more willing to address the issues of population explosion, pollution, destruction of renewable resources, soil erosion, depletion of rain forests, and overcrowding. Indeed, what hippies had to say about the dark underside of modern technological society—over-commercialization and overdevelopment—is even more valid and relevant today. A deep concern for the environment permeated the music, art, and literature of the hippie movement. Living green has become vogue.

Perhaps one of the most prominent hip themes currently resonating in American culture is the cult of the body, which permeates the lives of millions of citizens on a daily basis. Hordes of Americans run, swim, bicycle, do Pilates, yoga, and aerobic dancing at health/fitness clubs or in the great outdoors. Part and parcel of this commitment to maintaining youth and vitality is the whole or natural foods craze, reflecting yet another hippie throwback. No doubt much to the dismay of many hippie purists, eating organic has not only become mainstream, but big business as well with the proliferation of hundreds of health and organic food stores across the nation, most notably the multi-billion dollar enterprise of the Whole Foods chain. Eating healthy, organic foods is perhaps among the longest lasting of all hip innovations. Daily, millions of Americans eat yogurt, whole-wheat bread, free-range chicken and chicken eggs, hormone and antibiotic free milk, and thousands of other chemical-free, non-processed foods, all of which were once considered "hippie food." In 1971 New Jerseyite Alice Waters opened in Berkeley, California, what became one of the most influential food establishments in the 1970s: Chez Panisse. Waters' idea was to make the hippie's "macro-biotic" foods into meals all Americans would cheerfully eat. She used only locally grown, organic products, minimized red-meat selections, and her eatery became one of the first American restaurants to serve three-star meals in a room where a coat and tie *were not required*. Chez Panisse listed virtually every ingredient in a dish so that food-conscious diners would know exactly what they were eating. Waters' main objective, in which she more than succeeded in bringing to fruition, was to make palatable the hippie diet; to make healthy food not only tastier, but to introduce as well to the nation's restaurant scene, a uniquely American version of nouvelle cuisine that paid homage to its hippie progenitors.[24]

Last, but not least, and perhaps one of the greatest manifestations of the hip legacy can be found in contemporary pop music, modern rock and roll in particular, which has its foundation in the 1960s rock revolution; black rap and hip-hop remain distinct genres. Nineteen-sixties hip rock and roll, from the Beatles to the Rolling Stones to the Grateful Dead (before some of the band members passed away), and other bands of the San Francisco sound, and of course Bob Dylan, are not only popular with old hippies and aging baby boomers, but among millennials and other age-groups of the post-hip era as well. When the countercultural bands reunite and tour, they pack the house, as thousands of fans from across generational spectrums turn out for their concerts. Indeed, the Rolling Stones remain one of the hottest tickets in the business.

One of the more intriguing and increasingly popular contemporary hippie throwbacks is the annual Burning Man festival held in the late summer in northern Nevada's Black Rock desert. In 1986 bohemian Larry Harvey, accompanied by friends, burned a wooden statue on San Francisco's Baker Beach in a punk-pagan ritual to help Harvey heal a broken heart. For Harvey the spectacle was cathartic; for his friends it was a soul-energizing blast that should become an annual celebration. Harvey agreed but it had to be an event in which everyone participated; there would be no spectators. "A Disneyland in reverse," Harvey declared, "Everyone had to be a participant and march in the electric-light parade." How popular has Burning Man become since that night on Baker Beach? The 2014 jamboree attracted over 65,000 people from all walks of life; from no-collar Silicon Valley techno-geeks, to conservative Washington wonk Grover Norquist to entertainers such as Sean "Diddy" Combs, to Google founders Sergey Brin and Larry Page and Facebook's Mark Zuckerberg. Like the hippie tribal gatherings in the 1960s, the Burning Man festival has something for everyone. For some people the event is the biggest dance party in the world, while for others it is a week-long yoga and meditation retreat, or an opportunity to get totally wasted, or simply a challenging camping trip. For Grover Norquist, the appeal was Burning Man's promotion of "radical self-reliance and radical inclusiveness." Ironically, the ultra-liberal hippies would have been very comfortable using such terms to define the message of their events as well.[25]

Many see Burning Man as a modern compilation or fusion into one massive gathering of humanity of the 1960s countercultural happenings; a sort of "7 days of peace and music" à la Woodstock event. Perhaps so, and thus for some academics the celebration is a window to a new kind of hip community, complete with all the extravagant costuming, dancing, drugs, music, and general reckless abandon and revelry reminiscent of the hippie "happenings" of the 1960s. However, for some attendees such as Norquist, Burning Man *is not* Woodstock redux; the farthest thing from it. At Woodstock "a bunch of teenagers came to watch artists perform. At Burning Man, everyone is expected to be a participant. Burners [as attendees are called] bring their art work, their art cars, their personal dress and/or undress; everyone is on stage. The story of Woodstock was thousands of young people, without the sense to bring their own food and water, being rescued by the state police and sensible bourgeois rural folk."[26]

Although Norquist may see Burning Man as the quintessence of libertarian virtue, founder Harvey's view of the event reflects a much stronger connection to the hippie ethos, especially the idea of "decommodification"—everything at the festival is free, from whiskey to grilled cheese sandwiches to hair-washing—all are gifts provided by Burners—free of charge—for the enjoyment of others. No doubt such a philosophy would have delighted the Diggers. For Harvey, "Burning Man is like a big family picnic. Would you sell things to one another at family picnic? No, you'd share things." Harvey defines his Burning Man economic principle as "gifting"—the act of giving without the expectation of anything in return, which Harvey believes "alters the notion of value. What counts is the connection not the commodity." In a world of tech-driven isolation and high-speed consumerism, Harvey believes gifting acts as a much-needed antidote to what he calls "capitalism on steroids." Harvey is convinced that if the spirit of gifting "spread in the world" and was "widely adopted it would condition how people, as consumers in the marketplace, behave. If all your self-worth and esteem is invested in how much you consume, how many likes you get, or other quantifiable measures, the desire to simply possess things trumps our ability or capability to make moral connections with people around us." Fellow Burner Matt Schultz agrees: "We're trying to tell people to invest in things not because they'll get a profit, but because it's beautiful, because it's compelling." For Burner Tall Neil, "There are so many things at Burning Man we could do with more of in the outside world. The sense of community, open sharing of knowledge, actual communication instead of virtual, the joy of collective achievement and the simple abundance of love, compassion, and empathy." Schultz notes that Burning Man's mantra should be "We don't buy. We don't sell. We dream. We convene. We create. We make."[27] Any ex-hippie hearing such slogans or attending a Burning Man spectacle would surely believe that it was 1967 again and that he or she was about to experience another hippie gathering of the tribes à la 21st century.

These are just a few of the manifestations of the counterculture's positive legacy; as with any socio-cultural movement, there are negative remnants and ramifications as well. Hip behavior naturally caused a multitude of problems as the emphasis on experimentation often meant pushing life to extremes. There is little doubt that the hippies helped to intensify and expand the nation's drug culture, even though as the 1960s progressed, increasing numbers of hippies realized that drug usage had diminishing returns as they watched too many associates have bad trips or worse—overdose and die. Indeed, in the end for many hippies, the acid experience proved disappointing; just a hall of mirrors. Initially, however, hippie faith in LSD's potential knew no limits as they believed acid to be a gateway to experience itself, to spontaneity, to visions of unsuspected connections between things. They often referred to acid as a "de-conditioning" agent, capable of destroying the roots of war, racism, fascism, and a host of other evils that emerge as a result of narrow-mindedness and repression.

No doubt hippie advocacy of hallucinogenic drugs helped to open the door for the use of much harder drugs such as cocaine and heroin to attain the same consciousness delivered by LSD or marijuana, although cocaine and heroin use was not prevalent among hippies, who largely preferred acid or marijuana. Most hippies condemned cocaine and heroin but unfortunately both drugs entered the hip scene via the movement's more dissipated characters who simply added two more alternative substances hippies could use to get high. In the process, many hippies found heroin or cocaine a better kick than marijuana or LSD, became addicts, abandoned their use of psychoactive dope, and became lost, bereft souls to their quest for the visionary world of psychedelia. Hip permissiveness relative to drug use allowed hard drugs to penetrate the hip community, which contributed to hip's destruction as well as to problems elsewhere. For Christopher Swan, "the lessons of the [hip] drug culture were simple: people died, lives were ruined, and years were lost."[28]

Smack and crack use did not become popular or chic until the late 1970s and into the 1980s among those decade's post-hippie hipsters who were born toward the end of the baby boom era, roughly 1958–1964. Having missed the Sixties, they sought a high that had little to do with opening any "doors of perception"; "set and setting" for these hipsters became the bathroom stall of the clubs they frequented. Demand for those substances in the United States beginning in the 1970s and forward, has contributed to the current vicious and murderous drug wars along the U.S.-Mexican border. Not surprisingly on this issue, hippies would have argued that legalization would strip the drug lords of their enormous drug trade profit as well as end much of the violence spawned by drugs, which is the result of rivalry among sellers not users.

What was the impact of the hippies' carefree erotic energy? First, it must be remembered that the sexual revolution of the 1960s was *evolutionary* not *revolutionary*; thanks to the Pill, a change in attitudes towards sex and increasing premarital sexual activity, especially among the younger generation, was already well under way by the mid–1960s and did not really reach any sort of crescendo until the mid to late 1970s. Indeed during that decade many young women embraced feminist Germaine Greer's championing of promiscuity as a means to break women's "doglike" devotion to men.[29] Nonetheless the hippies were a major catalyst in this particular area of social change. More obsessed with but not necessarily enlightened by sex, hippies believed they were liberating white Americans from decades of Puritanical taboos that had made sex a shameful activity. Hippies believed they were in the vanguard of bringing about a *real* sexual revolution that would change the sexual behavior and frame of reference for white Americans for decades to come. Prior to the hippie movement white Americans obsessed over promiscuity, masturbation, premarital sex, and of having to repress sexual feelings and desires. The hippies declared such preoccupations to be the colossal "hang-ups" of a sexually shut-down, "uptight" white middle class. A truly free people should be able to express their sexuality at anytime and anywhere; sex was a naturally powerful, healthy, and pleasurable human instinct and necessity, not only for the purposes of procreation but for the sheer fun of it; for the intimacy and human bonding that occurs even if only for the moment, was worth the encounter. Indeed, restraint of sexual impulse became taboo in hippie culture. Thanks to the hippies, increasing numbers of white Americans over the course of the last four decades have released their anxieties about the issues of sex and sexuality. The hippie ethos relative to sex changed attitudes and to some extent practices in the nation as a whole—at least until the advent of AIDS and other sexually transmitted diseases—(STDs).[30]

Although certainly not the first generation to challenge sexual norms, the hippies did so with greater exhibition and passion. Although there was a lot of "making it"; "getting it on"; "balling," and "doing it," there was little genuine love, intimacy, sharing, or bonding, especially among young male hipsters who were driven solely by conquest and orgasm. The hippies' propagation of greater sexual openness did little to improve the quality of American life. Indeed, the sexual liberation of the 1960s and 1970s for which the hippies helped to ignite, is frequently hailed as a triumph for human freedom as momentous as the Declaration of Independence or the collapse of the Berlin Wall. But this upheaval had its victims. All too frequently hippie permissiveness promoted promiscuity, sexually transmitted diseases, illegitimacy, broken families, and countless numbers of desolated souls. The hippies helped pave the way for Americans to find more joy, delight and pleasure in their sexual relations, but as so often happens in the aftermath of revolutionary social change, especially in the United States, the promised bounties appear on hortatory billboards and advertisements put up by those absconders and co-opters of change, in this case the purveyors of jeans, underwear, and perfume. Despite such fallout, practitioners of alternative sexuality still exist in some former hippie outposts. Not surprisingly, one such enclave can be found in the Haight-Ashbury, in a commune that calls itself Kerista, whose dozen or so members engage in what they call "polyfidelity"—an arrangement of shared partners in which each individual is to remain absolutely faithful to the group but who can rotate within the group on a predetermined schedule to choose a new (but willing) sexual partner for a specific period of time.[31]

Finally, hip culture was overwhelmingly and fervently youth-oriented, regarding maturity and all that attends that stage of life as undesirable. The hip slogan "forever young," promoted an unrealistic and detrimental veneration of youth, generating hostility toward old age and a disparaging of the collective wisdom of experiences that usually accompanies getting older. Thus hippies pandered to "infantile attitudes, implicitly affirming the virtues of immaturity, instant gratification, self-centeredness, impulsivity, entitlement, and flights of fancy."

Bourgeois normality—"social responsibility, work, family, planning for the future, and rationality" were all to be avoided like the plague in the name of a truly liberated individual. As Abbie Hoffman told *Time* magazine before his death, "The world really began for us on August 6, 1945, when the atom bomb was dropped. So during the '60s we were all young. The whole world was going through its youth, its atomic youth. If you looked at the magazines at the time, they were all youth oriented, the culture was all youth oriented."[32] As Peter Braunstein has noted, the hippies' "forever young" mentality "presented the counterculture with its most intractable irresolution: how to plot the future of a movement that strives above all else to live in the moment." The mainstream media, especially the advertising industry for reasons of commodification and profit, reinforced such a mindset which further "inflated youth's sense of importance, producing an attitude that was at once self-confident and whimsical, holier-than-thou and smart-alecky, and occasionally smug and omnipotent," and always suspicious if not disdainful of "anyone over 30."[33] In short, hippies wanted to be treated on their own terms rather than judged by adult standards.

The attempts by early counterculture interpreters to ascribe greater meaning and purpose to the movement by exaggerated proselytizing and laudatory comments about hippie righteousness, proved to be naïve if not delusional. Hip exaltations to the contrary, from beginning to end, the movement lacked substance and direction; it amounted to little more than a temperament, a rebellious frame of mind and lifestyle choice. The hippie impulse was, according to Peter Braunstein and Michael William Doyle, "an inherently unstable collection of attitudes, tendencies, postures, 'lifestyles,' ideals, visions, hedonistic pleasures, moralisms, negations, and affirmations."[34] In sum the hippie phenomenon was so protean as to be virtually indefinable. To *Time*'s Timothy Tyler, "The counterculture began as an attitude, a radically new way of seeing life. Except on its political fringe, it was never translated into consciously conceived doctrine. It existed, in fact, mainly on the subconscious level, not so much a culture as a mass mental condition, a careless, peaceful state of arrested movement and introspection."[35] For some counterculture historians the movement's inchoate nature was the result of "a revolt of the un-oppressed. It [was] a response not to constraint but to openness" and "a search for new interactional norms in the widening, more diffuse margins of post-industrial societies." Most important, the hippies embarked on such an exploration because they were searching for "a range of experiences and exposures through which [they could find] a sense of significance."[36] Although inspired by the causes of some of the decade's other anti–Establishment movements for equal rights, cultural recognition, even cultural separatism, the hippies' inherent differences based on gender, class, or ethnicity, made it impossible for them to forge a common core ethos and united movement against the cultural mainstream.

The media and hip spokespersons such as Chester Anderson greatly inflated the disaffection and adversarial mood allegedly rampant among American white youth during the late 1960s. No doubt a high percentage of young folk at the time (those under 30) questioned the status quo and their parent's values and dabbled in some manifestation of hip culture and lifestyle, but such behavior and challenges to mainstream American life did not represent a tidal wave of generational change. In retrospect, the countercultural impact on the American polity and economic structure were marginal at best. Indeed, according to one ex-communard "The same people are in power and they've consolidated their power since the Sixties. They've gotten smarter. They saw the way the revolutionaries acted and they found ways to channel the revolutionary energy so that it wouldn't be dangerous to their power structure. The way things are now [the 1980s when this individual was interviewed by *Whole Earth Review*] in many ways parallel to how they were in the Sixties, except the oppressor is smarter, better equipped, and more popular now than in the Sixties. It's going to take many more years before the people get the idea of what's going on, if they ever do."[37]

As the movement gained momentum and followers, all too frequently the alleged purity and simplicity of hippie morality degenerated into sordid, misogynistic hedonism. Wanton, visceorgenic indulgence led to all manner of problems within the hippie community, from venereal diseases to drug overdoses to crime, and ultimately to thousands of disillusioned, betrayed, and abandoned souls. As Ed Sanders noted, although a noble experiment, the hippie movement attracted so many misfits and miscreants, mingling amongst the weak and the lost, that at times the hippie community looked "like a valley of thousands of plump white rabbits surrounded by wounded coyotes."[38] According to "hippie lawyer" Charlie Whitman of Lawrence, Kansas, by the early 1970s, "The wrong people, the wrong drugs," had "taken over" the hippie impulse. "The aggressive psychotic drunk has sprung up now in the drug culture. Heroin and speed have replaced marijuana and LSD. Hippie violence against hippie has become commonplace. It is numbers: too many hippies. We can only afford so many people alienated from society."[39]

Despite their many questionable behaviors and motivations, hippies nonetheless, in conjunction with other anti-establishment movements of their time, helped to alter the liberal consensus and ethos that had dominated the nation throughout the Cold War era. They helped to create a culture that fostered pluralistic lifestyle choices based on different notions of self-identity, liberation, and empowerment. Thus, for most hippies, participation in the movement was to be an individual experience and those encounters affected each participant differently. Some emerged out of their "trip" more aware, concerned, holistic individuals, while many others, from rock stars such as Jimi Hendrix, Jim Morrison, and Janis Joplin to countless numbers of teenage and young adult nobodies, overdosed on the experiment and committed the "ultimate downer." Some fled the chaos of the counterculture by searching for and embracing the opposite extremes of greater order and total discipline, with many subjecting themselves to the crazed authoritarianism of individuals such as the Rev. Jim Jones and his Jonestown inferno, which saw scores of individuals voluntarily commit mass suicide.

Initially the majority of hippies believed their movement contained the blueprint for a more harmonious world, and, ironically, as the assaults on their attempts to establish alternative lifestyles increased, the hippies became even more convinced that they had found a new way; it explained the rage and hostility toward them. They chose to blithely ignore or naively dismiss the powerful, insidious forces coming from a variety of unanticipated directions seeking either to undermine by co-optation or absorption, or outright destroy their vision of a new world order dawning in the Age of Aquarius. The slaughter and death of an escalating, unpopular Vietnam War, cities on fire caused by racial violence, and harshly enforced anti-drug laws, overshadowed and corroded the hippies' call for peace and love, the building of egalitarian communities, and expanded consciousness through the use of hallucinogenic drugs.

For many hippies, years of tripping had carried them to the edge of sanity and thus it was time to retreat and recover from thrill-seeking, either in isolated rural communes in New Mexico or Vermont, or back in the womb of the straight world. For many who joined the counterculture, the experience had been a frolic; a momentary romp through a Pinocchioesque "Donkey Island" with plenty of sex, and drugs, and rock and roll music to keep the party going until they got sick from all "the smoke." "For a lot of people" the fascination with hippiedom "lasted about six months. I mean some people left their home, went out, took a bunch of acid, got clap a couple of times, whatever, and in a few months were right back in college. 'Enough of that, whew!'"[40] It was easy, even vogue to revolt against the Establishment, smoke weed, engage in random, carefree sex, but then what? Many could never answer that question, and to them freedom simply meant "doing your own thing" regardless of how self-destructive, profligate, violent, or crazy. According to communard Richard Fairfield, freedom was "a difficult thing to handle. Give people freedom and they'll do things they thought they never had a chance to do. But that won't take very long. And after that? After that, my friend, it'll be time to make your life meaningful."[41]

Years after the counterculture had disappeared and he had become a multi-millionaire with his *Whole Earth Catalog* concept and enterprise, one of the Haight's original hippies and true-believers, Stewart Brand, explained to an interviewer why he had joined the hip counterculture. "Richard Alpert used to talk about the orange basketball. Psychologists raised some ducklings with a basketball and they imprinted on it as if it were the mother. Wherever the basketball rolled, they'd follow it. That's what the movement was to us. That was our orange basketball. Wherever it rolled, we'd follow."[42] Regardless of what motivated an individual to become a hippie and no matter what one may think of the hippies or the 1960s counterculture today, their impact on American society and culture, then and now, is undeniable. The counterculture permeated and affected mainstream America more profoundly than anyone suspected at the time. Beginning in the 1970s and down to the present, many socio-cultural norms and mores as well as many Americans' attitudes toward life, change, acceptance, and individual freedom in general, bear the mark of the 1960s youth culture. Thanks to the hippies, there will always be a countercultural element in American society, for "Whenever people courageously and passionately engage in rule-challenging behaviors that attempt to liberate humans from oppressive limitations (or limitations perceived as being oppressive), excitement, conflict, and scandal—and therefore engaging stories—are sure to follow."[43] As one ex-hippie declared, "Put any ideology to a contagious melody and beat and it will take root."[44] The hippies epitomized these observations par excellence. With all their foibles, child-like optimism, and narcissistic tendencies, they must be embraced, if for nothing else, as a wonderfully scandalous and engaging story of American youthful exuberance, idealism, and good, old-fashioned orneriness toward the status quo during one of the most pivotal decades in 20th century United States history. Few Americans would deny that there was an America before the 1960s hippies and a very different America afterwards.

Chapter Notes

Introduction

1. Allen J. Matusow, *The Unraveling of America: A History of Liberalism in the 1960s* (New York: Harper & Row, 1984); Adolf Reed, Jr., ed., *Race, Politics, and Culture: Critical Essays on the Radicalism of the 1960s* (New York: Greenwood, 1986); Howard P. Morgan, *The 60s Experience: Hard Lessons About Modern America* (Philadelphia: Temple University Press, 1991); David Farber, ed., *The Sixties: From Memory to History* (Chapel Hill: University of North Carolina Press, 1994); David Burner, *Making Peace with the Sixties* (Princeton, NJ: Princeton University Press, 1996); Maurice Isserman and Michael Kazin, *America Divided: The Civil War of the 1960s* (New York: Oxford University Press, 2004). In particular see Matusow, p. xiv, 277; Morgan, 212; and Burner, p. 5 and Chapter IV, 113–133. The reactionary crank Allen Bloom was especially harsh and vituperative in his assaults on both the 1960s New Left and counterculture, declaring that the decade did not produce "a single book of lasting importance." Allen Bloom, *The Closing of the Mind* (New York: Simon & Schuster, 1987), 314–322. Bloom is not alone in his condemnation of the 1960s youth uprising and the decade's "excesses" in general. Also see Peter Collier and David Horowitz, *Destructive Generation: Second Thoughts About the Sixties* (New York: Summit, 1989).

2. McDonald quoted in Sheila Weller, "Suddenly That Summer," *Vanity Fair*, July 2012, no. 623, p. 68.

3. Theodore Roszak, *The Making of a Counterculture: Reflections on the Technocratic Society and Its Youthful Opposition* (Berkeley: University of California Press, 1995 (1969)), p. xxvi. Also see Roszak, "The Misunderstood Movement," *New York Times*, December 3, 1994, A23–25.

4. See for example, William H. Whyte, *The Organization Man* (New York: Simon & Schuster, 1956); John Keats, *The Crack in the Picture Window* (New York: Ballantine, 1956); Sloan Wilson, *The Man in the Grey Flannel Suit* (New York: Four Walls Eight Windows, 2002 [1955]); Vance Packard, *The Hidden Persuaders* (New York: McKay, 1957).

5. Quoted in Roszak, "The Misunderstood Movement," A23; Burner, *Making Peace with the Sixties*, 6.

Chapter 1

1. Jack Kerouac, *The Dharma Bums* (New York: Viking, 1958), 10.

2. Barry Miles, ed., *Howl: Original Draft Facsimile, Transcript, and Variant Versions, Fully Annotated by Author, with Contemporaneous Correspondence, Account of First Public Reading, Legal Skirmishes, Precursor Texts, and Bibliography* (New York: Harper & Row, 1986), 165.

3. A description of the eclectic nature of the attendees as well as the Six Gallery's physical appearance along with photos can be found in poet Philip Whalen's "Notes," in the San Francisco Renaissance and Beat Collection (San Francisco, CA: San Francisco History Center, San Francisco Public Library). Hereafter cited as (SFHC-SFPL).

4. "Howl," reprinted in Gene Feldman and Max Gartenburg, eds., *The Beat Generation and the Angry Young Men* (New York: Citadel, 1958), 164–174; Preston Whaley, Jr. *Blows Like a Horn: Beat Writing, Jazz, Style, and Markets in the Transformation of U.S. Culture* (Cambridge, MA: Harvard University Press, 2004), 17–20; Michael Davidson, *The San Francisco Renaissance: Poetics and Community at Mid-Century* (New York: Cambridge University Press, 1989), 78–81; Maurice Isserman and Michael Kazin, *America Divided: The Civil War of the 1960s* (New York: Oxford University Press, 2000), 148–149.

5. Feldman and Gartenburg, eds., *The Beat Generation and the Angry Young Men*, 174.

6. Isserman and Kazin, *America Divided: The Civil War of the 1960s*, 149.

7. Feldman and Gartenburg, eds., *The Beat Generation and the Angry Young Men*, 174.

8. Miles, ed., *Howl*, 165; Bruce Cook, *The Beat Generation* (Westport, CT: Greenwood, 1983), 165; Glen Burns, *Great Poets Howl: A Study of Allen Ginsberg's Poetry* (New York: P. Lang, 1983), 332; Barry Miles, *Ginsberg: A Biography* (New York: Simon and Schuster, 1989), 196–197; Michael Schumacher, *Dharma Lion: A Biography of Allen Ginsberg* (New York: St. Martin's, 1992), 215–216.

9. City Lights was one of the first bookshops in the Bay Area (Ferlinghetti and his business partner Peter Martin opened their doors in June 1953), and in the country as well, to capture and promote the nascent paperback revolution, which at the time consisted mostly of tabloid literature distributed through drugstores and train and bus stations; the only quality paperbacks were published by British Penguin and Anchor-Doubleday of New York. Although supportive of the endeavor, few of

Ferlinghetti's fellow literati were sanguine about City Light's prospects for success. Kenneth Rexroth predicted, "There's no way they could ever make a success of that bookstore. Lawrence could stand at the door and hand out paperbacks as fast as he could and he still wouldn't make it." Fortunately, Rexroth's pessimism proved wrong; Ferlinghetti and Martin had found a niche in the burgeoning paperback revolution and there was no stopping it; they could not keep the racks filled or the doors closed. Indeed, City Lights stayed open until midnight on weeknights and 2 a.m. on weekends, and still does. Ferlinghetti had said he wanted to sell used books so that he could sit in the back room, wear a green eyeshade, and read, but he never got the chance. In 1955 Ferlinghetti bought out Peter Martin and added another dimension to his flourishing enterprise: publishing a series of paperbacks devoted to avant-garde literature. His press' first "Pocket Book" (he later named his publishing company Pocket Book Press) was his own *Pictures of the Gone World*, and later published a collection of poems by Kenneth Rexroth and Kenneth Patchen. All works were released in what became City Light's now classic signature look: nearly square format (4 by 5 inches), printed in black and white, collated and saddle-stitched, and sold for 75 cents to a dollar. Miles, *Ginsberg*, 197; John Tytell, *Paradise Outlaws: Remembering the Beats* (New York: William Morrow, 1999), 63; Steven Watson, *The Birth of the Beat Generation: Visionaries, Rebels, and Hipsters, 1944–1960* (New York: Pantheon, 1995), 207–209.

10. Jane Kramer, *Allen Ginsberg in America* (New York: Random House, 1969), 158–161; William Carlos Williams, "Introduction," in Allen Ginsberg's *Howl and Other Poems* (San Francisco: City Lights, 1956), vi; Lytle, *America's Uncivil Wars*, 49.

11. Schumacher, *Dharma Lion*, 260–263.

12. Theodore Roszak, *The Making of a Counterculture* (New York: Doubleday, 1969), 128.

13. Hermione Hoby, "Allen Ginsberg, Howl, and the Voice of the Beats," *The Guardian*, February 23, 2011, 26–27; *The Economist*, April 12, 1997, 87.

14. Ann Charters, *Kerouac: A Biography* (San Francisco: Straight Arrow, 1973), 127; Tytell, *Paradise Outlaws*, 136–138; Watson, *The Birth of the Beat Generation*, 104–108; Lytle, *America's Uncivil Wars*, 50.

15. Lytle; Tytell; Watson.

16. Gilbert Millstein, *New York Times*, September 5, 1957.

17. Christopher Gair, *The American Counterculture* (Edinburg, Scotland: Edinburgh University Press, 2007), 23. Also see Jack Kerouac, *Road Novels, 1957–1960: On the Road, The Dharma Bums, The Subterraneans, Tristessa; Lonesome Traveler, Journal Selections* (New York: Penguin-Putnam, 1984), *On the Road*, 3, 7, 278–279; Lytle, *America's Uncivil Wars*, 50–51; Tytell, *Paradise Outlaws*, 131–141; Allen J. Matusow, *The Unraveling of America: A History of Liberalism in the 1960s* (New York: Harper & Row, 1964), 285.

18. Tytell, *Paradise Outlaws*, 8–9; 45–50; Diggins, *The Proud Decades*, 263–268; Kenneth Leech, *Youthquake: the Growth of a Counterculture Through Two Decades* (Totowa, NJ: Littlefield, Adams, 1977), 29. Also see Lawrence Lipton, *The Holy Barbarians* (New York: Julian Messner, 1959), particularly pages 149–150. Lytle, *America's Uncivil Wars*, 51.

19. John Tytell, "An Interview with Herbert Huncke" in Arthur and Kit Knight eds., in *Unspeakable Visions of the Individual*, vol. 3, nos. 1 and 2 (California, PA: A. Knight, 1973), 3–15. Most of this issue is devoted to Huncke. Gregory Corso, "Variations on a Generation," in Ann Charters, *The Portable Beat Reader* (New York: Viking-Penguin, 1992), 183; Matusow, *The Unraveling of America*, 281–282; Allen Ginsberg in William Plummer, *The Holy Goof: A Biography of Neal Cassady* (New York: Paragon House, 1981), 46; John Clellon Holmes, "This Is the Beat Generation," *The New York Times Magazine*, November 16, 1952.

20. A valuable first-hand account of Harlem's and Chicago's black hipsters in the 1930s and 1940s and for a general assessment of the hipster persona as it developed in those decades is Milton Mezzrow and Bernard Wolfe's *Really the Blues* (New York: Random House, 1946), 44–233; Perhaps even more defining was Anatole Broyard's "A Portrait of the Hipster," first published in *Partisan Review*, June 1948. Complete text of the original article can be found at http://karakorak.blogspot.com/2010/11/portrait-of-hipster-by-anatole-broyard.html; Matusow, *The Unraveling of America*, 280. For an excellent synopsis of "the Dozens" see Lawrence W. Levine, *Black Culture and Black Consciousness: Afro-American Thought from Slavery to Freedom* (New York: Oxford University Press, 30th Anniversary Edition, 2007), 344–358; Broyard. On the development and importance of hipster jive language in the subterranean hipster world, see Norman Mailer, "The White Negro: Superficial Reflections on the Hipster," *Dissent* (Volume IV, Summer 1957).

21. Todd Gitlin, *The Sixties: Years of Hope, Days of Rage* (New York: Bantam, 1987), 345, 346.

22. Gair, *The American Counterculture*, 26–27.

23. Frank Tirro, *Jazz: A History* (New York: W.W. Norton and Company, 1977), 155; Marshall W. Stearns *The Story of Jazz* (New York: Oxford University Press, 1970), Chapter 18.

24. Gair, *The American Counterculture*, 56–64. Broyard, "A Portrait of the Hipster," 3–4. Also see Ross Russell, *Bird Lives: The High Life and Hard Times of Charlie (Yardbird) Parker* (Cambridge, MA: Da Capo Press, 1996), 85; Tytell, *Paradise Outlaws*, 135–136; Jon Panish, *The Color of Jazz: Race and Representation in Postwar American Culture* (Jackson: University Press of Mississippi, 1997), 39–44; Lewis MacAdams, *Birth of Cool: Beat, Bebop, and the American Avant-Garde* (New York: Free, 2001), 31–74.

25. For images of the new post-war hipster, see John Clellon Holmes' novel *Go* (New York: Scribner's, 1952); Russell, *Bird Lives*, 179–180; MacAdams, 183–214; Watson, *The Birth of the Beat Generation*, 121; Matusow, 281.

26. Norman Mailer, "The White Negro: Superficial Reflections on the Hipster." Mailer opens his article by citing another hipster assessment, that of Caroline Bird, titled "Born 1930: The Unlost Generation," which appeared in *Harper's Bazaar* in February 1957.

27. Mailer.

28. Ibid.

29. Watson, *The Birth of the Beat Generation*, 192–194; Snyder quoted on page 193.

30. Caen coined the word "beatnik" in an April 2, 1958, column in which he had lambasted *Look* magazine for producing yet another "picture spread of S.F.'s beat

generation (oh no, NOT AGAIN!)." As Caen remembered, the word "must have been spinning around in my subconscious and it just came out. I fell into it and to my amazement it caught on immediately." Jesse Hamlin, "How Herb Caen Named a Generation," *San Francisco Chronicle*, November 26, 1995.

31. Gair, *The American Counterculture*, 40.

32. Kenneth Rexroth in Ann Charters, ed., *The Dictionary of Literary Biography*, vol. 16 (Detroit: Gale Research, 1983), 462.

33. Holly George-Warren, *The Rolling Stone Book of the Beats: The Beat Generation and American Culture* (New York: Hyperion, 2006), 343, 362.

34. John Patrick Diggins, *The Proud Decades: America in War and Peace, 1941–1960* (New York: W. W. Norton, 1989), 180–181; William Chafe, *Unfinished Journey: American Since World War II* (New York: Oxford University Press, 2003), 107–109. For other works that stress the decade's affluence, especially that attained by white middle class Americans by the mid–1950s, with titles that reflect such a "glow," see William O'Neill, *American High: Years of Confidence, 1945–1960* (New York: Free, 1986); David Halberstam, *The Fifties* (New York: Ballantine, 1993); and Harold Vatter, *The American Economy in the 1950s* (New York: Praeger, 1963).

35. Robin Currie, "Children's Television, 1950s," *History Wired*. http://historywired.si.edu/detail.cfm?ID=132 (now inactive).

36. Chafe, *Unfinished Journey*, 122–124; 135–138; Diggins, *The Proud Decades*, 188–190; 229; Mark Kurlansky, *1968: The Year That Rocked the World* (New York: Ballantine, 2004), 109.

37. Chafe, 127. Also see Peter Biskind, *Seeing Is Believing: How Hollywood Taught Us to Stop Worrying and Love the Fifties* (New York: Pantheon, 1983), 44–56.

38. Karal Ann Marling, *As Seen on TV: The Visual Culture of Everyday Life in the 1950s* (Cambridge, MA: Harvard University Press, 1994), 87–126.

39. For the acceptance of various Caucasian ethnics/immigrants as *white* by WASP Americans in the post–World War II years, and thus their access to the post-war boom and entry into the middle class, see David R. Roediger, *Working Toward Whiteness: How America's Immigrants Became White* (New York: Basic, 2005); "Up from the Potato Fields," *Time* 61, no. 1 (July 3, 1950).

40. "Foreword" in John M. Gries and James S. Taylor, *How to Own Your Own Home* (Washington, D.C.: 1930). Also see Adam Rome, *The Bulldozer in the Countryside: Suburban Sprawl and the Rise of American Environmentalism* (New York: Cambridge University Press, 2001), 20–25.

41. W.W. Jennings, "The Value of Home Ownership as Exemplified in American History," *Social Science* (January 1938), 13.

42. FDR quoted in Cleo Fitzsimmons, *The Management of Family Resources* (San Francisco: W.H. Freeman, 1950), 38–39. Also see Rome, *The Bulldozer in the Countryside*, 28–32.

43. Chafe, *Unfinished Journey*, 117–119; James T. Patterson, *Grand Expectations: The United States, 1945–1974* (New York: Oxford University Press, 1996), 77–79; Richard A. Easterlin, *Birth and Fortune: The Impact of Numbers on Personal Welfare* (Chicago: University of Chicago Press, 1987), 48; Landon Jones, *Great Expectations: America and the Baby Boom Generation* (New York:

Coward, McCann & Geoghegan, 1980), 11, 23–35; Elaine Tyler May, "Cold War-Warm Hearth: Politics and the Family in Postwar America," in Steve Fraser and Gary Gerstle, eds., *The Rise and Fall of the New Deal Order, 1930–1980* (Princeton, NJ: Princeton University Press, 1989), 153–181; Todd Gitlin, *The Sixties: Years of Hope, Days of Rage* (New York: Bantam, 1987), 13.

44. Patterson; Easterlin, *Birth and Fortune*, 39–53; Arlene Skolnick, *Embattled Paradise: The American Family in the Age of Uncertainty* (New York: Basic, 1991), 64–67.

45. Patterson, *Grand Expectations*, 72–73; Richard Polenberg, *One Nation Divisible: Class, Race, and Ethnicity in the United States Since 1938* (New York: Penguin, 1980), 131–134; Jon Teaford, *The Twentieth Century American City: Problem, Promise, and Reality* (Baltimore: Johns Hopkins University Press, 1986), 100–102; Alexander Boulton, "The Buy of the Century," *American Heritage*, July/August 1993, 62–69; Kenneth Jackson, *Crabgrass Frontier: The Suburbanization of the United States* (New York: Oxford University Press, 1987), 58–64; Rome, *The Bulldozer in the Countryside*, 15–43; "Up from the Potato Fields," *Time*. Neither Levitt nor any of the other builders of the era could have accomplished such a feat without the aid of the federal government. It was through the generous policies of the Federal Housing Administration (FHA) and the Veterans Administration (VA) that GI's and millions of other Americans obtained home mortgages of up to 90 percent of the value of the home while allowing 30 years to pay off the debt. Interest rates on the loans ranged between 4 and 4.5 percent. Thanks to government largesse, compared to prewar homebuyers, Levittowners and other suburbanites got the buy of the century.

46. Polenberg, *One Nation Divisible*, 128, 131; O'Neill, *American High*, 15–18; Peter Muller, *Contemporary Sub/Urban America* (Englewood Cliffs, NJ: Prentice Hall, 1981), 51; Diggins, *The Proud Decades*, 181–182; Polenberg; Clifford E. Clark, Jr., "Ranch House Suburbia: Ideals and Realities," in Larry May, ed., *Recasting America: Culture and Politics in the Age of the Cold War* (Chicago: University of Chicago Press, 1989), 171–192; Rome, 1–2; "Birth of a City," *Time* 55, no. 16 (April 17, 1950); City of Lakewood, California—Lakewood History, Chapter 2, "A City as New as Tomorrow," http://www.lakewoodcity.org/about/history/history/ch2.asp.

47. Rome, 7.

48. For the *House Beautiful* quote and other contemporary comments about the Levittowns, see Ron Rosenbaum, "The House That Levitt Built," *Esquire* 100 (December 1983), 378–391; Malvina Reynolds, "Little Boxes," 1962, Columbia Records; Diggins, *The Proud Decades*, 181–182. For Levittown's restrictions on what homeowners could or could not do, see "Up from the Potato Fields," *Time*.

49. Diggins, 182–183. Also see Lewis Mumford, *The City in History: Its Origins, Its Transformations, and Its Prospects* (New York: Harcourt-Brace, 1961), 484–486; For suburbanization's negative impact on urban areas as well as suburbia's effect on the American character, see Teaford, *The Twentieth Century American City*, 98–112; Jackson, *Crabgrass Frontier*, 219–230; Robert Fishman, *Bourgeois Utopias: The Rise and Fall of Suburbia* (New York: Basic, 1987), 182–220; David Riesman, "The Suburban Sadness," in William Dobriner, ed., *The Suburban Community* (New York: Putnam and Sons, 1958), 375–

402; Chafe, *Unfinished Journey*, 116–117. A summary of many of these criticisms can be found in Richard Pells, *The Liberal Mind in a Conservative Age: American Intellectuals in the 1940s and 1950s* (Hanover, NH: Wesleyan University Press, 1985), 232–248. Also see John Keats, *The Crack in the Picture Window* (New York: Houghton Mifflin, 1956).

50. Galbraith quoted in Diggins, *The Proud Decades*, 251.

51. Diggins, 229–230, 246–247, 249, 252. Also see Irwin Unger, *The Movement: A History of the New Left, 1959–1972* (New York: Dodd, Mead, 1974), 22–24; Chafe, *Unfinished Journey*, 115–117, 135–137; Matusow, *The Unraveling of America*, 321–322; Gitlin, *The Sixties*, 19. There were a host of other critics of 1950s mass culture such as Paul Goodman, sociologists C. Wright Mills, Dwight MacDonald, William Whyte, historian Daniel Boorstin, journalist Vance Packard, and novelists Saul Bellow, John Cheever, and John Updike, to name but a few.

52. Quoted in Halberstam, *The Fifties*, 143. Levitt and Schaetzl quoted in "Up from the Potato Fields," *Time.*

53. Rome, *The Bulldozer in the Countryside*, 19.

54. Levitt quoted in Jackson, *Crabgrass Frontier*, 231.

55. Diggins, *The Proud Decades*, 187–188.

56. Matusow, *The Unraveling of America*, 287; Ginsberg quoted in McNally, *Desolate Angel*, 116.

Chapter 2

1. Judson Gooding and Malcolm Carter, "The Throbbing Three-Eights," in Joe David Brown, ed., *The Hippies: Who They Are; Where They Are; Why They Act That Way, and How They May Affect Our Society* (New York: Time, 1967), 30–31; David Talbot, *Season of the Witch: Enchantment, Terror, and Deliverance in the City of Love* (New York: Free, 2012), 27. Also see Frank Kavanaugh, "Dear Editor," San Francisco *Examiner*, July 7, 1966. Hippie Papers (San Francisco, CA: San Francisco History Center, San Francisco Public Library). Hereafter cited as Hippie Papers (SFHC-SFPL); Brian J. Godfrey, *Neighborhoods in Transition: The Making of San Francisco's Ethnic and Non-Conformists Communities* (Berkeley: University of California Press, 1988), 94–183.

2. Gene Anthony, *The Summer of Love: Haight-Ashbury at Its Height* (San Francisco: Last Gasp, 1980), 5; Gooding and Carter, "The Throbbing Three-Eights," 32; Sherri Cavan, *Hippies of the Haight* (St. Louis: New Critics, 1972), 43–44; Anthony Ashbolt, "'Go Ask Alice': Remembering the Summer of Love Forty Years On," *AustralAsian Journal of American Studies* 23 (June 2007), 36; Brian J. Godfrey.

3. Anthony, 6; Toynbee quoted in Judson Gooding, "Revolution or Revival?" in Joe David Brown, ed., *The Hippies*, 209; Ashbolt, 40.

4. Richard Alpert, interview, *San Francisco Oracle*, May 1967 (no. 12). Hippie Papers (SFHC-SFPL).

5. Gitlin, English, and Starr quoted in Mark Stein, "20 Years After the Hippie Invasion: The Summer of Love That Left Its Imprint on S.F.," *Los Angeles Times*, June 21, 1987.

6. Kevin Starr, *America and the California Dream* (New York: Oxford University Press, 1973), 51–61, 240–241, 264; Doris Muscatine, *Old San Francisco* (New York: Putnam and Sons, 1975), 11. Also see John Bernard McGloin, *San Francisco: The Story of a City* (San Rafael, CA: Presidio, 1978), 32.

7. Roger Lorchin, *San Francisco: 1846–1956* (New York: Oxford University Press, 1974), 342–347.

8. Howard Becker, ed., *Culture and Civility in San Francisco* (Chicago: Transaction, 1971), 6, 8–9. Also see Brian J. Godfrey, *Neighborhoods in Transition*, 86–90.

9. Starr, *America and the California Dream*, 61.

10. Scully quoted in Sheila Weller, "Suddenly Last Summer," *Vanity Fair*, July 2012, no. 623, 70. For the Haight's transformation from a random bohemian neighborhood to the most memorialized hippie ghetto, see *The Summer of Love*, DVD, directed by Gail Dogin and Vincent Franco. (New York: PBS American Experience, 2007).

11. Alice Echols, *Shaky Ground: The Sixties & Its Aftershocks* (New York: Columbia University Press, 2002), 19. Also see Ralph Gleason, "A Brief History of Those New Words," *San Francisco Chronicle*, August 9, 1967, 41.

12. Jerry Garcia quoted in Bill Graham with Robert Greenfield in *Bill Graham Presents: My Life Inside Rock and Out* (New York: Doubleday, 1992), 195.

13. Michael Fallon, "A New Paradise for Beatniks," *San Francisco Examiner*, September 5, 1965, 5; September 8, p. 10. Although Fallon is credited for coining the term "hippies," in his autobiography, Malcolm X stated that Harlem black folk were actually the first to refer to young whites who adopted the "hip" jive of black musicians and who frequented their borough in the 1940s, as "hippies." See *The Autobiography of Malcolm X* (New York: Ballantine, 1964), 94. Also see Jay Stevens, *Storming Heaven: LSD and the American Dream* (New York: Grove Atlantic, 1987), 304–305; Neil A. Hamilton, *The 1960s Counterculture in America* (Santa Barbara: ABC-CLIO, 1997), 148.

14. Seidemann and Getz quoted in Echols, *Shaky Ground*, 29. For the Garcia quote see Randy Groenke and Mike Cramer, "March 1967: Garcia Interview: One Afternoon Long Ago" which can be found at http://dead sources.blogspot.com/2013/05/march-1967-garcia-interview.html. Originally published in *Golden Road*, Summer 1985.

15. John Shaw, "Christ Was A Very Groovy Cat," in Joe David Brown, ed., *The Hippies: Who They Are*, 61.

16. Guy Strait, "What Is a Hippie?" *San Francisco Oracle*, May 27, 1967. Similar assessments can be found in the *Haight-Ashbury Eye*, June 1967 (vol. 1, no. 4), 2 and *Haight-Ashbury Maverick*, May 16, 1967 (vol. 1, no. 6), 4. Hippie Papers (SFHC-SFPL).

17. Henry David Thoreau, *Walden* in Carl Bode, ed., *The Portable Thoreau* (New York: Viking, 1947), 343. Also see Klaus Fischer, *America in White, Black and Gray: A History of the Stormy 1960s* (New York: Continuum, 2006), 295–296.

18. Undated "Broadside," Hippie Papers (SFHC-SFPL).

19. Quoted in Timothy Miller, *The Hippies and American Values* (Knoxville: University of Tennessee Press, 1991), 8, 117–118.

20. Hunter S. Thompson, "The 'Hashbury' Is the Capital of the Hippies," *New York Times Magazine*, May 14, 1967.

21. Quoted in Miller, *The Hippies and American Values*, 8.

22. *Ibid.*

23. Tuli Kupferberg, "The Politics of Love," *East Village Other* (May 1–15, 1967), 4–5. Also see Peter Braunstein, "Forever Young: Resurgent Youth and the Sixties Culture of Rejuvenation," in Peter Braunstein and Michael William Doyle, eds., *Imagine Nation: The American Counterculture of the 1960s & '70s* (New York: Routledge, 2002), 251–252.

24. *Haight-Ashbury Maverick*, August 1967 (no. 6). Hippies Papers (SFHC-SFPL).

25. Timothy Leary quoted in Martin Torgoff, *Can't Find My Way Home: America in the Great Stoned Age, 1945–2000* (New York: Simon & Schuster, 2000), 104.

26. Thompson, "The 'Hashbury' Is the Capital of the Hippies."

27. *The Rolling Stone Book of the Beats: The Beat Generation and American Culture*, edited by Holly George-Warren (New York: Hyperion, 2006), 353. Wolfe quoted in David P. Szatmary, *Rockin' in Time: A Social History of Rock and Roll* (Upper Saddle River, NJ: Pearson/Prentice Hall, 2007), 147–148.

28. George-Warren, 361.

29. Guy Strait interview with Ron Thelin, *San Francisco Oracle*, April 1967, 6; Peter Berg interview in Leonard Wolff, ed., *Voices from the Love Generation* (Boston: Little, Brown, 1968), 25; George-Warren, 361.

30. *The Summer of Love.*

31. Charles Perry, *Haight-Ashbury: A History* (New York: Random House, 1984), 78–88; Gene Anthony, *The Summer of Love*, 41–42; Helen Swick Perry, *The Human Be-In* (New York: Basic, 1970), 99–100; David Farber, "The Intoxicated State/Illegal Nation: Drugs in the Sixties Counterculture," in Peter Braunstein and Michael William Doyle, eds., *Imagine Nation: The American Counterculture of the 1960s and 1970s* (New York: Routledge, 2002), 29; Guy Strait interview with Ron Thelin, *Oracle*, April 1967.

32. Strait interview with Thelin. In every major city where a hippie community emerged, so did Thelin-inspired "psychedelicatessens." See *Time* (vol. 89, no. 8), February 24, 1967.

33. Perry, *Haight-Ashbury: A History*, 253; Gooding and Carter, "The Throbbing Three-Eights," 33–34. Before the hip takeover of the Haight, three countercultural enterprises existed and would continue operation until the early 1970s: The House of Richard, which sold Mexican ponchos and huarache sandals; Minasidika, a purveyor of mod clothing, and the famous Blue Unicorn bohemian café and bookstore located north of the Panhandle. See Perry, 6.

34. Thompson, "The 'Hashbury' Is the Capital of the Hippies." Also see Charles Perry, *The Haight-Ashbury: A History* (New York: Random House, 1984), 86.

35. Guy Strait, "What Is a Hippie?" in Alexander Bloom and Wini Breines, eds., *"Takin' It to the Streets": A Sixties Reader* (New York: Oxford University Press, 1995), 310–311.

36. Thelin interview, *San Francisco Oracle*.

37. *Ibid.*

38. *Ibid.* Also see, *The Haight-Ashbury Maverick* (vol. 1, no. 5, 1967), 6, 10.

39. Bowles quoted in Perry, *The Haight-Ashbury*, 157.

40. Thompson, "The 'Hashbury' Is the Capital of the Hippies."

41. http://www.fundinguniverse.com.

42. Theodore Roszak, *The Making of a Counter Culture* (New York: Anchor, 1969), 71, 72, 38.

43. Andy Warhol and Pat Hackett, *POPism: The Warhol Sixties* (New York: Harcourt Brace Jovanovich, 1980), 69; Fischer, *America in White, Black, and Gray*, 299.

44. Tom Wolf, *The Kandy-Kolored Tangerine-Flake Streamline Baby* (New York: Farrar, Straus & Giroux, 1965), 212; Fischer. Also see "Longer Hair Is Not Necessarily a Hippie," *Time* (vol. 90, no. 17), October 27, 1967.

45. Gooding and Carter, "The Throbbing Three-Eights," 30; Jerry Rubin, *We Are Everywhere* (New York: Harper & Row, 1971), 42; Fischer.

46. Guy Strait, "What Is a Hippie," in Bloom and Breines, eds., *"Takin' It to the Streets": A Sixties Reader*, 311–312.

47. Thomas Frank, *The Conquest of Cool: Business Culture, Counterculture, and the Rise of Hip Consumerism* (Chicago: University of Chicago Press, 1998), 20–33; 207–223; Macy's president quoted in Grace and Fred Hechinger, "In the Time It Takes You to Read These Lines the American Teen-Ager Will Have Spent $2,378.22," *Esquire*, July 1965, 65, 68, 113; Warhol and Hackett, *POPism*, 69.

48. Simpson quoted in Sheila Weller, "Suddenly That Summer," *Vanity Fair*, July 2012, no. 623, 74.

49. The best source for the Diggers is the Diggers themselves; their hundreds of printed leaflets, broadsides, announcements, and proclamations (courtesy of hipster/Digger Chester Anderson's Communication's Company), all reflecting in varying degrees the Digger philosophy as well as their various programs, zany activities, and "goofs." Scores of these items can be found in the Hippie Papers (SFHC-SFPL) as well as at http://www.diggers.org. A published version of the Digger manifesto can be found in Bloom and Breines, eds., *"Takin' It to the Streets": A Sixties Reader*, 316–322. Other accounts include Peter Coyote's *Sleeping Where I Fall* (Washington, D.C.: Counterpoint, 1998) and Emmett Grogan's *Ringolevio: A Life Played for Keeps* (New York: New York Review of Books, 1972). Grogan's book, however, should be used with caution. Todd Gitlin, *The Sixties: Years of Hope, Days of Rage* (New York: Bantam, 1987), 222–225; David Farber, *The Age of Great Dreams: America in the 1960s* (New York: Hill & Wang, 1994), 169–172; Farber, "The Intoxicated State/Illegal Nation," 29–30; Mark Hamilton Lytle, *America's Uncivil Wars: The Sixties Era from Elvis to the Fall of Richard Nixon* (New York: Oxford University Press, 2006), 212–213; Torgoff, *Can't Find My Way Home*, 200–205.

50. Farber, "The Intoxicated State/Illegal Nation," 30; Allan Matusow, *The Unraveling of America: A History of Liberalism in the 1960s* (New York: Harper & Row, 1984), 300; Lytle, 213.

51. Michael William Doyle, "Staging the Revolution: Guerrilla Theater as Countercultural Practice, 1965–1968," in Braunstein and Doyle, eds., *Imagine Nation*, 71–72; R.G. Davis, *The San Francisco Mime Troupe: The First Ten Years* (Palo Alto: Ramparts, 1975), 154.

52. Davis, *Mime Troupe*, 32, 39–40; Also see R. G. Davis, "Radical, Independent, Chaotic, Anarchic Theatre vs. Institutionalized, University, Little, Commercial, Ford, and Stock Theatre," in *Studies on the Left* (Spring 1964), 36–37. Pierre Biner, "The Living Theater," in Bloom and Breiners, eds., *"Takin' It to the Streets,"* 288–

293; Doyle, "Staging the Revolution," 73–76. On the history of mime and related issues see Anthony Caputi, *Buffo: The Genius of Vulgar Comedy* (Detroit: Wayne State University Press, 1978); on the Mime Troupe see "Mime Troup [sic] Always Set to Shuffle," *Berkeley Barb*, July 28, 1967, 9.

53. Robert J. Glessing, *The Underground Press in America* (Bloomington: Indiana University Press, 1972) 23–24; Abe Peck, *Uncovering the Sixties: The Life and Times of the Underground Press* (New York: Pantheon, 1985), 51; Eugene Alonzo Smith III, "Within the Counterculture: The Creation, Transmission, and Commercialization of Cultural Alternatives During the 1960s" (Ph.D. dissertation: Carnegie-Mellon University, 2001), 105–106. Smith claims that at its peak the *Oracle* had readers in Moscow, Prague, New Zealand, and South Vietnam, where U.S. soldiers would send back Vietnamese marijuana in return. "A Letter from a Digger," *San Francisco Oracle*, vol. 1, no. 3, November 10, 1966, 2. (SFHC-SFPL). Cohen quoted Szatmary, *Rockin' in Time*, 156.

54. Wilcock quoted in Thorne Dreyer and Victoria Smith, "The Movement and the New Media," 5. http://www.nuevoanden.com/rag/newmedia.html. Also see Charles Perry, *The Haight-Ashbury*, 88–90.

55. Matusow, *The Unraveling of America*, 300; The Digger Papers (SFHC-SFPL); Talbot, *Season of the Witch*, 38–39, 40. Grogan, *Ringolevio*, 318; Torgoff, *Can't Find My Way Home*, 203–204.

56. Allen Cohen, "Notes on the San Francisco Oracle," 4. Hippie Papers (SFHC-SFPL).

57. Strauch quoted in Wolff, *Voices from the Love Generation*, 187–187.

58. Lytle, *America's Uncivil Wars*, 213; Doyle, "Staging the Revolution," 83–85.

59. Doyle, 80–81; Steve Lieper, "At the Handle of Kettle," *San Francisco Oracle*, December 1966 (no. 4), 10.

60. Phyllis Willner's account can be found in the Hippie Papers (SFHC-SFPL) as well as in Gene Anthony, *The Summer of Love*, 21.

61. Anthony, 20; Ralph J. Gleason, "A Free Frame of Reference," *San Francisco Chronicle*, January 23, 1967; 37; Alice Echols, *Shaky Ground*, 21; Grogan, *Ringolevio*, 264; Talbot, *Season of the Witch*, 40.

62. Doyle, "Staging the Revolution," 81.

63. Hoffman quoted in Mark Kurlansky, *1968: The Year That Rocked the World* (New York: Ballantine, 2004).

64. Forman quoted in Joan Morrison and Robert K. Morrison, eds., *From Camelot to Kent State: The Sixties Experience in the Words of Those Who Lived It* (New York: Oxford University Press, 2001), 220.

65. Peter Coyote, *Sleeping Where I Fall*, 90.

66. Forman quoted in Morrison and Morrison, *From Camelot to Kent State*, 40.

67. Matusow, *The Unraveling of America*, 300; Lytle, *America's Uncivil Wars*, 213.

68. Quoted in Talbot, *Season of the Witch*, 40.

69. Hoffman quoted in Abbie Hoffman, *Soon to be a Major Motion Picture* (New York: Perigree, 1980), 122.

70. Forman quoted in Morrison and Morrison, eds., *From Camelot to Kent State*, 219.

71. Author interview with Larry Houchin, July 26–27, 2012.

72. *Ibid.*

73. Quoted in Stevens, *Storming Heaven*, 306.

Chapter 3

1. Author interview with Larry Houchin, July 26–27, 2012.

2. *Ibid.*

3. *Ibid.*

4. *Ibid.*

5. Quoted in Bruce Cook, *The Beat Generation* (New York: Scribner's 1971), 196.

6. Cohen quoted in David Farber, "The Intoxicated State/Illegal Nation: Drugs in the Sixties Counterculture," in Peter Braunstein and Michael William Doyle, eds., *Imagine Nation: The American Counterculture of the 1960s & 1970s* (New York: Routledge, 2002), 23, 29. Garcia quoted in David Szatmary, *Rockin' in Time: A Social History of Rock and Roll* (Upper Saddle River, NJ: Pearson/Prentice Hall, 2007), 161–162.

7. Coyote quoted in *The Summer of Love.* DVD. Directed by Gail Dogin and Vincent Franco. New York: PBS American Experience, 2007.

8. Timothy Miller, *The Hippies and American Values* (Knoxville: University of Tennessee Press, 1991), 25, 29–30. Also see Philip Mandelkorn, "The Drugs They Use," in Joe David Brown, ed., *The Hippies: Who They Are, Where They Are, Why They Act That Way, and How They May Affect Our Society* (New York: Time, 1967), 171.

9. Miller, 25

10. Quoted in Terry Anderson, *The Sixties* (New York: Longman, 1999), 137. Also see Miller, 42–43.

11. Quoted in Anderson, 137.

12. *Ibid.*, 138. Also see Mark Hamilton Lytle, *America's Uncivil Wars: The Sixties Era from Elvis to the Fall of Richard Nixon* (New York: Oxford University Press, 2006), 201.

13. "Behavior: Pop Drugs: The High as a Way of Life," *Time* (vol. 94, no. 13), September 26, 1969.

14. *Ibid.*

15. Philip Mandelkorn, "The Drugs They Use," Joe David Brown, ed., *The Hippies*, 181. Also see Miller, *The Hippies and American Values*, 27–28.

16. David Farber, "The Intoxicated State/Illegal Nation," *Imagine Nation*, 19–20. Also see Farber, *The Age of Great Dreams: America in the 1960s* (New York: Hill and Wang, 1994), 179; "Pop Drugs: The High as a Way of Life," *Time*, September 26, 1969.

17. Don Lattin, *The Harvard Psychedelic Club: How Timothy Leary, Ram Dass, Huston Smith, and Andrew Weil Killed the Fifties and Ushered in a New Age for America* (New York: HarperCollins, 2010), 64–66; Aldous Huxley, *The Doors of Perception* (New York: Harper & Row, 1964; paperback Perennial Library edition, 1970), 16, 24–25, 35–36, 56, 73. Also see Martin A. Lee and Bruce Shlain, *Acid Dreams: The C.I.A. and the Sixties Rebellion* (New York: Grove, 1985), 46–47.

18. Lattin, 66.

19. Huxley, *Doors of Perception*, 56, 73. Also see Matusow, *The Unraveling of America: A History of Liberalism in the 1960s* (New York: Harper & Row, 1984), 288; Farber, *Age of Great Dreams*, 180.

20. R. Gordon Wasson, "Seeking the Magic Mushroom." *Life* article available at www.imaginaria.org/wasson/life.htm.

21. Maurice Isserman and Michael Kazin, *America Divided: The Civil War of the 1960s* (New York: Oxford University Press, 2000), 155–156. For a more complete

recount of Hoffman's *first* trip, see Lee and Shlain, *Acid Dreams:* xiv. Lattin, *The Harvard Psychedelic Club,* 62–63.

22. Lattin.

23. Farber, "The Intoxicated State/Illegal Nation," 20–22; Lee and Shlain, *Acid Dreams,* 11, 30; Also see Isserman and Kazin, *America Divided,* 156; Farber, *The Age of Great Dreams,* 179. Also see Acid Dreams Time-Line at http://www.levity.com/aciddreams/timeline. html. LSD's potential as a truth serum or as a means of driving enemies insane is cleverly revealed in John Marks, *The Search for the Manchurian Candidate: The C.I.A. and Mind Control* (New York: Times, 1979). Also see Maia Szalavitz, "The Legacy of the CIA's Secret LSD Experiments on America," *Time,* March 23, 2012.

24. Lattin, *The Harvard Psychedelic Club,* 13–21.

25. Lee and Shlain, *Acid Dreams,* 73; Timothy Leary, *High Priest* (Oakland, CA: Ronin, 1995), 283; Lattin, *The Harvard Psychedelic Club,* 37–38, 40–41, 57. Also see Matusow, *The Unraveling of America,* 288–289.

26. Lattin, 61–62.

27. *Ibid.,* 68–72.

28. Timothy Leary, *Flashbacks: A Personal and Cultural History of the Era; an Autobiography* (Los Angeles: Jeremy P. Tarcher, 1983), 121; Lattin, 70–71; Farber, "The Intoxicated State/Illegal Nation," 23–24; Matusow, *The Unraveling of America,* 289.

29. Timothy Leary, "Turning on the World," in E.A. Swingrover, ed., *The Counterculture Reader* (New York: Pearson/Longman, 2004), 84–88; Matusow. For Ginsberg's first experience with LSD as a guinea pig, see Ginsberg quoted in Lee and Shlain, *Acid Dreams,* 59. Also see Matusow.

30. Swingrover, 90, 92; Matusow, 289–290.

31. Farber, "The Intoxicated State/Illegal Nation," 22; Information on Hollingshead and his desire to spread LSD to as many people as he possibly could, can be found at http://www.psychedelic-library.org/holl1.htm. Also see Leary, *High Priest,* 153, 253, and Chapter 12 as well as Leary's *Flashbacks,* 117–118; Matusow, 290.

32. Leary interview quoted in Lattin, *The Harvard Psychedelic Club,* 124.

33. *Ibid.,* 125. Also see Matusow, *Unraveling of America,* 290.

34. Quoted in Lattin, *The Harvard Psychedelic Club,* 86–87.

35. *Ibid.,* 88- 89; Timothy Leary, "Press Conference," *San Francisco Oracle* vol. 1 no. 4 (December 1966), 4, 17, 18, 19; Farber, "Intoxicated State/Illegal Nation," 22–24; Koestler quoted in Isserman and Kazin, *America Divided,* 158.

36. Richard Alpert (Ram Dass), *Be Here Now* (San Cristobal, NM: Lama Foundation, 1971), unpaginated.

37. Lattin, *The Harvard Psychedelic Club,* 87–95.

38. *Ibid.,* 97. Also see "Psychic Research: LSD," *Time* (vol. 81, no. 13), March 29, 1963.

39. Lattin, 105.

40. David Smith quoted in Tom Brokaw's *Boom: Voices of the Sixties: Personal Reflections on the '60s and Today* (New York: Random House, 2007), 245.

41. Farber, "Intoxicated State/Illegal Nation," 24.

42. Lattin, *The Harvard Psychedelic Club,* 111–112. Also see http://www.leary.com/Biography/Millbrook/millbrook.html (now inactive); John Cashman, *The LSD Story: The Drug That Expands the Mind* (New York: Gold Medal/Fawcett, 1969), 58–60; Martin Torgoff, *Can't*

Find My Way Home, 200–202. For an insider's view of Millbrook's antics and other issues, see Art Kleps, The Original Kleptonian Neo-American Church, *Millbrook: A Narrative of the Early Years of American Psychedelianism* at http://okneoac.org/millbrook/, 2005, particularly Chapters 1–14.

43. Lattin, 112; Torgoff, 203–205; Cashman, 60–61; Lytle, *America's Uncivil Wars,* 197.

44. Lattin, 116–118; Lytle.

45. Miller, *The Hippies and American Values,* 33; Art Kleps, *Millbrook* (Oakland, CA: Bench, 1975), 65–66, 243. Also see Kleps, *Millbrook: A Narrative of the Early Years of American Psychedelianism,* Chapters 14–41. Also see Kleps' Senate testimony 1966 about his as well as his church's purpose.

46. Lattin, *The Harvard Psychedelic Club,* 121. Also see "New York: Time to Mutate," *Time* (vol. 87, no. 17), April 29, 1966.

47. McLuhan and Leary quoted in Farber, "Intoxicated State/Illegal Nation," 32.

48. Lattin, *The Harvard Psychedelic Club,* 132–133.

49. *Newsweek* (vol. 67, May, 9, 1966); *Life* (vol. 60, March 25, 1966); *Saturday Evening Post* (vol. 239, May 21, 1966); *New York Times,* April 14, 1966, 35; April 6, pp. 1, 25; "Psychiatry: An Epidemic of Acid Heads," *Time* (vol. 87, March 11, 1966). Also see Farber, "The Intoxicated State/Illegal Nation," 31.

50. Farber, *Ibid.,* 32. Also see "The Dangers of LSD," *Time* (vol. 87, no. 16), April 22, 1966.

51. "LSD," *Time* (vol. 87, no. 24), June 17, 1966; "An Epidemic of Acid Heads"; "The Pros and Cons of LSD," *Time* (vol. 84, no. 26), December 18, 1964.

52. Snyder quoted in Isserman and Kazin, *America Divided,* 155.

53. *Ibid.*

54. "Bruce Hoffman" in Morrison and Morrison, ed., *From Camelot to Kent State,* 213.

55. "Jane DeGenaro" in Morrison and Morrison, 205.

56. *Ibid.,* 207. Also see, "LSD," *Time* (vol. 87, no. 24), June 17, 1966, and "Instant Mysticism," *Time* (vol. 82, no. 17), October 25, 1963.

57. Hippie quoted in *Aquarius Rising.* Online Database. Directed by Pierre Sogol. Psychedelic Archive, 1967. http://www.damer.com.

58. "Bruce Hoffman," in Morrison and Morrison, ed., *From Camelot to Kent State,* 212–213.

59. Author interview with Larry Houchin, July 26–27, 2012.

60. Leary, *High Priest,* 132; *Life,* 29; Lattin, *The Harvard Psychedelic Club,* 198–199, 202; Matusow, *The Unraveling of America,* 291.

61. Lattin, 203.

62. August Owsley Stanley III's harsh assessment of Leary can be found in Bruce Eisner, "Interview with an Alchemist: Bear Owsley Interview," https://ramblinjoe musicblog.files.wordpress.com/2011/10/owsley-stan ley-interview-with-an-alchemist.pdf . Also see Lattin, 203–204.

63. Kesey quoted in Farber, "Intoxicated State/Illegal Nation," 21. For a brief bio of Kesey see excerpt from Tom Wolfe's *The Electric Kool-Aid Acid Test* in Swingrover, ed., *The Counterculture Reader,* 95.

64. Swingrover, *Ibid.,* 95–96.

65. For an insightful recount of Kesey and friends' early explorations with LSD at Perry Lane, see Tom

Wolfe's chronicle of Kesey and the Pranksters' life and escapades in *The Electric Kool-Aid Acid Test* (New York: Farrar, Straus, & Giroux, 1968; Bantam paperback edition, 1999), Chapter IV. Also see Paul Perry and Ken Babbs, *On the Bus: The Complete Guide to the Legendary Trip of Ken Kesey and the Merry Pranksters and the Birth of the Counterculture* (New York: Thunder's Mouth, 1990), 30–41; Also see Kesey quoted Lytle, *America's Uncivil Wars,* 194–195; Farber, "Intoxicated State/Illegal Nation," 24; Matusow, *The Unraveling of America,* 291.

66. Wolfe, Chapter V; Lytle; Bowen quoted in *Newsweek* (vol. 69, February 6, 1967), 6. Bowen also quoted in Matusow, 292.

67. Wolfe, Chapter VI; Lytle, 194; Farber, "Intoxicated State/Illegal Nation," 26.

68. Wolfe quoted in Swingrover, *The Counterculture Reader,* 100.

69. Wolfe, *The Electric Kool-Aid Acid Test,* Chapter VI, 80; Perry and Babbs, *On the Bus,* 41–75.

70. Wolfe, 90. Also see Lytle, *America's Uncivil Wars,* 196; Perry and Babbs, 80–108.

71. Wolfe, Chapter 7.

72. Wolfe, Chapters 11 and 13.

73. Lattin, *The Harvard Psychedelic Club,* 128; Lytle, *America's Uncivil Wars,* 203–204; Lee and Shlain, *Acid Dreams,* 147; Isserman and Kazin, *America Divided,* 157; Farber, *The Age of Great Dreams,* 188; Mandelkorn, "The Drugs They Use," *The Hippies,* 177–178; Matusow, *The Unraveling of America,* 299.

74. "Pop Drugs: The High as a Way of Life."

75. Albert Hoffman quoted in Farber, "Intoxicated State/Illegal Nation," 22.

76. Mandelkorn, "The Drugs They Use," *The Hippies,* 184.

Chapter 4

1. Morris Dickstein, *Gates of Eden: American Culture in the Sixties* (New York: Basic, 1977), 185.

2. Sinclair quoted in Timothy Miller, *The Hippies and American Values* (Knoxville: University of Tennessee Press, 1991), 75.

3. McDonald quoted in Terry Anderson, *The Movement and the Sixties: Protest in America from Greensboro to Wounded Knee* (New York: Oxford University Press, 1995), 247.

4. Quoted in Miller, *The Hippies and American Values,* 77.

5. Robert Pattison, *The Triumph of Vulgarity: Rock Music in the Mirror of Romanticism* (New York: Oxford University Press, 1987), 33.

6. Maurice Isserman and Michael Kazin, *America Divided: The Civil Wars of the 1960s* (New York: Oxford University Press, 2000), 160; Christopher Gair, *The American Counterculture* (Edinburgh: Edinburgh University Press, 2007), 65–67; Carlo Rotella, *Good with Their Hands: Boxers, Bluesmen, and Other Characters from the Rust Belt* (Berkeley: University of California Press, 2000), 64; Rotella quoted in Gair, 67. Also see David P. Szatmary, *Rockin' in Time: A Social History of Rock and Roll* (Upper Saddle River, NJ: Pearson/Prentice Hall, 2007), 1–16.

7. Gair, 66.

8. Pattison, *The Triumph of Vulgarity,* 42.

9. Isserman and Kazin, *America Divided,* 160; Szatmary, *Rockin' in Time,* 16.

10. Greil Marcus, *Mystery Train: Images of America in Rock 'n' Roll Music* (New York: Penguin, 1997), 157, 163.

11. T.S. Eliot, *The Sacred Wood* (New York: Barnes & Nobles, 1928), 25.

12. Sinclair quoted in Miller, *The Hippies and American Values,* 75.

13. Paul Du Noyer, *The Illustrated Encyclopedia of Music* (London: Flame Tree, 2003) 14; John Tobler, *New Musical Express Rock 'n' Roll Years* (London: Reed International, 1992), 23. Freed and a host of other DJs proved invaluable to rock and roll's propagation. Indeed without them, to the delight of many parents, politicians, and clergymen, rock and roll might have faded away, but Freed and his compatriots helped keep the sound alive as long as they possibly could during the 1950s. One way they accomplished that objective was to take the most popular acts on the road, touring the country in a bus and stopping to perform in as many venues as allowed. However, much too frequently local townsfolk and the police who had hated the rock and rollers since the music's inception, tried manfully to shut the shows down but the kids refused to be cheated out of their fun, which often led to confrontations with local authorities. For such encounters see "Rock 'n' Riot," *Time* (vol. 71, no. 20). For the importance of radio DJs and other "discographers" who helped spread the new music, see "Tall, That's All," *Time* (vol. 74, no. 4); Szatmary, *Rockin' in Time,* 54–69.

14. Schaffer quoted in Robert Santelli, *Aquarius Rising: The Rock Festival Years* (New York: Dell, 1980), 7. Also see "St. Joan of the Jukebox," *Time* (vol. 81, no. 11), March 15, 1963; Szatmary, *Ibid.,* 21.

15. Peter Guralnick, *Last Train to Memphis: The Rise of Elvis Presley* (New York: Back Bay, 1994), 289; Szatmary, *Ibid.,* 29–35; Eddie Condon, "What Is an Elvis Presley?" *Cosmopolitan,* December 1956, 61, 35. On the rise of the teenage crooners see "Tuneless Tiger," *Time* (vol. 74, no. 4), July 27, 1959.

16. Guralnick, *Ibid.,* 338; Gary R. Edgerton, *The Columbia History of American Television* (New York: Columbia University Press, 2007), 187; Christine Gibson, "Elvis on Ed Sullivan: The Real Story, *American Heritage,* December 6, 2005.

17. Ralph J. Gleason, "The Times They Are a Changin'," *Ramparts* (April 1965), 47.

18. Stokes quoted in Miller, *The Hippies and American Values,* 74. Also see Szatmary, *Rockin' in Time,* 81–91; "Sibyl with Guitar," *Time* (vol. 80, no. 21), November 23, 1962; "The Folk Girls," *Time* (vol. 79, no. 22), June 1, 1962; "Like from Halls of Ivy," *Time* (vol. 76, no. 2), July 11, 1960; "The Faculty," *Time* (vol. 77, no. 25), June 16, 1961; "Take a Boy Like Me," *Time* (vol. 81, no. 13), March 29, 1963.

19. Isserman and Kazin, *America Divided,* 95–97. Also see Mark Hamilton Lytle, *America's Uncivil Wars: The Sixties Era from Elvis to the Fall of Richard Nixon* (New York: Oxford University Press, 2006), 206–208.

20. Allan J. Matusow, *The Unraveling of America: A History of Liberalism in the 1960s* (New York: Harper & Row, 1984), 294–295; Isserman and Kazin, 96. Teenager quoted in Gleason, "The Times They Are a Changin'," 48.

21. Gleason, 36, 37, 47, 48. As early as 1962 Baez had become a chart-buster, yet in that year she turned down $100,000 worth of concert dates, telling *Time* that "Folk Music depends on intent. If someone desires to make money, I don't call that folk music." Baez quoted in "The Folk Girls."

22. Dylan quoted in Isserman and Kazin, 96.

23. *Ibid.* 98.

24. Todd Gitlin, *The Sixties: Years of Hope, Days of Rage* (New York: Bantam, 1989), 197–198; Fischer, *America in White, Black, and Gray*, 319.

25. Dylan quoted in Jim Miller, *Flowers in the Dustbin: The Rise of Rock 'n' Roll, 1947–1977* (New York: Simon & Schuster, 1999), 223.

26. Szatmary, *Rockin' in Time*, 70–80. Also see, "Surf's Up!" *Time* (vol. 82, no. 6), August 9, 1963.

27. Quoted in Charles Kaiser, *1968 in America: Music, Politics, Chaos, Counterculture, and the Shaping of a Generation* (New York: Grove, 1988), 198–199. Also see Mark Hamilton Lytle, *America's Uncivil Wars*, 145. Also see Martha Bayles, *Hole in Our Soul: The Loss of Beauty and Meaning in American Popular Culture* (New York: Free, 1994), 171; Fischer, *America in White, Black, and Gray*, 324.

28. John Lennon quoted in Glen Frankel, "Nowhere Man," *Washington Post*, August 26, 2007. Also see "Singers: The New Madness," *Time* (vol. 82, no. 20), November 15, 1963; Szatmary, *Rockin' in Time*, 109–110.

29. Szatmary, 108–109.

30. Gillette quoted in Lytle, *America's Uncivil Wars*, 145. Also see Neil Hamilton, *The 1960s Counterculture in America* (Santa Barbara: ABC-CLIO, 1997), 256; Kaiser, *1968 in America*, 197.

31. Nicholas Schaffner, *The Beatles Forever* (New York: McGraw-Hill, 1978), Chapter One. Also see www.iamthebeatles.com/article1036.html.

32. Lytle, *America's Uncivil Wars*, 146.

33. Schaffner, *The Beatles Forever*, Chapter One. Sir Alec Douglas-Home quoted in Szatmary, *Rockin' in Time*, 111.

34. "Monkee Do," *Time* (vol. 88, no. 20), November 11, 1966; "Evolution," *Time* (vol. 89, no. 7), February 17, 1967; Szatmary, 118–120.

35. Quoted in Schaffner, 10. Also see Richard Corliss, "That Old Feeling: Meet the Beatles," *Time* (vol. 163, no. 6), February 7, 2004.

36. *Newsweek* quoted in Szatmary, *Rockin' in Time*, 114.

37. Allan Matusow, *The Unraveling of America*, 294.

38. Kesey quoted in Schaffner, *The Beatles Forever*, 75–76; For Kesey's take on the concert, see Thomas Wolfe, *The Electric Kool-Aid Acid Test* (New York: Farrar, Straus & Giroux, 1968; Bantam Paperback edition, 1999), Chapter 15; Patricia Oberhaus, "Artist Tells of Virgin Rites at Beatle Bacchanal," *Berkeley Barb* (vol. 1, no. 5), September 5; *The Beatles Anthology* (San Francisco: Chronicle, 2000), 223, 229, 321; Steve Turner, *A Hard Day's Write* (New York: HarperCollins, 1994), 99.

39. Dickstein, *Gates of Eden*, 210.

40. Quoted in Anthony Scaduto, *Dylan: An Intimate Biography* (New York: Tolmitch, 1973), 204.

41. Dylan quoted in Christopher Gair, *The American Counterculture*, 164.

42. Shelton quoted in Gair, 165.

43. Dylan "Friend" quoted in Lytle, *America's Uncivil Wars*, 207.

44. Gleason quoted in Miller, *The Hippies and American Values*, 79. The best assessment of Dylan's songs and lyrics is Michael Gray, *Song and Dance Man: The Art of Bob Dylan* (New York: E.P. Dutton 1972; paperback edition, London: Continuum, 2000).

45. *Don't Look Back*, DVD, directed by D.A. Pennebaker (New York: Pennebaker Films, 1967).

46. Joplin quoted Maurice Isserman and Michael Kazin, *America Divided*, 161. Also see in the same paragraph the account of the Hoffman incident at Woodstock.

47. McDonald quoted in Miller, *The Hippies and American Values*, 77.

48. Jarvis quoted in Miller, *The Hippies and American Values*, 74.

49. Gleason quoted in Miller, *The Hippies and American Values*, 78.

50. Quoted in Miller, *The Hippies and American Values*, 78.

51. Quoted in Gitlin, *The Sixties*, 195.

52. *Ibid.*, 196. Also see Scott Buchanan, ed., *Rock 'n' Roll: The Famous Lyrics* (New York: Harper Perennial, 1994), 189.

53. www.countryjoe.com/cheer.htm. Also see Buchanan, 70–71.

54. Lytle, *America's Uncivil Wars*, 208. Also see Peter Brown and Steven Gaines, *The Love You Make: An Insider's Story of the Beatles* (New York: New American Library, 2002), Chapter 11. Also see "Pop Music: The Messengers," *Time* (vol. 90, no. 12), September 22, 1967; Greil Marcus, "The Beatles" in *The Rolling Stone History of Rock and Roll*, Jim Miller, ed. (New York: Random House, 1976), 176; Lennon and Harrison quoted in Mark Hertsgaard, *A Day in the Life: The Music and Artistry of the Beatles* (New York: Delacorte, 1995), 198–199; Lennon quoted in Barry Miles, ed., *Paul McCartney: Many Years from Now* (New York: H.H. Holt, 1997), 293.

55. Chris Jones, "Review of the Beatles' Sgt. Pepper's Lonely Hearts Club Band," Review of Album, BBC News, 2007. http://www.bbc.co.uk/music/reviews/5dcz/.

56. Quoted in *Sergeant Pepper's Lonely Hearts Club Band* attachment to the compact disc (EMI Records, 1987), 4. Also see David Farber, *The Age of Great Dreams: America in the 1960s* (New York: Hill & Wang, 1994), 175; Lytle, *America's Uncivil Wars*, 218–219; Brown and Gaines, *The Love You Make*, Chapters 13 and 14; "Pop Music: The Messengers"; Jones. Also see Hertsgaard, *A Day in the Life*, 218 and Paul McCartney in *The Beatles Anthology* (San Francisco: Chronicle, 2000), 247.

57. Robert Christgau, "Secular Music," *Esquire*, December 1967, 283.

58. Richard Goldstein, "We Still Need the Beatles, but...," *The New York Times*, June 18, 1967, p. 104. Langdon Winner quoted in Greil Marcus, "The Beatles," *Rolling Stone Illustrated History of Rock and Roll*, 176.

59. Richard Goldstein, "I Blew My Cool Through The New York Times," *The Village Voice* (vol. 12, no. 40), July 20, 1967, pp. 4–8.

60. Leary quoted in Schaffner, *The Beatles Forever*, 71. Also see Brown and Gaines, Chapters 14–18.

61. Miller, *The Hippies and American Values*, 76. Also

see "Rock 'n' Roll: Open Up, Tune In, Turn On, *Time* (vol. 89, no. 25), June 23, 1967.

62. Holly George-Warren, ed., *The Rolling Stone Book of the Beats: The Beat Generation and American Culture* (New York: Hyperion, 1999), 363.

63. Joplin quoted in "Passionate and Sloppy," *Time* (vol. 92, no. 6), August 9, 1968.

64. Charles Perry, "The Sound of San Francisco," in Anthony DeCurtis and James Henke, eds., *The Rolling Stone Illustrated History of Rock and Roll* (New York: Random House, 1992), 362–369.

65. Richard Goldstein, "San Francisco Bray," in Alexander Bloom and Wini Breines, eds., *Takin' It to the Streets: A Sixties Reader* (New York: Oxford University Press, 1995), 294, 296.

66. Gene Anthony, *The Summer of Love: Haight-Ashbury at Its Height* (San Francisco: Last Gasp, 1980), 25–26. Also see Micah Issitt, *Hippies: A Guide to an American Counterculture* (Santa Barbara, CA: ABC-CLIO, 2009), 5–6.

67. Gleason quoted in Goldstein, "The San Francisco Bray," 295.

68. Anthony, *The Summer of Love,* 33–35; Also see Lytle, *America's Uncivil Wars,* 204, 214; Micah Issitt, *Hippies: A Guide to an American Subculture,* 84–87. Also see Sheila Weller, "Suddenly Last Summer," *Vanity Fair,* July 2012, no. 623, 72, 74.

69. Charles Perry, *The Haight-Ashbury: A History* (New York: Random House, 1984), 27.

70. Wolfe quoted in Anthony, *The Summer of Love,* 81.

71. Ralph Gleason, "Lesson for S.F. in the Mime Benefit." *San Francisco Chronicle,* December 13, 1965, 47.

72. Anthony, *The Summer of Love,* 76–77; Lytle, *America's Uncivil Wars,* 205.

73. Lytle, 202–203; Matusow, *The Unraveling of America,* 292; Wolfe, *Electric Kool-Aid,* Chapter 18; Mick Sinclair and John-Henri Holmberg, *San Francisco: A Cultural and Literary History* (Berkeley: Signal, 1995), 199–202. Also see Hamilton, *Counterculture in America,* 172 and Miller, *Flowers in the Dustbin,* 235, 237.

74. Anthony, *The Summer of Love,* 77.

75. Wolfe quoted in Anthony, 81. Also see Wolfe, *The Electric Kool-Aid Acid Test,* 234.

76. Ron Thelin quoted in Leonard Wolf, *Voices from the Love Generation* (Boston: Little, Brown, 1968), 228.

77. Goldstein, "San Francisco Bray," 296; Anthony, *Summer of Love,* 81; Weller, "Suddenly Last Summer," 74.

78. Wolfe quoted in Anthony, *The Summer of Love,* 81. Also see "Rock 'n' Roll: Open Up, Tune In, Turn On," *Time* (vol. 89, no. 25), June 23, 1967.

79. Anthony, 77.

80. Matusow, *The Unraveling of America,* 292.

81. Phillip H. Ennis, *The Seventh Stream: The Emergence of Rock 'n' Roll in American Popular Music* (Middletown, CT: Wesleyan University Press, 1992), 334–335; Hamilton, *Counterculture in America,* 126.

82. Garcia quoted in Lytle, *America's Uncivil Wars,* 205.

83. *San Francisco Chronicle,* January 18, 1966.

84. Quoted in Anthony, *The Summer of Love,* 58.

85. *Ibid.,* 86.

86. Gene Sculati and David Seay, *San Francisco Nights: The Psychedelic Music Trip, 1965–1968* (New York: St. Martin's, 1985), 63.

87. Quoted in Miller, *The Hippies and American Values,* 82.

88. Graham and Balin quoted in Szatmary, *Rockin in Time,* 163.

89. Jim Miller, *The Rolling Stone Illustrated History of Rock and Roll,* 2d ed. (New York: Rolling Stone, 1980), 196.

90. Albright quoted in George-Warren, ed., *Rolling Stone Book of the Beats,* 355, 356. Wilson and Conklin quoted in Szatmary, *Rockin' in Time,* 163.

91. George-Warren, 355.

92. Gair, *The American Counterculture,* 187–189.

93. *Ibid.,* 189. Also see Weller, "Suddenly Last Summer," 74.

94. A good, general biography/history of the period can be found in Michael Lobel, *James Rosenquist: Pop Art, Politics, and History in the 1960s* (Berkeley: University of California Press, 2010). Also see Jan Greenberg and Sandra Jordan, *Andy Warhol: Prince of Pop* (New York: Random House, 2004).

95. Goldstein, "San Francisco Bray," 294, 296. For the Garcia quote see Randy Groenke and Mike Cramer, "March 1967: Garcia Interview." http://deadsources. blogspot.com/2013/05/march-1967-garcia-interview. html.

96. Miller, *The Hippies and American Values,* 81. Kantner quoted in Szatmary, *Rockin' in Time,* 161.

97. Ralph J. Gleason, "Perspectives: A Power to Change the World," *Rolling Stone* (June 22, 1968), 10.

Chapter 5

1. "The Law and LSD," *Time* (vol. 87, no. 23), June 10, 1966.

2. "Affirming Humanness," *San Francisco Oracle,* vol. 1, no. 1 (September 1966), 2; "Lovin' Haight," *Berkeley Barb,* October 14, 1966, 3; Gene Anthony, *The Summer of Love: The Haight-Ashbury at Its Highest* (San Francisco: Last Gasp, 1980), 91.

3. Allen Ginsberg, "Demonstration or Spectacle as Example, as Communication, or How to Make a March/ Spectacle," originally published in the *Berkeley Barb,* November 19, 1965, and reprinted in the *San Francisco Oracle,* vol. 1, no. 1, September 1966, 2.

4. Anthony, *Summer of Love,* 92.

5. *Ibid.,* 93. Also see "Citizens for the Love Pageant Rally to Assemblyman Willie Brown," September 27, 1966. Hippie Papers (SFHC-SFPL).

6. Anthony. Also see "A Prophesy of a Declaration of Independence," *San Francisco Oracle,* vol. 1, no. 1 (September 1966), 14.

7. Anthony, *Summer of Love,* 97.

8. *Ibid.,* 98; "Lovin Haight," *Berkeley Barb,* October 14, 1966, 3.

9. Jay Stevens, *Storming Heaven: LSD and the American Dream* (New York: Grove Atlantic, 1987), 306–307.

Chapter 6

1. David Talbot, *Season of the Witch: Entertainment, Terror, and Deliverance in the City of Love* (New York: Free, 2012), 21.

2. *Ibid.*, 25. Also see Charles Perry, *The Haight-Ashbury: A History* (New York: Random House, 1984).

3. Talbot, 25, 30.

4. Allen Cohen, "A Gathering of the Tribes." Original broadside/press release undated, January 1967. Hippie Papers (SFHC-SFPL). Also see "Statement by the Inspirers of the Gathering of the Tribes," *Berkeley Barb,* January 13, 1967, p. 1.

5. Ron Thelin and Allen Cohen to Art Kunkin, January 1, 1967. Hippie Papers (SFHC-SFPL).

6. "Politics and Ecstasy," *San Francisco Oracle,* vol. 1, January 1967, pp. 1–2, Hippie Papers (SFHC-SFPL).

7. Perry, *The Haight-Ashbury,* 80. Also see Jane Kramer, *Allen Ginsberg in America* (New York: Random House, 1969), 25–26.

8. Ralph Gleason, "The Tribes Gather for a Yea-Saying," *San Francisco Chronicle,* January 16, 1967, 41. Also see Eugene Alonzo Smith III, "Within the Counterculture: The Creation, Transmission and Commercialization of Cultural Alternatives During the 1960s." (Ph.D. Diss., Carnegie-Mellon University, 2000), 130.

9. *San Francisco Chronicle,* January 20, 1967, 11; *Berkeley Barb,* January 13, 1967, 3.

10. Gleason, "The Tribes Gather for a Yea-Saying," 41.

11. *San Francisco Oracle,* vol. 1, no. 6, February 1967, p.1

12. Don Lattin, *The Harvard Psychedelic Club: How Timothy Leary, Ram Dass, Huston Smith, and Andrew Weil Killed the Fifties and Ushered in a New Age for America* (New York: HarperCollins, 2010), 119. Also see Mark Hamilton Lytle, *America's Uncivil Wars: The Sixties Era from Elvis to the Fall of Richard Nixon* (New York: Oxford University Press, 2006), 214–215; Burton H. Wolfe, *The Hippies* (New York: New American Library, 1968), 12–14. For contemporary accounts of Leary's LSD and his shows at the Village Theater, see *New York Times,* September 20, 1966, 33; September 21, 94; December 4, Section 2, pp. 5 and 9; "Talk of the Town," *The New Yorker* (Volume 42, October 1, 1966), 42–43.

13. Hunter S. Thompson, *Fear and Loathing in Las Vegas: A Savage Journey into the Heart of the American Dream* (New York: Random House, 1998, second Vintage edition), 179.

14. "A Gathering of the Tribes," original broadside. Hippie Papers (SFHC-SFPL).

15. Quoted in Perry, *The Haight-Ashbury,* 77.

16. Theodore Roszak, *The Making of a Counterculture: Reflections on the Technocratic Society and Its Youthful Opposition* (Berkeley: University of California Press, 1995 [1969]), 56.

17. Ed Denson, "What Happened at the Hippening," *Berkeley Barb,* January 20, 1967, p. 1,4,6. Also see in same edition, "Our Readers Rap: On Bein' at the Be-In," p. 7.

18. Denson quoted in Hunter S. Thompson, "The 'Hashbury' Is the Capital of the Hippies," *New York Times Magazine,* May 14, 1967, p. 121.

19. Decanio quoted in Thompson, "The 'Hashbury' Is the Capital of the Hippies," 124.

20. Talbot, *Season of the Witch,* 22.

21. "Statement by the Inspirers of the Gathering of the Tribes," *Berkeley Barb,* January 13, 1967, p. 1.

22. Talbot, *Season of the Witch,* 23. Also see Perry, *The Haight-Ashbury,* 80.

23. Helen Swick Perry, "The Human Be-In" in Alexander Bloom and Wini Breines, editors, *"Takin' It to the Streets": A Sixties Reader* (New York: Oxford University Press, 1995), 314.

24. Gleason, "The Tribes Gather for a Yea-Saying."

25. Perry, *The Haight-Ashbury,* 79. Also see Lytle, *America's Uncivil Wars,* 214; Emmett Grogan, *Ringolevio: A Life Played for Keeps* (New York: New York Review of Books, 1972), 267; Allen Matusow, *The Unraveling of America: A History of Liberalism in the 1960s* (New York: Harper & Row, 1984), 276.

26. Talbot, *Season of the Witch,* 23; Perry, *The Haight-Ashbury,* 81; Gleason, "The Tribes Gather for a Yea-Saying"; *San Francisco Chronicle,* January 20, 1967, 11; Helen Swick Perry, "The Human Be-In," 315; Matusow.

27. Helen Swick Perry.

28. Talbot, *Season of the Witch,* 23.

29. Helen Swick Perry, "The Human-Be-In," 316.

30. Lattin, *The Harvard Psychedelic Club,* 121–123.

31. *The Summer of Love,* DVD, directed by Gail Dogin and Vincent Franco. (New York: PBS: American Experience, 2007).

32. "Dropouts with a Mission," *Newsweek,* February 6, 1967, p. 92.

33. Timothy Miller, *The Hippies and American Values* (Knoxville: University of Tennessee Press, 1991), 9; Roszak, *The Making of a Counterculture,* xiii–xiv, 24; Charles A. Reich, *The Greening of America* (New York: Bantam, 1970), 2; Mark Kurlansky, *1968: The Year That Rocked the World* (New York: Ballantine/Random House, 2004), xviii–xix, 99–102; Jim F. Heath, *Decade of Disillusionment: The Kennedy-Johnson Years* (Bloomington: Indiana University Press, 1975), 242–243.

34. Quoted in Miller.

35. *Ibid.*, 10. Also see Maurice Isserman and Michael Kazin, *America Divided: The Civil War of the 1960s* (New York: Oxford University Press, 2000), 150. Moreover, age did not necessarily define a hippie. There were plenty of older hippies, many considered to be gurus by younger hipsters, such as former Beats-cum-hippies Allen Ginsberg, Michael McClure, Gary Snyder, Alan Watts, Timothy Leary and host of other over 30 bohemians, seekers, misfits, and vagabonds who believed to have "found themselves" in the new counterculture.

36. Ed Ward, Geoffrey Stokes, and Ken Tucker, *Rock of Ages: The Rolling Stone History of Rock & Roll* (New York: Simon & Schuster, 1986), 324.

37. Isserman and Kazin, 150–151.

38. James T. Patterson, *Grand Expectations: The United States, 1945–1974* (New York: Oxford University Press, 1996), 362; Klaus Fischer, *America in White, Black, and Gray: A History of the Stormy 1960s* (New York: Continuum, 2006), 61–63, 65; Todd Gitlin, *The Sixties: Years of Hope, Days of Rage* (New York: Bantam, 1967), 17–20; John Patrick Diggins, *The Proud Decades: American in War and Peace, 1941–1960* (New York: W.W. Norton, 1989), 201–202.

39. Miller, *The Hippies and American Values,* 17–18.

40. *Ibid.*, 17. Also see "Doctrines of the Dropouts," *Time* (vol. 91, no. 1), January 5, 1968.

41. Pike quoted in Judson Gooding, "Revolution or Revival?" in Joe David Brown, ed., *The Hippies: Who They Are, Where They Are, Why They Act That Way, and How They May Affect Our Society* (New York: Time, 1967), 205.

42. "Changes," or "The Houseboat Summit," *San*

Francisco Oracle, no. 7, February 1967, p. 10. Also see Peter Braunstein, "Forever Young: Insurgent Youth and the Sixties Culture of Rejuvenation," in Peter Braunstein and Michael William Doyle, eds., *Imagine Nation: The American Counterculture of the 1960s and 1970s* (New York: Routledge, 2002); 258–260. "Changes," in Braunstein and Doyle, eds., pp. 11–12. Also see Mandelkorn, "The Flower Children," in Joe David Brown, ed., *The Hippies,* 9; Brand quoted in John Luce, "Whither the Hippies?" *San Francisco Magazine,* May 1967, 39.

43. Robert Pattison, *The Triumph of Vulgarity: Rock Music in the Mirror of Romanticism* (New York: Oxford University Press, 1987), 123; Annie Gottlieb, *Do You Believe in Magic? The Second Coming of the 60s Generation* (New York: Times, 1987), 209–219; *Time,* "Doctrines of the Dropouts."

44. "The Hippies: Philosophy of a Subculture," cover story, *Time* (vol. 90, no. 1), July 7, 1967, 18–22. Although not quite as benign or sympathetic, both *Look* magazine and *Harper's* had similar assessments in their respective issues. For *Look* see the August 22, 1967, issue, "Inside the Hippie Revolution," pp. 58–61, and for *Harper's* "Turned On and Super Sincere in California," see the January 1967 edition, pp. 42–47. Also see, "The Hippies Are Coming," *Newsweek,* June 12, 1967, 28–29; "Dropouts with a Mission," *Newsweek,* February 6, 1967, 92.

45. "Turned on Way of Life," *Newsweek,* November 28, 1966, 72, 74; "The Hippies: Philosophy of a Subculture," *Time,* 18–22; Mandelkorn, "The Flower Children," 1, 10, 11; Judson Gooding, "Revolution or Revival," David Brown, ed., *The Hippies,* 204; William F. Marmon, Jr. "Man, I Dig Those Founding Fathers," in David Brown, ed., *The Hippies,* 125; Loudon Wainwright, "The Strange New Love Land of the Hippies," *Life,* March 31, 1967, 15–16; "Dropouts with a Mission," 92–93.

46. Mandelkorn, 1; "Dropouts with a Mission," 92–93; Gooding, 210; "The Hippies: Philosophy of a Subculture," 21; Martin Arnold, "Organized Hippies Emerge on Coast," *New York Times,* May 5, 1967, 8.

47. Ron Thelin quoted in an untitled interview with the *Haight-Ashbury Maverick,* vol. 1, no. 5 (1967), 6–7, 10–11, 13.

48. Causing hippie outrage and condemnation was Hinckle's narration of a supposed meeting between Ken Kesey's Pranksters and the Diggers, which he wrote in such a way that it appeared as fact. Hinckle also listed the names of the dozens of "hippie contributors" to his essay, implying that it was from such primary sources that he based his article's premise. Warren Hinckle, "A Social History of the Hippies," *Ramparts,* March 1967, 5–26; 9. For the controversy Hinckle's "research" engendered among the counterculture, as well as his chastisement, see "Ramparts' 'Hippie' Article Raises Row," *Berkeley Barb,* June 9, 1967, 7; "Inside Story on the 'Hippie' Tale," *Berkeley Barb,* June 6, 1967, 4; Charles Perry, *The Haight-Ashbury,* 90.

49. Earl Shorris, "Love Is Dead," *New York Times Magazine,* October 29, 1967, 114.

50. "Greying Hair," *Time* (vol. 91, no. 23), June 7, 1968; "New Plays: Hair," *Time* (vol. 91, no. 19), May 10, 1968; Richard Corliss, "That Old Feeling: 'Hair' Today," *Time* (vol. 157, no. 18), May 4, 2001.

51. "Changes" ("The Houseboat Summit"), *San Francisco Oracle,* no. 7, February 1967, 6–8. Also see Charles Perry, *The Haight-Ashbury,* 100–102; Braun-

stein, "Forever Young," Braunstein, Doyle eds., *Imagine Nation,* 258–260.

52. "Changes," 11.

53. *Ibid.,* 11, 16–17.

54. Jerry Rubin to Allen Cohen, July 6, 1967. Hippie Papers (SFHC-SFPL).

55. "Changes," *San Francisco Oracle,* 6. Ginsberg quoted in John Luce, "Whither the Hippies?" *San Francisco Magazine,* May 1967, 40.

56. Kenneth Keniston, *Young Radicals: Notes on Committed Youth* (New York: Harcourt, Brace, and World, 1968). Keniston quoted in William Braden, *The Age of Aquarius* (Cleveland: Quadrangle, 1970), 59.

57. Philip Deloria, "Counterculture Indians and the New Age," in Braunstein and Doyle, eds., *Imagine Nation,* 159–184; (166–169).

58. *Ibid.,* 166. For the Vietnam War correlation see Todd Gitlin, *The Sixties,* 261–282; and "You Don't Need a Weatherman to Know Which Way the Wind Blows," (1969) in William H. Chafe, Harvard Sitkoff, and Beth Bailey, eds., *A History of Our Time: Readings in Post War America,* 6th ed. (New York: Oxford University Press, 2003), 321–324.

59. "The American Indian Issue," *The San Francisco Oracle,* vol. 8 (Spring 1967); Deloria, "Counterculture Indians and the New Age," *Imagine Nation,* 164–166.

60. Deloria.

61. Charles McCabe, "Hippies and Indians," *San Francisco Chronicle,* May 27, 1967, 10.

62. Guy Strait, "The American Indian Issue," p. 5.

63. Ron Thelin, "The American Indian Issue," p. 9.

64. Deloria, "Counterculture Indians and the New Age," *Imagine Nation,* 163–164.

65. *Berkeley Barb,* May 12, 1967, 2; Emmett Grogan, *Ringolevio,* 381; Charles Perry, *The Haight-Ashbury,* 116; McCabe, "Hippies and Indians," 10.

66. Jeff Berner, "Astronauts of Inner Space: Hippies Are American Indians," *San Francisco Examiner,* June 18, 1967, Datebook, 30; Rupert Costo, "Hippies Are NOT American Indians," *San Francisco Examiner,* June 25, 1967, Datebook, 26.

67. Grogan, *Ringolevio,* 384.

68. Author's personal assessment of the two films after viewing them on YouTube. See *Hallucination Generation,* directed and written by Edward Mann, produced by Nigel Fox, and starring George Montgomery and Danny Stone; *The Trip: A Lovely Sort of Death,* produced and directed by Roger Corman, written by Jack Nicholson and starring Peter Fonda, Susan Strasberg, Dennis Hopper, and Bruce Dern, all young, up and coming actors at the time, all of whom will fortunately move on to bigger and better roles in "A" movies, especially Nicholson, who has since become a Hollywood icon.

69. J. Campbell Bruce, "Hippies at My Window," *San Francisco Chronicle,* April 6, 1967, 3; Arnold Toynbee's accounts of his many sojourns through the Haight while a visiting professor at Stanford, which he published in a series for the *London Observer* and were reprinted in the *San Francisco Chronicle,* May 16–18, 1967; "The Gossiping Guru: Will Success Spoil the Haight?" *San Francisco Oracle,* vol. 1 (March 1967), pp. 24, 39. Interestingly the *Oracle* predicted such tourist exploitation of the Haight would come sooner than later and that Grey Line would be the first to do so by creating a tour of "the tribes of urban gypsies in their natural state." Also see Horace

Sutton, "A Hippie Place to Blow the Mind," *San Francisco Chronicle,* July 2, 1967, 3. Also see Alonzo Smith, "Within the Counterculture," 269; George William Thiemann, "Haight-Ashbury: Birth of the Counterculture of the 1960s." (Ph.D. diss., Miami University, Oxford, Ohio, 1998), 133.

70. Haight resident "Ted," quoted in Thiemann, 133.

71. "Buslines Halt Haight Tours," *Berkeley Barb,* May 26, 1967; Charles Perry, *The Haight-Ashbury,* 120.

72. Perry, 83.

73. Dogin and Franco, *The Summer of Love,* DVD.

74. Adler and Scully quoted in Sheila Weller, "Suddenly That Summer," *Vanity Fair,* July 2012, no. 623, 77.

75. Ed Denson, "And a Thousand Shops Shall Bloom," *Berkeley Barb,* March 17, 1967, 6, 8; George Gilbert, "Diggers Preparing for the Invasion," *San Francisco Chronicle,* May 20, 1967, 1, 11; Talbot, *Season of the Witch,* 35; "The Gossiping Guru: Will Success Spoil the Haight?" 39.

Chapter 7

1. Lois Dickert Armstrong, "Christ Was a Very Groovy Cat," in Joe David Brown, ed., *The Hippies: Who They Are, Where They Are, Whey They Act That Way, and How They May Affect Our Society* (New York: Time, 1967), 47–55.

2. William F. Marmon, Jr., and Arlie Schardt, "Man I Dig Those Founding Fathers," 99–132. Also see "Love-In Boss Town, *Time* (vol. 92, no. 2), July 12, 1968; "The Great Hippie Hunt," *Time* (vol. 94, no. 15), October 10, 1969.

3. Jeff Hale, "The White Panthers' 'Total Assault on the Culture,'" in Peter Braunstein and Michael William Doyle, eds., *Imagine Nation: The American Counterculture of the 1960s & 1970s* (New York: Routledge, 2002), 126–127. Also see David A. Carson, *Grit, Noise & Revolution* (Ann Arbor: University of Michigan Press, 2005), 107–108.

4. Hale, 129.

5. Sinclair quoted in Christina Hill, "The Artists Workshop: John Sinclair and Others Sound Off," *The Detroiter,* September 9, 1986. http://www.thedetroiter.com/nov04/artistsworkshop.html (now inactive); Hale, 130; Carson, 113–114.

6. Hale.

7. *Ibid.,* 131.

8. For the formation of the underground press, its philosophy, purpose, and subsequent history see Abe Peck, *Uncovering the Sixties: The Life and Times of the Underground Press* (New York: Citadel Press: Carol, 1991); Robert J. Glessing, *The Underground Press in America* (Bloomington: Indiana University Press, 1970). Also see Thorne Dreyer and Victoria Smith, "The Movement and the New Media," at http://www.nuevoanden.com/rag/newmedia.html, 1–17.

9. Dreyer and Smith, 2, 7. Also see "Underground Alliance," *Time* (vol. 80, no. 5), July 29, 1966.

10. *Ibid.,* 1, 2, 6.

11. *Ibid.,* 1, 2.

12. John Leo, "Politics Now the Focus of the Underground Press," *New York Times,* September 1, 1968, 6; John Burks, "The Underground Press: A Special Report,"

Rolling Stone 43, October 4, 1969, 12. Also see James Lewes, *Protest and Survive: Underground GI Newspapers During the Vietnam War* (Westport, CT: Praeger, 2003), 38, 46, 67.

13. Hale, "The White Panthers," 132.

14. *Ibid.,* 133.

15. On the MC5's formation see Carson, *Grit, Noise & Revolution,* 101–106, 111. Bixby and McLeese quoted in Don McLeese, *The MC5's Kick Out the Jams (33⅓)* (New York: Continuum, 2005), 57; Ankeny quoted in James E. Perone, *Music of the Counterculture* (Westport, CT: Greenwood, 2004), 100. Also see Edwin Pouncey, "MC5 Meets Sun Ra: Motown City Burning," February 2007, in http://thewire.co.uk. Also see Wayne Kramer interview, published in online magazine *Addicted to Noise,* issue 1.02, parts I–IV, February 1995. http://www.addict.com/issues/1.02/Features/MC5/Wayne-Kramer (now inactive).

16. "The Story of the Mighty MC5-History -Part I," in http://www.punk77.co.uk/groups/mc5_history_1.htm,1; Hale, "The White Panthers' 'Total Assault on the Culture," 133.

17. McLeese, *The MC 5's Kick Out the Jams,* 65. Also see Mike Marino, "E=MC5: Kick Out the Jams, Motherfuckers!" http://www.rockandreprise.net/marino.html, 3; "The Story of the Mighty MC5—History Part II," 1. On the Grande Ballroom as Detroit's attempt to emulate Bill Graham's dancehall concept, see Carson, *Grit, Noise & Revolution,* 98–99; the MC5 becoming the "house band," 111–112..

18. Hale, "The White Panthers' 'Total Assault on the Culture," 133–134; Christina Hill, "The Artists Workshop: John Sinclair and Others Sound Off," *The Detroiter,* September 9, 1986. http://www.thedetroiter.com/nov4/artistsworkshop.html (now inactive). Robert Christgau, "The Continuing Saga of the MC-5" Original article appeared in the *Village Voice,* June 5, 1968. Reprinted at http://www.robertchristgau.com; Also see "The MC-5," in *The East Village Other* (vol. 4, no. 24), May 14, 1969, pp. 5, 17.

19. Kelley quoted in Hale, "The White Panthers," 137–138.

20. "Pun" Plamondon quoted in Frank Beaumier, "Man, I Dig Those Founding Fathers," in Joe David Brown, ed., *The Hippies,* 134; Hale, 138.

21. Hale.

22. Julie Morris and Jenny Nolan, "Sex, Drugs, Rock 'n' Roll and Plum Street," *The Detroit News,* September 12, 1997. Also see Marino, "E=MC5: Kick Out the Jams Motherfuckers!" 4–5.

23. Morris and Nolan.

24. "Love-In in Boss Town, *Time* (vol. 92, no. 2), July 12, 1968; "The Great Hippie Hunt," *Time* (vol. 94, no. 15), October 10, 1969.

25. Morris and Nolan, "Sex, Drugs, Rock 'n' Roll and Plum Street."

26. Marino, "E-MC5: Kick Out the Jams Motherfuckers!" 4–5.

27. Hale, "The White Panthers," 137; Morris and Nolan, "Sex, Drugs, Rock 'n' Roll and Plum Street," 3; Marino, "E=MC5: Kick Out the Jams Motherfuckers!" 5; Carson, *Grit, Noise & Revolution,* 114–115.

28. Wayne Kramer, "Riots I Have Known and Loved," originally published in *Left of the Dial,* magazine 4, http://makemyday.free.fr/wk1.htm, 1; Hale, 134; Marino;

Morris and Nolan, "Sex, Drugs, Rock 'n' Roll and Plum Street," 3; Carson, 115–116.

29. Sheila Salasnek, "Thousands of People Had a Love-In on Belle Isle," *The Fifth Estate* (vol. 11, no. 4), May 15–31, 1967.

30. Hale, "The White Panthers," 134; Kramer, "Riots I Have Known and Loved," 2; Morris and Nolan, "Sex, Drugs, Rock 'n' Roll and Plum Street," 3–4; Carson, *Grit, Noise & Revolution,* 115–116.

31. Kramer; Hale; Kramer; Morris and Nolan; Carson.

32. Kramer.

33. *Ibid.*

34. Hale, "The White Panthers," 134; Beaumier, "Man, I Dig Those Founding Fathers," 134.

35. Hale.

36. Hale, 142–143; Hill, "The Artists' Workshop," 2; Sinclair's manifesto was published in the *Fifth Estate* and then republished and quoted in the *Berkeley Barb,* November 29–December 5, 1968.

37. Hale, 145–146; Hill, 2; John Sinclair, "Rock and Roll Is a Weapon of Cultural Revolution," *The Story of the Mighty MC5—John Sinclair,* http://www.punk77.co.uk/groups/mc5_history_1.htm .

38. Hale, 151; *The Story of the Mighty MC5—John Sinclair,* 2. Also see John Sinclair, "Rock and Roll Is a Weapon of Cultural Revolution," in Alexander Bloom and Wini Breines, eds., *"Takin' It to the Streets: A Sixties Reader* (New York: Oxford University Press, 1995), 301–303. John Sinclair and D.A. Latimer, untitled interview, *East Village Other* (vol. 4, no. 25), June 4, 1969, 3.

39. Hale, 146–147, 149; Morris and Nolan, "Sex, Drugs, Rock 'n' Roll and Plum Street," 4.

40. Hale, 149–150.

41. Hale, 148,150; Morris and Nolan, "Sex, Drugs, Rock 'n' Roll and Plum Street," 5; Marino, "E=MC5: Kick out the Jams Motherfuckers!" 9.

42. Doug Rossinow, "The Revolution Is About Our Lives," in Braunstein and Doyle, eds., *Imagine Nation,* 106.

43. The University of Texas SDS Papers are a compilation of typed, double-spaced official reports, submitted by an undercover FBI agent to various university administrators, dating from 1966 to 1969. These reports can be found at the Dolph Brisco Center for American History at the University of Texas at Austin. Hereafter cited as (DBCAH-UT). The catalog title is Students for a Democratic Society Reports, 2J, Boxes 115–120.

44. Mariann Wizard quoted in Rossinow, "The Revolution Is About Our Lives," 107. Also see the Mariann Vizard (Wizard) Papers (DBCAH-UT), Boxes 3F 206 and 3 G7, years 1963–1970. Dreyer quoted in Abe Peck, *Uncovering the Sixties,* 59; also see Dreyer to "Editors," October 3, 1966, announcing the *Austin Rag's* first publication. Letter can be found in *The Rag* files at the (DBCAH-UT), which contain all the original *Rag* issues, dated October 1966 to the final edition, December 1977. Todd Gitlin, *The Sixties: Years of Hope, Days of Rage* (New York: Bantam, 1987), 213.

45. Rossinow; *The Rag,* January 2, 1967, Volume I. pp. 10–11, 18; Dreyer quoted in Peck; Jeff Shero, "Dallas Police Jail Banana Users," *The Rag,* March 27, 1967, vol. 1, pp. 7–8, 16.

46. Rossinow, 107–108; Kirkpatrick Sale, *SDS* (New York: Vintage, 1973), 204–205. For the emerging dis-

sension affecting the New Left and SDS by 1965 over a variety of issues as well as ideology, and the push by the more radical new members from the West to broaden SDS's focus and agenda, see Irwin Unger, *The Movement: The History of the American New Left, 1959–1972* (New York: Dodd, Mead, 1974), 88–91, 97–100. Also see Sale, 291–297.

47. Shero quoted in Sale, *SDS,* 205.

48. Rossinow, "The Revolution Is About Our Lives," 108–109; Also see Mariann Wizard, paper to be delivered at the National Conference for New Politics, in the Mariann Vizard Papers for the year 1967, 3F: 206. (DBCAH-UT).

49. Rossinow, 110, 111–112.

50. Dreyer and Smith, "The Movement and the New Media," 15.

51. Peck, *Uncovering the Sixties,* 58, 59, 75–76, 148–149, 287.

52. John McMillian, *Smoking Typewriters: The Sixties Underground Press and the Rise of Alternative Media in America* (New York: Oxford University Press, 2011). McMillian's renderings on *The Rag* can be found on pages 9, 53, 58–69, 62, 72–73, 91, 97–99, 129, 151, 162, 164, 171, 210, 222, 241.

53. Dreyer and Smith, "The Movement and the New Media," 14; Hermes Nye, "Texas Tea and Rainy Day Woman," in Francis Edward Abernethy, ed., *What's Going On?* (*In Modern Texas Folklore*) (Denton: University of North Texas Press, 1998), 118. First edition published in 1976 by Encino Press of Austin, Texas. Also see M. Keith Booker, ed., *Encyclopedia of Comic Books and Graphic Novels* (Santa Barbara, CA: Greenwood, 2010), 670.

54. Dugger quoted in *The Rag,* February 21, 1972, 3; also quoted in Rossinow, "The Revolution Is about Our Lives," 106.

55. Mark Hamilton Lytle, *America's Uncivil Wars: The Sixties Era from Elvis to the Fall of Richard Nixon* (New York: Oxford University Press, 2006), 199, 201; Iverson and Sanders quoted in Timothy Miller, *The Hippies and American Values* (Knoxville: University of Tennessee Press, 1991), 11.

56. Kenneth Keniston, "The Alienated: The Rejection of Conventional Adulthood," in Keniston, *Youth and Dissent: The Rise of a New Opposition* (New York: Harcourt Brace Jovanovich, 1971), 178.

57. "Marxist Scholar Opines on Hips," *Berkeley Barb,* May 12, 13, 16, 1967, 7, 9, 11, 12.

58. Carl Ogelsby, "The Hippies: Suburbanites with Beads, *Activist,* Fall 1967, 12.

59. "Changes" or "The Houseboat Summit," *San Francisco Oracle,* February 1967, no. 7, p. 10.

60. Wheelock, Mungo, and Finn, all quoted in Miller, *The Hippies and American Values,* 12–13.

61. Mark Kurlansky, *1968: The Year That Rocked the World* (New York: Ballantine, 2004), 180–181.

62. Kurlansky; James Kent Wilwerth, "The East Village Others," in Joe David Brown, ed., *The Hippies,* 80–81.

63. "…And the Yippies on St. Marks," in *The Local East Village,* http://localeastvillage.com/; Lytle, *America's Uncivil Wars,* 227–230; Kurlansky, *1968,* 95–97; For Hoffman's self-description see Abbie Hoffman, *Soon to Be a Major Motion Picture* (New York: Perigree, 1980), 127.

64. Katie Kelly, "The East Village Others," in Joe David Brown, ed., *The Hippies*, 88–92. Also see Mark Jacobson, "Long Hot Summer of Love," *New York Magazine*, June 25, 2007.

65. Todd Gitlin, *The Sixties: Years of Hope, Days of Rage* (New York: Bantam, 1987), 239–240; Allen Matusow, *The Unraveling of America: A History of Liberalism in the 1960s* (New York: Harper & Row, 1984), 337; Irwin Unger, *The Movement: A History of the American New Left, 1959–1972* (New York: Dodd, Mead & Company, 1974), 160–161.

66. Gitlin, *Ibid.*, 239; Hoffman quoted in Marty Jezer, *Abbie Hoffman: American Rebel* (New Brunswick, NJ: Rutgers University Press, 1992), 131–132; Ben Morea and Ron Hahne, *Black Mask & Up Against the Wall Motherfucker: The Incomplete Works of Ron Hahne, Ben Morea and the Black Mask Group* (Oakland, CA: PM, 2011), 133–140.

67. Kelly, "The East Village Others," 94.

68. Lewis Yablonsky, *The Hippie Trip: A First-Hand Account of the Beliefs, Drug Use, and Sexual Patterns of Drop-Outs in America* (New York: Pegasus, 1968), Part III, "Analysis," 250–265.

69. Don McNeill, "Central Park Rite Is Medieval Pageant," *Village Voice*, March 30, 1967, vol. 12, no. 24.

70. *Ibid.*

71. *Ibid.*

72. *Ibid.*

73. *Ibid.*

74. Kurlansky, *1968*, 98; Gitlin, *The Sixties*, 230–231; Michael William Doyle, "Staging the Revolution: Guerrilla Theater As A Countercultural Practice, 1965–68," in Braunstein and Doyle, eds., *Imagine Nation*, 85–86; "Talk of the Town," *The New Yorker*, October 14, 1967, 49.

75. Gitlin, *The Sixties*, 233; Doyle, "Staging the Revolution," 86–87; Lytle, *America's Uncivil Wars*, 244; Jezer, *Abbie Hoffman*, 111–112; Hoffman, *Soon to Be a Major Motion Picture*, 101; James Ledbetter, "The Day the NYSE Went Yippie," *CNNMoney*, http://money.cnn.com.

76. Hoffman, 108–110; 129–136; 101–102. "Clenched fist" quote, 99; Doyle, "Staging the Revolution," 88; Gitlin, *The Sixties*, 233.

77. Doyle, 88–89.

78. Matusow, *The Unraveling of America*, 412; Hoffman, *Soon to Be a Major Motion Picture*, 127, 128, 137; Jerry Rubin, *Do It: Scenarios of the Revolution* (New York: Simon and Schuster, 1970), 81; "The Yuppie and the Yippie: Jerry Rubin," in Joan Morrison and Robert K. Morrison, *From Camelot to Kent State: The Sixties Experience in the Words of Those Who Lived It* (New York: Oxford University Press, 1987), 281–283.

79. Hoffman, 137; Abbie Hoffman, *Revolution for the Hell of It* (New York: Dial, 1968), 102; Doyle, "Staging the Revolution," 89, 91.

Chapter 8

1. Charles Perry, *The Haight-Ashbury: A History* (New York: Random House, 1984), 119, 129–130. Also see original Summer of Love Council broadside in the Hippie Papers (SFHC-SFPL). Also see *The Summer of Love*, DVD. Directed by Gail Dogin and Vincent Franco. New York: PBS, American Experience, 2007.

2. Perry.

3. George Gilbert, "Diggers Preparing for the 'Invasion,'" *San Francisco Chronicle*, May 20, 1967, 1, 11. In its December 2, 1967, issue *Newsweek* contended that the total number of visitors to the Haight had been 50,000 while the *Chronicle* consistently claimed the number was much closer to 100,000. "Where Are They Now? The Haight-Ashbury Scene," *Newsweek*, December 2, 1967, 20.

4. Carolyn Garcia quoted in Joel Selvin, "Summer of Love: 40 Years Later: The Stuff That Myths Are Made Of," *San Francisco Chronicle*, May 20, 2007.

5. "Trouble in Hippieland," *Newsweek*, October 30, 1967, 84, 87–90; "The Hippies Are Coming," *Newsweek*, June 12, 1967, 28–29. Also see "The Ebb and Flow of the Hippie Tide," *San Francisco Chronicle*, June 23, 1967, 1, 18.

6. Nicholas von Hoffman, *We Are the People Our Parents Warned Us Against* (Chicago: Ivan R. Dee/Elephant, 1989), 218. Von Hoffman first published his account in 1968 with the title *We Are the People Our Parents Warned Us Against: A Close-Up of the Whole Hippie Scene* (Greenwich, CT: Fawcett, 1968). The original account contains some vital information omitted in the later publication, and thus when necessary citations from both versions will be used for documentation and will be duly noted.

7. "Youth: The Hippies: Philosophy of a Subculture," *Time*, July 7, 1967, 20. For the mainstream media blitz that enveloped the Haight that summer, see von Hoffman, 25–26.

8. Hedgepeth quoted in Alexander Bloom and Wini Breines, eds., *"Takin' It to the Streets": A Sixties Reader* (New York: Oxford University Press, 1995), 330. Also see Allen Matusow, *The Unraveling of America: A History of Liberalism in the 1960s* (New York: Harper & Row, 1984), 301–302; Robert Christgau, "Anatomy of a Love Festival," essay originally published in *Esquire* magazine, June 1969. Reprinted online at http://www.robert chrisgau.com.

9. Frank Kavanaugh to the *San Francisco Examiner*, "Dear Editor," original typed, two-page letter, dated July 7, 1966, can be found in the Hippies Papers (SFHC-SFPL).

10. Frank Kavanaugh, "A Personal Position Paper on the Future of the Haight-Ashbury," presented to the San Francisco Board of Supervisors, May 13, 1967, 2. Hippie Papers (SFHC-SFPL).

11. Kavanaugh, "Dear Editor," 2.

12. The Council for the Summer of Love to Mayor John Shelley, the San Francisco Board of Supervisors and Police Chief Tom Cahill, May 1967. Hippie Papers (SFHC-SFPL).

13. Kavanaugh, "A Personal Position Paper on the Future of the Haight-Ashbury," May 13, 1967, 3–4.

14. Allen Cohen, "Announcement Read to the Haight-Ashbury Round Table Conference and Addressed to the People of San Francisco, and To All Peoples of the World," undated document. Hippie Papers (SFHC-SFPL). Also see "'Love Community's Plea to 'Straights,'" *San Francisco Chronicle*, May 27, 1967, 2.

15. Author interview with several high school friends, all of whom wished to remain "anonymous," who either visited the Haight several times that summer, or who actually lived with relatives who lived very near

the neighborhood and thus frequented the Haight on a regular basis during the Summer of Love; a compilation and interpretation of their respected views about the Summer of Love in general and its impact on the Haight and its residents.

16. Dogin and Franco, *The Summer of Love.*

17. "Peace Corps 'Survival,'" *San Francisco Standard,* July 7, 1967, 2. Hippie Papers (SFHC-SFPL).

18. For the increasingly deteriorating situation in the Haight see A Statement of Concern to "The Executive Board of the Haight-Ashbury Neighborhood Council, Special Meeting, to the Mayor, the Board of Supervisors, Director of Public Health, and Chief of Police," June 25, July 3, 1967. Hippie Papers (SFHC-SFPL). Also see Chester Anderson broadside, "Unite or Die," July 16, 1967, Hippie Papers (SFHC-SFPL); *Berkeley Barb,* July 15–22, 1967. The July and August issues of the *San Francisco Oracle* exhorted hippies, especially the neighborhood's veteran hipsters to "supply free lodging. If you have food, share it. If you have money, give it, of you have room for pilgrims to rest, open your door." Also see "How to Survive in the Streets," a reprinted article from the *Los Angeles Free Press* that appeared in the *Oracle* and the Haight's other papers in June 1967. Also see, "Hepatitis Hits the Haight," *San Francisco Chronicle,* August 18, 1967, 14. For a contemporary account of Smith, his clinic, his work, and on how the community viewed him, see the *Haight-Ashbury Maverick,* vol. 5, August 1967, 2–3; and Chester Anderson, "A Man of Genuine Love Among Us," broadside, July 17, 1967, Hippie Papers (SFHC-SFPL). Also see David Talbot, *Season of the Witch: Enchantment, Terror, and Deliverance in the City of Love* (New York: Free, 2012), 51–59; Tom Brokaw, *Boom! Voices of the Sixties: Personal Reflections on the 60s and Today* (New York: Random House, 2007), 243–249; Charles Perry, *The Haight-Ashbury,* 124.

19. Smith quoted in Brokaw, 244; Talbot, 53.

20. Brokaw, Talbot.

21. Talbot, 54–56; Brokaw, 247.

22. Talbot, 56–57.

23. *Ibid.,* 57.

24. *Ibid.,* 56, 58.

25. Brokaw, *Boom!,* 247. Also see David Perlman, "'Meth Heads' Fantastic Drug Jolt," *San Francisco Chronicle,* July 29, 1967, 1, 4; "The STP Leak: A New Drug Mystery," *San Francisco Chronicle,* August 3, 1967, headline; "A New Mind Drug," *San Francisco Chronicle,* August 12, 1967, headline article. Also see David E. Smith and John Luce, *Love Needs Care: A History of San Francisco's Haight-Ashbury Medical Clinic and its Pioneer Role in Treating Drug Abuse Problems* (Boston: Little, Brown, 1971), 173–174. Smith asserts that STP hit the streets in early June 1967 and most users suffered from panic attacks, heart palpitations, and severe freak-outs. Also see Charles Perry, *The Haight-Ashbury: A History,* 122; von Hoffman, *We Are the People Our Parents Warned Us Against,* 36–41.

26. von Hoffman, *Ibid.,* 36–37.

27. *Ibid.,* 90, 93.

28. *Ibid.* 52.

29. *Ibid.,* 84.

30. The Diggers, Owsley, and others had distributed acid for free at the Be-In, while Country Joe and the Fish celebrated the release of their first album on Vanguard Records (May 1967), *Electric Music for Mind and Body,*

by giving away for free five kilos worth of joints to attendees at their Fillmore appearance. Charles Perry, *The Haight-Ashbury: A History,* 119. Perry also contends that the majority of pre–Summer of Love hippies who dealt in drugs such as grass often only made enough money to "underwrite their own stash of grass." 76.

31. "In Memoriam for Superspade and John Carter," *San Francisco Oracle,* vol. 1, no. 9, August 1967, 4.

32. David E. Smith and Alan J. Rose, "Health Problems in Urban and Rural 'Crash Pad' Communes," *Clinical Pediatrics* no. 9 (September 1970), 534–537; Leonard Wolf, ed., *Voices of the Love Generation* (Boston: Little, Brown, 1968), 34. Also see Brian Alexander, "Free Love: Was There a Price to Pay," June 22, 2007, MSNBC.

33. Joplin quoted in Robert Stephen Spitz, *Barefoot in Babylon: The Creation of the Woodstock Music Festival, 1969* (New York: Viking, 1979), 460. For other accounts of Joplin's legendary erotic blues singing and on-stage contortions, as well as her sexual romps, see Joel Selvin, *Summer of Love: The Inside Story of LSD, Rock and Roll, Free Love, and High Times in the Wild West* (New York: Cooper Square, 1994), 102, 134, 185–187, 253, 277–279. Also see Gretchen Lemke-Santangelo, *Daughters of Aquarius: Women of the Sixties Counterculture* (Lawrence: University Press of Kansas, 2009), 28; Allen Matusow, *The Unraveling of America: A History of Liberalism in the 1960s* (New York: Harper & Row, 1984), 303.

34. McDonald quoted in Gillian G. Gaar, *She's a Rebel: The History of Women in Rock and Roll* (Seattle: Seal, 1992), 106; Lemke-Santangelo, 28–29.

35. David Allyn, *Make Love Not War: The Sexual Revolution, an Unfettered History* (Boston: Little, Brown, 2000), 17–26, 40.

36. Warren Hinckle, "A Social History of the Hippies," *Ramparts,* March, 1967, 9–10, 11; *Time,* "The Hippies: Philosophy of a Subculture," 19.

37. Bill Osgerby, *Playboys in Paradise: Masculinity, Youth & Leisure Style in Modern America* (New York: Berg, 2001), 190.

38. Lemke-Santangelo, *Daughters of Aquarius,* 64–65. Keese quoted in Alexander, "Free Love."

39. *Ibid.,* 22, 73, 67.

40. Quoted in Wolf, *Voices from the Love Generation,* 71.

41. George Gilbert, "A Hippie's Day: The Flower Children's Society," *San Francisco Chronicle,* May 17, 1967, 1, 14.

42. "The Hippies: Philosophy of a Subculture," *Time,* July 7, 1967, 20.

43. Barbara La Morticella, "New Year's Day Wail—Visualities," *San Francisco Oracle,* vol. 1 no. 5 (January 1967), 5. Also see Beth Bailey, "Sex as a Weapon: Underground Comix and the Paradox of Liberation," in Peter Braunstein and Michael William Doyle, edited, *Imagine Nation: The American Counterculture of the 1960s and '70s* (New York: Routledge, 2002), 305–324.

44. Lemke-Santangelo, *Daughters of Aquarius,* 26; Bailey, 310–314.

45. Robert J. Glessing, *The Underground Press in America* (Bloomington: Indiana University Press, 1970), xiv; Bailey.

46. Lemke-Santangelo, *Daughters of Aquarius,* 24. Also see Bailey.

47. Abe Peck, *Uncovering The Sixties: The Life and Times of the Underground Press* (New York: Carol, 1985),

212–213. Also see *Dear Sisters: Dispatches from the Women's Liberation Movement*, Rosalyn Baxandall and Linda Gordon, eds. (New York: Basic, 2000), 53–57; Bailey, 316–317.

48. "The Ebb and Flow of the Hippie Tide," *San Francisco Chronicle*, June 23, 1967, 18.

49. Chester Anderson/The Diggers, "Uncle Tim'$ Children," *Communications Company Broadside*, July 1967. Hippie Papers (SFHC-SFPL). Also see Charles Perry, *The Haight-Ashbury*, 113.

50. Wolf, *Voices from the Love Generation*, 90; Lemke-Santangelo, *Daughters of Aquarius*, 59.

51. Wolf, 34; Lemke-Santangelo, 59–60.

52. Jane and Michael Stern, *Sixties People* (New York: Alfred Knopf, 1990), 156; Peter Coyote, *Sleeping Where I Fall* (Washington, D.C.: Counterpoint, 1998), 7–9, 132–133, 289; Lemke-Santangelo, 60.

53. von Hoffman, *We Are the People Our Parents Warned Us Against*, 203.

54. *Ibid.*, 200.

55. T.R. Wayne Hill, "Houston Homosexual Speaks Out," *Space City News*, October 11–25, 1969. (Houston, Texas: The Houston Metropolitan Research Center). Hereafter cited as HMRC. Also see Timothy Miller, *The Hippies and American Values* (Knoxville: University of Tennessee Press, 1991), 56–58; Lemke-Santangelo, *Daughters of Aquarius*, 69–70.

56. Emmett Grogan, *Ringolevio: A Life Played for Keeps* (New York: New York Review of Books, 1972), 280–286; *Berkeley Barb*, March 3, 1967, 10–12; Matusow, *Unraveling of America*, 304.

57. von Hoffman, *We Are the People Our Parents Warned Us Against*, 200.

58. Chester Anderson, February 9, 1967, "Two Page Racial Rap in Memorium [sic]: Malcolm X Who Died to Make *Us* Free, Too Baby." Hippie Papers (SFHC-SFPL).

59. *Ibid.*

60. Chester Anderson, undated broadside, "Freedom Now." Hippie Papers (SFHC-SFPL).

61. Anderson, "Two Page Racial Rap," 2.

62. *Ibid.*, 1.

63. Guy Strait interview with Ron Thelin, *San Francisco Oracle*, vol.1, no. 8 (April 1967), 7. Hippie Papers (SFHC-SFPL).

64. Chester Anderson, "Spades and Acid: Not a Good Mix," undated broadside. Hippie Papers (SFHC-SFPL).

65. Anderson, "Racial Rap," 2.

66. Quoted in Miller, *The Hippies and American Values*, 16.

67. "Merchant Denounces 'Plastic Hippies,'" *San Francisco Standard*, July 8, 1967, 1.

68. Judson Gooding and Malcolm Carter, *The Hippies: Who They Are*, 42.

69. "Merchant Denounces 'Plastic Hippies,'" *San Francisco Standard*, July 8, 1967, 1.

70. Jeff Jassen, "The Year of the Shuck: What Price Love?" *Berkeley Barb*, July 5, 1967, 5; George Gilbert, "Diggers Preparing for the Invasion," *San Francisco Chronicle*, May 20, 1967, 11; Charles Perry, *The Haight-Ashbury*, 132.

71. Chester Anderson, four-page broadside, "Uncle Tim$s Children," *Communication Company Broadside*, undated but probably released sometime in the early summer, 1967, 1.

72. *Ibid.*, 2–4.

73. Steve Tyler, "Some Time This Summer," broadside printed by the Communication Company, July 6, 1967. Hippie Papers (SFHC-SFPL).

74. "Beat The Heat," broadside, "gestetnered [sic] in the interests of Constitutional Liberty by the communication company, a member of the underground press syndicate, 8/24/67"; "Survive Baby," "Brothers: An Important Notice For Your Safety and Survival," undated broadside. Hippie Papers (SFHC-SFPL). Also see Charles Perry, *The Haight-Ashbury*, 133–135.

75. Anderson, "Uncle Tim$s Children," 3–4; *San Francisco Chronicle*, August 5, 1967, 5; *Berkeley Barb*, August 8, 1967, 4; *The Haight-Ashbury Maverick*, August 11, 1967, 3; Chester Anderson, "Trouble in Bohemia," *Berkeley Barb*, August 3, 1967, 3; John Luce, "Haight-Ashbury Today: A Case of Terminal Euphoria," *Esquire* (vol. 72, July 1969), 68; William Chapin, "A Day on the Hippieland Scene," *San Francisco Chronicle*, October 9, 1967, 14–15; "Daylight Raid on Haight," *San Francisco Chronicle*, October 10, 1967, 1; Charles Howe, "Hippies Say They Need Protection from the Police," *San Francisco Chronicle*, October 11, 1967, 3; "Frightened Hippies Are Arming," *San Francisco Chronicle*, August 10, 1967, 1; Matusow, *The Unraveling of America*, 302; "San Francisco: Wilting Flowers," *Time* (vol. 91, no. 19), May 10, 1968.

76. *The Haight-Ashbury Eye*, August 1967, vol. 1, no. 5, 2; *The San Francisco Oracle*, August 1967, vol. 1 no. 12, p. 2; Charles Perry, *The Haight-Ashbury*, 137–138; von Hoffman, *We Are the People Our Parents Warned Us Against*, Elephant edition, 176–177; "California: End of the Dance, *Time* (vol. 90, no. 7), August 18, 1967.

77. Jeff Berner, "Astronauts of Inner Space: The Haight-Ashbury Scene Is Finished!" *San Francisco Chronicle*, August 20, 1967, Datebook, 22.

78. "Haightians Thrill to Spacious Street," *Berkeley Barb*, September 15, 1967, 5.

79. Berner, "Astronauts of Inner Space"; "So Who Mutha'd the 'Hippies,'?" *Berkeley Barb*, October 6, 1967, 1.

80. Such are the recollections of the author who visited the Haight on Sunday, September 10, 1967. Labor Day was the previous Monday, September 4. Author had ventured with friends to the Haight during the Summer of Love (early August 1967) but barely got into the neighborhood, saw the crowds, and said "forget it," and decided to go to a San Francisco Giants baseball game instead of trying to persevere through the sea of humanity just to say he experienced the Haight during the Summer of Love.

81. Elaine May, quoted in Foreword, *It Happened in Monterrey: Rock's Defining Moment* (Culver City, CA: Britannia, 2002).

82. Joan Didion, *Slouching Toward Bethlehem* (New York: Farrar, Strauss and Giroux, 1968).

83. Harrison quoted in Barry Miles, *Hippie* (New York: Sterling, 2004), 206.

84. Hedgepeth quoted in Dogin and Franco, *The Summer of Love*.

85. Thelin quoted in Michael Grieg, "The Decline and Fall of Hippieland," *San Francisco Chronicle*, October 5, 1967, 1, 8. Also see "Death of Hip Birth of Free," *Berkeley Barb*, September 29, 1967, 3; *The Haight-Ashbury Eye*, October 1967, 5; von Hoffman, *We Are the People Our Parents Warned Us Against*, 261.

86. von Hoffman; *New York Times* and Hedgepath quoted in Bloom and Breines, eds., *"Takin' It to the Streets,"* 330.

87. Grieg, "Decline and Fall of Hippieland"; Also see Grieg, "Death of the Hippies: A Sad, Solemn Ceremony," *San Francisco Chronicle,* October 7, 1967, 2; Charles Raudebaugh, "Grateful Dead Hold Lively Wake," *San Francisco Chronicle,* October 6, 1967, 2; "A Wake for Hip, a Cheer for Free," *Berkeley Barb,* October 6, 1967, 3; "Death of Hip, Mixed Emotions," *Berkeley Barb,* October 13, 1967, 5; Charles Perry, *The Haight-Ashbury,* 147–148; "Hippies: Where Have All the Flowers Gone?" *Time* (vol. 90, no. 15), October 13, 1967.

88. Untitled editorial, *The Haight-Ashbury Eye,* undated but October issue, 1967, vol.1, no. 6., 3; Also see *Rolling Stone,* November 9, 1967, 11; *Berkeley Barb,* September 29, 1967, 3; October 6, 1967, 3.

89. von Hoffman, *We Are The People Our Parents Warned Us Against,* Elephant edition, 262.

90. Dogin and Franco, *The Summer of Love.*

91. "Wilting Flowers," *Time;* Guy Strait to Allen Cohen, February 18, 1968.

Hippie Papers (SFHC-SFPL).

Chapter 9

1. John Bassett McCleary, "Commentary: 40 Years Ago: The Monterey Pop Festival," *The Monterey County Herald,* Sunday Special commemorating the 40th Anniversary of the Monterey Pop Festival and the Summer of Love, June 10, 2007, 2–3.

2. Michael Hicks, *Sixties Rock: Garage, Psychedelic, and Other Satisfactions* (Urbana: University of Illinois Press, 1999), 60.

3. McCleary, "Commentary," 3.

4. Robert Santelli, *Aquarius Rising: The Rock Festival Years* (New York: Dell, 1980), 13, 17.

5. Maitland Zane, "Bash on Mt. Tam," *San Francisco Chronicle,* June 12, 1967, 3; Robert Hurwitt, "Magic Mountain Fervor," *Berkeley Barb,* June 16, 1967, 3; Mark Lomas, "Fantasy Fair & Magic Mountain Music Festival," *Marin History,* Marin Independent Journal. http://blogs.marinij.com/marinhistory/2008/9/fantasy_fair_magic_mountain_mu.html (now inactive).

6. Jeff Tamarkin, *Got A Revolution! The Turbulent Flight of the Jefferson Airplane* (New York: Astria, 2003), 128–157; "A Letter: The Lovin' Levis," *Berkeley Barb,* May 12, 1967, 6.

7. Adler quoted in Beth Peerless, "The Music," *The Monterey County Herald,* June 10, 2007, 4.

8. Robert Christgau, "Anatomy of a Love Festival," *Esquire,* January 1968. http://www.robertchristgau.com/xg/music/monterey-69.php, 3.

9. Ed Ward, Geoffrey Stokes, and Ken Tucker, *Rock of Ages: The Rolling Stone History of Rock & Roll* (New York: Rolling Stone, 1986), 374; Sarah Hill, "When Deep Soul Met the Love Crowd: Otis Redding: Monterey Pop Festival, June 17, 1967," in Ian Englis, ed., *Performance and Popular Music: History, Place, and Time* (Hampshire, England: Ashgate, 2006), 28–32; "Truth Be Told," *Monterey County Herald,* June 10, 2007, 4; "How the Happening Happened," *The Beat,* KRLA edition, Pop Festival Souvenir Issue (vol. 3, no. 9), July 15, 1967.

10. Santelli, *Aquarius Rising,* 23; Hill, 31.

11. Marc Cabrera, "The Father of 'Pop'," *The Monterey County Herald,* June 10, 2007, 12. Hereafter all citations from that issue will be simply *The Monterey County Herald.*

12. Phillips quoted in Robert Christgau, "Anatomy of a Love Festival," 6.

13. Goldstein quoted in Barney Hoskyns, "The Meeting of the Twain: Monterey and the Great California Divide," can be found in the booklet that accompanies *The Complete Monterey Pop Festival,* the DVD set, the Criterion Collection, 2002, 45.

14. Elaine Mayes, ed., *It Happened in Monterey* (Culver City, CA: Britannia, 2002), 27; Barney Hoskyns, *Waiting for the Sun: Strange Days, Weird Scenes, & the Sound of Los Angeles* (New York: St. Martin's, 1996), 143; Hill, "When Deep Soul Met the Love Crowd," 31.

15. Phillips quoted in John Glatt, *Rage & Roll: Bill Graham and the Selling of Rock* (New York: Birch Lane, 1993), 68.

16. Helms quoted in Mayes, *It Happened in Monterey,* 57.

17. Kantner quoted in Christgau, "Anatomy of a Love Festival," 6–7.

18. Hoskyns, "The Meeting of the Twain," 46.

19. Hoskyns, *Waiting for the Sun,* 142, 147; Reebee Garofalo, *Rockin' Out: Popular Music in the USA,* 2d ed. (Boston: Prentice Hall, 2002), 186.

20. "The Lou Adler Interview," *The Tavis Smiley Show,* June 4, 2007. http://www.pbs.org/kcet/tavissmiley/archive/200706/20070604_adler.html (now inactive).

21. Beth Peerless, "The Music," *The Monterey County Herald,* 4–9; Marc Cabrera, "The Father of 'Pop'," *The Monterey County Herald,* 12; "Truth Be Told," *Monterey County Herald,* 10. Also see *The Complete Monterey Pop Festival,* directed by D.A. Pennebaker, The Criterion Collection DVD set, 3 CDs, 2002. Hereafter cited as *The Complete Monterey Pop Festival.*

22. "Personal Memories: Talitha Stills, Jim Thomas, and Kathy Klawans Smith," *Monterey County Herald,* 13, 22, 23. I attended the Monterey Pop Festival, along with four of my closest high school friends, on the event's last day, Sunday, June 18. We had all read about the "scene" in our local newspapers but typical of teenage boys, we spontaneously decided to go that Sunday morning and by 11 a.m. we were headed down Highway 101 to Monterey, about a two to two and a half hour trip from our Santa Clara suburb. We arrived about 1:30 p.m. and had to walk about a mile to the Monterey County Fairgrounds where the event was being held. We arrived at the fairgrounds just as Ravi Shankar and his "Indian band" started to play. See subsequent note for more detail about the day's events. On Shankar see Michael Lydon, "Monterey Pop: The First Rock Festival," *Newsweek,* June 20, 1967, 31–32. A copy of Lydon's article can also be found in the booklet that comes with *The Complete Monterey Pop Festival.* For further documentation, the citation will be Lydon, "Monterey Pop: The First Rock Festival," *CMPF,* then page number. For Shankar's incredible performance see *The Complete Monterey Pop Festival,* disc 1, final act/scene; Christgau, "Anatomy of a Love Festival," 11–12.

23. As we maneuvered our way through the crowd to try to get as close to the stage as possible, our mouths

were in a perpetual "drop state" as we gaped at the throngs of humanity that seemed to be everywhere, especially the many scantily clad "hippie chicks." However, as we pulled ourselves together we noticed that the majority of the people looked like us; "straights." We had come of course for the music, but also for the good looking girls, the majority of whom were also straight. Naturally there were hippies, some dressed and behaving as outrageously as had become their stereotype. Dope was everywhere, particularly marijuana, which people smoked openly as the cops "looked the other way" at virtually all of the illicit activities taking place, from people having sex in their sleeping bags in the football field that had been opened for "campers," to people completely zonked on acid, talking to trees. By the time we arrived, the concert's promoters had stopped selling tickets (which originally sold for $6.50 for the "orchestra section"—simply chairs put around the stage—and $3 for the bleachers; we stood most of time for the rest of the shows, which did not end until around 1 a.m. with the Mamas and Papas, who were the finale. Ravi Shankar was incredible, playing virtually non-stop his "Indian music"—raga rock, for three hours. It was music the likes of which none of us had heard before. We and the other 60,000 to 90,000 people listened with rapt, mesmerized attention. He received a standing ovation. We also saw the Blues Project out of New York; Janis Joplin and Big Brother and the Holding Company's encore performance; Buffalo Springfield, The Who and Jimi Hendrix's legendary performances; the latter we had not heard about before Monterey. We all agreed that by far the most memorable performances were by Shankar, Janis Joplin, the Who, and Jimi Hendrix. Indeed, the Grateful Dead, whom three of us had heard on Easter weekend in March in the Haight, were unfortunately anti-climactic after first experiencing the Who. Nonetheless, the Dead were their usual outstanding selves, connecting with the audience as few of the other bands were able to do, "inciting" people to dance all around the stage and the fairgrounds. Also see Peerless; Christoph Grunenberg and Jonathan Harris, *Summer of Love: Psychedelic Art, Social Crisis and Counterculture in the 1960s* (Liverpool: Liverpool University Press, 2005), 347; Christgau, "Anatomy of a Love Festival," 8; Irene Larcher, "The Sunday Conversation: Lou Adler on Monterey Pop," *Los Angeles Times*, June 10, 2012; *The Complete Monterey Pop Festival*; "Did You Know?" *Monterey County Herald*, 13; Lydon, "Monterey Pop: The First Rock Festival," 2, 8–12.

24. Author recollection; *Complete Monterey Pop Festival*, disc 1; Ian Englis, *Performance and Popular Music: History, Place, and Time* (Aldershot-Hants, England: Ashgate, 2006), 28.

25. Lydon, "Monterey Pop," 3; Werner quoted in Lauren Onkey, "Voodoo Child: Jimi Hendrix and the Politics of Race in the Sixties," in Peter Braunstein and Michael William Doyle, eds., *Imagine Nation: The American Counterculture of the 1960s & 70s* (New York: Routledge, 2002), 200.

26. Lydon, "Monterey Pop," 31 (in *Newsweek*).

27. Irene Larcher, "The Sunday Conversation: Lou Adler on Monterey Pop," *Los Angeles Times*, June 10, 2012.

28. Christgau, "Anatomy of a Love Festival," 8; author recollection of seeing a number of Monterey cops

bedecked in flowers on the festival's last day as well as witnessing a young girl giving cops flowers.

29. Marinello quoted in Charles Perry, *The Haight-Ashbury: A History* (New York: Random House, 1984).

30. Cabrera, "The Father of 'Pop,'" *Monterey County Herald*, 12.

31. Sam Karas, Citizens Committee for Monterey Pop Festival, in "Quotable," *Monterey County Herald*, 10.

32. Perry, *The Haight-Ashbury*, 129.

33. Larcher, "The Sunday Conversation: Lou Adler on Monterey Pop."

34. Robert Christgau, "Anatomy of a Love Festival," 14.

35. *The Complete Monterey Pop Festival*, disc 1.

36. Shankar quoted in *The Monterey County Herald*, Sunday Special, June 10, 2007, 7.

37. Christgau, "Anatomy of a Love Festival," 10, 16–17; Onkey, "Voodoo Child," 199–200.

38. Christgau, 2, 4, 5.

39. Henderson quoted in Lauren Onkey, "Voodoo Child," 198.

40. *Ibid.*, 197–198; Clapton quoted on page 198.

41. *Ibid.*, 196. George quoted in Note 19, 211.

42. Author recollection of performance; Lydon, "Monterey Pop: The First Rock Festival," 6, 11; *The Complete Monterey Pop Festival*, disc 1; Christgau, "Anatomy of a Love Festival," 10–11.

43. Quoted in Onkey, "Voodoo Child," 204.

44. *Ibid.*

45. *Ibid.*

46. Christgau, "Monterey Pop: The First Rock Festival," 11. Also see "Wild, Wooly, & Wicked," *Time* (vol. 91, no. 41), April 5, 1968.

47. "Singers: Passionate and Sloppy," *Time* (vol. 92, no. 6), August 9, 1968.

48. *The Complete Monterey Pop Festival*, disc 1; Lydon, "Monterey Pop," 12.

49. Jasmine Tritten quoted in "Memories," *The Monterey County Herald*, 23.

50. Lydon, "Monterey Pop," 11.

51. Jacques Attali, *Noise: The Political Economy of Music* (Minneapolis: University of Minnesota Press, 1999), 11.

52. DeSoto quoted in "Quotable," *The Monterey County Herald*, 2.

53. Lydon, "Monterey Pop: The First Rock Festival," *CMPF*, 32–34.

54. "Personal Memories: Dan Chavez: Working Man from Salinas Still in Awe of His Experience," *The Monterey County Herald*, 16.

55. "Monterey—'It Was a Good Beginning' As Viewed by Eric Burdon," *The Beat*, 8.

56. Sinclair quoted in Timothy Miller, "The Cooling of America: Out of Tune and Lost in the Counterculture," *Time* (vol. 97, no. 8), February 22, 1971.

57. Lydon, "Monterey Pop" (*Newsweek*); Christgau, "Anatomy of a Love Festival"; Bergen quoted in *The Beat*, 4.

Chapter 10

1. John Stickney, "The Commune Comes to America," *Life*, July 18, 1969, 16–20. Also see Timothy Miller, "The Sixties Era Communes," Peter Braunstein and

Michael William Doyle, eds., *Imagine Nation: The American Counterculture of the 1960s & 1970s* (New York: Routledge, 2002), 327–328.

2. Miller, 329–330. For histories of some of the earlier communal experiments in the United States see Donald E. Pitzer, ed., *America's Communal Utopias* (Chapel Hill: University of North Carolina Press, 1997); Mark Holloway, *Heavens on Earth: Utopian Communities in America, 1680–1880*, 2d ed. (Mineola, NY: Dover, 1966); Kenneth Rexroth, *Communalism: From Its Origins to the Twentieth Century* (New York: Seabury, 1974); Everett Webber, *Escape to Utopia: The Communal Movement in America* (New York: Hastings House, 1959); and John Curl, *For All the People: Uncovering the Hidden History of Cooperation, Cooperative Movements, and Communalism in America*, 2d ed. (Oakland, CA: PM, 2012).

3. Timothy Miller, *The 60s Communes: Hippies and Beyond* (New York: Syracuse University Press, 1999), xviii. Also see Miller, *The Hippies and American Values* (Knoxville: University of Tennessee Press, 1991), 88; Hugh Gardner, *The Children of Prosperity: Thirteen Modern American Communes* (New York: St. Martin's, 1978), 3.

4. William Hedgepath quoted in Alexander Bloom and Wini Breines, ed., *"Takin' It to the Streets": A Sixties Reader* (New York: Oxford University Press, 1999), 332.

5. Bill Dodd, "Drop City," *San Francisco Oracle* April 1968, 24. Hippie Papers (SFHC-SFPL).

6. Quoted in Miller, *The Hippies and American Values*, 90.

7. Robert F. Jones, "Communes in the Country," in Joe David Brown, ed., *The Hippies: Who They Are, Where They Are, Why They Act That Way, and How They May Affect Our Society* (New York: Time, 1967), 63.

8. Hedgepath quoted in Bloom and Breines, ed., *"Takin' It to the Streets,"* 331.

9. Gwen Wheeler quoted in *Home Free Home: A History of Two Open-Door California Communes*, Chapter 9, pg. 5. *The Digger Papers.* http://www.diggers.org/homefree/hfh_int.html.

10. Peter Braunstein and Michael William Doyle, eds., *Imagine Nation: The American Counterculture of the 1960s & 1970s* (New York: Routledge, 2002), 12.

11. Miller, "The Sixties Era Communes," 329–330. Also see Helen Constas and Kenneth Weshues, "Communes: The Routinization of Hippiedom" in Kenneth Westhues, ed., *Society's Shadow: Studies of the Sociology of the Counterculture* (Toronto: McGraw-Hill Ryerson, 1972), 191–194; Maren Lockwood Camden, "Communes and Protest Movements in the U.S., 1960–1974: An Analysis of Intellectual Roots," *International Review of Modern Sociology*, vol. 6 (Spring 1976), 16.

12. Hedgepath quoted in Bloom and Breines, eds., *"Takin' It to the Streets,"* 330–331.

13. Jack Kerouac, *The Dharma Bums* (New York: Viking Penguin 1958, 1971; Buccaneer, 1986), 97–98. Allen Ginsberg agreed with his compatriots Kerouac and Snyder that the intellectual core of the Beat movement was "the return to nature and the revolt against the machine," Ginsberg quoted in Bruce Cook, *The Beat Generation: The Tumultuous '50s Movement and Its Impact on Today* (New York: Charles Scribner's Sons 1971; Westport, CT: Greenwood, 1983), 104.

14. For the impact of suburbia on the commune movement see Bennett M. Berger, *The Survival of a Counterculture: Ideological Work and Everyday Life Among Rural Communards* (Berkeley: University of California Press, 1981), 94. Many "boomers" eventually rebelled against both suburbia and the "multiversities" they attended, which for some intensified their commitment to the counterculture, the communal movement, and seeking harmony with nature. Many late 1960s and early 1970s Hollywood movies were about young people in revolt and thus many such pictures were shot on college campuses, where university administrators strongly encouraged filmmakers to make sure they showcased their school's majestic pastoral landscape, which even graced such urban universities as UC Berkeley, where director Mike Nichols filmed parts of *The Graduate*. On the importance of the physical, natural "set and setting" in university campus design, see Paul Venable Turner, *Campus: An American Planning Tradition* (Cambridge, MA: MIT Press, 1984).

15. Marcus and Tupferberg quoted in Timothy Miller, *The Hippies and American Values* 89–90.

16. *Ibid.*, 89.

17. *Ibid.*, 90.

18. Pam Hanna quoted in Timothy Miller, *The 60s Communes: Hippies and Beyond* (Syracuse, NY: Syracuse University Press, 1999), 153.

19. David [sic], "The Commune Movement in the Middle Seventies," *Communities*, September/October 1975, 22.

20. Communard quoted in Terry Anderson, *The Sixties* (New York: Addison Wesley Longman, 1999), 144.

21. Quoted in Keith Melville, *Communes in the Counter Culture: Origins, Theories, and Styles of Life* (New York: Morrow, 1972), 134–135.

22. Freedom Farm resident "Liz" quoted in Sara Davidson, "Open Land: Getting Back to the Communal Garden." Article originally appeared in *Harper's* 240 (June 1970), pp. 91–100, Reprinted and part of a collection of essays, written by Davidson over several decades that cover a wide range of topics. http://www.saradavidson.com.

23. Lew Welch, "Op-ed," *San Francisco Oracle*, vol. 2 (September 1968), 3–4 (SFHC-SFPL).

24. Communard quoted in Raymond Mungo, *Famous Long Ago: My Life and Hard Times with the Liberation News Service* (Boston: Beacon, 1970), 108. The vision held by many communards of impending urban/industrial demise because of the destruction of the land and depletion of natural resources is revealed in Paul Goodman's "Rural Life: 1984," in Goodman's collection of nine essays titled *People or Personnel and Like a Conquered Province* (New York: Vintage, 1968), 412–422.

25. Welch, "Op-ed," 4. Also see for a similar if not exact quote, Bill Voyd, "Funk Architecture," in Paul Oliver, ed., *Shelter and Society* (New York: Praeger, 1969), 159.

26. Williams and Steve quoted in Davidson, "Open Land: Getting Back to the Communal Garden."

27. "Morning Dew" can be found on the album *The Grateful Dead*, Warner Bros., 1967; Bonnie Dobson's version is on Various Artists, *The Best of Broadside, 1962–1988: Anthyms of the American Underground from the Pages of Broadside Magazine.* Produced, compiled and annotated by Jeff Place and Ronald D. Cohen, Smithsonian Folkways, 2000; Jefferson Airplane, *Crown of Creation*, RCA, 1968. Neil Young, *After the Goldrush*, Reprise,

1970; Crosby, Stills and Nash, *Crosby, Stills, and Nash*, Atlantic/WEA, 1969; Barney Hoskyns, *Waiting for the Sun: The Story of the Los Angeles Music Scene* (New York: Viking, 1996), 129; Frank Zappa with Peter Occhiogrosso, *The Real Frank Zappa Book* (New York: Touchstone, 1989), 255; Frank Zappa and the Mothers of Invention, *Ahead of Their Time*, Rykodisc, 1993.

28. Anderson, *The Sixties*, 144.

29. Hedgepath quoted in Bloom and Breines, eds., "*Takin' It to the Streets*," 332.

30. Anderson, *The Sixties*, 144.

31. George Fitzgerald, *Communes: Their Goals, Hopes, and Problems* (New York: Paulist, 1971), 8–9; Rosabeth Kanter, *Commitment and Community: Communes and Utopias in Sociological Perspective* (Cambridge: Harvard University Press, 1972), 176, 191–196; George Kozeny, "Intentional Communities: Lifestyles Based on Ideals," *Communities Directory: A Guide to Cooperative Living* (Langley, WA: Fellowship for Intentional Community, 1995), 18; Anderson, *The Sixties*, 144–145.

32. Quoted in Miller, "The Sixties Era Communes," 328. Also see Bill of Neverland [sic], "Commune Tripping," *Communitarian* (March/April 1972), 23.

33. Jones, "Communes in the Country," 63–64, 66; "Home Free Home," Chapters 1–2 and particularly Chapter 3, p. 8. On the Digger-Morning Star relationship see Chapter 3, pp. 3–4, and Chapter 4, p. 2. Also see Miller, "The Sixties Era Communes," 332–333; Miller, *The Hippies and American Values*, 92.

34. Stillman quoted in "Home Free Home," Chapter 3, page 7; Wheeler quoted in Chapter 13, page 7 and Chapter 21, page 3; and Gottlieb quoted in Chapter 3, page 8 and in Davidson, "Open Land."

35. Davidson.

36. Wheeler quoted in Davidson. "Near" quoted in "Home Free Home," Chapter 3, pp. 8–9.

37. Jones, "Communes in the Country, 64; "Home Free Home"; Gottlieb quoted "Home Free Home," Chapter 7, p. 3, and in Davidson, "Open Land"; Wheeler quoted in "Home Free Home," Chapter 10, p. 3; Stillman quoted in "Home Free Home," Chapter 2, pp. 1, 5. Also see Miller, *The Hippies and American Values*, 92.

38. "Home Free Home," Chapter 7, p. 3; Bentley quoted "Home Free Home," Chapter 2, p. 2; Davidson.

39. Gottlieb quoted in Davidson.

40. Sender quoted in "Home Free Home," Chapter 4, p. 1.

41. "Newcomer" quoted in Davidson, "Open Land."

42. "Home Free Home," Chapter 14, pp. 1–5, 8.

43. *Ibid.*, pp. 5, 7, 9.

44. Geoffrey O'Brien quoted in O'Brien, *Dream Time: Chapters from the Sixties* (New York: Viking Penguin, 1989), 74–76. For other country hippies who believed acid and nature "went together" see Leonard Wolf, ed., *Voices from the Love Generation* (Boston: Little, Brown 1968), 151–152; Stephen Diamond, *What The Trees Said: Life on a New Age Farm*, 2d ed. (New York: Delta 1971), 75–89; Nick Bromell, *Tomorrow Never Knows: Rock and Psychedelics in the 1960s* (Chicago: University of Chicago Press, 2000), 69–71; Zen Jack quoted in "Home Free Home," Chapter 14, page 8.

45. Quoted from Maurice Isserman and Michael Kazin, *America Divided: The Civil War of the 1960s* (New York: Oxford University Press, 2000), 158.

46. Davidson, "Open Land." Also see "Fruit n' Nuts

Nancy" discussing her children and their acid trips in "Home Free Home," Chapter 10, pp. 4–5.

47. Gottlieb quoted in "Home Free Home," Chapter 2, p. 11; Wheeler quoted Chapter 10, p. 6; Zen Jack quoted Chapter 10, p. 9.

48. "Home Free Home," Chapter 10, pp. 3–4; Chapter 7, pp. 9–10.

49. *Ibid.*, Chapter 6, p. 2; Chapter 10, pp. 6–7.

50. Coyote quoted in E.A. Swingrover, ed., *The Counterculture Reader* (New York: Pearson Longman, 2004), 48.

51. Davidson, "Open Land."

52. "Home Free Home," Chapter 9, pp. 5–6; Chapter 4, p. 3; Chapter 16, pp. 5–6.

53. Hanna (Read), "Infinite Points of Time," 10.

54. "Home Free Home," Chapter 23, pp. 7–8.

55. *Ibid.*, pp. 8–10.

56. *Ibid.*

57. *Ibid.*, Chapter 4, p. 4; Chapter 6, p. 9; Chapter 22, p. 2; Chapter 11, p. 3. For the list of grievances, complaints, and alleged violations of building codes and other laws leveled first against Morning Star and then later against Wheeler's Ranch, see Chapter 7, pp. 4–6. Also see Miller, *The Hippies*, 92

58. "Home Free Home," Chapter 22, pp. 1–2; Chapter 11, p. 11; Chapter 8, p. 8; Chapter 13, pp. 7–10.

59. *Ibid.*, Chapter 17, pp. 2–3; Chapter 21, pp. 5–8; Chapter 24, pp. 3–9.

60. Erin McCarley, "Remembering Stephen Gaskin: A Conversation with the Man Behind the Original Off-the-Grid Farm," *Yes Magazine*, November 2005, http://www.yesmagazine.org; Douglas Martin, "Stephen Gaskin, Hippie Who Founded an Enduring Commune, Dies at 79," *New York Times*, July 2, 2014. Robert and Diane Gilman, "The Farm Twenty Years Later: An Interview with Albert Bates," *Context Institute* (vol. 29, Summer 1991), 36; Steve Chawkins, "Stephen Gaskin Dies at 79; Founder of the Farm Commune," *Los Angeles Times*, July 5, 2014. Also see David Brill, "Down on the Farm," *Tennessee Illustrated* (January-February 1989), 29; "The Farm That Keeps Flowering, *Newsweek* (August 10, 1981), 14. On the transcendent importance of the Farm's midwifery program see Samantha M. Shapiro, "Mommy Wars: The Prequel: Ina May Gaskin and the Battle for Home Births," *New York Times Magazine*, May 23, 2012.

61. Douglas Stevenson, *Out to Change The World: The Evolution of the Farm Community* (Summertown, TN: Book, 2014), 5–10; Chris Simunek, "Stephen Gaskin, Creator of the Farm dies at 79," *High Times*, July 2, 2014, http://www.hightimes.com; John Coate, "The Caravan" in John Coate, "Life on the Bus and Farm: An Informal Recollection," 1987, http://cervisa.com; Also see Coate, "Farm Stories," *Whole Earth Review* (no. 60, Fall 1988), 86; Martin; *Mother Earth News* editors, "The Plowboy Interview: Stephen Gaskin and the Farm," May/June 1977. http://www.motherearthnews.com; Gaskin quoted in Pat LeDoux, "The History of a Hippie Commune: The Farm" (Ph.D. diss., Middle Tennessee State University, 1992), 23–24; 61.

62. Gaskin quoted in *Mother Earth News* editors, "The Plowboy Interview: Stephen Gaskin and the Farm," May/June 1977. http://www.motherearthnews.com. Also see LaDoux, 32–36.

63. Coate quoted in "Farm Stories," *Whole Earth Review* (no. 60, Fall 1988), p. 86.

64. Matthew McClure and Walter Rabideau in Kevin Kelly interview, "Why We Left the Farm," *Whole Earth Review* (no. 49, Winter, 1985), 57, 58–59.

65. Rabideau.

66. Stevenson, *Out to Change the World,* 142–143.

67. *Mother Earth News,* editors, "The Plowboy Interview"; Gaskin quoted in Albert Bates, "J. Edgar Hoover and The Farm," October 16, 1993. Paper presented at the International Communal Studies Conference on Culture, Thought, and Living in Community, New Harmony, Indiana, http://www.thefarm.org.

68. Gaskin quoted in Chawkins, "Stephen Gaskin Dies at 79," *Los Angeles Times,* July 5, 2014.

69. Gaskin quoted in Jim Windolf, "Sex, Drugs, and Soybeans," *Vanity Fair,* April 5, 2007. Also see LeDoux, "The History of a Hippie Commune," 45.

70. *Mother Earth News* editors, "The Plowboy Interview."

71. Coate, "Farm Stories," *Whole Earth Review,* 87; Stevenson, *Out to Change the World,* 24. Also see Rupert Fike, ed., *Voices from the Farm: Adventures in Community Living* (Summertown, TN: Book, 2012), 27–30.

72. Coate; Don Lattin, "Twilight of Hippiedom: Farm Commune's Founder Envisions Return to the Fold as Ex-Dropouts Age," *San Francisco Chronicle,* March 2, 2003.

73. Coate.

74. Bates, "J. Edgar Hoover and The Farm"; Graf and Ina May Gaskin quoted in Windolf, "Sex, Drugs, and Soybeans"; Kate Wenner, "How They Keep Them Down on the Farm," *New York Times Magazine,* May 8, 1977, 81.

75. *Mother Earth News* editors, "The Plowboy Interview."

76. Windolf, "Sex, Drugs, and Soybeans"; "Catherine" quoted in Editor, "Down on the Farm in Summertown, Tennessee: A Flower Child's Adventure," *2nd Sight Magazine.* secondsightresearch.tripod.com/cattales/id13html (now inactive) Also see Kevin Kelly on "soaking" in "Why We Left the Farm," *Whole Earth Review* (no. 49, Winter 1985), p. 59.

77. Coate quoted in "Farm Stories," *Whole Earth Review* (no. 60, Fall 1988), p. 87; Wenner, "How They Keep Them Down on the Farm," 81.

78. McCarley, "Remembering Stephen Gaskin"; Gaskin quoted in *The Tennessean,* October 11, 1981, in "Is Stephen Gaskin a Second Christ? Some Still Say Yes, Some Disagree"; Coate, 88; Walter Rabideau and John Seward in Kelly, "Why We Left the Farm," 64–65.

79. McCarley. Katherine Platt quoted in "Is Stephen Gaskin a Second Christ?"

80. Bonser quoted in "Is Stephen Gaskin a Second Christ?"

81. Seward and McClure quoted in Kelly, "Why We Left the Farm," 65–66. Also Coate, "Life on the Bus and Farm: An Informal Recollection." Another original Farmie, Michael Traugot, initially felt as personally responsible for the Farm's success as his compatriots. "I figured we were going to start something that was going to change America and do it by building something that was so graceful that everyone would follow it. I was into it because I thought it was the vanguard of the new way of doing things." Traugot quoted in LaDoux, "The History of a Hippie Commune," 46.

82. Walter Rabideau in Kelly.. Also see LaDoux, 71–72, for those Farmies who believed Gaskin was "the uni-
fying force in the community," "a father-figure to us all," "the energy that first pulled the Farm together," "the George Washington" of the community, and "theologian who knew how to breathe life into the ancient scriptures."

83. Walter Rabideau interview in Kelly, "Why We Left the Farm," 57; Coate, "Life on the Bus and Farm: An Informal Recollection"; John Coate and Cliff Figallo in "Farm Stories," 86. Else quoted in LeDoux, "The History of a Hippie Commune," 56–57.

84. Marilyn Friedlander in Fike, ed., *Voices from the Farm,* 26; Windolf, "Sex, Drugs, and Soybeans"; Matthew McClure in Kelly, 64; Stevenson, *Out to Change the World,* 41. On Gaskin's "bust," arrest, and sentencing see *Lewis County Herald,* September 2, 1971.

85. Rabideau and Cliff Figallo, in Kelly, 59–60; Stevenson, *Out to Change the World,* 34–36. Also see, "The Front Door" in Pike, ed., *Voices from the Farm,* 68–73.

86. Kelly, 63, 65.

87. Gaskin quoted in *The Tennessean,* October 22, 1973, p. 10.

88. Wenner, "How They Keep Them Down on the Farm," 84; Walter and Susan Rabineau and Kathryn McClure in Kelly, 63–64, 66; Kelly Luker, "Commune Sense, *Metroactive,* February 29, 1996, http://www.metroactive.com/papers/metro/02.29.96/hippie-9609.html.

89. *Mother Earth News* editors, "The Plowboy Interview"; Coate and Figallo quoted in "Farm Stories," *Whole Earth Review,* 88. Also see Jessica Bliss, "Stephen Gaskin, Founder of the Farm, Dies at 79," *The Tennessean,* July 2, 2014. Also see Doug Stevenson in Pike, ed., *Voices from the Farm,* 99–100.

90. Hippycommunekid, "Growing Up on a Hippy Commune." http://hippycommune.wordpress.com/tag/stephen-gaskin/.

91. Figallo, "Farm Stories," 93; Windolf, "Sex, Drugs, and Soybeans." Also see Gretchen Lemke-Santangelo, *Daughters of Aquarius: Women of the Sixties Counterculture* (Lawrence: University Press of Kansas, 2009), 76; Angela Aidala, "Communes and Changing Family Norms: Marriage and Lifestyle Choices Among Former Members of Communal Groups," *Journal of Family Issues* (vol. 10, Sept. 1989), 311–338; 322, 326; Stevenson, *Out to Change the World,* 49–50. For a breakdown of the Farm's human composition, i.e., the age, gender, religion, level of education, number of adults, children, married couples, non-married couples, and singles living on the Farm in 1974, see Peter Jenkins, *A Walk Across America* (New York: Fawcett Crest, 1979), 216–217. Although personally engaged and sanctioning alternative marital arrangements, Gaskin eventually believed such unions "created more crazies than one can deal with." Gaskin quoted in LaDoux, "The History of a Hippie Commune," 99.

92. Rachel Neunier, "Communal Living in the Late 60s and Early 70s: The Farm: Summertown, Tennessee, USA." http://www.thefarm.org; Windolf, "Sex, Drugs, and Soybeans."

93. Hippycommunekid, "Growing Up on a Hippy Commune"; Friedlander in Fike, ed., *Voices from the Farm,* 26.

94. Hippycommunekid; Friedlander, 25; Susan Rabideau in Kevin Kelly, "Why We Left the Farm," 62.

95. Hippycommunekid.

96. Simunek, "Stephen Gaskin, Creator of the Farm, Dies at 79"; "Stephen Gaskin—Obituary," *The Telegraph,* July 4, 2014, http://www.telegraph.co.uk; Interestingly as many of the neighbors got to know more and more Farmies, they tended to look the other way at the Farm's marijuana cultivation, with many even quaintly likening the plant to "moonshine" because it was, after all, "home grown." Some even teased Gaskin, telling him that they heard his "grass won first prize at the county fair." Quoted in LaDoux, "The History of a Hippie Commune," 74.

97. Windolf, "Sex, Drugs, and Soybeans." Also see John Coate, "Life on the Bus and Farm: An Informal Recollection."

98. Coate.

99. Goodman quoted in Windolf, "Sex, Drugs, and Soybeans." Also see Walter Rabideau and John Seward in Kelly, "Why We Left the Farm," 61.

100. Kelly. Also see "Year of the Commune," *Newsweek* (vol. 74, no. 7), August 18, 1969, p. 7; Zane Kesey quoted in Luker, "Commune Sense."

101. Windolf, "Sex, Drugs, and Soybeans"; Wenner, "How They Keep Them Down on the Farm," 86; Raymond Mungo, *Total Loss Farm* (New York: E.P. Dutton, 1970), 136–137; Communard quoted in Berger, *The Survival of a Counterculture,* 53.

102. Berger, 80–81; Mungo, 157; Luker, "Communal Sense"; Sara Beach, "Curse of the Hippie Parents," *Salon,* August 22, 2001.

103. Berger; Luker.

104. Matthew and Kathryn McClure in Kelly interview, "Why We Left the Farm," 64. Also see Kate Wenner, "The Technicolor Amish: Cult or Counterculture," 25; Stephen Gaskin, *The Caravan* (Summertown, TN: Book, 2007), 9; *Mother Earth News* editors, "The Plowboy Interview."

105. Kelly interview, 65.

106. Quoted in Timothy Miller, *The Hippies and American Values* (Knoxville: University of Tennessee Press, 1991), 99.

107. Kelly interview, "Why We Left the Farm," 61–62, 66.

108. Miller, *The Hippies and American Values,* 99–100; John Seward, Cliff Figallo, and Matthew McClure in Kelly, 57–58, 62.

109. Stevenson, *Out to Change the World,* 103–118; Bliss, "Stephen Gaskin, Founder of the Farm Dies at 79," *The Tennessean;* Martin, "Stephen Gaskin, Hippie Who Founded an Enduring Commune, Dies at 79," *The New York Times;* Chawkins, "Stephen Gaskin Dies at 79; Founder of the Farm Commune," *Los Angeles Times.* Margaret Mead quoted in Douglas Stevenson, *The Farm Then and Now: A Model for Sustainable Living* (Gabriola Island, BC: New Society, 2014), 219.

110. James Nix, "Trouble on the Farm," *Nashville Scene,* October 3, 2013.

111. *Ibid.*

112. Windolf, "Sex, Drugs, and Soybeans"; Don Lattin, "Twilight of Hippiedom"; Miller, *The 60s Communes: Hippies and Beyond,* 122–124. Also see Douglas Stevenson, *The Farm Then and Now,* not only for a thoughtful assessment of the Changeover's impact on the Farm community, but also for an equally insightful discussion of the Farm's present status and philosophy. See Chapters 6 and 11.

113. Kelly interview, "Why We Left the Farm," 65, 66.

114. *Ibid.*

115. "Design: The Dymaxion American," *Time* (vol. 83, no. 2), January 10, 1964. Miller, "The Sixties Era Communes," 331–332.

116. Barron Beshoar, "Communes in the Country," in Joe David Brown, ed., *The Hippies: Who They Are, Where They Are, Why They Act That Way, and How They May Affect Our Society* (New York: Time, 1967), 71.

117. J. Baldwin, "Alloy Report," in Stewart Brand, ed., *The Last Whole Earth Catalog* (New York: Random House, 1971), 112–117, 114.

118. On the mass media's "fascination" with Drop City, see Peter Rabbit, *Drop City* (New York: Olympia, 1971), 24–25; Miller, *60s Communes,* 38.

119. Beshoar, "Communes in the Country," 75.

120. Paul Voyd, "Funk Architecture," 156–157.

121. Douthit quoted in John Hendrickson, "Colorado's Dome on the Range," *The Denver Post,* June 16, 2009, http://www.denverpost.com.

122. Richert and Bernofsky quoted in Miller, "The Sixties Era Commune," 332.

123. "A Drop City Founder Speaks Out," Center for Land Use Interpretation, http://www.clui.org.

124. Richert quoted in Hendrickson, "Colorado's Dome on the Range."

125. Voyd, "Funk Architecture," 156.

126. Hendrickson, "Colorado's Dome on the Range."

127. Voyd, "Funk Architecture," 159.

128. Eryn Tomlinson, "An Interview with Clark Richert," zingmagazinewww, September 2009, http://www.zingmagazine.com/drupal/node/1005. Black Mountain College was an alternative liberal arts institution founded in 1933 by John Andrew Rice and Theodore Drier that placed particular emphases on curriculum that cultivated the avant-garde in the arts and letters as well as introducing and experimenting with an interdisciplinary approach to progressive education; John Dewey-inspired concepts for learning and knowledge acquisition.

129. Hendrickson, "Colorado's Dome on the Range." Also see Timothy Miller, "The Roots of the 1960s Communal Revival," *American Studies* 33 (October 1992), 73–93, 88.

130. Beshoar, "Communes in the Country," 75–6.

131. Voyd, "Funk Architecture," 156.

132. Bill Dodd, "Drop City," *San Francisco Oracle,* vol. 2 (September 1968), p. 4.

133. Bernofsky quoted in Timothy Miller, "The Roots of the 1960s Communal Revival," 88–89. Also see Beshoar, "Communes in the Country," 77, for Peter Rabitt's similar attitude toward "work."

134. Rabbit, *Drop City,* 33; Beshoar, "Communes in the Country," 73–75; Miller, "The Sixties-Era Communes," 332.

135. Beshoar, "Communes in the Country," 77–78.

136. Fuller, quoted in "The Dymaxion American."

137. Leder and Estellachild quoted in Miller, *The Hippies and American Values,* 96.

138. Quoted in William Hedgepeth, *The Alternative: Communal Life in America* (New York: Macmillan, 1970), 74.

139. Quoted in Davidson, "Open Land: Getting Back to the Communal Garden."

140. "Home Free Home," Chapter 20, p. 2; Chapter 10, p. 10; Chapter 21, p. 7.

141. "Corky" quoted in Davidson, "Open Land: Getting Back to the Communal Garden."

142. Quoted in Anderson, *The Sixties,* 145.

143. *Ibid.*

144. Hedgepeth quoted in *"Takin' It to the Streets,"* 333. On the Kerista, see Robert Anton Wilson, "The Religion of Kerista and Its 69 Positions," in *Fact,* July/August 1965, http://kerista.com/nkerdocs/raw.html.

145. "Hippies: Paradise Rocked," *Time* (vol. 93, no. 25), June 20, 1969; "American Notes: Closed Communes," *Time* (vol. 95, no. 13), March 30, 1970. Chicano quoted in Hugh Gardner, *The Children of Prosperity,* 113. Also see Miller, *The 60s Communes: Hippies and Beyond,* 222–224.

146. Miller; "American Notes: Closed Communes," *Time,* March 30, 1970.

147. Patsy Sun, "Why Our Commune Crumbled," *Mother Earth News,* May/June 1970, http://www.mother earthnews.com.

148. Elaine Sundancer, *Celery Wine: Story of a Country Commune* (Yellow Springs, OH: Community, 1973), 125.

149. Ron E. Roberts, *The New Communes* (Englewood Cliffs, NJ: Prentice Hall, 1971), 100.

Chapter 11

1. Paul Krassner, "60s Live Again Minus the LSD," *Los Angeles Times,* January 28, 2007, www.latimes.com.

2. Rubin quoted in Joan and Robert K. Morrison, eds., *From Camelot to Kent State: The Sixties Experience in the Words of Those Who Lived It* (New York: Oxford University Press, 1987), 284, 287. For a summation of the Yippie ethos that had evolved by 1968, see David Farber, *The Age of Great Dreams: American in the 1960s* (New York: Hill and Wang, 1994), 221.

3. Jerry Rubin, *Do It! Scenarios of the Revolution* (New York: Simon and Schuster, 1970), 113, 114, 116.

4. Abbie Hoffman, *Revolution for the Hell of It* (New York: Dial, 1969), 29–30.

5. New Leftist Henry Anderson quoted in Irwin Unger, *The Movement: A History of the American New Left, 1959–1972* (New York: Dodd, Mead, 1974), 143.

6. Lester quoted in Abe Peck, *Uncovering the Sixties: The Life and Times of the Underground Press* (New York: Citadel, 1991), 108.

7. Dana Beal, Steve Conliff, Grace Nichols, et al. *Blacklisted News: Secret Histories from Chicago 1968 to 1984; The New Yippies Book Collective* (New York: Bleecker, 1983), 514.

8. Hoffman quoted in Micah L. Issit, *The Hippies: A Guide to an American Counterculture* (Santa Barbara, CA: ABC-CLIO, 2009), 136; Hoffman, *Revolution for the Hell of It,* 74.

9. Jerry Rubin, *Do It,* 82.

10. Hoffman, *Revolution for the Hell of It,* 102. Also see "The Politics of Yip," *Time* (vol. 91, no. 41), April 5, 1968.

11. Hoffman, 80.

12. Rubin, *Do It!,* 83.

13. Hoffman quoted in David Farber, *Chicago '68* (Chicago: University of Chicago Press, 1988), 11.

14. Rubin quoted in Peck, *Uncovering the Sixties,* 103.

15. Abbie Hoffman, *Soon to Be a Major Motion Picture* (New York: Perigree, 1980), 146.

16. Hoffman quoted in Maurice Isserman and Michael Kazin, *America Divided: The Civil War of the 1960s* (New York: Oxford University Press, 2000), 233.

17. Jerry Rubin to Alan [sic] Cohen, February 14, 1968. Hippie Papers (SFHC-SFPL).

18. Rubin quoted in Michael William Doyle, "Staging the Revolution: Guerrilla Theater As a Countercultural Practice, 1965–68," in Peter Braunstein and Michael William Doyle, ed. *Imagine Nation: The American Counterculture of the 1960s and '70s* (New York: Routledge, 2000), 90.

19. Mobe was essentially an umbrella organization comprised of mainly temperate activist organizations, a "loose confederation of the Left wing, pacifist, and moderate antiwar groups," known for passive protest. Mobe encompassed a vast network of antiwar groups, such as Resist, a national conglomerate of activist who believed it was their moral duty to oppose the war and support draft resisters by raising money for bail funds and legal defense. Also part of the Mobe network were conscientious objectors affinity groups such as the Catholic worker, the Committee for Nonviolent Action, the Student Peace Union, and the War Resisters League. Norman Mailer described Mobe as "A respectable horde of respectable professionals, lawyers, accountants, men in hats wearing eyeglasses, Reform Democrats some of them members of SANE, or Women Strike for Peace—also American Friends Service Committee, CORE, W.E.B. Dubois Clubs, Inter-University Christian Movement, Catholic Peace Fellowship, Jewish Peace Fellowship, SDS, SNCC, National Lawyers' Guild, the Resistance, and National Conference for a New Politics." See Norman Mailer, *Armies of the Night,* 94; Resist, "A Call to Resist Illegitimate Authority in 1967," in Hugo Adam Bedau, ed. *Civil Disobedience: Theory and Practice* (New York: Pegasus, 1969), 162–164; Catholic Worker, "Declaration of Conscience Against the War in Vietnam," in Bedau, ed., *Civil Disobedience,* 160–161. In short, Mobe membership consisted of the young and old, professional men and female homemakers, white and black citizens, earnest, clean-cut students and scruffy hippies. With such a large and varied network, Mobe could produce thousands of participants for mass demonstrations for whatever the cause. It was the perfect organization for the Yippies to tap into for their madcap antics. Also see Andrew E. Hunt, *David Dellinger: The Life and Times of a Nonviolent Revolutionary* (New York: New York University Press, 2006), 142–143, 150–151; Fred Halstead, *Out Now! A Participant's Account of the American Movement Against the Vietnam War* (New York: Monad, 1978), 215; Douglas Robinson, "Scattered Peace Activists Seek to Unify Movement," *New York Times,* February 26, 1967, 3; Robinson, "100,000 Rally at U.N. Against Vietnam War," April 16, 1967, 2; Morrison and Morrison, *From Camelot to Kent State,* 284–285; Matusow, *The Unraveling of America,* 413–414; Irwin Unger, *The Movement: A History of the American New Left* (New York: Dodd, Mead, 1974), 142; Milton Viorst, *Fire in the Streets: America in the 1960s* (New York: Simon and Schuster, 1979), 429. "The Banners of Dissent," *Time* (vol. 90, no. 17), October 27, 1967.

20. Rubin quoted in Halstead, *Out Now!,* 316. Also see *Time,* "Banners of Dissent."

21. Halstead, 322.

22. Norman Mailer, *The Armies of the Night: History as a Novel, the Novel as History* (New York: New American Library, 1968), 108–109.

23. John Herbers, "Youths Dominate Capital Throng," *New York Times*, October 22, 1967, 58; E.W. Kenworthy, "Thousands Reach Capital to Protest Vietnam War," *New York Times*, October 21, 1967, 1; George C. Wilson, "Pentagon Mobilizes for March," *Washington Post*, October 21, 1967, A1. On the violent confrontations that ensued between the protesters, federal marshals and regular Army troops, see Jeremy Breslin, "Quiet Rally Turns Vicious," *Washington Post*, October 22, 1967, A1; William Chapman, "55,000 Rally Against War; GI's Repel Pentagon Charge," *Washington Post*, October 22, 1967, A1; Joseph Loftus, "Guards Repulse War Protesters at the Pentagon," *New York Times*, October 22, 1967, 1, 58; Laurence Stern, "Ugliness May Be Peace Protests' Lasting Image," *Washington Post*, October 22, 1967, A10; Tom Wells, *The War Within: America's Battle Over Vietnam* (Berkeley: University of California Press, 1994), 195–203; Ben. A. Franklin, "War Protesters Defy Deadline Seized in Capital," *New York Times*, October 23, 1967; Carl Bernstein and Robert G. Kaiser, "2000 Protesters Spend Night at Pentagon—Cold, Hopeful" *Washington Post*, October 22, 1967; Chapman, "Arrests End War Protest," *Washington Post*, October 23, 1967, A16; "The Banners of Dissent," *Time*.

24. Rubin quoted in Morrison and Morrison, *From Camelot to Kent State*, 287. Also see "The Banners of Dissent," *Time*.

25. J. Anthony Lukas, "Dissenters Focusing on Chicago," *New York Times*, August 19, 1968, 27.

26. Mark Kurlansky, *1968: The Year That Rocked the World* (New York: Ballantine, 2004), 273–274. Also see Allen Matusow, *The Unraveling of America: A History of Liberalism in the 1960s* (New York: Harper & Row, 1984), 413. Also see *Time*, "The Politics of Yip."

27. Rubin, quoted in Morrison and Morrison, *From Camelot to Kent State*, 287.

28. Rubin quoted Peck, *Uncovering the Sixties*, 109.

29. Mark Kurlansky, *1968*, 275–276; Todd Gitlin, *The Sixties: Years of Hope, Days of Rage* (New York: Bantam, 1987) 322; Matusow, *Unraveling of America*, 413; Also see Abbie Hoffman, *Soon to Be a Major Motion Picture* (New York: Perigee, 1980), 142–145; Mark Hamilton Lytle, *America's Uncivil War: The Sixties Era from Elvis to the Fall of Richard Nixon* (New York: Oxford University Press, 2006), 259–260; Maurice Isserman and Michael Kazin, *America Divided: The Civil War of the 1960s* (New York: Oxford University Press, 2000), 233; Hoffman, *Revolution for the Hell of It*, 106–108; Jerry Rubin, "Yippees are Coming, Coming, Coming to Chicago," *Liberation News Service* 48, March 1, 1968, 4 pages, p. 2; "Notes from a Yippizolean Era," *East Village Other*, vol. 3, no. 11, February 16–22, 1968, 8; Rubin, *Do It!*, 84. Lance Morrow, "1968: Like a Knife Blade: The Year That Severed Past from Future," *Time* (vol. 131, no. 2), January 11, 1988. Also see *Time*, "The Politics of Yip."

30. Gitlin, *The Sixties*, 328–329; Hoffman quoted in Kurlansky, *1968*, 275; The Walker Report: Daniel Walker, *Rights in Conflict: The Violent Confrontation of Demonstrators and Police in the Parks and Streets of Chicago During the Week of the Democratic National Convention of 1968* (New York: Bantam, 1968), 53; Farber,

Chicago '68, 170; Isserman and Kazin, *America Divided*, 233; Lytle, *America's Uncivil Wars*, 260–261. "Who Were the Protesters," *Time* (vol. 92, no. 10), September 6, 1968.

31. Hayden quoted in Matusow, *The Unraveling of America*, 415.

32. Robert Christgau, "Rock 'n' Revolution," essay originally published in *The Village Voice*, July 1969, http://www.robertchristgau.com/xg/bk-aow/revolut.php.

33. Royko quoted in Kurlansky, *1968*, 276.

34. Nicholas Von Hoffman, "Yippies Trot Out Candidate—A Pig," *Washington Post*, August 24, 1968, A5. Also see Hoffman, *Soon to Be a Major Motion Picture*, 144; Lytle, *America's Uncivil Wars*, 260.

35. Morrison and Morrison, *From Camelot to Kent State*, 288; "7 Yippies, Their Pig Seized at Rally," *Chicago Tribune*, August 24, 1968, A6.

36. Carl Ogelsby, *Ravens in the Storm: A Personal History of the 1960s Antiwar Movement* (New York: Scribner, 2008), 189.

37. Morrison and Morrison, *From Kent State to Camelot*, 289.

38. Farber, *Chicago '68*, 146; Gitlin, *The Sixties*, 321; Lytle, *America's Uncivil Wars*, 258–259; Frank Kusch, *Battleground Chicago: The Police and the 1968 Democratic National Convention* (Chicago: University of Chicago Press, 2008), 53, 55–56; Hoffman, *Soon to Be a Major Motion Picture*, 148; Walker, *Rights in Conflict*, 1.

39. Jackson quoted in Kurlansky, *1968*, 273.

40. Lockeridge quoted in Kusch, *Battleground Chicago*, 55.

41. "Dementia in the Second City," *Time* (vol. 92, no. 10), September 6, 1968.

42. On Daley, see Irwin Unger, *The Movement: A History of the American New Left* (New York: Dodd, Mead, 1974), 144.

43. Individuals quoted in Kusch, *Battleground Chicago*, 56.

44. Jean Genet, "The Members of the Assembly," in E.A. Swingrover, ed., *The Counterculture Reader* (New York: Pearson Longman, 2004), 121–122. For Daley's "defense preparations" see Kusch, *Battleground Chicago*, 52–53; Lytle, *America's Uncivil Wars*, 258; Walker, *Rights in Conflict*, 101–102; Farber, *Chicago '68*, 154; Isserman and Kazin, *America Divided*, 233; Adam Cohen and Elizabeth Taylor, *American Pharaoh: Mayor Richard J. Daley: His Battle For Chicago and the Nation* (Boston: Little, Brown, 2000), 462–463; *New York Times*, August 25, 1968, 4E. Also see *Time*, "Dementia in the Second City," and "Daley City Under Siege," *Time* (vol. 92, no. 9), August 30, 1968.

45. Peck, *Uncovering the Sixties*, 109.

46. Daley quoted in Isserman and Kazin, and also in Farber, *Chicago '68*, 160.

47. Tom Brokaw, *Boom! Voices of the Sixties: Personal Reflections on the '60s and Today* (New York: Random House, 2007), 97–98.

48. Colsky, Bellows, Latanzio, Grant Brown, and Norm Nelson, quoted in Kusch, *Battleground Chicago*, 50.

49. Peck, *Uncovering the Sixties*, 109.

50. *Ibid.*, 107.

51. Wenner quoted in Peck, 108.

52. *Ibid.*

53. Christgau, "Rock 'n' Revolution," 5.

54. Peck, *Uncovering the Sixties*, 118.

55. Walker quoted in Brokaw, *Boom*, 101.

56. Hayden quoted in Matusow, *The Unraveling of America*, 414. See p. 412 for his comment on the fractured New Left.

57. "The New Radical," *Time* (vol. 89, no. 17), April 28, 1967.

58. James T. Patterson, *Grand Expectations: The United States, 1945–1974* (New York: Oxford University Press, 2003), 633; Gitlin, *The Sixties*, 264–274. J. Edgar Hoover to the President, October 26, 1967 (Lyndon Baines Johnson Presidential Library, University of Texas at Austin), White House Central Files, Box 64C. Hereafter cited as (LBJL-WHCF). Reston and Mailer quoted in Lytle, *America's Uncivil Wars*, 245.

59."Who Were the Protesters?" *Time* (vol. 92, no. 10), September 6, 1968.

60. Dellinger quoted in Terry Southern, "Grooving in Chi," originally published in November 1968 and reproduced in Terry Southern, *Now Dig This: The Unspeakable Writings of Terry Southern, 1950–1995* (New York: Grove, 2001), 118–129. Dellinger quoted on p. 120. Also see Lytle, *America's Uncivil Wars*, 259. Brokaw, *Boom!*, 98.

61. Lytle, *America's Uncivil Wars*, 259. Also see Kirkpatrick Sale, *SDS* (New York: Random House, 1973), 473–475; Tim Findley, "Tom Hayden," Interview Part 1, *Rolling Stone*, October 21, 1972, 50–51; Hayden quoted in *Time*, "Daley City Under Siege."

62. Hoffman, *Revolution For the Hell of It*, 107; John Schultz, *No One Was Killed: The Chicago Democratic National Convention, August 1968* (Chicago: University of Chicago Press, 1969; 2009 edition used for this book), 4; Farber, *Chicago '68*, 151; Gitlin, *The Sixties*, 319, 323; Kusch, *Battleground Chicago*, 51–52; Walker, *Rights in Conflict*, 31–42; Lytle; Lowenstein quoted in Gitlin, *The Sixties*, 324.

63. Hoffman, *Soon to Be a Major Motion Picture*, 150; Hoffman, *Revolution for the Hell of It*, 107; Davis quoted in Kusch, *Battleground Chicago*, 55.

64. Gitlin, *The Sixties*, 327.

65. *Ibid.*, 327–328.

66. Schultz, *No One Was Killed*, 81–92; Southern, *Now Dig This*, 121–122; Matusow, *The Unraveling of America*, 418; "Hundreds of Protesters Block Traffic in Chicago," *New York Times*, August 26, 1968, 25.

67. Walker, *Rights in Conflict*, 147.

68. Von Hoffman and the *Washington Post* quoted in Terry Anderson, *The Sixties* (New York: Addison Wesley Longman, 1999), 122.

69. Patterson, *Grand Expectations*, 695–696; Kurlansky, *1968*, 278–279; Nancy Zaroulis and Gerald Sullivan, *Who Spoke Up? American Protest Against the War in Vietnam, 1963–1975* (Garden City, NY: Doubleday, 1984), 186–187; Walker, *Rights in Conflict*, 166, 182, 187; Southern, *Now Dig This*, 122–123.

70. Matusow, *The Unraveling of America*, 419; Gitlin, *The Sixties*, 331; Kurlansky, *1968*, 280–281; McCarthy quoted in Kusch, *Battleground Chicago*, 57.

71. Matusow.

72. Hayes quoted in Lewis Chester, Godfrey Hodgson, and Bruce Page, *An American Melodrama: The Presidential Campaign of 1968* (New York: Viking, 1969), 580.

73. Matusow, *The Unraveling of America*, 419.

74. Gitlin, *The Sixties*, 332; Kurlansky, *1968*, 281–282; Lytle, *America's Uncivil Wars*, 261; *New York Times* quoted in Matusow, *The Unraveling of America*, 419;

Ogelsby, *Ravens in the Storm*, 196; Farber, *Chicago '68*, 195–197; Walker, *Rights in Conflict*, 239; Anthony J. Lukas, "Hundreds Injured; 178 Are Arrested as Guardsmen Join in Using Tear Gas," *New York Times*, August 29, 1968, 1, 23; Southern *Now Dig This*, 128–129.

75. Gitlin, 333; Kurlansky, 282; Lytle, 261–262; Matusow, 420; Farber; Zaroulis and Sullivan, *Who Spoke Up?*, 194; Southern, 129; *Newsweek*, September 9, 1968, 24, 41; Lukas, "Hundreds,"1; "In The Streets: Tear Gas and Clubs," *Washington Post*, A1.

76. Quoted in Kusch, *Battleground Chicago*, 151.

77. Quoted in Peck, *Uncovering the Sixties*, 106.

78. Southern, *Now Dig This*, 123.

79. Larner quoted in Bloom and Breines, *"Takin' It to the Streets,"* 431.

80. Lance Morrow, "1968: Like a Knife Blade." Also see Morrow, "The Whole World Was Watching," *Time* (vol. 148, no. 1), August 26, 1996.

81. Huntley and others quoted in Anderson, *The Sixties*, 123; also see John C. McWilliams, *The 1960s Cultural Revolution* (Westport, CT: Greenwood, 2000), 55; White quoted in Lytle, *America's Uncivil Wars*, 263.

82. Wicker and *Newsweek* quoted in Michael W. Flamm, *Law and Order: Street Crime, Civil Unrest, and the Crisis of Liberalism in the 1960s* (New York: Columbia University Press, 2005), 158–159; "Dementia in the Second City," *Time*, September 6, 1968. Rather incident and Cronkite comment in Anderson, *The Sixties*, 122.

83. "A Week of Grievances," *Time* (vol. 92, no. 10), September 6, 1968.

84. Genet quoted in Swingrover, *The Counterculture Reader*, 124.

85. For the Ribicoff-Daley confrontation and exchange of words, see Zaroulis and Sullivan, *Who Spoke Up?"*; 196; Gitlin, *The Sixties*, 334; Matusow, *The Unraveling of America*, 421; Kurlansky, *1968*, 283.

86. Lowenstein quoted in Anderson, *The Sixties*, 123.

87. Severeid quoted in *Time*, "A Week of Grievances."

88. Genet quoted in Swingrover, *The Counterculture Reader*, 124.

89. Morrow, "The Whole World Was Watching."

90. Muskie quoted in Gitlin, *The Sixties*, 338.

91. Humphrey quoted in Kurlansky, *1968*, 285.

92. "Refighting Chicago," *Time* (vol. 92, no. 13), September 27, 1968.

93. Rubin quoted in Viorst, *Fire in the Streets*, 459; *Time*, "Who Were the Protesters?"

94. Genet quoted in Swingrover, *The Counterculture Reader*, 125.

95. Gitlin, *The Sixties*, 326 note; "Chicago Examined: Anatomy of a Police Riot," *Time* (vol. 92, no. 23), December 6, 1968.

96. Davis quoted in "Editorial: The Decline and Fall of the Democratic Party," *Ramparts*, vol. 7, no. 5, September 28, 1968, 20–42.

97. Albert quoted in Anderson, *The Sixties*, 124.

98. Walker Paine to the President, August 29, 1968, Box 66; Romney S. Philpott to the President, August 29, 1968, Box 67; Mrs. C.R. Gardner to the President, August 29, 1968, Box 67 (LBJPL-WHCF).

99. Kusch, *Battleground Chicago*, 155; Chicagoan and Wallace quoted in Anderson, *The Sixties*, 124.

100. Hayden quoted in Douglas Linder, "The Chicago Seven, 1969–1970." http://jurist.law.pitt.edu/trials2.htm (now inactive).

Chapter 12

1. Robert Santelli, *Aquarius Rising: The Rock Festival Years* (New York: Dell, 1980), 105–109, 266–67; Paul Beeman, "Music Fans Stay Orderly Despite Heat, Wine, Drugs," July 6, 1969, *The Atlanta Journal and Constitution*, 2; Beeman, "Pop's the Thing Despite Heat at Hampton," July 7, 1969, *The Atlanta Journal and Constitution*, 4; Tom Wilk, "Look Back: 1969's Atlantic City Pop Festival," August 17, 2011, *Atlantic City Weekly*, http://www.atlanticcityweekly.com; Guy Sterling, "The Atlantic City Pop Festival: The Festival That Time Forgot," August 1, 2004, *Atlantic City Press*; Paula Span, "40,000 Dance in Rain as Popfest Winds it Up," August 4, 1969, *Atlantic City Press*, 1–2; Jon Katz, "Hippies In and Out Like Breeze: Feared Trouble Didn't Come Off," August 5, 1969, *Atlantic City Press*, 2, http://atlanticcitypopfestival.com/webdoc_005.htm (now inactive).

2. Robert Stephen Spitz, *Barefoot in Babylon: The Creation of the Woodstock Music Festival, 1969* (New York: Viking, 1979), Chapters 1–3; Elliot Tiber, "How Woodstock Happened," Middletown, *New York Times Herald Record*, Woodstock Commemorative Edition, 1994. http://www.edjusticeonline.com/woodstock/history/index.htm, 1–2; Also see Tiber, "How Woodstock Happened: Part I—Woodstock Story. www.woodstockstory.com/how-woodstock-happened-1.html. "Rocky Road to Fame, if Not Fortune: Young Impresarios Drop a Bundle in Staging Biggest Rock-Music Festival, but Win a Place in the Business Scene, *Business Week*, August 20, 1969, 78–80.

3. Tiber, 3, 7, 8; Also see Louis Calta, "Peaceful Rock Fete Planned Upstate," *New York Times*, June 27, 1969, 24; "Woodstock Pop-Rock Fete Hits Snag," *New York Times*, July 17, 1969, 56; Richard F. Shepard, "Woodstock Festival Vows to Carry On," *New York Times*, July 18, 1969, 16; Shepard, "Pop Rock Festival Finds New Home," *New York Times*, July 23, 1969, 30; McCandlish Phillips, "Rock Festival at Bethel Defeats New Challenges," *New York Times*, August 13, 1969, 38; Roger Latzgo, "Woodstock: Two Score Years Ago," www.rogerlatzgo.com/pdf/woodstock.pdf. 1; Andrew Kopkind, "Coming of Age in Aquarius," in Alexander Bloom and Wini Breines, eds., *"Takin' It to the Streets: A Sixties Reader* (New York: Oxford University Press, 1995), 613.

4. Tiber, "How Woodstock Happened," 3, 7–8.

5. *Ibid.*, 5, 10.

6. Shepard, "Pop Rock Festival Finds New Home"; Tiber, 10.

7. Tiber, "How Woodstock Happened," 7, 12.

8. "Max Yasgur: Woodstock Patron," *Rolling Stone* (no. 130) March 15, 1973, 10.

9. Tiber, "How Woodstock Happened," 4.

10. Barnard Collier, "200,000 Thronging to Rock Festival Jam Roads Upstate," *New York Times*, August 16, 1969, 1, 31; B.J. Phillips, "Thousands Rolling in for Woodstock Rock," *Washington Post*, August 15, 1969, 12.

11. Lacey Fosburgh, "346 Policemen Quit Music Festival," *New York Times*, August 15, 1969, 22; David Fricke, "Woodstock Remembered: Minor Epiphanies and Momentary Bummer," *Rolling Stone*, August 24, 1989.

12. Phillips, "That Rocky Road," *Washington Post*, August 15, 1969, 6.

13. Joan Morrison and Robert K. Morrison, *From Camelot to Kent State: The Sixties in the Words of Those*

Who Live It (New York: Oxford University Press, 1987), 198.

14. Collier, "200,000 Thronging to Rock Festival Jam Roads Upstate," 31.

15. Jade Stone, "Woodstock 1969 Revisited," http://greenjadestone.com/Woodstock1969.pdf. 1 (now inactive).

16. Spitz, *Barefoot in Babylon*, 400–403; Tiber, "How Woodstock Happened," 6; Stone, 6; Morrison and Morrison, *From Camelot to Kent State*, 198; Collier, "200,000 Thronging to Rock Festival Jam Roads Upstate," 31; "Coming of Age in Aquarius," in Bloom and Wini Breines eds., *"Takin' It to the Streets*, 614; Collier, "300,000 at Folk-Rock Fair Camp Out in a Sea of Mud," *New York Times*, August 17, 1969, 80; "Promoter Baffled That Festival Drew Such a Big Crowd," *New York Times*, August 17, 1969, 80.

17. Tiber, 13.

18. Spitz, *Barefoot in Babylon*, 399–405; Richie Havens and Steve Davidowitz, *They Can't Hide Us Anymore* (New York: Spike/Avon, 1999), 126–127; Stone, "Woodstock 1969 Revisited," 10; The 60's Official Site, "Woodstock," http://the60sofficialsite.com.

19. Quoted in Terry Anderson, *The Sixties* (New York: Addison Wesley Longman, 1999), 146. Also see "Woodstock: Like It Was in Words of Participants at Musical Fair," *New York Times*, August 25, 1969, 30.

20. Anderson.

21. *Ibid.*

22. "The Message Of History's Biggest Happening," *Time* (vol. 94, no. 9), August 29, 1969. Also see Havens and Davidowitz, *They Can't Hide Us Anymore*, 126–127.

23. *Woodstock: 3 Days of Peace and Music: The Director's Cut.* Two-disc 40th Anniversary Edition, Warner Home Video, Disc 1; Stone, "Woodstock 1969 Revisited," 11.

24. Stone, 18; Bloom and Breines, eds., *"Takin' It to the Streets*, 611; Collier, "300,000 at Folk-Rock Fair Camp Out in a Sea of Mud," 80; Patrick Lydon, "'A Joyful Confirmation That Good Things Can Happen Here,'" *The Sunday New York Times*, Arts and Leisure, August 24, 1969, D16.

25. Hank Bordowitz, *Bad Moon Rising: The Unauthorized History of Credence Clearwater Revival* (Chicago: Chicago Review Press, 2007), 390.

26. Craig McGregor, "Woodstock: A Desperate Fear for the Future?" *New York Times*, Arts and Leisure, August 19, 1970, 99.

27. Ralph Marvin Abee, "Symbolism of Bethel," Letters to the Editor, *New York Times*, August 26, 1969, 46.

28. Herbert London, "Romantic Remembrances of Woodstock Misguided. *Newsmax*, August 31, 2009. www.newsmax.com.

29. William E. Farrell, "19-Hour Concert Ends Bethel Fair," *New York Times*, August 19, 1969, 1, 34; Lauren Onkey, "Voodoo Child: Jimi Hendrix and the Politics of Race in the Sixties," in Peter Braunstein and Michael William Doyle, eds., *Imagine Nation: The American Counterculture of the 1960s and 70s* (New York: Routledge, 2002), 189.

30. Onkey, 190; also see Note 3, 209; *Woodstock: 3 Days of Peace and Music*, disc 2; Morrison and Morrison, *From Camelot to Kent State*, 200.

31. Onkey; Morrison and Morrison.

32. "Woodstock: Like It Was," *New York Times*, August 25, 1969, 30.

33. Collier, "300,000 at Music Fair; Mud Plentiful and Food Scarce," *New York Times,* August 17, 1969, 80; Fosburgh, "346 Policemen Quit Music Festival," 22; "Woodstock: Like it Was in Words of Participants at Music Fair," 30; Morrison and Morrison, *From Camelot to Kent State,* 198; Stone, "Woodstock 1969 Revisited," 8, 12; Geoff Storm, "Historical Memory and the Woodstock Legacy," www.archives.nysed.gov.

34. Collier; "Woodstock Like It Was."

35. Wavy Gravy quoted in Geoff Storm, "Historical Memory and the Woodstock Legacy,"4; Collier.

36. Bloom and Breines, *"Takin' It to the Streets,"* 611.

37. Bonnie Packer and David Pactor, "The Importance of Woodstock," *The Quicksilver Times,* April 3–13, 1970, vol. 2, no. 6, p. 19.

38. "Nightmare in the Catskills," Editorial, *New York Times,* August 18, 1969, 34.

39. Fosburgh, "346 Policemen Quit Music Festival," 22.

40. Collier, "200,000 Thronging to Rock Festival Jam Roads Upstate," 31; Wavy Gravy (Hugh Romney) quoted in "Hog Farming at Woodstock," in Lynda Rosen Orbst, ed., *The Sixties: The Decade Remembered Now by the People Who Lived It Then* (New York: Rolling Stone, 1977), 274–279;

41. Collier; Bloom and Breines, *"Takin' It to the Streets,"* 614.

42. "Bethel Pilgrims Smoke 'Grass' And Some Take LSD to 'Groove,'" *New York Times,* August 18, 1969, 25; Collier, "200,000 Thronging to Rock Festival Jam Roads Upstate," 80; William E. Farrell, "19-Hour Concert Ends Bethel Fair," 34.

43. Bloom and Breines, *"Takin' It to the Streets,"* 615–616. Also see Stone, "Woodstock 1969 Revisited," 9; and "Woodstock: Like It Was in Words of Participants at Musical Fair," 30; and "Bethel Pilgrims Smoke 'Grass' and Some Take LSD to 'Groove.'"

44. "The Message of History's Biggest Happening, *Time,* August 29, 1969.

45. *Ibid.*; Collier, "300,000 at Folk-Rock Fair Camp Out in a Sea of Mud," 80; Collier, "Tired Rock Fans Begin Exodus from Rock Fair," *New York Times,* August 18, 1969, 1, 25; Stone, "Woodstock 1969 Revisited," 9; Farrell, "19-Hour Concert Ends Bethel Fair," *New York Times,* August 19, 1969, 1, 34.

46. Michael T. Kaufman, "Generation Gap Bridged as Monticello Residents Aid Courteous Festival Patrons," *New York Times,* August 18, 1969, 25; Farrell, 34.

47. Farrell; also see "Woodstock: Like It Was in Words of Participants at Musical Fair," *New York Times,* August 25, 1969, 80.

48. Quoted in Timothy Miller, *The Hippies and American Values* (Knoxville: University of Tennessee Press, 1991), 83.

49. *Ibid.*

50. Quoted in Anderson, *The Sixties,* 146–147.

51. Editorial, "Morning After Bethel," *The New York Times,* August 19, 1969, 42; "Nightmare in the Catskills," 34; Patrick Lydon, "A Joyful Confirmation that Good Things Can Happen Here," *The New York Times,* Arts and Leisure Section, August 24, 1969, D 16.

52. Storm, "Historical Memory and the Woodstock Legacy," 4, 5; Fricke, "Woodstock Remembered."

53. "The Message of History's Biggest Happening," *Time,* August 29, 1969.

54. Lerner and Marcus quoted in Miller, *The Hippies and American Values,* 82–83.

55. "The Message of History's Biggest Happening."

56. Geoff Storm, "Historical Memory and the Woodstock Legacy." Also see Jane Ganahl, "Woodstock '99: The Day the Music Died," *San Francisco Chronicle,* July 28, 1999. Ganahl asserted that although a variety of factors coalesced to produce the disaster, ranging from the heat to vendor price gouging, to "bad apples" in the crowd of 250,000, she contends that the most culpable for inciting the riots were the bands, most notably Kid Rock, Insane Clown Posse, Red Hot Chili Peppers, and most especially Limp Bizkit and the lead singer Fred Durst, who, in effect, almost single-handedly started the melee by encouraging fans to "mosh crazily" toward the stage. www.sfgate.com. Also see Rob Sheffield, "Woodstock '99: Rage Against the Latrine," *Rolling Stone,* September 2, 2009, http://www.rollingstone.com. For Woodstock 1994, see Christopher John Farley, "Woodstock Suburb," *Time* (vol. 144, no. 8), August 22, 1994.

57. Loder quoted in Donald Schwab, "Woodstock 1999." donaldschwab.com/Woodstock1999/Woodstock 1999.htm.

58. Storm, "Historical Memory and the Woodstock Legacy," 12.

59. Hilgardt quoted in Miller, *The Hippies and American Values,* 83.

60. Yasgur quoted in Farrell, "19-Hour Concert Ends Bethel Fair," *The New York Times,* August 19, 1969, 34.

61. Quoted in Morrison and Morrison, *From Camelot to Kent State,* 202; London, "Romantic Remembrances of Woodstock Misguided."

62. Gene Katz, "Woodstock at 25." http://magazine.14850.com.

63. Ellen Sander, "Woodstock Music and Art Fair: The Ultimate Rock Experience," *Saturday Review* (vol. 52, no. 39), September 27, 1969, 59, 65–66.

64. Ellen Willis, "Rock Etc.: Woodstock," *The New Yorker* (vol. 45, no. 6.), September 6, 1969, 121–124.

65. Jeff Samuels, "Another Woodstock Unlikely as Coin, Civic Problems Squeeze Promoters," *Variety* (vol. 258, no. 12), August 8, 1970, 85, 88; "Rock Festivals: Groovy but No Gravy," *Business Week* (no. 2136), August 8, 1970, 20–21; Thomas Barry, "Why Can't There Be Another Woodstock? After a Year the Music Business Learns How Hard It Is to Restage a Legend," *Look* (vol. 34), August 25, 1970, 28, 30; Bill Graham and Robert Greenfield, *Bill Graham Presents: My Life Inside Rock and Out* (New York: Doubleday, 1992), 289; John Glatt, *Rage & Roll: Bill Graham and the Selling of Rock* (New York: Birch Lane Press/Carol, 1993), 138–139; Rollo May, "An Opinion: On Bethel and After; The Catskillian Love Feast on the Couch," *Mademoiselle* (vol. 70), November 1969, 28, 40; Margaret Mead, "Woodstock in Retrospect," *Redbook Magazine* (vol. 124, no. 3), January 1970, 30, 32.

66. Jon Pareles, "Woodstock: A Moment of Muddy Grace," *New York Times,* August 5, 2009. www.nytimes.com/2009/08/09/arts/music/09pare.html?_r=0.

67. Ibid.

Chapter 13

1. Steven V. Roberts, "Charles Manson: One Man's Family," *New York Times Magazine,* January 4, 1970, 10.

2. Doug Linder, "The Charles Manson (Tate-LaBianca Murder) Trial." http://law2.unkc.edu/faculty/projects/trials/manson/mansonaccount.html (now inactive).

3. Manson quoted in David Talbot, *Season of the Witch: Enchantment, Terror, and Deliverance in the City of Love* (New York: Free, 2012), 132; also see Tom Snyder's 1981 interview with Manson, transcribed by Aaron Bredlau. http://www.charliemanson.com/tom-snyder-1981.htm (now inactive).

4. Talbot, *Season of the Witch,* 132; Vincent Bugliosi and Curt Gentry, *Helter Skelter: The True Story of the Manson Murders* (New York: W. W. Norton, 1974), 163–174. Also see Paul O'Neil, "The Wreck of a Monstrous 'Family,'" *Life,* December 19, 1969, 20–31.

5. O'Neil.

6. Roger Smith quoted in O'Neil.

7. "The Memoirs of Squeaky Fromme," *Time* (vol. 106, no. 11), September 15, 1975. Also see "The Girl Who Almost Killed Ford," same issue; O'Neil, "The Wreck of a Monstrous 'Family'"; Talbot, *Season of the Witch,* 133.

8. Roberts quoted in Olney, "Manson: An Oral History."

9. Quoted in O'Neil, "The Wreck of a Monstrous 'Family.'"

10. Smith quoted in O'Neil, "The Wreck of a Monstrous 'Family.'"

11. Charles Watson, *Will You Die for Me?* As told to Chaplain Ray Hoekstra, Cross Roads Publication online books, 1978. Chapter 8: "Magical Mystery Tour."

12. Roger Smith quoted in O'Neil, "The Wreck of a Monstrous 'Family.'"

13. Watson, *Will You Die for Me?* Chapter 8: "Magical Mystery Tour," Chapter 12: "Piggies."

14. Fromme quoted in "The Memoirs of Squeaky Fromme," *Time.*

15. Talbot, *Season of the Witch,* 133; Bugliosi and Gentry, *Helter Skelter,* 163–174; O'Neil, "The Wreck of a Monstrous 'Family.'"

16. Watson, *Will You Die for Me?* Chapter 11: "Revolution/Revelation."

17. Paul Watkins with Guillermo Soledad, *My Life with Charles Manson* (New York: Bantam, 1979), Chapter 12.

18. Share quoted in 2009 documentary *Manson,* Cineflix Productions, et al. http://www.cineflixproductions.com/shows/47-Manson. Interestingly, other than the *White Album,* all of the Beatles' previous and subsequent LPs were thematically all-you-need-is-love homilies, and thus the *White Album* was a momentary aberration but a tragically sufficient anomaly to excite an aberrant individual like Manson to go on a rampage. Ironically, if any band's music should have been an "inspiration" to Manson to bring Helter Skelter, that "honor" should have gone to the Doors, a group right in Manson's own backyard and a band dedicated to "anything about revolt, disorder, chaos, about activity that appears to have no meaning," as Jim Morrison told an interviewer. Thus, the Doors, not the Beatles, would seem to have been more in tune with Manson's acid theology and his Boschian-visions of a world run amok.

19. Watkins with Soledad, Chapter 13.

20. Watson, *Will You Die for Me,* Chapter 11: "Revolution/Revelation."

21. *Ibid.*; Watkins with Soledad, *My Life with Charles Manson,* Chapter Twelve.

22. Watson, *Will You Die for Me,* Chapter 11: "Revolution/Revelation.

23. Watkins with Soledad, *My Life with Charles Manson,* Chapter Fifteen; Watson, *Will You Die for Me,* Chapter 12: "Piggies."

24. Steven V. Roberts, "Actress Is Among 5 Slain at Home in Beverly Hills," *New York Times,* August 9, 1969; Marie Balfour, "Charles Manson and the Tate-La Bianca Murders: A Family Portrait," in Frankie Y. Bailey and Steven Chermak, eds., *Famous American Crimes and Trials,* vol. IV: 1960–1980. "The Demon of Death Valley," *Time* 94, no. 24, December 12, 1969; Watson, *Will You Die for Me?* Chapter 13: "You Were Only Waiting for This"; Bugliosi and Gentry, *Helter Skelter,* 33, 75–77; 91–96; 99–113; Susan Atkins with Bob Slosser, *Child of Satan, Child of God* (Plainfield, NJ: Logos, 1977), 94–120; Ed Sanders, *The Family* (New York: Avon, 1972), 184; Watson, *Will You Die for Me?* Chapter 14: "Helter Skelter I (August 8–9)." Although loaded on speed and obviously crazed out of his mind, the most accurate and graphic account of the murderous bloodbath at the Tate household was probably that of Tex Watson, who did most of the actually killing, "ably assisted" at times by the women, most notably Susan Atkins. Also see Roberts, "Actress Is Among 5 Slain at Home in Beverly Hills"; "The Demon of Death Valley," *Time;* Linder, "The Charles Manson (Tate-La Bianca Murder) Trial"; Balfour, "Charles Manson and the Tate-La Bianca Murders: A Family Portrait"; Olney, "Manson: An Oral History"; Bugliosi and Gentry, *Helter Skelter,* 28–38; 84–90; 176–184; 258–269; 341–344; 356–361; 463–468. For the La Bianca murders, again, the most gruesome but accurate retelling is Watson's. See Chapter 15: "Helter Skelter II (August 9–10.)" Also see all of the above accounts, except for Bugliosi and Gentry, see pages 22–25; 42–48; 206; 297; 380; 404; 406–407; 433.

25. Watson, *Will You Die for Me?* Chapter 6: "Gentle Children, with Flowers in Their Hair."

26. Andrea Sachs, "An Interview with Manson Prosecutor Vincent Bugliosi," *Time,* August 7, 2009. http://www.time.com.

27. "Hippie" quoted in Terry Anderson, *The Sixties* (New York: Addison Wesley Longman, 1999), 148.

28. "Hippies and Violence," *Time* (vol. 94, no. 24), December 12, 1969.

29. *Ibid.*

30. Karlene Faith, *The Long Prison Journey of Leslie Van Houten: Life Beyond the Cult* (Boston: Northeastern University Press, 2001), 9, 109–110.

31. Jess Bravin, *Squeaky: The Life and Times of Lynette Alice Fromme* (New York: St. Martin's, 1997), 112.

32. Quoted in Anderson, *The Sixties,* 148; *Express Times* quoted in Abe Peck, *Uncovering the Sixties: The Life and Times of the Underground Press* (New York: Citadel, 1991), 227.

33. Felton and Dalton, "Charles Manson: The Incredible Story of the Most Dangerous Man Alive: Year of the Fork, Night of the Hunter: Book One," *Rolling Stone,* June 25, 1970, 26.

34. David Dalton, "If Christ Came Back as a Con Man: Or How I Started Out Thinking Charles Manson Was Innocent and Almost Ended Up Dead," *Gadfly,* October 1998. Reprinted at *Gadflyonline.* http//www.gadflyonline.com/archive/October98/archive-manson.html.

35. *Ibid.*

36. Sanders quoted in Peck, *Uncovering the Sixties,* 228.

37. *Ibid.* Also see Rubin quoted in Todd Gitlin, *The Sixties: Years of Hope, Days of Rage* (New York: Bantam, 1987), 404.

38. Robert Christgau, "The Rolling Stones: Can't Get No Satisfaction." Original essay appeared in *Newsday,* July 1972, and in his collection of essays on rock and roll music, *Any Old Way You Choose It: Rock and Other Pop Music, 1967–1973* (New York: Cooper Square, 1973, 2000). http://www.robertchristgau.com/xg/bk-aow/altamont.php. Also see Todd Gitlin, *The Sixties: Years of Hope, Days of Rage* (New York: Bantam, 1987), 199; "The Stones and the Triumph of Marsyas," *Time* (vol. 100, no. 3), July 17, 1972. Oldham quoted in David P. Szatmary, *Rockin' in Time: A Social History of Rock and Roll* (Upper Saddle River, NJ: Pearson/Prentice Hall, 2007), 124; Harrison quoted on page 126.

39. Christgau; "The Stones and the Triumph of Marsyas."

40. *Ibid.*

41. *Ibid.* In this author's opinion, the best collection of Stones' songs, reflecting their evolution from a working-class, low-brow rhythm and blues band to the development of their own unique, unmistakably "Stones' sound," is the two–CD set, *The Rolling Stones: Hot Rocks, 1964–1971* (Abkco). Most books and articles on the band are anecdotal, uncritical, and campy. However, there are a few that have historical and socio-cultural substance, such as Stanley Booth's *Dance with the Devil: The Rolling Stones and Their Times* (New York: Random House, 1984) and *The True Adventures of the Rolling Stones* (New York: Vintage, 1985); Phillip Norman, *Sympathy for the Devil: The Rolling Stones Story* (New York: Simon & Schuster, 1984); and Tony Sanchez, *Up and Down with the Rolling Stones* (New York: American Library, 1979).

42. Talbot, *Season of the Witch,* 136.

43. Booth and Richards quoted in Rob Kirkpatrick, "The Day the Music Died? The Altamont Free Concert 40 Years Later," December 6, 2009, *The Huffington Post.* http://www.huffingtonpost.com.

44. Christgau, "Can't Get No Satisfaction."

45. Michael Lydon, "The Doors: 'You could call us erotic politicians,'" first published in the *New York Times,* December 1968. Republished in *The Guardian,* May 22, 2013. http://www.theguardian.com.

46. Quoted in Herbert London, *Closing the Circle: A Cultural History of the Rock Revolution* (Chicago: Nelson Hall, 1984), 11.

47. Lydon, "The Doors." Also see "Pop Music: Swimming to the Moon," *Time* (vol. 90, no. 21), November 24, 1967.

48. Lydon; "Pop Music: Swimming to the Moon."

49. Albert Goldman, "The Emergence of Rock," in Gerald Howard, ed., *The Sixties* (New York: Washington Square, 1982), 363, 360.

50. Jim Hopkins and Danny Sugerman, *No One Here Gets Out Alive: The Biography of Jim Morrison* (New York: Warner, 1980), 284.

51. www.youtube.com. Also see Sterling Whitaker, "42 Years Ago: Jim Morrison Plays Final Show with the Doors," December 12, 2012. ultimateclassicrock.com/jim-morrison-plays-final-show-with-the-doors/.

52. Stephen Davis, *Jim Morrison: Life, Death, Legend* (New York: Gotham, 2005), 472; Brad Olsen, *Sacred Places Europe: 108 Destinations* (San Francisco: CCC, 2007), 105.

53. Michael Lydon, *Rock Folk: Portraits from the Rock 'n' Roll Pantheon* (New York: Citadel, 2000), 308. Also see Mark Hamilton Lytle, *America's Uncivil War: The Sixties Era: From Elvis to the Fall of Richard Nixon* (New York: Oxford University Press, 2006), 336.

54. Benjy Eisen, "Rolling Stones Tour Manager Sam Cutler Finally Tells His Side of the Altamont Fiasco." www.spinner.com (now inactive). However, a similar if not at times verbatim interview Eisen did with Cutler in Altamont's aftermath can be found at rocksoff.org/cgi-bin/messageboard/YaBB.pl?num=1270342837/2.

55. Talbot, *Season of the Witch,* 122–130. For the concert promoters' difficulty in finding a venue, see Dennis McNally, *A Long Strange Trip: The Inside History of the Grateful Dead* (New York: Broadway, 2002), 332–342.

56. Lydon, *Rock Folk,* 307. Also see, Lester Bangs, Reny Brown, John Burks, Sammy Egan, Michael Goodwin, Geoffrey Link, Greil Marcus, John Morthland, Eugene Schoenfeld, Patrick Thomas, and Langdon Winner, "The Rolling Stones Disaster at Altamont: Let It Bleed," *Rolling Stone,* January 21, 1970.

57. Jagger quoted in Bangs, Brown, Burks.

58. Carter quoted in Bangs, Brown, Burks. Also see Robert Santelli, *Aquarius Rising: The Rock Festival Years* (New York: Dell, 1980), 168.

59. Kirkpatrick, "The Day The Music Died." Russell quoted in Ethan Russell, "The Rolling Stones at Altamont: The Day the Music Died," December 2, 2009. http://www.telegraph.co.uk.

60. Bangs, Brown, Burks, et al., "Let It Bleed."

61. Dryden quoted in Kirkpatrick, "The Day the Music Died."

62. Ralph Gleason, "Aquarius Wept," originally published in *Esquire,* August 1970 issue. Republished online August 12, 2009, at http://www.esquire.com/news-politics/a6197/Altamont-1969-aquarius-wept-0870.

63. Lydon, *Rock Folk,* 309. Also see Lester Bangs, Brown, Burks, et al., "Let It Bleed."

64. Scully quoted in David Curry, "Deadly Day for the Rolling Stones," December 5, 2009. Account republished in its entirety at http://davrosky.blogspot.com/2012/06/altamont-what-really-happened.html.

65. Eisen, "Sam Cutler."

66. Talbot, *Season of the Witch,* 137.

67. Curry, "Deadly Day for the Rolling Stones"; Rob Kirkpatrick, *1969: The Year Everything Changed* (New York: Skyhorse, 2009), 257.

68. Bangs, Brown, Burks, et al., "Let It Bleed."

69. Lydon, *Rock Folk,* 309–311. Also see Lydon quoted in Ethan Russell, *Let It Bleed: The Rolling Stones, Altamont, and the End of the Sixties* (New York: Springboard, 2009), 184.

70. Slick quoted in Barbara Rowes, *Grace Slick: The Biography* (New York: Doubleday, 1980), 155–157.

71. Richards quoted in John Burks, "Rock & Roll's Worst Day: The Aftermath of Altamont," originally published in *Rolling Stone,* February 7, 1970. Republished online July 22, 2008, at http://www.rollingstone.com.

72. Taylor quoted in Bangs, Brown, Burks, et al., "Let It Bleed."

73. Fine quoted in *ibid.*

74. *Ibid.*

75. Dodge quoted in P. Joseph Potocki, "Hippie Ar-

mageddon." http://sfbaytimeless.com/?p=5545. Also see Curry, "Deadly Day for the Rolling Stones"; Santana quoted in Bangs, Brown, Burks, et al., "Let It Bleed."

76. Kirkpatrick, "The Day the Music Died"; Curry, "Deadly Day for the Rolling Stones"; Bangs, Brown, Burks, et al., "Let It Bleed."

77. Talbot, *Season of the Witch*, 136; Lydon, *Rock Folk*, 311. Also see James Miller, *Flowers in the Dustbin: The Rise of Rock and Roll, 1947–1977* (New York: Simon & Schuster, 1999), 275–277.

78. Cutler quoted in Curry, "Deadly Day for the Rolling Stones." Also see Santelli, *Aquarius Rising*, 173.

79. Scully quoted in *ibid.*

80. David Dalton, "Altamont: End of the Sixties or Big Mix-up in the Middle of Nowhere?" *Gadfly*, November/December 1999.

81. Scully quoted in Curry, "Deadly Day for the Rolling Stones."

82. Richards quoted in Burks, "Rock & Roll's Worst Day."

83. Lydon, *Rock Folk*, 311.

84. Curry, "Deadly Day for the Rolling Stones"; Bangs, Brown, Burks, et al., "Let It Bleed"; Dalton, "Altamont: End of the Sixties"; Dodge quoted in Potocki, "Hippie Armageddon."

85. Curry; Mick Brown, "Stanley Booth Interview," *The Daily Telegraph*, April 19, 2012. http://www.telegraph.co.uk; Dalton, "Altamont: End of the Sixties."

86. Scully quoted in Curry.

87. Curry, "Deadly Day for the Rolling Stones"; Gleason, "Aquarius Wept"; Bangs, Brown, Burks, et al.

88. Graham quoted in Bangs, Brown, Burks, et al.

89. Wise quoted in "The Rolling Stones—Personal Accounts: Altamont." *UnCut: Music and Movies with Something to Say*. http://www.uncut.co.uk.

90. Angela Dellaporta and Joann Steck, *Best of Berkeley: The Daily Californian* (Berkeley: Independent Student, 1980), 23; Charles Perry, *The Haight-Ashbury: A History* (New York: Random House, 1984), 20; Peter Carlson, "Hell's Aging Angel," *Washington Post*, August 9, 2000, reprinted in *Biker Life*. http://www.nolimitsonline.com/biker_life1.htm. Altman quoted in Curry, "Deadly Day for the Rolling Stones"; Dalton, "Altamont: End of the Sixties"; Gleason, "Aquarius Wept"; Marcus quoted in Michael Sragow, "Gimme Shelter": The True Story of How a Free Rolling Stones Concert Turned into a Colossal Mass Bad Trip—and Spawned the Most Harrowing Rock 'n' Roll Movie Ever Made," *Salon*, August 10, 2000.

91. Cahill quoted in Abe Peck, *Uncovering the Sixties: The Life and Times of the Underground Press* (New York: Citadel, 1991), 226; For the Jewkes incident see Bangs, Brown, Burks, et al., "Let It Bleed," and Grover Lewis, "Viewing the Remains of a Mean Saturday," *The Village Voice*, December 18, 1969, vol. 14, no. 62. Tony Ortega republished the article with an addendum title, "In the Wake of Altamont: Who Hired the Hell's Angels," villagevoice.com. For the crowd/hippie response to the Angels' wanton violence, see The Rolling Stones, et al., *Gimme Shelter DVD*, 1970, Image Entertainment, Criterion Collection.

92. Zagaris quoted in Talbot, *Season of the Witch*, 138–139.

93. Talbot. Also see Bangs, Brown, Burks, et al., "Let It Bleed"; *Gimme Shelter*; Curry, "Deadly Day for the Rolling Stones."

94. Bangs, Brown, Burks, et al.; Curry; *Gimme Shelter*.

95. *Gimme Shelter*.

96. Dalton, "End of the Sixties."

97. Talbot, *Season of the Witch*, 139–140; Bangs, Brown, Burks, et al., "Let It Bleed."

98. *Ibid.*

99. Scully quoted in Curry, "Deadly Day for the Rolling Stones." Also see Talbot; Bangs, Brown, Burks. Also see Lydon, *Rock Folk*, 312–314; Dalton, "End of the Sixties"; Burks, "Rock and Roll's Worst Day." Russell, "The Rolling Stones at Altamont: The Day the Music Died."

100. Jagger quoted in Bangs, Brown, Burks. Richards quoted in Christgau, "The Rolling Stones: Can't Get No Satisfaction." Also see Gleason, "Aquarius Wept"; On the importance of the documentary as evidence for Passaro's eventual acquittal see "Movie of Slaying at Rock Fest Is Key Evidence in Coast Trial," *New York Times*, January 10, 1971; "Investigators Close Decades Old Altamont Killing Case, *USA Today*, May 26, 2005. Henry K. Lee, "Altamont's Cold Case Is Being Closed: Theory of Second Stabber Debunked by Sheriff's Dept.," *San Francisco Chronicle*, May 26, 2005.

101. Brand quoted in Talbot, *Season of the Witch*, 140–141.

102. Leary and *The Barb* quoted in Timothy Miller, *The Hippies and American Values* (Knoxville: University of Tennessee Press, 1991), 84.

103. Santana quoted in Bangs, Brown, Burks, et al., "Let It Bleed."

104. Lydon, *Rock Folk*, 310.

105. Crosby quoted in Bangs, Brown, Burks, et al., "Let It Bleed."

106. *Ibid.*

107. Peters quoted in Talbot, *Season of the Witch*, 141.

108. Gleason quoted in Bangs, Brown, Burks, et al., "Let It Bleed." Also see Gleason quoted in Lewis, "Viewing the Remains of a Mean Saturday." On the other deaths, see Kirkpatrick, *1969*, 263.

109. Graham quoted in Bangs, Brown, Burks, et al., "Let It Bleed."

110. George Paul Csiscery, "Stones Concert Now Ends It: America Now Up for Grabs," *Berkeley Tribe*, December 12–19, vol. 1, no. 15, pp. 1–3.

111. Bangs, Brown, Burks, et al., "Let It Bleed."

112. Quoted in Terry Anderson, *The Sixties* (New York: Addison, Wesley, Longman, 1999), 148.

113. Quoted in Miller, *The Hippies and American Values*, 83.

114. *Time*, "Hippies and Violence."

115. Quoted in Anderson, *The Sixties*, 148.

116. Dalton, "Altamont: End of the Sixties."

117. Ward quoted in Lytle, *America's Uncivil Wars*, 336.

118. Gitlin, *The Sixties*, 407. Also see Gitlin's original essay reprinted in Thomas King Forcade, ed., *Underground Press Anthology* (New York: Ace, 1972), 100–111.

Chapter 14

1. Robert Nisbet, *The Twilight of Authority* (New York: Oxford University Press, 1975), 67.

2. Barbara Ehrenreich, *Fear of Falling: The Inner Life of the Middle Class* (New York: Pantheon, 1998), 98,

101, 105. Also see "Business: The Blue Collar Worker's Lowdown Blues," *Time* (vol. 96, no. 19), November 9, 1970. According to the *Time* article, workers ranging from postal employees, who for the first time in history went out on strike, to city workers in Cincinnati stomping off the job to tugboat crewmen and gravediggers striking in New York; all joined with rubber workers in Akron and teamsters across the country in leaving their jobs. By January 1970, 400,000 General Motors workers were on strike as well. As a result, the United States had lost 41.5 million man-days of work.

3. Theodore Roszak, *The Making of a Counterculture* (New York: Doubleday, 1969), 69.

4. Jay Stevens, *Storming Heaven: LSD and the American Dream* (New York: Atlantic Monthly, 1987), 306.

5. Quoted in Jonathan Rieder, *Canarsie: The Jews and Italians of Brooklyn Against Liberalism* (Cambridge, MA: Harvard University Press, 1985), 133–134.

6. Quoted in Maurice Isserman and Michael Kazin, *America Divided: The Civil War of the 1960s* (New York: Oxford University Press, 2000), 202.

7. Quoted in Richard Polenberg, *One Nation Divisible: Class, Race, and Ethnicity in the United States Since 1938* (New York: Penguin, 1980), 228.

8. Deac quoted in "Man and Woman of the Year: The Middle Americans," *Time* (vol. 95, no. 1), January 5, 1970.

9. Roger Kimball, *The Long March: How the Countercultural Revolution of the 1960s Changed America* (San Francisco: Encounter, 2000), 102.

10. *Time,* "Man and Woman of the Year."

11. Peter Braunstein and Michael William Doyle, eds., *Imagine Nation: The American Counterculture of the 1960s & 1970s* (New York: Routledge, 2002), 9.

12. Clark Kerr, *The Uses of the University* (Cambridge: Harvard University Press, 1963), 23.

13. Charles Reich, *The Greening of America* (New York: Bantam, 1970), 7–8.

14. Isserman and Kazin, *America Divided,* 201–203; William H. Chafe, *Unfinished Journey: America Since World War II,* 5th ed. (New York: Oxford University Press, 2003), 326–328; Mark Hamilton Lytle, *America's Uncivil Wars: The Sixties Era from Elvis to the Fall of Richard Nixon* (New York: Oxford University Press, 2006), 340; Rieder, *Canarsie,* 102–104. Also see Rieder, "The Rise of the 'Silent Majority'" in Steve Fraser and Frank Gerstle, eds., *The Rise and Fall of the New Deal Order, 1930–1980* (Princeton: Princeton University Press, 1989), 243–268; On the class and racial bias of the Vietnam era draft, see Lawrence M. Baskir and William A. Strauss, *Chance and Circumstance: The Draft, the War, and the Vietnam Generation* (New York: Random House, 1978); Jeremy Engels, "The Politics of Resentment and the Tyranny of the Minority: Rethinking Victimage for Resentful Times," *Rhetoric Society Quarterly* (vol. 40), August 27, 2010, 313–317. Equally if not more appealing to many Middle Americans was the populist, race-baiting firebrand former governor of Alabama George Wallace, whose popularity reached beyond the South and deep into urban ethnic Northern working class neighborhoods. Indeed, Wallace won the most electoral votes—46—of any third-party candidate in the post–World War II era. On Wallace's Northern attraction see "Why They Want Him," *Time* (vol. 92, no. 16), October 18, 1968.

15. *Time,* "The Blue Collar's Worker's Lowdown Blues."

16. Rieder, *Canarsie,* 63–66, 139, 177, 26.

17. James Q. Wilson, *Thinking About Crime* (New York: Vintage, 1985), 5–7, 64–65.

18. Daniel Yankelovich, *The New Rules: Searching for Self-Fulfillment in a World Turned Upside Down* (New York: Random House, 1981), 98–99.

19. Lance Morrow, "1968: Like a Knife Blade: The Year Severed Past from Future," *Time* (vol. 131, no. 2), January 11, 1988.

20. Chafe, *Unfinished Journey,* 376–377; Lytle, *America's Uncivil Wars,* 342. Also see James T. Patterson, *Grand Expectations: The United States, 1945–1974* (New York: Oxford University Press, 1996), 749–752; Terry Anderson, *The Sixties* (New York: Addison Wesley Longman, 1999), 156–157; Patrick J. Hearden, *The Tragedy of Vietnam* (New York: Pearson Longman, 2004), 158–161.

21. Todd Gitlin, *The Sixties: Years of Hope, Days of Rage* (New York: Bantam, 1987), 377–391. Also see Chafe, *Unfinished Journey,* 394–396; Irwin Unger, *The Movement: A History of the American New Left, 1959–1972* (New York: Dodd, Mead, 1974), 180–183, 188; "At War with War," *Time* (vol. 95, no. 20), May 18, 1970.

22. Lytle, *America's Uncivil Wars,* 342; Anderson, *The Sixties,* 156–157.

23. Kissinger quoted in Lytle, *America's Uncivil Wars,* 341; for the antiwar protest Nixon's policies reawakened, see Lytle pages 347–349; Chafe, 391; Anderson, 157–158; Isserman and Kazin, *America Divided,* 268–270; Patterson, *Grand Expectations,* 753; Gitlin, *The Sixties,* 409–410. Also see "Parades for Peace and Patriotism," *Time* (vol. 94, no. 21), November 21, 1968; *Time,* "At War with War."

24. Gitlin. Also see Lytle, 353; *Time,* "At War with War."

25. John Kifner, "4 Kent State Students Killed by Troops," *New York Times,* May 5, 1970, 1; Anderson, 177–178; Mother and son exchange quoted on 178; Chafe, 393–394; Lytle, 353–355; Patterson, *Grand Expectations,* 754–755; Gitlin; Unger, *The Movement,* 183–188. The war was not the only issue affecting college campuses in 1970. Other concerns galvanized students as well to challenge university authority and policies but the war was always the initial catalyst. For other antiwar demonstrations as well as student protest against the university for other matters, see "Nation: Protest Season on the Campus," *Time* (vol. 95, no. 19), May 11, 1970.

26. Quoted in Joan Morrison and Robert K. Morrison, eds., *From Camelot to Kent State: The Sixties Experience in the Words of Those Who Lived It* (New York: Oxford University Press, 1987), 330.

27. *Ibid.,* 334–335. Also see Lytle, *America's Uncivil Wars,* 354, 356; Chafe, *The Unfinished Journey,* 394; "Investigations: Kent State Reopened," *Time* (vol. 102, no. 26) December 24, 1973. Also see "Kent State: Another View," *Time* (vol. 96, no. 17), October 26, 1970.

28. Homer Bigart, "War Foes Here Attacked by Construction Workers," *The New York Times,* May 9, 1970, 1; "Violence on the Right," *The New York Times Op Ed,* May 9, 1970; *Newsweek,* May 18, 1970, 50; Maurice Carroll, "Police Assailed by Mayor on Laxity at Peace Rally," *The New York Times,* May 10, 1970, 1. Also see Lytle, 355; Anderson, 178; Gitlin, *Years of Hope, Days of Rage,* 414; Woden Teachout, *Capture the Flag: A Political History of*

American Patriotism (New York: Basic, 2009), 185–190; Fred J. Cook, "Hard-Hats: The Rampaging Patriots," *The Nation,* June 15, 1970, vol. 210, 712–719; Harman quoted on page 715; E.E. LeMasters, *Blue Collar Aristocrats: Life-Styles at a Working-Class Tavern* (Madison: University of Wisconsin Press, 1975), 111–113. There were other incidents of women being assaulted during the hard-hat riots of that spring such as in the St. Louis rampage. See the *St. Louis Post Dispatch,* June 8, 1970. Blue collar worker quoted in Vincent Cannato, *The Ungovernable City: John Lindsay and His Struggle to Save New York* (New York: Basic, 2001), 452; Fanale quoted in Emmanuel Perlmutter, "Head of Building Trade Unions Here Says Response Favors Friday's Actions," *The New York Times,* May 12, 1970, 18; Agis Salpukas, "Unionists Say War Protestors Prompted a Backlash," *The New York Times,* May 16, 1970, 70.

29. Individuals quoted in "At War with War," *Time* (vol. 95, no. 20), May 18, 1970.

30. Eliot quoted in "Comments on Worker-Student Clash," *The New York Times,* May 19, 1970, 38.

31. Quoted in Cannato, *The Ungovernable City,* 451.

32. *Ibid.,* 452–453. Also see Homer Bigart, "Thousands Assail Lindsay in Second Protest by Workers, *The New York Times,* May 12, 1970, 1; "Thousands in City March to Assail Lindsay on War," *The New York Times,* May 16, 1970, 11; "Huge City Rally Backs Nixon's Indochina Policies," *The New York Times,* May 21, 1970, 1; Robert B. Semple, Jr. "Nixon Meets Heads of 2 City Unions," *The New York Times,* May 27, 1970, 2.

33. Jefferson Cowie, "'Vigorously Left, Right, and Center': The Crosscurrents of Working Class America in the 1970s," in Beth Bailey and David Farber, eds., *America in the Seventies* (Lawrence: University Press of Kansas, 2004), 88. Also see, Lytle, *America's Uncivil Wars,* 356. The majority of polls taken at the time revealed that almost 50 percent of blue collar workers favored immediate withdrawal from Vietnam; a higher percentage than among the more affluent members of the upper middle class, whose sons had obtained college deferments or other concessions and thus were not fighting and dying in Vietnam; further confirmation that the war had become by the early '70s, if not sooner, "a rich man's war but a poor man's fight."

34. Yankelovich, *New Rules,* 19.

35. Rieder, *Canarsie,* 157; Cook, "Hard Hats," 717.

36. Rosow quoted in "The Blue Collar Worker's Lowdown Blues." Also see "The Troubled American: A Special Report on the White Majority," *Newsweek,* October 6, 1969, 28.

37. *Time,* "Investigations: Kent State Reopened." Also see "Kent State Revisited," *Time* (vol. 98, no. 23), December 6, 1971.

38. Gregory H. Wierzynski, "The Cooling of America: The Students: All Quiet on the Campus Front," *Time* (vol. 97. no. 28), February 22, 1971.

39. Bruce Pollock, *By The Time We Got to Woodstock: The Great Rock 'n' Roll Revolution of 1969* (New York: Backbeat, 2009), 282.

Epilogue and Legacy

1. Anonymous reviewer of this manuscript, October 2014.

2. Holland Cotter, "Through Rose-Colored Granny Glasses," *New York Times,* May 25, 2007.

3. James T. Patterson, *Grand Expectations: The United States, 1945–1974* (New York: Oxford University Press, 1996), 751; Todd Gitlin, *The Sixties: Years of Hope, Days of Rage* (New York: Bantam, 1987), 430–431.

4. Jonathan Schell, "A Reporter at Large: History in Sherman Park," *The New Yorker,* January 12, 1987, 64.

5. Ken Gofman and Dan Joy, *Counterculture Through the Ages: From Abraham to Acid House* (New York: Villard, 2004), 311.

6. Roger Kimball, *The Long March: How the Cultural Revolution of the 1960s Changed America* (San Francisco: Encounter, 2000), 248–249.

7. Tom Wolfe, "These Radical Chic Evenings," and "Man-Mauing the Flak Catchers," in *The Purple Decades: A Reader* (New York: Berkley, 1987), 181–234. Daniel Yankelovich, *The New Rules: Searching for Self-Fulfillment in a World Turned Upside Down* (New York: Random House, 1981), 81.

8. Robert J. Ringer, *Looking Out for Number One* (New York: Funk & Wagnalls, 1977), x; Nena and George O'Neill, *Open Marriage* (Lanham, MD: M. Evans, 1972), 222.

9. Christopher Lasch, *The Culture of Narcissism: American Life in an Age of Diminishing Expectations* (New York: Warner, 1979), 4.

10. Jim Fixx, *The Complete Book of Running* (New York: Random House, 1977), 34. Fixx quoted in John Van Doorn, "An Intimidating New Class: The Physical Elite," *New York Magazine,* May 29, 1978, p. 38.

11. Lasch, *The Culture of Narcissism,* 73.

12. Rubin quoted in Paul Krassner, "Who Killed Jerry Rubin?" *The Realist,* Summer 1995, issue 130, 10; on Rubin's death, 11. Also see Eric Pace, "Jerry Rubin, 56, Flashy 60's Radical Dies; 'Yippies' Founder and Chicago 7 Defendant," *New York Times,* November 30, 1994; Joseph Berger, "Born to Be Wild. Scratch That. Born to Be Mild," *New York Times,* December 4, 1994; "Nation: Rubin Relents," *Time* (vol. 116, no. 6), August 11, 1980.

13. John J. Goldman, "Turbulent '60's Live Again at Funeral for Activist: Radicals, Friends Bid Hoffman Farewell," *Los Angeles Times,* April 20, 1989; Wayne King, "Mourning and Celebrating a Radical," *New York Times,* April 20, 1989; Richard Lacayo, "A Flower in a Clenched Fist: Abbie Hoffman: 1936–1989," *Time* (vol. 133, no. 17), April 24, 1989; Krassner, "Who Killed Jerry Rubin?" on Hoffman's death and its effect on Rubin, see page 2.

14. Peter Braunstein and Michael William Doyle, "Historicizing the American Counterculture of the 1960s and '70s," in Braunstein and Doyle, eds., *Imagine Nation: The American Counterculture of the 1960s & '70's* (New York: Routledge, 2002), 12.

15. Daniel Yankelovich, *The New Morality: A Profile of American Youth in the 1970s* (New York: McGraw-Hill, 1974), 103–111.

16. Jean Jacques Lebel, "Counter Culture: Hip Culture Ripped Off," *Spectator,* December 8, 1969, 12. Also see David Harvey, *The Condition of Postmodernity* (Cambridge, MA: Blackwell, 1989), 63; Thomas Frank, *The Conquest of Cool* (Chicago: University of Chicago Press, 1997), 4, 7, 9; Allen Matusow, *The Unraveling of America: A History of Liberalism in the 1960s* (New York: Harper

& Row, 1984), 306; Mark Hamilton Lytle, *America's Uncivil Wars: The Sixties Era from Elvis to the Fall of Richard Nixon* (New York: Oxford University Press, 2006), 211–212.

17. Interview with Dan and Theresa Gray, formerly "Ellen Bluestar" of the legendary northern California Morningstar commune, July 27, 2012.

18. Joseph Heath and Andrew Potter, *Nation of Rebels: Why Counterculture Became Consumer Culture* (New York: HarperCollins, 2004), 174, 206.

19. Hedgepeth quoted in Sheila Weller, "Suddenly Last Summer," *Vanity Fair,* July 2012, no. 623, 77.

20. *Ibid.,* 78.

21. "Resident" quoted in Jay Stevens, *Storming Heaven: LSD and the American Dream* (New York: Atlantic Monthly, 1987), 300.

22. Scully quoted in Weller, "Suddenly Last Summer," 79.

23. Sohnya Sayres, Anders Stephanson, Stanley Arnowitz, and Fredric Jameson, eds., *The 60s Without Apology* (Minneapolis: University of Minnesota Press, 1984), 254.

24. "Alice Waters: 40 Years of Sustainable Food." NPR books. http://www.npr.org/2011/08/22/139707078/alice-waters-40-years-of-sustainable-food. Also see Calvin Trillin, Michael Pollan, and Alice Waters, *40 Years of Chez Panisse: The Power of Gathering* (New York: Clarkson Potter, 2011).

25. Joel Stein, "The Man Behind Burning Man," *Time* (vol. 156, no. 12), September 18, 2000; Kevin Kelly, "Bonfire of the Techies," *Time* (vol. 150, no. 8), August 25, 1997; Grover Norquist, "My First Burning Man: Confessions of a Conservative from Washington," *The Guardian,* September 2, 2014. http://www.theguardian.com; Stuart Walmsley, "Behind the Burning Man Festival in Nevada," *The Herald Sun,* October 12, 2014. http://heraldsun.com.au.

26. Norquist. Also see Catherine Saillant, "Burning Man Becomes a Hot Academic Topic," *Los Angeles Times,* October 20, 2010.

27. Elizabeth Limbach, "The Wonderful, Weird Economy of Burning Man," *The Atlantic,* August 18, 2014; Walmsley, "Behind the Burning Man Festival in Nevada."

28. Christopher Swan, "Recalling Woodstock: Musical Emblem of an Era," *Christian Science Monitor,* March 8, 1985, 23.

29. Germaine Greer, *The Female Eunuch* (New York: Farrar, Straus and Giroux, 1971), 59.

30. Timothy Miller, *The Hippies and American Values* (Knoxville: University of Tennessee Press, 1991), 53–56.

31. *Ibid.,* 143

32. Hoffman quoted in Morrow, "1968: Like a Knife Blade: The Year That Severed Past from Future." Also see Klaus Fischer, *America in White, Black, and Gray: A History of the Stormy 1960s* (New York: Continuum, 2006), 315.

33. Peter Braunstein, "Forever Young: Insurgent Youth and the Sixties Culture of Rejuvenation," in Braunstein and Doyle, eds., *Imagine Nation,* 244, 249.

34. *Ibid.,* 10.

35. Timothy Tyler, "The Cooling of America: Out of Tune and Lost in the Counterculture," *Time* (vol. 97, no. 8), February 22, 1971.

36. Frank Musgrove, *Ecstasy and Holiness: Counterculture and the Open Society* (Bloomington: Indiana University Press, 1974), 19.

37. Matthew McClure in Kevin Kelly interview, "Why We Left the Farm," *Whole Earth Review* (Winter 1985), 65.

38. Sanders quoted in Anderson, *The Sixties,* 150.

39. Whitman quoted in Tyler, "The Cooling of America."

40. Walter Rabideau quoted in Kevin Kelly, "Why We Left the Farm," *Whole Earth Review* (Winter 1985), 57.

41. Fairfield quoted in Anderson, *The Sixties,* 150.

42. Brand quoted in Ben Austen, "Stewart Brand: The Last Prankster," *Men's Journal,* March 2013. http://www.mensjournal.com.

43. Gofman and Joy, *Counterculture Through the Ages,* 4.

44. Interview with former artist/bohemian Chris Moretta, February 28, 2015. Ms. Moretta dabbled for a while in the hip lifestyle while attending Humboldt State University in Arcata, California, in the early 1970s. At the time the university and surrounding area, in the heart of the California Redwoods, had become a favorite hangout for a variety of counterculturists. After a few months of "experiencing" hippiedom, Ms. Moretta opined that "There was always something that bothered me and it wasn't just the drugs. It seemed that by the early 1970s people became hippies just to say they had or were, when in reality they just wanted the dope and the sex and used the money their parents were sending them for the dope, the records, and the clothes. Many of them, particularly the ones who came from southern California, eventually went back home and became very successful business people, making tons of money. Many became yuppies in the 80s."

Bibliography *(Including Articles by Chapter)*

Archival Collections

The Digger Archives, www.diggers.org.

Freida Werden Papers, Briscoe Center for American History, University of Texas at Austin.

Hippie Papers, San Francisco History Center, San Francisco Public Library, San Francisco, California.

Mariann Wizard Papers, Briscoe Center for American History, University of Texas at Austin.

New Left Collection, 1964–1992, Hoover Institution Library and Archives, Stanford University, Palo Alto, California.

The Rag Files, 1966–1977, Briscoe Center for American History, University of Texas at Austin.

Ronald G. Davis Papers, University of California, Davis.

San Francisco Renaissance and Beat Collection, San Francisco History Center, San Francisco Public Library, San Francisco, California.

Sara Clark Social Justice Collection, Briscoe Center for American History, University of Texas at Austin.

Sexual Freedom League Records, Bancroft Library, University of California, Berkeley.

Social Protest Collection, Bancroft Library, University of California, Berkeley.

Space City News/Space City! Files, June 1969–August 1972, Houston Metropolitan Research Center, Houston Public Library, Houston, Texas.

Students for a Democratic Society Records, 1967–1971, Dolph Briscoe Center for American History, University of Texas at Austin.

Texas Observer Records, Briscoe Center for American History, University of Texas at Austin.

Texas Poster Art Collection, Briscoe Center for American History, University of Texas at Austin.

White House Correspondence Files, 1965–1969, Lyndon Baines Johnson Presidential Library, University of Texas at Austin.

Oral History Interviews

Ali, Deborah. October 2014
Evans, Dan, and Theresa Gray. July 2012.
Houchin, Larry. July 2012.
Ittner, Robert C. August 2013.
Martin, Roger. October 2013.
Moretta, Chris. February 2015.
Moretta, Michael. July 2014.

Phelps, Don and Sally. August 2012.
Poutous, George. August 2011.
Tycer, Lew and Gail. August 2011.

Books

Abernethy, Francis Edward, ed. *What's Going On? (In Modern Texas Folklore)*. Denton: University of North Texas Press, 1998.

Albert, Judith Clavir, and Stewart Edward Albert. *The Sixties Papers: Documents of a Rebellious Decade*. New York: Praeger, 1984.

Allywn, David. *Make Love Not War: The Sexual Revolution: An Unfettered War*. Boston: Little, Brown, 2000.

Alpert, Richard (Ram Dass). *Be Here Now*. San Cristobal, NM: Lama Foundation, 1971.

Anderson, Terry. *The Movement and the Sixties: Protest in American from Greensboro to Wounded Knee*. New York: Oxford University Press, 1996.

_____. *The Sixties*. New York: Pearson, 1999.

Anthony, Gene. *The Summer of Love: Haight-Ashbury at Its Height*. San Francisco: Last Gasp, 1980.

Atkins, Susan, with Bob Slosser. *Child of Satan, Child of God*. Plainfield, NJ: Logos International, 1977.

Attali, Jacques. *Noise: The Political Economy of Music*. Minneapolis: University of Minnesota Press, 1999.

Bailey, Beth, and David Farber, eds. *America in the Seventies*. Lawrence: University of Kansas Press, 2004.

Barayon, Ramon Sender, Gwen Leeds, Near Morningstar, Bill Wheeler, et al. *Home Free Home: A History of Two Open Door California Communes: Morningstar Ranch and Wheeler's (Ahisma) Ranch*. The Digger Archives. www.diggers.org.

Baskir, Lawrence M., and William A. Strauss. *Chance and Circumstance: The Draft, the War and the Vietnam Generation*. New York: Random House, 1978.

Baxandall, Rosalyn, and Linda Gordon, eds. *Dear Sisters: Dispatches from the Women's Liberation Movement*. New York: Basic, 2000.

Beal, Dana, Steve Conliff, Grace Michaels, et al. *Blacklisted News: Secret Histories from 1968 to 1984; the New Yippie Book Collective*. New York: Bleecker, 1983.

Becker, Howard, ed. *Culture and Civility in San Francisco*. Chicago: Transaction, 1971.

Bedau, Hugo Adam, ed. *Civil Disobedience: Theory and Practice*. New York: Pegasus, 1969.

Berger, Bennett M. *The Survival of a Counterculture: Ideological Work and Everyday Life Among Rural Communards.* Berkeley: University of California Press, 1981.

Biskind, Peter. *Seeing Is Believing: How Hollywood Taught Us to Stop Worrying and Love the Fifties.* New York: Pantheon, 1983.

Bloom, Alexander, and Wini Breines, eds. *"Takin' It to the Streets": A Sixties Reader.* New York: Oxford University Press, 1995.

Bloom, Allen. *The Closing of the American Mind.* New York: Simon & Schuster, 1987.

Bode, Carl, ed. *The Portable Thoreau.* New York: Viking, 1947.

Booker, M. Keith, ed. *Encyclopedia of Comic Books and Graphic Novels.* Santa Barbara, CA: Greenwood, 2010.

Booth, Stanley. *Dance with the Devil: The Rolling Stones and Their Times.* New York: Random House, 1984.

_____. *The True Adventures of the Rolling Stones.* New York: Vintage, 1985.

Bordowitz, Hank. *Bad Moon Rising: The Unauthorized History of Credence Clearwater Revival.* Chicago: Chicago Review Press, 2007.

Braden, William. *The Age of Aquarius.* Cleveland: Quadrangle, 1970.

Brand, Stewart. *The Last Whole Earth Catalog.* New York: Random House, 1974.

Braunstein, Peter, and Michael William Doyle, eds. *Imagine Nation: The American Counterculture of the 1960s and 1970s.* New York: Routledge, 2002.

Brevin, Jess. *Squeaky: The Life and Times of Lynette Alice Fromme.* New York: St. Martin's, 1997.

Brokaw, Tom. *Boom! Voices of the Sixties: Personal Reflection on the 60s and Today.* New York: Random House, 2007.

Bromell, Nick. *Tomorrow Never Knows: Rock and Psychedelics in the 1960s.* Chicago: University of Chicago Press, 2000.

Brown, Joe David, ed. *The Hippies: Who They Are, Where They Are, Why They Are That Way, and How They May Affect Our Society.* New York: Time, 1967.

Brown, Peter, and Steven Gaines. *The Love You Make: An Insider's Story of the Beatles.* New York: New American Library, 2002.

Bugliosi, Vincent, and Curt Gentry. *Helter Skelter: The True Story of the Manson Murders.* New York: W.W. Norton, 1974.

Burner, David. *Making Peace with the Sixties.* Princeton: Princeton University Press, 1996.

Burns, Glen. *Great Poets Howl: A Study of Allen Ginsberg.* New York: Peter Lang, 1983.

Canato, Vincent. *The Ungovernable City: John Lindsay and His Struggle to Save New York.* New York: Basic, 2011.

Caputi, Anthony. *Buffo: The Genius of Vulgar Comedy.* Detroit: Wayne State University Press, 1978.

Cashman, John. *The LSD Story: The Drug That Expands the Mind.* New York: Gold Medal/Fawcett, 1969.

Cavan, Sherri. *Hippies of the Haight.* St. Louis: New Critics, 1972.

Chafe, William. *Unfinished Journey: America Since World War II.* New York: Oxford University Press, 2003.

_____, with Harvard Sitkoff and Beth Bailey, eds. *A History of Our Time: Readings in Post-War America.* New York: Oxford University Press, 2003.

Charters, Ann. *Kerouac: A Biography.* San Francisco: Straight Arrow, 1973.

_____, ed. *The Dictionary of Literary Biography.* Detroit: Gale Research, 1983.

_____, ed. *The Portable Beat Readers.* New York: Viking-Penguin, 1982.

Chester, Lewis, Godfrey Hodgson, and Bruce Page. *An American Melodrama: The Presidential Campaign of 1968.* New York: Viking, 1969.

Christgau, Robert. *Any Old Way You Choose It: Rock and Other Pop Music, 1967–1973.* New York: Cooper Square, 1973, 2000.

Cohen, Adam, and Elizabeth Taylor. *American Pharaoh: Mayor Richard Daley: His Battle for Chicago and the Nation.* Boston: Little, Brown, 2000.

Collier, Peter, and David Horowitz. *Destructive Generation: Second Thoughts About the Sixties.* New York: Summit, 1989.

Cook, Bruce. *The Beat Generation.* Westport, CT: Greenwood, 1983.

_____. *The Beat Generation: The Tumultuous '50s Movement and Its Impact on Today.* New York: Charles Scribner's Sons, 1971.

Cowie, Jefferson R. *Stayin' Alive: The 1970s and the Last Days of the Working Class.* New York: New Press, 2012.

Coyote, Peter. *Sleeping Where I Fall.* Washington, D.C.: Counterpoint, 1989.

Curl, John. *For All the People: Uncovering the Hidden History of Cooperation, Cooperative Movements, and Communalism in America,* 2d ed. Oakland, CA: PM, 2012.

Davidson, Michael. *The San Francisco Renaissance: Poetics and Community at Mid-Century.* New York: Cambridge University Press, 1989.

Davis, R.G. *The San Francisco Mime Troupe: The First Ten Years.* Palo Alto, CA: Ramparts, 1975.

Davis, Stephen. *Jim Morrison: Life, Death, Legend.* New York: Gotham, 2005.

DeCurtis, Anthony, and James Henke, eds. *The Rolling Stone Illustrated History of Rock and Roll.* New York: Random House, 1992.

Diamond, Stephen. *What the Trees Said: Life on a New Age Farm.* New York: Delta, 1971.

Dickstein, Morris. *Gates of Eden: American Culture in the Sixties.* New York: W.W. Norton, 1977, 1997.

Didion, Joan. *Slouching Toward Bethlehem.* New York: Farrar, Straus and Giroux, 1968.

Diggins, John Patrick. *The Proud Decades: America in War and Peace, 1941–1960.* New York: W.W. Norton, 1989.

DuNoyer, Paul. *The Illustrated Encyclopedia of Music.* London: Flame Tree, 2003.

Easterling, Richard A. *Birth and Fortune: The Impact of Numbers on Personal Welfare.* Chicago: University of Chicago Press, 1987.

Echols, Alice. *Shaky Ground: The Sixties and Its Aftershocks.* New York: Columbia University Press, 2002.

Edgerton, Gary R. *The Columbia History of American Television.* New York: Columbia University Press, 2007.

Ehrenreich, Barbara. *Fear of Falling: The Inner Life of the Middle Class.* New York: Pantheon, 1998.

Eliot, T.S. *The Sacred Wood.* New York: Barnes and Noble, 1928.

Engless, Ian, ed. *Performance and Popular Music: History, Place, and Time.* Hampshire, England: Ashgate, 2006.

Ennis, Phillip H. *The Seventh Stream: The Emergence of*

Rock 'n' Roll in American Popular Music. Middletown, CT: Wesleyan University Press, 1992.

Faith, Karlene. *The Long Prison Journey of Leslie Van Houten: Life Beyond the Cult.* Boston: Northeastern University Press, 2001.

Farber, David. *The Age of Great Dreams: America in the 1960s.* New York: Hill and Wang, 1984.

_____. *Chicago '68.* Chicago: University of Chicago Press, 1988.

_____, ed. *The Sixties: From Memory to History.* Chapel Hill: University of North Carolina Press, 1994.

_____, with Beth Bailey, eds. *The Columbia Guide to America in the 1960s.* New York: Columbia University Press, 2001.

Feldman, Gene, and Max Gartenburg, eds. *The Beat Generation and the Angry Young Men.* New York: Citadel, 1958.

Fike, Rupert, ed. *Voices from the Farm: Adventures in Community Living.* Summertown, TN: Book, 2012.

Fischer, Klaus. *America in White, Black, and Gray: A History of the Stormy 1960s.* New York: Continuum, 2006.

Fishman, Robert. *Bourgeois Utopias: The Rise and Fall of Suburbia.* New York: Basic, 1987.

Fitzgerald, George. *Communes: The Goals, Hopes, and Problems.* New York: Paulist, 1971.

Fixx, Jim. *The Complete Book of Running.* New York: Random House, 1977.

Flamm, Michael W. *Law and Order: Street Crime, Civil Unrest, and the Crisis of Liberalism in the 1960s.* New York: Columbia University Press, 2005.

Frank, Thomas. *The Conquest of Cool: Business Culture, Counterculture, and the Rise of Hip Consumerism.* Chicago: University of Chicago Press, 1998.

Fraser, Steven, and Frank Gerstle, eds. *The Rise and Fall of the New Deal Order, 1930–1980.* Princeton: Princeton University Press, 1989.

Gaar, Gillian G. *She's a Rebel: The History of Women in Rock and Roll.* Seattle: Seal, 1992.

Gair, Christopher. *The American Counterculture.* Edinburg, Scotland: Edinburg University Press, 2007.

Garafalo, Reebee. *Rockin' Out: Popular Music in the USA,* 2d ed. Boston: Prentice Hall, 2002.

Gardner, Hugh. *The Children of Prosperity: Thirteen Modern Communes.* New York: St. Martin's, 1978.

Gaskin, Stephen. *The Caravan.* Summertown, TN: Book, 2007.

Gitlin, Todd. *The Sixties: Years of Hope, Days of Rage.* New York: Bantam, 1987.

Glatt, John. *Rage & Roll: Bill Graham and the Selling of Rock.* New York: Birch Lane, 1993.

Glessing, Robert J. *The Underground Press in America.* Bloomington: Indiana University Press, 1972.

Godfrey, Brian J. *Neighborhoods in Transition: The Making of San Francisco's Ethnic and Non-Conformist Communities.* Berkeley: University of California Press, 1988.

Gofman, Ken, and Dan Joy. *Counterculture Thought Through the Ages: From Abraham to Acid House.* New York: Villard, 2004.

Goodman, Paul. *Like a Conquered Province.* New York: Vintage, 1968.

Gottlieb, Annie. *Do You Believe in Magic? The Second Coming of the 60s Generation.* New York: Times, 1987.

Graham, Bill, with Robert Greenfield. *Bill Graham Presents: My Life Inside Rock and Out.* New York: Doubleday, 1992.

Gray, Michael. *Song and Dance Man: The Art of Bob Dylan.* New York: E. P. Dutton, 1972 [paperback edition].

Greenberg, Jan, and Sandra Jordan. *Andy Warhol: Prince of Pop.* New York: Random House, 2004.

Greer, Germaine. *The Female Eunuch.* New York: Farrar, Straus and Giroux, 2006.

Grogan, Emmett. *Ringolevio: A Life Played for Keeps.* New York: New York Review of Books, 1972.

Grunenberg, Christoph, and Jonathan Harris. *Summer of Love: Psychedelic Art, Social Crisis and the Counterculture in the 1960s.* Liverpool, UK: Liverpool University Press, 2005.

Guralnick, Peter. *Last Train to Memphis: The Rise of Elvis Presley.* New York: Back Bay, 1994.

Halberstam, David. *The Fifties.* New York: Ballantine, 1993.

Halstead, Fred. *Out Now! A Participant's Account of the American Movement Against the Vietnam War.* New York: Monad, 1978.

Hamilton, Neil. *The 1960s Counterculture in America.* Santa Barbara: ABC-CLIO, 1997.

Harvey, David. *The Condition of Post-Modernity.* Cambridge, MA: Blackwell, 1989.

Havens, Richie, and Steve Davidowitz. *They Can't Hide Us Anymore.* New York: Spike/Avon, 1999.

Hearden, Patrick J. *The Tragedy of Vietnam.* New York: Pearson-Longman, 2004.

Heath, Jim. *Decade of Disillusionment: The Kennedy-Johnson Years.* Bloomington: Indiana University Press, 1975.

Heath, Joseph, and Andrew Potter. *Nation of Rebels: Why Counterculture Became Consumer Culture.* New York: HarperCollins, 2004.

Hedgepeth, William. *The Alternative: Communal Life in America.* New York: Macmillan, 1970.

Hertsgaard, Mark. *A Day in the Life: The Music and Artistry of the Beatles.* New York: Delacorte, 1995.

Hicks, Michael. *Sixties Rock: Garage, Psychedelic, and Other Satisfactions.* Urbana: University of Illinois Press, 1999.

Hodgson, Godfrey. *America in Our Time: From World War II to Nixon: What Happened and Why.* New York: Vintage, 1976.

Hoffman, Abbie. *Revolution for the Hell of It.* New York: Thunder's Mouth, 1970.

_____. *Soon to Be a Major Motion Picture.* New York: Putnam, 1980.

Holloway, Mark. *Heavens on Earth: Utopian Communities in America, 1680–1880.* Mineola, NY: Dover, 1966.

Hopkins, Jim, and Danny Sugarman. *No One Gets Out Alive: The Biography of Jim Morrison.* New York: Warner, 1980.

Hoskyns, Barney. *Waiting for the Sun: Strange Days, Weird Scenes, and the Sound of Los Angeles.* New York: St. Martin's, 1996.

Howard, Gerald, ed. *The Sixties.* New York: Washington Square, 1982.

Hunt, Andrew. *David Dellinger: The Life and Times of a Nonviolent Revolutionary.* New York: NYU Press, 2006.

Huxley, Aldous. *The Doors of Perception.* New York: Harper and Row, 1964.

Issitt, Micah. *Hippies: A Guide to an American Counterculture.* Santa Barbara: ABC-CLIO, 2009.

Jackson, Kenneth. *Crabgrass Frontier: The Suburbaniza-

tion of the United States. New York: Oxford University Press, 1987.

Jezer, Marty. *Abbie Hoffman: American Rebel.* New Brunswick, NJ: Rutgers University Press, 1992.

Jones, Landon. *Great Expectations: America and the Baby-Boom Generation.* New York: Coward, McCann & Geoghegan, 1980.

Kaiser, Charles. *1968 in America: Music, Politics, Chaos, Counterculture, and the Shaping of a Generation.* New York: Grove, 1988.

Kanter, Rosabeth. *Commitment and Community: Communes and Utopias in Sociological Perspective.* Cambridge, MA: Harvard University Press, 1972.

Keats, John. *The Crack in the Picture Window.* New York: Houghton Mifflin, 1957.

Kenniston, Kenneth. *Youth and Dissent: The Rise of a New Opposition.* New York: Harcourt, Brace Jovanovich, 1971.

Kerouac, Jack. *The Dharma Bums:* New York: Viking, 1958.

_____. *Road Novels, 1957–1960: On the Road, the Dharma Bums, the Subterraneans, Tristessa, Lonesome Traveler, Journal Selections.* New York: Penguin-Putnam, 1984.

Kimball, Roger. *The Long March: How the Countercultural Revolution of the 1960s Changed America.* San Francisco: Encounter, 2000.

Kirkpatrick, Rob. *1969: The Year Everything Changed.* New York: Skyhorse, 2009.

Kleps, Art. *Millbrook.* Oakland, CA: Bench, 1975.

Knight, Arthur, and Kit Knight, eds. *Unspeakable Visions of the Individual.* California, PA: A. Knight, 1973.

Kurlansky, Mark. *1968: The Year That Rocked the World.* New York: Ballantine, 2004.

Kusch, Frank. *Battleground Chicago: The Police and the 1968 Democratic National Convention.* Chicago: University of Chicago Press, 2008.

Lasch, Christopher. *The Culture of Narcissism: American Life in the Age of Diminishing Expectations.* New York: Warner, 1974.

Lattin, Don. *The Harvard Psychedelic Club: How Timothy Leary, Ram Dass, Huston Smith, and Andrew Weil Killed the Fifties and Ushered in a New Age for America.* New York: HarperCollins, 2011.

Leamer, Lawrence. *The Paper Revolutionaries: The Rise of the Underground Press.* New York: Touchstone, 1972.

Leary, Timothy. *Flashbacks: A Personal and Cultural History of the Era; an Autobiography.* Los Angeles: Jeremy P. Tarcher, 1983.

_____. *High Priest.* Oakland, CA: Ronin, 1995.

_____. *The Politics of Ecstasy.* New York: Putnam, 1968.

Lee, Martin, and Bruce Shalin, eds. *Acid Dreams: The CIA and the Sixties Rebellion.* New York: Grove, 1985.

Leech, Kenneth. *Youthquake: The Growth of a Counterculture Through Two Decades.* Totowa, NJ: Littlefield, Adams, 1977.

LeMasters, E.E. *Blue Collar Aristocrats: Life-Styles at a Working Class Tavern.* Madison: University of Wisconsin Press, 1975.

Lemke-Santangelo, Gretchen. *Daughters of Aquarius: Women of the Sixties Counterculture.* Lawrence: University Press of Kansas, 2009.

Levine, Lawrence. *Black Culture and Black Consciousness: African American Thought from Slavery to Freedom.* New York: Oxford University Press, 2007.

Lewes, James. *Protest and Survive: Underground GI News-papers During the Vietnam War.* Westport, CT: Praeger, 2003.

Lipton, Lawrence: *The Holy Barbarians.* New York: Julian Messner, 1959.

Lobel, Michael, and James Rosenquist. *Pop Art, Politics, and History in the 1960s.* Berkeley: University of California Press, 2010.

London, Herbert. *Closing the Circle: A Cultural History of the Rock Revolution.* Chicago: Nelson Hall, 1984.

Lorchin, Roger. *San Francisco: 1846–1956.* New York: Oxford University Press, 1974.

Lydon, Michael. *Rock Folk: Portraits from the Rock 'n' Roll Pantheon.* New York: Citadel, 2000.

Lytle, Mark Hamilton. *America's Uncivil Wars: The Sixties Era from Elvis to the Fall of Richard Nixon.* New York: Oxford University Press, 2006.

MacAdams, Lewis. *Birth of Cool: Beat, Bebop, and the American Avant-Garde.* New York: Free, 2011.

Mailer, Norman. *The Armies of the Night: History as a Novel, the Novel as History.* New York: New American Library, 1968.

Malcolm X. *The Autobiography of Malcolm X.* New York: Ballantine, 1964.

Marcus, Greil. *Mystery Train: Images of America in Rock 'n' Roll Music.* New York: Penguin, 1997.

Marks, John. *The Search for the Manchurian Candidate: The CIA and Mind Control.* New York: Times, 1979.

Marling, Karal Ann. *As Seen on TV: The Visual Culture of Everyday Life in the 1950s.* Cambridge, MA: Harvard University Press, 2005.

Matusow, Allen J. *The Unraveling of America: A History of Liberalism in the 1960s.* New York: Harper and Row, 1984.

Mayes, Elaine, ed. *It Happened in Monterey.* Culver City, CA: Britannia, 2002.

McCleese, Don. *The MC 5's Kick Out the Jams (33 1/3).* New York: Continuum International, 2005.

McGloin, John Bernard. *San Francisco: The Story of a City.* San Rafael, CA: Presidio, 1978.

McMillan, John. *Smoking Typewriters: The Sixties Underground Press and the Rise of Alternative Media in America.* New York: Oxford University Press, 2011.

McNally, Dennis. *A Long, Strange Trip: The Inside History of the Grateful Dead.* New York: Broadway, 2002.

McWilliams, John C. *The 1960s Cultural Revolution.* Westport, CT: Greenwood, 2000.

Mezzrow, Milton, and Bernard Wolfe. *Really the Blues.* New York: Random House, 1946.

Miles, Barry. *Ginsberg: A Biography.* New York: Simon & Schuster, 1986.

_____, ed. *Howl: Original Draft Facsimile, Transcript, and Various Versions, Fully Annotated by Author with Contemporaneous Correspondence, Account of First Public Reading, Legal Skirmishes, Precursor Texts and Bibliography.* New York: Harper and Row, 1986.

Miller, Jim. *Flowers in the Dustbin: The Rise of Rock 'n' Roll, 1947–1977.* New York: Simon & Schuster, 1999.

_____, ed. *The Rolling Stone Illustrated History of Rock and Roll.* New York: Random House, 1976.

Miller, Timothy. *The Hippies and American Values.* Knoxville: University of Tennessee Press, 1991.

Morea, Ben, and Ron Hahne. *Black Mask & Up Against the Wall Motherfucker: The Incomplete Works of Ron Hahne, Ben Morea and the Black Mask Group.* Oakland, CA: PM, 2011.

Morgan, Howard P. *The 60s Experience: Hard Lessons About Modern America.* Philadelphia: Temple University Press, 1991.

Morrison, Joan, and Robert K. Morrison, eds. *From Camelot to Kent State: The Sixties Experience in the Words of Those Who Lived It.* New York: Oxford University Press, 2001.

Muller, Peter. *Contemporary Sub/Urban America.* Englewood Cliffs, NJ: Prentice-Hall, 1981.

Mumford, Lewis. *The City in History: Its Origins, Its Transformation, and Its Prospects.* New York: Harcourt Brace, 1961.

Mungo, Raymond. *Famous Long Ago: My Life and Hard Times with the Liberation News Service.* Boston: Beacon, 1970.

_____. *Total Loss Farm.* New York: E.P. Dutton, 1970.

Muscatine, Doris. *Old San Francisco.* New York: Putnam and Sons, 1975.

Musgrove, Frank. *Ecstasy and Holiness: Counterculture and the Open Society.* Bloomington: Indiana University Press, 1974.

Nisbet, Robert. *The Twilight of Authority.* New York: Oxford University Press, 1975.

Norman, Phillip. *Shout: The Beatles in Their Generation.* New York: Simon & Schuster, 1981.

_____. *Sympathy for the Devil: The Rolling Stones Story.* New York: Simon & Schuster, 1984.

O'Brien, Geoffrey. *Dream Time: Chapter from the Sixties.* New York: Viking-Penguin, 1989.

Ochiogrosso, Peter. *The Real Frank Zappa Book.* New York: Touchstone, 1989.

Ogelsby, Carl. *Ravens in the Storm: A Personal History of the 1960s Anti-War Movement.* New York: Charles Scribner, 2008.

Oliver, Paul, ed. *Shelter and Society.* New York: Praeger, 1969.

O'Neill, Nena, and George O'Neill. *Open Marriage.* Landon, MD: M. Evans, 1972.

O'Neill, William. *American High: Years of Confidence, 1945–1960.* New York: Free, 1986.

Orbst, Lynda Rosen, ed. *The Sixties: The Decade Remembered by the People Who Lived It Then.* New York: Rolling Stone, 1977.

Osgerby, Bill. *Playboys in Paradise: Masculinity, Youth and Leisure Style in Modern America.* New York: Berg, 2001.

Packard, Vance. *The Hidden Persuaders.* New York: McKay, 1957.

Panish, Jon. *The Color of Jazz: Race and Representation in Postwar American Culture.* Jackson: University Press of Mississippi, 1997.

Patterson, James T. *Grand Expectations: The United States, 1945–1974.* New York: Oxford University Press, 1996.

Pattison, Robert. *The Triumph of Vulgarity: Rock Music in the Mirror of Romanticism.* New York: Oxford University Press, 1987.

Peck, Abe. *Uncovering the Sixties: The Life and Times of the Underground Press.* New York: Pantheon, 1985.

Pells, Richard. *The Liberal Mind in a Conservative Age: American Intellectuals in the 1940s and 1950s.* Hanover, NH: Wesleyan University Press, 1985.

Perone, James E. *Music of the Counterculture.* Westport, CT: Greenwood, 2004.

Perry, Charles. *Haight-Ashbury: A History.* New York: Random House, 1984.

Perry, Helen Swick. *The Human Be-In.* New York: Basic, 1970.

Perry, Paul, and Ken Babbs. *On the Bus: The Complete Guide to the Legendary Trip of Ken Kesey and the Merry Pranksters and the Birth of the Counterculture.* New York: Thunder's Mouth, 1990.

Pitzer, Donald E., ed. *America's Communal Utopias.* Chapel Hill: University of North Carolina Press, 1997.

Plummer, William. *The Holy Goof: A Biography of Neal Cassady.* New York: Paragon House, 1981.

Polenberg, Richard. *One Nation Divisible: Class, Race, and Ethnicity in the United States Since 1938.* New York: Penguin, 1980.

Pollock, Bruce. *By the Time We Got to Woodstock: The Great Rock 'n' Roll Revolution of 1969.* New York: Backbeat, 2009.

Rabbit, Peter. *Drop City.* New York: Olympia, 1971.

Reed, Adolf, Jr. ed. *Race, Politics, and Culture: Critical Essays on the Radicalism of the 1960s.* New York: Greenwood, 1986.

Reich, Charles. *The Greening of America.* New York: Bantam, 1970.

Rexroth, Kenneth. *Communalism: Its Origins to the Twentieth Century.* New York: Seabury, 1974.

Rieder, Jonathan. *Canarsie: The Jews and Italians of Brooklyn Against Liberalism.* Cambridge, MA: Harvard University Press, 1985.

Ringer, Robert J. *Looking Out for Number One.* New York: Funk and Wagnalls, 1977.

Roberts, Ron E. *The New Communes.* Englewood Cliffs, NJ: Prentice Hall, 1971.

Roediger, David R. *Working Toward Whiteness: How American Immigrants Became White.* New York: Basic, 2007.

Rome, Adam. *The Bulldozer in the Countryside: Suburban Sprawl and the Rise of Environmentalism.* New York: Cambridge University Press, 2001.

Roszak, Theodore. *The Making of a Counterculture: Reflections on the Technocratic Society and Its Youthful Opposition.* Berkeley: University of California Press, 1969, 1995.

Rotella, Carlo. *Good with Their Hands: Boxers, Bluesmen, and Other Characters from the Rust Belt.* Berkeley: University of California Press, 2000.

Rowes, Barbara. *Grace Slick: The Biography.* New York: Doubleday, 1980.

Rubin, Jerry. *Do IT: Scenarios of the Revolution.* New York: Simon & Schuster, 1970.

_____. *We Are Everywhere.* New York: Harper & Row, 1971.

Russell, Ethan. *Let It Bleed: The Rolling Stones, Altamont, and the End of the Sixties.* New York: Springboard, 2009.

Russell, Ross. *Bird Lives: The High Life and Hard Times of Charlie (Yardbird) Parker.* Cambridge, MA: DaCapo, 1996.

Sale, Kirkpatrick. *SDS.* New York: Vintage, 1973.

Sanchez, Tony. *Up and Down with the Rolling Stones.* New York: New American Library, 1979.

Sanders, Ed. *The Family.* New York: Avon, 1972.

Santelli, Robert. *Aquarius Rising: The Rock Festival Years.* New York: Dell, 1980.

Sayres, Sohnya, Anders Stephanson, Stanley Arnowitz, and Fredric Jameson, eds. *The 60s Without Apology.* Minneapolis: University of Minnesota Press, 1984.

Scaduto, Anthony. *Dylan: An Intimate Biography.* New York: Tolmitch, 1973.

Schaffer, Nicholas. *The Beatles Forever.* New York: McGraw-Hill, 1978.

Schulman, Bruce J. *The Seventies: The Great Shift in American Culture, Society, and Politics.* New York: DaCapo, 2002.

Schultz, John. *No One Was Killed: The Chicago Democratic National Convention, August 1968.* Chicago: University of Chicago Press, 2009.

Schumacher, Michael. *Dharma Lion: A Biography of Allen Ginsberg.* New York: St. Martin's, 1992.

Sculati, Gene, and David Seay. *San Francisco Nights: The Psychedelic Music Trip, 1965–1968.* New York: St. Martin's, 1985.

Selvin, Joel. *Summer of Love: The Inside Story of LSD, Rock and Roll, Free Love, and High Times in the Wild West.* New York: Cooper Square, 1994.

Sinclair, Mick, and John Henri Holmberg. *San Francisco: A Cultural and Literary History.* Berkeley: Signal, 1995.

Skolnick, Arlene. *Embattled Paradise: The American Family in the Age of Uncertainty.* New York: Basic, 1991.

Smith, David E., and John Luce. *Love Needs Care: A History of San Francisco's Haight-Ashbury Medical Clinic and Its Pioneer Role in Treating Drug Abuse Problems.* Boston: Little, Brown, 1971.

Spitz, Robert Stephen. *Barefoot in Babylon: The Creation of the Woodstock Music Festival.* New York: Viking, 1979.

Southern, Terry. *Now Dig This: The Unspeakable Writings of Terry Southern, 1950–1995.* New York: Grove, 2011.

Starr, Kevin. *America and the California Dream.* New York: Oxford University Press, 1973.

Stern, Jane, and Michael Stern. *Sixties People.* New York: Alfred Knopf, 1990.

Stevens, Jay. *Storming Heaven: LSD and the American Dream.* New York: Grove Atlantic, 1987.

Stevenson, Douglas. *The Farm Now and Then: A Model for Sustainable Living.* Gabriola Island, BC: New Society, 2014.

_____. *Out to Change the World: The Evolution of the Farm Community.* Summertown, TN: Book, 2014.

Sundance, Elaine. *Celery Wine: Story of a Country Commune.* Yellow Springs, OH: Community Publications Cooperative, 1973.

Swingrover, E.A., ed. *The Counterculture Reader.* New York: Pearson-Longman, 2004.

Talbot, David. *Season of the Witch: Enchantment, Terror, and Deliverance in the City of Love.* New York: Free, 2012.

Tamarkin, Jeff. *Got a Revolution: The Turbulent Flight of the Jefferson Airplane.* New York: Astira, 2003.

Teaford, Jan. *The 20th Century American City: Problems, Promise, and Reality.* Baltimore: Johns Hopkins University Press, 1986.

Thompson, Hunter S. *Fear and Loathing in Las Vegas: A Savage Journey into the Heart of the American Dream.* New York: Random House, 1998.

Tobler, John. *The New Musical Express: The Rock 'n' Roll Years.* London: Reed International, 1992.

Torgoff, Martin. *Can't Find My Way Home: American in the Great Stoned Age, 1945–2000.* New York: Simon & Schuster, 2000.

Tirro, Frank. *Jazz: A History.* New York: W.W. Norton, 1977.

Turner, Paul Venable. *Campus: An American Planning Tradition.* Cambridge, MA: MIT Press, 1984.

Turner, Steve. *A Hard Day's Write.* New York: HarperCollins, 1994.

Tytell, John. *Paradise Outlaws: Remembering the Beats.* New York: William Morrow, 1999.

Unger, Irwin. *The Movement: A History of the New Left, 1959–1972.* New York: Dodd, Mead, 1974.

Vatter, Harold. *The American Economy in the 1950s.* New York: Praeger, 1963.

Viorst, Milton. *Fire in the Streets: America in the 1960s.* New York: Simon & Schuster, 1979.

Von Hoffman, Nicholas. *We Are the People Our Parents Warned Us Against: A Close-Up of the Whole Hippie Scene.* Greenwich, CT: Fawcett, 1968.

Walker, Daniel. *Rights in Conflict: The Violent Confrontation of Demonstrators and Police in the Parks and Streets of Chicago During the Week of the Democratic National Convention of 1968.* New York: Bantam, 1968.

Ward, Ed, Geoffrey Stokes, and Ken Tucker. *Rock of Ages: The Rolling Stone History of Rock 'n' Roll.* New York: Simon & Schuster, 1986.

Warhol, Andy, and Pat Hackett. *Popism: The Warhol Sixties.* New York: Harcourt, Brace and Jovanovich, 1980.

Warren-George, Holly. *The Rolling Stone Book of the Beats: The Beat Generation and American Culture.* New York: Hyperion, 2006.

Watkins, Paul, with Guillermo Soledad. *My Life with Charles Manson.* New York: Bantam, 1979.

Watson, Charles. *Will You Die for Me? As Told to Chaplain Ray Hoelkstra.* Crossroads, 1978.

Watson, Steven. *The Birth of the Beat Generation: Visionaries, Rebels, and Hipsters, 1944–1960.* New York: Pantheon, 1995.

Wells, Tom. *The War Within: America's Battle Over Vietnam.* Berkeley: University of California Press, 1994.

Westhues, Kenneth, ed. *Society's Shadow: Studies of the Sociology of the Counterculture.* Toronto: McGraw-Hill-Ryerson, 1972.

Whaley, Preston Jr. *Blow Like a Horn: Beat Writing, Jazz, Style and Markets in Transformation of United States Culture.* Cambridge, MA: Harvard University Press, 2004.

Whyte, William. *The Organization Man.* New York: Simon & Schuster, 1956.

Wilson, James Q. *Thinking About Crime.* New York: Vintage, 1985.

Wilson, Sloan. *The Man in the Grey Flannel Suit.* New York: Four Walls Eight Windows, 2002 [1955].

Wolf, Leonard, and Deborah Leonard, eds. *Voices from the Love Generation.* Boston: Little, Brown, 1968.

Wolfe, Burton H. *The Hippies.* New York: New American Library, 1968.

Wolfe, Tom. *The Electric Kool-Aid Acid Test.* New York: Farrar, Straus and Giroux, 1968.

_____. *The Kandy-Kolored Tangerine-Flake Streamline Baby.* New York: Farrar, Straus and Giroux, 1965.

_____. *The Purple Decades: A Reader.* New York: Berkeley, 1987.

Yablonsky, Lewis. *The Hippie Trip: A First-Hand Account of the Beliefs, Drug Use and Sexual Patterns of Young Drop-Outs in America.* New York: Pegasus, 1968.

Yankelovich, Daniel. *The New Rules: Searching for Self-Fulfillment in a World Turned Upside Down.* New York: Random House, 1971.

Zaroulis, Nancy, and Gerald Sullivan. *Who Spoke Up? American Protest Against the War in Vietnam, 1963–1975.* Garden City, NY: Doubleday, 1984.

Newspapers, Magazines and Journals (Mainstream and Underground)

Activist
American Heritage
American Studies
Atlanta Journal and Constitution
Atlantic City Press
Atlantic Monthly
Austin Rag
The Beat
Berkeley Barb
Berkeley Tribe
Business Week
Clinical Pediatrics
Communitarian
Communities
Denver Post
Detroit News
Detroiter
Dissent
East Village Other
Economist
Esquire
Guardian
Haight-Ashbury Eye
Haight-Ashbury Maverick
Harper's
High Times
International Review of Modern Sociology
Journal of Family Issues
Life
Look
Los Angeles Times
Marin Independent Journal
Monterey Count Herald
Mother Earth News
Nation
New York Times
New York Times Magazine
New Yorker
Newsweek
Partisan Review
Quicksilver Times
Ramparts
Realist
Rhetoric Society Quarterly
Rolling Stone
St. Louis Post Dispatch
Salon
San Francisco Chronicle
San Francisco Examiner
San Francisco Oracle
San Francisco Standard
Social Science
Space City News
Studies on the Left
Tennessean
Time
Vanity Fair
Village Voice
Washington Post
Whole Earth News
Yes Magazine

Articles by Chapter

INTRODUCTION

Roszak, Theodore. "The Misunderstood Movement." *New York Times,* December 3, 1994, A23–25.

CHAPTER 1

"Birth of a City." *Time* 60, no. 5 (April 17, 1950).

Boulton, Alexander. "The Buy of the Century." *American Heritage* (July/August 1969): 62–69.

Broyard, Anatole. "A Portrait of the Hipster." *Partisan Review* (June 1948): 721–728.

City of Lakewood, California—Lakewood History, Chapter 2. "A City as New as Tomorrow." http://www.lakewoodcity.org/about/history/ch2.asp.

Clark, Clifford E., Jr. "Ranch House Suburbia: Ideals and Realities." In *Recasting America: Culture and Politics in the Age of the Cold War,* edited by Larry May, 171–192. Chicago: University of Chicago Press, 1989.

Corso, Gregory. "Variations on a Generation." In *The Portable Beat Reader,* edited by Ann Charters, 183–186. New York: Viking-Penguin, 1992.

Currie, Robin. "Children's Television, the 1950s." *History Wired.* http://historywired.si.edu/detail.cfm?ID=132 (now inactive).

Hamlin, Jesse. "How Herb Caen Named a Generation." *San Francisco Chronicle,* March 26, 1995.

Hoby, Hermione. "Allen Ginsberg, Howl, and the Voice of the Beats. *The Guardian,* February 23, 2011, 26–29.

Holmes, John Clellon. "This Is the Beat Generation." *New York Times Magazine,* November 16, 1952.

Mailer, Norman. "The White Negro: Superficial Reflections on the Hipster." *Dissent* (Fall 1957).

May, Elaine. "Cold War—Warm Hearth: Politics and the Family in Postwar America." In *The Rise and Fall of the New Deal Order, 1930–1980,* edited by Steve Fraser and Gary Gerstle, 153–181. Princeton: Princeton University Press, 1989.

Riesman, David. "The Suburban Madness." In *The Suburban Community,* edited by William Dobriner, 375–402. New York: Putnam and Sons, 1958.

Rosenbaum, Ron. "The House That Levitt Built." *Esquire* 100 (December 1983): 378–391.

Tytell, John. "An Interview with Herbert Huncke." In *Unspeakable Visions of the Individual,* edited by Arthur and Kit Knight, 3–15. California, PA: A Knight.

"Up from the Potato Fields." *Time* 61, no.1 (July 3, 1950).

CHAPTER 2

Ashbolt, Anthony. "Go Ask Alice: Remembering the Summer of Love Forty Years On." *Austral-Asian Journal of American Studies* 23 (June 2007): 36–56.

Berkeley Barb. "Mime Troup [sic] Always Set to Shuffle." July 28, 1967, 9.

Biner, Pierre. "The Living Theater." In *"Takin' It to the Streets": A Sixties Reader,* edited by Alexander Bloom and Wini Breiner, 288–293. New York: Oxford University Press, 1995.

Davis, R.G. "Radical, Independent, Chaotic, Anarchic Theater Vs. Institutionalized, University, Little, Commercial, Ford, and Stock Theatre." *Studies on the Left* (Spring 1964): 36–46.

Doyle, Michael William. "Staging the Revolution: Guerrilla Theater as Countercultural Practice, 1965–1968," in *Imagine Nation: The American Counterculture of the 1960s and 1970s,* edited by Peter Braunstein and Michael William Doyle, 71–97. New York: Routledge, 2002.

Dreyer, Thorne, and Victoria Smith. "The Movement and the New Media." http://www.nuevoanden.com/rag/newmedia.html.

"Fads: The Psychedelicatessen." *Time* 89, no. 17 (February 24, 1967).

Fallon, Michael. "A New Paradise for Beatniks." *San Francisco Examiner.* September 5, 1965, 5; September 8, 1965, 10.

Farber, David. "The Intoxicated State/Illegal Nation." In *Imagine Nation: The American Counterculture of the 1960s and 1970s,* edited by Peter Braunstein and Michael William Doyle, 17–39. New York: Routledge Press, 2002.

Gleason, Ralph. "Brief History of Those New Words." *San Francisco Chronicle,* August 9, 1967, 41.

_____. "A Free Frame of Reference." *San Francisco Chronicle,* January 23, 1967, 37.

Gooding, Judson. "Revolution or Revival?" In *The Hippies: Who They Are, Where They Are; Why They Act That Way, and How They May Affect Our Society,* edited by Joe David Brown, 205–220. New York: Time, 1967.

_____, and Malcolm Carter. "The Throbbing Three-Eights." In *The Hippies,* edited by Joe David Brown, 28–42.

Kupferberg, Tuli. "The Politics of Love." *East Village Other.* May 1–15, 1967, 4–8.

Lieper, Steve. "At the Handle of the Kettle." *San Francisco Oracle* 4 (December 1966): 10.

"Longer Hair Is Not Necessarily a Hippie." *Time* 90, no. 17 (October 27, 1967).

Shaw, John. "Christ Was a Very Groovy Cat." In *The Hippies: Who They Are, Where They Are; Why They Act That Way, and How They May Affect Our Society,* edited by Joe David Brown, 58–71. New York: Time, 1967.

Stein, Mark. "20 Years After the Hippie Invasion: The Summer of Love That Left Its Imprint on S.F." *Los Angeles Times,* June 21, 1987.

Strait, Guy. "What Is a Hippie?" In *"Takin' It to the Streets": A Sixties Reader,* edited by Alexander Bloom and Wini Breines, 310–314. New York: Oxford University Press, 1995.

Thompson, Hunter S. "The 'Hashbury' Is the Capital of the Hippies." *New York Times Magazine,* May 14, 1967.

Weller, Sheila. "Suddenly Last Summer." *Vanity Fair* 623 (July 2012): 68–85.

CHAPTER 3

"The Dangers of LSD." *Time* 87, no. 16 (April 2, 1966).

"Degenaro, Jane." In *From Camelot to Kent State: The Sixties Experience in the Words of Those Who Lived It,* edited by Joan and Robert K. Morrison, 204–210. New York: Oxford University Press, 2001.

"An Epidemic of Acid Heads." *Time* 87, no. 10 (March 11, 1966).

"Hoffman, Bruce." In *From Camelot to Kent State: The Sixties Experience in the Words of Those Who Lived It,* edited by Joan and Robert K. Morrison, 211–216. New York: Oxford University Press, 2001.

"Instant Mysticism." *Time* 82, no. 17 (October 25, 1963).

Leary, Timothy. "Turning on the World." In *The Counterculture Reader,* edited by E.A. Swingrover, 84–88. New York: Pearson/Longman, 2004.

_____. "Press Conference." *San Francisco Oracle* 1 (December 1966); 4, 17, 18, 19.

"LSD." *Time* 87, no. 24 (June 7, 1966).

Mandelkorn, Phillip. "The Drugs They Use." In *The Hippies: Who They Are, Where They Are, Why They Act That Way, and How They May Affect Our Society,* edited by Joe David Brown, 171–185. New York: Time, 1967.

"Mushroom Madness." *Time* 61, no. 16 (June 16, 1958).

"Pop Drugs: The High as a Way of Life." *Time* 94, no.13 (September 26, 1969).

"The Pros and Cons of LSD." *Time* 84, no. 26 (December 18, 1964).

"Psychedelic Research: LSD." *Time* 81, no. 13 (March 29, 1963).

Szalavitz, Maia. "The Legacy of the CIA's Secret LSD Experiments on America." *Time,* March 23, 2012.

"Time to Mutate." *Time* 87, no. 17 (April 29, 1966).

Wasson, R. Gordon. "Seeking the Magic Mushroom." *Life* (June 10, 1957). www.imaginaria.org/wasson/life.htm.

CHAPTER 4

Christgau, Robert. "Secular Music." *Esquire* (December 1967): 283.

Corlisss, Richard. "That Old Feeling: Meet the Beatles." *Time* 163, no. 6 (February 9, 2004).

Frankel, Glen. "Nowhere Man." *Washington Post,* August 26, 2007.

Gibson, Christine. "Elvis on Ed Sullivan: The Real Story." *American Heritage* (December 6, 2005), http://www.americanheritage.com.

Gleason, Ralph. "Lesson for S.F. in the Mime Benefit." *San Francisco Chronicle* (December 13, 1967), 47.

_____. "Perspectives: A Power to Change the World." *Rolling Stone* (June 22, 1968): 10.

Goldstein, Richard. "I Blew My Cool Through the New York Times." *The Village Voice* 12 (July 20, 1967): 4–8.

_____. "San Francisco Bray." In *"Takin' It to the Streets": A Sixties Reader,* edited by Alexander Bloom and Wini Breines, 293–297. New York: Oxford University Press, 1995.

_____. "We Still Need the Beatles, but ..." *New York Times,* June 18, 1967, 104.

Groenke, Randy, and Mike Cramer. "March 1967: Garcia Interview." http://deadsources.blogspot.com/2013/05/march-1967-garcia-interview.html (now inactive).

Jones, Chris. "Review of the Beatles' Sgt. Pepper's Lonely Hearts Club Band." BBC News, 2007. http://www.bbc.co.uk/music/reviews/5dcz/.

"The New Madness." *Time* 82, no. 20 (November 15, 1963).

"The Messengers." *Time* 90, no. 12 (September 22, 1967).

"Passionate and Sloppy." *Time* 92, no. 6 (August 1968).

Perry, Charles. "The Sound of San Francisco." In *The Rolling Stone Illustrated History of Rock and Roll*, edited by Anthony DeCurtis and James Henke, 362–369. New York: Random House.

"Rock 'n' Roll: Open Up, Tune In, Turn On." *Time* 89, no. 25 (June 23, 1967).

CHAPTER 5

"Affirming Humanness." *San Francisco Oracle* 1 (September 1966): 1.

Berkeley Barb. "Lovin Haight." (October 14, 1966): 3.

Ginsberg, Allen. "Demonstration or Spectacle as Example, as Communication, or How to Make a March/Spectacle." *Berkeley Barb* (November 19, 1965): 2.

"A Prophesy of a Declaration of Independence." *San Francisco Oracle* 1 (September 1966): 14.

Time. "The Law and LSD." 87, no. 23 (June 10, 1966).

CHAPTER 6

"The American Indian Issue." *San Francisco Oracle* 1 (Spring 1967): 5–10.

Arnold, Martin. "Organized Hippies Emerge on Coast." *New York Times*, May 5, 1967, 8.

Berner, Jeff. "Astronauts of Inner Space: Hippies Are American Indians." *San Francisco Examiner*, June 18, 1967, 30.

Braunstein, Peter. "Forever Young: Insurgent Youth and the Sixties Culture of Rejuvenation." In *Imagine Nation: The American Counterculture of the 1960s and 1970s*, edited by Peter Braunstein and Michael William Doyle, 243–273. New York: Routledge, 2002.

Bruce, J. Campbell. "Hippies at My Window." *San Francisco Chronicle*, April 6, 1967, 3.

"Buslines Halt Haight Tours." *Berkeley Barb* (May 26, 1967): 2.

"Changes" or "The Houseboat Summit." *San Francisco Oracle* (February 1967): 10–20.

Corliss, Richard. "That Old Feeling: 'Hair' Today." *Time* 157, no. 18 (May 7, 2001).

Costo, Rupert. "Hippies Are Not American Indians." *San Francisco Examiner*, June 25, 1967, 26.

Deloria, Phillip. "Counterculture Indians and the New Age." In *Imagine Nation: The American Counterculture of the 1960s and 1970s*, edited by Peter Braunstein and Michael William Doyle, 159–184. New York: Routledge, 2002.

Denson, Ed. "And a Thousand Shops Shall Bloom." *Berkeley Barb* (March 17, 1967): 6.

_____. "What Happened at the Happening." *Berkeley Barb* (January 20, 1967): 1, 4, 6.

"Doctrines of the Dropouts." *Time* 91, no. 1 (January 5, 1968).

"Dropouts with a Mission." *Newsweek* (February 6, 1967): 92–95.

Gilbert, George. "Diggers Preparing for the Invasion." *San Francisco Chronicle*, May 20, 1967, 1, 11.

Gleason, Ralph. "The Tribes Gather for a Yea-Saying." *San Francisco Chronicle*, January 16, 1967, 41.

"The Gossiping Guru: Will Success Spoil the Haight?" *San Francisco Oracle* 1 (March 1967): 24, 39.

Hinckle, Warren. "A Social History of the Hippies." *Ramparts* (March 1967): 5–26.

"Hippie Article Raises Row." *Berkeley Barb* (June 9, 1967): 7.

"The Hippies: A Philosophy of a Subculture." *Time* 90, no. 1 (July 7, 1967): 18–22.

"The Hippies Are Coming." *Newsweek* (June 12, 1967): 28–30.

"Inside Story on the Hippie Tale." *Berkeley Barb* (June 6, 1967): 4.

"Inside the Hippie Revolution." *Look*. (August 22, 1967): 58–61.

Luce, John. "Whither the Hippies?" *San Francisco Magazine* (May 1967): 39–43.

Mandelkorn, Joel. "The Flower Children." In *The Hippies: Who They Are, Where They Are, Why They Act That Way, and How They May Affect Our Society*, edited by Joe David Brown, 1–24. New York: Time, 1967.

Marmon, William F., Jr., and Arlie Schardt. "Man I Dig Those Founding Fathers." In *The Hippies: Who They Are, Where They Are, Why They Act That Way, and How They May Affect Our Society*, edited by Joe David Brown, 99–132. New York: Time, 1967.

McCabe, Charles. "Hippies and Indians." *San Francisco Chronicle*, May 27, 1967, 10.

"Our Readers Rap: On Bein' at the Be-In." *Berkeley Barb* (January 20, 1967): 7

Perry, Helen Swick. "The Human Be-In." In *"Takin' It to the Streets": A Sixties Reader*, edited by Alexander Bloom and Wini Breines, 312–316. New York: Oxford University Press, 1995.

"Politics and Ecstasy." *San Francisco Oracle* 1 (January 1967): 1–2.

Shoris, Earl. "Love Is Dead." *New York Times Magazine*, October 29, 1967, 114–117.

"Statement by the Inspirers of the Gathering of the Tribes." *Berkeley Barb* (January 13, 1967): 1.

Sutton, Horace. "A Hippie Place to Blow the Mind." *San Francisco Chronicle*, July 2, 1967, 2–3.

"Talk of the Town." *The New Yorker* 42 (October 1, 1966): 42–43.

"Turned on and Super Sincere in California." *Harpers* (January 1967): 42–47.

"Turned on Way of Life." *Newsweek* (November 28, 1966): 72–74.

Wainwright, Loudon. "The Strange New Love Land of the Hippies." *Life* (March 31, 1967): 15–19.

CHAPTER 7

"…and the Yippies on St. Marks." *The Local East Village*. http://localeastvillage.com/.

Armstrong, Lois Dickert. "Christ Was a Groovy Cat." In *The Hippies: Who They Are, Where They Are, Why They Act That Way, and How They May Affect Our Society*, edited by Joe David Brown, 47–55. New York: Time, 1967.

Beaumier, Frank. "Man I Dig Those Founding Fathers." In *The Hippies: Who They Are, Where They Are, Why They Act That Way, and How They May Affect Our Society*, edited by Joe David Brown, 134–138. New York: Time, 1967.

Burks, John. "The Underground Press: A Special Report." *Rolling Stone* 43 (October 4, 1969): 12–34.

Christgau, Robert. "The Continuing Saga of the MC-5." *Village Voice* (June 5, 1968): http://www.robert

christgau.com/xg/rock/mc5–69.php. Also see "The MC-5" in *East Village Other* 4 (May 14, 1969): 5, 17.

"The Great Hippie Hunt." *Time* 94, No. 15 (October 10, 1969).

Hale, Jeff. "The White Panthers' Total Assault on the Culture." In *Imagine Nation: The American Counterculture in the 1960s and 1970s*, edited by Peter Braunstein and Michael William Doyle, 125–155. New York: Routledge, 2002.

Hill, Christina. "The Artists' Workshop: John Sinclair and Others Sound Off." *The Detroiter* (September 9, 1986). http://www.thedetroiter.com/nov04/artistswkshop.html (now inactive).

Jacobson, Mark. "Long Hot Summer of Love." *New York Magazine* (June 25, 2007.)

Kelly, Katie. "The East Village Other." In *The Hippies: Who They Are, Where They Are, Why They Act That Way, and How They May Affect Our Society*, edited by Joe David Brown, 88–92. New York: Time, 1967.

Kramer, Wayne. "Riots I Have Known and Loved." *Left of the Dial* #4: http://makeymyday.free.fr/wk1.htm (now inactive).

Ledbetter, James. "The Day the NYSE Went Yippie." *CNNMoney*, http://money.cnn.com.

Leo, John. "Politics Now the Focus of the Underground Press." *New York Times*, September 1, 1968, 6.

"Love in Boss Town." *Time* 92, no. 2 (July 12, 1968).

Marino, Mike. "E=MC5: Kick Out the Jams, Motherfuckers!" http://www.rockandreprise.net/marino.html.

"Marxist Scholar Opines on Hips." *Berkeley Barb* (May 12, 13, 16, 1967): 7, 9, 11, 12.

McNeil, Don. "Central Park Rite Is Medieval Pageant." *Village Voice* 24 (March 30, 1967).

Morris, Julie, and Jenny Nolan. "Sex, Drugs, Rock 'n' Roll and Plum Street." *The Detroit News*, September 12, 1997. detroitnews.com.

Nye, Hermes. "Texas Tea and Rainy Day Woman." In *What's Goin On? (In Modern Texas Folklore)*, edited by Francis Edward Abernethy, 118. Denton: University of North Texas Press, 1998.

Ogelsby, Carl. "The Hippies: Suburbanites with Beads." *Activist* (Fall 1967): 12–15.

Pouncey, Edwin. "MC5 Meets Sun Ra: Motown City Burning." (February 2007). http://thewire.co.uk/in-writing/interviews/p=12630 (now inactive).

Rossinow, Doug. "The Revolution Is About Our Lives." In *Imagine Nation: The American Counterculture of the 1960s and 1970s*, edited by Peter Braunstein and Michael William Doyle, 99–123. New York: Routledge, 2002.

Shero, Jeff. "Dallas Police Jail Banana Users." *The Rag* 1 (March 27, 1967): 7–8, 16.

Sinclair, John. "Rock and Roll Is a Weapon of Cultural Revolution." In *The Story of the MC5: John Sinclair*. http://www.punk77.co.uk/groups/mc5_sinclair.htm. Also see same declaration in *"Takin' It to the Streets": A Sixties Reader*, edited by Alexander Bloom Wini Breines, 301–303. New York: Oxford University Press, 1995.

_____, and D.A. Latimer. Untitled Interview. *East Village Other* 4 (June 4, 1969): 3.

"Story of the Mighty MC5—History-Part I." http://www.punk77.co.uk/groups/mc5_history_1.htm.

"Talk of the Town." *The New Yorker* (October 14, 1967): 49.

"Underground Alliance." *Time* 80, no. 15 (July 29, 1966).

"Yuppie and the Yippie: Jerry Rubin." In *From Camelot to Kent State: The Sixties Experience in the Word of Those Who Lived It*, edited by Joan Morrison and Robert K. Morrison, 281–289. New York: Oxford University Press, 1987.

"Wayne Kramer Interview." *Addicted to Noise* 1.02, parts I–IV (February 1995). http://www.addict.com/issues/1.02/Features/MC5/Wayne_Kramer (now inactive).

Wilwerth, James Kent. "The East Village Others." In *The Hippies: Who They Are, Where They Are, Why They Act That Way, and How They May Affect Our Society*, edited by Joe David Brown, 80–86. New York: Time, 1967.

Chapter 8

Alexander, Brian. "Free Love: Was There a Price to Pay?" *MSNBC* (June 22, 2007). http://www.nbcnews.com.

Anderson, Chester. "Trouble in Bohemia." *Berkeley Barb* (August 3, 1967): 3.

Bailey, Beth. "Sex as a Weapon: Underground Comix and the Paradox of Liberation." In *Imagine Nation: The American Counterculture of the 1960s and 1970s*, edited by Peter Braunstein and Michael William Doyle, 305–323. New York: Routledge, 2002.

Berner, Jeff. "Astronauts of Inner Space: The Haight-Ashbury Scene Is Finished!" *San Francisco Chronicle* (August 20, 1967): Datebook 22.

"California: End of the Dance." *Time* 90, no. 7 (August 18, 1967).

Chapin, William. "A Day on the Hippieland Scene." *San Francisco Chronicle*, October 9, 1967, 14–15.

Christgau, Robert. "Anatomy of a Love Festival." *Esquire* (June 1969). http://www.robertchristgau.com/xg/music/monterey-69.php.

"Daylight Raid on Haight." *San Francisco Chronicle*, October 10, 1967, 1.

"Death of Hip Birth of Free." *Berkeley Barb* (September 29, 1967): 3.

"Death of Hip, Mixed Emotions." *Berkeley Barb* (October 13, 1967): 5.

"The Ebb and Flow of the Hippie Tide." *San Francisco Chronicle*, June 23, 1967, 1, 18.

"Frightened Hippies Are Arming." *San Francisco Chronicle*, August 10, 1967, 1.

Gilbert, George. "A Hippie's Day: The Flower Children's Society." *San Francisco Chronicle*, May 17, 1967, 1, 14.

Grieg, William. "Death of the Hippies: A Sad, Solemn Ceremony." *San Francisco Chronicle*, October 7, 1967, 2.

_____. "The Decline and Fall of Hippieland." *San Francisco Chronicle*, October 5, 1967, 1, 8.

"Haightians Thrill to Spacious Street." *Berkeley Barb* (September 15, 1967): 5.

"Hepatitis Hits the Haight." *San Francisco Chronicle*, August 18, 1967, 14.

Hill, T. R. Wayne. "Houston Homosexual Speaks Out." *Space City News* (October 11–25, 1969): 4–5.

Howe, Charles. "Hippies Say They Need Protection from the Police." *San Francisco Chronicle*, October 11, 1967, 1.

"In Memoriam for Superspade and John Carter." *San Francisco Oracle* 1 (August 1967): 4.

Jassen, Jeff. "The Year of the Shuck: What Price Love?" *Berkeley Barb* (July 5, 1967): 5.

La Morticella, Barbara. "New Year's Day Wail—Visualities." *San Francisco Oracle* 1 (January 1967): 5.

"Love Community's Plea to Straights." *San Francisco Chronicle,* May 27, 1967, 2

Luce, John. "Haight-Ashbury Today: A Case of Terminal Euphoria." *Esquire* 72 (July 1969): 68–70.

"Merchant Denounces Plastic Hippies." *San Francisco Standard* (July 8, 1967): 1.

"A New Mind Drug." *San Francisco Chronicle,* August 12, 1967, Headline, 1–2.

"Peace Corps Survival." *San Francisco Standard* (July 7, 1967): 2.

Perlman, David. "Meth Heads' Fantastic Drug Jolt." *San Francisco Chronicle,* July 29, 1967, 1, 4.

Raudenbaugh, Charles. "Grateful Dead Hold Lively Wake." *San Francisco Chronicle,* October 6, 1967, 2.

"San Francisco: Wilting Flowers." *Time* 91, no. 19 (May 10, 1968).

Selvin, Joel. "Summer of Love: 40 Years Later: The Stuff That Myths Are Made Of." *San Francisco Chronicle,* May 20, 2007, www.sfgate.com.

Smith, David E., and Alan Rose. "Health Problems in Urban and Rural 'Crash Pad' Communes." In *Clinical Pediatrics* 9 (September 1970): 534–548.

"So Who Mutha'd the Hippies?" *Berkeley Barb* (October 6, 1967): 1.

"The STP Leak: A New Drug Mystery." *San Francisco Chronicle,* August 3, 1967, Headline, 1–3.

"Trouble in Hippieland." *Newsweek* (October 30, 1967): 84, 87–90.

"A Wake for Hip, a Cheer for Free." *Berkeley Barb* (October 6, 1967): 3.

"Where Are They Now? The Haight-Ashbury Scene." *Newsweek* (December 2, 1967): 20.

"Where Have All the Flowers Gone?" *Time* 90, no. 15 (October 13, 1967).

CHAPTER 9

Cabrera, Marc. "The Father of Pop." *Monterey County Herald: Sunday Special Commemorating the 40th Anniversary of the Monterey Pop Festival and the Summer of Love,* June 10, 2007, 12.

Hill, Sarah. "When Deep Soul Met the Love Crowd: Otis Redding: Monterey Pop Festival, June 17, 1967." In *Performance and Popular Music: History, Place, and Time,* edited by Ian Englis, 28–32. Hampshire, England: Ashgate, 2006.

Hoskyns, Barney. "The Meeting of the Twain: Monterey and the Great California Divide." *The Complete Monterey Pop Festival,* DVD set: Criterion Collection, 2002, 1–48.

"How the Happening Happened." *The Beat* 3, KRLA edition, Pop Festival Souvenir Issue (July 15, 1967): 1, 3–5.

Hurwitt, Robert. "Magic Mountain Fervor." *Berkeley Barb* (June 16, 1967): 3.

Larcher, Irene. "The Sunday Conversation: Lou Adler on Monterey Pop." (June 10, 2012): www..latimes.com.

"A Letter: The Lovin' Levis." *Berkeley Barb* (May 12, 1967): 6.

Lomas, Mark. "Fantasy Fair& Magic Mountain Music Festival." Marin History, *Marin Independent Journal.* http://blogs.marinji.com (now inactive).

Lydon, Michael. "Monterey Pop: The First Rock Festival." *Newsweek* (June 20, 1967): 28–32.

McCleary, John Bassett. "Commentary: 40 Years Ago: The Monterey Pop Festival." *Monterey County Herald,* June 10, 2007, 2–3.

Miller, Timothy. "The Cooling of America: Out of Tune and Lost in the Counterculture." *Time* 97, no. 8 (February 22, 1971).

"Monterey—'It Was a Good Beginning' as Viewed by Eric Burdon." *The Beat* 3, KRLA edition, Pop Festival Souvenir Issue (July 15, 1967): 8.

"Truth Be Told." *Monterey County Herald,* June 10, 1967, 4.

"Did You Know?" *Monterey County Herald,* June 10, 1967, 13.

"Quotable." *Monterey County Herald,* June 10, 1967, 10.

"Memories." *Monterey County Herald,* June 10, 1967, 23.

Onkey, Lauren. "Voodoo Child: Jimi Hendrix and the Politics of Race in the Sixties." In *Imagine Nation: The American Counterculture of the 1960s & 1970s,* edited by Peter Braunstein and Michael William Doyle, 189–213. New York: Routledge, 2002.

"Passionate and Sloppy." *Time* 92, no. 6 (August 9, 1968).

Peerless, Beth. "The Music." *Monterey County Herald,* June 10, 2007, 4.

The Tavis Smiley Show. "The Lou Adler Interview," June 4, 2007. http://:www.pbs.org/kcet/tavissmiley/archive/200706/20070604_adler.html (now inactive).

"Wild, Wooly & Wicked." *Time* 91, no. 41 (August 9, 1968).

Zane, Maitland. "Bash on Mt. Tam." *San Francisco Chronicle,* June 12, 1967, 3.

CHAPTER 10

Aidala, Angela. "Communes and Changing Family Norms: Marriage and Lifestyle Choices Among Former Members of Communal Groups." *Journal of Family Issues* 10 (September 1989): 311–338.

Baldwin, J. "Alloy Report." In *The Last Whole Earth Catalog,* edited by Stewart Brand, 112–117. New York: Random House, 1971.

Bates, Albert. "J. Edgar Hoover and the Farm." Paper presented at the International Communal Studies Conference on Culture, Thought, and Living in Community, New Harmony, Indiana. October 16, 1993. http://www.thefarm.org .

Beach, Sara. "Communal Sense." *Salon* (August 22, 2001). http://www.salon.com.

Beshoar, Barron. "Communes in the Country." In *The Hippies: Who They Are, Where They Are, Why They Act That Way, and How They May Affect Our Society,* edited by Joe David Brown, 70–83. New York: Time, 1967.

Bliss, Jessica. "Stephen Gaskin, Founder of the Farm, Dies at 79." *The Tennessean,* July 2, 2014, http://www.tennessean.com.

Camden, Maren Lockwood. "Communes and Protest Movements in the US, 1960–1974: An Analysis of Intellectual Roots." *International Review of Modern Sociology* 6 (Spring 1976): 13–22.

Chawkins, Steve. "Stephen Gaskin Dies at 79; Founder of the Farm Commune." *Los Angeles Times,* July 5, 2014. http://www.latimes.com.

"Closed Communes." *Time* 95, no. 13 (March 30, 1970).

Coate, John, and Cliff Figallo. "Farm Stories." *Whole Earth Review* 60 (Fall 1988): 84–105.

_____."Life on the Bus and Farm: An Informal Recollection." (1987). cervisa.com.

Constas, Helen, and Kenneth Westhues. "Communes: The Routinization of Hippiedom." In *Society's Shadow: Studies in the Sociology of Countercultures,* edited by Kenneth Weshues, 191–200. Toronto: McGraw-Hill Ryerson, 1972.

Davidson, Sara. "Open Land: Getting Back to the Communal Garden." *Harper's* 240 (June 1970): 91–100. http://www.saradavidson.com.

Dodd, Bill. "Drop City." *San Francisco Oracle* 2 (April 1968): 24–27.

"Down on the Farm in Summertown, Tennessee: A Flower Child's Adventure." *2nd Sight Magazine.* Secondsightresearch.Tripod.Com/Cattales/Id13html.

"The Dymaxion American." Time 83, no. 2 (January 10, 1964).

Gilman, Diane. "The Farm Twenty Years Later: An Interview with Albert Bates." *Context Institute* 29 (1991): 36–40.

Hendrickson, John. "Colorado's Dome on the Range." *The Denver Post,* June 16, 2009. http://www.denverpost.com.

Hippycommunekid. "Growing Up on a Hippy Commune." http://hippycommune.wordpress.com/tag/stephen-gaskin/.

"'Is Stephen Gaskin a Second Christ?' Some Still Say Yes, Some Disagree." *The Tennessean,* October 11, 1981.

Jones, Robert F. "Communes in the Country." In *The Hippies: Who They Are, Where They Are, Why They Act That Way, and How They May Affect Our Society,* edited by Joe David Brown, 63–75. New York: Time, 1967.

Kelly, Kevin. "Why We Left the Farm." *Whole Earth Review* 49 (Winter 1985): 56–66.

Lattin, Don. "Twilight of Hippiedom: Farm Commune's Founder Envisions Return to the Fold as Ex-Dropouts Age." *San Francisco Chronicle,* March 2, 2003. http://www.sfgate.com.

Luker, Kelly. "Commune Sense." *Metroactive* (February 29, 1996). http://www.metroactive.com/papers/metro/02.29.96/hippie-9609.html.

Martin, Douglas. "Stephen Gaskin, Hippie Who Founded an Enduring Commune, Dies at 79." *New York Times,* July 2, 2014. http://www.nytimes.com.

McCarley, Erin. "Remembering Stephen Gaskin: A Conversation with the Man Behind the Original Off-the-Grid Farm." *Yes Magazine* (November 2005). http://www.yesmagazine.org.

Miller, Timothy. "The Roots of the 1960s Communal Revival." *American Studies* 33 (October 1992): 73–93.

_____. "The Sixties Era Communes." In *Imagine Nation: The American Counterculture of the 1960s & 1970s,* edited by Peter Braunstein and Michael William Doyle, 32–351. New York: Routledge, 2002.

Mother Earth News editors. "The Plowboy Interview: Stephen Gaskin and the Farm." (May/June 1977). http://www.motherearthnews.com.

Meunier, Rachel. "Communal Living in the Late 60s and Early 70s: The Farm: Summertown, Tennessee, USA." http://www.thefarm.org.

"Paradise Rocked." *Time* 93, no. 25 (June 20, 1969).

Simunek, Chris. "Stephen Gaskin, Creator of the Farm, Dies at 79." *High Times* (July 2, 2014). http://www.hightimes.com.

Sun, Patsy. "Why Our Commune Crumbled." *Mother Earth News* (May/June 1970). http://www.motherearthnews.com.

Tomlinson, Eryn. "An Interview with Clark Richert." *Zing Magazine* (September 2009). http://www.zingmagazine.com/drupal/node/1005.

Voyd, Bill. "Funk Architecture." In *Shelter and Society,* edited by Paul Oliver, 155–166. New York: Praeger, 1969.

Welch, Lew. "Op-Ed." *San Francisco Oracle* 2 (September 1968): 3–4.

Wenner, Kate. "How They Keep Them Down on the Farm." *New York Times Magazine,* May 8, 1977, 80–88.

Windolf, Jim. "Sex, Drugs, and Soybeans." *Vanity Fair* (April 5, 2007). http://vanityfair.com/politics/features/2007/05/thefarm200705.

"Year of the Commune." *Newsweek* 74, no. 7 (August 18, 1969): 6–10.

CHAPTER 11

"The Banners of Dissent." *Time* 90, no. 17 (October 27, 1967).

Bernstein, Carl, and Robert G. Kaiser. "2000 Protesters Spend Night at Pentagon—Cold, Hopeful." *Washington Post,* October 22, 1967, A1-A2.

Breslin, Jeremy. "Quiet Rally Turns Vicious." *Washington Post,* October 22, 1967, A1.

"A Call to Resist Illegitimate Authority in 1967." In *Civil Disobedience: Theory and Practice,* edited by Hugo Adam Bedau, 162–164. New York: Pegasus, 1969.

Chapman, William. "Arrests End War Protest." (October 23, 1967): A16.

_____. "55,000 Rally Against War; GI's Repel Pentagon Charge." *Washington Post,* October 22, 1967, A1.

"Chicago Examined: Anatomy of a Police Riot." *Time* 92, no. 23 (December, 6, 1968).

Christgau, Robert. "Rock 'n' Revolution." *The Village Voice* (July 1969): http://www.robertchristgau.com.

"Daly City Under Siege." *Time* 92, no. 9 (August 30, 1968).

"Declaration of Conscience Against the War in Vietnam." In *Civil Disobedience: Theory and Practice,* edited by Hugo Adam Bedau, 160–161. New York: Pegasus, 1969.

"Dementia in the Second City." *Time* 92, no. 10 (September 6, 1968).

"Editorial: The Decline and Fall of the Democratic Party." *Ramparts* 7 (September 28, 1968): 20–42.

Findley, Tim. "Tom Hayden: Interview Part 1." *Rolling Stone* (October 21, 1972): 50–55.

Franklin, Ben A. "War Protesters Defy Deadline, Seized in Capital." *New York Times,* October 23, 1967, 1.

Genet, Jean. "The Members of the Assembly." In *The Counterculture Reader,* edited by E. A. Swingrover, 120–125. New York: Pearson-Longman, 2004.

Herbers, John. "Youths Dominate Capital Throng." *New York Times,* October 22, 1967, 58.

"In the Streets: Tear Gas and Clubs." *Washington Post,* August 29, 1968, A1.

Kenworthy, E. W. "Thousands Reach Capital to Protest Vietnam War." *New York Times,* October 21, 1967, 1.

Krassner, Paul. "60s Live Again Minus the LSD." *Los Angeles Times,* January 28, 2007. www.latimes.com.

Linder, Douglas. "The Chicago Seven, 1969–1970." http://jurist.pitt.edu/trials2.htm (now inactive).

Loftus, Joseph. "Guards Repulse War Protesters at the Pentagon." *New York Times,* October 22, 1967, 1, 58.

Lukas, J. Anthony. "Dissenters Focusing on Chicago." *New York Times,* August 19, 1968, 27.

_____. "Hundreds Injured; 178 Are Arrested a Guardsmen Join in Using Tear Gas." *New York Times,* August 29, 1968, 1, 23.

Morrow, Lance. "1968: Like a Knife Blade: The Year That Severed Past from Future." *Time* 131, no. 2 (January 11, 1988);

_____. "The Whole World Was Watching." *Time* 148, no. 10 (August 26, 1996).

"The New Radical." *Time* 89, no. 17 (April 28, 1967).

"Notes from a Yippizolean Era." *East Village Other* 3 (February 16–22, 1968): 6–8.

"The Politics of Yip." *Time* 91, no. 41 (April 5, 1968).

"Refighting Chicago." *Time* 92, no. 13 (September 27, 1968).

Robinson, Douglas. "100,000 Rally at U.N. Against Vietnam War." *New York Times,* April 16, 1967, 2.

_____. "Scattered Peace Activists Seek to Unify Movement." *New York Times,* February 26, 1967, 3.

Rubin, Jerry. "Yippees Are Coming, Coming, Coming to Chicago." *Liberation News Service* 48 (March 1, 1968): 1–4.

Stern, Laurence. "Ugliness May Be Peace Protesters Lasting Image." *Washington Post,* October 22, 1967, A10.

"A Week of Grievances." *Time* 92, no. 10 (September 6, 1968).

"Who Were the Protesters?" *Time* 92, no. 10 (September 6, 1968).

Von Hoffman, Nicholas. "Yippies Trot Out Candidate—A Pig." *Washington Post,* August 24, 1968, A5.

Wilson, George C. "Pentagon Mobilizes for March." *Washington Post,* October 21, 1967, A1.

CHAPTER 12

Abee, Ralph Marvin. "Symbolism of Bethel." Letters to the Editor of the Times. *New York Times,* August 26, 1969, 46.

Barry, Thomas, "Why Can't There Be Another Woodstock? After a Year the Music Business Learns How Hard It Is to Restage a Legend." *Look,* 34 (August 25, 1970), 28–30.

Beeman, Paul. "Music Fans Stay Orderly Despite Heat, Wine, Drugs." *The Atlanta Journal and Constitution,* July 6, 1969, 2.

_____. "Pop's the Thing Despite Heat at Hampton." *The Atlanta Journal and Constitution,* July 7, 1969, 4.

"Bethel Pilgrims Smoke Grass and Some Take LSD to Groove." *New York Times,* August 18, 1969, 25.

Calta, Louis. "Peaceful Rock Fete Planned Upstate." *New York Times,* June 27, 1969, 24.

_____. "Woodstock Pop-Rock Fete Hits Snag." *New York Times,* July 17, 1969, 56.

Collier, Barnard. "Promoter Baffled That Festival Drew Such a Big Crowd." *New York Times,* August 17, 1969, 80.

_____. "300,000 at Music Fair Mud Plentiful and Food Scarce." *New York Times,* August 17, 1969, 80.

_____. "200,000 Throng to Rock Festival Jam Roads Upstate." *New York Times,* August 16, 1969, 1, 31.

_____. "Tired Rock Fans Exodus Rock Fair." *New York Times,* August 18, 1969, 1.

Farrell, William E. "19-Hour Concert Ends Bethel Fair." *New York Times,* August 19, 1969, 1, 34.

Fosburgh, Lacy. "346 Policemen Quit Festival." *New York Times,* August 15, 1969, 22.

Ganahl, Jane. "Woodstock '99: The Day the Music Died." *San Francisco Chronicle,* July 28, 1999. www.sfgate.com.

"Hog Farming at Woodstock." In *The Sixties: The Decade Remembered Now by the People Who Lived It Then,* edited Lynda Rosen Orbst, 274–279. New York: Rolling Stone, 1977.

Katz, Gene. "Woodstock at 25." http://magazine.14850.com.

Katz, Jon. "Hippies in and Out Like Breeze: Feared Trouble Didn't Come Off." *Atlantic City Press,* August 5, 1969, 2. http://atlanticcitypopfestival.com/webdoc_005.htm (now inactive).

Kopkind, Andrew. "Coming of Age in Aquarius." In *"Takin' It to the Streets: A Sixties Reader,* edited by Alexander Bloom and Wini Breines, 610–615. New York: Oxford University Press, 1995.

Kaufman, Michael T. "Generation Gap Bridged as Monticello Residents Aid Courteous Festival Patrons." *New York Times,* August 18, 1969, 25.

Latzgo, Roger. "Woodstock: Two Score Years Ago." http://www.rogerlatzgo.com/pdf/woodstock.pdf.

London, Herbert. "Romantic Remembrances of Woodstock Misguided." *Newsmax,* August 31, 2009. http://www.newsmax.com/HerbertLondon/woodstock-anniversary/2009/08/31/id/334720/.

Lydon, Patrick. "A Joyful Confirmation That Good Things Can Happen Here." *The Sunday New York Times, Arts and Leisure,* August 24, 1969, D16.

May, Rollo. "An Opinion: On Bethel and After; the Catskillian Love Feast on the Couch." *Mademoiselle,* 70 (November 1969), 28, 40.

McGregor, Craig. "Woodstock: A Desperate Fear for the Future?" *New York Times,* August 19, 1970, 99.

Mead, Margaret. "Woodstock in Retrospect." *Redbook Magazine,* 124, no. 3 (January 1970), 30–32.

"The Message of History's Biggest Happening." *Time* 94, no. 9 (August 29, 1969).

"Morning After Bethel." *New York Times,* Editorial, August 19, 1969, 42.

"Nightmare in the Catskills." *New York Times,* Editorial, August 18, 1969, 34.

Packer, Bonnie, and David Pactor. "The Importance of Woodstock." *The Quicksilver Times* 2 (April 3–13, 1970): 19.

Pareles, Jon. "Woodstock: A Moment of Muddy Grace." *New York Times,* August 5, 2009. www.nytimes.com/2009/08/09/arts/music/09pare.html?_r=0.

Phillips, B.J. "That Rock Road." *Washington Post,* August 15, 1969, 6.

_____. "Thousands Rolling in for Woodstock Rock." *Washington Post,* August 15, 1969, 12.

Phillips, McCandlish. "Rock Festival at Bethel Defeats New Challenges." *New York Times,* August 13, 1969):, 38.

"Rocky Road to Fame, if Not Fortune: Young Impresarios Drop a Bundle Staging Biggest Rock Music Festival, but Win a Place in the Business Scene." *Business Week,* August 20, 1969, 78–80.

"Rock Festivals: Groovy but No Gravy." *Business Week,* 2136 (August 8, 1970), 20–21.

Samuels, Jeff. "Another Woodstock Unlikely as Coin, Civic Problems Squeeze Promoters." *Variety,* 258, no. 12 (August 8, 1970), 85, 88.

Sander, Ellen. "Woodstock Music and Art Fair: The Ultimate Rock Experience." *Saturday Review* 52 (September 27, 1969): 59–67.

Schawab, Donald. "Woodstock 1999." donaldschwab. com/Woodstock1999/Woodstock1999.htm.

Sheffield, Rob. "Woodstock '99: Rage Against the Latrine." *Rolling Stone* (September 2, 2009): www.rolling stone.com.

Shepard, Richard F. "Pop Rock Festival Finds New Home." *New York Times,* July 23, 1969, 30.

_____. "Woodstock Festival Vows to Carry On." *New York Times,* July 18, 1969, 16.

Span, Paula. "40,000 Dance in Rain as Popfest Winds It Up." *Atlantic City Press,* August 4, 1969, 1–2.

Sterling Guy. "The Atlantic City Pop Festival: The Festival That Time Forgot." *Atlantic City Press,* August 1, 2004.

Stone, Jade. "Woodstock 1969 Revisited." http://green-jadestone.com/Woodstock1969.pdf (now inactive).

Storm, Geoff. "Historical Memory and the Woodstock Legacy." www.archives.nysed.gov.

Tiber, Elliot. "How Woodstock Happened." *New York Times Herald Record,* Middletown. Woodstock Commemorative Edition, 1994. http://www.edjustice online.com/woodstock/history/index.htm.

Wilk, Tom. "Look Back: 1969's Atlantic City Pop Festival." (August 17, 2011): URL address: http://www. atlanticcityweekly.com.

Willis, Ellen. "Rock Etc. Woodstock." *New Yorker* 45 (September 6, 1969): 121–124.

"Woodstock: Like It Was in Words of Participants at Music Fair." *New York Times,* August 25, 1969, 30.

CHAPTER 13

Balfour, Marie. "Charles Manson and the Tate-La Bianca Murders: A Family Portrait." In *Famous American Crimes and Trials,* edited by Frankie Y. Bailey and Steve Chermak, Vol. IV, 1960–1980.

Bangs, Lester, et al. "The Rolling Stones' Disaster at Altamont: Let It Bleed." *Rolling Stone* 50 (January 21, 1970).

Brown, Mick. "Stanley Booth Interview." *The Daily Telegraph* (April 19, 2012): http://www.telegraph.co.uk.

Burks, John. "Rock & Roll's Worst Day: The Aftermath of Altamont." *Rolling Stone* 51 (February 7, 1970).

Carlson, Peter. "Hell's Aging Angel." *Washington Post,* August 9, 2009.

Christgau, Robert. "The Rolling Stones: Can't Get No Satisfaction." *Newsday,* July 1972.

Csiscery, George Paul. "Stones Concert Now Ends It: America Now Up for Grabs." *Berkeley Tribe* 1 (December 12–19): 1–3.

Curry, David. "Deadly Day for the Rolling Stones." *The Canberra Times,* December 5, 2009.

Dalton, David. "Altamont: End of the Sixties or Big Mix-Up in the Middle of Nowhere?" *Gadfly* (November/ December 1999).

_____. "If Christ Came Back as a Con Man: Or How I Started Out Thinking Charles Manson Was Innocent and Almost Ended Up Dead." *Gadfly* (October 1998).

"The Demon of Death Valley." *Time* 94, no. 24 (December 12, 1969).

Eisen, Benjy. "Rolling Stones Tour Manager Sam Cutler Finally Tells His Side of the Altamont Fiasco." www. spinner.com.

Felton, David, and David Dalton. "Charles Manson: The Incredible Story of the Most Dangerous Man Alive: Year of the Fork, Night of the Hunter: Book One." *Rolling Stone* 61 (June 25, 1970): 25–40.

"The Girl Who Almost Killed Ford." *Time* 106, no. 11 (September 15, 1975).

Gleason, Ralph. "Aquarius Wept." *Esquire* (August 1970).

Goldman, Albert. "The Emergence of Rock." In *The Sixties,* edited by Gerald Howard, 360–363. New York: Washington Square, 1982.

"Hippies and Violence." *Time* 94, no. 24 (December 12, 1969).

"Investigators Close Decades Old Altamont Killing Case." *USA Today,* May 26, 2005.

Kirkpatrick, Rob. "The Day the Music Died? The Altamont Free Concert 40 Years Later." *The Huffington Post,* December 6, 2009. http://www.huffingtonpost. com.

Lee, Henry K. "Altamont's Cold Case Is Being Closed: Theory of Second Stabber Debunked by Sheriff's Dept." *San Francisco Chronicle,* May 26, 2005.

Lewis, Grover. "Viewing the Remains of a Mean Saturday." *The Village Voice* 14 (December 18, 1969).

Linder, Doug. "The Charles Manson (Tate-La Bianca Murder) Trial." http://law2.umkc.edu/faculty/proj ects/ftrials/manson/mansonaccount.html.

Lydon, Michael. "The Doors: 'You Could Call Us Erotic Politicians.'" *New York Times,* December 1968; republished in *The Guardian* (May 22, 2013), www.the guardian.com.

"The Memoirs of Squeaky Fromme." *Time* 106, no. 11 (September 15, 1975).

"Movie of Slaying at Rock Fest Is Key Evidence in Coast Trial." *New York Times,* January 10, 1971.

O'Neil. Paul. "The Wreck of a Monstrous Family." *Life* (December 19, 1969): 20–31.

Ortega, Tony. "In the Wake of Altamont: Who Hired the Hells' Angels." www.villagevoice.com.

P. Joseph Potocki. "Hippie Armageddon." http://sfbay timeless.com/?p=5545.

Roberts, Steven V. "Actress Is Among 5 Slain at Home in Beverley Hills." *New York Times,* August 9, 1969.

_____. "Charles Manson: One Man's Family." *New York Times Magazine,* January 4, 1970.

Russell, Ethan. "The Rolling Stones at Altamont: The Day the Music Died." *The Telegraph,* December 2, 2009. http://www.telegraph.co.uk.

Sachs, Andrea. "An Interview with Manson Prosecutor Vincent Bugliosi." *Time* (August 7, 2009).

Sragow, Michael. "'Gimme Shelter': The True Story of How a Free Rolling Stones Concert Turned into a Colossal Mass Bad Trip—And Spawned the Most Harrowing Rock 'n' Roll Movie Ever Made." *Salon* (August 10, 2000).

"The Stones and the Triumph of Marsyas." *Time* 100, no. 3 (July 17, 1972).

Swimming to the Moon." *Time* 90, no. 21 (November 24, 1967).

Whitaker, Sterling. "42 Years Ago: Jim Morrison Plays Final Show with the Doors." (December 12, 2012). ultimateclassicrock.com/jim-morrison-plays-final-show-with-the-doors/.

CHAPTER 14

"At War with War." *Time* 95, no. 20 (May 18, 1970).

Bigart, Homer. "Huge City Rally Backs Nixon's Indochina Policies." *New York Times,* May 21 1970, 1.

_____. "Thousands Assail Lindsay in Second Protest by Workers." *New York Times,* May 12, 1970, 1.

_____. "Thousands in City March to Assail Lindsay on War." *New York Times,* May 16, 1970, 11.

_____. "War Foes Here Attacked by Construction Workers." *New York Times,* May 9, 1970, 1.

"The Blue Collar Worker's Lowdown Blues." *Time* 96, no. 19 (November 9, 1970).

Carroll, Maurice. "Police Assailed by Mayor on Laxity at Peace Rally." *New York Times,* May 10, 1970, 1.

"Comments on Worker-Student Clash." *New York Times,* May 19, 1970, 38.

Cook, Fred J. "Hard-Hats: The Rampaging Patriots." *The Nation* 210 (June 15, 1970): 712–719.

Cowie, Jefferson. "'Vigorously Left, Right, and Center: The Crosscurrents of Working Class American in the 1970s." In *America in the Seventies,* edited by Beth Bailey and David Farber, 75–105. Lawrence: University Press of Kansas, 2004.

Engels, Jeremy. "The Politics of Resentment and the Tyranny of the Minority: Rethinking Victimage for Resentful Times." *Rhetoric Society Quarterly* 40 (Fall 2010): 303–325.

"Kent State: Another View." *Time* 96, no. 17 (October 26, 1970).

"Kent State Revisited." *Time* 98, No. 23 (December 6, 1971).

"Kent State Reopened." *Time* 102, no. 26 (December 24, 1973).

Kifner, John. "4 Kent State Students Killed by Troops." *New York Times,* May 5, 1970, 1.

"Man and Woman of the Year: The Middle Americans." *Time* 95, no.1 (January 5, 1970).

"My God! They're Killing Us." *Newsweek* (May 18, 1970).

"Parades for Peace and Patriotism." *Time* 94, no. 21 (November 21, 1968).

Perlmutter, Emmanuel. "Head of Building Trade Unions Here Says Response Favor's Friday's Actions." *New York Times,* May 12, 1970, 18.

"Protest Season on the Campus." *Time* 95, no. 19 (May 11, 1970).

Rieder, Jonathan. "The Rise of the 'Silent Majority.'" In *The Rise and Fall of the New Deal Order, 1930–1980,* edited by Steve Fraser and Frank Gerstle, 243–268. Princeton: Princeton University Press, 1989.

Salpukas, Agis. "Unionists Say War Protesters Prompted a Backlash." *New York Times,* May 16, 1970, 70.

Semple, Robert B. Jr. "Nixon Meets Heads of 2 City Unions." *New York Times,* May 27, 1970, 2.

"The Troubled American: A Special Report on the White Majority." *Newsweek* (October 6, 1969): 1–30.

"Violence on the Right." *New York Times,* May 9, 1970, 1–3.

"Why They Want Him." *Time* 92, no. 16 (October 18, 1968).

Wierzynski, Gregory H. "The Cooling of America: The Students: All Quiet on the Campus Front." *Time* 97, no. 28 (February 22, 1971).

EPILOGUE AND LEGACY

Berger, Joseph. "Born to Be Wild. Scratch That. Born to Be Mild." *New York Times,* December 4, 1994.

Braunstein, Peter, and Michael William Doyle. "Historicizing the American Counterculture of the 1960s and '70s." In *Imagine Nation: The American Counterculture of the 1960s & '70s,* edited by Braunstein and Doyle, 1–15. New York: Routledge, 2002.

Cotter, Holland. "Through Rose-Colored Granny Glasses." *New York Times,* May 25, 2007.

Goldman, John J. "Turbulent '60s Live Again at Funeral for Activist: Radicals, Friends Bid Hoffman Farewell." *Los Angeles Times,* April 20, 1989.

Kelly, Kevin. "Bonfire of the Techies." *Time* 150, no. 12 (September 18, 2000).

King, Wayne. "Mourning and Celebrating a Radical." *New York Times,* April 20, 1989.

Krassner, Paul. "Who Killed Jerry Rubin?" *The Realist* 130 (Summer 1995): 2–12.

Lacayo, Richard. "A Flower in a Clenched Fist: Abbie Hoffman, 1936–1989." *Time* 133, no. 17 (April 24, 1989).

Lebel, Jean Jacques. "Counter Culture: Hip Culture Ripped Off." *Spectator* (December 8, 1969).

Limbach, Elizabeth. "The Wonderful, Weird Economy of Burning Man." *The Atlantic* (August 18, 2014.

Norquist, Grover. "My First Burning Man: Confessions of a Conservative from Washington." *The Guardian* (September 2, 2014).

Pace, Eric. "Jerry Rubin, 56, Flashy '60s Radical Dies; 'Yippies' Founder and Chicago 7 Defendant." *New York Times,* November 30, 1994.

"Rubin Relents." *Time* 116, no. 6 (August 11, 1980).

Saillant, Catherine. "Burning Man Becomes a Hot Academic Topic." *Los Angeles Times,* October 20, 2010.

Schell, Jonathan. "A Reporter at Large: History in Sherman Park." *New Yorker* (January 12, 1987).

Stein, Joel. "The Man Behind Burning Man." *Time* 156, no. 12 (September 18, 2000).

Tyler, Timothy. "The Cooling of America: Out of Tune and Lost in the Counterculture." *Time* 97, no. 8 (February 22, 1971).

Van Doorn, John. "An Intimidating New Class: The Physical Elite." *New York Magazine* (May 29, 1978).

Walmsley, Stuart. "Behind the Burning Man Festival in Nevada." *The Herald Sun,* October 12, 2014. http://heraldsun.com.au.

Index

Abbey Road 103
acid tests 106–108
Adler, Lou 138, 199–200, 203–4
African Americans 15–17, 18, 83–5, 100, 185–88, 190, 191, 203, 222–3 260, 268–9; 292–3, 306–7, 333
Albright, Thomas 111
Allyn, David 178
Alpert, Richard 34, 67–8, 69, 74, 75, 77, 114, 115, 134, 365
Altamont 5, 6, 318–319, 320–1, 321–3, 335, 349, 351
American Civil Liberties Union 10
Anderson, Chester 171, 181, 185, 186, 187, 189, 215
Ankeny, Jason 143
"Ann Arbor Riots" 150
Anthony, Gene 106, 108–9
antiwar movement 263–5; *see also* march on the Pentagon; Mobe
Armstrong, Louie 17
Atlanta, hippies in 145
Austin, Texas 152; hippies in 152–5, 156
Austin Rag 152–53, 155–56
Avalon Ballroom 105–106

Babbs, Ken 77–8
Baby Boom 26
Baez, Joan 88, 89, 90, 292
Balin, Marty 10, 327
Ball, Lucille 22
Baraka, Amiri 160
Barayon, Ramon Sender 218, 220–21
Barger, Sonny 174–75, 327, 329
Beach Boys 91, 111
Beat movement 4, 9, 12, 14–15, 20, 30–31, 35, 40–2, 158
the Beatles 91–4, 95–6, 1001, 103, 305–6
Beatniks 19–20
Bell, Daniel 273
Belle Isle Love-in 146–9

Berg, Peter 41, 55
Bergen, Candice 210
Berkeley, California 121
Berkeley Barb 95, 122, 141, 157–8, 191, 331, 334, 338
Big Brother and the Holding Company 36, 103, 104, 105, 143, 168, 175
birth control (the pill) 178
Bixby, Robert 142–3
Black Mask Revolution 159–60
Black Panthers 149, 187–8
Black Power 159
Boo-Hoos 70
Booth, Stanley 315
Boston, hippies in 145
Boston Herald 67–8
Bowen, Michael 77, 114–16, 118
Brand, Stewart 106, 128, 330, 365
Brokaw, Tom 270, 273–4
Buffalo Springfield 113
Bugliosi, Vincent 307
Burdon, Eric 138, 209
Burning Man festival 359–61
the Byrds 99

Caen, Herb 19
Cahill, Tom (San Francisco chief of police) 137–8, 190
California 23, 24, 26, 27, 28, 33–4, 42
Carmichael, Stokely 159
Carter, Shob 191
Casady, Neal 13–14, 77
Castalia Foundation 69
censorship 11–12
Central Intelligence Agency (CIA) 63–4, 150
the Charlatans 104
Chicago 17, 84, 131, 166, 260, 262, 265–66, 267, 274–5, 283–4 335, 351; *see also* the Democratic National Convention (1968)
Christgau, Robert 169–70, 199, 202, 204, 205, 207, 210, 267, 272, 313, 314, 315

City Lights Bookstore 9
Clark, Ramsey 281
Cleaver, Eldridge 151, 293
clothing *see* High Costume
Coate, John 229–30, 231, 232–33, 234, 236, 237, 240, 242
Cobb, Robert 144–5
coffeehouses 19
Cohen, Allen 51, 58–9, 114–16, 118, 121, 171, 185, 194, 262
Cohen, Dr. Stanley 72
Cold War 8, 15, 21, 30, 41, 63, 106
Coltrane, John 17
communes 212–216, 217–18, 246, 247, 253–4, 256–7; *see also* Barayon, Ramon Sender; Davidson, Sara; Drop City; The Farm; Gaskin, Ina May; Gaskin, Stephen; Gottlieb, Lou; Hedgepath, William; Morningstar; Wheeler, Bill
Conklin, Lee 111
Corso, Gregory 15
Costo, Rupert 135
Council for the Summer of Love 171, 190
Cox, Harvey 127
Coyote, Peter 54–5, 59, 124, 183, 221, 224, 320
Crawford, J.C. 143
Cream 143
Cronkite, Walter 279
Crosby, David 331
Crosby, Kathryn 175
Cutler, Sam 317, 318, 320, 323

Dahlstrom, Eric Frank 191
Daley, Richard 263, 265, 268–70, 273–4, 279, 280–1
Dalton, David 309–10, 324, 325, 334
dance halls, ballroom concerts at 104–106
dancing 106
Davidson, Sara 216, 219, 222, 253

Davis, Rennie 282
Davis, Ron, and the San Francisco
    Mime Troupe 49–51
Death of Hippy Ceremony/March
    193–4
DeCanio, Steve 122
Dellinger, David 263, 273–4
Democratic National Convention,
    Chicago (1968) 265, 274–80
Denson, Ed 122
Detroit 140–1, 144–6; see also the
    Motor City Five; Sinclair, John;
    Trans Love Energies
Didion, Joan 192–3
the Diggers: New York City East
    Village 163–65; San Francisco
    6, 49–55, 123, 135, 138, 167–
    68; 172, 181, 183, 190, 218
Disney, Walt 23
Disneyland 23, 136
Distant Drummer 98
Doegler, Henry 27
Donovan 138
the Doors 315–17
Doyle, Michael William 54
"Dozens" 16
Dreyer, Thorne 141–42, 152–55
Drop City 249–252
drugs 7, 8, 15, 16, 18, 19, 36, 42,
    44, 46, 56, 57–81, 175–77, 215,
    361; see also Alpert, Richard;
    Cohen, Allen; Coyote, Peter;
    Garcia, Jerry; Ginsberg, Allen;
    Houchin, Larry; Kesey, Ken;
    Leary, Timothy; Stanley,
    Augustus Owsley; Zappa, Frank
Duncan, Gary 41

East Village (NYC): Beats 19;
    hippies 45, 54, 69, 158–9
East Village Other 141, 150, 207,
    258, 300
The Economist 12
The Ed Sullivan Show 87, 93, 314
Eisenhower, Dwight David 21
Emerson, Ralph Waldo 14–15, 68
Epstein, Brian 92, 103

Fallon, Michael 35–6
Farber, David 77
The Farm 228–49
Father Knows Best
Federal Bureau of Investigation
    (FBI) 150
Ferlinghetti, Lawrence 9
Fifth Estate 141–42, 147–8
Figallo, Cliff 240, 247
First Amendment 10
Fisher, Donald 46
Fisher, Doris 46
Fishman, Marvin 159–60
Fogerty, John, and Credence
    Clearwater Revival 292
Folk music 87–8
Ford, Henry 30

Four Freshmen 91
Fouratt, Jim 161
Frank, Thomas 48
Free Clinic 172–74, 176; see also
    Smith, Dr. David
Freed, Allen 85, 110
French Quarter 19
Fromme, Squeaky 304, 305
Fuller, Richard Buckminster 249,
    252

Galbraith, John Kenneth 29
The Gap 46
Garcia, Jerry 36, 41, 59, 77, 105,
    109, 113, 197, 216, 328
Gaskin, Maggie (Ina May) 182,
    233, 239
Gaskin, Sam 248
Gaskin, Stephen 228–37, 238–9,
    240–2, 243–5, 247
Generation Gap 124–6
Genet, Jean 270, 280, 281
Gentlemen's Quarterly 48
Getz, Dave 36
Gibb, Russ 143
Gillespie, Dizzy 17
Gillett, Charlie 93
Ginsberg, Allen 7–9, 12, 31, 71,
    74, 112–4, 120, 123–4, 132, 134,
    137, 155, 185, 277
Gitlin, Todd 34, 153, 267, 274,
    334
Gleason, Ralph 87, 89–90, 97–
    98, 106, 113, 120, 123, 319, 332
Golden Gate Park 33, 117, 124,
    168
Goldstein, Richard 102–3, 104,
    108, 113, 200
Gooding, Judson 128, 129, 139,
    145
Gottlieb, Lou 108–110, 218, 219,
    220, 222, 227
Graham, Bill 106, 109–10, 112,
    175, 198, 326, 332–3
Grande Ballroom (Detroit) 143–
    44
Grateful Dead 104, 105, 106, 107,
    108, 109, 113, 168, 208, 315,
    319–20, 328
Great Society 5, 49, 138
Great Speckled Bird 60
Grey Line Bus Company and
    Tours of the Haight 136–7
Grogan, Emmett 50, 55, 167, 184
Guthrie, Woody 89

Haight-Ashbury ("Hashbury")
    32–3, 42–3, 44, 45, 46, 49, 50,
    51, 55, 56, 52, 129, 136, 137,
    138, 167–172, 188–9, 190, 191–
    2, 195, 304
Haight-Ashbury Eye 194
Haight-Ashbury Maverick 129
Hair 130
HALO (Haight-Ashbury Legal

Organization) 118
Hallinan, Vince 117
Ham, Bill 104
Hamilton, Neil 93
Hanrahan, William 9
Hard Day's Night 94
Harrington, Alan 58
Harrison, George 193, 313
Harvard Crimson 67–8
Harvard University 29, 57, 64, 65,
    67–9
Harvey, Larry 359–60,
Havens, Richie 290–1
Hayden, Tom 267, 272–3, 274,
    277, 284
Hedgepath, William 169, 193,
    194, 213, 214, 217, 253, 254, 357
Hefner, Hugh 66
Hells' Angels 79, 114, 146, 174–5,
    184, 315, 318, 323–6, 326–8,
    329–30, 331, 332, 333
Helms, Chet 104, 105–6, 112, 198
Hendrix, Jimi 6, 205–7, 293–4
High costume (hippie clothing
    and appearance) 35, 47–49,
Hill Country, Texas 152
Hinckle, Warren 129–130
H.I.P. (Haight Independent Pro-
    prietors) 51, 116, 137, 181, 188,
    189
Hippie women 53, 179, 180, 181–
    84, 252–3
"Hippieland" 43, 46
Hipsters 15–16, 17–18
Hitchcock, Peggy 69
Hitchcock, Tom 69
Hitchcock, William 69
Hoffman, Abbie 54, 159–160,
    162–165, 259, 260, 261, 262,
    274, 354, 363
Hofmann, Albert 63–64, 81
Hollingshead, Michael 66
Hollywood 23, 135–6
homosexuality 67, 184
Hoover, J. Edgar 150–51, 273
Hotel Catalina 57–58
Houchin, Larry 56–58, 74
Houseboat Summit 130–2
Howe, Irving 273
Howl 7–9
Human Be-In 116, 117–124,
Humphrey, Hubert 266, 275–6,
    280
Huncke, Herbert 15
Hunter, Meredith 329–30
Huxley, Aldous 61–62

I Love Lucy 22
individualism 15, 28, 37, 39
Inobsky, Mark 104
International Foundation for
    Human Freedom 57
Isserman, Maurice 298, 300
"It" 14

Jazz (bebop) 17, 140
Jefferson Airplane 59, 98, 105, 108, 113, 198, 216, 315, 32–8
Jerome, Daric 188
Johnson, Jack 16
Johnson, Lyndon Baines 5, 49, 275–6
Joplin, Janis 46, 98, 103–4, 177, 207–8, 291

Kaiser, Henry J. 27
Kandel, Leonor 123, 182–3
Kantner, Paul 113, 122, 200
Kavanaugh, Frank 170–1
"Keith Decision" 151
Kelley, Ken 144
Kennedy, John F. 65, 87, 93
Kennedy, Robert F. 268
Kent State 344–45, 346, 348
Kerouac, Jack 13–15, 31, 78, 214
Kesey, Ken 14, 75–77, 95, 106–7, 109, 239, 349
Khrushchev, Nikita 65
King, Martin Luther, Jr. 159
Kingston Trio 88
Klep, Arthur 70
Knauth, Lothar 64
Koestler, Arthur 67
Kopkind, Andrew 297
Kornfeld, Artie 286, 287, 290, 291
Kramer, Wayne 142–3, 148–9
Krassner, Paul 162, 164, 165, 258
Kunkin, Art 119
Kupferberg, Tuli 39, 215

La Honda, California 77, 79
Lakewood, California 27
Lang, Michael 286, 287, 291
Lawrence, D.H. 38
Leary, Timothy 39, 57–8, 64, 72, 74–5, 103, 120–1, 131, 157, 189, 330–1
Leave It to Beaver 22
Levitt, William 26–7, 29–30
Liberation News Service (LNS) 142, 158
Liddy, G. Gordon 72
Life magazine 19–20, 62, 74, 211, 308
Limeliters 88
Lipton, Lawrence 39
Long Island, NY 27
Look magazine 68, 169
Los Angeles 19, 26, 139
Los Angeles Free Press 119, 125, 141, 157
"Love Generation" 137
Lowenstein, Allard 274, 280
LSD 36, 39, 50, 56, 57–58, 59, 60, 61, 63, 64–5, 66–9, 72–74, 75, 77–80, 123, 175, 177, 189, 191, 221
Lydon, Michael 202, 203, 206–7,

208–9, 210, 318, 320–21, 324, 331
Lydon, Patrick 298

MacPhee, Chester 9
Magic Mountain Festival 199
Mailer, Norman 18, 140, 264, 273, 293
Maloney, George D. 125
Manson, Charles 303–11, 335, 351
March on the Pentagon (October 1967) 263–5
Marcus, Greil 85, 214–5, 299
Marcuse, Herbert 29, 155
marijuana 16, 18, 36, 42, 44, 56, 59, 60–1, 80, 242
Marinello, Frank 204
Marrakech 1–3
Martin, George 95, 103
Matusow, Alan 95
Mayes, Elaine 192
McCabe, Charles 133–4
McCarthy, Eugene 276, 277
McClesse, Don 143
McCloskey, Jason 48
McClure, Kathryn 239, 246
McClure, Matthew 231, 237, 238, 247, 249
McClure, Michael 9, 123
McDonald, Country Joe 3, 71, 82–3, 98–9, 100, 177–78, 292
McGuire, Barry 99
McKenzie, Scott 138, 200, 208
McLuhan, Marshall 71
"Me Generation" 352–3
Merry Pranksters 77–9
Mexico 57–58, 62, 64, 69, 72
middle class backlash 336–9, 342, 346–7, 347–8
Millbrook 69–70, 72
Miller, Timothy 103, 126–7
Millstein, Gilbert 14
"Mitchell Doctrine" 151
Mobe 263–5
Moby Grape 105
Monk, Thelonious 17
the Monkees 94
Monterey International Pop Festival 198–200, 201–5, 208–10
Morgan, Robin 181
Morningstar (Open Land) 218–228
Morocco 1–3
Morrow, Lance 278, 280
Mother Earth News 234, 239
Motor City Five (MC5) 142–44, 146, 147–8, 150, 267
Mountain Girl (Carolyn Garcia) 168
Moynihan, Daniel Patrick 129
Mumford, Lewis 28–9
Mungo, Raymond 39, 158, 243
Murao, Shigeyoshi 9–10

music festivals 197–198, 285–6, 296, 299–300, 301
Muskie, Edmund J. 280

National Guard 5
National Institute of Mental Health 61, 80
Native Americans and hippies 131–35
Neo-American Church 70
New Christy Minstrels 88
the New Left 4, 5, 52, 121–22, 149, 152–4, 153–55, 157–8, 258–60, 272–3, 343; *see also* Students for a Democratic Society
New Mexico communes 255
New York City 12, 17, 18, 34, 70, 346, 347
New York Times 12, 14, 129, 161, 194, 233, 265, 269, 273, 277, 283, 289, 290, 293, 296, 297, 346, 347, 351
Newport Folk Festival 96
Newsweek 95, 124, 128–9, 169, 202, 243, 279
Nixon, Richard 151, 341, 342–4, 346, 347, 352
North Beach (SF) 9, 19, 32, 35, 45, 56

Ochs, Phil 99
Ogelsby, Carl 157, 268
On the Road 13–14, 41
Ono, Yoko 103
the *Oracle* 36, 41, 43, 51, 52, 115, 119, 120, 130, 133, 134, 157, 177, 180, 213, 251
Osmond, Humphrey 61–2
the Outlaws 146–8
Ozzie and Harriet 22

"Papa Al" 174–5
Pardun, Robert 154–55
Parker, Charlie "the Bird" 17
Peace Corps 172
"Peacock Revolution" 48
Peck, Abe 155, 270, 271, 272, 277
Pennebaker, D.A. 97, 202, 207, 208
Perry, Helen Swick 123
Perry Lane 77
Peter, Paul, and Mary 88–9, 96
Phillips, John 138, 199–200
Pike, James (Episcopal Bishop of California) 127
Plamondon, Lawrence Robert "Pun" 144, 150, 151
Playboy 66–7
Plum Street 144–5, 146
police: in Atlanta 145; in Austin 153; in Chicago 265, 270–1, 276–9, 281–2, 283; in Detroit 147–9, 151; in San Francisco 190

poster/pop art 112
Presley, Elvis 86–7
Psychedelic Shop 42–3, 115, 194

Quicksilver Messenger Service 41, 105, 168
Quicksilver Times 295–6

Rabideau, Walter 231, 236, 238, 239, 243
Reagan, Ronald 130
Red Dog Saloon 104
Redding, Otis 203
Reich, Charles 124, 340–1
Reston, James 273
Revolver (Beatles' LP) 100
Rexroth, Kenneth 9, 20
Reynolds, Malvina 28, 89–90
Richards, Keith 315, 321, 324, 329
Roberts, John 286, 287, 290, 295
rock and roll 16–17, 82–6, 97, 100–1, 103, 197–8
Rohan, Brian 117–8
Rolling Stone 318–19, 320, 327
Rolling Stones 311–315, 320, 329
Romantics 4, 14–15, 37
Romney, Hugh ("Wavy Gravy") 295, 296, 298
Rosenman, Joel 286, 287
Roszak, Theodore 3, 46–7, 73, 122, 124
Royko, Mike 267
Rubin, Jerry 47, 74, 162–5, 258–9, 260, 261, 262, 263, 264, 265, 266, 268, 272, 281, 310–11, 354
Russin, Joseph 67–8

Sadler, Staff Sergeant Barry 99
San Francisco 6, 7, 9, 18–19, 26, 31, 32, 34–5, 167, 168–9, 170–1
San Francisco Chronicle 19, 97, 106, 108, 110, 167, 175, 191
San Francisco Mime Troupe 50–1
"San Francisco Renaissance" 9, 18–19
"San Francisco Sound" 103, 104, 113
San Francisco Standard 172
Sanders, Ed 157, 158, 310, 364
Santana, Carlos 322, 331
Schlesinger, Arthur, Jr. 94
Sculati, Gene 110
Scully, Rock 138, 324, 325, 329, 358
Scully, Tim 79–80
Sergeant Pepper's Lonely Hearts Club Band 101–2
sex and hippies 177–180, 183, 184, 253, 361–2
sexual revolution 16

Seward, John 235, 238, 243, 246–7, 249
Shankar, Ravi 201–2, 205, 292
Shapiro, Sherman 144–5, 146
Sheep Meadow Be-In (Central Park, NYC) 161–2
Shelley, John (mayor of San Francisco, 1964–8) 115, 138
Shero, Jeff 152, 154
Shoriss, Earl 130
Sinclair, John 82, 85, 140–1, 142–44, 146, 148, 149–52, 210
Six Gallery 1, 12
Slick, Grace 41, 321
Smith, Dr. David 69, 172–74, 175, 176, 177, 304–5
Smith, Dr. Roger 304, 305
Snyder, Gary 19, 72, 131
Southern, Terry 278
Sox, Ellis 173
Space City 98
Sparks, Randy 88
Spock, Benjamin 126
Stanley, Augustus Owsley III 79–80, 106–7, 202
Stepanian, Michael 117–8
Stevens, Jay 116
Stevenson, Adlai III 281
Stevenson, Douglas 231, 232
Stills, Stephen 113
Stokes, Geoffrey 88
Strait, Guy 43, 47–8
Student Non-violent Coordinating Committee (SNCC) 159
Students for a Democratic Society (SDS) 5, 152–55, 156, 157
Suburbia 24, 28, 29, 170–1
Summer of Love (documentary) 42, 195
Summer Solstice Do-In 167–8
Superspade 191
Swanson Company 22

"Teddybear" 176, 195
teenage crooners 86
television 22–3
Thelin, Ron 41–44, 108, 118–19, 129, 134, 186–7, 193–4
Thompson, Hunter S. 39–40, 43, 45, 79, 121
Thoreau, Henry David 14–15, 37
Tiber, Elliot 288, 290
Time (magazine) 29, 36, 60, 61, 72, 80, 114, 121, 128–9, 145, 149, 169, 178, 191, 207, 210, 213, 218, 249–50, 264, 278, 279, 281, 291, 297, 298, 299, 308, 316, 348, 363
Trips Festival 107–10
"TV dinners" 22

underground comix 180

underground press 141–2
universities 340–41, 345, 348–9

Variety 92
Vietnam War 5, 37–8, 41, 99, 126, 132, 231, 262, 272, 273, 290, 341, 342–44, 345, 352, 364
Village Voice 102, 161, 162, 163, 164, 200
Virginia City, Nevada 104
Von Hoffman, Nicholas 169, 183, 191, 195, 267, 275, 357

Wadleigh, Michael 290
Wainright, Loudon 128
Walden Pond 15, 37
Walker, Daniel 272, 275, 281–2
Walker Commission 272, 275, 281–2
Wallace, George 283
Warhol, Andy 48, 112
Warren, Holly George 41
Washington Post 169, 195, 267, 275, 289, 357
Wasson, R. Gordon 62–3
"Wasteland" 12
Watson, Tex 305
Watts, Alan 131–2
Wavy Gravy 295, 296, 298
Wayne State University 140–1
Weathermen 309
Weil, Andrew 67–8
Weir, Bob 113
Wenner, Jann 271–72
Wenner, Kate 233–34
Wheeler, Bill (Wheeler's Ranch) 218, 219–220, 222, 225–6, 227–8, 253
White Panther Party 149–51
"White Rabbit" 113
Whitman, Walt 12
Whole Earth Review 363–4
Whyte, William 4
Wicker, Tom 279
Williams, William Carlos 10
Wilson, Sloan 4
Wilson, Wes 111–12
Wolfe, Burton 40
Wolfe, Tom 78–9, 106, 108
Woodstock 6, 285–302; *see also* music festivals
Woodstock 1999 299–300

Yablonsky, Lewis 161, 308
Yasgur, Max 286, 287–88, 300
Yippies 165–66, 258–263, 265–266, 281, 283
Yogi, Maharishi Mahesh 101
Young, Neil 216–17
Youngbloods 98
Yuppies 353–4

Zappa, Frank 60, 217